Frommer's

CHINA

THE 50 MOST MEMORABLE TRIPS

The Lunan Stone Forest near Kunming

Aerial view of Hong Kong

Kowloon night market

The First Emperor's terra-cotta warriors in Xi'an

The Li River at Guilin

Sunset in the Li River Valley at Yangshuo

View of the Great Wall

Palace and moat in Beijing's Forbidden City

Statues in the Longmen Buddhist Caves in Luoyang

Workers leaving the rice paddy fields in the evening in Guizhou

Winter palace in Xi'an

The Pamir Mountains on the Silk Road

Frommer's

CHINA

THE 50 MOST MEMORABLE TRIPS

by J. D. Brown

IDG Books Worldwide, Inc.
An International Data Group Company
Foster City, CA • Chicago, IL • Indianapolis, IN • New York, NY

About the Author

J.D. Brown has lived and worked in China and has written about China as a literary traveler, a travel writer, and a guidebook author. His work has appeared in such diverse publications as the *New York Times,* the *Washington Post,* the *Michigan Quarterly Review, Islands,* and *National Geographic Traveler.* When he is not traveling in the Far East, he lives in Eugene, Oregon.

IDG BOOKS WORLDWIDE, INC.
An International Data Group Company
919 E. Hillsdale Blvd.
Suite 400
Foster City, CA 94404

Find us online at **www.frommers.com**

ISBN 0-02863673-2

Editor: Jeff Soloway
Production Editor: Scott Barnes
Photo Editor: Richard Fox
Design by designLab, Seattle
Staff Cartographers: John Decamillis, Elizabeth Puhl, and Roberta Stockwell

Front cover photo: Terraced rice fields in Longsheng.
Back cover photo: The Li River near Yangshuo.

SPECIAL SALES

For general information on IDG Books Worldwide's books in the U.S., please call our Consumer Customer Service department at 1-800-762-2974. For reseller information, including discounts, bulk sales, customized editions, and premium sales, please call our Reseller Customer Service department at 1-800-434-3422.

Manufactured in the United States of America

5 4 3 2 1

CONTENTS

Southwest China: Searching for Shangri-La

Silk Road China: Cities of Sand

Mountain China: Pinnacles & Sacred Peaks

List of Maps

Southwest China: Searching for Shangri-La

Silk Road China: Cities of Sand

Mountain China: Pinnacles & Sacred Peaks

China by River: Up and Down the Yangzi

A Quick History

An Invitation to the Reader

In researching this book, we discovered many wonderful places—hotels, restaurants, shops, and more. We're sure you'll find others. Please tell us about them, so we can share the information with your fellow travelers in upcoming editions. If you were disappointed with a recommendation, we'd love to know that, too. Please write to:

Frommer's China: The 50 Most Memorable Trips
Frommer's Travel Guides
909 Third Avenue
New York, NY 10022

An Additional Note

Please be advised that travel information is subject to change at any time—and this is especially true of prices. We therefore suggest that you write or call ahead for confirmation when making your travel plans. The author, editors, and publisher cannot be held responsible for the experiences of readers while traveling. Your safety is important to us, however, so we encourage you to stay alert and be aware of your surroundings. Keep a close eye on cameras, purses, and wallets, all favorite targets of thieves and pickpockets.

What the Symbols Mean

The following abbreviations are used for credit cards:

AE	American Express	JCB	Japan Credit Bank
DC	Diners Club	MC	MasterCard
EC	EuroCard	V	Visa

Photo Credits

1. Lunan Stone Forest: Kelly/Mooney Photography
2. Aerial view of Hong Kong: Glen Allison/Tony Stone Images
3. Kowloon night market: Shaun Egan/Tony Stone Images
4. Terra-cotta warriors: Christopher Liu/China Stock
5. Li River at Guilin: Robert Everts/Tony Stone Images
6. Sunset in the Li River Valley: Catherine Feng/Viesti Associates
7. View of the Great Wall: D.E. Cox/Tony Stone Images
8. Palace and moat in the Forbidden City: Flip Chalfant/ The Image Book
9. Statues in the Longmen Buddhist Caves: Glen Allison/ Tony Stone Images
10. Workers leaving the rice paddy fields: Yann Layma/ Tony Stone Images
11. Winter palace in Xi'an: Suzanne Murphy/Tony Stone Images
12. The Pamir Mountains: David Sanger Photography

Why Go to China?

China has been my destination of choice for 2 decades. The reasons are various. No other place on Earth quite possesses such an intensity of beauty and strangeness, no other nation has a longer or richer historical legacy, and no other nation is likely to be as important in the 21st century. When I try to explain my own continuing fascination with the China of the past, present, and future, I remember a remark made by a China scholar, Marcel Granet: "By its extent, its duration, its mass, Chinese civilization is one of the most powerful creations of mankind," he wrote. "None other is richer in human experience."

Over the last 2 decades I have left home often and traveled through China's ancient capitals, fabled cities, and countryside villages and towns; crossed its rivers, lakes, and seas; admired its ancient stone monuments, from the Great Wall to the Great Buddha; followed the Silk Road across the deserts to the West; and stood on the summits of its nine sacred mountains. Along the way I have traveled by every available conveyance, from jet to train, from bicycle to camel; stayed in five-star international hotels and no-star mountain inns; eaten the most delightful creations of one of the world's great cuisines and gulped down some of the most dismal, too. Travel has been hard at times, but it is growing increasingly easy. Each time I return to the Middle Kingdom, I find large-scale changes and I discover more about China's culture, which remains exotic despite rapid modernization and growing Western influences. At some rare junctures, I even discover something about myself.

What fascinates me first about China is its past, so unlike and so often at odds with the heritage of the West. These contrasts, visible in temples and museums, city walls and pagodas, and in enduring social customs, provide a means to see my own culture from a larger perspective. Chinese art and history are a continual delight, and to see China's past made visible, whether in the vaults where the First Emperor died among his terra-cotta armies or in the Forbidden City where the last emperor was born, brings the dreamy Middle Kingdom to life.

Present-day China also has enormous appeal, although the sheer beauty of the past seldom shines through. Modern China, particularly

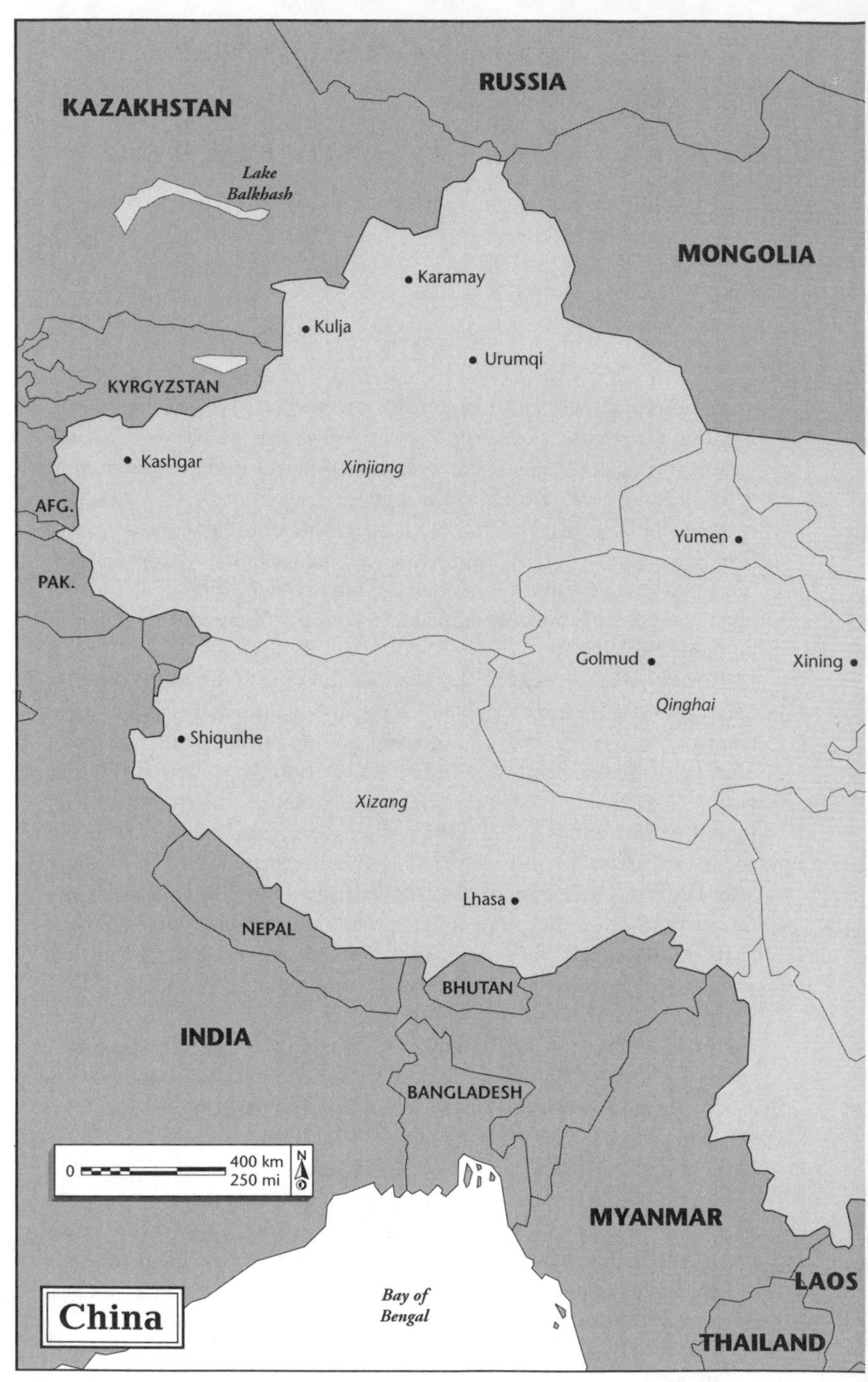
RUSSIA
KAZAKHSTAN
Lake Balkhash
MONGOLIA
Karamay
Kulja
Urumqi
KYRGYZSTAN
Kashgar
Xinjiang
AFG.
Yumen
PAK.
Golmud
Xining
Qinghai
Shiqunhe
Xizang
Lhasa
NEPAL
BHUTAN
INDIA
BANGLADESH
0
400 km
250 mi
N
MYANMAR
LAOS
Bay of Bengal
THAILAND
China

Lake Baikal
Hailar
Heilongjiang
Qiqihar
Harbin
Changchun
Nei Mongol
Jilin
Shenyang
Liaoning
NORTH KOREA
Hebei
Hohhot
Beijing
Dalian
Tianjin
SOUTH KOREA
Taiyuan
Shijiazhuang
Yantai
Yinchuan
Ningxia
Qingdao
Jinan
Shanxi
Lanzhou
Shandong
Yellow Sea
Zhengzhou
Jiangsu
Gansu
Xi'an
Henan
Anhui
Shaanxi
Nanjing
Hefei
Shanghai
Sichuan
Hubei
Hangzhou
Wuhan
Chengdu
Zhejiang
Chongqing
Nanchang
East China Sea
Changsha
Jiangxi
Hunan
Guizhou
Fuzhou
Guiyang
Fujian
Xiamen
Kunming
TAIWAN
Guangdong
Guangxi
Yunnan
Guangzhou
Nanning
Hong Kong
VIETNAM
Haikou
Hainan
South China Sea

its urban centers, is shockingly gray and dismal, unexpectedly so for most first-time visitors who arrive with a vision of old China. But the cities of China, as ugly and monotonous as they often are, are undergoing a metamorphosis, and this has its own fascination. No large country has ever boomed so rapidly and decisively since the Industrial Revolution began in the West 2 centuries ago. Much of China looks like a construction zone today, but this raw reconstruction lends a vibrancy to the cityscapes. China has its sights locked on the coming century. If you want to visit the next superpower as a work in progress, China is your ticket—the new Pacific Century begins in Shanghai, Beijing, Chongqing, and a dozen other Chinese boomtowns.

Nor is this new China simply an overpopulated carbon copy of the Western world. China is charting its own course, holding tenaciously to the tattered strands of its own cultural identity. The new and old China are in collision, and the fireworks illuminate a vast and various stage. Present changes as well as the ancient monuments make China one of the most dynamic destinations on any traveler's map—an open gallery of treasures and traditions in vivid transition, beautiful but ugly, new but old, an imperial dragon but a modern phoenix.

It is now possible to travel to most of the interesting places in China in a style not dreamed of 10 years ago, barely possible even 5 years ago. Major cities have enough Western amenities and foreign tourism facilities in place to make travel on one's own a viable option even for the less adventurous traveler. It's no longer necessarily a choice between hitting the road via ramshackle local buses with backpack and water purification system firmly in hand or spending a small fortune for a grueling 7-day, 8-city, 9-banquet luxury tour. These options still exist—they are still sometimes the best means to see a place—but China has finally begun to make touring on one's own a more amenable and comprehensible process, even if one doesn't speak the language.

In this guide I've recorded in as frank detail as possible 50 of my most memorable travels in China. You should be able to follow in my footsteps if you choose to do so, or make your own detours. I steer you to the best sights I know at each stop, both those on everyone's tour and those that aren't, and I warn you about what to avoid, too. I've certainly made my share of poor choices and seen more than my share of boring sights, but I have also had the most amazing experiences along the way, sometimes by sheer accident. I try to point out your options at each destination, listing the best hotels as well as more economical choices when possible; explaining how and where to hire local tour guides, if needed; and pointing out the most interesting sights and how to reach them.

In all cases, I've sampled what I list myself, although I can't guarantee they'll all be there in the same condition they were for me. China is changing so rapidly. Not only are prices rising but hotels and cafes are constantly opening, closing, and reinventing themselves, and fresh new competitors are emerging every few months in some places. The same warning must be extended even to matters of transport. New roads, new rail connections, and new airport routes open constantly, usually without fanfare. Cable cars are going in at remote mountain peaks. Inexpensive, informative tours—many of them offered by new private companies—are added every year.

This is all to your advantage, of course. There's almost no place in China where I wouldn't welcome a new cafe with an English menu, a new three-star hotel with clean, modern rooms at a reasonable rate, or a new private tour agency that makes getting to a site easier.

As in most guidebooks, you'll also find a chapter on Chinese history and culture and a chapter on the practical matters of travel. In both, I take a personal approach, explaining what I've found most useful to know while traveling in China, from what dynasties really matter to what you absolutely must pack. I've added a chapter on Chinese temples, mosques, and churches, and what to look for when touring them.

Whether you choose to see China on your own or book a tour, you should find something useful in the following chapters. My tastes, responses, and adventures in China may differ from yours, of course, but I've endeavored to give you a full account of my actual experience at each destination rather than a bare recital of facts and statistics. This should help you decide if a place is your cup of tea or simply a bowl of gruel. In each account, I also weave in considerable strands of history and lore, which I always find makes a destination much more interesting. China, of course, is not the place to tour if you're seeking relaxation, pampering, or a week in the mellow tropics. It's an education—mostly a pleasant and unusual one—but it can require determination and patience. Think of it, perhaps, as a puzzle in which the pieces you're working with are not always what they appear to be and the rules are not always logical. If the picture that emerges is that of a looking-glass world, you're probably on the right track. China is different, but it's no longer an alien world. Traveling through it has never been easier for an outsider, in part because China—long the self-contained Middle Kingdom mesmerized by its own reflection—is becoming more and more like the outside world.

China is one of the world's largest countries, as well as the most populous. Ethnically and culturally, it is not as diverse as North America or Europe, but its sights, its landscapes, and its history are quite various. Beijing is a city quite unlike Kunming. The Great Wall bears little resemblance to the First Emperor's underground realm of terra-cotta soldiers, horses, and chariots. The southern Chinese act and speak differently than the northern Chinese and eat some foods no one else in the world would touch. In fact, each region of China has its own identity, so experiencing Chinese culture, seeing its treasures, and viewing its natural wonders require considerable travel.

China travel is a movable feast of sights and sensations, new and old. The following pages are a taste of what to expect, culled from one traveler's long, memorable banquet in the Middle Kingdom.

NORTHEAST CHINA: TRADITIONS & TREASURES

BEIJING: THE UNFORBIDDEN CITY

北京

BEIJING HAS MORE ATTRACTIONS than any other city in China. At one time, these cultural highlights were about all that appealed to travelers. Otherwise, China's capital was a sprawling metropolis of long, flat, monotonous avenues inhabited by uninspired socialist architecture, snarled traffic, and frightful levels of pollution. Beijing was also subject to shattering dust storms from the Gobi Desert. It was devoid of nightlife and lacking in pleasant neighborhoods for strolling. This atmosphere has begun to change in the last few years, as Beijing has blossomed into a city that an international traveler can enjoy. New shops and restaurants have spread across the city: The 13,661 restaurants counted in 1990 had nearly tripled to 39,196 by 1995 and may now have tripled once again. Beijing has become one of China's trendiest cities. Pubs and coffeehouses are displacing discos. Teahouses are opening by the score. Bowling, billiards, and swimming are increasingly popular. All-girl rock bands have appeared. Since July 1, 1997, only unleaded fuel has been sold in Beijing, the first Chinese city to mandate such a cleanup. And on a recent annual Tree-Planting Day, over two million Beijingers pitched in to help the capital build its much-needed greenway. The building and beautification programs initiated by the 50th anniversary of the founding of the People's Republic, celebrated on October 1, 1999, have further transformed many of Beijing's once dismal neighborhoods.

Beijing is by no means a paradise, but it is a more vibrant and interesting city. Dreariness no longer defines the cityscape. The first task of visitors, however, is unchanged: to partake of those places for which the Middle Kingdom, and Beijing, are celebrated. The Forbidden City, the Summer Palace, the Temple of Heaven, Tiananmen Square, and the Great Wall should not be missed. Nor should some of the dozens of lesser historical and cultural draws. At the same time, exploring Beijing's modern delights and side streets has also become a pleasure.

I have been to Beijing many times under many circumstances, as teacher, tourist, vagabond, and business writer. In this chapter, I'll concentrate on those places most worth exploring, and I'll try to tell you not

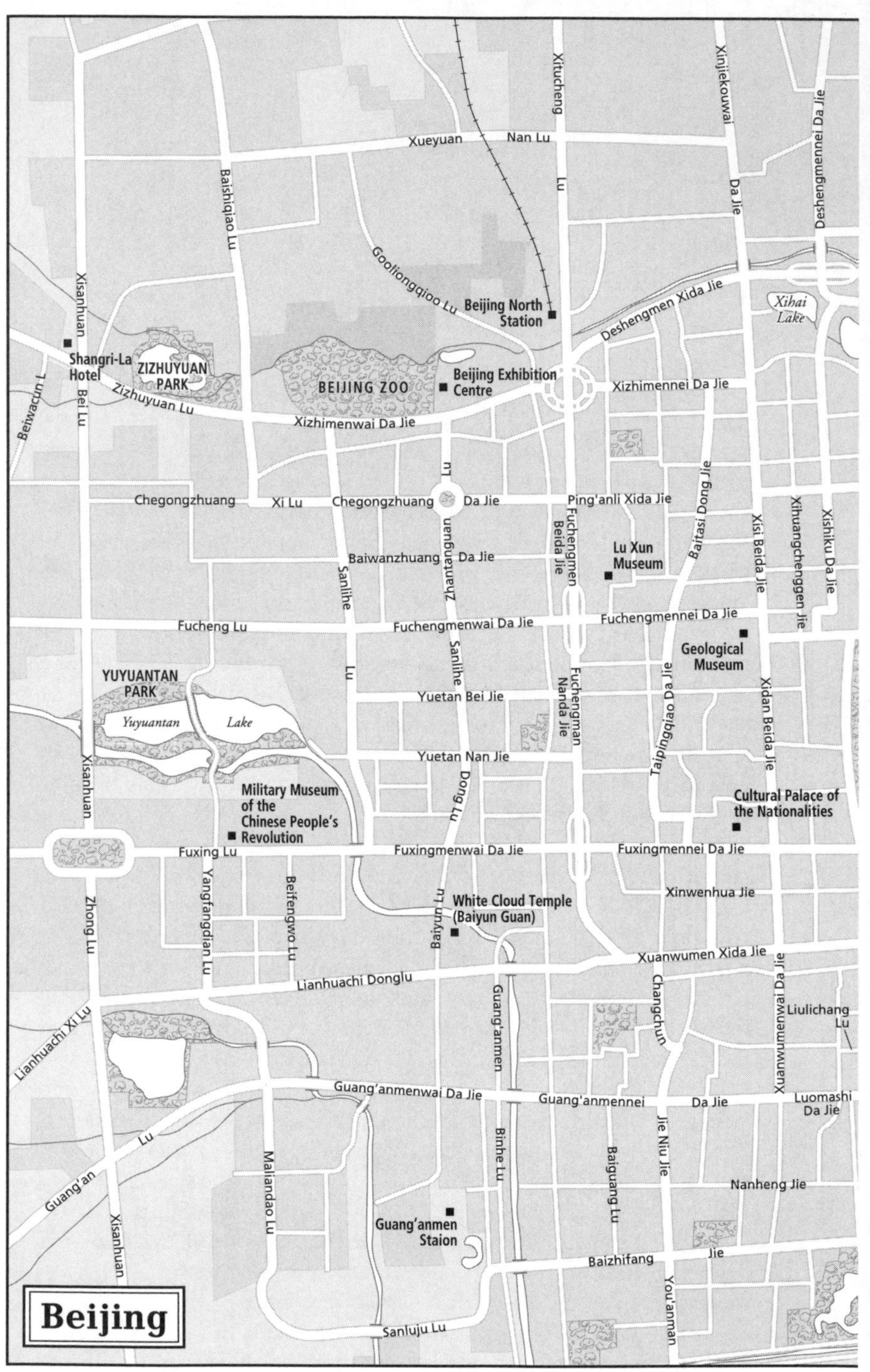
Beijing
Xueyuan
Nan Lu
Xituchen
Lu
Xinjiekouwai
Da Jie
Deshengmennei Da Jie
Baishiqiao Lu
Gooliongqioo Lu
Beijing North Station
Deshengmen Xida Jie
Xihai Lake
Xisanhuan
Shangri-La Hotel
ZIZHUYUAN PARK
BEIJING ZOO
Beijing Exhibition Centre
Xizhimennei Da Jie
Beiwacun L
Bei Lu
Zizhuyuan Lu
Xizhimenwai Da Jie
Chegongzhuang
Xi Lu
Chegongzhuang
Da Jie
Ping'anli Xida Jie
Fuchengmen Beida Jie
Baitasi Dong Jie
Xisi Beida Jie
Xihuangchenggen Jie
Xishiku Da Jie
Lu Xun Museum
Baiwanzhuang
Da Jie
Sanlihe
Zhantanguan
Lu
Fucheng Lu
Fuchengmenwai Da Jie
Fuchengmennei Da Jie
Geological Museum
YUYUANTAN PARK
Yuyuantan
Lake
Yuetan Bei Jie
Fuchengman Nanda Jie
Taipingqiao Da Jie
Xidan Beida Jie
Yuetan Nan Jie
Sanlihe
Dong Lu
Military Museum of the Chinese People's Revolution
Cultural Palace of the Nationalities
Fuxing Lu
Fuxingmenwai Da Jie
Fuxingmennei Da Jie
Zhong Lu
Yangfangdian Lu
Beifengwo Lu
Baiyun Lu
White Cloud Temple (Baiyun Guan)
Xinwenhua Jie
Xuanwumen Xida Jie
Lianhuachi Donglu
Guang'anmen
Changchun
Xuanwumenwai Da Jie
Liulichang Lu
Lianhuachi Xi Lu
Guang'anmenwai Da Jie
Guang'anmennei
Da Jie
Luomashi Da Jie
Lu
Guang'an
Maliandao Lu
Binhe Lu
Jie Niu Jie
Baiguang Lu
Nanheng Jie
Xisanhuan
Guang'anmen Staion
Baizhifang
Jie
You'anman
Sanluju Lu

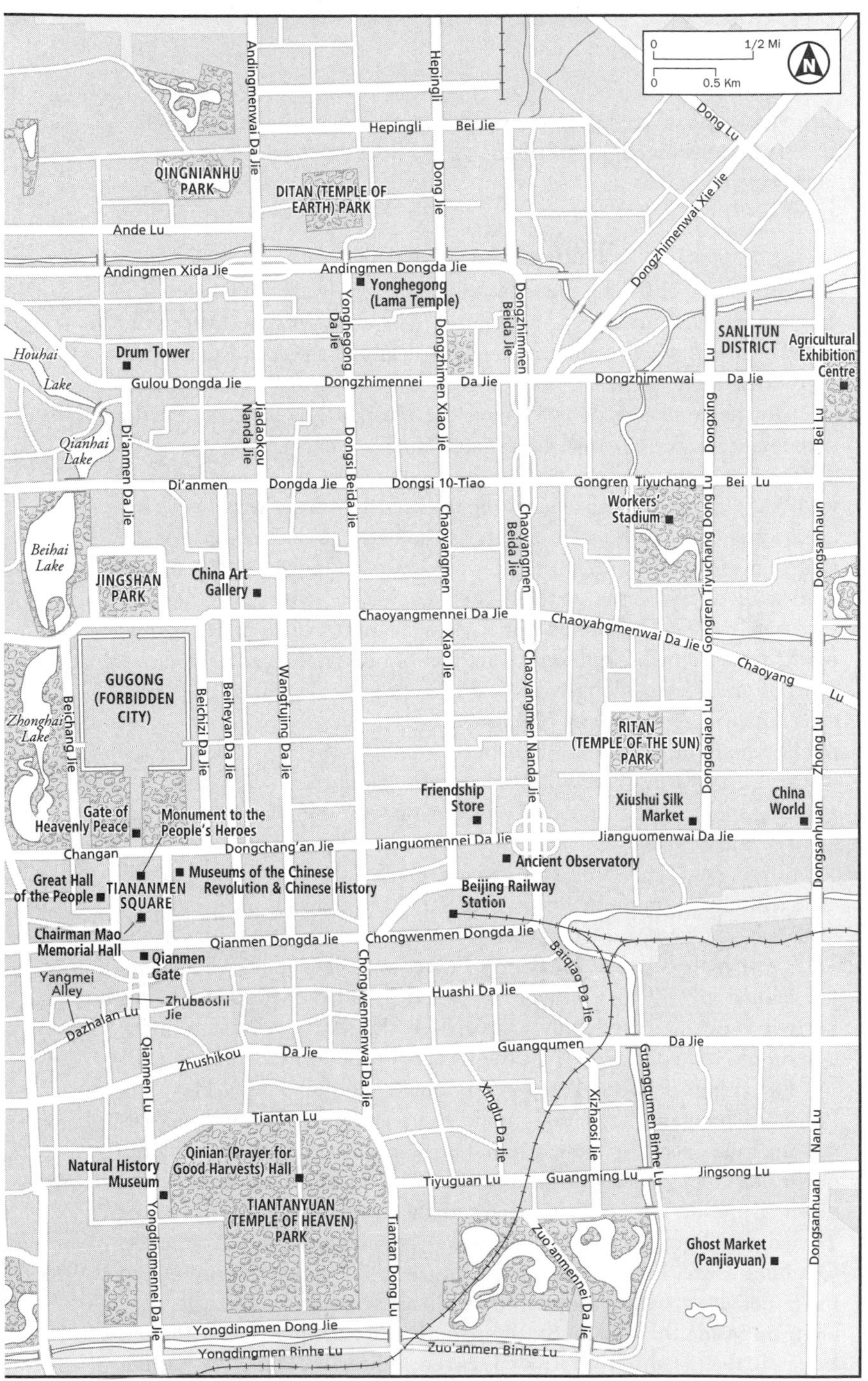

0
1/2 Mi
0
0.5 Km
N
QINGNIANHU PARK
DITAN (TEMPLE OF EARTH) PARK
Yonghegong (Lama Temple)
Drum Tower
Houhai Lake
Qianhai Lake
Beihai Lake
Zhonghai Lake
JINGSHAN PARK
China Art Gallery
GUGONG (FORBIDDEN CITY)
Gate of Heavenly Peace
Monument to the People's Heroes
Great Hall of the People
TIANANMEN SQUARE
Museums of the Chinese Revolution & Chinese History
Chairman Mao Memorial Hall
Qianmen Gate
Yangmei Alley
Zhubaoshi Jie
Dazhalan Lu
Zhushikou Da Jie
Natural History Museum
Qinian (Prayer for Good Harvests) Hall
TIANTANYUAN (TEMPLE OF HEAVEN) PARK
Friendship Store
Ancient Observatory
Beijing Railway Station
SANLITUN DISTRICT
Agricultural Exhibition Centre
Workers' Stadium
RITAN (TEMPLE OF THE SUN) PARK
Xiushui Silk Market
China World
Ghost Market (Panjiayuan)
Andingmenwai Da Jie
Hepingli
Hepingli Bei Jie
Dong Jie
Dong Lu
Dongzhimenwai Xie Jie
Ande Lu
Andingmen Xida Jie
Andingmen Dongda Jie
Yonghegong Da Jie
Dongzhimen Xiao Jie
Dongzhimen Beida Jie
Gulou Dongda Jie
Dongzhimennei Da Jie
Dongzhimenwai Da Jie
Dongxing Lu
Bei Lu
Jiadaokou Nanda Jie
Di'anmen Da Jie
Dongsi Beida Jie
Di'anmen Dongda Jie
Dongsi 10-Tiao
Gongren Tiyuchang Bei Lu
Chaoyangmen Xiao Jie
Chaoyangmen Beida Jie
Gongren Tiyuchang Dong Lu
Dongsanhuan Zhong Lu
Chaoyangmennei Da Jie
Chaoyahgmenwai Da Jie
Chaoyang Lu
Beichang Jie
Beichizi Da Jie
Beiheyan Da Jie
Wangfujing Da Jie
Chaoyangmen Nanda Jie
Dongdaqiao Lu
Changan
Dongchang'an Jie
Jianguomennei Da Jie
Jianguomenwai Da Jie
Qianmen Dongda Jie
Chongwenmen Dongda Jie
Baiqiao Da Jie
Chongwenmenwai Da Jie
Huashi Da Jie
Guangqumen Da Jie
Qianmen Lu
Guangqumen Binhe Lu
Xinglu Da Jie
Xizhaosi Jie
Tiantan Lu
Tiyuguan Lu
Guangming Lu
Jingsong Lu
Dongsanhuan Nan Lu
Yongdingmennei Da Jie
Tiantan Dong Lu
Zuo'anmennei Da Jie
Yongdingmen Dong Jie
Yongdingmen Binhe Lu
Zuo'anmen Binhe Lu

just what sights to see but how to experience them as deeply as possible. I won't skip the highlights of Beijing, but I do want to take you on some unexpected detours.

Tiananmen Square

This is the Eye of China, the focus of the nation. In the 20th century, it truly became the middle of the Middle Kingdom. In the 21st century many believe it will become the symbolic center of the Asia Pacific, perhaps even of the world.

Most foreigners recognize Tiananmen instantly as the stage for the democratic movement that culminated in the events of June 4, 1989. Tiananmen Square had been the focal point of earlier movements as well, and officials are no doubt hopeful that its image worldwide has been softened by such recent events as the national celebrations for the return of Hong Kong to Chinese sovereignty on July 1, 1997, and the 50th anniversary of the birth of the People's Republic, held here on October 1, 1999. Tiananmen Square was renovated in 1999, its cement blocks replaced by 1.7 million square feet of pink granite and some sections of green lawn, along with 4,535 lamps and a legion of blue trash cans. Chewing gum is now prohibited on the plaza. This is the largest public square in the world, as befits the most populous nation in the world. Every paving block of the square is numbered, partly so that a standing spot can be assigned to each person who attends one of China's great public forums.

Striking out across this wide expanse gives visitors the chance to orient themselves to monuments on every horizon, allowing the immensity of the place to become a microcosm for the immensity of China. On the north side is the **Gate of Heavenly Peace,** a viewing stand where Mao proclaimed in 1949 that China had stood up on the world stage. His portrait is on the gate, easily visible from the square. Under it is the entrance to the Forbidden City, the palaces of the former emperors.

The avenue between Tiananmen Square and the Gate of Heavenly Peace is **Changan,** the capital's main thoroughfare. It was widened, as was the square itself, in a massive public works program initiated by the new ruler, Mao Zedong, beginning in 1950. The city walls also came down. Opposite Changan Avenue and the Gate, on the south side of Tiananmen Square, is a monumental remnant of the city walls, **Qianmen Gate,** built in the 15th century as the southern entrance to the imperial city within Beijing, its two massive stone arches easily visible from inside the square. Straight south from the gate along the old Imperial Way is the **Temple of Heaven,** where the Ming and Qing emperors made annual sacrifices to Heaven.

On the east side, Tiananmen Square is bordered by the **Museum of Chinese History** and the **Museum of the Revolution.** On the west side is the **Great Hall of the People,** China's national hall of Congress, where the world's envoys meet China's leaders. Both these architectural giants are open to visitors, but both are a bit dull.

The **Monument to the People's Heroes** is in the center of the square. This granite obelisk was erected in 1958 to honor soldiers, farmers, and other patriots who became martyrs to the Communist Revolution. Ironically, it became the focal point of the martyrs to the democratic student movement in 1989. Bullet holes and other blemishes from that night have been removed, surveillance cameras remain on surrounding poles, and the marble platform can seem a haunted place even now.

From Tiananmen Square all roads radiate out, north to the Forbidden City, south to the Temple of Heaven, northeast to downtown shopping and the diplomatic missions, and northwest to the summer palaces. Tiananmen Square is open dawn to dusk daily. Admission is free.

Chairman Mao's Mausoleum

In the center of Tiananmen Square, aligned with the north–south axis that runs through the square and links the Forbidden City to the Temple of Heaven, is the **Chairman Mao Memorial Hall (Mao Zhuxi Jinian Bei).** It was completed in 1977, the year after Mao's death. You can join the long line outside, facing south, for a 60-second look at Mao lying in state in a crystal sarcophagus. He rests on a black granite slab from Mount Tai, recalling one of Mao's favorite quotations from China's Grand Historian: "Although death befalls all men alike, in significance it may be weightier than Mount Tai or lighter than a swan's down." Every evening Mao is lowered into the floor, to be refrigerated underground. At dawn, he rises with the sun in the east. The mausoleum reopened in 1998 after a 6-month cleanup. In its first 20 years, it chalked up 110 million visitors.

This is the quietest, cleanest, and most revered room in China. Cameras and handbags must be checked in booths outside, at a cost of RMB 8 ($1) per item. The Chairman Mao Mausoleum is open mornings Monday through Saturday 8:30 to 11:30am and on Monday, Wednesday, and Friday afternoons 2 to 4pm. Admission is free.

The Forbidden City

Site of the palaces of the Ming and Qing dynasties from 1421 to 1924, the Forbidden City (Gugong) is the work of one million laborers. The wall that encompasses its 9,000 rooms consists of 12 million bricks.

Another 20 million bricks ended up in the walls of pavilions and the surfaces of courtyards. Such is the scale of the Forbidden City, with its gorgeous glazed rooftops, red wooden columns, and uplifted eaves. It is a bewildering complex that defines the very word *imperial.* Deep, treeless courtyards are strung between the successive pavilions, with mazes of halls and walls inserted on either side. This is the largest palace enclosure in China, home to 24 emperors, closed off to all but members of the royal court and official delegations for 500 years.

Vastness, beauty, and pleasant confusion are the usual responses once you're inside the compound, and these might be all you take away, too, on the first visit. The best way to navigate and make some sense of this collection is by renting a tape machine as your guide at the entrance. This recorded walk-through hits the high points, identifying the major halls and important museum pieces on display inside, and helps you bring some sense to the welter of sights within the once-forbidden walls and the grand pavilions—the thrones, the furniture, the porcelains, the costumes.

It's important to hit the stop button often, however, and explore some of the side streets of the palace city. New exhibits open in different halls year-round, offering a chance to actually go inside one of the original buildings (entrances to the main interiors are now blocked off). There are exquisite gardens and lovely courtyards all along the main track, and special exhibits culled from the millions of artifacts owned by the Palace Museum are often placed on temporary display. Making your own detours is also a good way to get away from the newest entrepreneurs to be loosed upon the common visitor: the roving bands of vendors interrupting you, even grabbing your arm, in the hopes you'll buy postcards, souvenir albums, and other bounty.

The basic layout unfolds along a north–south axis (conceived of as beginning and ending at the center of the world, here where the second Ming emperor, Yongle, set to work on the Forbidden City in A.D. 1407). Enter under the **Gate of Heavenly Peace** (Tiananmen) on Changan Avenue, doff your worker's cap to Mao, and proceed straight ahead over the moats to **Meridian Gate** (Wumen), where emperors once reviewed their armies. It now houses the ticket booths for entrance into the Forbidden City. Five marble bridges cross the expanse of the first great courtyard, which leads to the final great entryway, the **Gate of Supreme Harmony (Tai He Dian),** guarded by stone lions. The immense space beyond is where the entire imperial court, 100,000 strong, was once convened, prostrate before the Son of Heaven who lived within. It's not difficult to imagine a crowd that immense these days, as the Forbidden City is one of the most popular attractions in the world. The best time to go is early in the morning before the crush begins.

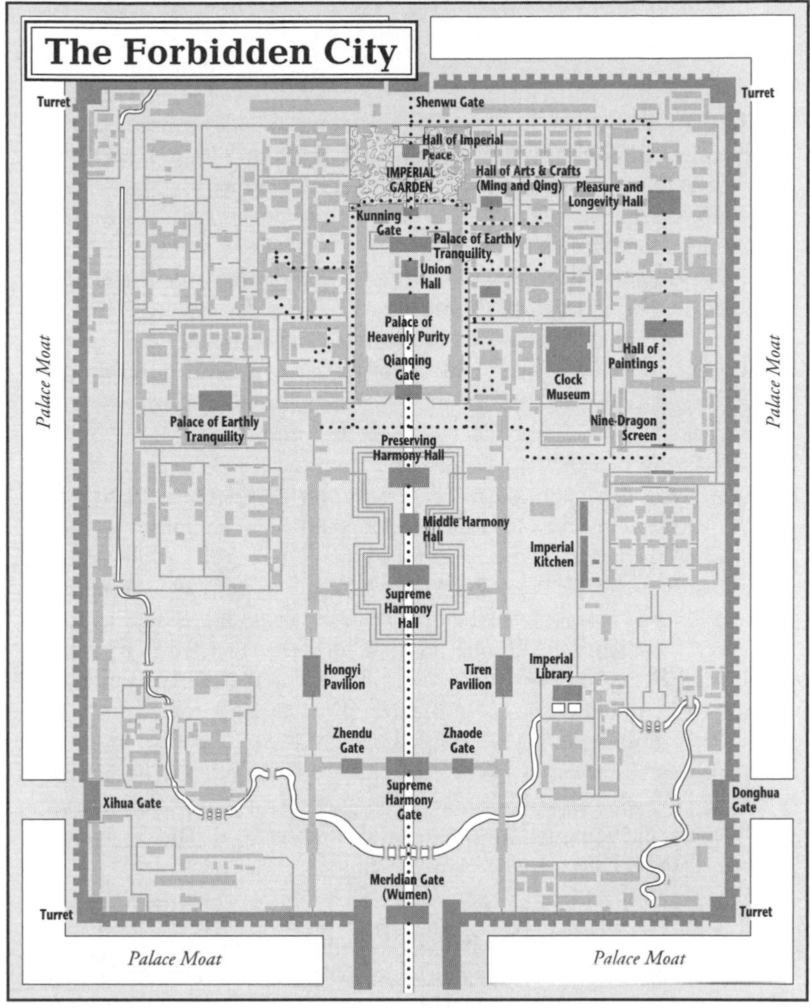

The first ceremonial hall, **Taihedian (Hall of Supreme Harmony),** raised upon a triple-tiered terrace and entered via a marble ramp with carved dragons, was the route followed by the emperor's sedan chair. Inside you can glimpse his golden dragon throne. The massive red columns are covered in a formula of tung oil, clay, hemp, and pig's blood. The **Hall of Middle Harmony (Zhonghedian),** a lesser throne room, is next in line. The third great hall, **Baohedian (Preserving Harmony),** was the venue for the state civil service examinations and royal banquets. Inside is a 250-ton marble block carved with dragons and clouds from the Ming Dynasty.

Beyond these three ceremonial halls are the three main living quarters of the rulers, retainers, and thousands of eunuchs. The first, the

Palace of Heavenly Purity (Qiangingong), once contained the emperor's bedroom; the second, the **Hall of Union (Jiaotaidian),** the throne of the empress; and the third, the **Palace of Earthly Tranquility (Kunningong),** the red wedding chamber where the last emperor, Pu Yi, was wedded as a child groom in 1922.

The emperors spent most of their time in the palaces along the west side of the Forbidden City. On the east side are palaces now serving as galleries to display the museum treasures of the Ming and Qing dynasties. One, Juxiandong, now houses the **Clock Museum,** probably the most fascinating small gallery in the Forbidden City, filled with old timepieces from the West collected by a Qing emperor.

Near the rear of the complex, the Kunning Gate opens onto the **Imperial Garden**'s ponds, halls, and rockeries. This is the place to rest, buy a drink or snack, and decide if you want to work your way back south into the heart of the palaces for a second look. You can always tag along with one of the dozens of tour groups that continually throng the courtyards and pavilions, their guides chanting facts and recounting lore in every major language. If you're overwhelmed or exhausted by your initial march, head to the exit just north of here, by the **Hall of Imperial Peace (Qinandian),** a shrine to Xuanwu, Daoist god of fire.

The Forbidden City is China's Grand Canyon, the nation's most magnificent spectacle, but it's so vast it numbs the mind. The Forbidden City is open 8:30am to 5pm daily (last tickets sold at 3:30pm). Full admission, including entrance to special exhibits, is RMB 55 ($6.60); audio rental of "acoustiguide" is RMB 25 ($3).

Summer Palace

In the summer, the emperors pulled up stakes, left the Forbidden City behind, and encamped in the pavilions on the lakeshores of Yiheyuan to the northwest. Summer palaces have existed here for at least 8 centuries, but Emperor Qianlong created the present one in the 18th century.

The Summer Palace is the loveliest imperial park in China, landscaped with gardens and graceful pavilions along the shores of Kunming Lake. It became the pleasure grounds of Empress Dowager Ci Xi (1835–1908), who ruled China during the decline of the Manchus. She rebuilt and restored the palace at a time when China needed the funds for its own defense. Particularly shocking was the construction of the infamous Marble Boat on the northern shore of the Summer Palace grounds. Local guides have dozens of stories describing Ci Xi's ruinous extravagances and Machiavellian political maneuvers, though it is doubtful that the empress dowager was really such a witch.

The main entrance is at the East Gate, site of the new **Cultural Relic Archive,** with 40,000 historic pieces displayed in a two-story Ming/Qing-style pavilion. The original palaces line **Longevity Hill (Wanshou Shan).** The empress dowager's throne is in the **Hall of Benevolence and Longevity (Renshoudian),** now something of a 19th-century furniture museum. Nearby is the **Palace of Virtue and Harmony (Deheyuan),** containing a three-level theater where the empress dowager sometimes played the role of Guanyin, Goddess of Mercy. **Jade Waves Palace (Yulantang)** was the residence of young Emperor Guangxu, in whose name Ci Xi was said to rule for 10 years. In the **Cloud-Dispelling Hall (Pianyundian),** Ci Xi received birthday greetings from her advisors. If you're curious about what she looked like, you can look at her famous portrait in oil here, painted by Hubert Voss in 1903.

The most delightful construction of the Summer Palace, the **Long Corridor (Changlang),** links these palaces to the Marble Boat. Running about a half mile along the lake, this undulating covered walkway is a gallery of scenes that forms an outdoor encyclopedia of Chinese geography, zoology, botany, and myth. Emperor Qianlong saw to its creation in 1750, the British and French burned it down in 1860, and the Empress Dowager resurrected it in 1888. The paintings that decorate the ceiling, beams, columns, and the four intersecting pavilions are crude but bright, like century-old cartoons that map the treasures of the Middle Kingdom. Group tours herd visitors the length of the Long Corridor without a break, but if there is anywhere to pause in Beijing, it is here. The lake scenery is fetching and the painted arcade is a naive and fascinating window on classic Chinese culture. Unfortunately, the crowds usually spill out of the Long Corridor, making peaceful contemplation impossible. Early mornings and evenings bring the only respites. Beijingers say that the Long Corridor is so long that couples who fall in love after they enter set the wedding date by the time they exit.

Beyond the **Marble Boat (Shifang),** looking like a sad cement pavilion in an old amusement park, is a dock where a large ornate ferry takes visitors back to the main gate, for RMB 10 ($1.20). The view of the hills and pavilions from the lake is almost as magical as the views from West Lake in Hangzhou, after which the empress dowager modeled many of the bridges, causeways, and pagodas of the New Summer Palace.

The Summer Palace is open 7am to 6:30pm (or until sunset) daily. Admission is RMB 30 ($3.75). Starting in late 1999, it became possible to travel to the Summer Palace the way the empress dowager did a century ago, by pleasure boat over the original waterway that led to the Forbidden City. At present there are two routes to the Summer Palace's

South Gate, one leaving eight times a day from Bayi Hu in Yuyuantan Park, the other leaving twice a day from the Exhibition Centre (Beizhan Houhu). Both voyages take about 50 minutes. Ordinary river boats cost RMB 40 ($5) one-way, RMB 70 ($8) round-trip; deluxe pleasure boats, RMB 50 ($6) one-way, RMB 80 ($10) round-trip. For exact schedules and new routes, contact hotel tour desks.

Old Summer Palace

Far less crowded is the Old Summer Palace (Yuanmingyuan), which was leveled by British and French troops in 1860 to punish the Chinese during the Opium Wars. The ruins, however, are haunting. Emperor Kangxi built this original summer palace on an even grander scale than his grandson, Emperor Qianlong, built the present Summer Palace. Kangxi's original contained over 200 pavilions, halls, gazebos, miradors, and man-made lakes stocked with goldfish and lotus. Deer and ducks inhabited the grounds. Curiously, some of the architecture was not Chinese but European; Jesuit missionaries in the Qing court were pressed into providing blueprints. Foreigners called the Old Summer Palace the Versailles of China, an apt comparison. In its day, it was the largest imperial garden in the world.

Time is running out on these ruins. Every year there's a new proposal to restore the Old Summer Palace, a tremendous mistake in my opinion, as these bare ruined choirs give voice to the splendors of the past far more eloquently than any modern copy could. Nevertheless, in 1999, a partial renovation was completed. Now there are pleasure boats for hire in the Fuhai Scenic area, Qichunyuan Square has new working fountains, and the labyrinth near Jianbi Pavilion has been restored.

The Old Summer Palace is just over a mile east of the New Summer Palace, but they are worlds apart. The ruins of the European gardens and Grand Fountains are in the easternmost sector, known as the **Garden of Eternal Spring (Changchunyuan).** Built between 1747 and 1759, these European buildings included a concert chamber, an aviary, a maze, and several kiosks, in addition to the fountains where water spouted from 12 stone animals that once constituted an ingenious water clock. The looting of the Old Summer Palace augmented the collections of the British Museum, as well as the private collections of Queen Victoria and Napoleon. The New Summer Palace was also looted, but the empress dowager rehabilitated it in 1888. Yet for all its beauty, it evokes little of the dark romance so palpable in the ruins of the Old Summer Palace.

My own visit there remains vivid in my mind, particularly because of one superb ruin, the **Hall of Tranquility**—the most perfect spot in all of Beijing for a picnic. The tumbled-down remains of the stone-and-marble arches and Greek columns that once graced the Grand Fountains, decorated in rococo and Qing patterns, elicit like no other ruins I've seen—even those in Ireland and Greece—the impermanence of man's grandest achievements. The Old Summer Palace is open from 6:30am to 7pm daily. Admission is RMB 10 ($1.25).

Temple of Heaven

Beijing's grand collection of Ming Dynasty architecture is in the **Temple of Heaven Park (Tiantanyuan),** about a mile due south of the old Qianmen Gate on Tiananmen Square. This was conceived of as the exact meeting point of Heaven and Earth by Emperor Yongle and his geomancers when they completed the round tower on its high square base in 1420. Here the Son of Heaven was obliged to perform sacrifices after praying for the year's good harvest. The annual procession to the Temple of Heaven was so sacred that the people of Beijing could not cast their eyes upon it, and the Temple of Heaven complex was itself a forbidden city until China became a republic in 1912.

The main entrance was traditionally from the south. The **Round Altar (Huanqiutan),** three marble tiers representing Earth, Man, and Heaven, was the Center of the World. It is said that an orator's voice originating from these tiers was magnified and could be heard for miles. Today, the acoustically inclined hasten to the next monument, **Echo Wall (Huiyinbi),** another round-walled platform where even a whisper directed into the wall is broadcast around the whole circle. I tested this several times, and it was possible to hear the words whispered from the opposite side. Of course, this phenomenon is transformed into babbling once Echo Wall is engulfed by visitors, all intent on using the wall phone at once.

The primary temple in this heavenly park is the **Hall for Prayer for Good Harvests (Qiniandian),** located to the north. It is one of the most remarkable buildings in China; a round tower capped by a magnificent three-tiered blue-tiled dome, paneled in the most ornate carvings ever produced in China. The vault, 120 feet high, is so perfectly fitted together that not a single nail was used. Fifty thousand glazed tiles coat the conical roof. Four inner columns (the Dragon Well Pillars), representing the four seasons, and two concentric sets of 12 outer pillars, for the months and the 2-hour units of the day, provide the support. The ceiling is a bright, dazzling dragon design. In 1889, a bolt of lightning destroyed the tower, but it has been faithfully reconstructed. These days, visitors can only peer into the grand interior. A decade ago, it was possible to walk inside and feel the full pull of the ancient cosmos.

The park is most heavenly these days in the early morning, before the tour buses pull up. Locals gather for morning exercises: *tai ji quan* (shadow boxing), sword practice, and strange forms of *qi gong* (a channeling of internal energies). The retired men stake out benches and display their caged songbirds and crickets. College students, seeking solitude and space for study, pore over their books on benches under an old cypress grove inside the western gate. There the main road (Qianmen Lu) leads straight back the 3 miles to Tiananmen Square. The Temple of Heaven is open daily from 5am to 9:30pm in summer and from 8am to 5:30pm in winter. Admission is RMB 30 ($3.75).

Lama Temple

Beijing's premier temple, locals agree, is the Lama Temple (Yonghegong), northeast of Tiananmen Square, just inside the Second Ring Road. It first served as Emperor Yongzheng's mansion. Emperor Qianlong, his successor, consecrated it as a lamasery in 1744 and hired 500 lamas from Mongolia to run it. In the early 20th century it served as the Bureau of Mongolian and Tibetan Affairs, reverting in recent times to its original functions.

Part of its attraction is its grand scale. The **Hall of the Heavenly Kings** contains Maitreya, the Buddha of the Future, smiling broadly on all visitors. Four celestial guardians, one for each cardinal direction, each accompanied by eight of his top generals, protect the Buddha from a horde of demons. Next in line is the **Hall of Harmony (Yonghedian),** with Buddhas of the past, present, and future. The layout is a lengthy one. In the fourth hall, **Falundian,** the eastern wing contains statuary locked in amorous embraces. They are usually covered in scarves that serve as fig leaves. These and other draped statues in the Lama Temple are regarded as China's Kama Sutra, reputedly serving as an illustrated sex manual for the sons of emperors. As late as the 1930s, the Lama Temple still had an aura of the forbidden about it. "Devil dances," which included rituals imitating human sacrifice, were regularly performed.

The final great hall is the tallest: the **Tower of the Great Buddha (Wangfuge).** Inside is a second rendition of the Buddha of the Future, standing 75 feet tall. This sandalwood colossus, a gift to Emperor Qianlong from the seventh Dalai Lama, is considered the largest sculpture ever carved from a single piece of wood. It was here that the Dalai Lama's followers once held sway.

The Lama Temple is open from 9am to 4pm Tuesday through Sunday, with admission RMB 15 ($1.85). The temple is always busy not only with local visitors and Chinese worshippers but with at least 70 monks in brown robes, heads shaven. If this complex doesn't leave you "templed out," nothing will. My favorite retreat from the crowds is a side tower, the **Pavilion of Perpetual Peace,** which contains a large prayer wheel suspended from its ceiling. The Lama Temple has enough diversions and pavilions scattered through its five courtyards to provide hours of quiet diversion. Sometimes you can still hear bronze bells suspended from the yellow-tiled eaves singing in the breeze that rocks the swaying bamboo.

White Cloud Temple

Less touristy and more fascinating than the Lama Temple is the White Cloud Temple (Baiyun Guan) in the western Xuanwu District. This is Beijing's most popular Daoist shrine, a favorite of locals, who flock here to burn incense and perform a number of curious rites in the hopes that the gods will answer their prayers. There are pavilions, halls, and temples that cater to a variety of desires, from passing the college entrance exam to having a healthy baby boy. There's even a hall dedicated to eyes and curing the problems of failing eyesight. The faithful will rub their hands on various golden statues and other images and relics, kowtow before the temple statues, and check on their life expectancy at a hall of the zodiac. This is a very active temple, far more local and vital than many of the other temples in Beijing; at the rear of the complex is a rock garden where I've often seen novice monks in training. The very best time to drop in on this colorful scene is on a festival day, which occurs on the first and 15th of every lunar month. The White Cloud Temple, at 6 Baiyuguan Lu, is open daily from 8:30am to 4:30pm. Admission is RMB 8 ($1).

Star Gazing

In 1422, just after the Forbidden City was finished, a celestial observatory was built on a corner of the city wall. The Chinese were keen observers of the heavens (of whom the emperor was the son). The observatory in Beijing became the most important in the Middle Kingdom. In the early 1600s, Jesuit missionaries in the capital introduced Western methods of astronomy, hoping to attract converts to Christianity through their ability to predict eclipses. Several of the instruments designed by the Jesuits remain on the roof of the **Ancient Observatory (Guguanxiangtai)** today. The observatory is located on the south side of Jianguomenwai Dajie—the eastern portion of Changan Avenue—where it seems like a stranded piece of history, a Ming Dynasty terrace clinging to the last surviving block of the old city wall.

The Ancient Observatory is an incongruity, located as it is in the heart of Beijing's heaviest traffic and newest office complexes, but it is also a graceful reminder of the imperial past. The eight bronze astronomical instruments on the open roof are visible for better than a mile up and down the busy avenue. Displays inside the two-story museum are usually replicas rather than originals, but the gold foil atlas of the stars, based on Tang Dynasty observations, shows how the Chinese mapped the sky, creating constellations unknown to the West.

This is the ideal place to take a break, both in time and space, if you're walking the seemingly endless street east from Tiananmen Square. The dragon quadrant, celestial globe, ecliptic armilla, theodolite, sextant, zodiac, and other instruments date from the early Qing Dynasty. Whether they are originals or copies isn't clear—not that it matters. The effect is of an antique world, its eyes fixed on the cosmos and its instruments, mounted on a garden terrace, as beautiful as a starry, unpolluted night. The Ancient Observatory is open Wednesday through Sunday from 9 to 11:30am and from 1 to 4:30pm. Admission is RMB 10 ($1.20).

Streets & Alleys

Once you gorge yourself on the highlights of old Beijing, you're ready to wander its streets. There are dozens of other museums, temples, and parks to visit, but time quickly runs out. To miss out on exploring the streets is to miss the experience of China's modern capital.

The essential architecture of Beijing is not that of the temple or palace but of the courtyard homes and the narrow alleyways, called *hutongs.* The most interesting group to join in Beijing is the **Hutong Tour,** first organized by a local photographer devoted to urban preservation. Bicycle rickshaws do the heavy work, slicing through the impossible traffic snarls from the back entrance of Beihai Park, along Shisha Lake, down to the old **Drum Tower.** The Drum Tower contains an exhibit of hutong photographs. The tour group finishes up with tea in an elaborate courtyard mansion. The **Beijing Hutong Tourist Agency** (☎ 010/6615-9097) handles two tours daily, starting at 9am and 2pm. They cost RMB 240 ($30) and can be booked directly or through hotel travel desks.

The backstreets of old Beijing are fast disappearing, but the **Qianmen District** on the south end of Tiananmen Square is a fine place to wander in search of traditional shops, lanes, and hutongs. Start on the southwest side of the traffic circle, walk southeast through the sidewalk vendors, and turn straight down Jewelry Street (Zhubaoshi Jie). The entrance to Jewelry Street is marked by a large bicycle billboard. This street runs north and south parallel to Qianmen Dajie—the old Imperial Way—and constitutes one of the more crowded outdoor markets in

Beijing. After about 4 blocks, take a right west on Dazhalan Lu (Dahalar Street). Behind the Qing Dynasty facades lining this old theater street are traditional pharmacies and silk shops. At no. 18 Dazhalan Lu is Beijing's **Underground City,** the remains of the elaborate air-raid shelter system, built by hand, that Chairman Mao initiated during the Cold War standoff with the Soviet Union more than 30 years ago. There's not only shopping down there these days but also an underground hotel.

Meanwhile, back on Earth, go about a quarter mile west on Dazhalan Lu, past tea shops and herbal medicine stores, and take a turn north and then west along Yangmei Alley, a hutong of crowded courtyards. The alley soon joins **Liulichang Lu,** Beijing's most famous avenue of antiques. Most of the buildings along here were rebuilt in recent times to resemble an old shopping district. The curio shops, bookstores, musical instrument showrooms, and art galleries here are among the best in China. **Rongbaozhai,** at 64 Liulichang, is the most highly regarded art store in the country.

Markets

While the shops are fascinating in the Liulichang District, the prices are far better east of Tiananmen Square at the **Xiushui Silk Market** and the **Friendship Store.** Changan Avenue turns into Jianguomenwei Dajie as it heads east toward the Ancient Observatory. Keep on the north side for the Friendship Store, the largest in China, with its floors of gifts, crafts, foods, and sundries. The Silk Market is located between the Friendship Store and the Jianguo Hotel. It is a series of stalls pinched into several narrow alleyways. You won't find much silk here, but you will find plenty of sportswear. Get there early to avoid the rush. Prices on clothing of all sorts, including designer labels, can be very low, but be sure to pay no more than half the vendor's initial asking price.

A far more interesting market is **Panjiayuan,** known locally as the Ghost Market, the Dirt Market, or the Sunday Market—because shortly after dawn every Sunday morning is the best time to visit. The market is a ways south of downtown, just inside the Third Ring Road on Huaweiqiaoxi Nan Dajie; take a cab. The emphasis here is on collectibles, which includes family heirlooms, antique furniture, ceramics, statues, and scrolls. In aisles under canvas canopies, several thousand vendors spread out their wares and upwards of 100,000 browsers take a look. There are special aisles for jade, teapots, and folk crafts. Last time I visited on a Sunday morning there was even an upright piano for sale, as well as treadle sewing machines.

Wangfujing Shopping Street

My favorite shopping ramble is into the heart of the city on **Wangfujing Street,** which runs north off Changan Avenue a few blocks east of Tiananmen Square. Begin this jaunt by cutting through the **Beijing Hotel.** If you walk through its main corridor from west to east, you'll be walking through an innkeeper's time capsule of grand accommodations in Beijing. The oldest section, in the middle of the long edifice, dates from 1917. The rooms here are in the French style with brocade wallpapers. The west wing, conjoined in 1954, has a magnificent dining hall up the north stairs. The east wing, added in 1974 and remodeled in 1990, contains 600 modern luxury rooms (but not with service to match). The cathedral ceilings and sweeping staircases run the length of this landmark. On its east corner is Wangfujing Street.

Before Liberation in 1949, Wangfujing Lu (Goldfish Lane) was known as Morrison Street. It catered to China's richest Westerners. Nowadays, Wangfujing caters to China's richest Chinese. The new **Sun Dong An Plaza,** one of China's largest shopping and office complexes, 11 stories of steel and glass and underground parking, intended as a "reconstruction" of the century-old Dong An Market, epitomizes the upscale shopping along Wangfujing. Actually, the street contains a wide range of shops and restaurants, from McDonald's to hole-in-the-wall steamed-dumpling shops, from Louis Vuitton to a local specialty shop selling nothing but stuffed animals. The farther you push up Wangfujing, the more traditional and varied the stores. The **Chinese department stores** are particularly worth browsing. They feature an increasingly large range of imported commodities, always have an immense uniformed sales staff on the floor, and frequently put on good old-fashioned demonstrations of their goods right in the aisles. I've seen salespeople try out the latest electronic acupressure devices on shoppers, and I've seen both men and women sitting beside counters receiving demonstration hair dyes, their friends and everyone else crowding in for a closer look. Wangfujing received a face-lift late in 1999, complete with fresh new granite slabs on its sidewalks, golden placards identifying its most famous stores, and special police patrols levying heavy fines for littering and spitting. At night it is ablaze with neon lights, much like Hong Kong.

Bars & Teahouses

Beijing's most international neighborhood these days is the **Sanlitun District,** northeast of Tiananmen Square, on the west side of the Third

Ring Road, not far from the congregation of foreign-based hotels and businesses (Sheraton Great Wall, Kempinski Hotel, Lufthansa Centre, Hard Rock Cafe). To reach the outdoor cafes, bars, and small shops that cater to foreigners and hip Beijingers, walk west from the Kunlun Hotel to the Huadu Hotel, turn south (left) on Sanlitun Bei Lu, and follow this tree-lined boulevard past Embassy Row a good 6 blocks. Just north of Gongrentiyuchang Bei Lu, Sanlitun is occupied by dozens of cafes with outdoor seating. Clothing stalls, cheese shops, and other private businesses are booming along here, too.

This is Beijing's best (and perhaps only) real place to hang out. When the weather is good, hundreds of expatriates and foreign travelers drop by, unwind in one of the cafes, and enjoy life as it passes. The German-style **Kebab Cafe,** with plenty of outdoor seating, a full international menu, and imported beers (all at imported prices), is my favorite. Stacks of pirated music tapes and CDs are hawked from table to table all along Sanlitun, priced at about $2 (with no guarantee of quality, of course). New eating and drinking outlets spring up every few weeks, as the demand for international venues continues to outrun supply. Ten years ago, finding an English-language menu, let alone a German beer, outside of the big hotels in Beijing was something of a fool's errand. Today it's a hot business.

Equally trendy in this surprisingly trendy city are the teahouses, which are more in keeping with the legacies of the capital. Teahouses once drew in Beijing's literate and wealthy residents, its mandarins, for an evening devoted to the arts and spirited conversation. **Tian Hai Tea House** (located in a hutong just north of Gongrentiyuchang Bei Lu, off Sanlitun; ☎ 010/6416-5676) is among the newest attempts to return to that tradition. The interiors of the teahouse, designed by Beijing artist Son Xiao Hong and his daughter, Song Hui Bin, evoke Qing Dynasty days with their dark woods, bamboos, and wall paintings. Waiters and waitresses dress up in royal costumes. On weekends, musicians take up traditional instruments, such as the *erhu* and *pippa,* and Peking opera stars drop in to conduct sing-alongs. The teas of the teahouse are green and jasmine, but fruit flavors have been added, and the menu of northern Chinese steamed snacks and noodles is augmented by salads and ice-cream treats.

Curiously, these new teahouses, based on old traditions, embody the rising spirit of modern Beijing. In this city, East seems more comfortable with West than ever before, the past keeps finding new ways into the present, and people seem confident of playing a leading role in the future not just of China but of the world.

PRACTICAL INFORMATION

ORIENTATION & WHEN TO GO

Beijing, located in northeast China, is the country's capital and its most popular tourist destination. It's also its own municipality, not part of a province. Summers are quite hot, winters quite cold. Visit in late April, May, October, or November for warm, dry weather. Early spring brings dust storms from the Gobi Desert.

The most popular day trip from Beijing is the **Great Wall** (see the next chapter), 2 hours by bus or car to the north. **Chengde** (see separate chapter in this section), an imperial city 4 hours to the northeast, requires an overnight stay. Arrangements to visit these sites are provided by hotel tour desks and China International Travel Service (CITS).

GETTING THERE

By Plane Beijing's **Capital Airport** (☎ 010/6456-3604) has connections to major destinations inside and outside of China. The new terminal opened here on November 1, 1999, with improved services. Over 30 international airlines serve Beijing, including **United Airlines** (☎ 800/241-6522 in the U.S., 010/6463-8551 in China), **Qantas Airlines** (☎ 800/227-4500 in the U.S., 010/6467-4794 in China), **Northwest Airlines** (☎ 800/225-2525 in the U.S., 010/6505-3505 in China), **British Airways** (☎ 800/247-9297 in the U.S., 010/6512-4070 in China), and **Canadian Airlines** (☎ 800/426-7000 in the U.S., 010/6463-7906 in China). The city's hotels have service desks at the main airport exit. Several branches of the Bank of China will exchange foreign currencies for **renminbi** (RMB). The airport is only 17 miles northeast of the city, but allow at least an hour for the transfer. Airport buses directly outside the main entrance serve several downtown hotels and the central train station; they cost RMB 16 ($2). Inquire about their routes at the Air Bus service counter, as these can change. Taxis cost RMB 100 ($12) or more. Red cabs charge more than yellow cabs. Many hotels provide free airport shuttles, especially if you send a request ahead by fax with your arrival time.

By Train From Beijing's **Main Railway Station (Beijing Zhan)** or **West Station (Xi Zhan),** the largest train station in the world, there are trains to virtually every city and town in China. The newest rail service is the train route launched to celebrate Hong Kong's return to sovereignty in 1997, connecting Beijing and Hong Kong via China's most deluxe train (Train no. 97 to Hong Kong; Train no. 98 return).

GETTING AROUND

Equipped with a map, you can see most of the attractions yourself by foot, by taxi, or by subway. The **subway system** is modern, clean, easy to navigate, and impervious to traffic jams. Hours of operation are 5:30am to 11pm daily. Tickets are RMB 2 (25¢) per trip. Station arrivals are announced in English and Chinese. The crosstown line (Line no. 2 running east and west along Changan Avenue) has just opened. If you use a **taxi** instead, make

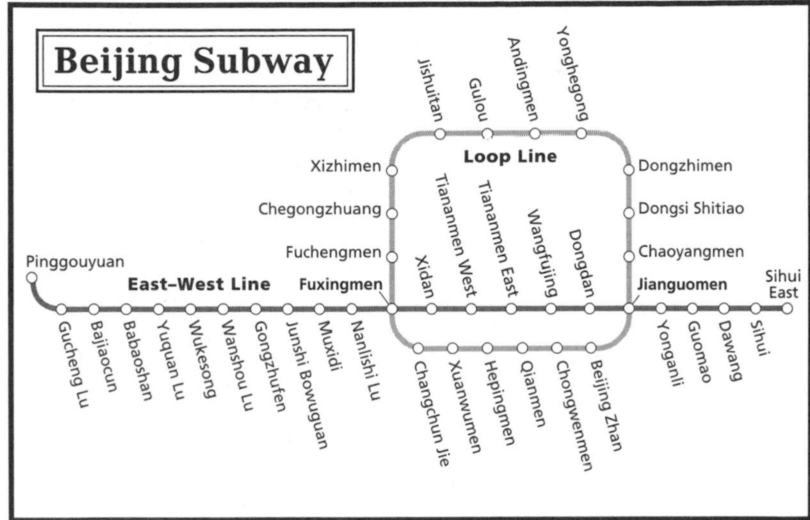

sure it has its meter running (say "da biao"). The best taxis (usually new Volkswagen "Santanas") charge RMB 12 ($1.50) for the first 4 kilometers and RMB 2 (25¢) for each additional kilometer, making taxis a fairly economical way of getting about the city. Many hotels rent **bicycles** (about $3 per hour). Beijing has millions of bikes on the streets at any one time, and there is safety in numbers. If you stay off the big streets and follow the bike flow, you'll be surprised how easy bike riding is in Beijing.

TOURS & STRATAGEMS

Tours China International Travel Service (CITS), with headquarters at 28 Jianguomenwai Dajie (☎ 010/6515-8652; fax 010/6515-8603), arranges guided tours (available in 12 languages) to all major sites. CITS maintains convenient branches in most hotels, and has also opened a second office at 103 Fuxingmennei Dajie, Room 417 (☎ 010/6607-1575; fax 010/6608-7124), open Monday to Friday from 8:30am to 5:30pm. Hotel tour desks can book airline and train tickets. **American Express,** with offices in the China World Trade Center, Tower 1, Room 2101, 1 Jianguomenwai Dajie, can be contacted at ☎ 010/6505-2888, but American Express travel services are now handled at the new CITS office on Fuxingmennei Dajie. The 24-hour Beijing **tourist hot line** number is ☎ 010/6513-0828.

WHERE TO STAY

Beijing has a fuller range of hotels than any other city in China except Hong Kong, featuring such international chains as Shangri-La, Holiday Inn, Sheraton, Hilton, New Otani, Kempinski, Movenpick, and Radisson. Top choices are listed here. Note that, although hotels frequently list room rates in U.S. dollars, they generally only accept credit cards or Chinese currency as payment.

Beijing Hilton Hotel (Xierdun Fandian). *1 Dongfang Lu, Dongsanhuan Beilu (west side of Third Ring Rd. N., north of Xinyuan Nanlu), Beijing 100027.* ☎ *800/445-8667 in U.S. and*

Canada, or 010/6466-2288. Fax 010/6465-3052. 363 units, including 24 suites. A/C MINIBAR TV TEL. $200 double. AE, DC, JCB, MC, V. This hotel is justifiably noted for its international atmosphere, efficient services, and fine restaurants—it's a favorite of many Western business travelers. The rooms are well kept up; bathrooms are equipped with separate showers and tubs. There are two rooms for travelers with disabilities and three nonsmoking floors. Jazz is a theme woven through the hotel's restaurants and bars.

Dining: The Louisiana, with Cajun dishes and a fine wine list, is often cited as the best Western restaurant in Beijing. There are also restaurants specializing in Japanese, Cantonese, and international dishes.

Amenities: Indoor swimming pool, Clark Hatch fitness club, massage, Jacuzzi, sauna, two squash courts, one outdoor tennis court, bicycle rentals, small 24-hour business center, conference rooms, tour desk, beauty salon, newsstand, boutique, brandy shop, concierge, valet, 24-hour room service, same-day laundry and dry cleaning, nightly turndown, newspaper delivery, baby-sitting, wheelchairs.

Beijing International Club Hotel (Guoji Julebu Fandian). *21 Jianguomenwai Dajie (entrance 1 block north on west side of Xiushui Jie), Beijing 100020.* ☎ *800/325-3589 in U.S. and Canada, 0800/973-119 in U.K., 1800/814-812 in Australia, 0800/44 5309 in New Zealand, 1800/597-000 in Ireland, or 010/6460-6688. Fax 010/6460-3299.* www.sheraton.com. *287 units, including 145 suites. A/C MINIBAR TV TEL. $390 double. AE, DC, JCB, MC, V.* The lobby of this 19-story boutique hotel is the most spectacular in Beijing. This Sheraton-managed property presently shares health and athletic facilities with the neighboring (and historic) Beijing International Club, but its own swimming pool and other hotel facilities are to be constructed in the future. Guest rooms are large; bathrooms sport separate bathtubs and showers; and there's 24-hour butler service on all floors. Everything is highly stylish.

Dining: Danieli's is a southern Italian brasserie; Tokyo Aoyama Mangetsu does sushi and teppanyaki; Celestial Court offers Cantonese; the palm tree-lined Garden Lounge does afternoon teas; and the Press Club Bar, decorated with mementos of diplomats and international correspondents, changes its snacks daily.

Amenities: Small fitness center, 24-hour business center, conference rooms, beauty salon, newsstand, concierge, 24-hour room service, same-day laundry and dry cleaning, newspaper delivery, nightly turndown, twice-daily maid service, 24-hour personal butler service.

Beijing Song He Hotel (Songhe Da Jiudian). *88 Dengshikuo Jie (just off Wangfujing Dajie, south from the Holiday Inn Crowne Plaza), Beijing 100006.* ☎ *010/6513-8822. Fax 010/6513-9088. 310 units. A/C MINIBAR TV TEL. $90 double. AE, MC, V.* This three-star hotel is now under local management. Its rooms are clean and modern, but its amenities are simple (no hair dryer, no coffeemaker, no CNN). The top floor (11) is for nonsmoking guests. The downtown location and adequate maintenance make it a good buy.

Dining: The Sawasdee Restaurant has some of Beijing's best Thai buffets (lunch and dinner). The Song He Coffee Shop serves inexpensive buffet breakfasts and à la carte lunch and dinner choices (Western and Asian cuisines).

Amenities: Small health club, sauna, massage, small business center, conference rooms, tour desk, beauty salon, shops, newsstand, 24-hour room service, same-day laundry and dry cleaning services.

China World Hotel (Zhongguo Da Fandian). *1 Jianguomenwai Dajie (on northwest corner of Third Ring Rd.), Beijing 100004.* ☎ *800/942-5050 in U.S. and Canada, 1800/222-448 in Australia, 0800/442-179 in New Zealand, 181/747-8485 in London, or 010/6505-2266. Fax 010/6505-3167.* www.shangri-la.com. *738 units, including 56 suites. A/C MINIBAR TV TEL. $230 double. Children under 18 stay free in parents' room. AE, DC, JCB, MC, V.* China World, managed by Shangri-La, is frequently rated by international business magazines as one of the top 100 hotels in the world and is still the best in Beijing. It combines attentive service with deluxe facilities. Its newly expanded business center is the best in the capital. There are 221 nonsmoking guest rooms. All rooms contain plenty of counter space, a writing desk, bright lighting, and data ports for PCs. This is the hotel of choice for many CEOs and world leaders.

Dining/Diversions: The Summer Palace is one of the top Cantonese restaurants in Beijing, and Nadaman is one of the top Japanese restaurants as well. A classical orchestra performs at Sunday brunch in the lobby. Aria, with its jazz and wine bar, is one of the trendiest new dining spots. Henry J. Bean's, an American bar and grill, is across the street, and China's first Starbucks coffee bar is in the shopping center basement.

Amenities: Large indoor swimming pool (22 meters), extensive health and fitness club, Jacuzzi, sauna, solarium, three indoor tennis courts, squash courts, aerobic dance studio, bowling alley, jogging routes, two driving ranges, one putting green, two golf-simulator machines, 24-hour business center (Beijing's largest), conference rooms, beauty salon, newsstand, crafts shop, shopping plaza, concierge, valet, 24-hour room service, same-day laundry and dry cleaning, newspaper delivery, nightly turndown, twice-daily maid service.

Holiday Inn Crowne Plaza (Guoji Yiyuan Huangguan Jiari Fandian). *48 Wangfujing Dajie (corner of Dengshikou Dajie), Beijing 100006.* ☎ *800/465-4329 in U.S. and Canada, 1800/221-066 in Australia, 0800/442-222 in New Zealand, 1800/553-155 in Ireland, 0800/897-121 in U.K., or 010/6513-3388. Fax 010/6513-2513.* www.crowneplaza.com. *E-mail:* HICPB@public3.bta.net.cn. *385 units. A/C MINIBAR TV TEL. $220 double. Children under 19 stay free in parents' room. AE, DC, JCB, MC, V.* This hotel features a skylit atrium open to all nine floors and an art theme underlined by a sales gallery of contemporary Chinese work off the lobby and an art salon on the second floor mezzanine. The staff is very helpful. Rooms are small for a five-star hotel, but stuffed with lavish amenities, and the city-center location is convenient.

Dining: The Atrium Coffee Shop serves international buffets, the Pearl Garden specializes in Cantonese dishes and dim sum, and the elegant Plaza Grill on the atrium mezzanine is one of Beijing's top French restaurants.

Amenities: Indoor swimming pool (with city view), small health club, Jacuzzi, sauna, solarium, bicycle rental, small 24-hour business center (e-mail, PC rental), conference rooms, tour desk (Panda city tours), beauty salon, shops (antiques, souvenirs, sundries), 24-hour room service, same-day laundry and dry cleaning services, newspaper delivery, nightly turndown, baby-sitting.

Holiday Inn Downtown (Jindu Jiari Fandian). *98 Beilishi Lu (Xicheng District, northwest corner of Fuchengmenwai Dajie and Second Ring Rd. W.), Beijing 100006. ☎ 800/465-4329 in U.S. and Canada, 1800/221-066 in Australia, 0800/442-222 in New Zealand, 1800/553-155 in Ireland, 0800/897-121 in U.K., or 010/6833-8822. Fax 010/6834-0696.* www.holiday-inn.com. *346 units, including 20 suites. A/C MINIBAR TV TEL. $130 double. Children under 19 stay free in parents' room. AE, DC, JCB, MC, V.* Formerly Beijing's best three-star international hotel hands-down, the Holiday Inn Downtown has been upgraded to four stars, which better describes its service level. The rooms are spacious, clean, and well equipped; bathrooms are small but spotless. This is an American-style hotel with good service.

Dining: Beijing's first Indian restaurant, Shamiana, serves superb lunches and dinners. The Oasis Coffee House has Western and Asian buffets and à la carte selections.

Amenities: Small indoor swimming pool, health club, Jacuzzi, sauna, business center, conference rooms, tour desk, air ticket office, beauty salon, shops, newsstand, 24-hour room service, same-day laundry and dry cleaning services, newspaper delivery, nightly turndown, baby-sitting.

Holiday Inn Lido (Lidu Jiari Fandian). *Jichang Lu, Jiangtai Lu (Chaoyang District, east side of Airport Expressway, 10.5 miles southwest of Capital Airport), Beijing 100004. ☎ 800/465-4329 in U.S. and Canada, 1800/221-066 in Australia, 0800/442-222 in New Zealand, 1800/553-55 in Ireland, 0800/897-121 in U.K., or 010/6437-6688. Fax 010/6437-6237.* www.holiday-inn.com. *E-mail:* lido@ht.rol.cn.net. *720 units, including 76 suites. A/C MINIBAR TV TEL. $190 double. Children under 19 stay free in parents' room. AE, DC, JCB, MC, V.* The world's largest Holiday Inn, located beyond the Fourth Ring Road on the expressway to the airport, is a city within a city. It's a four-star hotel, but its facilities—ranging from bank and shoe repair to drugstore and supermarket—exceed those of most five-star hotels. The rooms are large, the bathrooms tidy. The Lido provides a free downtown shuttle bus with four stops from 7:40am to 7:30pm daily, and also an airport shuttle with service roughly every hour.

Dining/Diversions: The Lido offers excellent Thai (Borom Piman), Mexican (Texan Bar and Grill), Shanghainese (Lao Shanghai), Cantonese, Beijing fast food, German, and Italian restaurants. Galateria is Beijing's first ice cream parlor. Nightlife outlets include an English-style pub, a sports bar, and a disco.

Amenities: Indoor swimming pool (14 meters), health club, 20-lane bowling center, Jacuzzi, sauna, tennis courts, 24-hour business center, conference rooms, tour desk, United/Lufthansa air ticket office, beauty salon, large shopping arcade, newsstand, Watson's Drug Store, Lido Supermarket, Bank of China, post office, Kodak express film developing shop, medical clinic, shoe repair, florist, 24-hour room service, same-day laundry and dry cleaning services, newspaper delivery, nightly turndown, baby-sitting, bicycle rental.

Jianguo Hotel (Jianguo Fandian). *5 Jianguomenwai Dajie (north side of street, 1 block east of Silk Alley), Beijing 100020. ☎ 800/223-5652 in U.S. and Canada, 0800/898-852 in U.K., 1800/ 553-549 in Australia, or 010/6500-2233. Fax 010/6500-2871.*

www. hoteljianguo.com. *E-mail:* exec@ hoteljianguo.com. *399 units, including 67 suites (some with kitchenette). A/C MINIBAR TV TEL. $190 double (including breakfast), $115 in winter. AE, DISC, JCB, MC, V.* This landmark spot was the first joint venture hotel in China (built in 1982). For 2 decades it was the expatriate community's favorite meeting place in Beijing. The hotel still maintains a lively lobby under its golden chandelier.

Dining/Diversions: Justine's is a romantic spot for fine French and continental dishes. Four Seasons presents Cantonese cuisine in elegant surroundings. Charlie's American Bar is a mainstay for drinks. The lobby is the setting for buffets, afternoon tea, and an elaborate Sunday brunch with live classical music.

Amenities: Indoor swimming pool, health club, Jacuzzi, sauna, acupuncture and massage parlor, conference rooms, 24-hour business center, tour desk, beauty salon, shopping arcade, 24-hour room service, same-day laundry and dry cleaning services, bicycle rental.

Jinglun Hotel (Jinglun Fandian). *3 Jianguomenwai Dajie (next to Jiangguo Hotel, north side of street), Beijing 100020.* ☎ *800/645-5687 in U.S. and Canada, 0800/282-502 in U.K., or 010/6500-2266. Fax 010/6500-2022.* www.jinglunhotel.com. *E-mail:* jinglun@ public3.bta.net.cn. *558 units, including 22 suites. A/C MINIBAR TV TEL. $180 double. AE, DISC, JCB, MC, V.* The former Beijing-Toronto Hotel (Jinglun means Toronto) is now managed by Nikko Hotels International, which maintains its high levels of service and upkeep. Rooms are modern and clean, with hot water thermoses (no coffeemakers); bathrooms are compact. The hotel maintains an airport shuttle bus.

Dining: The Si He Xuan features Beijing's best local cuisine.

Amenities: Indoor swimming pool, health club, Jacuzzi, sauna, massage, conference rooms, business center, tour desk, air ticket counter, beauty salon, shops, 24-hour room service, same-day laundry and dry cleaning services, bicycle rental.

Kerry Centre Hotel (Beijing Jiali Zhongxin Fandian). *1 Guanghua Lu (2 blocks north of China World, 1 block west of the Third Ring Rd.), Beijing 100004.* ☎ *800/942-5050 in U.S. and Canada, 1800/222-448 in Australia, 0800/442-179 in New Zealand, 181/ 747-8485 in London, or 010/8529-6999. Fax 010/8529-6333.* www.shangri-la. com. *487 units, including 51 suites. A/C MINIBAR TV TEL. $220 double. Children under 18 stay free in parents' room. AE, DC, JCB, MC, V.* One of Beijing's newest hotels, and the third sister in the Shangri-La hotel cluster on Jianguomenwai Dajie, the Kerry is a four-star hotel with five-star facilities and service. The rooms possess a high-tech edge, with steel trim, data plugs, and large, curving desk tops (they also have duvets). Bathrooms contain separate tubs and showers.

Dining: The Kerry has three restaurants: a lobby lounge serving continental fare; a 24-hour coffee shop; and a Chinese restaurant featuring Hong Kong chefs.

Amenities: A roof garden encircled by a track for jogging and in-line skating, children's play area, health club, 25-meter lap pool, Jacuzzi, sauna, two indoor tennis courts, one mixed-used court, sundeck, 24-hour business center, conference rooms, tour desk, newsstand, concierge, valet, 24-hour room service, same-day laundry and dry cleaning, nightly turndown, babysitting.

Movenpick Hotel Beijing (Guodu Da Fandian). *Xiao Tianzhu Village, Capital Airport (Shunyi County, within 1.5 miles of airport), Beijing 100621.* ☎ *800/344-6835 or 010/6456-5588. Fax 010/6456-5678.* www.all-hotels.com. *E-mail:* bjmphtlc@iuol.cn.net. *408 units, including 35 suites. A/C MINIBAR TV TEL. $140 double. Children under 16 stay free in parents' room. AE, DC, ER, JCB, MC, V.* A true airport hotel, about a 15-minute drive via the free Movenpick shuttle (but too far to walk), this is also Beijing's only hotel with a resort atmosphere and outdoor recreational facilities. The service is highly efficient, and there's a comfortable, European atmosphere. Rooms are spacious. This airport hotel-cum-resort features the capital's only natural thermal hot springs pool, interconnected indoor and outdoor swimming pools, and courtyard chess board with resident master. The free airport shuttle runs every half hour from 6am to 11pm, and the free downtown shuttle bus makes 10 runs daily from 8am to 10pm.

Dining: The Mongolian, located in a yurt, serves steaming hot pots. The Boulevard has a continental breakfast and ice cream and sandwiches until midnight.

Amenities: Indoor/outdoor swimming pool, hot springs pool, health club, solarium, Jacuzzi, sauna, two outdoor tennis courts, one indoor squash court, beach volleyball, children's summer programs, playground, horseback riding stables nearby, 24-hour business center, conference rooms, tour desk, beauty salon, shopping arcade, newsstand, 24-hour room service, same-day laundry and dry cleaning services, baby-sitting, bicycle rental.

The Palace Hotel (Wangfu Fandian). *8 Jingyu Hutong (1 block east off Wangfujing Dajie), Beijing 100006.* ☎ *800/262-9467 or 010/6512-8899. Fax 010/6512-9050. E-mail:* tph@peninsula.com. *530 units, including 52 suites. A/C MINIBAR TV TEL. $300 double. AE, DC, JCB, MC, V.* The most luxurious of Beijing's city center hotels, the Palace flashes with its fleet of Rolls-Royces and its stunning red marble lobby and waterfall. Its services are also top of the line. The two basement floors contain China's most exclusive designer-name shops and boutiques. The gold-trimmed rooms are spacious, and the large marble bathrooms are equipped with safe drinking water dispensers.

Dining: Four swank restaurants specialize in Italian, German, Cantonese and Chaozhou (Southern Chinese) cuisines.

Amenities: Indoor swimming pool, large health club with superb exercise machines and weights, Jacuzzi, sauna, solarium, large 24-hour business center (e-mail, PC rental), conference rooms, tour desk, beauty salon, upscale shopping arcade, concierge, 24-hour room service, same-day laundry, dry cleaning and pressing services, newspaper delivery, nightly turndown, massage, twice-daily maid service, baby-sitting, limousine fleet.

Radisson SAS Hotel (Huangjia Da Fandian). *6A Beisanhuan Donglu (south side of the Third Ring Rd. E., 1 block from Airport Expressway overpass, at the China International Exhibition Centre), Beijing 100028.* ☎ *800/333-3333 in U.S. and Canada, 1800/333-333 in Australia, 0800/44-3333 in New Zealand, 1800/55-7474 in Ireland, 0800/374411 in U.K., or 010/6466-3388. Fax 010/6465-3186.* www.radisson.com. *362 units, including 16 suites. A/C MINIBAR TV TEL. $225 double. Children under 12 stay free in parents' room. AE, DC, ER, JCB, MC, V.* This 15-story international hotel has large stylish rooms in three decors (Oriental, High-Tech, and Art Deco). Spotless throughout, it maintains a modern European atmosphere and highly efficient service. A 5-year renovation plan began in 1999.

Dining: The LaxenOxen is a good Scandinavian grill. Rooftop barbecues are popular on summer evenings.

Amenities: Indoor swimming pool (17.6 meters), Jacuzzi, sauna, solarium, exercise machines, one outdoor tennis court, two indoor squash courts, sundeck, business center, conference rooms, tour desk, newsstand, shopping arcade, florist, concierge, valet, 24-hour room service, same-day laundry and dry cleaning, nightly turndown, newspaper delivery, free cribs, baby-sitting.

Shangri-La Beijing Hotel (Xiangge Lila Fandian). *29 Zizhuyuan Lu (northwest corner of Third Ring Rd.), Beijing 100081.* ☎ *800/942-5050 in U.S. and Canada, 1800/222-448 in Australia, 0800/442-179 in New Zealand, (44 181) 747-8485 in London, or 010/6841-2211. Fax 010/6841-8002.* www.shangri-la.com. *640 units, including 21 suites. A/C MINIBAR TV TEL. $190 double. Children under 18 stay free in parents' room. AE, DC, JCB, MC, V.* The number one luxury hotel in northwest Beijing, this 24-story hotel is noted for its high service levels and elegance. The large traditional garden is a serene focal point for the open lobby. Rooms are also elegant, among the largest in Beijing, and two guest rooms are designed for travelers with disabilities. The service is worthy of the five-star rating, and the distant location is ameliorated by free shuttle service to downtown locations.

Dining: Shang Palace, with chefs from Hong Kong, turns out excellent dim sum for lunch and fine Cantonese specialties for dinner, accompanied by performances of traditional Chinese music. Peppinos, with a resident Italian chef, has oven-baked pizzas and a strolling musician. Nishimura is an excellent Japanese restaurant with Beijing's first Robatayaki.

Amenities: Health club (in the basement) with exercise machines, large swimming pool, sauna, solariums, massage, recreation center with indoor tennis courts, squash courts, billiards, basketball court, 24-hour business center, conference rooms, tour desk, beauty salon, florist, newsstand, shopping arcade, concierge, valet, 24-hour room service, same-day laundry and dry cleaning, nightly turndown, baby-sitting.

Traders Hotel Beijing (Gumao Fandian). *1 Jianguomenwai Dajie (north side of China World, west of the Third Ring Rd.), Beijing 100004.* ☎ *800/942-5050 in U.S. and Canada, 1800/222-448 in Australia, 0800/442-179 in New Zealand, (44 181) 747-8485 in London, or 010/6505-2277. Fax 010/6505-0818.* www.shangri-la.com. *564 units, including 20 suites. A/C MINIBAR TV TEL. $140 double. Children under 18 stay free in parents' room. AE, DC, JCB, MC, V.* Sister hotel to the China World, to which it is now joined via a new underground shopping center complete with an ice-skating rink, Traders is highly rated by foreign business travelers for its large rooms and efficient service. When you stay at Traders, you have full guest privileges at the adjoining five-star China World, including use of its superb fitness and health facilities. This hotel is in high demand most of the year. Rooms in the recently remodeled west wing are the best, but all rooms are quite spacious.

Dining: Traders Cafe has international buffets. The Oriental Restaurant employs an open kitchen where excellent Cantonese and Beijing dishes are prepared.

Amenities: Fitness center, sauna, Jacuzzi, exercise machines, guest access to China World swimming pool and tennis courts, large business center, conference rooms, tour desk, newsstand, souvenir shops, concierge, valet, 24-hour room service, same-day laundry and dry cleaning, nightly turndown, baby-sitting, bicycle rental, bookstore.

WHERE TO DINE

There are scores of good restaurants and bars in Beijing. I can list but a few tried-and-true favorites. For up-to-date information on dining and for a larger current listing, check the free local newspapers, such as *Welcome to China: Beijing, Beijing This Month,* and *Beijing Scene,* or the new *Frommer's Beijing.*

Aria. *In the China World Hotel, Levels 2–3, 1 Jianguomenwai Dajie (at the intersection with the Third Ring Rd. E.). ☎ 010/6505-2266. Main courses RMB 80–RMB 200 ($10–$25). AE, DC, JCB, MC, V. Daily 11am–midnight. AMERICAN/CONTINENTAL.* This plush grill with its open kitchen and rotisserie, where the chefs love to put on "showtime" performances, is one of Beijing's trendiest new night spots. Jazz is the focus (there's a piano bar). The spiral staircase of polished wood is honeycombed with shelves for storing wines. The Western menu ranges from lobster potstickers and baked oysters Rockefeller to grilled fish and imported steaks.

Bleu Marine. *5 Dongdaqiao Lu (2 blocks north of Jianguomenwai Dajie). ☎ 010/6500-6704. Reservations recommended on weekends. Main courses RMB 80–RMB 350 ($10–$44). AE, JCB, MC, V. Mon–Sat 11:30am–3pm and 6:30–10:30pm. Closed Sun. SOUTHERN FRENCH.* Sidewalk dining is available under the blue awning of this trendy cafe when the sun shines; inside, the decor is Mediterranean. The emphasis is on seafood. Set dinners change with the season and are dependent on what's available in the local markets. The waiters keep the supply of sliced baguette replenished throughout.

Borom Piman. *In the Holiday Inn Lido, Jichang Lu, Jiangtai Lu (east side of Airport Expressway). ☎ 010/6437-6688, ext 2899. Reservations recommended on weekends. Main courses RMB 80–RMB 160 ($10–$20). AE, DC, JCB, MC, V. Daily 11am–2pm and 5–10pm. THAI.* Unfailingly flavorful, this Thai food is Beijing's best. You can choose between Western-style seating or mat-covered platforms with leg wells hidden underneath the low tables. The *tom yam goong* (prawn in hot-and-sour soup) is justly renowned, and the *khow ob sub-parod* (fried rice with pork and shrimp in fresh pineapple) is unforgettable. The chefs hail from Bangkok.

The Courtyard. *95 Donghuamen Lu (east side of Forbidden City Moat, look for lions and glass doors). ☎ 010/6526-8881. Reservations recommended on weekends. Main courses RMB 160–RMB 320 ($20–$40). AE, JCB, MC, V. Daily 6am–10:30pm. NOUVELLE FRENCH.* This upscale fusion bistro is a perfect place to relax with a flute of Moët & Chandon. Fresh salads blend Western and Chinese ingredients; entrees include blackened salmon, filet mignon, and Chinese noodle dishes; desserts range from chocolate mousse to steamed dumplings stuffed with fruit. A gallery in the basement features contemporary Chinese artists; a cigar divan upstairs offers exceptional views of the Forbidden City.

Fangshan Restaurant. *Inside Beihai Park on the northern shore of Beihai Island, Xicheng District. ☎ 010/6401-1879. Main courses RMB 150–RMB 250 ($18–$30). AE, JCB, MC, V. Daily 11am–1:30pm and 5–7pm. IMPERIAL.* A special Beijing culinary treat is the city's Imperial cuisine, the meals being based on the banquet menus of the Qing Dynasty. The park setting of the venerable Fangshan, founded by former cooks from the old Forbidden City, is delightful, replete with elaborate dynastic decorations and costumed waitresses.

Green Tian Shi. *57 Dengshi Xikou Lu (east of the Holiday Inn Crowne Plaza, 1 block off Wangfujing Dajie). ☎ 010/6524-2349. Main courses RMB 150–RMB 200 ($18–$25). AE, JCB, MC, V. Daily 11am–9pm. VEGETARIAN.* There's a vegetarian grocery at the entrance and a gaudy dining room upstairs serving Beijing's tastiest and trendiest vegetarian fare. The menu (in English) is filled with Chinese dishes made entirely without meat or dairy products (although some egg and milk dishes are available). The cuisine employs legumes, grains, and tuber stalks, along with artfully disguised chunks of *doufu* (bean curd) to achieve the appearance, texture, and sometimes the taste of fish, flesh, and fowl. This cafe has a more "new age" atmosphere than the bigger State-run vegetarian emporium, Gongdelin, which uses a heavier hand (and more oil) in preparing its more extensive menu.

Henry J. Bean's. *West wing of the China World Trade Center, 1 Jianguomenwai Dajie (near the Third Ring Rd. E.). ☎ 010/6505-2266, ext 6334. Main courses RMB 58–RMB 120 ($7–$15). AE, DC, JCB, MC, V. Sun–Thurs 11:30am–1am, Fri–Sat 11:30am–2:30am. AMERICAN.* This particularly comfortable place is one of the many flashy new spots for beer, sandwiches, grilled steaks, and live music.

Li Family Restaurant (Li Jia Cai). *11 Yangfang Hutong, Deshengmennei Dajie, Xicheng District (south of Xihai and Houhai lakes). ☎ 010/6618-0107. Reservations required. Set menus RMB 200, 300, 360, 480, and 560 ($25–$70). No credit cards. Daily 6–10pm. IMPERIAL BEIJING.* This restaurant has taken Beijing by storm. Located in a traditional hutong courtyard complex near the historic Back Lakes, the humble dining rooms serve the very recipes that were created for the Qing Dynasty Empress Dowager herself during the twilight of the Forbidden City. The great grandfather of the restaurant's founder (Ms. Li Li) commanded the Palace Guard before the fall of the last dynasty, and he was able to walk away with a number of the royal recipes, now re-created on the spot in the Li family kitchens. Ingredients are simple and healthful, and the dishes are rustic. The waiting list here sometimes stretches for weeks.

Louisiana. *In the Beijing Hilton Hotel, 2nd floor, 1 Dongfang Lu (east side of Third Ring Rd. E.). ☎ 010/6466-2288, ext 7420. Reservations recommended on weekends. Main courses RMB 200–RMB 500 ($25–$50). AE, DC, JCB, MC, V. Mon–Sat 11:30am–2:30pm and 6–10pm, Sun 6–10pm. AMERICAN/CAJUN.* Frequently named the best American restaurant in Beijing, Louisiana features a Cajun and Creole menu with touches of new American cuisine and Pacific Rim fusions. The elegant decor is highlighted by wall posters of Louisiana and statuettes of leading jazz and blues performers.

Shang Palace. *29 Zizhuyuan Lu (Level 1, Shangri-La Beijing Hotel). ☎ 010/6841-2211, ext 2732. Reservations* *recommended. Main courses $10–$50. AE, DC, JCB, MC, V. Daily 11:30am–2pm and 5:30–10pm. CANTONESE/BEIJING.* Long famous for its dim sum and Cantonese-style seafood dishes, Shang Palace is also the best place in town for Beijing's specialty, Peking duck, which is less greasy here than in the duck restaurants downtown. The large, open dining area with red columns is decorated tastefully in Qing Dynasty dragons and clouds.

Sihexuan. *In the Jinglun Hotel, 4th floor, 3 Jianguomenwai Dajie ☎ 010/6500-2266, ext 8116. Meals RMB 50–RMB 120 ($6–$12.50). AE, JCB, MC, V. Daily 11:30am–2pm and 5:30–10pm. BEIJING.* This is the best place in town to sample Beijing specialties. The fine setting employs red lanterns, long-spout teapots, and photographs of old Beijing streets and pavilions. The open kitchen turns out dumplings, and trolley carts thread their way between tables. The showstopper is the Spring Pie, a roll-your-own pancake with onion strips and pork, but even the spring rolls are delicious.

Summer Palace. *In the China World Hotel, Level 2, 1 Jianguomenwai Dajie (at intersection of the Third Ring Rd. E.). ☎ 010/6505-2266, ext 34. Reservations recommended on weekends. Main courses RMB 160–RMB 300 ($20–$37). AE, DC, JCB, MC, V. Daily 11:30am–2:30pm and 6–10:30pm. CANTONESE.* China World Hotel's signature restaurant offers superb southern Chinese dishes in a bright, airy dining hall, surrounded by eight private dining rooms. Chefs are from Hong Kong. The dim sum here is the best in Beijing. Seafood dishes are particularly tasty.

Peking Duck Restaurants Probably the most popular dish with foreigners, at least until they try it, is Peking duck. It's a brash dish, and certainly worth sampling. The two most popular places to do so are Bianyifang and Qianmen, but the Wangfujing outlet is the best. Expect slices of duck skin and meat, the crunchier the better—and the less fat the better—with a generous assortment of Shandong Province vegetable side dishes. Peking duck is served banquet style around a table, and you should get a group together to enjoy it (4 to 12 people is best).

Beijing Wangfujing Quanjude Roast Duck Restaurant. *13 Shuaifuyuan, Wangfujing Lu. ☎ 010/ 6525-3310. Reservations recommended. Main courses $15–$25. No credit cards. Daily 10:30am–1:30pm and 4:30–9:30pm. PEKING DUCK.*

Bianyifang Roast Duck Restaurant. *2 Chongwenmenwai Dajie. ☎ 010/6712-0505. Reservations recommended. Main courses $15–$25. No credit cards. Daily 11am–2pm and 5–8:30pm. PEKING DUCK.*

Quanjude Hepingmen. *14 Qianmen Xi Dajie, Xuanwu District (on the southeast corner at the intersection with Nanxinhua Jie, within sight of the Hepingmen subway station). ☎ 010/6301-8833. Main courses $9–$15. AE, JCB, MC, V. Daily 10:30am–1:30pm and 4:30–8:30pm. PEKING DUCK.*

Quanjude Kaoyadian. *32 Qianmen Dajie, Chongwen District (a few blocks straight south of Tiananmen Square, east side). ☎ 010/6511-2418. Main courses $13–$25. AE, JCB, MC, V. Daily 10:30am–1:30pm and 4:30–8:30pm. PEKING DUCK.*

The Great Wall: Four Views from Beijing

万里长城

The Great Wall is China's most renowned monument, frequently heralded as the only man-made object visible from space. That is a dubious, if compelling, claim. I have not orbited the Earth, but I do know that the Great Wall, despite its combined 6,200-mile length, is not only slim but is more broken than whole (in fact, it's rife with gaps the size of small countries) and varies in both color or contour. More than half of the wall has been demolished over the centuries. Much of it lies in ruined, earthen strips that are barely distinguishable from the hills and valleys out of which it was formed. Still, this dragon's spine of Old China, every inch laid by hand, was a massive project, certainly worthy of heavenly praise.

The Chinese call it *Wan Li Chang Cheng,* "the long wall of 10,000 li." A li is an ancient unit of measure, roughly equivalent to one-third of a mile. The wall's origins go back to the 5th century A.D. (and perhaps even earlier), when the rival kingdoms of the Warring States Period (453–221 B.C.) built walls in central China as defensive ramparts against their enemies, including barbarian tribes. The first emperor of unified China, Qin Shi Huang Di, fortified the barriers in the 3rd century B.C. Over a 10-year period, 300,000 conscripted laborers, many of them slaves, knit the walls into a continuous rampart to protect the northern frontier. New sections extended the wall east 1,700 miles to the Yellow Sea.

The Great Wall was constantly repositioned and extended along new routes as successive dynasties rose and fell. In the year A.D. 607 alone, more than a million workers toiled on this line of defense, but thereafter the Great Wall was largely abandoned. The conquest by the Mongols from the north and their establishment of the Yuan Dynasty (A.D. 1271–1368) rendered the wall obsolete. After China reverted to native rule under the Ming Dynasty (1368–1644), however, the rulers became fearful of another barbarian onslaught and set in motion the last great phase of wall building. This was not enough to keep out the Manchurians, who overran the Ming defenses and created China's last dynasty, the Qing (1644–1911).

Today, the Great Wall can be visited where it meets the sea in the east (at Old Dragon Head near the town of Shanhaiguan), where it disappears into the desert on the Silk Road to the west (at Jiayuguan), and at several junctures in between. But by far the most popular approaches are near Beijing, where there is a choice of four dramatic sections. All four—at Badaling, Mutianyu, Simatai, and Juyongguan—are within an easy day trip of Beijing, and all four are appealing. **Badaling** is where most tourists walk on the Great Wall. **Mutianyu** is a fine alternative, beautifully restored and often less crowded with visitors. **Simatai** is a wild, nearly unrestored segment, farther from Beijing and thus far less inundated with tour buses. **Juyongguan,** the newest section to open, is near the Ming Tombs on the road to Badaling. All four sections are 300 to 500 years old, dating from the Ming Dynasty, and all four are beautiful stretches of the Great Wall, coiling up and down impossibly steep terrain. Each section is a fitting representative of the greatest wall ever built by man—what one 19th-century traveler called a "fantastic serpent of stone."

The Great Wall at Badaling

Almost everyone who tours China, from heads of state to backpackers, pays a call on the Great Wall at Badaling, 42 miles northwest of Beijing. This is a grand section of the wall, set in a steep, forested mountain range. The wall, its stairs, and the magnificent watchtowers were carefully restored beginning in 1957. While many a traveler pooh-poohs Badaling as a deplorable tourist trap, crowded beyond all endurance, I have never been disappointed by it. The Great Wall is China's number-one tourist attraction, after all, and China is the world's most populous country. The Great Wall at Badaling, then, is the prime site for immersion into the Chinese world, past and present.

Construction of the Ming Dynasty Great Wall began in 1368 and continued for almost 200 years. Built of stone, it stretched 2,484 miles east to west and averaged 24 feet in height, 21 feet in width at its base, and 18 feet wide on top. The interior was a mixture of tamped earth and rubble. The sides were covered in stone, the top in layers of brick. The brick we associate with the Great Wall wasn't introduced until the Ming builders set to work. Gateway arches and watchtowers run the length of the wall, which served as a highway through the mountains. Five horses could ride abreast, drawing carriages.

The wall at Badaling has been restored to reflect its Ming Dynasty grandeur. The main parking lot and squares, filled with vendors these days, reflect China's modern economic boom. A long stairway runs up to the wall. You can turn left (north) or right (south) and walk a mile or

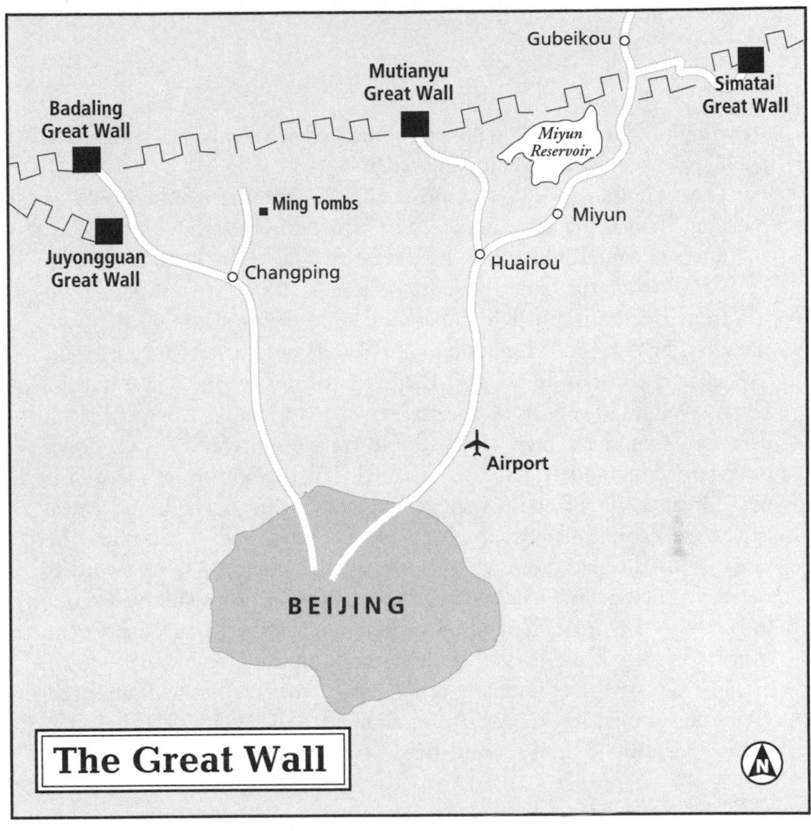

so in either direction. The segment on the left is a bit steeper, but I find it more scenic, so that's the way I usually head.

The incredible steepness of the Great Wall and the high rise of its stair treads always astound visitors. Walking up to the highest watchtower is often enough to exhaust a traveler thoroughly, especially on a hot day. There's no reason to hurry. The scenery is splendid. The two-story watchtowers, consisting of a guardroom below and an observation house above, are fine places to recuperate.

The northern section of the wall rises to the highest watchtower at Badaling, then runs down to the south. If you walk it to the end, about two-thirds of a mile from the entrance, you can head north again on an unrenovated spine of the wall that has a much more primitive feel. Few tourists venture out this far. The stairs are crumbling and the sides of the wall are broken, exposing the earthen filling.

If you choose to walk Badaling in the other direction, south atop the wall, the trek is longer, more than a mile. At the far end there's a terminal for the Great Wall cable car. Beyond this point, the Great Wall reverts to its former ruins, which one is free to explore. (Liability laws are weak in China, meaning broken bones and other mishaps suffered in public places are seldom compensated.)

The Qinglongqiao West train station is near the southern end of Badaling. This is the first railroad to be built entirely with Chinese labor and funds (1909). It tunnels under the Great Wall. Locals tell me that in the winter, when the Great Wall at Badaling is dusted with snow, a train trip from Beijing is a delight. There are almost no tourists on the wall, the sun is bright, and the mountain peaks and guard towers are gorgeous.

Since most of us do not visit Beijing in winter, we must descend the Great Wall in the heat of tourist season—and it is a fiercely steep descent down these high stairs. Some travelers prefer to walk down backward. The modern handrails can help. At the bottom of the wall is the "Great Mall" of endless souvenir stands, a movie hall, and cafes. Prices are exceptionally high for trinkets, crafts, and "I Climbed the Great Wall" T-shirts, even when you bargain. I bought a tacky sword at Badaling once, paying half what the vendor asked, which still turned out to be twice the price charged by Beijing and Hong Kong department stores. Oh well, I told myself, it did come from the Great Wall.

The Great Wall at Badaling is open daily from 6am to 6:30pm (until 10pm on summer weekends). Admission is RMB 30 ($3.75). The cable car is RMB 100 ($12.50) round-trip.

The Great Wall at Mutianyu

The Great Wall at Badaling proved so popular that authorities restored a second section of the wall in 1986, at Mutianyu (55 miles northeast of Beijing). Mutianyu was supposed to relieve the overcrowding at Badaling, particularly on weekends. The ploy has not really succeeded, but I'm glad that Mutianyu is open. Its setting is more rough and rugged than that at Badaling, even if it now has summer traffic jams of its own.

The mile-long segment of the Great Wall of Mutianyu was among the first built during the Ming Dynasty, beginning well over 500 years ago. As at Badaling, a long stairway leads up to the wall. The hike can take up to 30 minutes, so you might want to use the nearby cable car. If you turn right at the top of the entrance, you can walk the ramparts for over a half mile. At the end, there is a barrier; visitors are not permitted to venture beyond this point. All you can do is contemplate the wall in ruins, which gives one an excellent idea of what most of the Great Wall, even those sections built just a few hundred rather than a few thousand years ago, looks like now.

Returning on the wall in the other direction leads to the cable-car station, which is the kindest way back down (in respect to your knees and thighs).

The Great Wall at Mutianyu is open daily 6:30am to 6pm (until 10pm on summer weekends). Admission is RMB 30 ($3.60). The cable car is RMB 100 ($12.50) round-trip, and a new roller train, which winds up and down the hillsides, is the same price.

The Great Wall at Simatai

The Great Wall at Simatai is quiet, remote, and virtually unreconstructed. Fortification aficionados consider Simatai the most beautiful section of the Great Wall. It is beautiful, but its main aesthetic attraction is its state of ruin. This is how the Great Wall really looks 500 years after the Ming constructed it. Simatai is also a paradise for hikers and hill walkers, with its dramatic natural scenery. The view of the sharp peaks is heightened by the outline of the Great Wall and its crumbling watchtowers.

I visited Simatai twice recently, first by hiring a car with driver and guide, then by just hiring a car. This put Simatai within 2 hours of downtown Beijing. The cheaper but rougher alternative is the public bus that leaves the Dongzhimen bus station in Beijing at 7am and arrives at Simatai 3 or 4 hours later.

The Chengde Highway to Simatai is smooth, the countryside green. At Miyun Reservoir, the terrain steepens. The roadside is clotted with fishing families selling their catch, enormous reservoir trout, many 3 feet long, sheathed in plastic and suspended on posts like lanterns. At Gubeikou, 70 miles northeast of Beijing, a country lane winds 7 more miles through the foothills to Simatai Village and the entrance to the wall. The town at the base is tiny. The main street leading to the wall has a few beef noodle cafes, souvenir shops, and vendor shelters stocked with T-shirts and Great Wall tablecloths, but this is a mere minnow pond of sellers compared to the ocean of hawkers flooding the gates to Badaling and Mutianyu. Towering high over the village is the formidable outline of the Great Wall, slithering like a dragon's back over a series of sharp, clipped peaks.

Beyond the village there is a half-mile walk up to the first stairway and watchtower. The sandy path rises and skirts the small Simatai Reservoir, where in the heat of summer, tourists from Beijing board pleasure boats for a sail along the Great Wall. But from the water the wall remains high and remote. The reservoir lies in a deep crease dividing two sections of the wall: Simatai to the east, Jinshanling to the west.

Ascending the stairs to the first watchtower at Simatai is a matter of pounding a few hundred stone steps, the treads of this staircase often just half as deep as an average foot length. The climb is a struggle, but the view from the first of the ascending towers, taken through open cannon archways, is magnificent: endless mountain chains to the deserted north; watchtowers crowning the ridgelines east and west; and the reservoir, village, and farmlands far below, rolling southward toward Beijing.

This first portion of the Great Wall at Simatai has been restored, as have virtually all the walkways and towers that tourists see along Badaling and Mutianyu—but from here on at Simatai, the wall has been left to crumble. A sign at the entrance boasts that Simatai is the most dangerous segment of the Great Wall, and indeed it is. The grand stairways disappear. The pathway becomes a ledge of rock and sand along the outside of the rising wall, narrowing to sheer drop-offs. Sometimes there are no footholds at all. At times the path, grown smooth over the centuries, is as treacherous to scale as a slide of gravel.

The wall bricks, each with its own stamped number, date from the Ming Dynasty. Many of the bricks have fallen away, exposing the original earthen core with which the large work gangs capped the mountain peaks. From the towers on the wall, signals of fire and smoke once alerted those inside the wall to impending invasions from without.

At Simatai one can still see the results of the Ming building program. The toll taken by 5 centuries of weather and civilization is substantial, but far from complete. Simatai survives as a wild run of ruins, its main outline intact, stretching from peak to chiseled peak on ridges sometimes pitched to 70-degree inclines. Best of all for the traveler, Simatai is as peaceful as it is untouched and as beautiful as the mountains it dances across.

Coming down Simatai is more daunting than going up. Locals recount stories of visitors who have broken into tears during the descent, unnerved by the steepness, the lack of stairs, the unstable footings. Some come down on the stairless top of the wall backward, on all fours. The name *Simatai* shares the same sounds in Chinese as the words for *dead horse platform,* a reference to a horse that fell in a famous battle fought beneath the wall here. So far, no tourists have added their names to this venerable tradition.

In fact, there is a safer way to scale Simatai. East of the entrance is a **gondola.** Visitors can hop a ride partway up and climb a new, safer set of steep stairs to the 2,624-foot-high eighth tower on the wall. From here, it is said that on a clear evening you can see the lights of Beijing. You can also get far away from the city. When I first visited Simatai, in the spring, only four other visitors arrived, and it was only a little busier in the early summer when I returned.

There are 14 watchtowers at Simatai, stationed at quarter-mile intervals and strung across the peaks until the wall dissolves into scattered bricks, piles of sand, and fragments of bone from the workers who were buried within the wall. "To think that these walls, built in apparently inaccessible places, as though to balance the Milky Way in the sky, a walled way over the mountaintops, are the work of men," one 19th-century traveler gasped, "makes it seem like a dream." Indeed, Simatai is magical, but beauty transcends ordinary reality wherever one walks today along the Great Wall of China.

The Great Wall at Simatai is open daily 8am to 5pm. Admission is RMB 20 ($2.40). The cable car is RMB 60 ($7.50) round-trip.

The Great Wall at Juyongguan

Opened in 1998, the section of the Wall at Juyongguan is the nearest to Beijing (36 miles northwest). Here a 2.5-mile section of the old Wall was renovated under an extensive 5-year program. The name means "Tower that bestrides the road," and Juyongguan lives up to that image. The wall undulates over the ridges of the Taihang range. The site of a famous mountain pass, Juyongguan boasts some impressive restored guard towers, as well as several temples and a garden. There are also some grand Buddhist carvings here, rendered in six languages, including Chinese, Tibetan, and Sanskrit. This section of the wall was erected in A.D. 1345, predating the Ming Dynasty and thus making it one of the oldest Great Wall monuments near Beijing.

Lying just 6 miles south of the Great Wall at Badaling, Juyongguan has become a popular alternative to the more crowded sections of the old Wall. CITS arranges some tours here, and the site is also served by Tourist Buses no. 1 through 5. Juyongguan is open daily 8am to 5pm, with an admission of RMB 20 ($2.50).

PRACTICAL INFORMATION

ORIENTATION & WHEN TO GO

From Beijing, the four main sites to visit the Great Wall are at Badaling (42 miles northwest), Mutianyu (55 miles northeast), Simatai (77 miles northeast), and Juyongguan (36 miles northwest). To avoid the crowds, visit the Great Wall on weekdays rather than weekends, early in the morning if possible. Springtime is the most pleasant time to go to the wall; June through September is high tourist season.

All four sites are day trips from **Beijing** (see previous chapter).

GETTING THERE

To Badaling A new expressway connects Beijing to the Great Wall at Badaling. **Tour buses** make the trip in about 90 minutes, unless the expressway is clogged with other buses or there's been an accident (which is not uncommon). Government-sponsored tour buses (the green no. 1 buses) make the run every 20 minutes in the morning, beginning at 6am and leaving from in front of Qianmen Gate (at the south end of Tiananmen Square), costing RMB 9 ($1) each way. For information, contact the Beijing CITS office (see below). The **train** from Beijing to Hohhot stops near the Badaling section of the wall at Qinglongqiao West train station. The rail journey (no. 527 train) takes about 3 hours from Beijing's Yongdingmen train station, departing at 9:40am (one-way fare RMB 20/$2.40). There are many other trains as well.

To Mutianyu If you are not on a tour, you can catch a **minibus** to Mutianyu in front of the Great Hall of the People. A kiosk sells tickets (RMB 10/$1.20 each way) the day before. Morning departure times vary, so check ahead. There is no train service.

To Simatai To reach the Great Wall at Simatai, book a **tour** at the hotel or through CITS (see below), hire a **taxi** (about RMB 400/$48), or book a **minibus** (RMB 100/$12 round-trip) at the tourist office in the **Jinghua Hotel,** Nansanhuan Xi Lu (☎ 010/6722-2211).

To Juyongguan This section of the Great Wall is located on the same new expressway that runs to Badaling, and can be reached by bus or taxi in about 80 minutes. The government-sponsored Tour Buses depart every morning at 8:30am from five locations in the city (no. 1 from Qianmen, no. 2 from the Beijing Railway Station, no. 3 from Dondaqiao, no. 4 from the Beijing Zoo, no. 5 from Qianmen Xi Dajie), costing RMB 8 ($1) each way.

TOURS & STRATAGEMS

Tours to Badaling & Mutianyu **China International Travel Service (CITS),** with headquarters at 28 Jianguomenwai Dajie in Beijing (☎ 010/6515-8566; fax 010/6515-8602), arranges guided tours to the Great Wall. CITS maintains convenient branches in most hotels.

CITS group tours to the Great Wall at Badaling leave from various hotels at 8:30am daily and cost about RMB 400 ($48) per person, including lunch and a tour of the uninspiring Ming Tombs. CITS group tours to the Great Wall at Mutianyu leave at noon on Tuesday, Thursday, and Saturday from various hotels and cost about RMB 300 ($37) per person.

Tours to Simatai There are no group tours to the Great Wall at Simatai, although private guided tours can be arranged by CITS and hotel tour desks. I booked a tour with a private car and English-speaking guide, for RMB 1,200 ($145), at the tour desk of the **Trader's Hotel,** 1 Jianguomenwai Dajie (☎ 010/6505-2277). I later returned to Simatai by hiring a taxi for the day on my own, costing RMB 400 ($48).

Tours to Juyongguan Check with your hotel tour desk or CITS to see if tours have begun to the newest section of the Wall.

WHERE TO STAY

As the Great Wall is a day trip from the capital, consult the chapter on Beijing for lodging choices. Adventurous visitors have been known to take sleeping bags and tents, dodging officials to camp out on the Great Wall. Rustic accommodations (cabins and dormitories) are offered at **Simatai Village**

(☎ 010/6903-1221) at the Simatai section of the Great Wall. The cabins sleep four, have their own bathrooms/ showers, and rent for RMB 606 ($75) a day; dorms cost RMB 96 ($12) per person.

WHERE TO DINE

All four Great Wall sites have **food stands** (beef noodles for $2 a plate) and **cafes.** If your tour includes lunch, you'll dine at one of the restaurants catering to foreigner groups with fixed-price set Chinese lunches. The Great Wall at Badaling even has a branch of Kentucky Fried Chicken. If you're on your own for food, it's best to pack a lunch in Beijing and enjoy it on the wall.

CHENGDE: SUMMER HOME OF THE EMPERORS

承德

ON SEPTEMBER 14, 1793, EMPEROR Qianlong received the first delegation from a Western government ever to set foot in China, a British group headed by Lord Macartney. Matters did not get off to a promising start. The British lord refused to kowtow to the emperor, a ceremony that all visitors to the Middle Kingdom had performed for centuries, bowing deeply and banging their heads upon the ground. The emperor agreed to no treaties with England that day and declared that requests to open up trade were pointless. "We possess all things," Emperor Qianlong declared. "I set no value on objects strange or ingenious, and have no use for your country's manufactures."

The site of this historic meeting of East and West took place not in the Forbidden City in Beijing but 155 miles northeast in a remote imperial retreat built by Qianlong's grandfather, Emperor Kangxi. This summer palace in the wilderness, located in the country town of Chengde (formerly called Jehol in the West), was by no means a primitive outpost. Befitting the station of the Qing rulers, it was a grand summer palace, larger than Beijing's summer palace and Forbidden City combined, with numerous halls, pavilions, lakes, and hunting grounds. The retreat has survived, largely intact, and today Chengde is a summer resort open to all the people of China as well as sightseers from abroad. City-dwellers seem as anxious as the royal courts of 2 centuries past to escape the heat of Beijing and partake of the splendors of the countryside.

The stunning temples and the palaces of the Imperial Summer Villa are the last grand expression of the power and wealth wielded by China's final imperial dynasty at its height. The Qing Dynasty was little over a century away from complete collapse. Largely emptied of monks and worshippers, the pavilions of Chengde today serve delegations of tourists.

Mountain Villa for Escaping the Summer Heat

The road from Beijing is in excellent condition and the scenery is often spectacular, with sharp wooded peaks and valleys. Chengde is surrounded

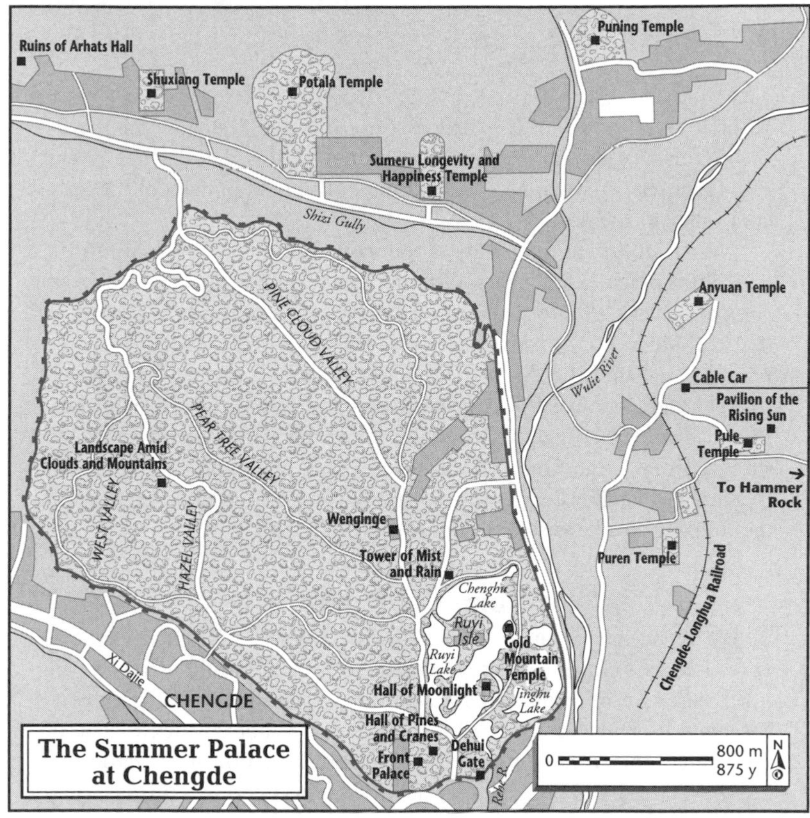

The Summer Palace at Chengde

by green mountains—no doubt one reason the emperors favored this place. The town of Chengde, which grew up around the parklands, has become a resort center, but it is still no more than a village by Chinese standards, with a population of merely 150,000. Tourism has brought some prosperity, although in the nearby fields I saw farmers pulling rounded stones on ropes, used to level the strips between furrows, and I also saw furrows being dug with wooden plows harnessed to the bent backs of peasants, no other beasts of burden being available.

Before the era of automobiles and trains, the journey from the capital to Chengde would have been a formidable undertaking. In 1703, Emperor Kangxi ordered the construction of the "Mountain Villa for Escaping the Summer Heat" (Bishushanzhuang). From the first, it was China's court away from court. Even the throne was transported from Beijing so that the emperor could wield full power while he enjoyed the sports of the privileged. Kangxi was intensely dedicated to the horsemanship and hunting of his Manchu ancestors, and Chengde became his passion. For the next 117 years, this summer retreat was expanded and enriched, the Qing emperors holding court here 6 months of the year. In 1820, however, Emperor Jiaqing died at Chengde, reportedly the victim of a lightning bolt, a bad omen. It was decades before the court again began its annual decampment of Beijing in favor of the lush, cool valley to the north.

What's most striking today is the vast scale of the imperial retreat, which fills much of the great valley of Chengde, and its rustic setting. In comparison with the ornate and elaborate pavilions and courtyards of the Forbidden City and summer palaces in Beijing, Chengde's compound is raw and wild. Most of Chengde's retreat is given over to water, rock, and grasslands—the grasslands that the once-nomadic Manchus, who had grown civilized as the masters of the Chinese empire, called their spiritual home. One of the first foreigners to see the retreat, a Jesuit missionary living in Beijing, wrote that the enclosure was so extensive it required an hour to survey on horseback.

Imperial Palace

Today, Bishushanzhuang is surrounded by a wall 6 miles in circumference. The **east entrance gate (Dehuimen)** is at the Wulie River, on the northwest edge of town, near an intriguing footbridge where locals congregate with long bamboo fishing poles and vendors stock towers of glass aquariums with the fresh catch. No matter that the water under the bridge is turgid and clogged with debris, or that the resort town is noisy and uninviting. The park the emperors built is beautiful and spacious, consisting of enormous fields, lakes, pavilions, and pagodas; this is the largest imperial garden in China.

West of the entrance gate, atop a small rise, is the old palace (Zhenggong), now the **Bishushanzhuang Museum.** The **Front Palace** complex is where diplomatic business was conducted. For several centuries, China in the summertime was ruled from nine courtyard halls, each fashioned from unpainted wood. These are plain, linear buildings, more like imperial lodges than palaces, landscaped in mighty pines, graveled walkways, and convoluted rockeries. The interiors are sparsely decorated with the furniture and armaments of the time, as well as life-sized waxen figures representing emperors, concubines, court advisors, and foreign diplomats. Envoys were once received in the Hall of No Worldly Lust But True Faith, constructed of fragrant nanmu wood from southwestern China. The royal bedroom is located in the Refreshing Mist Veiled Waters Pavilion. In the Landscape Amid Clouds and Mountains Hall, visitors can reach the second floor by climbing the rockery in front.

The Imperial Summer Villa is open from 5:30am to 6pm daily (until 10pm in summer). Admission is RMB 50 ($6).

Royal Garden

Outside the main palace grounds is a set of interlinked **lakes,** woven with paths, arched bridges, and viewing pavilions, where the Chinese enjoy themselves, rowing boats and splashing each other as they pass. Family picnics and games are popular here. Across the flat grasslands, adults and children together play what looks like blind man's bluff and rover-red-rover. Teens circle up for versions of hacky-sack. The last great private preserve of emperors has become a genuine people's park. Courtyards are commandeered by martial arts demonstrations featuring retired citizens in white uniforms and red sashes. In another courtyard in front of the emperor's palace, preschool children flash swords in formation, some of them barely old enough to walk.

The circular tents known as **yurts,** which the nomadic tribes of the north erected and dismantled as they traveled the grasslands, and which the Manchu emperors also employed during their long summer vacations, have returned to Chengde, albeit in strictly modern fashion. In one large grassy field, several dozen of these Manchurian tents are rented out as overnight accommodations at the Yurt Holiday Inn. The modern models are fitted out with air conditioners, private baths, and color televisions. It was on this lawn, in the emperor's yurt, that England's first envoy to China refused to bow.

Many pavilions from the days of the emperors have survived. The **Literary Nourishment Pavilion (Wenjinge),** once one of China's four great imperial libraries, is northwest of the lakes on a secluded wooded hill. It resembles the classic gardens of Suzhou and Ningbo, with an immense rockery facing a graceful wooden pavilion across a goldfish pool. The rockery has its own caves, paths, and overlooks, and one of its rocks has been shaped and stationed so that from the pavilion those who linger can see the silver image of the moon continuously reflected on the waters.

Along the lakeshores are several dazzling towers and halls, including the **Temple of Eternal Blessing,** a golden birthday gift from Emperor Qianlong to his mother. On **Changlang Isle,** Emperor Qianlong constructed a copy of Suzhou's Changlang Garden. Even prettier is the **Tower of Mist and Rain (Yanyulou),** perched on a hill and reached by a bridge, favored by emperors for its views of the lake in the fog. On the northeast shore is a stunning three-story pavilion, **Gold Mountain Temple (Jinshan Si),** bordered by lower halls, which Emperor Kangxi in a poem likened to a mountain rising from the lake. "To ascend it," he sang, "is like climbing a magical peak."

Lord Macartney rode through the park during his diplomatic mission in 1793 and was charmed by the lake scenes: "The shores of the lake have all the varieties of shape which the fancy of a painter can delineate . . . one marked by a pagoda, or other building, one quite destitute of ornament, some smooth and level, some steep and uneven and others frowning with wood or smiling with culture."

North of the lakes, the grasslands and hills fan out and the walkways become secluded hiking trails stretching beyond the **Garden of Ten Thousand Trees (Wanshun Wan)** and the **Horse Testing Ground (Shima Da),** where emperors once reviewed archers and horsemen. The Imperial Summer Villa at Chengde essentially re-creates the wild grasslands of the Manchus north of the Great Wall but softens them with the garden arts and sweeping pavilions of south China.

Little Tibet

Emperor Kangxi had a political motive in moving his summer court to Chengde. He hoped to impress, to beguile, and to subdue the unruly legions to the north, and to placate restive religious and ethnic factions throughout China. This ploy produced a legacy visible today in the hillsides north and east of the Imperial Summer Villa, a string of Eight Outer Temples built in honor of Tibetans, Kazaks, and other peoples. As fascinating as this Summer Palace of the Wild West is, the array of distant hillside temples is even more striking.

A dozen were built from 1713 to 1779. Eight remain open. Two of the neighboring northern temples, Tibetan in style, are the grandest and most unusual. Built 10 years apart, they are the work of Kangxi's grandson, Emperor Qianlong.

The **Mount Sumera Longevity and Happiness Temple (Xumifushou Miao)** was built in 1779 in honor of the sixth Panchen Lama's visit to Chengde. The design is based on the lama's residence in Shigatse, Tibet. At the rear of this lavish uphill enclosure is a yellow-and-green pagoda erected to celebrate Emperor Qianlong's 70th birthday. At the entrance are two white stone elephants kneeling on bent legs. In the center is the high red wall of the main temple, decorated with Tibetan windows. The walls enclose a massive squarish four-story hall with a copper-tiled roof gilded in a ton of gold, decorated with eight ridge-running dragons, each weighing 1 ton. The inside of the red walls is lined with tiers of galleries, affording inward views of the square hall and outward views of the valley of Chengde. This was the last copy temple built at Chengde.

The **Small Potala Temple (Putuozongsheng Miao),** a mile to the east, was built by Emperor Qianlong 10 years earlier, partly to celebrate his 60th birthday and his mother's 80th. It is the largest temple at Chengde, its 60 halls and terraces covering 54 acres.

To reach the main hall requires a long, steep climb up the hillside. Prayer flags and banners drape its golden beams. The great red wall at its rear evokes the wall of the Dalai Lama's Potala Palace in Lhasa. In the front courtyard, a massive four-sided stone tablet inscribed, respectively, in Tibetan, Manchurian, Mongolian, and Chinese, proclaims the temple's links to the Potala. Whitewashed outer buildings, capped with dagobas, are empty shells, built for show rather than worship. Even the richly decorated Tibetan windows on the red wall are blank, serving as pure decorative flourishes to impress the visiting Mongol dignitaries who practiced Lama Buddhism. The stairs up to the red wall are so steep that sedan chair carriers now do a steady business ferrying visitors to the top.

Within the mammoth red walls is a large square pavilion, now empty of its Buddha statue, but capped with an extraordinary tiled roof gilded bright gold. Many of the buildings, such as the Hall of All Laws Falling into One, are gradually being filled with religious artifacts and Chinese porcelains. The arcades in the red wall contain hundreds of images of the Buddha. But perhaps the strangest of the displays is in the **East Hall (Donggang Zi Dian),** situated beneath the red facade, where images of the Red Hat sect perform "esoteric" rituals under cover of their yellow gowns. Such expressions of sexuality, more common in certain holy places in India, are rarely manifested in the temples of China, although at Chengde there are other examples.

All the temples are open daily from 8am to 5pm. Admission is RMB 20 to RMB 25 ($2.50 to $3).

A Strange Rock

Standing above the wealth of imperial and religious ruins in Chengde's outdoor museum to the glories of the last dynasty is one of the most peculiar natural monuments in China, **Hammer Rock (Bangchui Shan).** It can be seen atop the distant eastern hills from nearly anywhere in Chengde, a forlorn stone pinnacle jutting straight up from a flat ridge, its base narrower than its rounded top. Its shape was suggestive of another object altogether—one the modest tourism authorities would never suggest—and I was sure it had a more provocative local nickname.

Hammer Rock is connected to a parking lot on the east side of Chengde by hiking trails and a ski lift. I decided to take the ski lift up (RMB 31/$3.90) and walk back down. The lift is a 20-minute ride over quiet hills and valleys where farmers and horsemen tended the fields. At Hammer Rock, the view down into the valley is wide and peaceful, the arc of the eight temples neatly outlined on the lower hills.

Hammer Rock is at the far end of a terrifyingly narrow ledge with sheer drop-offs on either side. Moreover, when I went, it was teeming with visitors and no railings or path had been provided. One misstep or shove could be fatal. The 60-foot monolith is barely 10 feet wide at its base, and at its base everyone gathered for a moment and touched the rock. I inched my way across the flat ledge and touched the rock myself, discovering later that to do so ensured I would live to the age of 130.

The trail back to the valley runs south past another formation, **Toad Rock,** then down through desolate country to the **Temple of Universal Joy (Pule Si),** which is open daily 8am to 5pm and costs RMB 20 ($2.50) to enter. It was built by Emperor Qianlong in 1766 as a place for yet more Mongol envoys to worship while paying their respects to China's ruler. At the rear of this west-facing temple, more active with monks than the Tibetan-style northern complexes, is a round tower, the **Pavilion of the Rising Sun (Xuguang Ge),** reminiscent of Beijing's Temple of Heaven. The altar holds a Tantric mandala in the form of a cross and a copper Buddha of Happiness. What's being portrayed in this theater is cosmic sexual union, a theme typical of Tantric Buddhism. The Temple of Joy is aligned perfectly with Hammer Rock to the east—there's definitely something more pagan than divine afoot on these fringes of Chengde.

PRACTICAL INFORMATION

ORIENTATION & WHEN TO GO

Chengde, in northern Hebei Province, is 155 miles northeast of Beijing. Most visitors include the sights of Chengde on an overnight trip from Beijing, often booking a tour from there. April to November, the weather is warm. Winters are too cold for comfortable sightseeing.

GETTING THERE

Chengde is 5 hours by **train** from Beijing. There are frequent trains connecting Beijing and Chengde, but no commercial airline service. By **car, taxi,** or **tour bus,** the trip takes 3½ hours over an excellent paved highway.

TOURS & STRATAGEMS

China International Tourist Service (CITS) in Chengde has its offices at 6 Nanyuan Dong Lu, next door to the Yunshan Hotel (☎ 0314/202-6827). CITS in Chengde can arrange day tours (with English-speaking guides) of the palace grounds and the surrounding temples. CITS in Beijing also offers 2-day bus tours of Chengde with English-speaking guides (call ☎ 010/6515-8566 in Beijing or check with your Beijing hotel tour desk).

Accompanied by two German students studying Chinese, I hired a taxi from Beijing at a total cost of RMB 1,600 ($195), including all excursions in Chengde and return to Beijing. Lodging, meals, and admissions were extra.

WHERE TO STAY

The **Yunshan Hotel,** 6 Nanyuan Dong Lu (☎ 0314/202-6171; fax 0314/202-4551), and the **Chengde Guesthouse for Diplomatic Missions (Waijiao Renyuan Binguan),** Wulie Lu (☎ 0314/202-1970; fax 0314/202-2269), are the two best hotels in town. Both are three-star, modern facilities, but neither is fully up to international standards of service and maintenance. Doubles are RMB 420 ($50) at both. I stayed at the Chengde Guesthouse for Diplomatic Missions—which is located on the river, within walking distance of the Summer Palace entrance—and I was reasonably comfortable. It has a business center, a beauty parlor, three dining rooms, and a bar. The rooms have televisions and clean bathrooms.

The two-star **Yurt Holiday Inn (Menggu Bao Fandian),** Wanshu Yuan (☎ 0314/202-3094), located on the Summer Palace grounds, is open April to November. It consists of 50 tents (yurts) with televisions, carpets, and private bathrooms. It has a superb location, but the management and facilities need improvement. The cost is RMB 350 ($43) for a yurt.

WHERE TO DINE

The **Yunshan Hotel** and the **Chengde Guesthouse for Diplomatic Missions** both have adequate Chinese restaurants with wide-ranging menus in English. Both are inexpensive (RMB 34 to RMB 75/$4 to $9). Local specialties, which include exotic wild game dishes (rabbit, camel, venison, boar), are served at the **Fangyuan Restaurant** (☎ 0314/ 202-3429), located inside the Imperial Summer Villa, north of the main palace on the west shore of the lake.

I had a cheap, tasty lunch of *jiaozi* (steamed dumplings) at one of the **cafes** located under the large canvas awning at the entrance to the Small Potala Temple (Putuozongsheng Miao) north of Chengde. While dining, I watched our taxi driver shell and consume a large goose egg with chopsticks without spilling a single morsel.

DATONG: TEMPLE SUSPENDED OVER THE VOID

大同

DATONG IS THE COAL FIELD OF China, a northern outpost on the Mongolian frontier that stood for centuries as the Middle Kingdom's barrier against the barbarians. It is still something of a frontier town, rough-edged and lagging behind China's cities to the south and east, modern cities that Datong still fuels with its coal. Datong's name comes from the phrase in a Tang Dynasty poem that means the "Big Same," and indeed the town seems to be a vast sameness, a desert plateau scorched with coal pits and riddled with slow-moving coal trucks, the air a black sackcloth of dust.

The great tourist attraction here is the **Yungang Buddhist Caves,** carved into the nearby cliffs in the 5th century A.D., but Datong also has other historic treasures. The gray streets yield some of the largest temples in China, and the **Temple Suspended over the Void** makes the forbidding countryside south of Datong worth crossing. At times, Datong was the supreme city in northern China, capital to dynasties that have all but turned to dust, save for a few monuments—monuments which are nonetheless spectacular.

The Buddhist Grottoes at Yungang

Just 10 miles west of downtown Datong is the most spectacular array of ancient stone carvings, the Yungang caves. Here, 40,000 workers and artists set to work on a sandstone cliff, beginning in A.D. 460, chiseling out caves and sculpting huge Buddhist statues from stone on a scale not attempted previously. Datong was then capital of the Northern Wei Dynasty (A.D. 386–534). More than 51,000 statues remain at Yungang today, most of them completed by the time the rulers moved their capital south to Luoyang, in A.D. 494, where they set about carving another major Buddhist grotto at Longmen, although the work at Yungang continued until A.D. 525.

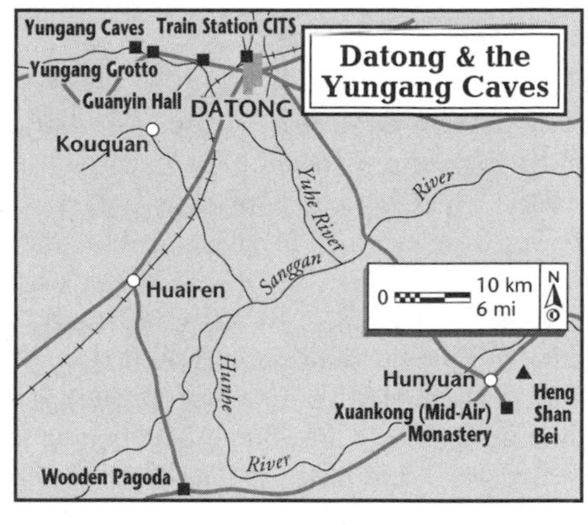

The massive figures carved into the cliffs at Yungang are rounded, lively human images. Many have sharp noses and beards, features of Indian and Persian, rather than Chinese, origin. Many of the craftsmen came to Datong from Central Asia, crossing the Silk Road into northern China over the same route that Buddhism itself traveled. The first caves, however, were finished under the direction of a brilliant local monk, who is credited with creating the most monumental images of Buddha and with initiating the earliest stone-carved caves in China. Emperor Wen Cheng had appointed this monk, named Tan Hao, as China's religious leader, and Tan Hao responded by ordering five statues carved in the cliffs representing the emperor's five predecessors, who had been regarded as living Buddhas. These five monuments are located today in the center of the Yungang grottoes (Caves 16–20), barely changed after 15 centuries.

The Yungang caves were built as an illustration of the Northern Wei Dynasty's power and its dedication to Buddhism as the state religion. Confucians, who dominated the class of scholars and officials for nearly 1,500 years after the Yungang caves were completed, sneered at the carvings as the height of folly, dismissing them as if the caves were a big comic book for the superstitious. The carvings were created by a non-Chinese dynasty (the "barbarian" Toba tribe from north of the Great Wall) and based on a foreign religion (Buddhism, from India). Thus, the sculptures at Datong were ignored for centuries, not studied seriously until a scholar from Japan, Isoto Chuta, arrived in 1903. Western art dealers followed, crating up several dozen statues and the heads of nearly 700 Buddhas and their religious attendants for shipment to Europe, America, and Japan, where they still remain in various collections. Even so, most of the art is still in place at Yungang.

The caves face south. On the bluff above, there are earthen sections of the Great Wall, plowing across the sands like ocean liners stranded in a desert. *Yungang* means "Cloud Hill." Centuries of wind-blown sand and dust have eroded the openings of the caves, once protected by wooden pavilions. The statues inside are open to the elements and to the eyes of visitors. The 53 major caves cover a half mile of the weathered cliff face.

The Eastern Grottoes I began my tour of Yungang along its eastern cliffs, to the right side of the main entrance. Local guides proved unnecessary: There are plenty of signs in English and even a large signpost with a bilingual map of Yungang. The first four caves **(Caves 1–4),** set apart from the rest by a ravine that slashes through the cliff, are not spectacular. **Cave 3,** however, is the largest at the site, 43 feet high inside (the cliff looms to a height of 80 feet at this point). The Monastery of the Enchanted Cliff once stood inside, and Tan Hao himself taught Buddhism here. Three Buddhas remain in **Cave 3.** The central Buddha, seated, one hand raised to his chest, is 30 feet tall. The carving of these statues may have occurred during the Sui Dynasty (A.D. 589–618) as an act of contrition by an emperor who murdered his father.

The Central Grottoes **Caves 5, 6,** and **7** are more dramatic than the first four. The Old Monastery of the Stone Buddhas, built in 1652, is located here, and three wooden towers cover the cliffside, protecting the cave entrances. At one time, many temples fronted the cliff, but only this monastery remains. I wandered through its small courtyards, where monks and vendors had pitched their prayer bead and soda stands, and entered **Cave 5,** where a 55-foot-tall Buddha with red eyes, blue hair, and a gold face illuminates the shadows. The image is arresting, even terrifying. Yungang's largest Buddha—with ears 10 feet long—was probably built to honor one of the Northern Wei emperors. The bas-relief sculptures that decorate the walls of the cave are delicately carved, and their abundance is typical of the Yungang style.

Cave 6 is equally impressive. At the entrance, Emperor Kangxi, who visited in 1697, inscribed four characters meaning "the grand unity of all doctrines." Inside, there is a 49-foot-high square tower carved from rock in the center of the square chamber. The wall and the pillar are densely decorated in ornate carvings with stories from the life of Buddha, vividly rendered in deep relief. **Caves 7** and **8** form a pair that fuses Indian and Chinese art. The Indian gods Shiva, with five faces and six arms, and Vishnu, with three faces and eight arms, ride an eagle and a bull, popular figures from Han Dynasty Chinese sculpture. Shiva and Vishnu are posted at the entrance to **Cave 8;** two carved lions lie contentedly at the foot of Buddha in **Cave 7.**

The remaining caves along the central wall **(Caves 9–15)** are richly adorned in a sea of fine bas-relief and statuary, all carved from stone and often painted in bright colors applied by a 19th-century donor. Hundreds of *apsareses* (Buddhist angels) swirl up the cave walls and across the ceilings. Buddha's followers ride elephants and meditate atop lotus flowers in a universe of plants, animals, and flowing designs. **Cave 12** contains wall carvings of 5th-century palaces and a splendid mural of musicians accompanying Buddha on ancient flutes, drums, and lutes. The large Buddha sitting cross-legged in **Cave 13** has his right arm supported by a four-armed figure standing on his knee, an innovation in Chinese sculpture found first at Yungang. **Caves 14** and **15** are heavily eroded, their front walls crumbling over the centuries, but both retain thousands of carved figures in their niches.

The Western Grottoes The most striking caves are on the western side but near the center: **Caves 16 to 20,** the first five caves carved at Yungang, their large Buddhas inside commemorating the first five emperors of the Northern Wei. These caves form a unified cluster. **Cave 16** on the right is filled with a 43-foot-high standing Buddha, one arm flung outward. The figure has a heavy appearance. His face is round, his eyes set deep. The lower portions of his body have suffered severe erosion; he seems to be emerging from the dust. **Cave 17** contains an even more massive Buddha, 50 feet tall, sitting with legs crossed, with a smaller attendant on either side. In **Cave 18,** the most impressive of the five Buddhas stands on a lotus flower, symbol of beauty flowering out of the muck that constitutes the earthly realm. His legs are short and massive, contributing to his aura of power. The folds of his robe are carved with processions of *bodhisattvas* (followers who have achieved enlightenment but chosen to return to Earth to inspire others). The four bodhisattvas who attend the Buddha are the most fully humanized and lively figures at Yungang. The monstrously divine and the merely human seem to meet in this shrine. **Cave 19** consists of three chambers. A 55-foot-tall Buddha sits in the middle, where surrounding walls, their niches filled with bodhisattvas, resemble the cells of a beehive. The caves to either side are elevated 16 feet off the ground and open like enormous second-story windows to reveal the 26-foot bodhisattvas inside.

The final cave on the west side of this cluster, **Cave 20,** is scarcely a cavern at all. An earthquake removed the front of this cave. The Buddha sits exposed in a huge halo-shaped niche, his hands on his legs. This 35-foot image has shoulders 20 feet wide. He seems set in an immobile eternity, his huge drooping ears a symbol of the worldly decorations he has cast off. A student from Datong, noticing me as I eyed the smiling statue, said this was the Buddha of the Present. On the right, he said, the Buddha of the Past stands against the surviving wall, one hand raised. On the left, there was no figure. The Buddha of the Future, the student said, has been erased. That would be fitting. The carved figures of Yungang reflect the glories of the past as resoundingly as any monument in China.

The caves at the far western end of the cliff are small and far less magnificent than those to the east. Many of them are badly eroded inside. **Cave 21** is the most impressive of the group. A tapered five-story pagoda stands in the center, its peak a lotus flower touching the ceiling. **Cave 50,** a hike up the end of the sandstone ridge, is worth a peek, too. Its walls are carved with acrobats and its ceiling with angels, birds, and flying elephants, making it a kind of stone Big Top.

Located just 10 miles west of Datong, Yungang is open daily from 9am to 5pm. Admission is RMB 25 ($3).

The no. 2 bus, with frequent departures from Datong's northern train station, takes more than 30 minutes to cover this short distance, but costs just RMB 8 (95¢). Taxis are quicker and cost about RMB 20 ($2.40). CITS offers convenient guided tours. If you are going to be at the caves during lunch, you're best off packing food purchased ahead of time at the Yungang Hotel. There are no cafes at the cave site, although Chinese snacks and drinks are sold at kiosks.

Temple of the Liao

The remains of Datong's imperial past can be discovered on foot. The streets are those of a city a decade behind the rest of urban China, lacking glass-and-steel department stores and international hotel towers. The wide avenues carry bicycles and donkey carts instead of imported automobiles and motorcycles. No lawns, few fountains, no sumptuous greenery under blue skies—this is a hard city of a million workers toiling in the basin of a sea of coal.

It's hard to believe that Datong once housed the royal palaces of the Northern Wei Dynasty, from A.D. 398 to 493. The Northern Wei were barbarians, Toba people from the northern plains beyond the nearby Great Wall, thought to be of Turkic origin. They finally abandoned Datong and moved their capital south to Louyang, but Datong would become China's capital again. The Kingdom of the Liao (A.D. 907–1125), consisting of nomadic Khitan people, ruled China until they were overrun here by yet another band of northern invaders, the Jin, ancestors of the Manchu, who would one day create China's last imperial dynasty. Out of this chaos of invading northern kingdoms, one great temple has survived in Datong: the Huayan Monastery, ancestral temple of the Liao kings.

Huayan Monastery is west of the old drum tower along Da Xijie in downtown Datong. Several of its halls date from before A.D. 1100, but the complex was finished under the Jin Dynasty 40 years later. Every hall and pavilion faces east, not south as in traditional Chinese constructions—a reflection of the sun-worshipping traditions of the Khitan conquerors.

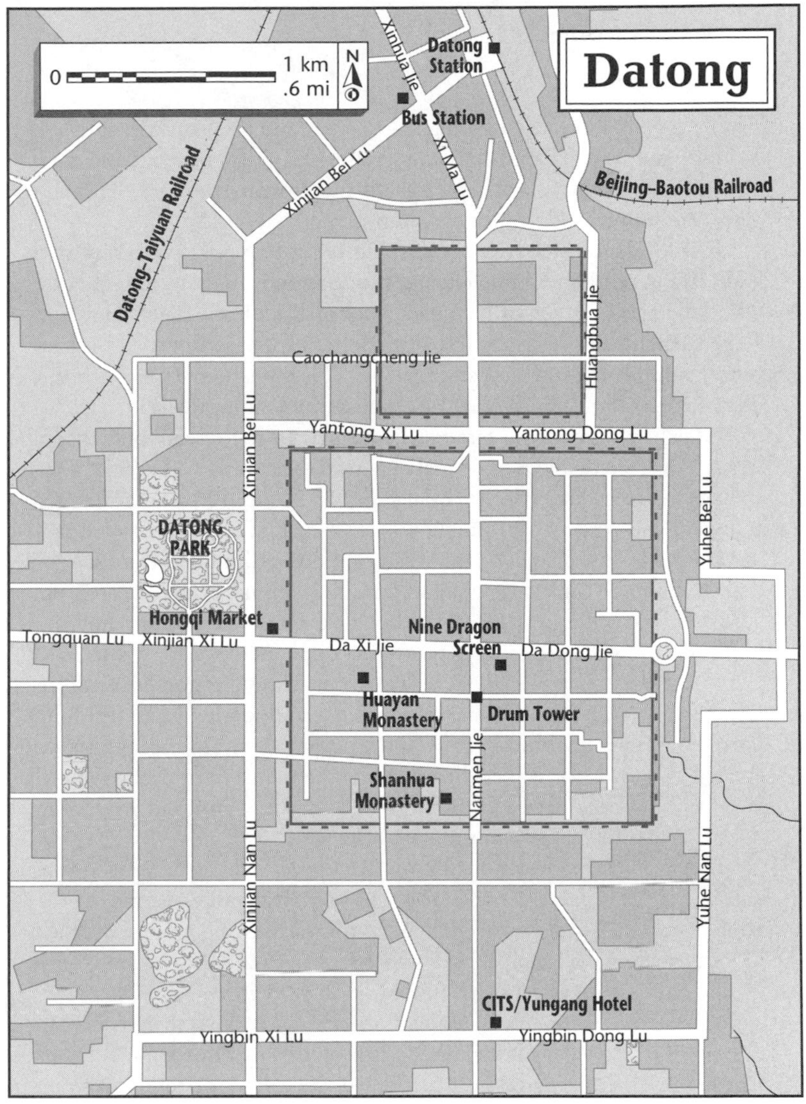

If you walk through the heart of Huayan's halls, you'll reach the main building, one of the two largest Buddhist temples in China, the **Powerful Treasure Hall (Da Xiong Bao Dian).** Set on a platform of stone 14 feet high, it shatters the horizon. Its walls are 3 feet thick. The courtyard contains strange altars on pedestals in the shape of dollhouses. These are used to hold scriptures. Inside, the hall is dark, cool, and spacious. Its centerpiece is the Five Buddhas of the Five Directions, some fashioned from wood, some from clay, and all occupying high thrones. They were made during the Ming Dynasty. The ceilings of the great temple are embellished with dragons, flowers, and the Sanskrit alphabet. When I was here, shaven monks in yellow leggings, brown pants, and gray gowns were pacing the courtyards and crossing through the moon gates. Some were old, some very young.

It is a remarkable temple, quiet and unassuming, but survives on a scale rare in modern China. During the Liao and Jin dynasties, Huayan was the central temple of its own school of Buddhism (later known as Kegon Buddhism in Japan). Huayan Buddhism, based on the Garland Sutra, upholds the essential sameness of all things. In keeping with this doctrine, the temple in Datong takes austerity to a high level.

After my visit to the temple, I returned to the streets of Datong, where I overtook handcarts of coal pucks on their way to makeshift sidewalk ovens consisting of loose bricks. At the **Hongqi Market,** I bought soda pop and strawberries from a bicycle cart. Lucky toddlers were racing around Post Office Square on electric-powered miniature army jeeps and jet fighters, their grandparents running behind them to catch up. The dust was whipping up, and although the sun was shining hot and hard, I felt as if I were moving through a dirty snowstorm.

I next passed by the wooden gate to the **Nine Dragon Screen (Jiu Long Bi),** the city's most famous sight—a ceramic mural 150 feet long portraying nine dragons rising from the sea in pursuit of the sun. It was created in A.D. 1392 as the spirit wall for the mansion of the provincial viceroy, Zhu Gui, 13th son of the first Ming emperor, but its setting doesn't suit it (it's in a vacant unkempt lot).

I turned east down an odorous backstreet and came out at the entrance to the old city wall. The **Datong city wall** is as old as the famous city wall of Xi'an. A general of the early Ming empire oversaw its construction, of stamped yellow earth, in A.D. 1372. Much of the 4-mile circumference remains, though most of it is neglected, exposed, and subject to erosion. Here, renovation is under way. New stairs lead to the top of a section of the wall that has been freshly bricked in. Sections that haven't are often used by locals as storage cellars, earthen caves dug into the walls of the city.

On the wall is a newly restored eight-sided seven-story brown-brick pagoda, **Yan Tower.** Suspended from its eaves are golden bells with velvety clappers. Here I inadvertently flushed out a pair of Chinese lovers in a secret embrace. All of us were embarrassed. We smiled and left in different directions.

The brick soon runs out, and the wall reverts to packed earth. On the southeast corner of old Datong broken ramparts of a guard tower survive, its archways collapsing. South of the city wall is a uniform housing development a half-mile wide and 15 blocks deep. Each gray-tiled rooftop is punctuated by a half-dozen regularly spaced smokestacks.

Touches of life slop over the edges. The rooftops are littered with laundry, logs, sticks of firewood, rolls of sheet metal, tool handles, oil drums, baskets, and a few cats patrolling for rats or scraps.

Back in the hotel, I met a young clerk who spoke excellent English. She had just graduated from Beijing's top university with a degree in international business, but rather than follow her classmates to the money-cities on the eastern seaboard, she obeyed her parents. They wanted her close to home, in Datong. This is still the traditional way, although to me it seemed like finishing Harvard, heading home, and landing a job at McDonald's.

She didn't seem to mind. When she spoke of Datong and its future in China, she beamed. She pointed out that uptown there's some new development now: big modern department stores, a Crocodile boutique, a California Beef Noodle outlet. She laughed when I asked her what locals call the tiny, gleaming red, two-cylinder taxis with long snouts that dart hither and yon through the streets. Rats, she said. What do people like to eat in Datong? I asked. Dog meat is extremely popular, she said, but quite expensive at RMB 20 ($2.50) per kilogram in the street stalls. She was looking forward to a special graduation dinner of the same at a friend's house. She revealed the secret to cooking dog: Boil it in a pot, she said, but don't forget to throw in one new brick.

She also suggested that I book a tour to the Temple Suspended over the Void and see something of how the people live in the countryside. Many of them, she said, still live in caves.

Temple Suspended over the Void

The next morning, I met our group: taxi driver, guide, and two Austrian geologists who have been working in Xi'an. We traveled for 2 hours over the barren rolling hills south of Datong, a plateau of sandstone, coal, and soda ash, a desert shaved down to a stubble. Villages sprout like oases, built of the same dried earth on which they squat. The two vacationing geologists were not impressed with the "Big Sameness" of the landscape.

Forty twisting, bumpy miles later we reached the town of Hunyuan, where concrete and brick replace mud and straw. Ahead is Heng Shan Bei, a high ridge of limestone, parted by the Mouth of the Dragon, the opening in the **Magnet Gorge.** This gorge was bored out in A.D. 397 by a Wei Dynasty emperor and his 10,000 troops to ease passage through the mountains. On its west wall is **Xuan Kong Si,** the Temple Suspended over the Void. It was constructed in the 6th century by a team of Daoist monks known as the Feathered Scholars, because to reach the heights of the temple fastened to the immense cliff face must have required wings.

The suspended temple is spectacular from a distance. It consists of 40 cave rooms carved into limestone, fronted with wooden facades, columns, and tiled roofs, all connected by a series of catwalks and bridges perched on jutting beams and posts socketed into solid rock. A mountain gazetteer describes the Temple Suspended over the Void this way: "The Air-Temple is very steep to come up to, without steps. The Temple Tied Up in Emptiness hangs alone in the Gorge of Porcelain and gets scarcely any sunlight. It contains many shrines and is the abode of ox-riding, sword-bearing immortals. Looking over the side, the scene is like a great ocean; only birds can fly over or monkeys climb out."

These days, of course, visitors come to climb up to the temple. There are concrete steps to its entrance, there's a toll booth, and the way along the river in the gorge is lined with souvenir stands selling polished rocks and charms. The temple retains much the same form it possessed for centuries. The wooden catwalks and stairways still appear dilapidated and dangerous. Each small cave hall is festooned with a sacred figure or two, most of them fashioned from plaster and brightly painted. The central altar features a shrine to three religions, with statues of Buddha, Lao Zi, and Confucius in a black beard.

The temple has been rebuilt many times over 14 centuries, but the triple-storied main sections of the temple are still pinioned to the rock with simple timbers. Though a new parking lot and suspension bridge have been completed in the last few years, the catwalks of the temple still creak as you walk from shrine to shrine. Above, I could make out evidence of earlier cave altars and footholds. In earlier times, I suspected, the Temple Suspended over the Void sprawled elsewhere, or perhaps hermits pulled up their ladders there as they entered their own cliff-side nests.

Today there was only one monk in attendance, but I did spot the same vendor I saw years ago, wearing a green Mao cap and pacing at the entrance, an eagle perched on his shoulder. The eagle is for hire (RMB 5/60¢) if you want a snapshot.

The Temple Suspended over the Void is dwarfed by a modern shrine of sorts, a dam and reservoir suspended higher yet at the end of the gorge and hidden from view. But the temple remains as startling as ever, a fairy castle of yellow tiles and red wooden columns pinned impossibly to a face of rock.

Cave Houses & Coal

We headed back on the long winding road to Datong, stopping on the shoulder to visit one of the cave houses dug out of the steep earthen bluffs. The whole family came out to greet us: grandpa, mom and pop, a toddler dressed in a red embroidered suit and plastic orange thongs. The patriarch was burnt black by the sun. His few remaining teeth were sharp and yellowed. He has occupied the house "only 50 years," he said. The inside of the cave consisted of two large curving earthen chambers tamped smooth. The entry room was used for storage. The second room, the family's living quarters, was lighted by a single bare electric bulb and a six-paned glass window and contained a small coal-burning stove in one corner and no running water. Niches had been scraped out of the walls to shelve shoes and clothing and sturdy wicker baskets of empty green bottles awaiting refunds. The walls were decorated with garish posters of pop stars and teen idols; with scrolls, calendars, liquor bottles, and packages of cookies; with bags of rice and bowls of fruit set on a wooden altar under a mirror. Under the window was a *kang,* a wide communal bed built of mud and brick, covered by a rattan mat and heated underneath by coal fire.

This cave house was a neat, homey, warm, cheerful abode. Many are 2 centuries old. Outside, even the family dog had a matching mud dog house, its own semidetached cave. The earthen walls were smooth but flaked at my touch. The toddler was selling tiny cloth horses his mother had stuffed and stitched together. I bought two ornaments for a Christmas tree.

The fields are mean here, their plowed furrows dry. The villages are clusters of hand-shaped earth. Ancient earthen signal towers, left over from the Western Wei Dynasty, tower like massive shanks. The camel caravans that might have passed this way have been replaced by ranks of 60-ton double-trailered coal trucks, some of them produced by Steyr, an Austrian joint-venture corporation. All these trucks are as slow as dinosaurs after a feast, limping up the hills at no more than 5 miles per hour. The drivers wear leafy branches around their necks. Whenever they have to stop on the road—breakdowns are frequent—they hang branches from the back and front of their trucks as a warning. Our guide told us that recently a truck accident caused a traffic logjam that went on for miles and took 2 days to free up.

As we approached Datong, we saw coal stations, fields with brick shacks where the trucks stop and unload. The coal is sized by hand and restacked. Oxen and donkeys hitched to wooden plows clear rocks from the fields. Nomads on horseback sweep across the valleys between sandstone buttes. The north is a hard region and Datong is a hard city, racked by wind, its air scratchy with coal dust and desert silt, which makes the survival of its imperial temples all the more precious.

PRACTICAL INFORMATION

ORIENTATION

Datong is located between two sections of the Great Wall on a 4,000-foot plain in northern Shanxi Province, 200 miles west of Beijing. The city can be toured on foot if you stay on the southern side, far from the railroad station. To see the Temple Suspended over the Void, however, a guided tour is recommended. For many visitors, the main reason to visit Datong is to see the ancient Buddhist caves carved at Yungang, 10 miles north of the city.

Datong is also the gateway to one of the Five Sacred Mountains of China, the northern Daoist peak of **Heng Shan Bei,** a 2-hour drive south of the city. See the separate chapter on Heng Shan Bei.

GETTING THERE

There is no airport. The express **train** to Beijing is a pleasant 7-hour journey.

TOURS & STRATAGEMS

China International Travel Service (CITS) has efficient offices in the Yungang Hotel (☎ 0352/502-4176) and at the train station (☎ 0352/502-2265; fax 0352/502-2046). I used the train station office, managed by Gao Jin Wu, where day tours were easily arranged, train tickets booked, and hotel reservations secured. If you are not intercepted by a CITS employee at the train station, go into the main entrance on the eastern side and turn left; the office is labeled in English.

For RMB 100 ($12) CITS offers a guided tour (with car and driver) that includes both the Temple Suspended over the Void and the Yungang Buddhist Caves, an excellent value. Lunch and two admissions, a total of RMB 85 ($10), are not included. "Panda Bus Tours" for groups are also available from CITS to the Great Wall and the Steam Train factory for the same price. All tours leave the Yungang Hotel at 8:30am, the train station at 9am.

WHERE TO STAY

The energetic CITS guides are quite likely to pick you up as you come out of the Datong train station and book you a hotel on the spot. Their economy choice is the new 11-story **Fei Tian Hotel** next door, with doubles costing RMB 190 ($23). It is already run-down, however, and the location is too far from downtown. The rooms have a view of a large beer factory and two huge brick smokestacks about an arm's length away. Strongly insist on the Yungang Hotel.

Yungang Hotel (Yungang Binguan). *21 Yingbin Dong Lu.* ☎ *0352/502-1601. Fax 0352/209-0006. 240 units. TV TEL. RMB 420 ($51) double. JCB, MC, V.* The good news is that this is Datong's best hotel. The bad news is the same. This two-star monstrosity has a good location, modest but modern facilities, and a few extra services, including a business center, two restaurants, and a small lobby bar. The Yungang is not a luxury hotel—there's no pool or turndown service—but the rooms and bathrooms are Western style (although not well maintained) and the television receives some satellite stations.

WHERE TO DINE

The best restaurant in town has no name, but it is on the south side of **Yingbin Xi Lu,** across from the Yungang Hotel (one door west of the glitzy Hongqi Restaurant). You'll recognize it by the Christmas tree lights on the outside and the sparkling clean chairs and tables inside. It's a comfy little cafe with an English menu, run by a helpful young staff. Main courses cost RMB 25 to RMB 42 ($3 to $5). The big **Hongqi Restaurant** next door is more formal and twice as expensive. The Chinese dishes in both restaurants are good.

The **Yungang Hotel** (☎ 0352/502-1601) has its main restaurant off the lobby. This is the best place to go for a Western fixed-price breakfast. You can also get fairly inexpensive—RMB 34 to RMB 85 ($4 to $10)—and quite average Chinese lunches and dinners, featuring hot pots and mutton stews.

HARBIN: TIGERS & ICE
哈尔滨

HARBIN, CAPITAL OF HEILONGJIANG (Black Dragon River), China's most northerly province, is best known these days for its **Harbin Ice and Snow Festival,** a world-famous ice sculpture display held annually each winter. I visited Harbin in late March, however, after the ice had melted, primarily to see Harbin's newest attraction, its **Siberia Tiger Park,** where 30 of these endangered animals were freely roaming and being trained for eventual release into the wild.

Harbin is a fascinating city even without its tigers and ice. It's located on the endless Manchurian plains, known for vast forests, among the largest left in the Far East. The province borders the former Soviet Union, with the Black Dragon River (better known by its Russian name, the Amur) serving as the northeastern dividing line between China and Siberia. Harbin was occupied by Japanese forces in 1931, seized by Russian armies in 1945, and retaken by the Chinese with the establishment of the People's Republic of China in 1949.

Daoli Old Town

The Russian influence is still strong in Harbin, especially in the city's unusual architecture. Onion domes outnumber upturned tile-roofed eaves along Harbin's main street, giving Harbin a cityscape unique among China's major cities. Walking down Zhongyang Dajie to the Songhua River in the old town, **Daoli District,** a mile's stroll from the Holiday Inn, I passed dozens of these old buildings with their spires and cupolas, now converted to offices, restaurants, and department stores. The street is made of cobblestones. Several of the side streets are devoted to pedestrian-only outdoor markets. The largest market is on the street labeled **Xi-11-Dao Jie,** unmistakable because of its crowds and the large Russian-style turrets at its entrance. Clothes, food, pine-nut stands, and beggars line both sides of this alleyway.

A number of the Russian facades on Zhongyang Street are being removed, but their modern replacements are tasteful European-style

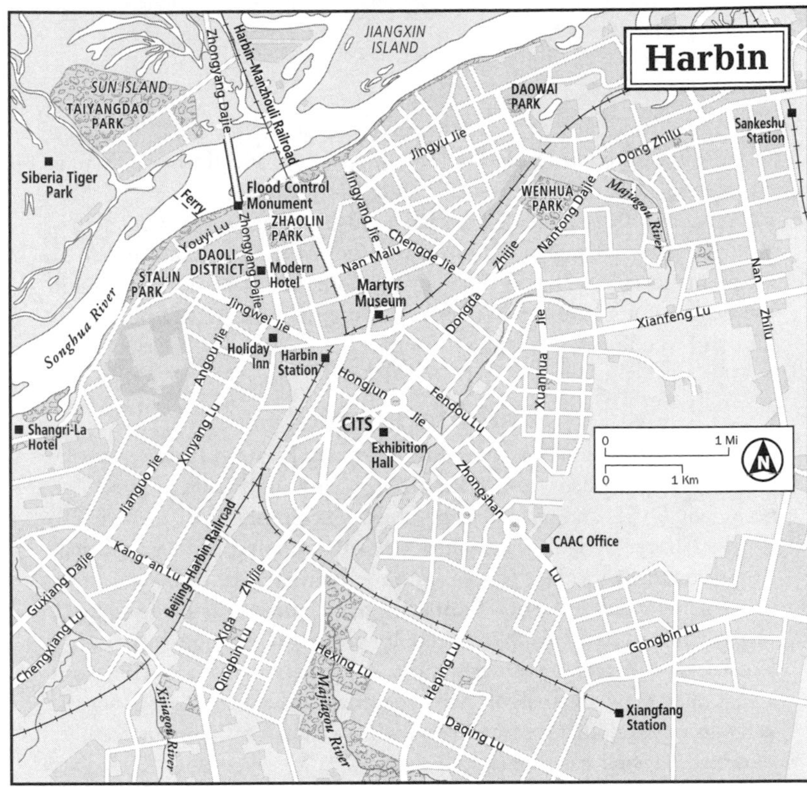

buildings, much in keeping with the old-town atmosphere. One old building worth taking a peek inside is the ironically named **Modern Hotel,** at 89 Zhongyang Dajie, a Russian-style building opened in 1903 whose lobby has been colorfully, if a little shabbily, restored.

On my slow walk down this street in the Chinese city once called "Little Moscow," I also came across a more modern trend: Western commercialization. Amid onion towers, cupolas, and painted plaster columns are a Kentucky Fried Chicken outlet (complete with a white statue of the Colonel), a TCBY cafe, a Playboy logo store, and Bossini and Crocodile boutiques. These signs of Western encroachment are eating into the heart of most Chinese cities, so I was not entirely surprised to find them even in this northern outpost.

The leading foreign presence in Harbin remains Russian, however, as it has since Russians began building a train line linking Harbin to Vladivostok in 1896. Later, in 1917, White Russians fleeing the Communist Revolution arrived in Harbin by the thousands, settling in and erecting scores of Russian-style buildings and churches. During the 1930s, half the 200,000 residents of Harbin were Russian. Although most of them left after China's own Communist Revolution in 1949, Harbin is still a major trading post for consumer goods bound for the north. Most of the Russians come to Harbin on business, not for sightseeing, hoping to pick up items that are scarce enough in Siberia to command high prices. Some Russians trade Siberian goods, such as furs, straight across, with no cash exchanged. Harbin is a center of the fur trade, and there are plenty of coat, hat, and stole outlets along the main street, although these are outnumbered by Western wedding salons featuring photo studios and wedding-gown rentals.

Parks & Temples

Harbin has attractions apart from its old town. **Zhaolin Park,** where the ice festival is held, is just a long block east of the main street, on Shangzhi Dajie, and even though the ice sculptures had melted into giant ice cubes by late March, it was worth trooping through the spacious grounds, with their gardens and rock formations.

The splendid, red-brick **Santa Sophia Church** (on Dong Da Zhi Jie, admission RMB 10/$1.25) no longer hosts religious services in Russian; it now serves as an arts and crafts gallery with a retail outlet. It is jammed into an area of new construction, most notably several karaoke entertainment complexes with monumental Roman statuary mounted on their garish facades.

Harbin's Confucian Temple, **Wen Miao,** also on Dong Da Zhi Jie in the Nangang District, is worth browsing through (admission RMB 30/$3.75). The grounds are large, with a dozen pavilions. Golden dragons emblazon the roofs. Although this complex was not built until 1926, the Confucian grounds contain steles (stone tablets), dated A.D. 551 and A.D. 587, as well as three ornate triple-footed gates and one yurt (whose purpose I could not determine).

A more interesting complex, the **Temple of Bliss (Jile Si),** admission RMB 6/75¢, is situated at 9 Dong Da Zhi Jie. It contains a small statue of the god Puxian on an elephant, along with the familiar likenesses of Maitreya, Buddha, and Guanyin. A fair number of monks and nuns inhabit this temple, which is in the shadow of the Qiji Futu pagoda. Although built recently, in 1924, this is the largest temple in the entire province. The street outside is one of the liveliest in town, filled with stalls selling golden Buddhas and glass shrines to the faithful.

War Crimes

One afternoon I got up my courage, hired a taxi, and paid a call on the **Exhibition Hall for the Ruins of the Japanese Troops Invading China,** a war crimes exhibit opened in 1982 at the site of a secret germ warfare research center 12 miles south of Harbin. Here, starting in 1939, the Japanese performed unimaginably horrible experiments on citizens (employing frostbite, bomb explosions, biological agents, and surgical procedures), comparable to those conducted in Nazi Germany's concentration camps. Its existence was covered up until the 1980s.

The exhibit, mercifully, is not so horrifying as the crimes. It consists mainly of a few artifacts from the Manchurian occupation, telltale documents, an incinerator smokestack, and a re-creation of a gruesome operation using life-sized wax figures.

Songhua River

It was a relief after a detour through the horrors of the past to return to the cobblestone main street of Harbin and resume my pleasant stroll down to the swift-flowing Songhua River. A 26-mile embankment was constructed along the river after the floods of 1933, and a spacious promenade, now lined with trees and statuary, was developed on the shore. The promenade retains its original name: **Stalin Park (Jiangpan Gongyuan).**

The most prominent statue is the **Flood Control Monument,** built the year after one of Harbin's most notable floods, which covered the downtown streets in up to 9 feet of water. The monument is now a popular gathering point for visitors and locals. Vendors circle the monument, selling hot pine nuts and kites in the shape of birds.

Like Zhongyang Dajie, the Stalin Park promenade is a prime location for a leisurely stroll, fronting the river for miles. In the summer, scores of tour boats of every possible description (including an all-metal enclosed vessel in the shape of a fish with fins) take passengers out on the river or across to **Sun Island (Taiyang Dao).** Fishermen also beach their open boats on the sandy banks and ice-cream vendors ply their trade along the walkway—it's quite a festive spot when the sun is shining and sailboats are for rent. In the deep of winter, the river freezes solid—often remaining so for half the year—and ice-skating is popular. This is also the place for winter swimmers to take the plunge. Thirty swimmers braved the icy river in 1982, when this ritual began, and nowadays as many as 300 brave the water each winter, plunging into a special 60-foot-long lane carved out of the ice.

Tigers of Siberia

The **Siberia Tiger Park** (open daily 9am to 5pm, admission RMB 30/$3.75) is located across the Songhua River on Sun Island, where a large recreational district is under development, featuring gardens, swimming lakes, cafes, and a hunting range. I hired a car at the Holiday Inn to reach Sun Island via a bridge south of town. Siberia Tiger Park has plans to expand into a large preserve, with areas for deer, bears, and swans, as well as shops, a fishing pond, a restaurant, and a fairy-tale theme village. At present, only a museum and large fenced tiger reserve are finished. The museum is a dark, uninspiring cavern of a building with photographic displays (captions are in Chinese), a motley stuffed tiger with its kittens, and an informational film about the tigers projected on a screen through a very dirty lens.

Visitors board a variety of vehicles for an extended drive through the tiger reserve. I was placed on an old bus with sliding windows, filled with Russian teenagers on spring vacation. There was no guide on the bus and no effort was made to keep us from sliding open the unbarred windows during the tour, but there were numerous tigers stalking the grounds. We had plenty of close encounters. At one point, a caged jeep appeared and the gamekeeper placed a live chicken on the roof. A tiger promptly leaped on top and pounced on its prey. All the tigers, including some cubs, looked healthy and seemed at ease on the sandy reserve. The Siberia Tiger Park's mission is to save, study, and breed these great cats in captivity and eventually release them into their native habitat. In order to complete this mission, the tigers must be trained to hunt live prey. I should not have been surprised, therefore, when I learned that a few weeks earlier the Holiday Inn had donated a live cow to the park. Hotel employees were invited out that day and bused into the reserve to watch the tigers tackle and devour the poor creature, a spectacle not likely to be offered to visitors at Western zoos!

But then, Harbin is not like most places in the West—indeed, not much like most places in China.

The Far North

Having reached the northern edge of the Middle Kingdom at Harbin, I was struck by the variety of culture and landscape that China encompasses. Returning to the airport, I passed a dozen magazine-cover photo opportunities: a plethora of donkey and horse carts driven by dark-faced peasants in floppy-eared hats, crude vegetable markets on the roadsides, piles of straw heaped high by hand in the flat fields, cold rivers running swiftly through avenues of wiry trees, and, incongruously, clusters of Chinese theme parks awaiting summer visitors with their Disneyesque, Sino-Rococo, Magic Middle-Kingdom turrets and spires.

These were amusements seemingly at odds with the harsh climate and country life of the Black Dragon province—this once distant Manchuria of tigers and ice.

PRACTICAL INFORMATION

ORIENTATION & WHEN TO GO

Harbin (urban population about four million) is 860 miles northwest of Beijing in one of the coldest regions of China. In 1900, over 60,000 foreigners from 16 countries called Harbin home. While most of the foreign population is gone, there are still 40 ethnic minorities in the city, including people who migrated here from Mongolia, Manchuria, and Korea. Harbin's province, Heilongjiang, shares a border with Siberia. Spring is often a pleasant, sunny season, and in summer the Songhua River comes alive with boat tours and swimmers. Two events worth taking in are the celebrated **Harbin Ice and Snow Festival,** officially conducted from January 5 through February (and into early March if the weather stays cold), and the 12-day **Harbin Music Festival** in July (exact dates vary from year to year).

GETTING THERE

By Plane The flight from Beijing to **Yanjiagang International Airport** requires just 90 minutes. A taxi into town is another 40 minutes, but Holiday Inn will provide a transfer in its van if you fax ahead your arrival time—a wise tactic, since taxi drivers often charge foreigners triple the going rate after claiming their meter is "broken." For airport information, call ☎ 0451/289-4114.

By Train The train ride from Beijing is an 18-hour overnight affair through mountains and into the virtual desert lands of Heilongjiang Province.

TOURS & STRATAGEMS

Tours Two tourist offices organize tours, including extended trips through the province: **Heilongjiang China International Travel Service (CITS),** 95–1 Zhongshan Lu (☎ 0451/230-2601; fax 0451/230-2476), and **Harbin Overseas Tourism Company,** located in the Harbin Modern Hotel, 89 Zhongyang Dajie (☎ 0451/461-5846; fax 0451/461-4997). Guided tours, as well as air and rail tickets, can also be booked at hotel desks.

WHERE TO STAY

Holiday Inn City Centre Harbin (Wanda Jiari Jiudian). *90 Jingwei Lu (downtown).* ☎ *800/465-4329 or 0451/422-6666. Fax 0451/422-1661. 144 units. A/C MINIBAR TV TEL. $110 double. AE, DC, JCB, MC, V.* This well-established four-star hotel is conveniently located at the downtown end of Zhongyang Dajie, the main street to the river in the old Daoli District. There's an English-speaking staff, a chef from France, and a new general manager who is dedicated to keeping this the best international hotel in Harbin. A local quintet plays light classical music in the lobby each evening.

Amenities: Health club, sauna, business center, room service (6am–midnight), next-day dry cleaning and laundry, nightly turndown, beauty salon, shopping arcade, free airport shuttle.

Modern Hotel (Madie'er Binguan). *129 Zhongyang Dajie (downtown).* ☎ *0451/661-5846. Fax 0451/461-4997. 160 units. A/C MINIBAR TV TEL. $80 double. JCB, MC, V.* This turn-of-the-century monument to Harbin's Russian past is superbly located in the heart of Daoli old town, a few blocks from the river. The lobby is right out of *Casablanca.* The hotel was renovated in 1990, achieved three-star ranking, and raised its prices but not its service level. The rooms are not as well maintained as at the Holiday Inn. The staff speaks some English and is cheerful. Plenty of Russian businesspeople stay here.

Shangri-La Hotel Harbin (Harbin Xiangge Lila Fandian). *555 You Yi Lu, Dao Li District (southwest of downtown, near the Songhua River Bridge).* ☎ *800/942-5050 or 0451/485-8888. Fax 0451/462-1777. 346 units. A/C MINIBAR TV TEL. $180 double. AE, DC, JCB, MC, V.* One of Harbin's newest hotels (built in 1999), and its most luxurious, the Shangri-La offers spacious rooms trimmed in rich wooden moldings, with executive desks, sofas, data plugs, in-room safes, and a host of five-star amenities.

Dining: The Shang Palace serves Cantonese dishes. The Coffee Garden has international buffets (Asian, American, European) and an extensive imported wine list.

Amenities: Health and fitness club, indoor swimming pool, tennis court, sauna, Jacuzzi, massage, 24-hour room service, same-day laundry and dry cleaning, beauty salon, business center, tour desk, newsstand, conference rooms, valet, concierge.

WHERE TO DINE

The Holiday Inn's **Phoenix Restaurant** serves excellent dim sum, and its **Le Petit Coffee Shop** (☎ 0451/422-6666) has a fine buffet with Western and French dishes. Reservations aren't necessary. Main courses cost $5 to $14; the buffet is $12. Ice-cream desserts at Le Petit are quite good.

The **Gloria Inn Hotel,** 257 Zhongyang Dajie (☎ 0451/463-8855), just a block from the Songhua River, has an elegant street-level dining room with an international buffet. It serves one of the largest hamburgers I've ever eaten (although I wondered halfway through if it were really beef).

Across the street from the Gloria Inn is a new locally run **Hanns Burger** joint, and across the street from the Modern Hotel is the **Huamei Western Restaurant** (142 Zhongyang Dajie), which serves good Russian dishes, with main courses running RMB 30 to RMB 60 ($3.75 to $7.50).

Local restaurants often specialize in Muslim dishes or wild game, and their quality and price usually correspond to the number of red lanterns suspended from the rafters outside (I've counted up to 10 of these at one site).

For American fast food with peppery seasoning, try the big **Kentucky Fried Chicken** on Zhongyang Dajie at Xi-7-Dao Jie, which is better than the similar **Brownie's Chicken** (a Canadian chain) on Shangzhi Dajie, opposite Zhaolin Park. Expect to pay the same prices you pay outside of China.

QINGDAO: BEACHES & BEER

青岛

QINGDAO, A MODERN CITY ON THE Yellow Sea in southeast Shandong Province, is China's fourth busiest shipping port, and the site of many foreign joint-ventures, especially factories financed by German and Korean corporations. It's internationally famous for its *Tsingtao* beer, one of China's leading exports. Unfortunately, the great brewery for some reason is not open for public tours. Instead, Qingdao lures Chinese visitors to its summertime beaches, some of the best in China. For foreign travelers, however, it is Qingdao's legacy as a German concession that makes the city worth seeing. (A "concession" was a district of the city surrendered to foreign colonial control as a result of trade treaties China was compelled to sign following the Opium Wars of the 1840s.) Large sections of Qingdao retain whole neighborhoods of turn-of-the-century Western architecture, adjacent to traditional and modern Chinese development—a mixture that makes this hilly and green city on the coast an invigorating refuge from the noisy, polluted, often ugly modern metropolises. The presence of old Western residences and tree-lined avenues in Qingdao are startling and surprising and there's no equivalent in the West: you won't see large neighborhoods of Chinese temples and tile-roofed shop houses in downtown London or New York.

German Town

I headed immediately for the greatest concentration of Qingdao's German legacy, the **Badaguan District** on Taiping Bay near Beach Number 2. A sign in English on Zhengyangguan Lu (the same street called Zhanshan Da Lu as it continues east) directs visitors south into lovely, quiet lanes, each planted with a different tree or flower. There's a maple lane, peach lane, and snow-pine lane, each fronted by Western mansions and landscaped lawns—the area closely resembles an upper-class neighborhood on Lake Geneva. The grand houses with their spacious yards and gardens also reminded me of those at Pebble Beach. A number of these old estates have become exclusive summer beach resorts for workers and party bosses of the government agencies and companies that now own them. Many of the houses are rented out as vacation villas. The **Badaguan Hotel,** at 19 Shanhaiguan, began as a German hotel in 1903, was expanded by the Spanish and Japanese in the 1920s, and became a Chinese hotel in 1953. Its main building dates from 1988.

The largest structure in Badaguan is right on the coastline. This **palace,** an immense castlelike fortress of stone, was once the German governor's lodge. It's now open to visitors. Beneath its wall is a rugged beach.

Qingdao's German influence began in 1897, when Kaiser Wilhelm annexed portions of the city and developed it as a railway terminus, deep-water port, and naval station. The brewery went up in 1903. The Germans controlled Qingdao until 1914, when it fell to the Japanese, and the Japanese occupied Qingdao until 1922, when the Chinese regained it.

The Pier

From Badaguan it's easy enough to walk down to the **Number 1 Beach,** Qingdao's longest, with its strip of wooden beach houses and changing rooms. From there, I continued west along the white sands through Lu Xun Park toward **Beach Number 6** (the beaches are not numbered in geographical order). This is the location of Qingdao's harbor landmark, **Qianhai Zhangqiao Pier,** which extends 1,300 feet into the bay to **Huilan Ge,** an eight-sided pavilion. Dating from 1891 and expanded in 1931, it remains the prime gathering point for locals, visitors, and a tidal wave of vendors hawking ice cream, shells, pearls, and photographs. The beachfront by the Pier is rocky, and plenty of people comb those rocks for edible seafood and plants. Overlooking this beach is an esplanade that after dark becomes a lively strolling area for locals. Even here, the pace of life is far more relaxed than in most Chinese cities.

Two Churches

Directly north of the Pier is **Zhongshan Lu,** Qingdao's main street, which now rips through a rapidly modernizing downtown of new department stores, small boutiques, and a mixture of old and new shops, some selling designer-name fashions and Swiss watches. I stopped for lunch at one of many hole-in-the-wall cafes and ordered the local hot pot, as well as clams, bite-sized octopuses, and a 6-inch-wide crab. (The price was a bit steep; the crab alone was RMB 35/$4.20.)

Back on the big avenue, I followed Zhongshan Lu north until I could see the **Catholic church (Tianzhu Jiaotong),** located up a steep

cobblestone lane to the east (on Sifang Lu). This large stone edifice with its two towering spires was built by the Germans in the early 1930s. Still quite active with Chinese worshippers, it is also open to foreigners, who can attend mass here. The curious can take a look around from 8:30am to 4pm daily for RMB 5/65¢. The surrounding streets are lined with German concession buildings, their black iron balconies draped in drying laundry.

East of city center, at 15 Jiangsu Lu, near the entrance to Xinhao Park, is the **Protestant Church (Jidu Jiaotong),** also built by the German community in the first decade of the 20th century. Look for its high clock tower, which still keeps time. Visitors can tour the interior daily from 8:30am to 5pm (admission RMB 3/35¢). Both the Protestant and Catholic churches underwent extensive interior renovations in 1999. Most of the windows and statues are new. Both the big churches come into splendid view, along with the red-roofed Western neighborhoods and white-sand harbor beaches, from the top of **Xinhao (Marker) Hill,** a steep trek up from the Protestant church. On the peak are three domes in the shape of mushrooms, stuffed with vendors and panoramic viewpoints. The park is open daily dawn to dusk and charges RMB 2 (25¢) admission.

Mao Slept Here

The most curious treasure in **Xinhao Park,** however, is down toward the harbor on its grassy flanks, where a magnificent residence was built for the German governor in 1903. This mansion has been converted into a hotel, the **Qingdao Welcome Guest House** (also called the Safety Hotel), located at 26 Longshan Lu (☎ 0532/286-1985). Its interior is a museum of the high life enjoyed by colonials during the days of the Qingdao Concession. The stained glass, dark woods, and plush furnishings have survived, perhaps because Chairman Mao and Premier Zhou En-Lai met here in 1957, and Chairman Mao and his wife occupied one of the suites for a month. You can rent the Chairman Mao suite today for RMB 1,600 ($192) a night (although it's a little musty and the bathroom facilities are old). A Chinese family occupying the suite invited me in for a look. They proudly showed off Chairman Mao's green felt-top desk and revealed that it contained a hidden compartment in the right-hand drawer. The hotel's lobby and dining rooms are the original living rooms and dining halls of the mansion, with carved woods, massive chandeliers, and velvet curtains still intact. A German grand piano, built in 1876, occupies one corner of this immense chamber.

A favorite park among locals is **Little Fish Hill (Xiaoyushan),** a short walk south of the mansion. The three-story pagoda (Lanchao Ge) on its peak is stocked with souvenir salespeople and offers an unfettered view of Badaguan to the east and the Pier to the west. This pavilion was once used as a marine observation post. It's a quiet place to survey this seaside city.

Sea Mountain

Next to Qingdao's beaches, which swell with upward of 100,000 vacationers in the summer, the most popular outdoor attraction is **Mount Lao (Lao Shan),** about 25 miles directly east along the rocky coastline of the Yellow Sea. The highway to Lao Shan runs by one of Qingdao's newest attractions, its **International Beer City,** which is seldom open except for Qingdao's International Beer Festival. The festival begins its 2-week run on August 12, when the grounds host one of the biggest beer gardens outside of Bavaria, supplemented by fireworks, beach volleyball, motorcycle races, sailing and swimming competitions, beer-drinking contests, and whatever else the local promoters can dream up.

The coastal highway is charming any time of year. Stone cutting is a large industry here, where granite dominates the landscape. The Lao mountains rise abruptly to 3,000 feet from the white-boulder shoreline.

A trail of stone stairs leads to the peaks (or you can hitch a ride on the chairlift). The path is steep but quite scenic, with increasingly dazzling views down empty abysses to the tiny fishing villages below. Vendors here specialize in strings of **pearls,** the product of those fishing villages, with prices under $5. (The price drops further the higher you hike.) Another popular trailside commodity is a package of three sea treasures: a dried turtle, a tiny "sea-dragon" eel, and a seahorse. Lao Shan mineral water, the most famous in China and the basic ingredient in Tsingtao beer, originates in the springs of the Lao mountains, where there were once 72 Daoist temples.

There are still a few temples in these mountains. In Daoist legends, this is the home of the Eight Immortals, who could fly with the clouds. Qin Shi Huang, the first emperor of unified China, is reputed to have visited here more than two thousand years ago in search of the elusive potion of immortality. His visit is commemorated in the sprawling **Taiqing Temple,** a Song Dynasty complex spread across the cliffs on the eastern shore of the mountain range.

A Temple by the Sea

Lacking time to make a comprehensive trek of this vast sea mountain park, I contented myself with a climb up to **Peach Peak** (along the chairlift line) and then a descent to the **Xiaqinggong Temple,** located on the southern beachfront. This complex, consisting of three temples and courtyards, was established in 14 B.C. and rebuilt during the Song Dynasty 900 years ago. The western temple, **Sanhuang Hall,** contains a copy inscribed in stone of Genghis Khan's edict of A.D. 1271 calling for the protection of Daoist culture. The courtyards are home to ancient cypress trees. There's also a statue of the ever-popular Guanyin, Goddess of Mercy, who the locals tell me has the face of a woman but the body of a man. When I asked why, I was told that the goddess was really a man but took on the face of a woman to show a compassionate face to petitioners.

The seaside temple is surrounded by ancient specimens of elms and cypress, a bamboo field, cafes, shops selling sea turtle shells, and a parking lot. A few monks wander about, but I doubt this is a vigorous Daoist temple these days. Certainly it is overrun with Chinese visitors in the summer, and money-making has become a major religion.

I returned to the city and to the Badaguan District for a farewell stroll one afternoon in the late spring, finding it the quietest neighborhood I'd ever encountered in China, a green island of parks, beaches, and architecture—if not an elixir of immortality, certainly an ingredient.

PRACTICAL INFORMATION

ORIENTATION & WHEN TO GO

Qingdao, located in southeast Shandong Province on the Yellow Sea, is one of China's best-known seaside resorts. It was occupied by the Germans in 1897, and its architecture still bears a remarkably foreign stamp. In the summer, Qingdao is crowded with Chinese visitors. The rest of the year, it's a quiet retreat, with mild days and plenty of sunshine.

Among annual events, there's the **Qingdao International Beer Festival,** August 12 to 18, which coincides with a "Love of the Sea" carnival and a city arts fair. This annual festival now attracts about one million visitors, who consume a total of 600 tons of beer. The Beer City Hall resembles an Octoberfest drinking hall with its long tables and 1.5-liter pitchers of beer (RMB 30/$3.75 each), but the stage shows are strictly Chinese, with disco performers, fashion shows, and beer-drinking contests. The Beer City Hall seats 2,000. Also during the summer, several hundred thousand Chinese tourists head for the Qingdao beaches daily, considerably altering this island of tranquility.

GETTING THERE

By Plane The airport is 21 miles north of the city. Airport taxis charge up to RMB 150 ($19) for the trip. **Dragonair,** with an office in the Grand Regency Hotel, 1 Taiwan Lu (☎ 0532/589-6809), has service between Hong Kong and Qingdao. Air tickets on regional airlines can be booked from hotel service desks; there are flights between Qingdao and many Chinese cities, including Beijing and Shanghai.

By Train There is a direct but slow overnight train from Shanghai and an express train from Beijing (which nonetheless consumes 18 hours), but the best way to reach Qingdao is by plane.

By Ship Overnight ferries connect Qingdao to Dalian and Shanghai, at prices comparable to train travel (about $40), but this service usually operates only from May to October.

GETTING AROUND

The city can be toured on foot, but taking a taxi to and from hotels is a good idea. Taxis within Qingdao should charge about RMB 10 to RMB 20 ($1.20 to $2.40) per ride. Inexpensive minibuses link the Qingdao train station (on Tai'an Lu, north of Beach Number 6) with Lao Shan scenic spots. Show the driver where you want to go on a map if you don't speak Chinese.

TOURS & STRATAGEMS

Qingdao Overseas Tourist Corporation, located at the Huiquan Dynasty Hotel, 9 Nanhai Lu (☎ 0532/286-1513; fax 0532/287-0983), can sometimes be persuaded to put together special tours for independent travelers, particularly if you have three or four people. This is about the only way to get inside the Tsingtao Brewery and do some beer tasting. Hotel tour desks can offer more convenient tour options. The **tourist hot line** number is ☎ 0532/387-5345. The **Qingdao Tourism Administration,** 16 Guanhai Lu (☎ 0532/288-2420; fax 0532/288-2407), can also assist independent travelers.

WHERE TO STAY

Gloria Inn. *21 Donghai Lu. ☎ 0532/387-8855. Fax 0532/386-4640. 238 units. A/C MINIBAR TV TEL. $125 double. AE, DC, JCB, MC, V.* This sparkling three-star hotel is a block closer to the sea than the Shangri-La, but its view is blocked by seaside apartments. The rooms are spacious, bright, and well maintained. The business center in the lobby is efficient. Though the hotel lacks a swimming pool and some other amenities, it is far better managed and maintained than most three-star hotels in China.

Haitian Hotel. *39 Zhanshan Da Lu. ☎ 0532/387-1888. Fax 0532/387-1777. 641 units. A/C MINIBAR TV TEL. $175 double. AE, DC, JCB, MC, V.* This massive four-star, 15-story, two-building edifice east of the Badaguan District is a favorite of expatriates. Service and maintenance are good. In terms of facilities, it ranks between the Shangri-La and the Gloria Inn. It's located closer to downtown Qingdao and the beaches.

Amenities: Outdoor swimming pool, health club, sauna, two tennis courts, bowling, 24-hour business center, concierge, 24-hour room service, next-day dry cleaning and laundry, tour desk, beauty salon, shopping arcade, newsstand.

Hotel Equatorial Qingdao (Gouji Guidu Da Fandian). *28 Xiang Gang Zhong Lu. ☎ 0532/572-1688. Fax 0532/571-6688. 463 units, including 18 suites. A/C MINIBAR TV TEL. $130 double. AE, DC, JCB, MC, V.* Qingdao's newest luxury hotel, the four-star Equatorial offers a full range of services, second only to those of the Shangri-La.

Dining: The Golden Phoenix offers a variety of Chinese dishes, the Kampachi features Japanese cuisine, and the Coffee Shop and the Etoile Pastry Shop serve Western foods.

Amenities: Indoor swimming pool, health club, sauna, Jacuzzi, massage center, free shuttle to Huashan Golf Resort, bicycle rental, conference rooms, business center, 24-hour room service, 24-hour laundry and dry cleaning, in-room safe, coffeemaker, hair dryer, beauty salon, florist, nonsmoking rooms, free airport shuttle.

Shangri-La Hotel Qingdao (Qingdao Xiangge Lila Fandian). *9 Xiang Gang Zhong Lu. ☎ 800/942-5050 or 0532/388-3838. Fax 0532/388-6868. 502 units, including 25 suites. A/C MINIBAR TV TEL. $160 double. AE, DC, JCB, MC, V.* This is Qingdao's most luxurious hotel. There are 101 executive-floor rooms and two rooms for travelers with disabilities. All rooms are spacious and are equipped with desks, sofas, electronic safes, and data ports. The location is east of downtown and the German quarter, about a 40-minute walk along the sea. There's also a German pub off the lobby.

Amenities: Indoor swimming pool, health club, Jacuzzi, sauna, two outdoor tennis courts, concierge, 24-hour room service, same-day dry cleaning and laundry, nightly turndown, coffeemaker, in-house movies, business center, tour desk, beauty salon, shopping arcade, newsstand.

WHERE TO DINE

Qingdao is renowned for its seafood. To sample the catch, prepared in Cantonese style, head to **Hsin Kuang,** 19 Zhanshan Da Lu, on the eastern edge of the Badaguan District. The dining room has a touch of elegance (linen tablecloths), and the prices are moderate to fairly expensive, RMB 100 to RMB 200 ($12.50 to $25 per person). There's an extensive menu in English.

But probably the best meal I sampled in Qingdao was lunch at the new **Korea Town** restaurant, located a mile east of the Shangri-La Hotel on Zhanshan Da Lu. Again, the prices are fairly expensive—RMB 85 to RMB 250 ($10 to $30)—but the Korean and Chinese dishes, cooked on grills at the table, are superb.

Among other choices, the **House of Sichuan,** on the sixth floor of the Gloria Inn Hotel, is a cheery setting for a fine chili-laced dinner buffet ($12). Chinese specialties and local dishes are exquisite at the very expensive **Shang Palace** restaurant in the Shangri-La Hotel. The best venue for cocktails is the lounge bar at the **Haitian Hotel** (in the western building), which has a breathtaking view of the sea.

Weifang: Kingdom of the Kite

A Chinese adage proclaims that "on the ninth day of the ninth moon, the howl of the wind fills the sky." This is a call to fly kites in the land where kites, according to tradition, were invented over 2,000 years ago. In modern China, kite-flying is a common pastime on city squares, in parks, and across country fields whenever the wind rises; but in the city of Weifang, in Shandong Province, south of Beijing, it has become an annual rite and passion. Since 1984, Weifang has staged an annual international kite festival, an event that has grown by leaps and bounds to become China's premier kiting gala.

Every April 20 and 21, this city of 338,000, otherwise renowned for China's largest reserve of sapphire and a third of the nation's crude salt, doubles its population for a few days of friendly kite flying, open to all nations, drawing both the casual hobbyist and the dedicated aficionado of paper and twine. Venturing across Shandong Province in the spring, drawn by the better-known sites there (such as the city of Qingdao, the birthplace of Confucius at Qu Fu, and the sacred mountain of Tai Shan), I happened to reach Weifang just as the skies were to fill—as perhaps nowhere else in the world—with kites.

Museum & Kite Factory

On the eve of the great kite-flying event, visitors whet their appetites first by paying a morning visit to the **Weifang Kite Museum,** 66 Xingzheng Lu (☎ 0536/823-7313; fax 0536/888-0099), located downtown. It's open daily from 8am to 6pm; admission is RMB 20 ($2.50). The museum consists of 12 exhibition halls which display (without benefit of signs in English) a vast array of Chinese kites of every size and shape imaginable, from miniatures the size of thimbles to stately hand-painted silk box kites to groups of kites strung together, creating a delicate flying centipede of wood, paper, and string as long as a football field. There are also displays here chronicling the history of the kite in

China and the West, as well as honoring foreign competitors from around the world who have flown their kites in the Weifang festival. The oldest type of kite here is the Luban Kite, which is said to have originated in China some 2,400 years ago.

From the museum it's a 20-minute ride by taxi or bus eastward to Weifang's most famous kite factory at the print-making village of **Yangjiabou** (☎ 0536/752-2050). The factory consists of a series of workrooms where the villagers assemble and paint by hand the kites which one may purchase in the salesroom (prices range from RMB 40 to RMB 240 or $5 to $30, including a box). It's open from 8am to 4pm daily except Sundays. Yangjiabou is even more famous for its woodblock prints, with scenes from Chinese operas, used to adorn windows and walls during the Chinese New Year. These are printed by hand on presses in the workshop and can also be purchased in the salesroom. The workshops also include a museum which displays historic sets of the New Year prints and the old carved blocks used to print them.

One can also wander the grounds of the Yangjiabou workshops, where elaborate gates and historic monuments, such as a model of the Temple of Heaven, are constructed out of woodblock prints and kites. On a field above these colorful creations, locals are usually engaged in kite-flying, and don't mind if you watch or even join in.

A Village Lunch

Those on a day tour, as I was, can also partake of one of the most interesting lunch stops in China, in a farm house at **Shijia Village,** south of Weifang, where a family prepares a lavish banquet in their tiny kitchen. Our lunch consisted of mounds of *jiaozi* (steamed buns filled with vegetables and meats) and big bottles of local beer, served up at the kitchen table by Mr. and Mrs. Shi. Shijia Village contains all of 304 households, with a per capita income of about RMB 5,000 ($600). The village also maintains a dozen different small factories and vegetable farms. We each had to sign a temporary resident permit before the meal. The village also offers visitors overnight stays with families, arranged by the Weifang CITS.

Most day visits also include a lively **circle dance** put on by the villagers, who, donning capes and costumes, stilt walk and ride stick horses around the main square. Foreigners are free to join in, and some try out the stick horses. All in all, this is one of the happier lunchtimes I've spent in China.

In the evening, Weifang conducts lavish opening ceremonies in its new Olympic-size outdoor stadium, which seats 50,000. Entertainment

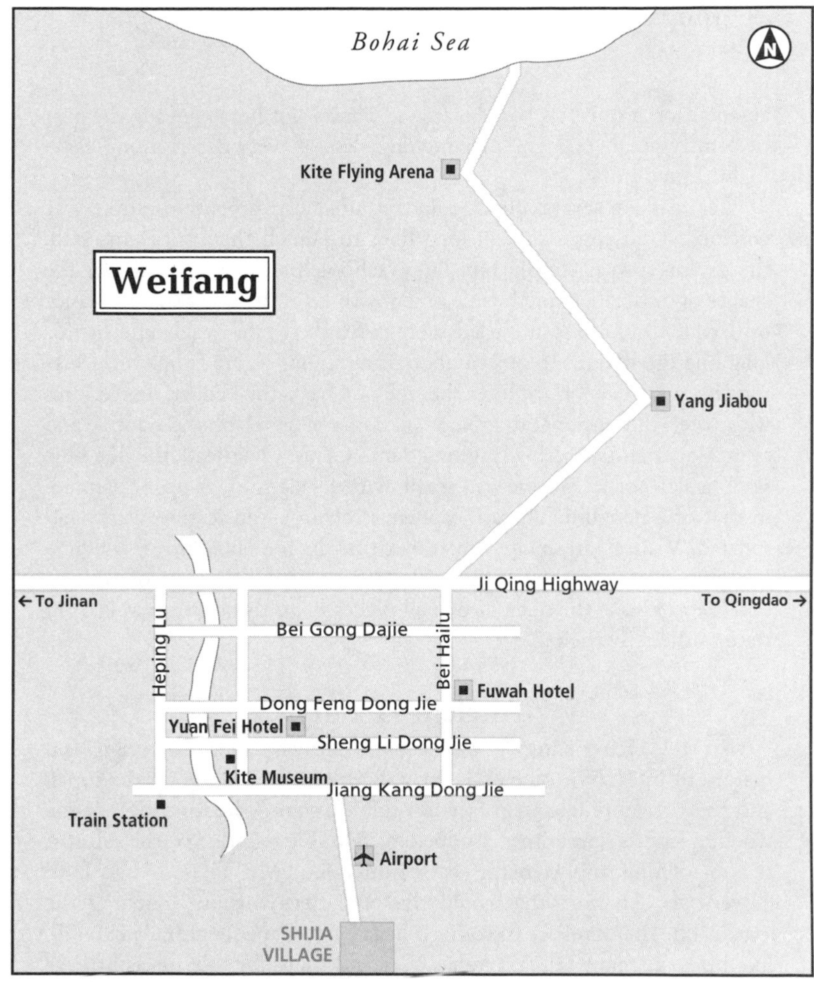

consists of a parade of colorful floats and marching bands, a soccer match featuring local celebrities, and a fireworks show.

Weifang International Kite Festival

On the morning of April 21 buses and taxis converge on the International Kite Flying Arena, a 20-minute journey north from downtown Weifang. I knew beyond doubt that we were closing in on the competition grounds when I spotted troupes of schoolchildren flying kites near powerlines in the surrounding fields. The festival viewing stands overlook a large, flat, sandy field filled with thousands of kite fliers. Happily enough, visitors are not confined to the stands for this competition; rather, everyone is free to wander for hours among the participants who are engaged in launching kites of every description, seemingly at random.

Teams from several dozen countries unstack immense multiple-kite ensembles and spread out in long lines to launch them; peasants stalk the grounds with simple box kites, schoolchildren with kites in the shapes of butterflies, and businessmen with kites the exact size and color of hawks. One group unfurled scores of linked kites, each kite in this long line the life-size representation of a famous figure from world history. I saw splashy bright kites the size of a basketball court, linked kites with three-dimensional dragon heads as large as telephone booths, and even a kite painted with a laughing Santa Claus. Overhead, the dull blue sky is a slash of kites large and small, with forms from that of a samurai to that of a penguin. The atmosphere is chaotic and festive, warm and spirited. Visitors are invited to take a turn in the launchings, which is not always an easy chore; the field is jammed with kite-lofters and observers. This is the one place of all places to go fly a kite, or at least to watch others fly theirs.

Ancient History

A visit to Weifang naturally evokes one's curiosity about the origin and history of kites. Not much scholarly work has been done on the topic, and there is more lore than fact to wade through. The invention of the wooden kite is sometimes ascribed to Mo Ti, founder of the Mohist School of philosophy in the 4th century B.C. Mo Ti is said to have carved wooden kites that could fly for 3 days without touching the Earth. The first kites are thought to have been shaped, naturally enough, like birds, as many are still today. You find them for sale for as little as $3 at the road stands surrounding Weifang.

Many a story is also told of a Han Dynasty General, Han Xin, who tied a string to his hat to retrieve it in the wind and unwittingly invented the first kite. The same general was later credited with using a kite trailing a tail of thin bamboo strips that shrieked in the wind to scare off his enemies, and he is also said to have used a kite to measure the distance into enemy territory his troops would need to dig a secret tunnel to lay siege on a fortified palace.

In Marco Polo's *Travels* we find a description of a man-lifting kite used to forecast the fortunes of sea journeys undertaken in certain Chinese ports. A sailor, Polo wrote, is lashed to a wicker frame kite and sent aloft in a gale. If he returns alive from his flight, it is a harbinger of a profitable voyage for a merchant ship. In fact, man-lifting kites do seem to have been used to carry spies over enemy territory in ancient

China. Their constant use is verified in an anecdote related by Joseph Needham, the West's leading scholar of Chinese science and technology. "About the year 1911," Needham tells us, "an old gentleman taking a stroll in Peking had his attention drawn to an aeroplane flying overhead, but with perfect sang-froid remarked, 'Ah, a man in a kite!'"

I'm not sure that kites are solely the invention of China. The Malaysians may also have invented them about the same time. And the oldest kite festival in the world is not at Weifang, but at Ahmedabad in India, where every January a hundred thousand fighting kites tear up the sky at a festival called Makar Sankranti. But the Chinese have as good a claim to kite originality as anyone, and it is probable that some Marco Polo-like explorer or Silk Road merchant did introduce kites to Europe, where they are first mentioned in 1589 and first pictured in a Dutch engraving in 1618. It could be said that without the Chinese invention of the kite, Ben Franklin would never have discovered electricity in the sky.

While the history of the kite is long and mysterious in China, nowhere is its heritage as resplendent at the present time as at Weifang, truly the "Kite Capital of the World," as it likes to boast. It's the perfect town in which to watch, to fly, and to buy a kite—but don't ever pick up a kite lost by others here. Since the last dynasty, it has been widely believed in China that letting go of a kite means letting go of bad luck or illness, and that is never what one wants to pick up on one's travels.

PRACTICAL INFORMATION

ORIENTATION & WHEN TO GO

Weifang is located in central Shandong Province south of the Bohai Sea. The best time to visit is during the Weifang International Kite Festival, an annual event held on April 20 and 21. The rest of the year, this is an interesting area, off the beaten track, with sunshine all summer, but fairly chilly winters.

GETTING THERE

By Plane The modern Weifang airport is in the southern outskirts, 6 miles from the city center. Airport taxis charge up to RMB 80 ($10) for the trip. Various Chinese airlines provide service to and from Beijing, Guangzhou, Shanghai, Harbin, Chengdu, and Hangzhou. Air tickets on these regional airlines can be booked from hotel service desks.

By Train There is a daily train service from Jinan, the capital of Shandong Province (located on the main Shanghai-to-Beijing train line) via the Jiaoji Railway, which connects Jinan and Qingdao. The train takes 2 to 3 hours from Jinan, and the afternoon express train from Beijing to Jinan takes under 5 hours.

By Bus Many tourists book tour groups from Jinan to Weifang. The bus trip via the new Jinan-Qingdao Expressway covers about 75 miles and takes 2 hours.

GETTING AROUND

The main sites require a taxi to and from hotels. Taxis should charge RMB 15 to RMB 30 ($2 to $4) per ride.

TOURS & STRATAGEMS

Tours It is best to book a guided tour of Weifang, particularly during the Kite Festival, when the population of urban Weifang doubles. These tours can be booked at CITS branch offices all over China, including those in Beijing, Jinan, and Weifang. The **Weifang CITS** is located at 381 Dongfeng Dong Lu (☎ 0536/823-8119; fax 0536/823-3854); it offers group bus tours and special tours for independent travelers, both with English-speaking guides. I booked my Weifang tour (including transportation, hotel, and tours) through the **Shandong CITS,** 88 Jingshi Lu, in Jinan (☎ 0531/296-5858; fax 0531/296-5651), where service was superb. The contact there is Zhai Baoping (English name: Joy). The Shandong CITS in Jinan can set up a 15-day China tour that originates in Beijing, takes in the Weifang International Kite Festival, visits Suzhou, and departs from Shanghai, for $698 per person (based on double occupancy), including virtually everything (ground transport, accommodations, most meals, guides, sightseeing) except the international airfare to Beijing. In the U.S., comprehensive arrangements for travel in Shandong Province can be arranged through **Rim-Pac,** Suite 1812, 51 East 42nd Street, New York, NY 10017 (☎ 212/ 986-2090; fax 212/986-1783).

Recreation The **Fuhua Amusement Park,** next door to the Fuwah Hotel on the east end of Dongfeng Lu (☎ 0536/888-5230; fax 0536/888-0970), is a modern Chinese Disneyland, with 30 rides imported from America, Italy, and Japan, including water rides, go-carts, a merry-go-round, a Ferris wheel, and a double-ring roller-coaster. The "fantasy architecture" is highlighted by a large "castle" and a shopping city. Restaurants, discos, snack bars, video games, and other diversions abound. There's even a bumper car ride. Not a bad place to take the kids or simply watch the locals enjoy themselves in a Western-style theme park located, rather improbably, in a small Chinese city.

WHERE TO STAY

Fuwah Hotel (Fuhua Fandian). *168 Fuso Dong Lu (off Beihai Lu). ☎ 0536/888-1988. Fax 0536/888-0766. 246 units including 26 suites. A/C MINIBAR TV TEL. $110 double. AE, DC, JCB, MC, V.* Weifang's only five-star hotel, the nine-story triangular-shaped Fuwah is luxurious and well-equipped. This is Weifang's grand hotel. It's located east of downtown, adjacent to the town's Convention Center and the Fuhua Amusement Park (see above). The large rooms come with safes, hair dryers, satellite TV, coffeemakers, and marble-walled bathrooms. Service is adequate, on a par with the less expensive but more experienced Yuan Fei Hotel.

Dining: The 10 upscale restaurants and bars include outlets serving Korean, Japanese, Cantonese, and Western specialties.

Amenities: Concierge, room service (24-hour), dry cleaning and laundry (next day), indoor swimming pool, health club, sauna, Jacuzzi, massage, billiards, aerobics room, outdoor tennis courts (two), 12-lane bowling alley, business center, conference rooms, tour desk, beauty salon, florist, shopping arcade, newsstand, baby-sitting.

Yuan Fei Hotel (Yuan Fei Dajiudian). *31 Siping Lu. ☎ 0536/ 823-6901. Fax 0536/823-3840. 368 units. A/C MINIBAR TV TEL. $65 double. MC, V.* This hotel is located near the kite museum, only 3 miles from the Weifang Airport. The newer 21-story wing is rated at four stars; the old wing is three-star rated and not the place to stay if upkeep and a high level of service are required (although it is cheaper). The new wing has all the trappings of a modern luxury hotel, including a dazzling marble lobby and plenty of amenities. The service is constantly improving; the staff is eager to please. Rooms are clean and well-equipped. Local tours can be arranged at the front desk.

Dining: Western buffets are provided in the bright and shiny lobby restaurant. Shandong Province specialties are served upstairs in a number of dining rooms. There are also Japanese and Korean restaurants.

Amenities: indoor swimming pool, fitness center, billiards, four-lane bowling alley, outdoor tennis court, sauna, massage, business center, conference rooms, beauty salon, souvenir shops, newsstand, ticket office, concierge, tour desk.

WHERE TO DINE

Stick to the hotels, where the food is quite good. The city restaurants are cheaper than the hotel restaurants, but they lack experience serving Westerners, and their menus are in Chinese only.

Qu Fu: Birthplace of Confucius

The hometown of Confucius (B.C. 551–479), China's great philosopher and social thinker, is a charming spot devoted to honoring its most famous son, although there is no doubt it is equally devoted these days to cultivating the tourist dollar. Despite its legions of hawkers, vendors, and postcard sellers, I found Qu Fu well worth a stopover. The historic and monumental sites associated, however tenuously, with Confucius are undeniably grand, and one can still come across a degree of small-town innocence and reverence that recalls the Old Cathay that was China for centuries, from the birth of Confucius to the 20th century. The old part of the city is made up of newly constructed shophouses in the Qing Dynasty style.

The three great sights of Qu Fu are within walking distance of each other (although the walk can stretch for several miles). The **Temple of Confucius,** the **Confucian Mansion,** and the **Cemetery of Confucius** were all inscribed on the UNESCO World Heritage List in 1994 and as a result are well-maintained.

The Socrates of China

As for the Great Sage himself, he is known in China as Kong Fu Zi, and scores of his descendants, members of the Kong clan, still reside in Qu Fu. He was the Socrates of China in some ways, a teacher rather than a writer (his followers, led by Mencius, would later put his words to paper in a canon known as the *Analects*), who received little in the way of acclaim or wealth in his lifetime. His teachings constitute a code of social conduct, rather than a religion, but he was deified nonetheless. Thousands of Temples of Confucius eventually spread throughout China, where the literati, the wealthy, and the bureaucrats worshipped the Great Sage and promoted his rules. The rules are those dear enough to many a bureaucrat, since they established a rigid hierarchy of ruler over subject, society over the individual, boss over employee, man over woman, and father over son. These "harmonious" relationships were

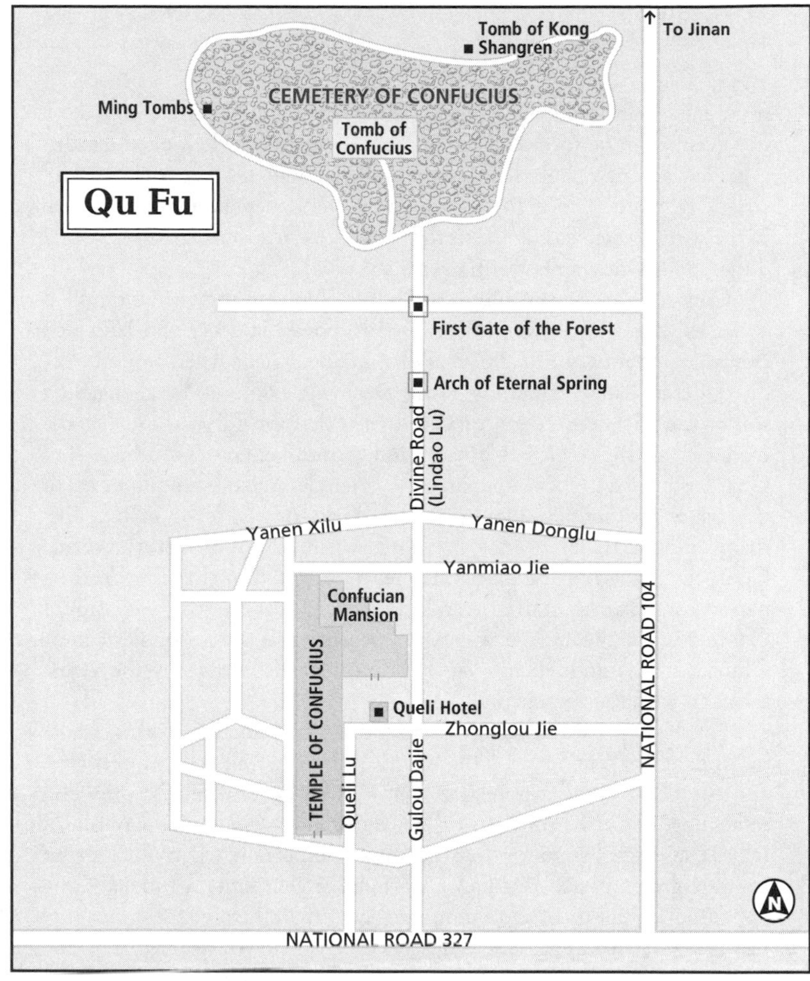

considered cosmic—even the emperor was a Son of Heaven and subject to its fateful decrees.

Among the more dramatic developments of Confucian thought put into practice over the centuries in China were the rites of **filial piety,** in which children mourned for departed parents to extremes that could last a lifetime; **ancestor worship,** in which respect was extended to all the previous generations of the clan; and the **Imperial Examination system,** which persisted in China for almost 2,000 years and was used to select those who worked for the government at nearly all levels, including the Imperial Court itself. The basis of the examination was knowledge of the Confucian *Analects* and one's skill in the traditional arts of China, from calligraphy to poetry. The teachings of Confucius were conservative even when he formulated them 2,500 years ago. He looked back to a golden age of enlightened emperors, wise and selfless advisors, and strictly regulated family life, in which everyone, depending on his place in the social order, was obedient to those above, respectful of all laws and duties, and selfless in bettering society.

Confucius's followers fell in and out of favor, but they never tumbled so far as when the Communists came to power in 1949 and launched campaigns to root out feudal ways of thinking. That's when a number of direct descendants (including Kong Decheng, Duke of Yansheng, first son of the 77th generation of Confucius) fled for Taiwan. During the madness of the Cultural Revolution, contingents of youthful Red Guards stormed Qu Fu, attacking and often demolishing monuments to the Sage. Fortunately, Confucius has been slowly rehabilitated, like many another fallen leader in more recent Chinese history. While Confucianism is not the party line, neither is the thought of his leading persecutor, Chairman Mao; and in fact in Qu Fu the worship of Confucius is quite in line with the free enterprise philosophy of New China, as thousands of money-spending tourists, drawn by the Great Sage, enrich local merchants.

For the past 2 decades, Qu Fu has busily gone about restoring, refurbishing, and re-creating a Confucian Qu Fu for tourists and devotees, and they have done a good job. Qu Fu can be beautiful, exotic, and refreshing, and the grounds of the Confucian mansion, the Confucian temple, and the Confucian forest cemetery, especially when not overrun by tour groups, have the flavor of a dreamy, antique China. Of the 650,000 inhabitants of Qu Fu, more than 125,000 claim the Kong surname, but far fewer are direct descendents of the Master, living members of the 69th through 78th generations of the Confucius clan.

Temple of Confucius (Kong Miao)

The heart of Qu Fu is the Temple to Confucius, a 50-acre complex said by local boosters to be the largest temple complex in China. Experts regard this as one of China's three greatest imperial residences (along with Beijing's Forbidden City and Chengde's Summer Retreat). It dates from B.C. 478, but has been rebuilt many times. Some of the pavilions and monuments date from the Ming Dynasty (A.D. 1513), but most are from the more recent Qing Dynasty. There are nine courtyards running on a south-to-north axis for well over half a mile, so it takes some time to tour. You enter at the **Star Gate (Lingxingmen).** The many halls, pavilions, and temples are fully restored and grand, with yellow and green tiled roofs and red columns. The courtyards are teeming with large incense burners, ancient gnarled trees, and over 2,000 historic carved stone tablets. Women were long forbidden to set foot on the temple grounds.

North of the Star Gate are two arches and an inner gate, followed by a long courtyard with stone carvings from the Han Dynasty on the left, and the Bi River, crossed by three arched bridges. More gates and a three-tiered wooden library come next, followed by 13 small pavilions containing commemorative stone tablets, some inscribed over 1,500 years ago. The most important temple, **Dacheng Hall,** rebuilt in 1724, has its own gate and side halls. In the courtyard on the right is an ancient **cypress tree,** believed by many to have been planted by Confucius himself. It is perhaps the most venerated tree in China, whatever its real age. In front of the grand temple is the **Apricot Terrace,** where Confucius is said to have delivered lectures. The temple itself is supported by 28 magnificent columns, carved with twisting dragons and set on white marble; the 10 dragon columns on the front, enhanced with inscribed clouds and pearls, constitute one of the most stunning sets of stone columns in Asia. Dacheng Hall contains traditional drums, musical stones, and bronze bells once used in Confucian festivals; Confucius was enamored with ancient musical instruments. Here one finds the main statue of Confucius and those of 12 of his chief followers. To the east side of Dacheng Hall is a pavilion honoring the many descendants of Confucius, and at the rear of the complex is a hall displaying 120 tableaux in stone illustrating the life of China's number one Sage.

Altogether, this is one of the most magnificent and, at dawn or dusk, one of the most beautiful and peaceful temples in China. It's open from 8am to 4:30pm (from dawn to dusk in summer); admission is RMB 20 ($2.50) at the southern gate.

Confucian Mansion (Kong Fu)

Just northeast of the rear of the Temple of Confucius, along Queli Lu, which is chockablock these days with souvenir vendors and two-story tile-roofed shophouses, is the historic residence of the Sage's family, the Kong clan. The clan claims to have resided here through 77 generations, up until 1948, although the mansion grounds were not constructed on this site until the late 14th century under the Ming Dynasty. The grounds are nearly as large as those of the nearby temple. Its 463 halls are ample testimony to its former status; it is one of the most lavish private estates in Chinese history, surpassing that of many an emperor.

Today, the Confucian Mansion is something of a family museum, with plenty of relics in its halls (which served the family and its servants as offices, libraries, studies, bedrooms, and ancestral shrines). Artifacts range from old furniture and scrolls to personal clothing and ceremonial robes. The first son of the direct descendants of Confucius for each generation, known as the Duke of Yansheng, ruled this mansion and much of Qu Fu in the old days; by the time of the last dynasty, this duke had powers and privileges second only to those of the emperor.

The first section of the grounds contains various offices; the second, the family residences; the rear, a rock garden. There were scores of offices and local ministries here, since the mansion served as Qu Fu's "Forbidden City." In the first of the three great halls, the duke, seated on a tiger skin, delivered his edicts; in the second hall, he received officials; and in the third he dealt with family matters and the affairs of his 500 servants.

The inner mansions beyond these halls were the clan's private residences, studies, and ancestral halls, once restricted only to the relatives of Confucius and the duke's concubines. They now contain a fine collection of Qing Dynasty furniture and ceramics. At the north end of the grounds is the Iron Hill Garden, dating from 1503 and decorated with fine rockeries and ancient trees. It makes a serene conclusion to a walk through one of Old China's greatest mansions, through the confines of an aristocratic life that endured even longer than the imperial dynasties. The Confucian Mansion is open daily 8am to 4:30pm (dawn to dusk in the summer). Admission is RMB 20 ($2.50).

Cemetery of Confucius (Kong Lin)

More properly known as the Kong Forest, this huge grove—the largest and oldest cemetery park in China—serves as the Confucian burial grounds. The grave of Confucius himself is here. The 500-acre park is an old man-made forest, a large island of towering trees surrounded by farms and the northern outskirts of the town. It is a 2-mile walk from downtown, and there are plenty of bicycles for rent on the way (about $2 for a morning or afternoon excursion). The road itself is lined with graceful cypress trees, and the great forest of pine and oak that is the cemetery grounds, enclosed within thick, 10-foot-high stone walls, is dotted with gravestones, small temples, arched bridges, and scores of carved stone animals. In ancient times, admission was barred to all but the Kong family and visiting emperors, who came here frequently. Women, except for Confucian wives, were restricted to burial outside the forest walls.

This is a fine place to wander on a sunny afternoon. The main southern gate (Arch of Eternal Spring, built 1594) leads along the Divine Road to the First Gate of the Forest, the formal entrance. Turn left at the second gate, and stroll west about 200 yards along the

Imperial Carriageway to the arched bridge over the Zhu River. Then follow the stone path north to the main tomb, that of Confucius. Along the way there are small courtyards and halls, which were once used by participants to cleanse themselves for the Confucian rites of burial and worship.

The **grave of Confucius** is in the last courtyard on the west side. It is a simple mound of green earth, walled off, with an inscribed 15th-century stone tablet as marker, nearly lost from view in the thick, lush forest. The tomb on the left is that of the grandson of Confucius; on the right is that of Confucius's son; in the center, the final resting place of the Sage. The courtyard that leads to the Great Sage's tomb is lined both with statues and, when I was last there, with a few vendors, including a skilled painter who unrolled his sheets on the cobblestones and turned out colorful, traditional paintings one after the other, all snapped up by the tourists.

Thousands of the descendants of Confucius are buried in this graveyard forest—perhaps as many as 200,000—and the grounds are quite haunting. Many of the graves established here date back over 2,000 years and are but simple mounds among the old trees. If there's time, take an interesting walk that begins back at the Zhu River. There, the western bridge joins a road that follows the river west and north to a haunting collection of Ming Tombs and stone statues, seemingly discarded into the forest from the Heavens. Follow this road as it circles inside the cemetery walks until you reach another group of stone animals at the grave of Madame Yu, daughter of a Qing Dynasty emperor who married the head of the 72nd generation of the Confucian clan. Her tomb is followed by that of Kong Shangren (1648–1718), a celebrated dramatist and 64th generation descendant, and those of the 76th generation duke, too. In fact, those in the line of Confucius are still being buried here today, in a forest cemetery that has no equal, in beauty or scale, in China.

The Cemetery of Confucius is open from dawn to dusk and costs RMB 10 ($1.25) to tour.

PRACTICAL INFORMATION

ORIENTATION & WHEN TO GO

Qu Fu, about 90 miles south of Jinan, capital of Shandong Province, is a small city, but it receives over 2.5 million visitors yearly. Its major sites are conveniently located in the charming old city center, within a few blocks of the main hotel (the Queli Hotel, see listing below). A taxi or even one of the horse or donkey carts, especially designed and decorated for tourists, might be necessary for a trip to the Cemetery of Confucius (about 2 miles north); expect to pay about RMB 20 to RMB 30 ($2.50 to $3.75) for the trip. The best times to visit are spring and fall, when the temperature is mild. Summers are hot and dry, and wintertime is chilly.

For those who love celebrations and costumes, as well as big, big crowds, the best time to visit Qu Fu is on the **Birthday of Confucius,** every September 28th. The festival actually runs from September 26 through October 10, with lots of parades in the streets and music and dancing at the temple and mansion. Qu Fu is jammed during the festive season; be sure to book well ahead through CITS.

GETTING THERE

By Train Qu Fu is not disturbed by a railway station. The nearest one is in Yanzhou (8 miles west), with connections from there to Jinan, the Shandong capital. From Jinan, it is about 5 hours by train north to Beijing.

By Plane There is no airport in Qu Fu. The nearest major airport is in Jinan.

By Bus The Qu Fu bus station is located 3 blocks directly south of the Temple of Confucius, on Jingxuan Lu, and offers many buses to Jinan. The ride takes 1 to 2 hours and costs RMB 20 to RMB 40 ($2.50 to $5). Minibuses and taxis link Qu Fu to the railway station in Yanzhou.

TOURS & STRATAGEMS

Tours The easiest way to tour Qu Fu is to make arrangements at the CITS office in Jinan, where you have many choices, from an "independent" tour, including just transport and accommodations, to a group tour with an English-speaking guide. A guide is not absolutely necessary here, since the town is small and the sights are easy to find, especially with help from the hotel desk and a map. Qu Fu is quite used to foreign tourists, although Western tourists make up a small minority of visitors here. But because getting to Qu Fu is not simple, many Western visitors book tours (including transportation, hotel, and guides) through the **Shandong CITS,** 88 Jingshi Lu, in Jinan (☎ 0531/296-5858; fax 0531/296-5651), where the service is good (contact: Zhai Baoping; her English name, Joy). In Qu Fu itself you can book tours and transportation at the **Qu Fu CITS office,** 1 Xuequan Lu (☎ 0537/441-2491; fax 0537/441-2492), located near the south entrance of the Temple of Confucius.

Entertainment Any time of year the Queli Hotel presents Confucian musical performances every evening on its second floor. Tickets are for sale in the hotel lobby (RMB 50 to RMB 100/$6 to $12).

WHERE TO STAY

Queli Hotel (Queli Binshe). *1 Queli Jie. ☎ 0537/441-1300. Fax 0537/441-2022. 160 units. A/C MINIBAR TV TEL. $48 double. MC, V.* This is the best place to stay in Qu Fu, and it's not terribly expensive. The hotel is located within a few minutes' walk of both the temple and the mansion of Confucius. It's one of the few hotels in China designed to blend in with traditional dynastic architecture (courtyard style, low, with tile roofs). Upkeep and maintenance, however, are not what they should be, and some Western visitors have trouble finding English-speaking staff. One couple I spoke with complained of mice in their room one night, although they admitted they had left the window cracked (because the heat was too much). Nonetheless, despite some service and hygiene problems, I found it perfectly adequate. Perhaps I was bewitched by its old-fashioned look, handy location, and the charm of the nearby buildings and pavilions. This two-story hotel is rated by the government at three stars, meaning it has modern rooms and some Western-style amenities. There are Confucian musical performances in the evenings, shops in the lobby, and the best Western and Confucian-style restaurants in town.

Amenities: Small fitness center, business center, beauty salon, next-day laundry and dry cleaning, shopping arcade, conference rooms.

WHERE TO DINE

Queli Lu, which runs north along the east wall of the Temple of Confucius, has dozens of small outdoor food stands featuring very basic fare, as well as such local Confucian specialties as roasted nuts and bean curd; but for hygienic fare, stick to the **Confucius Restaurant** and the Western Dining Room in the **Queli Hotel** (see above). So far, Qu Fu has not developed an acceptable choice of restaurants for Western visitors.

However, two of the most popular products in Qu Fu do keep some thirsty travelers happy these days: the **Confucius Family liquor** (pure fire) and the **San Kong (Three Confucius) beer,** both produced here by Confucian descendants and sold nationwide in China.

SOUTHEAST CHINA: COMMERCE & CULTURE

SHANGHAI: BACK TO THE FUTURE

上海

SHANGHAI'S JOURNEY TO THE FUTURE is underpinned by its colonial and indigenous past, as one can still see in the old architecture of the city and the watery villages on its edges. The dominant thrust today, however, is that indicated by the new area of Pudong. Shanghai is clearly one of Asia's most powerful cities, perhaps soon to be its most powerful economically. No one can say how long its spectacular growth will continue, although its population shows no signs of slowing. With 13 million residents, Shanghai is China's most populous city, and the United Nations estimates that by the year 2015 Shanghai's population will reach the unimaginable figure of 23.4 million. One population figure Shanghai relishes is its visitors' census. Seven of every ten visitors to China now pay a visit here, and the sum of foreign visitors is approaching two million yearly.

Shanghai is still something of a construction site over which a blueprint is spread like a dream. But if any city can link China to the outside world on equal terms, it will be Shanghai. Aware of its past, but always outward-looking, Shanghai is determined to have a preeminent role on the world stage. In few other cities in the world can you feel that future pressing so relentlessly.

The best way to take the pulse of Shanghai is to make a long circuit on foot. I always begin uptown on **Nanjing Road,** China's greatest shopping street, and walk a few miles east to the edge of the **Huangpu River,** presided over by the green towering roof of the historic Peace Hotel. There, I turn south down the spacious promenade that runs between the river and that remarkable architectural museum known as the **Bund,** where the neoclassical business offices of Shanghai's colonial period form an unforgettable skyline. Then I head back uptown, dropping by the splendid teahouse and garden in the **old Chinese Quarter.** Continuing west, I pay a visit to the new **Shanghai Museum,** then swing through the French Concession back to where I started. It's a long walk with plenty of distractions—sometimes I spend 2 days covering

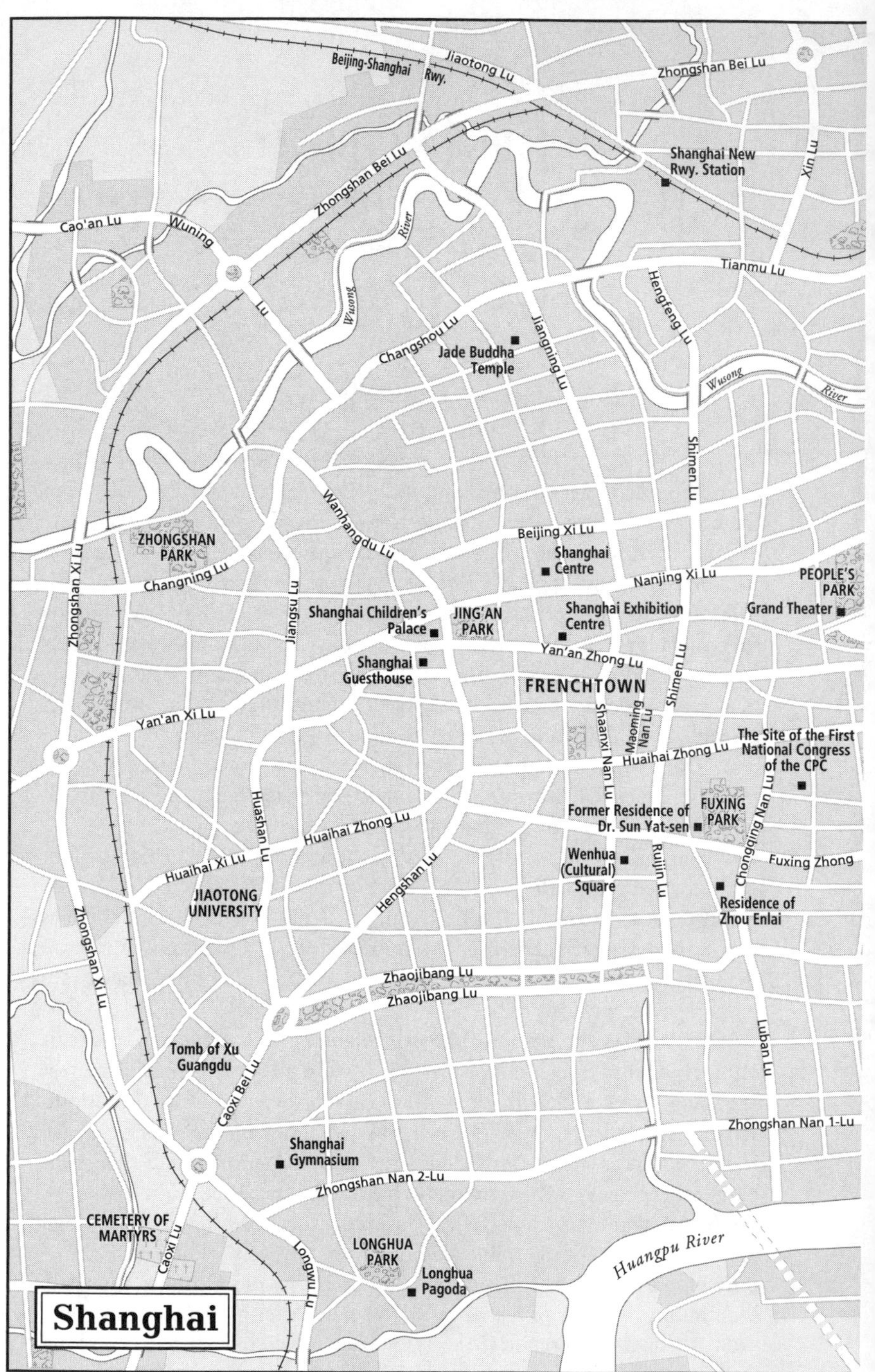
Shanghai
Beijing-Shanghai Rwy.
Jiaotong Lu
Zhongshan Bei Lu
Shanghai New Rwy. Station
Xin Lu
Cao'an Lu
Wuning Lu
Wusong River
Tianmu Lu
Hengfeng Lu
Changshou Lu
Jade Buddha Temple
Jiangning Lu
Shimen Lu
Wanhangdu Lu
Beijing Xi Lu
ZHONGSHAN PARK
Changning Lu
Shanghai Centre
Nanjing Xi Lu
PEOPLE'S PARK
Grand Theater
Zhongshan Xi Lu
Jiangsu Lu
Shanghai Children's Palace
JING'AN PARK
Shanghai Exhibition Centre
Yan'an Zhong Lu
Shanghai Guesthouse
FRENCHTOWN
Yan'an Xi Lu
Shaanxi Nan Lu
Maoming Nan Lu
Huaihai Zhong Lu
The Site of the First National Congress of the CPC
Huashan Lu
Former Residence of Dr. Sun Yat-sen
FUXING PARK
Chongqing Nan Lu
Huaihai Xi Lu
Wenhua (Cultural) Square
Ruijin Lu
Fuxing Zhong
JIAOTONG UNIVERSITY
Hengshan Lu
Residence of Zhou Enlai
Zhaojibang Lu
Luban Lu
Tomb of Xu Guangdu
Caoxi Bei Lu
Zhongshan Nan 1-Lu
Shanghai Gymnasium
Zhongshan Nan 2-Lu
CEMETERY OF MARTYRS
Caoxi Lu
Longwu Lu
LONGHUA PARK
Longhua Pagoda
Huangpu River

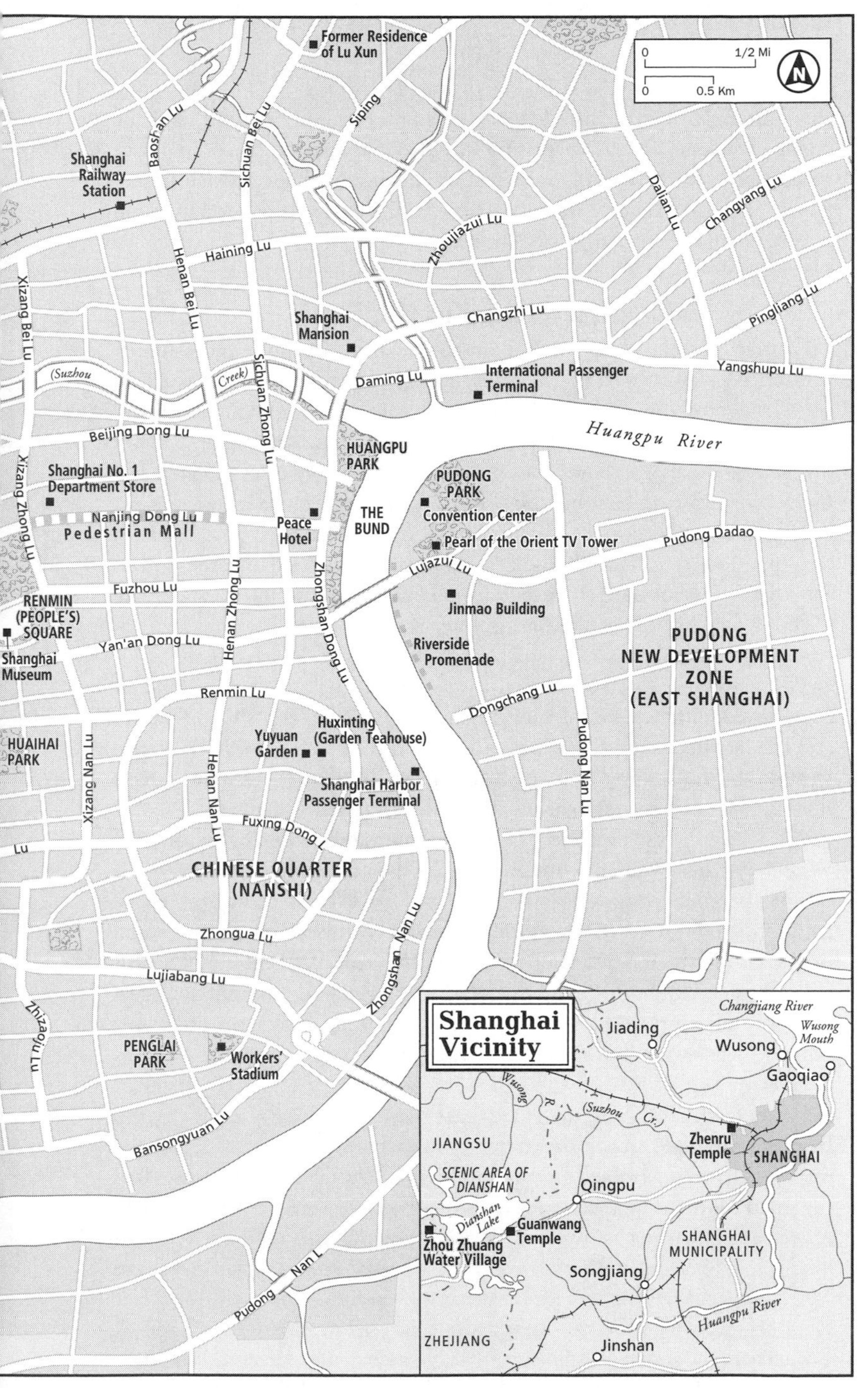
Former Residence of Lu Xun
Shanghai Railway Station
Baoshan Lu
Sichuan Bei Lu
Siping
Haining Lu
Henan Bei Lu
Xizang Bei Lu
Zhoujiazui Lu
Dalian Lu
Changyang Lu
Shanghai Mansion
Changzhi Lu
Pingliang Lu
Yangshupu Lu
(Suzhou Creek)
Sichuan Zhong Lu
Daming Lu
International Passenger Terminal
Huangpu River
Beijing Dong Lu
HUANGPU PARK
Shanghai No. 1 Department Store
PUDONG PARK
Xizang Zhong Lu
Nanjing Dong Lu
Pedestrian Mall
Peace Hotel
THE BUND
Convention Center
Pearl of the Orient TV Tower
Pudong Dadao
Lujazui Lu
Fuzhou Lu
Jinmao Building
RENMIN (PEOPLE'S) SQUARE
Henan Zhong Lu
Zhongshan Dong Lu
Shanghai Museum
Yan'an Dong Lu
Riverside Promenade
PUDONG NEW DEVELOPMENT ZONE (EAST SHANGHAI)
Renmin Lu
Dongchang Lu
Huxinting (Garden Teahouse)
Yuyuan Garden
HUAIHAI PARK
Xizang Nan Lu
Henan Nan Lu
Shanghai Harbor Passenger Terminal
Pudong Nan Lu
Fuxing Dong L
Lu
CHINESE QUARTER (NANSHI)
Zhongshan Nan Lu
Zhongua Lu
Lujiabang Lu
Zhizaoju Lu
PENGLAI PARK
Workers' Stadium
Bansongyuan Lu
Pudong Nan L
0 1/2 Mi
0 0.5 Km
N
Shanghai Vicinity
Changjiang River
Jiading
Wusong
Wusong Mouth
Gaoqiao
Wusong R.
(Suzhou Cr.)
JIANGSU
Zhenru Temple
SHANGHAI
SCENIC AREA OF DIANSHAN
Qingpu
Dianshan Lake
Guanwang Temple
Zhou Zhuang Water Village
SHANGHAI MUNICIPALITY
Songjiang
Huangpu River
ZHEJIANG
Jinshan

this route—but by the time I finish, Shanghai is under my skin and the crowded, hectic, always surprising streets of congested Shanghai have swallowed me. These days, there's a detour for any Shanghai visitor, too, a new Shanghai, called **Pudong,** rising on the east side of the Huangpu River, which can no longer be ignored.

Nanjing Road to the Bund

Of course even the old Shanghai, on the west side of the river, has modernized considerably in the past few years, and this is still the place to spend the most time, largely because it has a romantic past that is still accessible. Until 1999, old Shanghai was nearly impassable, a patchwork of torn streets and detours, demolitions and new construction sites, but today downtown Shanghai no longer resembles a giant erector set dropped from the sky. Ian Buruma, writing for the *New York Times* in the mid-1990s, called Shanghai's reconstruction "perhaps the greatest urban transformation since Baron Haussmann rebuilt Paris in the 19th century." Much of the preliminary work, at least, has already been completed.

Shanghai is again a city to walk. I begin my explorations at **Shanghai Centre,** a complex of offices, apartments, and shops that are still the most prestigious business address in the city. It's located 2 miles west of the Huangpu River up Nanjing Road, Shanghai's main street. Shanghai Centre is a city within the city, a joint venture opened in 1990 that has become the emblem of the new international Shanghai. Its 472 Western-style apartments house many of the city's high-rolling foreign businesspeople, requiring rents that used to exceed those in Tokyo, London, and New York, although recent competition has lowered prices. Inside you'll find a shopping mall, supermarket, preschool, health club, theater, exhibition hall, and plenty of pricey restaurants, lounges, and even an espresso bar. Some foreign residents scarcely venture out into the city streets, but they are missing nearly everything the city has to offer.

The length of Nanjing Road east from Shanghai Centre to the **Bund promenade** on the riverfront shows what's happened. I know the road well, having strolled it frequently since 1984, but it now looks like the main route through an entirely different city. There are plenty of new office and shopping complexes, most following the modern Western model inside and out. Within minutes I passed the massive **Westgate Mall** and a sidewalk arcade featuring fast-food chicken from KK Roasters, as well as pizza and cappuccino from the Gino Cafe. A Burberrys of London is followed by a Nautica outlet store and finally a shop that a decade earlier would have been unthinkable anywhere on

Nanjing Road, anywhere in China: a thriving Playboy Store, its bunny logo gracing a variety of upscale merchandise.

I shouldn't be taken aback. This is no longer Mao's fashion show. The younger women in the streets are cavorting in the latest Western styles: high heels, short skirts, black tights, flashy earrings, and curly, red-tinted coiffures. Shanghai has long been China's capital of fashion, and it always looks outward with intensity. Young couples flock to Western wedding parlors. A KFC occupies the entrance to People's Park.

The venerable department stores that made Nanjing Road the most famous shopping street in China have undergone glitzy face-lifts. The **New World Department Store** was one of the first to take the leap into the 21st century, with its bubble-glass walls, curving escalators, and refrigerated photographic film, but now everyone is getting into the act.

The great change on Nanjing Street is focused on the new **Nanjing East Pedestrian Mall,** which runs for nearly a mile between Xizang Zhong Lu and Henan Zhong Lu, right through the heart of the great shopping route. Traffic is banished (except at cross streets); red granite walking stones have replaced the pavement; park benches, lampposts, kiosks, and scores of new shop fronts and department stores have been added; and the mall is as flashy and as easy to walk and as lively as any built in the center of any downtown capital in Europe or North America. The sole difference is perhaps the persistence and outcroppings of Shanghai's colonial legacy, the brick and stone towers of its early 20th century colonial cityscape. From the pedestrian overpasses, one can still glimpse the old in the stranglehold of the new, all the way to the Bund. There's the historic 1934 Park Hotel, once the tallest building in the Far East and Chairman Mao's favorite (now with a nicely restored lobby); the Number One Department Store, built in 1934 (with the first elevator in China); and the Wing On (1918) and Sincere buildings (1917), former homes of top Chinese clothing stores (now stuffed with new Western-style wares).

All the way along the mall, if one looks carefully, there are examples of newborn outlets hunkering down into their 75-year-old shells. Friendship Europe City, which replaced the "old-fashioned" Donghai Shopping Centre in September 1999, has four floors of elite European fashions. The Xinhua Bookstore, which has served Chinese cities for decades, has been surpassed here by Shanghai's City of Books, a multi-storied vendor that has plastered its front windows with its Web site. At the eastern end of the mall there's a commemorative plaque and one of those life-size iron statues of a family pushing a baby carriage, as well as a line forming to board the gaudy little electric trolleys which whisk visitors up and down the mall for RMB 1 (12¢).

This giant mall, designed by Arle Jean Marie Carpentier and Associates of France, opened on September 20, 1999, and it has transformed the shopping scene of old Shanghai so thoroughly that by the time I finished exploring it I wondered if I would find the historic Bund on the riverfront intact or repackaged as a Western amusement park. At least the easternmost 2 blocks of Nanjing are largely unremodeled. One returns abruptly to the congested, grimy streets, to the narrow, irregularly surfaced, shoulder-pinching sidewalks, to the pockets of earthy odors from no-holds-barred cooking and waste. The new has not entirely erased the old. Not as long as the historic Peace Hotel still stands on the Bund like a sentinel, even if across the river now is Pudong with its 88-story Jin Mao skyscraper and the Pearl of the Orient TV Tower, a gargantuan Tinkertoy visible over the rooftops of both old and new Shanghai.

Peace Hotel

Before strolling down the Bund promenade at the east end of Nanjing Road, I always make a circuit of the lobby of the Peace Hotel. It is Shanghai's grand monument to art deco, and some of the original design still clings to its walls, columns, furnishings, and carved woodwork.

It was originally the Sassoon House, built in 1929 by one of Shanghai's legendary immigrant tycoons, Victor Sassoon, a Jew from Baghdad, who ended up owning thousands of city properties. It included the redoubtable Cathay Hotel, one of the finest in Asia. Sassoon kept his offices in its famous pyramid tower. Noel Coward did some writing in one of its suites. And Steven Spielberg filmed a scene of *Empire of the Sun* here, re-creating the view that a hotel guest would have had of the Japanese bombing of Shanghai during World War II.

In the north wing the hotel, a jazz band plays swing music every evening. One or two of the members started out in the late 1930s, when this was the number one jazz club in China. Today, it's simply the place for a nostalgic evening of fun. The lobby, a gorgeous reminder of the Jazz Age, is worth gawking at. Sometimes I can find a hotel worker willing to take me on a tour of the hotel rooms; they retain their grand art deco form and decor. Otherwise I just take the elevator up to floor 8, take a look for myself at the old parlor rooms there, each done in a different international style, then walk upstairs to the roof. The rooftop lounge recently reopened. One can now walk outside, right up to the Peace Hotel's triangular dark green tower, and enjoy one of Shanghai's most romantic views, south down the Bund into the romantic past and east across the river into China's high-rise future.

East Shanghai (Pudong)

In the late 1990s, at any given moment, fully one-fifth of the world's high-lift cranes were at work in the city of Shanghai. In one massive convulsion, the urban landscape was being erased and redrawn. As the smoke clears now, China's largest city is slated to assume the position occupied by Hong Kong as the nation's commercial center. The plan has been to make Shanghai China's first fully modernized metropolis, a Pearl of the Orient for the 21st century, and much of that plan is nearing completion.

Meanwhile, traces of Shanghai's past—its cultural relics, its quaint architectural monuments to Western colonial days, and its legacy of poverty and pollution—remain at the margins. If Shanghai is where this new century begins, then the future has been nurtured in the craters of 25,000 construction sites.

When you come to Shanghai these days, you really find two cities: the romantic Shanghai of old, still peeking out along Nanjing Road, and the new Shanghai that's remaking itself in Pudong. The dividing line is the Huangpu River, the eastern shore of historic downtown Shanghai and the western shore of the new development zone called Pudong.

Shanghai's monument to new development is the **Pearl of the Orient TV Tower,** Asia's tallest structure at 1,535 feet. It's visible for miles, even back across the river in old downtown Shanghai. Its neighborhood is the Pudong New Development Zone, directly east of the Bund, which is a museum of European customhouses, banks, and taipan clubs that memorializes Shanghai's business success when foreigners ran the city. Old Shanghai has certainly modernized itself here, too, but to see the full extent of Shanghai's economic boom, you need to cross under the river via the new subway line, walk there via the moving sidewalk in the new underground tunnel, or cross over by taxi or bus via two long bridges or the underground vehicle tunnel. Whatever your choice, all roads now lead east in Shanghai.

Pudong is the new city's leading edge, its heart of trade, bordered by the river that feeds the interior of China and the ocean that links it to the Western world. It's not what ordinarily attracts visitors to China, but it's the essence of Shanghai. The TV tower is a genuine tourist attraction, open daily from 8am to 9pm. You buy a ticket outside the gate for RMB 50 to RMB 100 ($6 to $12), depending on how high you want to go; check handbags and cameras; and then enter an elevator that lifts off like a rocket. The uniformed elevator operator recites the TV Tower statistics from memory in Chinese and English as you ascend a quarter of a mile to the observation deck. There, you have a 360-degree view of all of Shanghai, east and west, new and old, and everything that's being squeezed in between.

From the observation deck in the Pearl of the Orient TV Tower, Pudong looks like a fresh new urban hub of massive skyscrapers. The main developments are concentrated within an easy stroll. The tallest structure is the modern pagoda of Shanghai, the 88-story **Jin Mao Building,** currently the world's third tallest building, which has its own public observation deck and 79 high-speed elevators (admission RMB 50/$6), affording an even higher view of Shanghai than the TV Tower, not to mention a high-tech new Grand Hyatt Hotel, starting on floor 54. Nearby is the Shanghai Securities and Exchange Building, home to China's most vibrant stock exchange; the new Shanghai International Convention Center, with its glass world globes on either side; and the stately new Customs House. At the foot of these and the office towers going up daily are two brand-new parks.

The first is **Lujiazui Central Garden** (admission RMB 5/65¢), just east of the TV Tower, with its white magnolias, piped-in outdoor music system, and its own lake with snack stands. The entrance is on the north side. On the southeast side is the Lujiazui Development Exhibition Room, actually a large orange and black brick mansion built as a private residence by a foreign tycoon in 1914. This mansion is a museum in its own right, with carved doors, wooden windows, archways, brass door pulls, and green and marble tile floors from the colonial period. Displays of a few artifacts, maps, and photographs record the transformation of Pudong into a 21st-century Manhattan of the East.

The **Riverside Promenade (Binjiang Dadao)** is on the river side of the TV Tower, running parallel to the Bund for well over a mile. Former site of the Li Xin Shipbuilding Yard, it affords a view the Bund doesn't, a view of old Shanghai on the river. At night, when the Bund is lit up, it's the grandest view in Shanghai. By day it is also dramatic, particularly from its northern section, where the "Wave-Viewing Platform" is just a yard above the busy waterline. Admission is RMB 5 (65¢)

This tip of Pudong is developing its own shopping and eating centers, too, although these do not rival those of the Shanghai to the west. The **Lujiazui Food Square,** located between the TV Tower and the Jin Mao Building, contains dozens of restaurants in a "shophouse mall" design encircling a large courtyard fountain. Painted in muted pink, this food mall has sparkling new cafes serving Shanghainese, Korean, and Japanese cuisine, as well as a coffeehouse and a microbrewery named the "Jenny Brewing Club." Heading south into the more densely packed streets of downtown Pudong, you'll reach **Times Square,** a shopping complex that boasts the largest department store in Asia, Nextage/Yaohan (second biggest in the world after Macy's). But presiding over it all is the TV Tower, Pudong's chief sightseeing draw, its 11 blue-and-green spheres the pearls in a flashy string of Shanghai's sudden wealth, glittering night and day, winking at the streets of the elder city across the river.

Shanghai's Mississippi

The Huangpu River, which divides the two Shanghais, east and west, past and future, serves as the city's shipping artery both to the East China Sea and the mouth of the Yangzi River, which the Huangpu joins 18 miles north of downtown Shanghai.

The "bunds" of Shanghai refer to the mudflats on its shores, secured by dikes of stone and earth. The Bund and its promenade are landmarks of Shanghai's 19th-century struggle to reclaim a waterfront from the bogs of the Huangpu.

The Huangpu's 36 miles of wharves are the most fascinating in China. The port handles the cargo coming out of the interior of China, from Nanjing, Wuhan, and other Yangzi River ports, including Chongqing, the rice bowl of China, 1,500 miles deep into Sichuan Province. From Shanghai, which produces plenty of industrial and commercial products in its own right, as much as a third of China's trade with the rest of the world is conducted each year—a substantial part of it flowing up and down the Huangpu River. Mile for mile, this is the most important river in China.

Mornings and afternoons tour boats make the $3^1/_2$-hour voyage up the Huangpu to the Yangzi River delta. From the river, there are unrivaled views of Shanghai's port facilities, the ships of the world that dock there, and the junks and Chinese barges that clot the narrow river avenue. Unrivaled, too, are the postcard views of Shanghai's celebrated European skyline to the west and the booming cityscape of Pudong to the east.

After buying a ticket one Saturday morning on the Bund promenade, I was able to board a tour boat before noon, settling into a soft chair on the upper deck. Surrounded by picture windows, served hot tea and nuts, I leaned back as we pulled away from the Shanghai waterfront. But I couldn't sit still. I went out on deck as we pulled away. The monumental granite offices, banks, consulates, and hotels of Shanghai's past colonial masters formed a stately panorama to the west, while the Pearl of the Orient TV Tower and the new skyscrapers commanded the east bank, forming the tallest and most expensive building project in the world. I tried to scan both banks at once, as well as keep my eye on the river traffic itself.

We headed north, passing **Huangpu Park** where the Bund begins, across from the **Peace Hotel** and its stunning green pyramid roof, still the loveliest piece of architecture in Shanghai, east or west. The park borders **Suzhou Creek** and is dominated by a new monumental sculpture, soaring ribbons of marble that rise like Shanghai's economic expectations. Huangpu Park was once the British Public Gardens. It is widely reported today that a sign was once posted at its entrance reading DOGS AND CHINESE NOT ALLOWED. In fact, dogs were not allowed in the garden, and according to a separate ordinance, neither were Chinese except by permission of their foreign employers. This insult stung the Shanghainese for a century, until they regained sovereignty over their city in 1949.

Suzhou Creek is spanned by **Waibaidu Bridge,** which once linked the American and British concessions. The Americans staked out the northern shore; the British claimed the downtown waterfront. Waibaidu Bridge was originally a wooden toll bridge built in 1856 by an enterprising Englishman. Steel girders replaced timber in 1906. Sixty feet wide, with two 171-foot-long spans, the bridge was regularly crossed by human-powered rickshaws, introduced to Shanghai from Japan by a Frenchman. Trams were soon routed across the bridge, too, as were motorcars, which have been driving the streets of Shanghai since 1901.

Less than a mile north of Suzhou Creek is the **International Passenger Terminal** where luxurious cruise ships tie up. The Huangpu River jogs sharply east at this point on its way to the Shanghai shipyards, where cranes and derricks load and unload a logjam of freighters. The freighters are interesting in that they are stamped with the country names of the world's shipping giants: America, Japan, Holland, Russia, Norway. I have seen vessels registered to archenemies unload side by side in Shanghai.

Across the river on the eastern shore, vast coal yards crop up, along with petroleum storage facilities. At the **Yangshupu Power Plant,** the stacks are tipped with flames night and day. Here, one begins to sense fully Shanghai's industrial might. The river seems endless and its industrial ranks—the dry docks, factories, and power plants—equally unlimited, like an army of millions massed on both shores of a worldwide economic battlefield.

The Bund and the Pearl of the Orient TV Tower rapidly fade from view as the Huangpu slowly begins to curve northward again. We crossed under **Yangpu Cable Bridge,** and then **Nanpu Cable Bridge** to the south, two of the largest such structures in the world, both completed just a few years ago. Shanghai's modern boom is accelerating on both sides of the Huangpu, which is still its main shipping link to the world and into the rich interior of China.

What overwhelms river passengers even more than the long industrial shoreline is the traffic slinking up and down the waterway. The Huangpu is, on the average, just 600 feet wide. It's like a superhighway

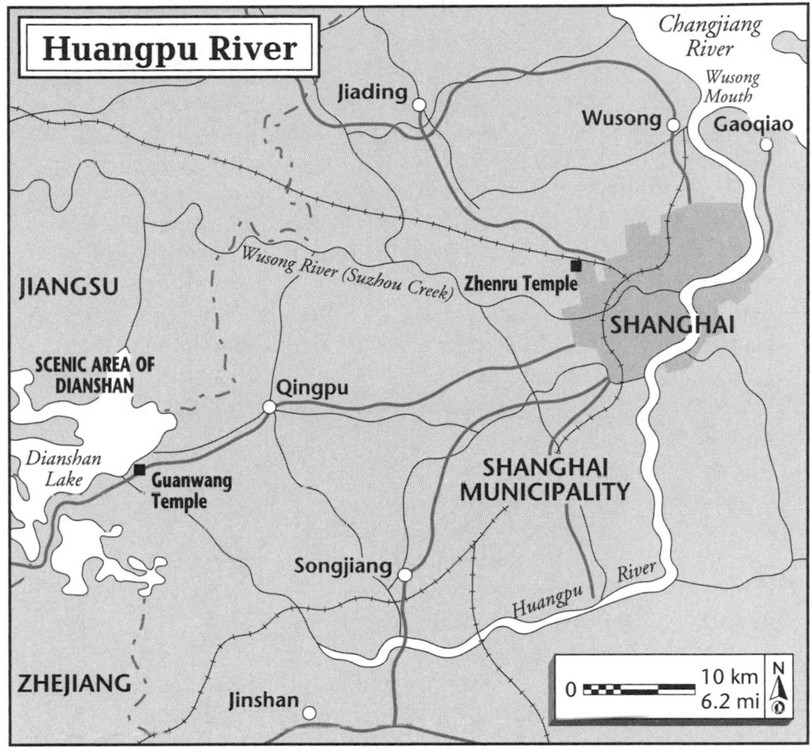

without visible lanes, glutted with gigantic freighters, tugs, tiny sampans, and above all the undulating trains of unpainted wooden barges, tied together to save fuel, forming serpentine dragons on the river. Flotillas of these heavily laden barges, their gunwales just above the waterline, usually number a dozen or more. Their open holds are stuffed with coal, lime, brick, produce, scrap metal, and a thousand other commodities in transit. The rear cabins are homes to families who sleep and cook and work and play on the Huangpu. The family bicycle is often parked on deck. Potted flowers festoon the cabin roofs. Noisy outboard engines, often in teams of four or five, propel the barges from the stern. Laundry lines stretch from cabin roof to prow. Dishes are washed and meals are cooked with water scooped from the brown river. More than 2,000 oceangoing ships compete with the 20,000 barges, fishing junks, and rowboats that stalk the Huangpu every year.

There are also navy gunboats and even an occasional submarine anchored on the shores. A sign in English nailed to the railing of our tour boat deck sternly warned that photographs of military craft and installations are strictly forbidden, but there was no one this morning to enforce the ordinance. A decade ago I spotted a pre–World War II submarine lounging alongside a pier on the Huangpu River. This time, after passing a dozen gray gunboats, looking less than threatening, I spotted the same U-boat as before.

I spent most of the cruise outside on the upper deck, leaning over the rail, absorbed by the continuous parade of barges, ships, and factories. Our northern destination was **Wusong Kuo,** where the harbormasters wait beneath a ghostly pale clock tower, its hands frozen. This marks the Yangzi River delta, where the Huangpu disappears into the convergence of far mightier waterways: the Yangzi River and the Pacific Ocean. The estuary seems as vast as an ocean, although it is neither ocean nor river here but a netherworld of water moving in contrary directions on crisscrossing tides, salted and silted, muddied and fresh. The river currents churn against the implacable wall of the East China Sea. An armada of vessels, large and small, waits in the estuary for a sea change, for shipments to be readied, for a turn at the Shanghai docks. On this watery tarmac, the population of boats surpasses that of any man-made marina. The vessels wait and bob up and down, moving nowhere on their anchors as if time itself has stopped.

Our tour boat ventured only far enough out into this twilight zone of tides and currents to pivot slowly and turn back into the narrowing passageway of the Huangpu. For the return trip I pulled up a wicker deck chair, sipped my hot tea, nibbled on the fruit, nuts, and a chocolate bar I packed, and watched the procession of barges as endless as the silk shops and clothing stores on Shanghai's Nanjing Road, where the human traffic is just as thick.

Our boat eventually sailed into Shanghai, as countless clipper ships and ocean steamers have over the past 160 years, bearing outsiders for their first glimpse of the great colonial skyline of the Bund. The 1920s neoclassic edifices, built by Shanghai's conquering taipans, still dominate the waterfront, but new skyscrapers of the 21st century are crowding in on them from behind now. And across the Huangpu, on the eastern shore, there's an entirely fresh skyline mounting the stage, more imposing, soaring far higher, the product of Shanghai's modern taipans who are enterprising local Chinese rather than carpetbagging Westerners. Nevertheless, the architecture of East Shanghai is also strictly international, a Western import—but now an import rather than an imposition. Our ferry slowly parted this divided architectural curtain of old brick and stone, of new glass and steel, coming to rest at its quay on a river of commerce and industry that has few rivals East or West—a waterway not of China's past but of its future.

Huangpu River cruises depart from a wharf on the south end of the Bund promenade. The day-tour tickets can be purchased from a hotel tour desk or from offices on the wharf. I purchased my ticket from the ticket office at 229 Zhongshan Dong Lu (on the lower-level sidewalk that runs alongside the promenade, south of the pyramidal Diamond Restaurant looming overhead). The booking office (☎ 021/6374-4461; fax 021/6374-4882) is well marked in English and the clerks can figure out what you want. Check for times. The long cruises usually depart at 9am, 11am, and 2pm, with a shorter evening cruise at 7pm (great for the light show along the Bund). Tickets for Special Class A (a soft seat, no-smoking lounge with tea service, wraparound picture windows, and private deck on the bow) are RMB 100 ($12) on weekdays, RMB 118 ($14) on weekends. The river tour boats are wide two-deckers, about 150 feet long, with a kiosk selling snacks; a bar selling tea, coffee, sodas, and beer; and a buffet dining room used for weekend and evening voyages.

The Bund

By the Bund, most everyone means the long promenade along the shores of the Huangpu (its proper street name is Zhongshan Nong Yi Lu). This is indeed a fine place to stroll, north to south, taking in the views of skyscrapers across the river and the old architecture of Shanghai across the street. Despite the city's incredible development, the Bund's stately skyline still defines Shanghai, setting it apart from any other city in China. The monumental European architecture here is what interests me most. It is more out of place in Shanghai than ever before. These were once the triumphant seats of power of Shanghai's Western masters—the banks, private clubs, and grand offices of the taipans who ran Shanghai for nearly a hundred years, beginning in the 1840s when Shanghai became a treaty port. In the twilight of the colonial period, in the 1930s, there was a popular saying in Shanghai that anywhere within a 10-mile radius you'd see a foreign face.

All of these rock-solid old buildings have new owners and tenants today, mostly financial institutions from inside China. The old occupants included the **British Consulate** and the **Jardine & Matheson trading company,** as well as the stately **Cathay Hotel,** the **Shanghai Customhouse,** the **Hong Kong and Shanghai Bank** (built in 1921), and the **Tung Feng Hotel** (once the site of the Shanghai Club and its celebrated Long Bar). Other buildings in this lineup include former consulates, brokerage houses, chambers of commerce, and banks from Japan, India, Denmark, France, Belgium, Britain, and Canada. Several are worth walking into, as they have been restored recently to their original splendor.

From north to south along the west side of the Bund, there are over 20 distinct specimens of colonial architecture. Those with the most dramatic lobbies include the current **Agricultural Bank Building (at no. 26),** a 1916 office building; the Peace Hotel (no. 20) with the pyramid roof, built by Sassoon in 1929; the **Palace Hotel (no. 19),** built in red and white brick in 1906; the current **New China Merchants Bank (no. 16),** which was rebuilt in 1924 in a Western/Japanese style to serve as the Bank of Taiwan; the massive **Customs House (no. 13)** with its stately bell tower, built in 1927; and the current **Pudong Development Bank (no. 12),** which has the Bund's most astounding interior. Some of the old hulks are still unoccupied, awaiting new tenants who must preserve and restore them now by law; others are of peculiar note. The **China Foreign Exchange Trade System Building (no. 15),** for example, houses the Three Gun Monopoly Shop. This odd name refers to China's largest underwear manufacturer; it comes from Gan Tinghui, who launched the company in 1937 to alleviate undergarment dependence on archenemy Japan. Gan had previously won renown for his marksmanship, winning three competitions and receiving the prize of a gun each time. The most famous building on the southern Bund, until recently the **Dongfeng Hotel (no. 2),** was the location of the exclusive Shanghai Club when it was built in 1910. It was empty during my last visit (the run-down hotel and even the KFC outlet had been removed), and its Long Bar, once the haunt of every well-to-do businessman and adventurer in Shanghai, had disappeared as well.

A word about the Bund's most splendid lobby, at no. 12: This great building, with its marble walls and arches, massive wooden revolving doors, and two bronze lions guarding the wide entrance, has a breathtaking dome, newly restored, over its lobby. The dome is an eight-sided mural of Greek-styled gods and heroes posing in eight great world capitals: Bangkok, Hong Kong, Tokyo, New York, London, Paris, Calcutta, and of course, Shanghai. The bank and its lobby beyond the dome are also exquisitely restored in leather and carved wood. The building was opened by the British Minister to China on June 23, 1923, to house the Hong Kong and Shanghai Bank.

These days, the Bund promenade is filled with far more visitors from inside China than out. This is the place to be for morning exercises, before the working day starts. Hundreds of residents do their morning *tai ji quan* workouts along the riverside, escaping for an hour into their own slow, quiet worlds before entering the maelstrom of work and commerce. Some of that commerce takes place on the promenade. Tour boats depart for Huangpu River tours, outdoor cafes sell sodas and snacks, ferries cross the river to the Pearl of the Orient TV Tower, and peddlers push their wagons of ice-cream treats up and down the walkway. Artists also wade through the stream of visitors. One enterprising artist, armed with scissors, struck up a conversation with me as we sauntered along the river. As we walked, he swiftly captured my likeness, cutting out two paper silhouettes, mounting both when we paused, and selling them to me on the spot. A moment later, he vanished, a step ahead of the licensing authorities.

The Best Little Old Teahouse in China

From the Bund it's a short walk southwest to the **old Chinese Quarter.** Throughout Shanghai, everyone seems to believe that if you build a modern city, wealth will beat a path to your door. Even **Nanshi,** Shanghai's Old Town, harbors this hope. Yu Yuan, the city's classic garden, and Huxintang Teahouse, with its zigzag Bridge of Nine Turnings, remain intact in the heart of old Shanghai. But these two delightful tourist stops are now surrounded by a new shopping mall. Mo's Burgers and Church's Chicken rub shoulders with Lu Bo Lang restaurant and the Tong Han Chun Traditional Medicine Store. What's surprising is that the commercial remodeling blends in with the old neighborhood of shophouses, pavilions, and the Temple to the Town God. Shanghai seems aware of the need to preserve the look and essence of its endangered past, even when redeveloping a tourist zone.

Many feel they already know the garden teahouse, **Huxinting Teahouse,** at the heart of Old Town the first time they see it; it could well have served as the model for classic Blue Willow tableware. This five-sided, two-story pavilion, with its dramatic upturned eaves and gray-tiled double roof, dates from 1784. It was built by merchants in the cotton trade as a place to broker their products, but become a teahouse a century later. Today it is the most visited teahouse in China, and a wonderful spot to rest from the surrounding frenzy. It's open 8:30am to 10pm, with tea and snacks served all day upstairs.

But even this island of tranquillity is responding to the construction mania currently shaking China's greatest metropolis to its foundations. The alleyways surrounding the teahouse, once lined with small shops and stalls, have fallen to the bulldozer of progress, replaced by a modern shopping mall of department stores and fast-food outlets featuring hamburgers as well as dumplings.

This arena of commercial development, officially known as the **Yu Yuan Shopping Centre,** located in the oldest inhabited section of Shanghai, reflects the classic Chinese low-rise style. The structures that now hug the shores of the pond where the teahouse floats like a lotus flower are faithful to the architecture of a century past. Sweeping tiled rooflines, ornately carved entryways, and massive wooden columns are the rule. The look of the traditional shophouse is preserved, even when these antique-style facades house outlets for fast food. Another old-fashioned aspect of the Shopping Centre is that it is for pedestrians only. Taxis and tourist buses line up blocks away on the fringes.

Next door to the teahouse, on the south shore, the picturesque **Lu Bo Lang** Restaurant is still serving local Shanghai specialties, including spicy hot eel and shrimp dishes. Perhaps the cuisine most often associated with Old Town, however, is snack food. For decades, visitors to the teahouse and garden gorged themselves on a variety of pastries and dumplings, from wheat flour muffins with a variety of fillings to glutinous rice balls with pigeon eggs. This Chinese-style "fast food" (fast to eat but slow to prepare) remains the most popular fare, although hamburgers, milk shakes, fried chicken, and mashed potatoes are catching on.

A few years ago, visitors with a taste for Chinese snacks might have stood in line at the Moslemo Restaurant, located on the west shore of the teahouse lake. Crowded and unkempt, this place afforded a splendid view of the bridge and teahouse, but the food was, at best, hearty. Today, the old cafe has been expanded and cleaned up (and is currently named the Lake De Delicate Food Restaurant), but it still lines the western shore of the teahouse lake. From a picture window outside you can watch the cooks preparing thousands of little pastries in the kitchen. This establishment serves traditional steamed snacks that are delicately fashioned and appealing to the palate.

The entire shopping area, which radiates out several blocks from the teahouse, is far more appealing than in the past. Many of the shops continue to offer the small native commodities that made the old bazaar one of China's most famous marketplaces. Chopsticks fill one specialty store, silk cloth another. The newly expanded **Tong Han Chun Medicine Store** dispenses traditional remedies. Other shops stock bamboo products, fans, and incense sticks, and there are larger emporiums that dispense a full range of regional arts and crafts. Two of old Shanghai's best-known products are available at little shops within a block of the teahouse: spiced beans and pear syrup (the latter is Shanghai's answer to the cough drop).

There is up-to-date shopping, too. A new department store a few steps from the zigzag bridge does a brisk business in handbags and luggage, including the latest roll-on suitcases embossed with likenesses of Mickey Mouse. The **World Shopping Centre** on the mall's southwest corner carries plenty of Western imports. The largest new structure is an amusement center teeming with the latest electronic and video games. A vending machine invasion has been launched as well. Coca-Cola machines, automatic teller machines, digital height and weight machines, even a brigade of shiny new portable toilets are moving into Old Town Shanghai.

Because of the tasteful remodeling of the teahouse shopping area, the old and the new do coexist neatly. Traditional Chinese dining and shopping mix with the latest from the West. One notable beneficiary of redevelopment has been the **Temple to the Town Gods (Cheng Huang Miao).** Built on the grounds of a 15th-century temple, its back garden became the southern section of Yu Yuan Garden in 1709. During this century, the Temple of the Town Gods often fell on hard times, once even serving as a warehouse. It is now an active place of worship. In the old days, the temple was the center of seasonal flower shows (plum blossoms in spring, chrysanthemums in autumn), street fairs, and lively markets.

Today, the temple's marketplace atmosphere has returned, particularly on Sunday, when Shanghai's largest **antique market** takes over the temple square. Weekdays are only slightly less crowded. Visitors number up to 200,000 a day. The Huxinting teahouse is the sole refuge—a fine place to sip tea at one's leisure while contemplating the frantic pace of life on every side.

The festive atmosphere of the area recalls the era of the temple bazaar, and the style of the remodeled shops enhances one's enjoyment of older pleasures. The newest addition to this quarter of old Shanghai Chinese-style is **Shanghai Old Street,** a half-mile stretch of Fangbang Zhong Lu, which is the east-west street marking the southern border of Old Town. It was remodeled in 1999 as an antique shopping street. Now lined with charming shophouses and wine shops, colorful antique and jewelry stores, and traditional theaters and teahouses, it is designed to recapture the atmosphere of Shanghai shopping under the Qing Dynasty.

Like the teahouse, **Yu Yuan Garden** is unchanged—a solid, beautiful monument from the past that doesn't require updating. Its undulating dragon walls still shelter its pavilions, pools, rookeries, and winding paths from a changing world outside, making it Shanghai's 16th-century retreat in the center of a city readying itself for the 21st century. After my most recent visit to Yu Yuan, I am confident in pronouncing it the single most beautiful classical garden in China, surpassing even those of Suzhou. Don't miss it, especially in the morning or late afternoon when the crowds are somewhat less pressing. And don't worry about the name or function of each pavilion. This is a garden to lose yourself in, a maze of delights. It's open daily from 8:30am to 5pm; admission is RMB 20 ($2.50).

French Concession

From 1842 on, Europeans carved up Shanghai into concessions, large neighborhoods where they built villas and residential blocks in the architectural styles of the West. The French Concession, often called **Frenchtown,** with its art deco and Tudor town houses and its neo-Gothic office blocks, survives to this day south of Nanjing Road and west of the Bund.

To reach Frenchtown from the Chinese Old Town, I walk west along **Huaihai Road,** which runs parallel to Nanjing Road and is also a major shopping street. Locals usually check it out before Nanjing Road these days, as the trendiest new shops and shopping centers open here.

Frenchtown is over a mile from the Bund, and the walking can be slow owing to the crush of pedestrians—your shoulders may well be sore by the end of the day. But Frenchtown's architecture is worth the trouble. The cityscape is another page from Shanghai's colonial days. The best-preserved area is along Maoming Nan Lu at the **Jin Jiang Hotel,** a massive complex of dark marble. This is where President Nixon stayed after signing the Shanghai Communiqué, the document that reopened China to the West in 1972, and it's also in the heart of the French District. Across the street is the **Garden Hotel,** a modern tower that contains a unique cultural treasure: the original stained glass, carved ceiling, and staircase of the entrance to the Cercle Sportif Francais, once the exclusive social center of well-to-do foreigners in Shanghai's age of decadence, the 1920s and 1930s.

Many traces of notorious Shanghai remain here, even with relentless modernization. The French Quarter still has some avenues lined with the shops and houses of its heyday. Many are being cleaned up and refitted with boutiques for the tourist trade. Several dozen mansions also exist, although few are open to the public. Still, well over 1,400 monumental Western-style buildings have been documented recently in Shanghai, and the major European-built hotels, churches, mansions, private residences, garden villas, and public buildings from the past 2 centuries will probably be preserved for the next century—with an eye to capturing the growing tourism dollar, if nothing else, as more and more of these sites are being converted into upscale restaurants. One of the finest examples is the **La Na Thai Restaurant** on the exquisite grounds of the old Ruijin Guest House (118 Ruijin Er Lu, just south off Maoming Lu in Frenchtown).

To see the gentrification of Shanghai close-up, the combining of old and new at its best, take a stroll down **Hengshan Lu,** just west of Frenchtown. It is the most fashionable area these days among locals, chock-full of upscale eateries, bars, and teahouses. Cafes such as **Sasha's** (in a mansion once owned by the Soong family, at 9 Dongping Lu) and teahouses like **Harn Sheh** (at 2A Hengshan Lu) are dazzling.

Shanghai Museum

There's a great historical legacy in Shanghai as well, and it is being preserved, although the chief treasures have moved into modern quarters. The new oval-shaped Shanghai Museum, on the south side of

People's Square, is China's most up-to-date museum. When I visited it on a Sunday morning, the plaza was teeming with skateboarders, in-line skaters, and children flying paper kites purchased from roving vendors.

Inside, the galleries are as modern as any in the world: the floors carpeted, the explanatory signs in English as well as Chinese, the track lighting precise and illuminating. There are four floors of exhibits, each floor looking down on an immense atrium. Stalls on each floor sell gifts and museum reproductions, and there are two larger gift shops on the ground floor. Galleries devoted to bronzes and stone sculpture are on the first floor. Ceramics dominate the second floor. Paintings, calligraphy, and seals (chops) have separate galleries on the third floor, and coins, jade, furniture, and minority displays are on the top floor. The two most impressive galleries are those of sculpture and of jade, featuring artifacts that span all the major dynasties back to the New Stone Age.

Using the audiophone (included in the admission price) literally throws light on some of the exhibits. The phone is keyed by number to certain exhibits. When you press the number of the selected exhibit, a light beam is activated to highlight that display and an explanatory tape is played on the earphone.

While the museum's 120,000 treasures are not on the scale of those collected in Beijing, Taipei, or even Xi'an, Shanghai shows that it knows how to display its past to a sophisticated international audience. On the second floor there's a fine tearoom for refreshment, with traditional Chinese furniture and a choice of cookies, four different teas, mineral water, and even Brazilian coffee. The museum is open daily from 9am to 5pm (until 10pm Saturdays). Admission is RMB 60 ($7.25) with audio tour, RMB 20 ($2.50) without; free admission 5 to 7pm Saturdays only.

Newly opened across the street from the Shanghai Museum (on the north side) are the **Grand Theater** (where daily tours cost RMB 50/$6), Shanghai's premier performance venue, and the **Shanghai Urban Planning Exhibition Hall,** which showcases on five floors the history of the city's explosive development.

Other Attractions

Shanghai has a surprising number of sights for a commercial city. Many of them are included on typical group tours, but most of them are of special interest, of limited interest, or too often of no interest at all. Among the best temples to visit are the **Jade Buddha Temple,** with its Buddha of white jade (170 Anyuan Lu), and the **Longhua Temple,** with its wooden pagoda (2853 Longhua Lu). The **Jingan Temple** (1700

Nanjing Lu) is small but active, and the **Confucian Temple** (Wenmiao Lu) is recently restored.

Among the homes and museums of local luminaries, those that most reward a visit are the Former Residence of **Soong Qingling** at 1843 Huaihai Zhong Lu and the memorial park and museum of writer **Lu Xun** at 146 Jiangwan Dong Lu. Shanghai is also the site of a small Jewish museum, the **Ohel Moshe Synagogue** at 62 Changyang Lu, the **Shanghai Arts and Crafts Research Institute** at 79 Fenyang Lu, the 19th-century **Xujiahui Cathedral** at 158 Puxi Lu, the extensive **Shanghai Botanical Gardens** at 1100 Longwu Lu, and the **Shanghai Zoo** at 2381 Hongqiao Lu, with its pandas. These and other attractions are covered in detail in *Frommer's Shanghai.*

Zhou Zhuang Water Village

Tour operators offer an array of day trips from Shanghai, even to Suzhou and Hangzhou (see separate chapters), but the best 1-day excursion is to the 900-year-old water village of **Zhou Zhuang,** a 90-minute bus ride (50 miles) southwest of city center. The tour gives you a good chance to see the flatlands that encircle Shanghai, with their mix of farms and factories, and a rare opportunity to see a small village that owes its origins to the Venice-like canals that interlace this vast delta. Tours usually include a stop on Lake Dingshan, one of China's largest lakes, 37 miles from Shanghai, for a tour of a new theme park, **Grand View Garden,** a reconstruction of the old estate that is the setting for a famous Chinese novel. Few Westerners find this literary amusement park of much interest.

The water village, however, is fascinating, as this canal village resembles an illustration from an antique Blue Willow plate with waterways, Chinese gondolas, arched stone bridges, and tile-roofed wooden houses. Several of the 200-to-400-year-old residences of village leaders are open to tour; there's a village museum; and there are hundreds of quaint shops all along the canal promenade. The two-story traditional wooden courtyard houses, decorated with Qing Dynasty furniture, consist of a formal meeting room, separate villas for men and women, workshops, bedrooms, and ancestral shrines.

The highlights of a village tour include lunch in one of a dozen canal-side dining rooms (where pork roast and fish are the local specialties), topped off by a gondola ride up the village canal, which costs RMB 60 ($7.50) per eight-person boat. The gondolas are "rowed" by long tillers at the stern, which are expertly maneuvered by the women of Zhou Zhuang. This is perhaps as close to the "Venice of the East" as a traveler to China can get these days. Zhou Zhuang is extremely crowded on weekends, so aim for a weekday if possible.

PRACTICAL INFORMATION

ORIENTATION & WHEN TO GO

Shanghai, which means "Above the Sea," is located near the East China Sea and the Yangzi River Delta, midway between Beijing (700 miles to the northwest) and Hong Kong (750 miles to the southwest). Summers are blisteringly hot, humid, and rainy, and winters are lengthy and cold. Spring brings unsettled weather, making autumn the best time to visit, as days then are generally warm but not humid. Hangzhou, Suzhou, and Lake Tai (each the subject of a separate chapter in this guide) are just a few hours away by road or rail.

GETTING THERE

By Plane There are now two airports in Shanghai, the old one to the west, the new one in Pudong. Shanghai's **Hongqiao Airport** (☎ 021/6253-6530) has connections to major destinations inside and outside of China, although as the "old" airport, it is beginning to serve fewer international destinations. The airport is 12 miles west of downtown Shanghai; transfers take 20 to 40 minutes with improved highways. Taxi queues form just outside to the right; ignore touts, as they overcharge. Taxi rates should be RMB 60 to RMB 100 ($7.25 to $12), depending on the downtown destination. An airport shuttle bus (RMB 3/35¢), run by China Eastern Airlines, goes to an office at 200 Yan'an Xi Lu, not far from Shanghai Centre, 2 miles west of the Huangpu River. Many hotels provide free airport shuttles, especially if you fax a request ahead, with your arrival time. Or, inquire at the hotel desks just inside the Hongqiao terminal on the left.

The new **Pudong International Airport** is about 30 miles east of the Pudong New Area, but until the new highways are complete, transfer takes an hour and more. A number of international carriers have signed up to use this airport, moving their operations from the Hongqiao. **United Airlines** (offices in Shanghai Centre, Room 204, West Wing, ☎ 021/6279-8009) was the first to move its flights to Pudong. It began direct Shanghai–San Francisco flights on April 1, 2000. Most flights that originate in China, however, continue to use the old airport. The subway line to the new airport won't be completed for a few years. Taxis charge over RMB 120 ($15) for the trip to downtown Shanghai; hotels are beginning to set up cheaper shuttle services. The new French-designed terminal can handle up to 60 million passengers yearly and offers excellent last-minute shopping.

By Train From Shanghai's massive main **train station** (☎ 021/6317-9234), now fronted by metal detectors, there are trains to most cities and towns in China. Hotel tour desks can book onward tickets. Particularly easy to reach by train from Shanghai are the nearby towns of Hangzhou, Suzhou, and Wuxi (Lake Tai), which are covered in separate chapters, as well as the major overnight destinations of Hong Kong and Beijing, which are served by train nos. 99 and 100, China's most luxurious.

By Ship Three passenger ships, the *Haixin,* the *Shanghai,* and the *Jin Jiang,* ply the Shanghai–Hong Kong route.

First-class tickets cost about $150 one-way. It's a 3-night voyage with meals (but little else) included. Book passage from CITS or a hotel tour desk.

GETTING AROUND

To get around Shanghai on your own, use an English-language map and set off on foot, by subway, or by taxi. Many of the 40,000 registered **taxis** now print out customer receipts from their meters; they charge RMB 10 ($1.25) for the first kilometer, RMB 2 (25¢) for each additional kilometer. For river tunnels and bridges, add RMB 15 ($2). Most taxi rides through the city cost from RMB 15 to RMB 25 ($1.80 to $3).

The Shanghai **subway** is a fairly clean, highly efficient means for navigating the crowded distances of the city. The no. 1 line connects the train station in the north to Jinjiang amusement park in the south, a 10-mile run. The most central stop is at Renmin Park (Renmin Shangchang Station), where transfers can be made to the new no. 2 line that runs east-west, including under Nanjing Road and across to Pudong (but not yet as far as the new airport). Tickets for 12 stops or less cost RMB 3 (37¢), RMB 4 (50¢) if you travel farther; purchase tickets at the platform window. The subway's hours of operation are 5am to 11pm daily.

TOURS & STRATAGEMS

China International Travel Service (CITS) arranges guided tours in English to all major sites. Their main office is located at 2 Jinling Dong Lu (☎ 021/6321-7200), near the Bund. I have not always found this office helpful, preferring the CITS office near Shanghai Centre at 1277 Beijing Xi Lu (☎ 021/6289-7827 or 6289-8899; fax 021/6289-7838). Hotel tour desks provide the same services. Hotels can also book air, train, and boat tickets. **Spring Travel Service,** 1556 Dingxi Lu, maintains a 24-hour tourist information line (in English) at ☎ 021/6252-0000.

The most efficient tour office I have used is the **Jin Jiang Optional Tours Center** near the Jin Jiang and Garden hotels at 191 Changle Lu (☎ 021/6445-9525; fax 021/6472-0184). It offers a brochure with itineraries and prices, and the staff at the back desk speaks English. Group bus tours with English-speaking guides and lunch cost RMB 250 ($30). You can also book 1- and 2-day group tours to Suzhou and Hangzhou and a day tour to Zhou Zhuang Water Village (for RMB 350/$43) including lunch. Jin Jiang also offers English-speaking guides and private tours (with car, driver, and guide) at set rates; hotel reservations; Pudong River cruise tickets; and tickets to evening entertainment (acrobatics, opera, Peace Hotel jazz).

The **Tourism Hot Line** number is ☎ 021/6439-0630. **American Express,** 1376 Nanjing Xi Lu, Room 206, Shanghai Centre (☎ 021/6279-8082), offers traveler's assistance, but does not book tours or transportation, although with an American Express card you can cash personal checks at a number of Bank of China branches in Shanghai. **Thomas Cook** has a liaison office with China Travel Service at 881 Yanan Zhong Lu (☎ 021/6247-6390).

The best selection of **books** on Shanghai and China is in the bookstore in the shopping arcade just inside the walls of the **Jin Jiang Hotel,** 59 Maoming Nan Lu, in Frenchtown. For reading up on Shanghai before arrival, try Pan Ling's *In Search of Old Shanghai,* Nien Cheng's *Life and Death in Shanghai,* Vicki Baum's *Shanghai '37,* J. G. Ballard's *Empire of the Sun,* and Sterling Seagrave's *The Soong Dynasty.* Shanghai even has two English-language **radio stations,** 101.7 FM and 103.7 FM.

WHERE TO STAY

Shanghai is filled with top hotels, so travel agents can usually come up with room rates far below the official rates posted below. Unfortunately, like the rest of China, Shanghai lacks mid-range, economical three-star accommodations.

Grand Hyatt Shanghai (Jinmao Kaiyue Dajiudian). *54th floor, Jin Mao Tower, 2 Shiji Da Dao, Pudong (near Pearl of the Orient Tower).* ☎ *800/233-1234 or 021/5049-1234. Fax 021/5049-1111. 555 units including 45 suites. A/C MINIBAR TV TEL. $300 double. AE, DC, JCB, MC, V.* This trendy Grand Hyatt is indeed grand. It has Shanghai's highest room rate, in addition to some of the highest hotel rooms in the world (54th through 88th floor of the Jin Mao Tower). Even the technology is high: These are some of the spaciest, most inventive hotel rooms anywhere, down to their solid, see-through glass washbasins and post-modern designs with Chinese decor. The tubs have an outer wall of glass looking out over Shanghai; the separate showers have three nozzles. The furniture is traditional Chinese, but the enormous cascading hotel swimming pool is definitely not: It stretches from window to window, 57 floors up, and is aptly described as "swimming in the sky."

Amenities: Indoor lap pool with cascades, highest fitness center in the world, Jacuzzi, sauna, business center, conference rooms, beauty salon, newsstand, shops, concierge, valet, 24-hour room service, same-day laundry and dry cleaning, newspaper delivery, nightly turndown, baby-sitting, airport shuttle.

Holiday Inn Crowne Plaza (Yinxing Jiari Fandian). *400 Panyu Lu (west Shanghai).* ☎ *800/465-4329 or 021/6280-8888. Fax 021/6280-3353. 534 units, including 28 suites. A/C MINIBAR TV TEL. $230 double. AE, DC, JCB, MC, V.* Large guest rooms stand out in this five-star luxury hotel, a favorite of many Western travelers. Data ports, work desks, safes, high ceilings, a superb range of satellite TV channels, and sparkling marble bathrooms are standard. There are also nonsmoking and handicapped rooms, as well as six executive floors.

Amenities: Indoor swimming pool, fitness club, Jacuzzi, sauna, squash court, billiards, business center, conference rooms, beauty salon, newsstand, shops, concierge, valet, 24-hour room service, same-day laundry and dry cleaning, newspaper delivery, nightly turndown, baby-sitting, free airport shuttle.

Holiday Inn Pudong (Pudong Jiari Fandian). *899 Dong Fang Lu (southwest Pudong).* ☎ *800/465-4329 or 021/5830-6666. Fax 021/5830-5555. 320 units, including 39 suites. A/C MINIBAR TV TEL. $160 double. AE, DC, JCB, MC, V.* A recently opened 32-story four-star hotel in the downtown area of Pudong, this Holiday Inn is sleek and clean, with reliable service. Once favored largely by business travelers with nearby operations, it now appeals to others, since the new subway line is within walking distance. Rooms are spacious enough for couches, and bathrooms are covered in spotless white tile. There are three nonsmoking floors and three executive floors.

Amenities: Outdoor swimming pool, fitness club, Jacuzzi, sauna, billiards, table tennis, business center, conference rooms, beauty salon, newsstand, valet, 24-hour room service, same-day laundry and dry cleaning, newspaper delivery, nightly turndown, baby-sitting, free airport shuttle.

Novotel Shanghai Yuan Lin (Nuo Fute Yuan Lin Binguan). *201 Baise Lu (southwest Shanghai). ☎ 800/221-4542 or 021/6470-1688. Fax 021/6470-0008. 183 units. A/C MINIBAR TV TEL. $120 double. AE, DC, JCB, MC, V.* This small (six-story) complex, affiliated with the French chain Accor, is the best three-star hotel in Shanghai. Rooms are small and basic, but modern and clean. The grounds contain a small garden and goldfish pond and 40 two-story "Canadian-style" lodges for long-term guests. The staff is friendly. The chief drawback is location: It's far from everything else, except the Shanghai Botanical Garden next door.

Amenities: Indoor swimming pool, fitness club, Jacuzzi, sauna, two tennis courts (outdoors), billiards, darts, aerobics gym, table tennis, bowling alley, indoor shooting range, business center, conference rooms, beauty salon, newsstand, concierge, valet, 24-hour room service, next-day laundry and dry cleaning, tour desk, medical clinic, free shuttle to airport and subway station.

Peace Hotel (Heping Fandian). *20 Nanjing Dong Lu (on the Bund). ☎ 021/6321-6888. Fax 021/6329-0300. 279 units. A/C TV TEL. $160 double. AE, DC, JCB, MC, V.* This is the classic hotel of Shanghai, with art deco touches still in place. Some of the rooms have been modernized, but the rest are spacious and contain original woodwork and furnishings, though they're somewhat rundown. There are some grand suites, such as the elaborate India Room, but these are priced at well over $400. The service is inefficient and the cleanliness is not quite up to international standards, but the hotel's location is superb and it has the romantic, nostalgic feel of pre-revolutionary Shanghai.

Amenities: Health club, sauna, billiards, conference room, beauty salon, shops, newsstand, next-day laundry and dry cleaning, 24-hour room service, concierge, jazz bar.

Regal International East Asia Hotel (Fuhao Huanqiu Dong Ya Jiudian). *516 Hengshan Lu (southwest Shanghai). ☎ 800/222-8888 or 021/6415-5588. Fax 021/6445-8899. 300 units, including 22 suites. A/C MINIBAR TV TEL. $220 double. AE, DC, JCB, MC, V.* Along with top service and lavish amenities, this 22-story hotel boasts the best health and fitness facilities in the city. The rooms are medium-sized and modern, with a full range of amenities. The European-inspired lobby looms large.

Amenities: Indoor swimming pool (25 meters), large fitness club, Jacuzzi, sauna, 10 tennis courts (two indoors), indoor squash court, billiards, simulated golf range, aerobics gym, 12-lane bowling alley, business center, conference rooms, beauty salon, newsstand, shops, concierge, valet, 24-hour room service, same-day laundry and dry cleaning, newspaper delivery, nightly turndown, baby-sitting, tour desk, free airport shuttle.

Ritz-Carlton Portman Hotel (Boteman Dajiudian). *1376 Nanjing Xi Lu (inside the Shanghai Centre).*

☎ *800/241-3333 or 021/6279-8888. Fax 021/6279-8800. 564 units. A/C MINIBAR TV TEL. $250 double. AE, DC, JCB, MC, V.* Fully renovated in 1999, the city's number-one business hotel comes with large guest rooms containing writing desks, sofas, three phones, hair dryers, and in-room safes. The adjacent Shanghai Centre (☎ 021/6279-8009) includes a supermarket and deli (open 8am to 10:30pm), a Watson's drugstore, and an Espresso Americano coffee bar (☎ 021/6279-8518). Excellent service throughout.

Amenities: Heated indoor-outdoor lap pool, large health club, Jacuzzi, sauna, tennis court, two squash courts, 24-hour business center, tour desk, beauty salon, shopping arcade, newsstand, concierge, valet, room service (24-hour), dry cleaning and laundry (same day), newspaper delivery, nightly turndown, twice-daily maid service, express checkout, free airport shuttle, World Link medical clinic.

Shanghai Hilton International (Jinan Dajiudian). *250 Huashan Lu.* ☎ *800/445-8667 or 021/6248-0000. Fax 021/6248-3848. 772 units, including 56 suites. A/C MINIBAR TV TEL. $180 double. AE, DC, JCB, MC, V.* Located at the west end of the French Quarter, this 43-story tower has outstanding services and features. It is completely foreign-owned and managed, and very popular with visiting businesspeople. The lobby is spacious and busy. There are three nonsmoking floors.

Amenities: Indoor pool, health club, sauna, tennis court, two squash courts, business center, conference rooms, tour desk, beauty salon, florist, drugstore, shopping arcade, newsstand and bookstore, concierge, room service (24-hour), dry cleaning and laundry (24-hour, same day), nightly turndown, express checkout, free airport shuttle, medical clinic.

Shangri-La Pudong Hotel (Xiangge Lila Fandian). *33 Fu Cheng Lu (Pudong, east Shanghai).* ☎ *800/ 942-5050 or 021/6882-8888. Fax 021/ 6882-6688. 612 units, including 25 suites. A/C MINIBAR TV TEL. $240 double. AE, DC, JCB, MC, V.* With a spectacular view from the east shore of the Huangpu River, this new (1998) five-star 28-story tower, within walking distance of the new subway and underground river tunnel, is surprisingly convenient to the heart of old Shanghai. Service is good; amenities are excellent. Guest rooms are very large, with marble-top desks, glass coffee tables, and separate bathtubs and showers.

Amenities: Indoor swimming pool, fitness club, Jacuzzi, sauna, tennis court, free access to Riverside Park, business center, conference rooms, newsstand, shops, concierge, valet, 24-hour room service, same-day laundry and dry cleaning, newspaper delivery, nightly turndown, baby-sitting, free airport shuttle.

Westin Tai Ping Yang (Weisiting Taipingyang). *5 Zunyi Nan Lu (Hongqiao area, west Shanghai).* ☎ *800/ WESTIN-1 or 021/6275-8888. Fax 021/ 6275-5420. 578 units, including 39 suites. A/C MINIBAR TV TEL. $240 double. AE, DC, JCB, MC, V.* This fine 27-story luxury hotel has excellent service, and a "home away from home" warmth that insures repeat business. Its rooms are plush and sizable, its chairs and desks very comfortable. There are four nonsmoking floors and rooms for the handicapped. Golf reservations and transport to the Shanghai International Country Club are assured.

Amenities: Indoor swimming pool, fitness club, Jacuzzi, sauna, tennis court, billiards, business center, conference rooms, beauty salon, newsstand, shops, concierge, valet, 24-hour room service, same-day laundry and dry cleaning, newspaper delivery, nightly turndown, baby-sitting, tour desk, free airport shuttle.

Yangtze New World Marriott Hotel (Yangzijiang Dajiudian). *2099 Yanan Xi Lu (Hongqiao area, west Shanghai).* ☎ *800/321-2211 or 021/6275-0000. Fax 021/6275-0750. 544 units, including 25 suites. A/C MINIBAR TV TEL. $185 double. AE, DC, JCB, MC, V.* An excellent four-star hotel newly under Marriott management, this 33-story tower is slated for renovations in 2000. Its present rooms are small and plain, but include deluxe amenities (data ports, safes, large desks, slippers and robes). Known in Shanghai for its catering, the hotel has cooked for many world leaders.

Amenities: Outdoor swimming pool, fitness club, Jacuzzi, sauna, business center, conference rooms, beauty salon, florist, newsstand, shops, concierge, valet, 24-hour room service, same-day laundry and dry cleaning, newspaper delivery, nightly turndown, baby-sitting, tour desk, free airport shuttle.

YMCA Hotel (Qian Nian Hui Binguan). *123 Xizang Nan Lu (2 blocks south of Nanjing Rd., 1 mile west of the Bund).* ☎ *021/6326-1040. Fax 021/6320-1957. 150 units. A/C TV TEL. $64 double. Dorm rooms (4 people) $15. AE, DC, JCB, MC, V.* For budget accommodations—and for those who don't expect too much—this will do. This 11-story hotel, fronted by columns and topped by a traditional tiled roof, really was Shanghai's YMCA when it was built in 1929. The service is friendly, the rooms small and drab. There's a 24-hour cafe in the lobby that serves Western dishes, a beauty salon, exercise machines, a massage room, a karaoke ballroom, a small business center, and even a free airport shuttle. Most guests are Chinese, but the clerks at the counter can speak some English.

WHERE TO DINE

Shanghai has its own distinct cuisine, featuring river eel, crabs, and other seafood in light, sweet sauces. In addition, there are many international choices in this most international of Chinese cities.

One local specialty you probably won't want to try is **snake,** valued for its ability to increase vitality. There's been a recent boom in snake restaurants, which now number 6,000, most illegal. Snakes come in live to cafes from the snake market in West Shanghai. One cafe that charges diners $20 per pound for cobra, $35 per pound for pit viper, and $4 per pound for the more common water snake, is said to be packed every night of the week. Sorry, I don't know its address.

The international hotels have excellent, often expensive restaurants, and these are beginning to be rivaled in quality by independent restaurants in the streets. International fast-food chains are also proliferating, with McDonald's leading the charge. I happened to try one located north of the Jin Jiang Hotel in the French Quarter, finding it to be the best-run outlet of its type I'd ever seen in China. Some English was even spoken. While I ate lunch, a local business executive came in, guiding his frail mother by the arm. She'd clearly heard about these fast-food places from the West, but she'd never ventured into the barbarian's den until that afternoon. Her son dutifully steered her through the maze of tables (the place was packed) to the counter, where he pointed to the pictures of foreigners' food. She didn't order, but she was clearly amazed by every shining detail of this strange wokless, riceless restaurant.

Today there are now several hundred good restaurants to choose from. Here's a handful of the best bets:

Cafe Bistro. *5 Zunyi Nan Lu (in the Westin Tai Ping Nan Hotel, Level 1, on the way to the airport in the Hongqiao Development Zone). ☎ 021/6275-8888. Reservations required. Sun brunch RMB 137 ($16). AE, JCB, MC, V. Brunch 11:30am–2:30pm. BRUNCH/ INTERNATIONAL.* Shanghai's hotels (the Hilton most notably) put up elaborate brunches every Sunday, but this champagne brunch remains a particularly outstanding deal. Children (12 years and under) eat for just RMB 80 ($10). The buffets usually feature a specific cuisine (such as Thai) as their monthly special. There are views of an intimate garden.

Dragon and Phoenix Restaurant. *20 Nanjing Dong Lu (8th floor, Peace Hotel). ☎ 021/6321-6888, ext 5201. Reservations recommended for dinner. Main courses $20–$35. AE, DC, JCB, MC, V. Daily 11:30am–2pm and 5:30–10pm. SHANGHAI.* This is a return to the Shanghai of glitz and kitsch, and a perfect place to enjoy Shanghai cuisine. Dragons and bats are carved into the ceiling, and everything else is painted green, except the columns, which are red and gold. The English menu has plenty of choices, from river eel to whole barbecued duck. There are Cantonese and Sichuan choices, too. Pork chops are a specialty here, as are the basket of steamed dumplings ("Palace Under the Sea") and the seafood hot pot. Be sure to reserve a window table on the river side.

Gino's Cafe. *2nd Floor, 66 Nanjing Dong Lu (just west of the Bund, a few doors down from the Peace Hotel). ☎ 021/6361-2205. Reservations not accepted. Main courses $2.50–$5. AE, DC, JCB, MC, V. Daily 9am–11pm. ITALIAN (FAST FOOD).* If you must succumb to a desire for Western fast food in Shanghai (and most travelers do), then go for something a step above the hamburger joint. Gino's is an international chain that delivers fine fast food in a clean bistro setting at a low price. Minestrone soup with garlic bread is just RMB 15 ($2); fresh tossed salad RMB 15 ($2); and lasagnas, fettucines, and pennes under RMB 40 ($5). The pan pizza is the best I've had in China. The service is efficient. Gino's has seven locations in Shanghai, including branches in Hongqiao (at the Friendship Shopping Centre) and Pudong (in the Yaohan Department Store).

Gongdelin. *445 Nanjing Xi Lu (west Shanghai). ☎ 021/6327-0218. Reservations recommended on weekends. Main courses $7–$15. No credit cards. Daily 6:30–9:30am, 11am–2pm, 5–9pm. VEGETARIAN CHINESE.* Shanghai's best vegetarian restaurant has over a half century of experience, and it frequently plays to packed houses with its meatless (often tofu-filled) imitations of fish and fowl, pork and beef—best of all is its faux duck. Its present location, not the original one, offers basic dining facilities that contrast with the inventive creations on the plate.

Grand Hyatt's Grand Cafe. *54th floor, Jin Mao Tower, 2 Shiji Dadao (Grand Hyatt Hotel, Pudong). ☎ 021/5049-1234. Reservations recommended on weekends. Main courses $10–$18. AE, DC, JCB, MC, V. Daily 6am–midnight. WESTERN.* The Grand Cafe provides not only the best view of any hotel lobby restaurant in Shanghai, but also some of the best food. The stylish show kitchen creates different specialties for each meal. This is buffet paradise. The mix-it-yourself salad at the granite-top salad bar is very fresh, as are the antipasti and European cheeses. Main courses come from the grill, with Shanghai homecooked dishes an alternative. The dessert bar is decadent. The lunch buffet currently costs RMB 168 ($20) and the dinner buffet is RMB 188 ($23).

Lan Na Thai. *2nd floor, Building no. 4, Ruijin Guesthouse, 118 Ruijin Er Lu (French Quarter).* ☎ *021/6466-4328. Reservations recommended on weekends. Main courses $10–$18. AE, DC, JCB, MC, V. Daily 5:30–11pm. THAI.* Tucked down a lush, twisting lane in the northwest corner of this elegant 1930s estate, Building no. 4 is actually the former mansion of a colonial, left gloriously intact. The cuisine, prepared by Thai chefs and served with care and skill, is equal to the fine setting. Downstairs there's a posh Indian restaurant (Hazara) with the same hours, fairly high prices, and excellent food and service, as well as a stylish bar and lounge (Faces). This is a sweet, nostalgic, but hip place to dine.

Lu Bo Lang. *115 Yu Yuan Lu (on the northwest corner of the teahouse lake, Old Town Shanghai).* ☎ *021/6328-0602. Main courses $10–$20. AE, DC, JCB, MC, V. Daily 11am–1:45pm, 5–10pm. Morning tea daily 7–10am, afternoon tea daily 2–4:30pm. SHANGHAI.* This towering traditional Chinese pavilion, with its uplifted black tile eaves and bold red balustrades, blends in perfectly with the nearby Nine-Turns-Bridge and old teahouse. Lu Bo Lang is known for its Shanghai dishes (including its crab), its shark's fin creations, and its delicate snacks, and has served its share of heads of state, more than 40 of whom (from Queen Elizabeth to Fidel Castro) are remembered in the photographs on second- and third-floor corridors. U.S. President Bill Clinton's favorite snack here was *mei mao su* (eyebrow-shaped shortcakes). Reservations required here for dinner.

M on the Bund. *7th floor, 20 Guangdong Lu (entrance on this side street off the Bund).* ☎ *021/6350-9988. Reservations required. Main courses $15–$35. AE, DC, JCB, MC, V. Daily 11am–2pm, 5–10pm. CONTINENTAL.* This is the restaurant that put Shanghai back on the world dining map. It remains the city's classiest, with European-level service, facilities, and dishes. The emphasis is on Mediterranean cuisine and fine wines, presented casually. From its spacious balcony M has a knock-out view of the Bund running north to the Peace Hotel and of the TV Tower, Jin Mao Tower, and other skyscrapers across the river. A three-course weekend brunch is priced at RMB 218 ($26), a great bargain here.

Mei Long Zhen. *no. 22, 1081 Nanjing Xi Lu (west Shanghai).* ☎ *021/6253-5353 or 6256-6688. Reservations required. Main courses $12–$20. AE, DC, JCB, MC, V. Daily 11am–1:30pm, 5–9pm. SHANGHAI/SICHUAN.* One of the city's oldest (1938) and most famous restaurants, Mei Long Zhen harks back to strictly local traditions for its cooking. The current decor has an elegant air, highlighted by the Qing Dynasty furnishings (dark mahoganies, marble chair backs, carved wood). The top dish on the 1930s menu is a sweet-and-sour deep-fried Mandarin fish in chili sauce and noodles; the top dessert, a red bean paste–filled pancake, cut in strips. English menus are available.

Park 97. *2 Gaolan Lu (inside west entrance of Fuxing Park, central Shanghai).* ☎ *021/6318-0785. Reservations* *required. Main courses $12–$25. AE, DC, JCB, MC, V. Mon–Thurs 5pm–2am, Fri–Sun 11am–2am. CONTINENTAL.* This park restaurant and lounge is very chic, with its art gallery and art deco touches. The dishes are mostly gourmet, although for cafe lunches, one can order a ham pizza or fish and chips. The panfried salmon fillet (in warm potato salad, carrot spaghetti, and lemon capers) is more typical of what's served for dinner in the more formal, more expensive restaurant. With its mirrors, lighted columns, oil paintings, and wall of windows on the park's rose garden, this is one of Shanghai's smartest places to be seen.

Sasha's. *House 11, 9 Dongping Lu (at Hengshan Lu, west Shanghai).* ☎ *021/6474-6166. Reservations recommended on weekends. Main courses $12–$25. AE, DC, JCB, MC, V. Daily 11:30am–2pm and 5:30–11:30pm (but hours seem less than reliable). CONTINENTAL.* This three-story mansion from the 1920s, located in the former Soong family compound, has been beautifully converted into an airy, informal, but upscale international restaurant. The first floor is a lounge, with a patio in the back. The second floor forms a large dining room. The third floor has verandas and specializes currently in serving cheese and chocolate fondues. The soups and grilled fish are excellent, as are the summer weekend barbecues (RMB 130/$16) and express lunches (RMB 85/$11).

Tandoor. *59 Maoming Nan Lu (in the New South Building of the Jin Jiang Hotel).* ☎ *021/6472-5494. Reservations required. Main courses $15–$20. AE, DC, JCB, MC, V. Daily 11:30am–2pm and 5:30–10:30pm. INDIAN.* Local expatriates voted this Shanghai's best foreign restaurant in 1998, and it hasn't slipped. It has a fine fixed-price lunch of tandoori specialties. The staff comes from India, as do the classical dancers (evenings 6:30 to 10:30pm). Service is prompt, unobtrusive, and professional. The decor is traditional, and so is the food, from the starters (such as chicken *chat,* a barbecued chicken with lemon juice) to the tandoori breads (baked in a clay oven) through the tandoori chicken itself, marinated in yogurt and known as *murgh malai kebab.*

Zips. *46th Floor, Senmao Building, 101 Yin Cheng Dong Lu (near the Pearl of the Orient TV Tower, Pudong).* ☎ *021/6431-3300. Reservations not necessary. Main courses $12–$18, set dinners $15–$22. AE, DC, JCB, MC, V. Daily 11:30am–2pm and 5:30–8:30pm. Closed Sun. CONTINENTAL.* Superb views of barges and the Bund, at 600 feet above the Huangpu River, make this an appealing spot for lunch or dinner. The theme is marine, with bulkhead partitions and porthole lighting. Main courses come off the grill: cod, jumbo prawns, teriyaki beef fillet. Styles vary from American to Malaysian.

SUZHOU: THE GARDEN CITY

苏州

THERE IS "HEAVEN ABOVE, SUZHOU and Hangzhou below," according to a popular adage. Unlike Hangzhou, whose beauty is of a broad, natural nature, Suzhou is intimate and artistic. More than 170 bridges arch over the 20 miles of slim waterways within the moated city. The poetic private gardens number about 70, with a dozen of the finest open to public view. Suzhou's interlocking canals, classic gardens, and embroidery and silk studios are the chief surviving elements of a cultural capital that dominated China's artistic scene for long periods during the Ming and Qing dynasties. Even the women of Suzhou, with their rounded faces and pale skin, became the model of traditional beauty in China.

Members of England's first official mission to China (1792–94) summed up Suzhou as the home of China's "greatest artists, the most well-known scholars, the richest merchants" and as the ruler of "Chinese taste in matters of fashion and speech." To this day, Suzhou retains something of its stylish legacy. Its downtown is a pleasant array of tree-lined lanes, many of them running alongside canals. I must warn you, however, that the city's narrow, soupy canals are not quite those of Venice. Old Suzhou certainly contains an element of decay. But in this decay there is a certain charm and authenticity not found in other old cities that have been remodeled and reconstructed into hygienic picture postcards of their former selves. Even with its darkening patina, Suzhou remains one of the most beautiful cities in China.

The focus of the city's beauty is its magnificent collection of private classic **gardens.** These small, exquisite jewels of landscaping art are the finest surviving examples of the tradition. Their enchantment is of a nature both philosophical and sensuous. The closest equivalent in the Western tradition might be Walden Pond, where Henry David Thoreau escaped the confines of city and civilization in order to confront his essential self. For Western romantics, the natural retreat opens ever outward in a widening circle of grass and field—the cosmos of an untamed New World. But for the Chinese mystic, the natural retreat closed ever

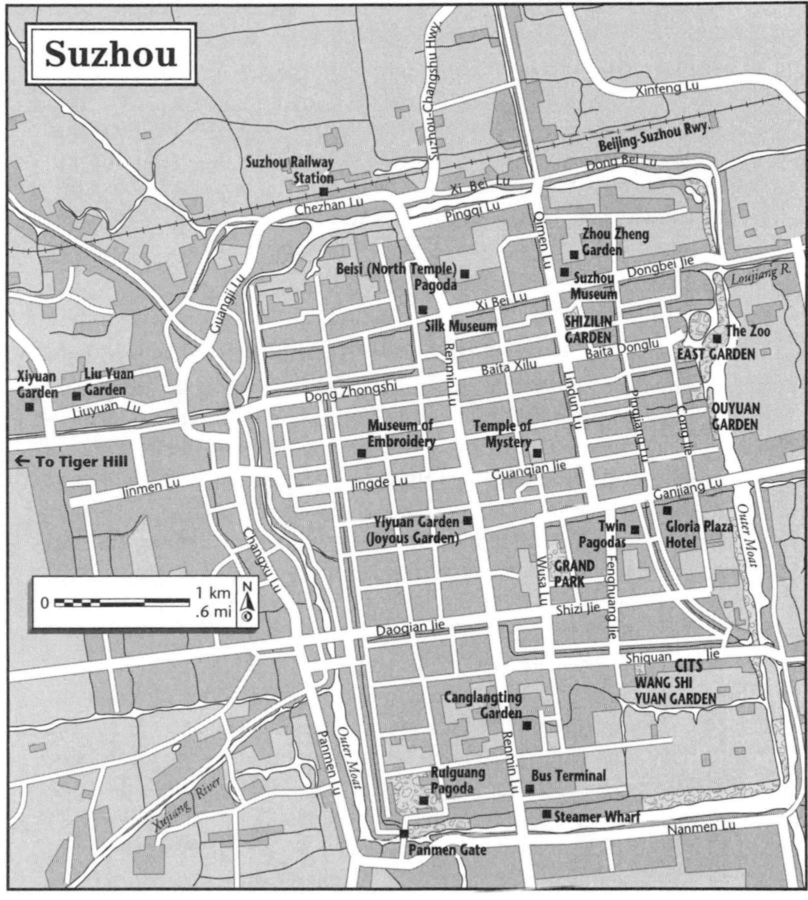

more inwardly upon itself within the perfect garden—a microcosm of the unchanging ancient Way.

The gardens are often choked with visitors, making a slow, meditative tour difficult, but it is only by taking enough time to lose oneself in them that their power and essence can be discovered. The gardens of Suzhou are unlike those we are familiar with in the West—even unlike the Japanese gardens for which they once served as models. When Ch'i Piao-chia, a 17th-century scholar, became obsessed with building a garden, he likened himself to both "a master painter at his work, not allowing a single dead stroke" and "a great writer writing essays, not permitting a single inharmonious sentence." A Chinese garden fuses landscape painting and literary composition to create an art of its own in which nature is shaped but not tamed.

Old Suzhou, surrounded by remnants of a moat and canals linked to the Grand Canal, has become a protected historical district, 2 by 3 miles across, in which little tampering and no skyscrapers are allowed. Suzhou, in other words, is one of those rare places in China where the ravages of modernization have been severely restricted and new industrial development has been shifted to suburban zones. In Suzhou's case, what's preserved is all the more remarkable because the downtown was spared destruction during World War II, and its private classic gardens, as well as its canals, have survived over the centuries.

Forest of Lions Garden

When I first saw the private gardens of Suzhou, they looked to me like large estates consisting of pavilions and open halls, unpaved and irregular pathways, small labyrinths of walls and screens, and heaps of grotesque rocks. There were few flower beds, no manicured lawns, and an absence of logical order. While I could immediately admire their quiet beauty, any deeper design or effects remained obscure. A quick tour of a celebrated garden can be disappointing to an inexperienced visitor from abroad, but with a little patience a Suzhou garden opens up an entirely new vision of the world.

The first Suzhou garden I ever toured was **Shi Zi Lin** (Forest of Lions) at 23 Yulin Lu. It was founded in 1336 by a Buddhist monk and last owned by relatives of the renowned American architect I. M. Pei. The garden consists of four small lakes, a multitude of buildings, and random swirls of rockeries. Its elements are strange to those unaccustomed to Chinese gardens.

The principles of garden landscape design in China are often the reverse of those in the West. A classic Chinese garden expresses man's relation to nature, not his control over it. The symmetry and regularity we expect in a garden have been replaced by an organic, spontaneous pattern. The Chinese garden is a manifestation of the essential (even mystical) order of nature, in all its shiftings of vitality and vista. This is the way of nature itself, expressed by the garden at every turn. For this reason, the cult of the lawn never developed in China because the emphasis was always on the spirit of nature, uncultivated and various. As one Chinese critic wrote, the large lawns in an English garden, "while no doubt pleasing to a cow, could hardly engage the intellect of human beings."

Neat flower beds and trimmed hedge borders are likewise eschewed in the traditional Chinese garden, since they are too obviously artificial, too "unnatural." The many human elements in the garden—the halls, verandas, and bridges—are regarded as points of intersection with the natural realm rather than the interventions of a superior human hand. It is ultimately the task of the garden artist to arrange courtyard and screen, lake and path, rock and shadow organically, in obedience to the rhythms and patterns of a purely natural world, heightened in a garden for human contemplation.

While Tai Hu rocks and honeycombed rockeries seem more bizarre than evocative at first, the Chinese landscape artist regards them as an essential component of nature. The Forest of Lions Garden contains the largest rocks and most elaborate rockeries of any garden in Suzhou. This garden was designed specifically to emphasize the role of mountains in nature. These miniature monoliths recall the sacred mountains of China's past and the twisted, gouged-out morphology of the quintessential Chinese landscape common to scroll paintings. Mountains are also emblems of the Way (Dao), that process of transformation and transcendence in nature that Daoist monks and hermits achieve in their quests for immortality.

It took repeated visits to Chinese gardens before I developed a feel for these rocks, which I can now contemplate with interest. The Qing Dynasty emperors Kangxi and his grandson Qianlong were far more knowledgeable in such matters: They valued the rockeries of the Forest of Lions so highly that they used them as a model for those in the Old Summer Palace in Beijing.

The finest of the expressionistic slabs in Suzhou's Forest of Lions Garden came from nearby Lake Tai (Tai Hu). Since the Tang Dynasty (A.D. 618–907), connoisseurs have been selecting the best Tai Hu rocks for the gardens of emperors, high officials, and rich estate owners. During the Song Dynasty (A.D. 960–1126), rock appreciation reached such extremes that the expense of hauling stones from Lake Tai to the capital is said to have bankrupted the empire.

The Forest of Lions Garden is open daily 8:30am to 5pm; admission is RMB 10 ($1.25).

Lingering Garden

The single finest specimen of Tai Hu rock is located in **Liu Yuan,** the Lingering Garden, a spacious Ming Dynasty estate at 80 Liuyuan Lu. Its centerpiece is a 20-foot-high, 5-ton, contorted castle of rock called Crown of Clouds Peak. Lingering Garden is also notable for its viewing pavilions, particularly the **Mandarin Duck Hall,** which is divided into two sides: an ornate southern chamber for men and a plain northern chamber for women.

Suzhou's contemporary painters maintain a sales gallery in this garden, which is planted in osmanthus and willow, varieties that are not known for their brilliant flowerings, in keeping with a traditional prejudice for plain, unshowy vegetation. The Lingering Garden's name is derived from the original owner's family name, which sounds like the character for the word *lingering*. Subsequent owners continued to use the old name, after they discovered that their own family name for the garden did not catch on with the people of Suzhou.

The Lingering Garden is open daily 8:30am to 5pm; admission is RMB 20 ($2.50).

Humble Administrators & Stupid Officials

While these first two gardens are celebrated for their rockeries, other Suzhou gardens emphasize different elements. **Zhou Zheng Garden,** at 178 Dong Bei Jie, one of Suzhou's largest and most popular gardens, makes complex use of waters. Zhou Zheng Garden is usually translated as "Humble Administrator's Garden," but garden scholar Maggie Keswick points out that the characters in the name have an ambiguous meaning that can be translated either as "Garden of the Unsuccessful Politician" or "Garden of the Stupid Officials." This garden, which dates from the 16th century, is located off Dong Bei Jie, just a few blocks northeast of the Lingering Garden.

In Zhou Zheng garden, Tai Hu rocks are not as prominent as the maze of connected pools and islands. This watery maze is in fact an illusion, since there is only a single, long, meandering lake. It's impossible to tell where the water begins or ends; it even seems to flow under waterside pavilions. The creation of multiple vistas and the dividing of spaces into distinct segments are the artist's means of expanding the compressed spaces of the garden. As visitors stroll through the small space, new vistas open up at every turn. Such constant change can be confusing, producing what Maggie Keswick calls "that magical confusion which is the essence of garden architecture." Ideally, one walks through a garden not simply to contemplate nature and learn about its underlying patterns but to feel its disorienting power—to break down logical, social, and human definitions of order and enter a state of direct communion with the natural order.

Zhou Zheng garden is open daily 8:30am to 5pm; admission is RMB 30 ($3.75).

Master of the Nets Garden

While many rich officials and merchants built garden estates simply to entertain, the more scholarly and poetic among the rich wanted to create contemplative retreats. They conceived of the garden as an enclosed series of spaces within spaces, each parcel inviting heightened contact with nature. The human world outside the garden walls was deliberately held at bay. The most perfect of these retreats is **Wang Shi Yuan,** the Master of the Nets Garden, a masterpiece of landscape compression.

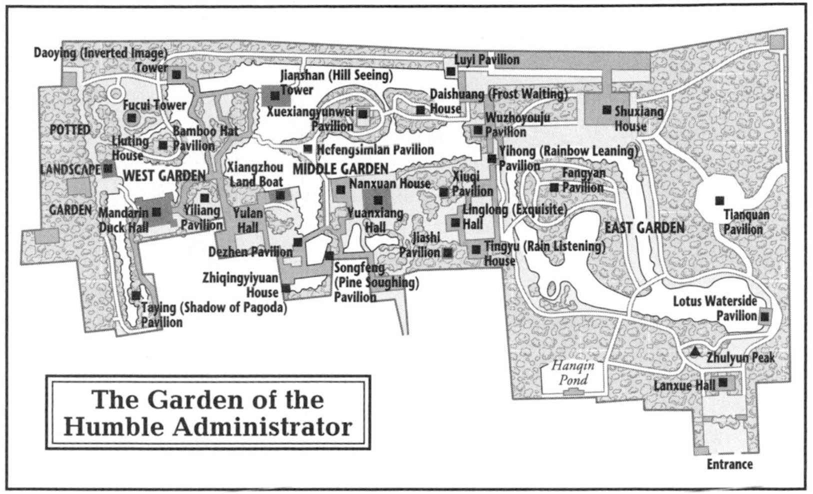

The Garden of the Humble Administrator

Hidden at the end of a blind alley (11 Kuotao Xiang) off Shiquan Jie, a busy street of scroll and handicraft shops, the tiny grounds of the Master of the Nets Garden have been cleverly expanded by the placement of innumerable walls, screens, and pavilion halls, producing a seemingly limitless maze. The eastern sector of the garden is a cluster of three interlinked buildings, the residence of the former owner and his family. At the center of the garden is a pond, just 1 square *mu* (about 2,700 square feet), encircled by verandas, pavilions, and covered corridors, and crossed by two arched stone bridges. Set back from this watery "mirror of heaven," with its proportionate rockeries and bamboo, is a complex of halls and inner courtyards: a garden within a garden. The halls invite rest and meditation. The most lavish hall, **Dianchun Cottage,** furnished in palace lanterns, dark chairs and tables, and hanging scrolls, served as the model for Mingxuan Garden, the Astor Chinese Garden Court and Ming Furniture Room constructed in 1980 in the Metropolitan Museum of Art in New York City. The original, owing to its setting, has a much more open feel than its museum version.

No longer in the hands of a privileged family or restricted to a few upper-class Confucian scholars, officials, and poets, the Master of the Nets Garden has become a favorite retreat of Suzhou's own citizenry. Grandparents bring their grandkids here on inaugural outings to pose for ceremonial snapshots. Workers snack on seeds and fresh fruits. Lovers dangle their feet in the motionless pond waters. Children chase each other around the rockeries. Rimmed by galleries of carved stone tablets and poetic inscriptions on wooden plaques, the garden is a relic of Old China. Paths meander like wild geese, pavilions unfold like lotus leaves, rocks rise as sharply as mountain peaks, and the gates open in the shape of a full moon. Nature becomes a living poem.

Master of the Nets Garden is open daily 8am to 5pm; admission is RMB 10 ($1.25).

Tiger Hill

Even Suzhou's best park, **Tiger Hill (Hu Qiu Shan),** 2 miles northwest of the city at 8 Huqiu Shan, contains classic gardens, although I was stunned on a recent visit to find that large, bright plots of flowers, planted and potted, had become a major feature, as had dozens of robotic figures of the sort one normally sees at theme parks or in department store windows at Christmas. These modern additions have jazzed up the park and appeal to young children and their parents, it seems, but they are really just so much garish frosting.

Today there is a new trail from the entrance that passes by a number of the park's historic sights, including **Han Han Spring** (used since A.D. 500, when it cured a monk of blindness) and several mythic rocks. At the very top of Tiger Hill is its remarkable leaning pagoda **Yunyan Ta (Cloud Rock Pagoda),** a seven-story work dating from A.D. 961, now safely shored up by modern engineering, although it still leans. Under the pagoda is the grave of Suzhou's legendary founder, He Lu, a 6th-century B.C. leader whose arsenal of 3,000 swords is also said to be buried in the park and protected by a white tiger. The artificial hill on which the pagoda stands was once an island. To one side is a stone tablet engraved by Qing Emperor Qianlong, as well as the plain Great Hall Temple. Down below is a large bonsai garden with over 600 specimens and a big tree said to be over 500 years old.

The most remarkable site at the foot of the Tiger Hill pagoda is a natural ledge, the **Ten Thousand People Rock,** where according to legend a rebel delivered an oratory so fiery that the rocks lined up to listen. A deep stone cleavage, the **Pool of Swords (Jianchi),** runs along one side of it, reputedly the remnants of a pit dug by order of the First Emperor (Qin Shi Huang) 2,000 years ago in a search of the 3,000 swords.

All these legends of Tiger Hill are simply colorful stories, of course; the historic sites of China are decked in many such legends. Sometimes the truth is even more interesting. In the 1950s, excavations of pits at Tiger Hill revealed a three-door passageway with tunnels 30 feet into the hill, heading directly under the leaning pagoda. Although unexplored, the tunnels are thought to lead to a major tomb, a hollow creating unstable foundations that might explain why the pagoda tilts.

Tiger Hill is open daily 8am to 5pm; admission is RMB 25 ($3).

Water Gates & Canals

Another leading historical site in old Suzhou is **Panmen Gate,** at 2 Dong Da Lu, which once operated as a water gate and fortress when the Grand Canal was the most important route linking Suzhou to the rest of China. Panmen, built in A.D. 1351, is the only major piece of the Suzhou city wall to survive. Nearby is a large arched bridge, **Wumen Qiao,** over the Grand Canal—the finest place to view the ever-changing traffic—and a small arched bridge over a feeder canal that connects to Panmen. Panmen also has excellent views of the old city, including a view of Ruiguang Ta, a 122-foot pagoda built in A.D. 1119.

When I visited Panmen, it was teeming with visitors and with an aggressive army of vendors, fortune-tellers, and painters. At the top of the bridge to Panmen, a local street musician was stroking out the refrains of "Oh! Susanna" on his *erhu,* a traditional two-stringed instrument. When he spotted me, he grabbed my arm, attempting to shake a few coins into his basket, and he was quite outraged that I, an American, refused to cough up a donation for my traditional song. The Panmen fortification today charges an admission of RMB 15 ($2), which includes entrance to an uninteresting, recently restored royal mansion and an equally uninspiring new amusement park.

The Panmen district and the southern streets of old Suzhou are excellent places to walk at one's leisure. Traditional shophouses with galleries predominate; the streets are narrow and shaded by trees; and bridges and lanes provide an excellent vantage from which to watch the canal traffic, an endless stream of barges propelled by hand-held poles as well as motors. Near Panmen, the old city moat widens and the water traffic thickens.

Uptown, the canals narrow, but the backs of the white houses are still open to the water and quite a bit of commerce is conducted on the water. The canal scenes are unsanitized. The arched bridges are pocked and mud splattered. The canal houses are coated with a stubble of moss and dirt. Scores of cement barges move from outhouse to outhouse to extract the night soil for use in suburban farms. The gondoliers of Suzhou evoke little of the romance of vanished dynasties, but they do reveal the rough-edged world of labor that hundreds of millions of Chinese do each day. And there is something beautiful still in the canal scene of Suzhou when the arched bridges and simple stucco houses and floating barges line up just right.

The Art of Silk

Suzhou is known for more than its garden arts. Its silk fabrics have been among the most prized in China for centuries, and the art of silk embroidery is still practiced at the highest levels. Silk is what made Suzhou a city of importance in China. The **Museum of Suzhou Embroidery** on Jingde Lu (open 9am to 5pm daily, admission free) is both a factory and sales outlet. It contains the most accomplished silk embroideries I have seen in China. The best work on display there, some of it for sale, are canvases of traditional scenes (landscapes, birds, flowers, bamboos) stitched by one artist over the course of 3 years. A few of the embroidery masters have international reputations, and the price of their works soars once they retire. The artists working upstairs in this factory stitch with bare hands, depending only on natural light, without magnifying lenses or other aids. They work 2-hour stretches and take 10-minute tea breaks. The embroidery factory also produces double-sided embroideries on a canvas of thin silk gauze, using a method developed here, in which two different figures, front and reverse, are stitched with two needles simultaneously—the factory guide calls this "a secret technique." The finished embroidery is mounted in a mahogany frame carved in Ming or Qing Dynasty style.

A less commercial display of Suzhou's silk industry is offered by the **Suzhou No. 1 Silk Mill,** at 94 Nan Men Lu (open 9am to 6pm daily, free admission; ☎ 0512/525-1047), site of a 60-year-old silk factory where you can still see the old looms in operation. The complete history of silk and the process of its manufacture are explained by English-speaking guides. This factory hasn't changed since I first saw it in the mid-1980s, including its extensive sales rooms of silk clothing and souvenirs.

Temple of Mystery

One of Suzhou's least visited monuments is the Temple of Mystery (Xuan Miao Guan), located in the heart of the old city on Guanqian Jie, engulfed by Suzhou's largest street market. Constructed in the 3rd century A.D., the temple's 31 halls are reduced today to the singular, massive three-eaved **Hall of the Three Pure Ones (San Qing),** which dates from A.D. 1179. This is the largest early Daoist temple in China, almost 50 yards wide. Its courtyard, bordered by a carved stone Song Dynasty railing, is a favorite hangout for older citizens. Inside is a golden statue of Guanyin, Goddess of Mercy, and some 60 Daoist figures in glass cases. South of this is another large building that clearly belonged at one time to the Temple of Mystery. Unchanged on the outside, this runaway hall is now devoted to souvenirs, musical instruments, and other commodities, all displayed in glass-and-metal counters. Meanwhile, the east and west walls of this emporium are still festooned with the massive statues of warriors and gods of the original Daoist hall.

Suzhou's Temple of Mystery is emblematic of the state of China's legacies. Hanging on by a thread in the center of a rapidly modernizing city, the temple has been altered, divided, and gutted by time, politics, and economics. Yet something visible remains. The old bazaar has been reincarnated. Small, simple stalls still hug the temple grounds, but the newest sort of shopping bazaar is shouldering its way nearer the Temple of Mystery. A spick-and-span pedestrian mall has sprung up within a block of the old temple, with deluxe department stores, cinemas showing the latest action films from America, two Kentucky Fried Chicken emporiums, and boutiques hawking the logos of Crocodile and Playboy.

The Temple of Mystery is open daily 9am to 6pm; admission is RMB 10 ($1.25).

PRACTICAL INFORMATION

ORIENTATION & WHEN TO GO

Suzhou is 18 miles east of Lake Tai, 50 miles northwest of Shanghai, in Jiangsu Province. Surrounded by suburbs and new industrial development zones, the old city of Suzhou has a population of 700,000. Most travelers stay several days in Suzhou, reaching the city from Shanghai (which is less than an hour south via a new expressway). Suzhou is one of China's busiest tourist destinations, receiving several million visitors a year, making it third in tourism-derived income in China, trailing only Beijing and Xi'an. The city's hot, humid summers, cold winters, and rainy springs mean that the best time to visit is from September to November.

GETTING THERE

By Train Suzhou has no airport, but it is served by many trains each day from Shanghai. The trip takes less than 90 minutes. The Suzhou Train Station is at the beginning of Renmin Lu, on the north side of the canal, 1 block east of the bridge.

By Boat Suzhou is also linked to Hangzhou to the south by overnight passenger boats on the Grand Canal and to Wuxi and Lake Tai to the north. Overnight passage to Hangzhou on the Grand Canal costs RMB 60 to RMB 125 ($7.25 to $14.75), depending on the cabin class. The top cabin class is a compartment consisting of bunkbeds and little else. Tickets may be purchased at hotel tour desks.

TOURS & STRATAGEMS

China International Travel Service (CITS), with headquarters in the Suzhou Hotel, 115 Shiquan Jie (☎ 0512/522-3175; fax 0512/523-3593), can arrange tours of the city with English-speaking guides. I used their helpful branch in the lobby of the Gloria Plaza Hotel to book a day-long "Panda Car Tour" of the city, which cost RMB 260 ($31), with an English-speaking guide and lunch included. The tour visited two classic gardens, Tiger Hill, Panmen Gate, and the Silk Embroidery Factory.

With this tour as introduction, first-time visitors to Suzhou can then use the map that CITS hands out and tour other sites on their own. Taxis and pedicabs are both good ways to get around; they cost RMB 10 to RMB 20 ($1.20 to $2.40) per trip. CITS also books tickets for trains, boats on the

Grand Canal and, in the summer, evening performances of classical Chinese music in the Master of the Nets Garden.

WHERE TO STAY

Bamboo Grove Hotel (Zhu Hui Fandian). *168 Zhu Hui Lu (in the south of the city, near Master of the Nets Garden).* ☎ *0512/520-5601. Fax 0512/520-8778. 405 units. A/C MINIBAR TV TEL. $150 double. AE, DC, JCB, MC, V.* The rooms in this five-story, four-star, three-unit hotel were last renovated in 1994 and are showing some wear. But the hotel's international management is efficient, and the place is popular with expatriates as a place to dine and drink. Foreign tour groups often stay here. Bicycle rental is available. The attached garden is a peaceful retreat.

Amenities: Swimming pool, fitness club, sauna, tennis courts, 24-hour room service, next-day dry cleaning and laundry, nightly turndown, medical clinic, beauty salon, shopping arcade, newsstand, bicycle rental, tour desk.

Gloria Plaza Hotel Suzhou (Kailai Dajiudian). *535 Ganjiang Dong Lu (east of city center).* ☎ *0512/521-8855. Fax 0512/521-8533. 300 units. A/C MINIBAR TV TEL. $150 double. AE, DC, JCB, MC, V.* This luxury hotel offers spacious rooms with a desk, sofa, and safe. It is within easy walking distance of the downtown Temple of Mystery and the Twin Pagodas, built in A.D. 982, one of the few examples of identical pagodas still standing in China. From the south side of the hotel there is a splendid view of a lively old neighborhood of courtyard houses, including backyard fish ponds.

Amenities: Fitness club, sauna, 24-hour room service, next-day dry cleaning and laundry, nightly turndown, 24-hour business center, beauty salon, shopping arcade, CITS tour desk.

Sheraton Suzhou Hotel & Tower (Kailai Dajiudian). *388 Xin Shi Lu (near Pan Men, southwest Suzhou).* ☎ *800/325-3535 or 0512/510-3388. Fax 0512/510-0888. 328 units. A/C MINIBAR TV TEL. $175 double. AE, DC, JCB, MC, V.* The five-story Sheraton is the city's top hotel and its newest, with five-star facilities, three restaurants, and an excellent location, as well as beautiful classical gardens and traditional architecture. It overlooks its own ponds, a lake, and the Grand Canal. Guests frequently rate it above any hotel in Shanghai, particularly for its grounds and the beauty of its lavish interiors. Rooms (including nonsmoking and handicapped rooms) are spacious and well-appointed, the best in Suzhou.

Amenities: Indoor and outdoor swimming pools, fitness center, sauna, Jacuzzi, business center, concierge, 24-hour room service, same-day dry cleaning and laundry, shops, newsstand, tour desk.

WHERE TO DINE

Hotels offer the best fare in town and accept credit cards. The fresh and bright **Atrium Cafe** in the Gloria Plaza Hotel has excellent breakfast, lunch, and dinner buffets with a choice of Western, Chinese, and Asian dishes (☎ 0512/521-8855). Four Hong Kong chefs work in the Gloria, which operates two excellent dinner restaurants as well, the **Suzhou Express,** with its

1920s decor, and the **Sampan Seafood Restaurant.**

The **Bamboo Grove Hotel** has good Western and Cantonese food in its restaurants (☎ 0512/520-5601). Efficient service, English-language menus, and reasonable prices ($10 to $25 per person) characterize the fare.

The best local food is at the **Songhelou (Pine and Crane Restaurant),** 141 Guanqian Jie (☎ 0512/727-7006), a downtown establishment that claims to have been in business since Emperor Qianlong visited Suzhou in the 18th century. The menu is strictly Suzhou, with braised eel, sea cucumber, and duck and pork dishes. Foreigners are seated in a special room and given menus in English. Prices range from RMB 30 to RMB 120 ($3.60 to $14.45) per dish. I found the food rather oily. East of this restaurant along Guanqian Jie and south on Taijian Long, an alley, is the vegetarian cafe **Gongdelin,** which is cheaper and tastier.

There are plenty of other cafes, as well as a **Kentucky Fried Chicken** outlet on Guanqian Jie, the pedestrians-only street east of Renmin Lu near the Temple of Mystery, where Suzhou's newest and some of its oldest establishments commingle and a lively night market convenes at dusk.

HANGZHOU: TEA ON WEST LAKE

杭州

ARRIVING IN HANGZHOU 7 CENturies ago, Marco Polo pronounced it "the finest, most splendid city in the world . . . where so many pleasures may be found that one fancies oneself to be in Paradise." Today, Hangzhou's claim to paradise does not lie in its streets, which are ordinary, but in its lake, its shoreline, and the surrounding countryside, where the strolling and biking are the best you'll find in the Middle Kingdom. As many as 20 million visitors throng Hangzhou yearly, a vast number in a city of little more than one million residents. Yet perhaps because the lake is large enough, the walkways wide, and the causeways long, one does not feel as crowded strolling here as when strutting elbow-to-elbow in the streets of Shanghai or upon the Great Wall near Beijing.

The focus of Hangzhou's exceptional beauty is **West Lake (Xi Hu).** It's a small lake, about 3 miles across and 9 miles around. You can walk the circumference in under 4 hours—longer if you linger at a temple, pavilion, cafe, or park. Two causeways—one running on the north shore, the other on the west shore—vary and shorten the journey. The shallow waters of West Lake are sufficient to fill and beguile the eye's compass but not to overwhelm it. Hangzhou's West Lake remains to this day what one 12th-century visitor proclaimed it: "a landscape composed by a painter."

I've visited Hangzhou's West Lake often, finding each time a serenity that I associate with the Middle Kingdom days of mandarins and moonlit courtyards. Strolling the promenades and crisscrossing the causeways of West Lake, I've entered Old China as in a dream. The islets and temples, pavilions and gardens, causeways and arched bridges of this jade-like lake have constituted the supreme example of lakeside beauty in China ever since Hangzhou served as China's capital during the Southern Song Dynasty (A.D. 1127–1279).

Solitary Island

I like to begin my early morning rambles at the aptly named Hangzhou Shangri-La Hotel, situated on the lake's northwest shore, where at dawn the mists wrap the willow-draped shoreline. Crossing **Xiling Bridge,** dedicated to poet Su Xiaoxiao, who was entombed here in A.D. 501, I am quickly transfixed by the lush scenery and old architecture of Solitary Island (Gushan), the largest of the four main islands in West Lake. A roadway sweeps eastward across Solitary Island toward the city skyline, past monumental tile-roofed halls built in the style of Qing Dynasty palaces.

As a matter of fact, it was on this very island that the two most traveled emperors of the last dynasty, Kangxi (1662–1723) and Qianlong (1736–95), stayed during their own vacations on West Lake. Sailing down the Grand Canal to its terminus at Hangzhou, these emperors hastened to Solitary Island, staying at pavilions erected solely for their royal excursions. These 18th-century emperors, grandfather and grandson in the Manchu line, came strictly as sightseers. They established a viewing platform on the southeastern tip of the island for a connoisseur's view of sunrise and moonlight. Qianlong named the viewing pavilion "Autumn Moon on a Calm Lake," and today there's a fine teahouse in its place, perfect for sipping green tea. The view is the same today as that which enthralled generations of emperors.

It's worth returning to Solitary Island later to tour the **Zhejiang Provincial Museum** not only to see the oldest grains of cultivated rice in the world (discovered 7,000 years ago in a nearby Hemudu village) but also to survey the skeleton of a whale beached at Hangzhou centuries ago when it, like West Lake, was connected more spaciously to the East China Sea. West Lake was once a river lagoon, until sedimentation removed it from its source and a series of scholar-administrators designed the causeways and islands that have made West Lake a work of art. The museum is open daily from 8:30am to noon and 2 to 5:30pm; admission is RMB 20 ($2.50).

Shadow-Boxing & Ballroom Dancing

Solitary Island is connected to downtown Hangzhou by Baidi, one of the two great man-made causeways that divide West Lake into three parts. These two causeways are the finest stretches to walk on West Lake. Both are scenic and serene. The **Bai Causeway** is named after a Tang Dynasty poet, Bai Juyi, who served as prefectural governor here in A.D. 822 to 824 and saw to its construction. Composed of silt dredged from the lake, this causeway runs east for half a mile, rejoining the north

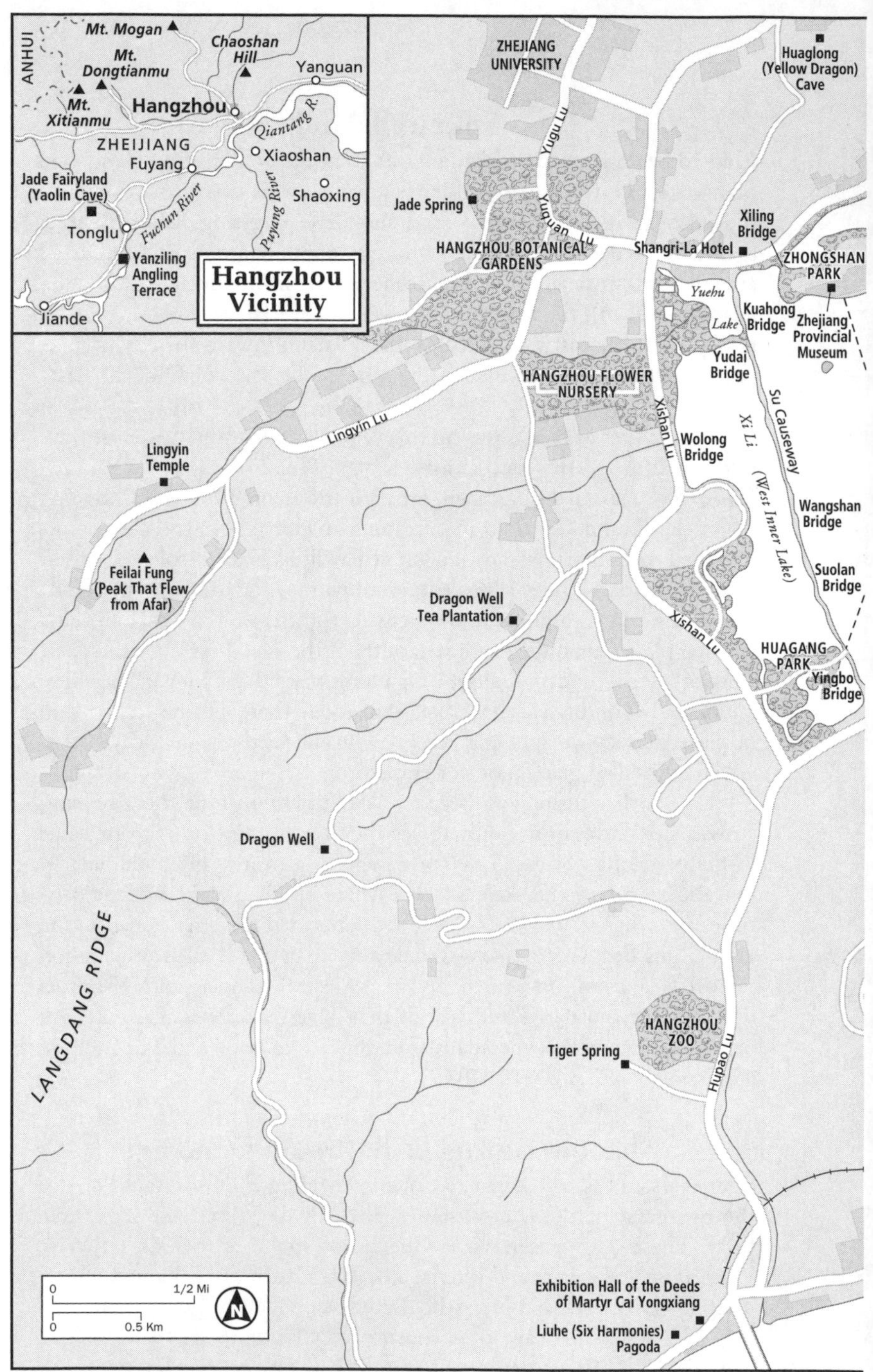

Hangzhou Vicinity
ANHUI
Mt. Mogan
Chaoshan Hill
Mt. Dongtianmu
Yanguan
Mt. Xitianmu
Hangzhou
Qiantang R.
ZHEIJIANG
Xiaoshan
Fuyang
Jade Fairyland (Yaolin Cave)
Fuchun River
Puyang River
Shaoxing
Tonglu
Yanziling Angling Terrace
Jiande
ZHEJIANG UNIVERSITY
Huaglong (Yellow Dragon) Cave
Yugu Lu
Jade Spring
Yuquan Lu
Xiling Bridge
HANGZHOU BOTANICAL GARDENS
Shangri-La Hotel
ZHONGSHAN PARK
Yuehu Lake
Kuahong Bridge
Zhejiang Provincial Museum
Yudai Bridge
HANGZHOU FLOWER NURSERY
Su Causeway
Xi Li (West Inner Lake)
Xishan Lu
Lingyin Lu
Wolong Bridge
Lingyin Temple
Wangshan Bridge
Feilai Fung (Peak That Flew from Afar)
Suolan Bridge
Dragon Well Tea Plantation
HUAGANG PARK
Yingbo Bridge
Dragon Well
LANGDANG RIDGE
HANGZHOU ZOO
Tiger Spring
Hupao Lu
Exhibition Hall of the Deeds of Martyr Cai Yongxiang
Liuhe (Six Harmonies) Pagoda
0 1/2 Mi
0 0.5 Km
N

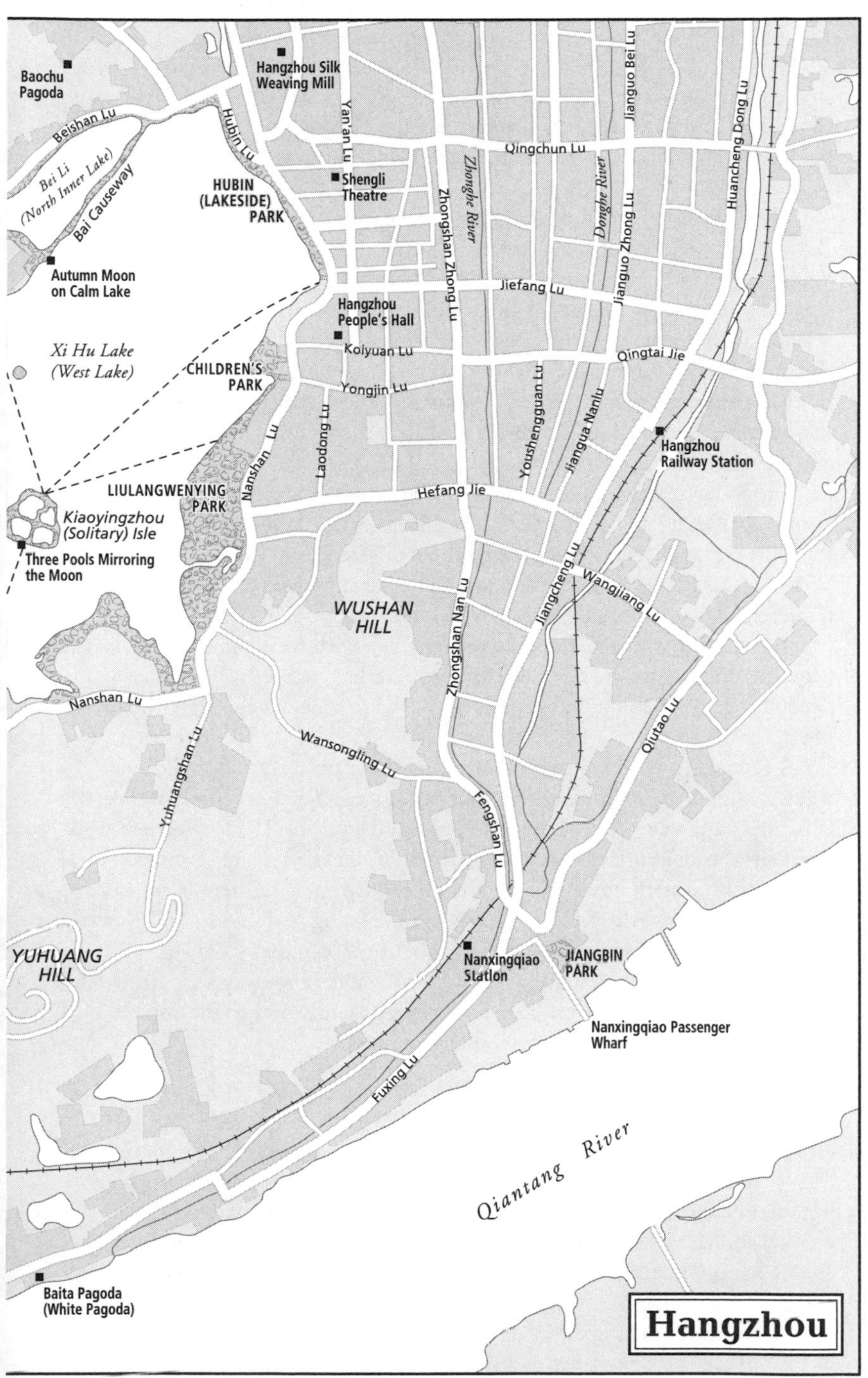
Hangzhou
Baochu Pagoda
Hangzhou Silk Weaving Mill
Beishan Lu
Bei Li (North Inner Lake)
Bai Causeway
Hubin Lu
Yan'an Lu
HUBIN (LAKESIDE) PARK
Shengli Theatre
Qingchun Lu
Zhonghe River
Donghe River
Jianguo Bei Lu
Huancheng Dong Lu
Zhongshan Zhong Lu
Jianguo Zhong Lu
Autumn Moon on Calm Lake
Jiefang Lu
Hangzhou People's Hall
Koiyuan Lu
Qingtai Jie
Xi Hu Lake (West Lake)
CHILDREN'S PARK
Yongjin Lu
Youshengguan Lu
Jiangua Nanlu
Laodong Lu
Nanshan Lu
Hangzhou Railway Station
LIULANGWENYING PARK
Hefang Jie
Kiaoyingzhou (Solitary) Isle
Three Pools Mirroring the Moon
Jiangcheng Lu
Wangjiang Lu
WUSHAN HILL
Zhongshan Nan Lu
Nanshan Lu
Qiutao Lu
Wansongling Lu
Yuhuangshan Lu
Fengshan Lu
YUHUANG HILL
Nanxingqiao Station
JIANGBIN PARK
Nanxingqiao Passenger Wharf
Fuxing Lu
Qiantang River
Baita Pagoda (White Pagoda)

shore road, **Beishan Lu,** at **Broken Bridge (Duan Qiao),** so-named because when winter snows first melt the bridge appears from a distance to be broken.

The **lakeshore promenade** that encircles West Lake widens at Broken Bridge where it joins the Bai Causeway and runs parallel to the western edge of downtown Hangzhou. Along the way, I always find the pavilions, with their octagonal tiled roofs and upturned eaves, jammed at dawn with devotees of the latest recreational craze, Western ballroom dancing. At the same time the walkway teems with a more Eastern, more ancient form of exercise, *tai ji quan* (shadow-boxing). Tai ji is a formal exercise designed to promote health and spirit by directing and enhancing an inner stream of energy called the *qi.* It has become so popular in China that its basic forms have been systematized by the government, creating an official tai ji form. But just as there are dialects in the Chinese language, so there are regional differences in exercise. Along West Lake, various tai ji schools conduct their prebreakfast classes. Tai ji masters tack up their insignia on trees, and their students (women slicing the crisp air with red-tasseled swords, men with bare palm and fist) begin practice, ignoring the pedestrians, bicyclers, baby strollers, street sweepers, and occasional foreign visitors who squeeze through their ranks.

A few paces away ballroom dancers spill out onto the sidewalk in a waltz straight out of Strauss. Partner swings partner until their step-close-step merges with the slow push-and-pull of shadow-boxers. Across the widening avenue, at the Children's Palace square, hundreds of workers toil with mass calisthenics. It's worth getting here early to take in the action. All of China seems to be moving its joints.

The ballroom dancing commences about 6:30am every day, finishing up 2 hours later. If you know a few steps, you'll be warmly welcomed if you join in. I did some tai ji exercises here recently and found myself the recipient of advice from Hangzhou's masters.

Lakeside Avenue

At Hubin Lu (Lakeside Avenue) the promenade turns south. Along the lake is a delightful encampment of boat launches, souvenir stands, restaurants, Qing-style mansions, and outdoor cafes. This spacious shore retreat, known as Lakeside Park, is just the spot for tea, snacks, and ice cream. Meanwhile, the city shops across the main street have undergone extensive redevelopment in the last few years. You can edge into the downtown rush at Hangzhou's new TCBY (The Country's Best Yogurt) or for a pastry at Croissants da France. On the lakefront itself there's a Joe Eagles fast-food restaurant, with hamburgers, outdoor seating, and a menu in English. Lakeside Park is also the place for a beer, served at a fashionable new pub in an old mansion, the Casablanca Country Bar.

In some ways Hangzhou's downtown shoreline is coming to resemble a Western shopping mall, but the lake remains as it has for centuries, a gem best explored by foot, bicycle, or boat. In fact, the true heart of West Lake is only reached by water. There are no sailboats, canoes, or kayaks to rent on West Lake, but you can hire your own 10-foot, heavy wooden rowboat. There are also small junks propelled by the owner's single oar that will take you out to the islands, as well as ferries—flat-bottomed launches seating 20 under an awning—that pick up passengers along the Lakeside Park shore. For the small junks, you have to bargain for the fare, usually about RMB 40 ($4.80) for 2 hours on the water. The passenger ferries usually sell tickets at roughly twice the price ($10). The touts will find you if you don't get to a ticket booth first, but the easiest place to purchase your ticket for a cruise is back where this morning ramble began, at a dock across the street from the Shangri-La Hotel. Here, many a fairly comfortable and sizable motorized launch, its bowsprit the head of a dragon, departs for a 2-hour lake tour, with stops at several of the islands.

Boats on West Lake have a venerable history. Emperors were rowed across these waters in elaborate dragon-headed craft. Even Marco Polo took a cruise. "A voyage on this lake," he wrote, "offers more refreshment and pleasure than any other experience on earth. On one side it skirts the city so that your barge commands a distant view of all its grandeur and loveliness . . . On the lake itself is an endless procession of barges thronged with pleasure seekers." Although the downtown skyline has certainly been transformed over the centuries and the boats for hire today are mere reproductions of the royal barges, West Lake still enthralls pleasure seekers, foreign and Chinese.

Three Pools Mirroring the Moon

The island you should not miss is the **Island of Little Oceans,** at the center of West Lake. This man-made atoll was formed during a silt-dredging operation in 1607. It is, as another Chinese saying goes, "an island within a lake, a lake within an island." Its form is that of a wheel with four spokes, its bridges and dikes creating four enclosed lotus-laden ponds. The main route into the hub of this wheel is the **Bridge of Nine-Turnings,** built in 1727. Occupying the center is the magnificent **Flower and Bird Pavilion,** one of the most graceful structures I have ever visited in China, notable for its intricate wooden railings, lattices, and moon gates. It isn't an ancient work, dating only from 1959, but it's a superb rendition of the best in traditional Chinese architecture. There always seem to be crowds here, although weekday mornings before 10am are the most peaceful times to arrive.

On the southern rim of the Island of Little Oceans is West Lake's defining monument: **Three Pools Mirroring the Moon,** which consists of three water pagodas, each about 6 feet tall. They have "floated" like buoys on the surface of West Lake since 1621. Each pagoda has five openings. On evenings when the full moon shines on the lake, candles are placed inside. The effect is of four moons shimmering on the waters. Even by daylight, the three floating pagodas are a startling touch, the grand flourish of ancient engineers and scholar-administrators who shaped the lake into a work as artful as any classical garden. Local legends portray the three pagodas as the feet of an upturned stone tripod plunked into the water to clamp down on a dark monster of the deep.

The floating pagodas were the creation of Hangzhou's most famous governor, the poet Su Dongpu (A.D. 1036–1101), who placed the original trio of pagodas here, at the deepest point in the lake, to stake out an area where water plants were forbidden to grow. Lily, lotus, and a host of other plants had repeatedly strangled West Lake and still pose a threat. Several times I've seen keepers in skiffs weed the island pools as if they were overgrown gardens.

Su Causeway

The best view from land of the Three Pools Mirroring the Moon is from the Su Causeway (Sudi), the great dike that connects the north and south shores along the western side of West Lake. This pathway across West Lake has vistas as rewarding as those along the east–west Bai Causeway, but the Su Causeway is three times as long (nearly 2 miles). Lined with weeping willows, peach trees, and shady nooks, it crosses six arched stone bridges. Locals fish and picnic along its hems. The Su Causeway is named for the poet Su Dongpu, who, as the official in charge, set some 200,000 workers to dredging the lake. Su also composed a poem naming West Lake after a stunning young woman, Xi Zi, whose beauty, like that of the lake itself, shone through in laughter or in tears: "Rippling water shimmering on a sunny day/Misty mountains gorgeous in the rain/Plain or gaily decked out like Xi Zi/The West Lake is ever alluring," Su wrote.

The Su Causeway begins on the north shore at a small park, **Lotus Stirred by the Breeze,** across from the patriotic monument to Yue Fei, a 12th-century general. Favored by Emperor Kangxi, this park became the best spot for viewing lotus blossoms. More recently, it has been fronted by a modern shopping center, featuring local crafts and several restaurants specializing in the West Lake carp, considered a great delicacy here.

The carp of West Lake are famous in China. Nine hundred years ago, carp in this province (Zhejiang) mutated into the first goldfish and Hangzhou rapidly became the capital of goldfish cultivation, a reputation it enjoys to this day. (It wasn't until 1782 that goldfish were introduced to the West, first reaching London from China.) One of the two best places to observe the giant ornamental carp and goldfish is Jade Spring in the **Hangzhou Botanical Garden,** about a mile west of the Shangri-La Hotel; it's open 8am to 5pm and charges RMB 10 ($1.20). The other is **Huagang Yuan** (Flower Harbor Park), at the south end of the Su Causeway, a delightful array of paths and flower gardens; its pavilions and fish ponds date back to the Qing Dynasty. Admission is RMB 12 ($1.50).

Besides West Lake carp, another celebrated local dish is Beggar's Chicken, discovered by Emperor Qianlong during an 18th-century jaunt along West Lake. The emperor, it is said, chanced upon a Hangzhou peasant who, lacking a proper pan, baked his chicken by coating it in mud and tossing it into a fire. The modern version of Beggar's Chicken is more refined, of course, being carefully seasoned and slowly cooked in clay. The best place to savor this moist invention is in the Shangri-La Hotel's **Shang Palace Restaurant.**

Baochu Pagoda

Hikes on either of the two great causeways usually take up a morning or an afternoon, depending on one's pace. A boat ride and island walk consume another pleasant half day. A shorter but more strenuous ramble is up the green hillside of the lake's north shore to Hangzhou's most famous landmark, the needlelike Baochu Pagoda, which is visible everywhere from West Lake and adds yet another subtle element to the composition. This pagoda dates from A.D. 968, but has exhibited a tendency to collapse, requiring rebuilding most recently in 1933. Young or old, Baochu Pagoda is an irresistible symbol of West Lake; one morning I set out to see it close up.

Maps didn't give me clear directions, so I simply set out early, walking toward downtown along Beishan Lu from the Shangri-La Hotel. After a 20-minute stroll, I pulled even with the pagoda on the hill and chose a likely looking, rather steep road up. The road petered out into a well-worn trail, which after 10 minutes brought me to the top of the ridge, face-to-face with the solitary 125-foot-high pinnacle. The vista was worth the climb, even though the pagoda, fashioned from solid stone and brick, was devoid of an inner stairway that might have afforded a still better view.

The real interest here, as is often the case when one wanders a bit off the tourist track, was the crowd of ordinary people who had gathered that morning. There was a group of housewives, each in a hand-knit sweater, practicing tai ji with a master. Zigzagging through their ranks was a troupe of school kids, dressed like flowers, on a field trip. When they spotted me, they couldn't take their eyes off this unexpected visitor from afar. I rested on a stone wall and watched them play. An old man emerged from the steep path to the pagoda, cane in hand. His mobility was terribly hampered, but he did not pause to rest. He stamped both feet and strode forward, circling the pagoda courtyard in ever-widening circles, determined to keep moving. Then one little girl broke from her schoolmates, ran up to me, and opened her hand. In her palm lay a single white Chiclet. I thanked her and placed it in my mouth. She ran back, laughing in delight.

Undertaking such rambles in any Chinese city is a sure way to discover the accidentally strange and beautiful, as well as to gain a feeling for the daily life of China. The visitors' sights you've set out to see are quite often secondary.

Laughing Buddha

China is the land of the **bicycle,** of course. Everyone seems to own one and to use it constantly. Nowadays, automobiles, particularly taxis, are dominating the streets, but bicycles often have their own wide lanes. For one not in a hurry, particularly for a visitor, the bicycle is a superb form of movement in the city, and in Hangzhou, out of the city as well. The Shangri-La Hotel rents good multispeed mountain bikes at reasonable hourly and daily rates. Their gears are useful for mounting the green hillsides surrounding West Lake on three sides. To the west reside two of Hangzhou's greatest treasures—the great Buddhist temple of Lingyin and the tea village of Dragon Well—and both lie within an hour's countryside bike ride. From the hotel, the roads are well marked to both locations, and any city map shows the way clearly.

Lingyin Temple (Temple of the Soul's Retreat) took me just 20 minutes to reach from the hotel, an easy ride through parklands forested in bamboo and larch, the last 10 minutes on a slight uphill incline. The temple parking lot proved to be extremely crowded, heaped with vendor stalls, buses, visitors, and beggars, but the bicycle parks were clearly marked with pictorial signs. I selected one and paid a small fee, locked up my bike, took my ticket from the vendor, and followed the crowds across a stream to the temple entrance.

Lingyin Temple has been rebuilt a dozen times since its creation in A.D. 326. The path to the temple complex is lined with attractions, including a new park to the left (Fei Lai Feng Zaoxiang), a sculpture garden of statuary, reproductions of famous Buddhist statues from all over China—tacky for the most part and worth skipping.

The real attraction on the road to the temple is the limestone cliff called the **Peak That Flew from Afar (Feilai Feng),** so named because it resembles a holy mountain in India seemingly transported to China. The peak, nearly 500 feet high, contains four caves and about 380 Buddhist rock carvings, most of them created over 600 years ago during the Yuan Dynasty. The most famous carving here is of a Laughing Buddha, carved in the year A.D. 1000. This Buddha of the Future is laughing with joy at the ultimate glorious fate of the world and with amusement at the childish vanities of the unenlightened. His elongated earlobes symbolize his wisdom. His round bulging belly is a manifestation of his inner powers.

Scholars consider these stone carvings the most important of their kind in southern China. They are more animated, realistic, and gaudy than the Buddhist sculptures done earlier on a more extensive scale in northern China and along the Silk Road, where Buddhism entered the Middle Kingdom from India. Although you will find much grander Buddhist rock carvings in those more remote regions of China, the flying peak is worth a look.

So are the temples. The small pagoda at the temple entrance, built in 1590, is the burial marker for a monk named Huili, who founded Lingyun 16 centuries ago. The present buildings go back decades rather than centuries, but they are immense—some of the grandest temples in China. The Front Hall and the Great Hall beyond it have the typical Chinese Buddhist layout. The **Front Hall** contains the Four Guardians of the Four Directions, two on either side, protecting a rotund image of Maitreya (the Laughing Buddha). Lingyin's Maitreya dates from the 18th century, and behind this image is a statue in camphor wood of Skanda, another protector, which dates from the Southern Song Dynasty when Hangzhou was China's capital. The even larger **Great Hall** contains an image of Buddha crafted in 1956 from 24 sections of camphor and gilded with 104 ounces of gold—not a bad modern re-creation. Behind this grand Buddha is a fairyland relief of clay figures, with Guanyin, the Goddess of Mercy, at its center. Guanyin, China's most venerated goddess, is still petitioned by those seeking a male child or a miraculous cure. In Lingyin Temple, she is portrayed as standing on a fish with a bottle of merciful waters in her hand (as she is also a protector of mariners). When I was last in this temple I saw two old women and one young man kneeling with lighted incense before the goddess.

Lingyun Temple is always crowded, very popular with Chinese visitors, as is all of Hangzhou. It's open from dawn to dusk; admission is RMB 26 ($3).

Dragon Well Tea

A less frantic jaunt by bicycle is toward the village of **Dragon Well,** known for Hangzhou's famous **Longjing tea,** grown only on these hillsides and revered throughout China as cool and refreshing—a favorite summertime thirst quencher. Longjing tea is said to be a supreme vintage with four special characteristics: its green color, smooth appearance, fragrant aroma, and sweet taste. When Emperor Qianlong came to these hills (perhaps after discovering Beggar's Chicken down by the lake), he picked tea at Dragon Well Village and returned to Beijing with leaves for his mother. Thereafter, yearly tributes of Longjing tea were shipped via the Grand Canal to the Forbidden City. The best tea at Dragon Well is still picked and processed by hand. The villagers begin picking in late March or early April. The first of the 30 pickings is by far the best of the 16 grades of Longjing tea now produced. At Dragon Well and in nearby Tiger Spring, where the best spring water for tea brewing was first discovered by a Tang Dynasty monk, you can buy the tea directly from the source.

The bike ride to Dragon Well Village requires nearly an hour and the road is sometimes steep, but the journey is an exceptional one. This is pure countryside, inundated with large tea plantations. On the way, you can stop at the **Dragon Well Tea Plantation (Cha Yuan Chun),** open 8:30am to 4:30pm, and comb through its extensive displays of Chinese teas, pots, cups, and ceremonial tea implements. The RMB 20 ($2.50) admission includes a tea sampling and demonstration of the Chinese tea ceremony in a private tea room. The first small glass of tea, a sign of friendship, is only served for its aroma; a second fuller glass is then poured, with tips of the pot, for tasting. The Longjing tea served here is very clear, and the leaves have the smell of a fresh field. There's a large sales room, too, which seems to be the main purpose of this "museum."

Dragon Well Village, a few miles beyond the Tea Plantation, is where the best tea is grown and processed. Plenty of local grandmas are on hand to kidnap independent travelers, take them into their homes and kitchens, ply them with hand-picked tea, and sell them a few pounds at inflated prices. They can be resisted, but you may not want to. Though three-quarters of China's population lives in the country, few visitors ever get a chance to see their homes. Here you can.

Ten years ago, when I first visited Hangzhou, I boarded a public bus (no. 27) to Dragon Well Village. A peasant woman latched onto me at once and refused to let go. She couldn't speak a word of English, but she had mastered the jingle, "Longjing tea, Longjing tea," and with this mantra she made many a convert. She promised to guide me to the tea hills. When we arrived, she conducted me on a whirlwind tour of the grounds of the village, where to this day there is a stream of rippling waters and an old pool where tossed coins float on its tense surface.

Of course her true objective was to whisk me through the village amongst clumps of tea bushes and into her house, where she brewed up some Longjing and launched into her hard sell. An old man sitting out front, drawing on a long, narrow pipe, was exhibited as proof of the amazing benefits of said tea, one of which is said to be longevity. He was 80, the woman said (and I thought at the time, by god, he looks it). Meanwhile, a neighbor lady dropped in hoping to sell me her tea as well. I managed to escape with a pound of Longjing tea in a plastic bag but not before my host went so far as to point out her children's badly worn shoes and patched clothing. This Dragon Well tea lady was a terrific operator, a harbinger of the entrepreneurial 1990s, certainly not the last of her kind. Today the village still peddles its wares to visitors as aggressively as ever—but there are few places in China where foreigners are so openly and easily invited into a village home. This village is one place where I didn't mind the vendors. As for price, what you should pay for a bag of loose tea in these circumstances depends of the tea's quality (which can vary greatly). Generally, if you pay more than half of what's initially asked or more than RMB 80 ($10), you've paid too much.

Eden of the East

Hangzhou is a rarity in China: a city in a beautiful setting that's made for strolling and biking. You can do the usual things here, too, and they are pleasant enough fillers: Visit the **museums** (there are new ones devoted to silk, traditional medicines, and pottery, as well as tea); tour the **factories** (the Hangzhou Silk and Satin Printing and Dyeing Complex is China's largest); and patronize the **shops** (tea, silk, and painted fans are nationally famous products). But Hangzhou's essence is outside, on the lake, on the walkways, and in the folds of the green tea-laden hills. At the end of the Southern Song Dynasty, in 1279, just 4 years after Marco Polo became the first foreign visitor, Hangzhou was the largest urban center in the world, and probably the most refined. Its Heavenly Avenue was China's main street, lavish and pulsating, a thoroughfare so ripe with splendors it even contained shops for the wealthy featuring fish for pet cats. The imperial glitter has long faded from its more ordinary streets, but the beauty of West Lake endures.

PRACTICAL INFORMATION

ORIENTATION & WHEN TO GO

Hangzhou is located in northern Zhejiang Province, near the East China Sea, 115 miles southwest of Shanghai. Most visitors arrive by rail or bus from Shanghai, although some come by plane directly from Hong Kong or Beijing. Via the new Hu Hang Expressway, with its 65 mph speed limit, the road journey has been reduced from over 5 hours to under 2 hours. Downtown Hangzhou is concentrated on the east and north shores of West Lake. Summers are quite hot and humid, making spring and autumn the times to visit, although winters are mild with only occasional snowfalls.

GETTING THERE

By Plane **Dragonair** offers direct service from Hong Kong (a 2-hour flight). Dragonair's office in Hangzhou is in the east lobby of the Dragon Hotel, 7 Shuguang Road (☎ 0571/799-8833, ext 6061; fax 0571/798-7902). In the United States, Cathay Pacific handles Dragonair reservations; call ☎ 800/233-2742. Various Chinese airlines connect Hangzhou to most major mainland cities (2 hours to Beijing, 25 minutes to Shanghai). The Hangzhou airport is 9 miles from downtown; taxi fare is about RMB 50 ($6). For airport information, call ☎ 0571/514-1010.

By Train The most common way to reach Hangzhou is via train (2 to 3 hours) from Shanghai. Soft-seat train tickets on the Hangzhou–Shanghai cost about RMB 40 ($5) when purchased from hotel tour desks. The no. 7 bus connects the train station to downtown and to the Shangri-La Hotel. For train information, call ☎ 0571/702-3729.

By Ship Hangzhou is also served by overnight passenger boats on the Grand Canal from Suzhou (see the chapter on the Grand Canal).

GETTING AROUND

If you stay out of downtown, **bike riding** in Hangzhou can be a pleasure. The multispeed mountain bikes for rent at the **Shangri-La Hotel** (see below) are in top condition (brakes work, tires don't flatten, locks function). Rates are RMB 20 ($2.40) per hour, RMB 50 ($6) per half day, RMB 100 ($12) per full day.

TOURS & STRATAGEMS

China International Travel Service (CITS) provides tours only for prearranged groups and has been unable to assist me as an individual traveler. CITS is located on the northeast corner of West Lake at 1 Shihan Lu (☎ 0571/515-2888; fax 0571/515-6667). For local guided tours, you'll have to rely upon the tour desk in your hotel (which is usually a middleman for CITS or another tour agency that can't seem to deal with foreigners directly).

The business center in the West Building of the **Shangri-La Hotel** offers escorted half-day and full-day tours of Hangzhou, conducted by local

AT&T

AT&T Direct® Service

AT&T Access Numbers

Aruba	800-8000	**Czech Rep. ▲**	**00-42-000-101**
Australia	**1-800-551-155**	Egypt ●(Cairo)‡	510-0200
Austria ●	**0800-200-288**	**France**	**0-800-99-0011**
Bahamas	1-800-872-2881	**Germany**	**0800-2255-288**
Barbados ✚	1-800-872-2881	**Greece ●**	**00-800-1311**
Belgium ●	**0-800-100-10**	Guam	1-800-2255-288
Bermuda ✚	1-800-872-2881	**Hong Kong**	**800-96-1111**
Cayman Isl. ✚	1-800-872-2881	**Hungary**	**06-800-01111**
China, PRC ▲	10811	**India ✖, ➤**	**000-117**
Costa Rica	0-800-0-114-114	**Ireland ✓**	**1-800-550-000**

AT&T

AT&T Direct® Service

AT&T Access Numbers

Aruba	800-8000	**Czech Rep ▲**	**00-42-000-101**
Australia	**1-800-551-155**	Egypt ●(Cairo)‡	510-0200
Austria ●	**0800-200-288**	**France**	**0-800-99-0011**
Bahamas	1-800-872-2881	**Germany**	**0800-2255-288**
Barbados ✚	1-800-872-2881	**Greece ●**	**00-800-1311**
Belgium ●	**0-800-100-10**	Guam	1-800-2255-288
Bermuda ✚	1-800-872-2881	**Hong Kong**	**800-96-1111**
Cayman Isl. ✚	1-800-872-2881	**Hungary**	**06-800-01111**
China, PRC ▲	10811	**India ✖, ➤**	**000-117**
Costa Rica	0-800-0-114-114	**Ireland ✓**	**1-800-550-000**

Israel	**1-800-94-94-949**	**Philippines** ●	**105-11**
Italy ●	**172-1011**	**Portugal** ▲	**0800-800-128**
Jamaica ●	1-800-872-2881	Singapore	800-0111-111
Japan ● ▲	**005-39-111**	**Spain**	**900-99-00-11**
Malaysia ●	**1800-80-0011**	**Switzerland** ●	**0-800-89-0011**
Mexico ● ▽	**01-800-288-2872**	Thailand ❮	001-999-111-11
Neth. Ant. ○	001-800-872-2881	**Turkey** ●	**00-800-12277**
Netherlands ●	**0800-022-9111**	**U.K.**	**0800-89-0011**
New Zealand ●	**000-911**	**U.K.**	**0800-013-0011**
Panama	800-001-0109	**Venezuela**	**800-11-120**

FOR EASY CALLING WORLDWIDE

1. Just dial the AT&T Access Number for the country you are calling from.
2. Dial the phone number you're calling. *3.* Dial your card number.

For access numbers not listed ask any operator for **AT&T Direct®** Service. In the U.S. call 1-800-331-1140 for a wallet guide listing all worldwide AT&T Access Numbers.

Visit our Web site at: www.att.com/traveler
Bold-faced countries permit country-to-country calling outside the U.S.

- ● Public phones may require coin or card deposit to place call.
- ✝ Outside of Cairo, dial "02" first.
- ▲ May not be available from every phone/payphone.
- ✚ Public phones and select hotels.
- ✓ Use U.K. access number in N. Ireland.
- ❮ When calling from public phones, use phones marked "Lenso."
- ▽ When calling from public phones, use phones marked "Ladatel."
- ✖ Not available from public phones.
- ➤ Available from phones with international calling capabilities or from most Public Calling Centers.
- ○ From St. Maarten or phones at Bobby's Marina, use 1-800-872-2881.

When placing an international call ***from*** the U.S., dial 1 800 CALL ATT.

Israel	**1-800-94-94-949**	**Philippines** ●	**105-11**
Italy ●	**172-1011**	**Portugal** ▲	**0800-800-128**
Jamaica ●	1-800-872-2881	Singapore	800-0111-111
Japan ● ▲	**005-39-111**	**Spain**	**900-99-00-11**
Malaysia ●	**1800-80-0011**	**Switzerland** ●	**0-800-89-0011**
Mexico ● ▽	**01-800-288-2872**	Thailand ❮	001-999-111-11
Neth. Ant. ○	001-800-872-2881	**Turkey** ●	**00-800-12277**
Netherlands ●	**0800-022-9111**	**U.K.**	**0800-89-0011**
New Zealand ●	**000-911**	**U.K.**	**0800-013-0011**
Panama	800-001-0109	**Venezuela**	**800-11-120**

FOR EASY CALLING WORLDWIDE

1. Just dial the AT&T Access Number for the country you are calling from.
2. Dial the phone number you're calling. *3.* Dial your card number.

For access numbers not listed ask any operator for **AT&T Direct®** Service. In the U.S. call 1-800-331-1140 for a wallet guide listing all worldwide AT&T Access Numbers.

Visit our Web site at: www.att.com/traveler
Bold-faced countries permit country-to-country calling outside the U.S.

- ● Public phones may require coin or card deposit to place call.
- ✝ Outside of Cairo, dial "02" first.
- ▲ May not be available from every phone/payphone.
- ✚ Public phones and select hotels.
- ✓ Use U.K. access number in N. Ireland.
- ❮ When calling from public phones, use phones marked "Lenso."
- ▽ When calling from public phones, use phones marked "Ladatel."
- ✖ Not available from public phones.
- ➤ Available from phones with international calling capabilities or from most Public Calling Centers.
- ○ From St. Maarten or phones at Bobby's Marina, use 1-800-872-2881.

When placing an international call ***from*** the U.S., dial 1 800 CALL ATT.

© 1/2000

English-speaking guides, with the price based on the number of participants. Half-day tours cost RMB 470 ($57) for a lone individual, RMB 300 ($36) per person for groups of two to five people, RMB 200 ($24) per person for groups of six to nine, and RMB 160 ($19) per person for groups of 10 or more. Full-day tours cost RMB 696 ($84) for a lone individual, RMB 420 ($51) per person for groups of two to five people, RMB 320 ($38) per person for groups of six to nine, and RMB 240 ($29) per person for groups of 10 or more.

If you are staying in Shanghai and want a day-tour of Hangzhou, book at the **Jin Jiang Optional Tours Center** near the Jin Jiang and Garden hotels at 191 Changle Lu (☎ 021/6445-9525; fax 021/6472-0184), in Shanghai's French District. The center offers full-day group tours to Hangzhou for RMB 350 ($43), including guide, admissions, and lunch, and a more extensive overnight tour for RMB 850 ($105).

WHERE TO STAY

Holiday Inn Hangzhou (Hangzhou Jiari Fandian). *Fengqi Lu and Jianguo Bei Lu (in new central business district, northeast Hangzhou). ☎ 800/465-4329 or 0571/527-1188. Fax 0571/527-1199. 294 units. A/C MINIBAR TV TEL. $110 double. AE, DC, JCB, MC, V.* Holiday Inn's 24th hotel in China (opened in 1999) is not located near the lake shore, but its facilities are top-notch. The 26-story tower includes an extensive health and fitness center, executive floors, and rooms for the handicapped. All rooms are spacious, with spotless bathrooms, the service is friendly, and there are three restaurants, serving Western, Cantonese, and local cuisines.

Amenities: Indoor swimming pool, health and fitness center, sauna, Jacuzzi, eight-lane bowling alley, billiards, business center, conference rooms, deli, 24-hour room service, next-day dry cleaning and laundry, newsstand, tour desk, free airport shuttle.

Lily Hotel. *45 Shuguang Lu (northwest of West Lake). ☎ 0571/799-1188. Fax 0571/791-1166. 152 units. A/C MINIBAR TV TEL. $60 double. AE, DC, JCB, MC, V.* A modest three-star hotel just a short taxi hop from West Lake, this is a basic, inexpensive, Chinese-managed hotel with few amenities, but with clean, modern rooms. The staff is familiar with foreign guests (although they may have difficulties with English). There is a restaurant serving Hangzhou specialties, a coffee shop with a Western menu, and a lobby bar with pastries, coffees, and liquor. Rooms have satellite TV and full bathrooms.

Amenities: Outdoor swimming pool, fitness center, billiards, mahjong, souvenir shop, business center, conference rooms, beauty salon.

Shangri-La Hotel Hangzhou (Hangzhou Xiangge Lila Fandian). *78 Beishan Rd. (north shore of West Lake). ☎ 800/942-5050 or 0571/797-7951. Fax 0571/799-6637. 387 units. A/C MINIBAR TV TEL. $185 double (hillside view), $235 double (lakeside view). AE, DC, JCB, MC, V.* There's no doubt that the Shangri-La Hotel Hangzhou is the number one address in the city, as it has been for the past 2 decades. Its location is ideal for exploring West Lake. Though it was constructed as a Soviet-style hotel in the 1950s, the Shangri-La has been extensively remodeled and modernized. An elaborate covered walkway connects the hotel's East and West buildings.

Rooms in both wings are clean, modern, spacious, and well equipped. The lakeside view rooms are worth the extra money for the splendid view. The service is what one expects from a five-star international hotel: thorough and efficient. The business center handles tours and the luggage counter arranges bicycle rental; both are in the West Building.

Amenities: Fitness club, Jacuzzi, sauna, tennis courts, business center, conference rooms, concierge, 24-hour room service, same-day dry cleaning and laundry, nightly turndown, beauty salon, shopping arcade, tour desk, free airport shuttle.

Wang Hu Hotel (Wanghu Binguan). *2 Huancheng Xi Lu (downtown, 2 blocks from lakeshore). ☎ 0571/ 707-1024. Fax 0571/707-3027. 364 units. A/C MINIBAR TV TEL. $125 double. AE, DC, JCB, MC, V.* This downtown hotel doesn't offer the service and facilities of the Shangri-La, but it's a good, less-expensive alternative. The staff is not proficient in English. The rooms are large and clean, and have safes. There's not much of a view and the streets are noisy, but it's only a 2-block walk to Lakeside Avenue. If you're on a budget, inquire about cheaper rooms, since rooms in the old building have not been upgraded yet.

Amenities: Swimming pool, health club, sauna, 24-hour room service, business center, tour desk.

Zhejiang World Trade Center Grand Hotel (Zhejiang Binguan). *15 Shuguang Lu (one-half mile north of West Lake). ☎ 0571/799-0888. Fax 0571/795-0088. 330 units. A/C MINIBAR TV TEL. $175 double. AE, DC, JCB, MC, V.* One of Hangzhou's newest luxury hotels, this sleek ultra-modern tower offers a full range of facilities and spacious, well-appointed rooms. It caters to business travelers, with data plugs and work desks in every room (as well as safes, robes, and slippers), and executive floors (as well as nonsmoking and handicapped rooms). There are six restaurants, including Western and Japanese outlets. A buffet breakfast is included in the room rates.

Amenities: Indoor and outdoor swimming pools (in adjacent health club), fitness center, sauna, Jacuzzi, massage, billiards, business center, conference rooms, concierge, valet, baby-sitting, 24-hour room service, same-day dry cleaning and laundry, newsstand, shops, medical clinic.

WHERE TO DINE

My two favorite Chinese restaurants in Hangzhou are both expensive, but neither requires reservations or fancy dress. The **Lou Wai Lou (Pavilion Beyond Pavilion)** restaurant is located at 30 Gushan Lu (☎ 0571/ 796-9023; fax 0571/702-9023), on Solitary Hill Island, between the Xiling Seal Engraving Society and the Zhejiang Library. Its dining halls are a bit garish, reminiscent of Qing Dynasty decline, and the service is not always tip-top, but the dishes are fine examples of local specialties, such as Beggar's Chicken, West Lake Carp, Shelled Shrimp with Longjing Tea Leaves, Dongpo Pork, and Bamboo Shoots. Expect to pay about RMB 150 ($18) per person for four moderate courses here (no credit cards accepted). Open daily 11:30am to 2pm, and 5 to 8pm. In past summers, Lou Wai Lou has offered dinner cruises on West Lake.

For a full range of Chinese dishes, including some Hangzhou specialties, in a more elegant setting with better service, try the Shangri-La Hotel's signature restaurant, **Shang Palace** (☎ 0571/797-7951). It's superb. Full dinners cost from $12 to $25 and up, depending on what you order.

Humbler fare is available one-half block west of the Shangri-La Hotel at the **Have-A-Bite Cafe** (the sign is in English), a Chinese fast-food venue that's used to serving up rice and noodle concoctions to Westerners at reasonable prices, RMB 25 to RMB 60 ($3 to $5).

For Western-style fast foods, there are (at last count) three **Kentucky Fried Chicken** outlets, including a big one downtown on Renhe Lu, 2 blocks from West Lake, and a new branch a few blocks west of the Shangri-La Hotel at the intersection of Beishan and Lingyin roads.

For beer, snacks, and late-night entertainment, check out the **Casablanca Country Bar,** 23 Hubin Lu, in Lakeside Park (☎ 0571/702-5934). It opens around 7pm on weekdays and about noon on weekends, and it stays open until well past midnight.

The best Western dinners in town are at **Peppino's,** Shangri-La Hotel, East Building, second floor (☎ 0571/797-7951), where the Italian pastas, breads, and brick-oven pizzas are fresh and expertly seasoned, the ice creams and cappuccinos rich, and the prices bearable—RMB 80 to RMB 110 ($10 to $14) for main courses.

LAKE TAI: THE GREAT LAKE OF CHINA

太湖

LAKE TAI (TAI HU) IS THE MOST fabled body of fresh water in China, a vast natural mirror embracing two ancient kingdoms: the Kingdom of Wu and the Kingdom of Yue. Tai Hu is often draped in mists, likened by poets to the clouds between water and mountain. On its shores are the ancient garden city of Wuxi and the pottery town of Yixing, famous for its caves. In the lake itself are scattered temple islands.

Lake Tai has always had its curiosities, first and foremost the massive limestone boulders that its lathing waters shape and scrape. The Chinese pulled them out of the water for centuries for use in the rockeries of classic gardens. Emperor Huizong, who ruled China from 1101 to 1126, emptied most of the Middle Kingdom's treasury in pursuit of more and more fantastical Tai Hu rocks.

The Gardens of the Grand Canal

The city of **Wuxi,** set on the northeast shore of Lake Tai, has a history of 3,000 years, but it is largely a center of industry today, lacking the natural and cultural beauty of nearby Suzhou and Hangzhou. Nevertheless, Wuxi does retain a few beauty spots apart from Lake Tai. **Xihui Park,** bordered on the east by the Grand Canal, for instance, is Wuxi's chief downtown attraction (open daily from 8:30am to 5pm, admission RMB 25/$3). The park is topped by the seven-story Dragon Light Pagoda (Long Guang), first built during the Ming Dynasty. It's attractive enough, but the real treasure within Xihui Park's sprawling, well-manicured grounds is **Jichang Garden,** the most famous of Wuxi's private gardens.

Built on the site of a Buddhist temple, Jichang Garden became the retirement villa of an official who finished the original landscaping in 1520. Jichang is laid out much like the famous gardens of Suzhou, replete with fish ponds, halls with slim columns and upturned eaves, old steles (carved stone tablets), and rockeries consisting of massive Tai Hu

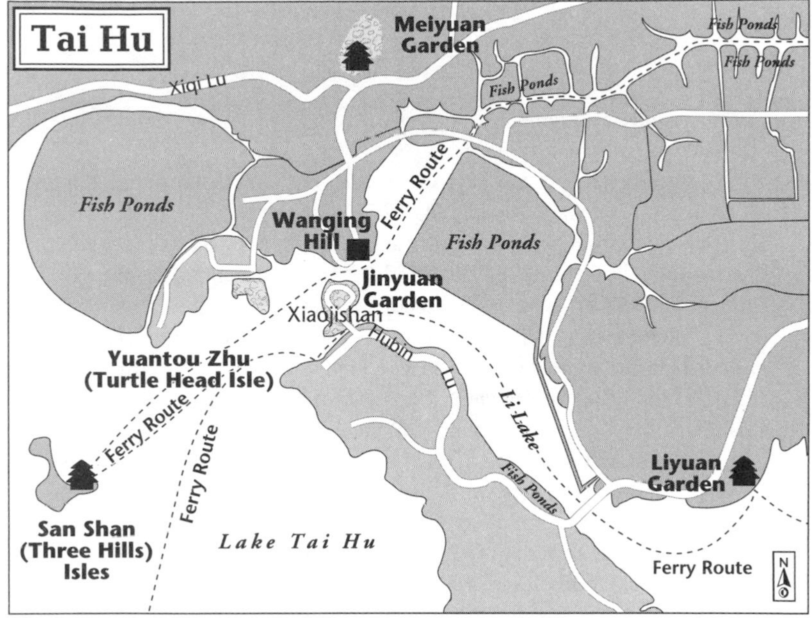

stones, whose bizarre shapes and indentations are the result of long dunkings in the great lake. Jichang Garden was a favorite of Emperor Qianlong, who in 1750 ordered the construction of a similar garden in Beijing's Summer Palace. The covered walkways of Jichang Garden lead to higher vantage points in which the terrain of the surrounding Xihui Park becomes the "borrowed scenery" of this small garden, a fundamental "expansion" technique of Chinese garden design.

Jichang Garden also contains a display of Wuxi's most famous handicraft, **Huishan clay figures,** which are miniature sculptures of plump little children and rotund characters from operas and plays. They were first fashioned 4 centuries ago by local peasants and now are made at the adjacent **Clay Figurine Research Institute** at 8–1 Xiahetang (open daily 8am to 4pm). Clay for these figurines, which are produced both by hand and by mold, comes from Hui Shan, a mountain connected to Xihui Park by a cable car. I find them a bit hideous, but there's no accounting for taste.

Also in Xihui Park is **Erquan Pool,** a Tang Dynasty spring that Lu Yu, author of the *Classic of Tea (Cha Jing),* immortalized as the "Second Spring of the World"—he said that its superb sweetness and viscosity made it perfect for the brewing of tea. During the Song Dynasty, Yixing clay and Wuxi spring water became the emperor's cup of tea, and both are still found on the shores of Lake Tai. It is also said that the reflection of the moon in Erquan Pool is exquisite beyond all words. Indeed, when the blind folk musician Abing heard about the moon mirrored in this pool, he was inspired to compose one of China's most enduring and plaintive songs, another echo, faint as mist on a great lake, of the hidden depths of China's history.

Another pretty garden, **Liyuan,** lies in southern Wuxi on Li Lake, which is actually a back bay of Lake Tai. Celebrated as the garden of Xi Shi, a legendary beauty of the Spring and Autumn period (403–221 B.C.), Liyuan was rebuilt between 1927 and 1930 and expanded by the government in 1952. It actually consists of two older gardens built along the shore. Noted for its peach blossoms in the spring, this complex of watery gardens features a veranda with 89 windows that frame changing views of fish ponds, rockeries, flowering bushes, and the Pavilion of the Four Seasons. A long, covered cement corridor hugs the lakeshore, ending at a floating restaurant modeled and named after Jumbo, Hong Kong's famous culinary barge. Liyuan is not one of the more beautiful gardens in the region, and I cannot say I was that enthralled when I toured it. I felt it more or less lived up to its name, translated as the Garden Eaten by the Worms. Admission is RMB 20 ($2.50).

Sailing Lake Tai

The best reason to visit Wuxi is Lake Tai. The finest views are at Wuxi's Turtle Head Isle (Yuantouzhu), a turtle-shaped peninsula into the lake. Turtle-Head began as a garden in 1918 and grew into a large park of teahouses, halls, walkways, and vistas. Entrance costs RMB 50 ($6), which includes the ferry ride described below. The lake viewpoints along the peninsula's shoreline are equipped with pavilions. The best view of all is from a small modern lighthouse.

North of the lighthouse is a large pier with ferries to **Three Hills Island (San Shan Dao),** a 20-minute boat ride west into Tai Hu. When I boarded the vessel, it was packed with hundreds of local schoolchildren. The view back to Turtle Head Isle and the Wuxi lakeshore was splendid. A light fog rose from the shallow, glassy surface where fishermen glided past in their boats. Three Hill Island has been developed recently as a walk-through amusement park with an artificial cave, brand-new pavilions, sedan-chair rides, and groups of wild monkeys. Its local name translates as Fairy Island, which befits its new theme-park atmosphere. Views of the lake, its other islands and distant shores, were once reason enough to cross Lake Tai—reason enough still for me. The center of the island park is a four-story mock temple with the gargantuan, garish plaster statue of an ancient emperor inside its atrium. Again, the views from the top are superb. The return journey on the ferry can be soothing, too. For a moment, skimming the waters, I have a glimpse of the Lake Tai that the old poets celebrated: vast, flat, misty, a contemplative vacuum quietly reflecting the heavens.

The Teapots of Yixing

Another aspect of Tai Hu is contained in the area of Yixing, the town west of Wuxi that is the most famous center of teapot production in China. Though the town itself isn't much of an attraction, the surrounding villages are well worth a visit. Yixing teapots are available in any large souvenir shop worth its salt in China. Pottery production began in Yixing more than 3,000 years ago. For the last 2,000 years, Yixing has turned out the finest glazed china in China, relying on a local clay known as purple sand. Tea sets from Yixing are said to impart a taste to brewed tea that is essential for complete enjoyment. The pots are now mass-produced in this region, some in factories employing over 10,000 workers. Even the lakeside freeway from Wuxi is lined with ceramic: with ceramic light poles, with retail yards of glazed roof tiles and garden ornaments, with huge ceramic pots.

The road to Yixing is a superhighway through two Chinas: one old, one new. In one respect, the road resembles an old avenue, its median strip decorated in trimmed hedges, its light poles arranged like brown-and-yellow ceramic columns decorated in dragon coils, glass globes suspended on either side like lanterns. Dozens of old canals feed Lake Tai, and slabs of marble and newly raised Tai Hu rocks fill the courtyards of roadside merchants.

In another respect, the road reminds one of China's feverish economic boom. Scores of smokestacks boil over day and night, coughing out black-and-yellow coils of pungent smoke, thick as carpets. This is one of the most visibly polluted areas I have visited in China, sharply at odds with a serene lake and ancient teapots. Officials are aware of environmental problems in the region and they are taking action. Cleaning up Lake Tai was a major priority under the ninth Five-Year Plan (1996–2000); efforts have now been redoubled as we begin the 21st century. Wuxi residents pay a monthly RMB 2 to RMB 4 (25¢ to 50¢) sanitation fee for waste treatment, but more is needed. By the year 2010, 90% of city and township sewage discharges will be treated (as will 30% of the rural sewage)—substantial increases over what we see today. So far the venerable waters of Lake Tai are not drinkable.

At Dingshu, a small town 15 miles south of Yixing, I stop off at **Purple Sand Village,** a model town of nice new two-story villas with patios, sales rooms, and workshops. Some of China's best-known potters, having made enough to give up their factory jobs, live here. In this model teapotters' village, I met members of some of the most celebrated artisan families and watched them at work, molding the clay by hand on small tables, shaping pots, cups, and saucers, and applying decorative touches with their fingertips. The pots are fired for 24 hours in small kilns, then shipped to galleries or patrons or kept at home on sales shelves. Signed, such sets sometimes command prices above $1,000. Photographs on the walls often show a potter in the embrace of an illustrious visitor such as Chinese Premier Li Peng. Less refined, far less expensive Yixing teapots and cups are for sale at the stalls along Dingshu's main street. A visit to the town's **Ceramic Exhibition Hall** is also worth a half hour, as it features exquisite pots from several dynasties, modern creations by today's artists, and such everyday ceramics as bathroom fittings.

Underground Yixing

Yixing's reputation for teapots is international, while its reputation for limestone caverns is still confined to China. I visited two of Yixing's caverns, both in the countryside east of Lake Tai on roads leading out of Dingshu. I'm not a devotee of caves, but the caves of China are unusual, almost always fronted by temples and imbued with ancient stories of hermit monks or Romeo-and-Juliet tragedies from feudal times. The caves are not brilliant affairs. They are rough-edged and poorly lit, but the roads that lead to them are interesting. Large tea plantations and hulking rock quarries punctuate the flat fields that encircle much of Lake Tai and the lower Yangzi River basin. Women in straw hats stuff handbaskets with tea leaves. The dusty roads are clogged with small tractor-trailers hauling rock from quarry to crusher.

The first cavern I visited, **Shanjuan Cave,** was named for a legendary ancient poet who refused an offer to become king, preferring utter freedom. He lived as a recluse in the cave. Open to the public since 1935, Shanjuan contains a large chamber called Lion and Elephant Hall after its size, the texture of its ceiling, and two large stalagmites that resemble the creatures. In its deepest recesses, an underground river winds for a quarter mile through the Crystal Palace. There, I boarded a small wooden flat-bottomed boat. The oarsman planted his feet on the deck and pushed off using a long pole, propelling us into the dark. The water chamber is lined with 75 tiny caves, most of them unfathomable, even when our pilot attempted to illuminate them with his flashlight.

Outside Shanjuan Cave, a walkway along a stream leads to a temple complex that commemorates China's Romeo and Juliet, two young lovers who met as students 15 centuries ago. Since women were not allowed to attend schools in those days, the girl disguised herself as a lad. At school, she fell in love with another student. By the time this misadventure was disentangled, the boy, learning that the girl was betrothed to another, had taken his life. The girl, about to wed an older man chosen by her parents, threw herself into his grave. They emerged together as butterflies. Their tomb is said to be at this temple, which has dolled itself up with painted wall murals recounting the story. I have heard the same story recounted at two other locations in China, both claiming to be the place of its origin.

The second cavern I visited, **Zhanggong,** fronted by a sprawling Daoist temple rising up a terraced hillside, proved to be larger and more intricate, with 72 interlinked chambers. Entrance required a local guide with a flashlight and the purchase of an RMB 19 ($2.30) ticket (with RMB 1/12¢ added as a "safety insurance fee"). Zhanggong's bewildering mile of passageways resembles a labyrinth for fairies. The largest room, Hall of the Sea Dragon Kong, opens through a long funnel of twisting rock to the sky, and the sky in turn is reflected in a pool on the rock floor below. I was glad to emerge into the light, failing to find either of these caves conducive to meditation.

World's Largest Buddha

The newest attraction on Lake Tai is the most massive of all—the largest Buddha in Asia. Erected on Ling Shan, a forested hill 11 miles west of Wuxi, and unveiled in October 1997, the **Ling Shan Buddha** presides over two new temples and a large wall mural engraved with a pictorial map of the Western Paradise. This is something of a Chinese Land of the Giants. In the shrine's main courtyard there is an enormous golden hand sprouting from the Earth, Buddha's hand (37 feet tall, 17 feet wide, and weighing in at 13 tons). The Big Buddha is fashioned from bronze—from 1,638 sheets of bronze—each sheet 5 yards square. Standing atop a hefty 28-foot platform, the statue is 240 feet tall and tips the scale at 700 tons. By comparison, the Buddha on Hong Kong's Lantau Island, completed by the same company in 1993 and heralded as the largest in its class (seated, outdoor, bronze), is a mere 81-foot, 250-ton child. Construction of the Big Buddha at Ling Shan was initiated in the fall of 1994. Twenty chanting monks arrived to bless the undertaking. Wuxi and Lake Tai tourism officials are no doubt hoping that a million times that many tourists come to make their own offerings—tickets cost RMB 20 ($2.40)—at the feet of the world's biggest standing Buddha.

PRACTICAL INFORMATION

ORIENTATION

Lake Tai (Tai Hu) is China's third largest freshwater lake, bordering Jiangsu and Zhejiang provinces. Wuxi, a Grand Canal port, is on the northwest tip of Tai Hu. Shanghai lies nearby, directly east. Yixing, the pottery region, is on the west shore. Summers are uncomfortably hot and humid here, winters chilly and gray, and springs windy and wet. Late autumn is the ideal time to visit the Lake Tai region.

GETTING THERE

Wuxi is located on the Beijing–Shanghai train line. It's 25 minutes by bus or rail from Suzhou and less than 2 hours from Shanghai. There is an airport, but it has few flights. Hotel tour desks can book train tickets.

TOURS & STRATAGEMS

China Travel Service (CTS), 59 Chezhan Lu (☎ 0510/230-4906; fax 0510/230-2743), offers custom individual tours. I arranged a 2-day tour for one person with private car and guide, lunches included, that took in the gardens of Wuxi, Lake Tai, and the pottery shops, caves, and monuments of Yixing County for RMB 1,200 ($145). The best contact at CTS is Ms. Chen Yue Fen (English name, Celina). The main CTS office is directly across from the train terminal (☎ 0510/230-2574); it has the first automated information kiosk I have seen in China.

Wuxi's **taxi** drivers are friendly. A cross-town taxi should cost less than RMB 20 ($2.40).

WHERE TO STAY

Lakeview Park Resort Wuxi (Shanshuicheng Dajiudian). *Lake Tai Tourism Zone (on Lake Tai, across from the new Three Kingdoms theme park).* ☎ *0510/555-5888. Fax 0510/555-6909. 151 units. A/C MINIBAR TV TEL. $80 double. AE, DC, JCB, MC, V.* This four-star, five-story resort on Lake Tai is not quite as well-managed or luxurious as the new Sheraton, but it's the second- or third-best choice in Wuxi. Its four-star facilities include unusual recreational activities (rock climbing, archery). Guest rooms are of average size and above-average upkeep.

Amenities: Indoor swimming pool, fitness club, sauna, rock climbing, four tennis courts, archery, billiards, business center, meeting rooms, 24-hour room service, next-day dry cleaning and laundry, concierge, tour desk, free shuttle bus.

Milido Hotel Wuxi (Meilidu Dajiudian). *2 Liangxi Lu.* ☎ *0510/ 586-5665. Fax 0510/580-1668. 219 units. A/C MINIBAR TV TEL. $105 double. AE, DC, JCB, MC, V.* Located on the banks of the Grand Canal, 3 miles from Lake Tai, the nine-story Milido is now managed by the Huating group based in Shanghai. Upkeep and service have slipped, making it a bit over-priced for a three-star hotel, but it still maintains many of its former amenities and has added new sports and fitness facilities.

Amenities: Swimming pool, fitness center, squash court, business center, 24-hour room service, next-day dry cleaning and laundry.

Pan Pacific Wuxi Grand Hotel (Wuxi Dafandian). *1 Liangqing Lu.* ☎ *800/327-8585 or 0510/580-6789. Fax 0510/270-0991. 342 units. A/C MINIBAR TV TEL. $110 double. AE, DC, JCB, MC, V.* At 20 stories one of the tallest buildings in Wuxi, the Pan Pacific provides plenty of luxury, from its soaring atrium to its Chinese carpets and ceramics. The rooms (including rooms for the disabled) were recently renovated; they are spacious and clean. The hotel has plenty of facilities (including a clinic, post office, and four restaurants) and a free shuttle bus to the rail station.

Amenities: indoor swimming pool, fitness club, sauna, concierge, 24-hour room service, next-day dry cleaning and laundry, nightly turndown, business center, beauty salon, shopping arcade, medical clinic, tour desk.

Sheraton Wuxi Hotel & Towers (Shi Lai Tun Dafandian). *443 Zhongshan Lu (at Garden City Mall, downtown Wuxi). ☎ 800/325-3535 or 0510/272-1888. Fax 0510/275-2781. 396 units. A/C MINIBAR TV TEL. $160 double. AE, DC, JCB, MC, V.* This hotel, Wuxi's finest, has an array of five-star facilities and good restaurants, as well as dependable service. The rooms are large and comfortable, equipped with desks, comfortable chairs, good lighting, robes and slippers, and Wuxi's best selection of satellite TV stations (CNN, HBO).

Amenities: Indoor/outdoor swimming pool, health and fitness club, sauna, Jacuzzi, massage, 24-hour room service, same-day dry cleaning and laundry, business center, conference rooms, shopping center, newsstand, beauty salon, concierge, valet, tour desk.

WHERE TO DINE

The **Jumbo Floating Restaurant** at Li Garden (☎ 0510/670-8888) is owned by the nearby Lakeside Hotel (Hubin Fandian) and features Tai Hu specialties (mainly eels, shrimp, and lake crab) for RMB 20 to RMB 50 ($2.40 to $6). There's an English menu, and credit cards are accepted. The **Wuxi Roast Duck** at 222 Zhongshan Lu (☎ 0510/272-9435) is a popular local restaurant in the heart of downtown serving big plates of local specialties, including lake fish, eels, and crabs, for about $10 a person (no credit cards, no English menu). The Sheraton's **Someplace Else** (☎ 0510/272-1888) has Wuxi's best Western comfort food (pizza, burgers), for about $10 a plate.

The Grand Canal: The Infinite Waterway

大运河

China's Grand Canal, measuring 1,112 miles north to south from Beijing to Hangzhou, is the longest canal in the world, and one of the oldest. Its first section was dug in 486 B.C. by the king of Wu in order to dispatch soldiers and grain during a campaign of conquest. In 361 B.C., extensive canals were dug from Kaifeng, connecting it to Beijing. During the Han Dynasty (206 B.C. to A.D. 220) and the Southern and Northern dynasties (A.D. 420–589), weirs and dams were built on the canals that served as locks. Winch systems were also developed, the earliest employment of ship-lifting mechanisms in the world. In 984, the first double-lock was built on the Grand Canal; the first double-lock built in the West, in Italy, was not completed until 1481. During the Song Dynasty (1127–1279), the new capital of Hangzhou hooked itself up to the Grand Canal as far as the Yangzi River. And finally, under the Yuan Dynasty (1271–1368), when the capital moved up to Beijing, the Grand Canal reached its final form, linking Beijing in the north and Hangzhou in the south, as it does to this day.

Yangdi, second emperor of the Sui Dynasty (A.D. 589–618), made the longest single contribution to the Grand Canal, conscripting one million workers to construct a shipping channel linking his capital at Luoyang in central China to the Yangzi River basin and to northern China as far as Beijing. In 611, Emperor Yangdi sailed to Beijing from central China aboard a four-deck, 180-foot-long royal barge with a carved dragon's head as its mast. A thousand vessels attended the emperor. To haul this procession, 80,000 coolies in harness were employed, and 40 new palaces were built along the way. Yangdi died on the Grand Canal during his third excursion, hanged by rebellious members of his own court.

Like the Great Wall, the Grand Canal has fallen into ruins at many places, although long segments are still in use, particularly in the Shanghai region of eastern China, where many lakes and rivers were

realigned and joined over the centuries. The most active segment for modern travelers is now between **Suzhou** and **Hangzhou,** the southern terminus of the Grand Canal for over 13 centuries. It was this stage that I wanted to sail, hoping to trace something of China's long history where it is still deeply carved into the Earth.

Emperors on the Canal

The motive to build a grand canal on the scale of the Great Wall was chiefly imperial greed. The capitals of successive dynasties always required a water route to the regions that produced not only necessities such as rice but luxuries such as tea and silk. Since the major rivers of China flow from the west to the east, the emperors built an entirely new river over the centuries, as massive as the Yellow River or the Yangzi River, in order to create a flow of goods on a north–south axis that bisected their palaces and treasure houses. As they cut the various channels, they encountered an engineering problem. Differences in terrain and water flow led to varying water speeds. To harmonize the Grand Canal, water gates were constructed. The Panmen Water Gate still stands in Suzhou. It was just east of this monument on the city moat that I boarded one of the dozens of passenger ferries that sail the Grand Canal to Hangzhou.

For the last 6 centuries the primary function of the Grand Canal has been to transport grain and other articles as tax and tributes north to the capital of Beijing. There is a saying that it was the Grand Canal that brought the city of Beijing into existence. The moat that once surrounded the Forbidden City connected directly to the Grand Canal. The bricks in the Forbidden City, the Temple of Heaven, and the Ming

Tombs all came up the Grand Canal. Two hundred thousand tons of rice were required by the rulers in the north, but owing to waste, traveling expenses, and the tenacious middle men of the Middle Kingdom, twice that much grain had to set out from the south. More than 10,000 rice barges, replaced every 10 years, plied the Grand Canal. Other ships carried cloth, food, salt, porcelain, lacquerware, bricks, bamboo, and timber to Beijing. Scholars used the canal to reach the capital for the imperial examinations. A special bureaucracy evolved to regulate and maintain the canal, repairing the earthen embankments, planting trees, dredging waterways, and arresting pirates. Laborers were stationed every mile, 10 per outpost. In 1902, many of the officials in charge of water management were dismissed and canal transport was officially abandoned. Rail service had come into play.

Smaller boats continued to use segments of the canal for local shipping. In the 1950s, the canal was dredged and enlarged in the south, where it is now open year-round. The section that runs through Suzhou down to Hangzhou contains 20 locks, as well as culverts and water-pumping stations. It is also so thick with ships and barges that I doubt canal travel will ever be a thing of the past in China, the anachronism it has become in America.

Water City of the East

Suzhou is a romantic place to begin a Grand Canal cruise (see the Suzhou chapter). Known as the "Water City of the East," Suzhou rose to prominence by shipping its silk embroidery up the canal to China's imperial courts, establishing a high reputation in the arts that it never relinquished. Square bricks from Suzhou's kilns paved the Forbidden City. An inner moat encases this city of interlaced canals; a gated outer waterway connected Suzhou to the Grand Canal.

Panmen, the old water gate in southwest Suzhou, consists of two sections: an inner brick gate 12 feet wide and an outer granite gate 9 feet wide. The walls between were used to entrap and inspect canal ships that called upon the city. The **Panmen Water Gate** is still in place, as is the nearby **Wumen Bridge,** one of the largest arched stone bridges on the canal and now the entryway to Suzhou's wharves. Suzhou has everywhere the marks of a Grand Canal city. The whitewashed houses of Suzhou still have crimson doors that open on the inner waterways that feed the Grand Canal. You can cross more than a hundred bridges in Suzhou: arched stone bridges, ladder-shaped bridges, even house-spanning bridges *(lian jia qiao)* that connect two parts of a dwelling.

Two miles west of the city, the Grand Canal sweeps by **Cold Mountain Temple,** jogging inland to join Suzhou's city moat to the southeast. This is where poet Zhang Ji, arriving at the temple by canal boat during the Tang Dynasty, wrote this delicate passage:

Moon sets and crows caw in the frosted sky
River maples and the lights of fishing boats break into
my troubled sleep.
Beyond Suzhou lies Cold Mountain Temple;
At midnight the clang of the bell reaches the
traveler's boat.

I did not hear the clear bell in the frosted sky clanging in Cold Mountain Temple as I embarked on the canal boat at Suzhou. Instead, I heard the horns of two dozen nearly identical canal boats as they backed out from the piers to begin their journeys to Hangzhou. These are not dainty vessels, outfitted to resemble the elegant dragon boats of the emperors who once sailed the Grand Canal. Nor are they modern ferries, comfortably tailored for the international tourist. They are rusty steel double-deckered passenger boats that have worked hard and long. Their deluxe staterooms are simple, crude, deteriorating closets with a set of narrow bunk beds, a nightstand, an oil heater, and a spittoon on the floor. They have windows to let in the breeze and glass doors that open directly onto the outside deck. Although the knob was missing from my door, I could still lock it from the inside. But alas, the real drawback is that these ferries cruise by night. We departed in the late afternoon, with only a few hours of daylight on either end. I tried to make the most of the light, clinging to the railing above the bow.

The **city moat** where we pushed off is exceedingly narrow. The ship must pivot neatly and precisely to begin the journey. I was surprised but fascinated when three of these bargelike flat-bottomed passenger ships undocked together. The vessel on our port side was the only one using its engines. The deck hands, leashing and unleashing the ropes that held the three ships together, maneuvered us into the middle of the canal so that we drifted into a staggered line. Then the crew hooked us together, end to end, using an iron pole on a swivel to lash stern to bow. My canal boat was second in line. The lead boat does all the work. We were gently towed forward, the black smoke of the first canal boat streaming back on us.

Night Passage

The Grand Canal is not beautiful, but it is as fascinating as the work-a-day canal boats, themselves just a step up from the barges that surrounded our small flotilla. These barges, each about 60 feet long, with simple cabins on their sterns and open holds running forward to rounded stems, also like to hold hands. They too are often linked end to end in the tow of small tugs. Those barges that choose to go it on their own are powered by outboard engines with long, straight shafts. Often, a single barge will have four or five of these engines mounted in a row across the stern.

We passed scores of fishing junks tied up at docks, white flags fluttering on their sterns, then turned south, passing under a long, blackened bridge. We were on the Grand Canal. Sunset was already coloring the sludge of the sky. The barges were low in the water, crushed by loads of brick, coal, and sand to feed the factories that line the canal. The passage is narrow at times, although once out of Suzhou it widens to 300 feet or more. The only scenery on the banks is of flat farmlands and grime-coated factories. The chimneys of coal-powered factories ignite with orange flames. Several discharge effluents into the canal, colored a thoroughly unearthly blue. The Grand Canal is an industrial river, made and run by humans, and it is black with discharges. I could smell from the railing a powerful mixture of diesel oil and diarrhea—it's the smell of an open sewer.

Many waterways cut in and out of the Grand Canal, which is the main artery for farms and factories all across the vast plain of rapeseed and rice that radiates out from Shanghai. The Grand Canal cuts straight and true. Scores of low bridges span it. Thousands of vessels run up and down its length, stopping to load or unload at factories and towns and farms on the embankments, or to head down a side canal to towns and businesses that are still served by waterways. There must be hundreds of villages that depend on canal barges, places no tourist ever sees.

The passing barges were also homes. I saw dogs, cats, bicycles, plants, and laundry lines. On deck a woman cooked the family dinner on a small coal stove. Fourteen barges linked together were the most I saw, and I saw that number often. Perhaps it's the maximum allowed on the Grand Canal.

In the southern outskirts of Suzhou, the Grand Canal embankment is straddled by **Precious Belt Bridge,** which consists of 53 stone arches. At over a half mile, it is the longest arched bridge on the canal. It was finished in A.D. 819, after the prefect's governor donated his precious belt to fund its completion. I barely noticed it in passing. I was watching the barges coming at us in the darkness. The running lights I saw turned out to be a son or daughter standing on the bow waving a flashlight.

I lay back on the hard bunk. It was too hot for a quilt. I couldn't sleep long. The oncoming traffic was continuous. Ships passed within a few feet, like apartment buildings hurtling through the night. The engines rattled and screamed, the ship horns blasted away, and the larger vessels such as ours swept the water and canal banks with searchlights. Sometimes I heard shouts.

End of the Grand Canal

After 5am, I didn't sleep another wink. A faint sun crept into overcast skies. I rubbed my eyes, but the panorama of gray factories, coal yards, smokestacks, and cranes did not brighten. The fishermen were up. They were trolling the waters with baskets for shrimp. I wondered how these people can survive on the Grand Canal. It is a severe world. Even this voyage seemed little better than a 13-hour Greyhound bus tour of a sewer.

Yet as we neared Hangzhou (see the Hangzhou chapter), last stop on the Grand Canal, the banks became stone, neatly laid by hand, and the promenades were shaded by groves of willow and maple. We docked at Genshan Harbor near the tripled-arched **Gongchen Bridge,** the last ancient stone crossing on the Grand Canal. The lead boat angled in and cut us loose. We drifted into the dock. "Above there is Heaven," goes the popular saying; "Below are Suzhou and Hangzhou." And between these rivers there is still the Grand Canal, reaching across the land like the dark, powerful arm of an ancient warrior, a palpable link with the China of the emperors.

PRACTICAL INFORMATION

CRUISES

June and July are the best months to make this voyage, particularly since sunset is at its latest, so you'll have more time to view the Grand Canal.

Canal boat passage can be booked through **China International Travel Service (CITS)** in Suzhou. The main office is in the Suzhou Hotel, 115 Shiquan Jie (☎ 0512/522-3175; fax 0512/523-3593). I booked my ticket to Hangzhou at the tour desk (a branch of CITS) in the **Gloria Plaza Hotel.** The price for the entire two-berth cabin was RMB 256 ($31), which included an RMB 60 ($7.25) service charge. This was a first-class ticket. Second-class tickets (four berths to a room) are considerably cheaper, about RMB 80 ($10 per person). Cabins are crude, without sinks or private baths. In fact, these canal ships have no showers or tubs whatsoever. Toilets are unisex and Chinese style (hole in the floor). Dinner is served aboard, but I avoided it by packing a picnic lunch in Suzhou, including bottled water. All other passengers were Chinese, some from overseas, and all were quite friendly.

Canal boats depart Suzhou at 5:30pm and arrive in Hangzhou the next morning at about 7:30am. The boat is docked in Suzhou at the **Nanmen Passenger Boat Terminal,** northeast of the bridge that crosses the moat on Renmin Nan Lu. The reverse voyage (Hangzhou to Suzhou) is also an overnight affair, leaving in the evening, costing the same amount. The **passenger wharf** in Hangzhou, where tickets are sold, is in the north part of the city at 138 Huancheng Bei Lu (near Zhongshan Bei Lu; ☎ 0571/505-8458). You can also buy tickets through a hotel tour desk.

XIAMEN: AMOY MON AMOUR

厦门

BETTER KNOWN TO THE WEST AS Amoy, its name in the local Fujian dialect, Xiamen is among the most charming cities in China, and it was recently voted the cleanest as well. An ordinance forbids the honking of horns, mitigating yet another aspect of pollution common to developing cities in China—and Xiamen is every bit a boomtown. Owing to its location on the East China Sea, directly across from Taiwan, Xiamen has benefited for years from its connections with overseas Chinese. When I first visited in 1987, Xiamen showed signs of being the single most developed place in China, if crates of imported appliances, throngs of motorbikes, and jungles of television antennas were any indication. Every other resident of Xiamen seemed to have relatives abroad and thus a ready conduit to the foreign luxury goods, which until quite recently few in China had the means to procure.

Xiamen is still prosperous, but it has had the good sense not to turn its downtown and harbor into a microcosm of Manhattan or Hong Kong. Rather, the old town is still old and the island in its harbor, Gulangyu—once the stronghold of foreigners—remains a resort of mansions, parks, and pedestrian-only streets that is simply China's most charming reliquary of its colorful colonial past.

Old Town Xiamen

The key intersection in Xiamen is on the inner harbor at the crossroads of **Lujiang Lu** and **Zhongshan Lu,** near the stately Lujiang Hotel, with its sea-view balconies. This is where the local buses congregate, the conductors leaning out the windows, shouting their destinations and banging the side of the bus with a wrench. The ferries to Gulangyu, the gorgeous island of red-roofed mansions and green hills just west across the waterfront, depart from here. The square is the liveliest place in Xiamen, the congregating point for visitors, vendors, shoppers, and fishermen working the docks and wharves.

To explore the **old downtown,** just walk east past the curving facade of the Lujiang Hotel on Zhongshan Lu. This is main street, filled these days with shops large and small, old and new. Many of the side streets are as they have been for decades, consisting of row upon row of shop-houses, their columns and colonnades covering the sidewalks.

One of the first treks I ever made in Xiamen was southward from the main ferry dock along **Minzu Road.** The quays are a feverish sprawl of fishing boats unloading their catches, warehouses shuffling pallets of imported electronics, and factory yards piled with coal and dried fish. One morning I came across two little children frolicking in one factory yard, running and leaping on the other side of the gate, both of them stark naked and laughing.

Temple, School & Disputed Strait

If you're up for a long walk, you can stroll all the way down the east shore of Xiamen (which is itself an island, not joined to the mainland until a causeway was constructed after Liberation in 1949). Eventually, Siming Nan Lu leads to **Nan Putuo Temple,** Xiamen's greatest place of worship (open daily 8:30am to dusk, admission RMB 10/$1.25). Nan Putuo, built into a rocky hillside, is an active Buddhist complex of grand halls, bell towers, inscribed rocks, and pavilions, striking for its white marble and upswept tiled roofs. The temple dates from the Tang Dynasty, but it has been extensively rebuilt in the thousand years since. This is a fine place to watch locals pray for riches and burn incense (which is collected for reuse by numerous monks). At the highest hall there is a magnificent red character, meaning Buddha, carved into a massive boulder. The outcroppings beyond this point, the **Peaks of the Five Old Men (Wulao Shan),** make for excellent day hikes.

When I visited Xiamen 10 years ago, much of the Nan Putuo halls and courtyards were undergoing another renovation. A small city of stonecutters was encamped at the temple gates. Today, Nan Putuo has been put back together. It teems with visitors, drawn to this southern "home" of China's most popular divinity, Guanyin, Goddess of Mercy.

Just south of the temple is one of China's best schools, **Xiamen University,** founded in 1921 by Tan Kah-kee (Chen Jiageng), a native of the area who moved to Singapore and made his fortune in rubber plantations. If you've never strolled a campus in China before, this might be your best chance. Ask at the gate if you may enter or wait for helpful students to approach you to practice their English. Lu Xun (1881–1936), China's most famous modern essayist, taught here for a term in 1926 to 1927, and there's a small exhibit in his memory just inside the main gate. One of Xiamen's students befriended me when I visited here. He gave me a tour of the campus, told me about the inner workings of student dorm life, and took me to lunch at a nearby student cafe.

South of the temple and university is the **Huli Mountain Cannon Platform,** the remnants of German artillery placed here in 1891 (open daily dawn to dusk, admission RMB 5/65¢). Looking across the Formosa Strait, it's just a few miles to two islands, Jinmen and Mazu, that were once much in dispute between China and Taiwan. For years they taunted each other across this strait with loudspeakers, propaganda balloons, and live explosives. The islands figured in the Kennedy–Nixon presidential debates in 1960, when Jinmen and Mazu (now being opened to tourism by Taiwan) were better known to Cold Warriors as Quemoy and Matsu.

Garden Island

Xiamen's most engrossing attraction is **Gulangyu,** the small island in its harbor that is served by innumerable ferries. The main ferry to Gulangyu is across from the Lijiang Hotel. Look for the two big entryways to the pier. There's no charge on the way out to Gulangyu, and it's just RMB 2 (25¢) to return. The voyage requires just 10 minutes. These old two-deck ferries have almost nowhere to sit down. With their sliding screen doors, they look rather like cattle cars.

The island fathers have wisely ordered all new buildings to conform in spirit and style to its graceful colonial legacy. Evenings, walking the twisting lanes, I've passed more than one garden villa emitting the soothing sounds of a pianist in rehearsal or a private concert. Many of China's best musicians come from here, and the locals, who number barely 12,000, sometimes call Gulangyu by another name, not on the maps: Piano Island.

Gulangyu is an island for walking. Cars and even bicycles are banned. A few electric carts are permitted; some give tours. The island is quite hilly but also quite compact. Straight up from the dock is the town, packed with shops and seafood cafes. The streets are cobbled or paved, and they twist and turn like pretzels. You'll probably get lost, but it's easy to find the way back to the town and ferry dock.

The newest attraction, and the one least worth seeing, is the **Underwater World** (2 Longtou Lu, north of the ferry terminal; ☎ 0592/206-7825), an aquarium highlighted by a walk through a 250-foot-long viewing tunnel. Admission is RMB 60 ($7.50) for adults, half-price for children 12 and under.

South of the ferry dock is the way to turn: Here, a number of the grand buildings and villas occupy the hillside, survivors of Gulangyu's days as a foreign quarter. Western traders moved onto Gulangyu in 1842. The foreigners built the villas, sanitation system, consulates, schools, churches, hospitals, and roads that remain today. In 1903, Gulangyu became Xiamen's official foreign concession. The British and Germans had their consulates on the east side of the little island, as did the Amoy Telephone Company. The **old British Embassy building** still stands atop the first hill on your left as you leave the ferry. It burned a few years ago and is being restored. The towering whitewashed **Roman Catholic church,** on a quiet lane rising above the southeastern shore, is over a century old now (1882) and still used on Sunday, as is the **Sanyi Protestant church,** which the English built in 1904.

Gulangyu seems to be blanketed in hundreds, even thousands, of old villas, many of them now the residences of locals. The original coats of arms in enamel have been removed from the stucco doorways, but the Corinthian columns, two-story porches, plaster curlicues, and immense verandas recall many foreign architectural styles, especially the Portuguese types still prevalent in Macau. Mature banyans, bougainvillea, and bauhinia overhang the winding, walled lanes that enclose luxuriant gardens. Gulangyu seems like a slice of the tropics with only a few Chinese intrusions.

Placed on the southeast cusp of Gulangyu like a beacon is a mesmerizing statue of the robed warrior **Koxinga (Zheng Chenggong),** who commanded Xiamen with his pirate armada said to consist of 8,000 war junks and 250,000 fighting men. Koxinga expelled the Dutch from Taiwan in 1661. He died there the next year, but he has been remembered ever since. His statue surveys the sea from atop a sea pillar, which visitors reach via a bridge from a lovely seaside garden. This rounded image of Koxinga is as memorable as New York's Statue of Liberty, if less dramatic. Its form also mirrors that of the summit of Gulangyu itself, Sunlight Rock.

Near the Koxinga statue, up Tian Wei Lu, is the **Gulangyu Guesthouse compound,** with its 1920s billiard room and seaside terraces, where U.S. President Nixon stayed in 1972 when opening up relations with the People's Republic.

The island's best **beach** is due west of Koxinga, on the southern shores. The sands are inviting and a new graceful portico has been built on the shore, but the most interesting areas to explore are along the fringes of the beach, where pathways wind through stone pinnacles that rise from the shore.

Overlooking the beach is one of the island's best-known gardens, **Shuzhuang,** built in 1913 by Lin Er-jia, a wealthy merchant who fled his home in Taiwan when the Japanese occupied it in 1895. It is a small seaside garden that has recently been refurbished with a zigzag bridge, a large goldfish pond, and a massive honeycombed wall of lake rock. Locals seem to like lingering here, and they make a great deal of the pond in a garden on the sea ("A garden in the sea, a sea in the garden," they say). For me it has an artificial, sterile look—an amusement park garden. It's open daily from 7am to 6pm; admission is RMB 20 ($2.50).

Gulangyu's finest overlook is **Sunlight Rock (Riguangyan),** nearly 300 feet above the harbor, the highest of the island's peaks. Surrounding its base is Yanping Park (admission RMB 40/$4.80). The summit of Sunlight Rock is a short, steep climb along rock paths dotted with flower gardens, old cannons, small cafes, and a number of amusement arcades, yurts, and contemporary metal sculptures. Sunlight Rock has taken on a carnival atmosphere, but at its higher levels it is simply a beautiful landform of granite boulders and outcroppings rising to a rounded summit of smooth, bare rock. From the top the outlines of Gulangyu, the harbor, and downtown Xiamen to the east are in full view. Gulangyu is particularly fetching from this height, an island garden of villas in red brick and tile.

Gulangyu's most prominent building is the **Xiamen Museum,** a spacious, colonnaded edifice crowned with a large red dome (admission

RMB 2/25¢). I was determined to see its interior on my most recent visit, so I retraced my steps back into Gulangyu town and at the ferry dock followed the shore northward up Yanping Lu. I turned up a nearby street and after a few blocks and a few false turns found the museum's gate. It is a curiously hollow, unadorned old hall inside, its four floors divided in the center by a circular atrium. The exhibits are not splashy. The first floor is decorated with photographs of Gulangyu's colonial architecture. Various rooms have different exhibits: relics of recent wars, printing presses, a set of handcuffs. The second floor contains a collection of painted porcelains dating back to the Tang Dynasty; a room devoted to gifts sent by Xiamen's sister cities from around the world (including Baltimore and Sutter Creek, California); tributes from a number of foreign countries; a hall displaying Iron Age weapons, scrolls, wooden rifles, and pieces from a cart; and a Trophy Room festooned with the prizes of local sports heroes. The top two floors were closed. The staff was drinking tea in the staff rooms, and the doors were swung wide open to the tropical sea breezes.

PRACTICAL INFORMATION

ORIENTATION & WHEN TO GO

Xiamen, population about 600,000, is an island port city in southern Fujian Province located on the Formosa Strait, opposite Taiwan. As one of China's Special Economic Zones (SEZ), it receives considerable outside investment (especially from neighboring Taiwan). Xiamen is warm most of the year, owing to its southern location. Summers are particularly humid, however, and late springs and early autumns bring rainstorms. October, November, March, and early April are the most comfortable times to visit.

GETTING THERE

By Plane The international airport is 11 miles from downtown. Airport taxis cost about RMB 50 ($6). **Dragonair,** 8 Jianye Lu, Marco Polo Hotel (☎ 0592/511-7702), has regular flights to Hong Kong. **Xiamen Airlines** (☎ 0592/602-2961) has service to most cities in China. **Philippine Airlines** (☎ 0592/509-4451) serves Manila.

By Train There are trains to Shanghai (26 hours), but Xiamen is not located on the main Guangzhou–Shanghai–Beijing rail line. For northern destinations, such as Beijing, air transport is more efficient.

By Ship Passenger ships connect Hong Kong and Xiamen, docking at the **Passenger Station** of Amoy Port Administration, Heping Pier, Tongwen Lu (a 15-minute walk south from the Lujiang Hotel/Ferry Station). Call ☎ 0592/202-2517 for information. I've returned to Hong Kong several times by ship. It's a pleasant excursion, leaving Xiamen in the afternoon (usually at 3pm) for the 19-hour voyage.

The terminal is notable for its luggage escalator, a belt of wooden bars and catches, where you set down your carry-ons; they roll along with you to the second-floor customs desk. My ship, rechristened the *Min Nan*, was formerly a member of the Brittany Ferries fleet. My first-class cabin cost RMB 452 ($54). Facilities were adequate: a private bathroom and shower, cinema, buffet restaurant, duty-free shop, disco lounge—but no towels in the cabins. Passengers are Chinese, loaded down with luggage and shopping bags.

GETTING AROUND

You can tour Xiamen on your own by foot. Buy a map from the hotel or a street vendor and set out from the ferry terminal south to Nan Putuo Temple, east to old town Xiamen, or west on the ferry to Gulangyu.

TOURS & STRATAGEMS

China International Travel Service (CITS) (☎ 0592/505-1825) has many branches in Xiamen—but none are useful for setting up a tour. Rely upon the tour desks in the **Marco Polo Hotel** or the **Holiday Inn** for air, rail, and boat tickets and for city tours. **American Express** has an office in the Holiday Inn (☎ 0592/212-0268).

WHERE TO STAY

Holiday Inn Crowne Plaza Harbourview (Haijin Jiari Dajiudian). *12–8 Zhenhai Lu (downtown). ☎ 800/465-4329 or 0592/202-3333. Fax 0592/203-6666. 367 units. A/C MINIBAR TV TEL. $160 double. AE, DC, JCB, MC, V.* This 22-story tower is Xiamen's top downtown hotel. The rooms are spacious and clean and have safes. No-smoking rooms are available. There are two executive floors and an American Express office. Service is highly efficient.

Amenities: Outdoor swimming pool, health club, sauna, business center, concierge, 24-hour room service, same-day dry cleaning and laundry, nightly turndown, tour desk, medical clinic, beauty salon, shopping arcade, newsstand, free airport shuttle.

Marco Polo Xiamen. *8 Jianye, Hubin Bei Lu (north of city center on Yuandong Lake). ☎ 800/524-0500 or 0592/509-1888. Fax 0592/509-2888. 350 units. A/C MINIBAR TV TEL. $160 double. AE, DC, JCB, MC, V.* The guest rooms of this grand luxury hotel are arranged on tiers looking down on its eight-story atrium lobby. The top floor, its Continental Club, caters to business executives. Services are first-rate. Taxis downtown cost RMB 12 ($1.50). All rooms come with a large desk, sofa, and safe. No-smoking rooms are available, as are a medical clinic and delicatessen.

Amenities: Outdoor swimming pool, health club, sauna, business center, concierge, 24-hour room service, same-day dry cleaning and laundry, nightly turndown, tour desk, beauty salon, shopping arcade, newsstand, free airport shuttle.

WHERE TO DINE

The Marco Polo Hotel's **Lotus Court** (☎ 0592/509-1888) on the second floor has the best Chinese food I've eaten in Xiamen, as well as impeccable service. The Marco Polo's lobby restaurant, **Cafe Marco,** provides good breakfast and lunch buffets (Western and Asian fare).

Downtown, the **Holiday Inn** has excellent Sichuan, Cantonese, and Western dining in its restaurants, including the best dim sum breakfasts in town (☎ 0592/202-3333).

The **Lujiang Hotel's rooftop restaurant,** overlooking the ferry to Gulangyu (54 Lujiang Lu), has an English menu, hot local Fujian and Cantonese dishes, live seafood, and the city's best evening view (☎ 0592/202-2922).

For fast food, there's a **Pizza Hut** on the harbor 1 block north of the ferry dock in Haibin Park.

On Gulangyu, I tried several hole-in-the-wall **seafood cafes.** All of them were pleasant, bright, moderately expensive, and marginally clean. Most had no English menus or posted prices, but all had plenty of helpful proprietors used to foreign visitors. Just point at the live seafood of your choice in the plastic pans on the sidewalk and settle on a price before ordering. Xiamen is celebrated for its delicacies from the sea, some of them quite expensive, many of them dried and for sale at stands.

Guangzhou (Canton): The Gate to China

广州

Guangzhou, better known by its old Western name, Canton, is the center of all things Cantonese—that is to say, south China's people, language, and cuisine. It is also among my least favorite Chinese cities. Hardly a stone's throw from Hong Kong, Guangzhou is all business and industry these days, all freeways and skyscrapers and factories—hardly a major tourist stop like Beijing and Shanghai, eastern seaboard metropolises comparable in size and wealth to noisy Guangzhou. All the same, I've discovered, after repeated visits, that old Canton has its pleasurable treasures, too, several of them unique.

First impressions of Guangzhou are seldom promising, unless one is driven into raptures by construction noise and modern expressways. Guangzhou has some of the most advanced elements anywhere in urban China, some of the highest salaries and most efficient corporations, and its network of new roads and elevated freeways is the most impressive in China. Its traffic is the swiftest and best regulated—or so I thought until I noticed that the on-ramps to these towering expressways are filled with cars using them as off-ramps as well. The pace in Guangzhou is feverish, and its drivers have learned to swerve with the flow, even when that flow instantaneously reverses itself, heedless of head-on collisions, unannounced U-turns, illegal stops in busy traffic lanes, and other unpredictable detours. This is Cantonese life in the fast lane, without the impediments imposed by common sense, courtesy, or police on most other city streets in the world. The sheer energy, of course, is contagious, and it defines the Cantonese way as it drives full-throttle into the 21st century. Already, the Pearl River Delta region accounts for more than half of China's commerce.

Canton's Central Park

At the heart of the city there are older, quieter islands of repose and culture. The city's largest park, **Yuexiu Yuan,** is its best (open daily 8am to

10pm, admission RMB 3/35¢). Built on a grand scale, the green, hilly 247-acre grounds possess a number of boring features, such as three artificial lakes and a 40,000-seat stadium. For most foreign visitors, the **Sun Yat-sen Memorial Hall (Zhongshan Jiniantang),** with a separate admission of RMB 10 ($1.25), located at the southern foot of the mountain that gives the park its name, isn't that exciting, either. Finished in 1931, 6 years after Dr. Sun Yat-sen's death, the hall and its blue-tiled tower host lectures, plays, and other cultural offerings. It's a grand but simple edifice, engineered so that no interior pillars are required for support. Sun Yat-sen is the province's most beloved native son, credited with leading the overthrow of China's last imperial dynasty and the establishment of China's first republic. He founded the Guomindang (Nationalist Party) in 1923 in Canton, the political party that later tried to unite China under Chiang Kai-shek but fell to the victorious Communist revolutionaries under Mao Zedong. Still, Sun Yat-sen is claimed by both Nationalists (who fled to Taiwan in 1949) and Communists as the founder of modern China, and almost invariably the main street in China's cities today bears Sun Yat-sen's Chinese name (Zhongshan).

Guangzhou's reputation as a hotbed of revolutionary activity was enhanced not only by Sun Yat-sen's Republican Revolution but by Mao's early Communist movement. From 1924 to 1927, Mao, Zhou En-lai, and other Communist Party founders trained future firebrands at Canton's **Peasant Movement Institute,** located in the former Temple of Confucius. Chairman Mao's spartan bedroom is still on view there, in yet another of Guangzhou's politically correct but touristically dull attractions.

What's interesting in Yuexiu Park is, of all things, the **Guangzhou Museum** (daily 8:30am to 5pm, admission RMB 5/65¢). By the time I actually came to look inside, I'd visited Guangzhou enough times to expect yet another display of photographs and letters tracing the history of the Communist Party or recording one of several massacres of martyrs to China's revolution. Instead, within the graceful **Pavilion Overlooking the Sea (Zhen Hai Luo),** which European traders called the Five-Story Pagoda, there are fine, well-displayed historical exhibits, arranged chronologically by floor, with signs in English and Chinese. First built during the Ming Dynasty in 1380 and rebuilt as a Pearl River lookout in 1686, this pavilion (Guangzhou's oldest building) is an ideal venue for a historical museum, capped by an elegant teahouse on the fifth floor. My favorite item is a Ming Dynasty water clock, dated A.D. 1316, consisting of three large barrels arranged like stairs that employed a large dipstick to measure the correct time. The museum is open Tuesday to Sunday from 9am to 4pm; admission is RMB 5 (75¢).

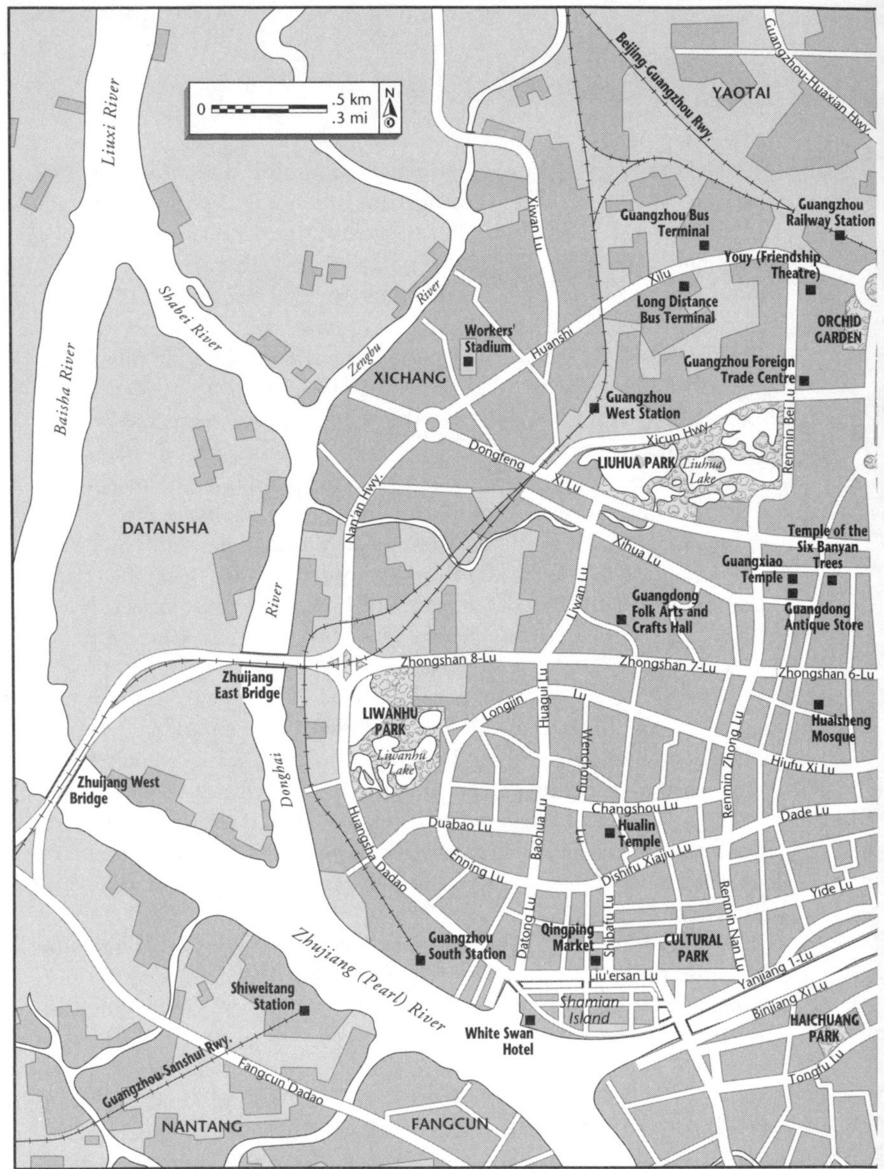

The centerpiece of Yuexiu Park is its **Statue of Five Rams.** The five rams recall the story of Guangzhou's founding, when five fairies from the Celestial Realm rode their goats into town to present the Cantonese with their first grains of rice. I expected this oft-photographed emblem of the city—a modern sculpture always dismissed as of little artistic merit—to be

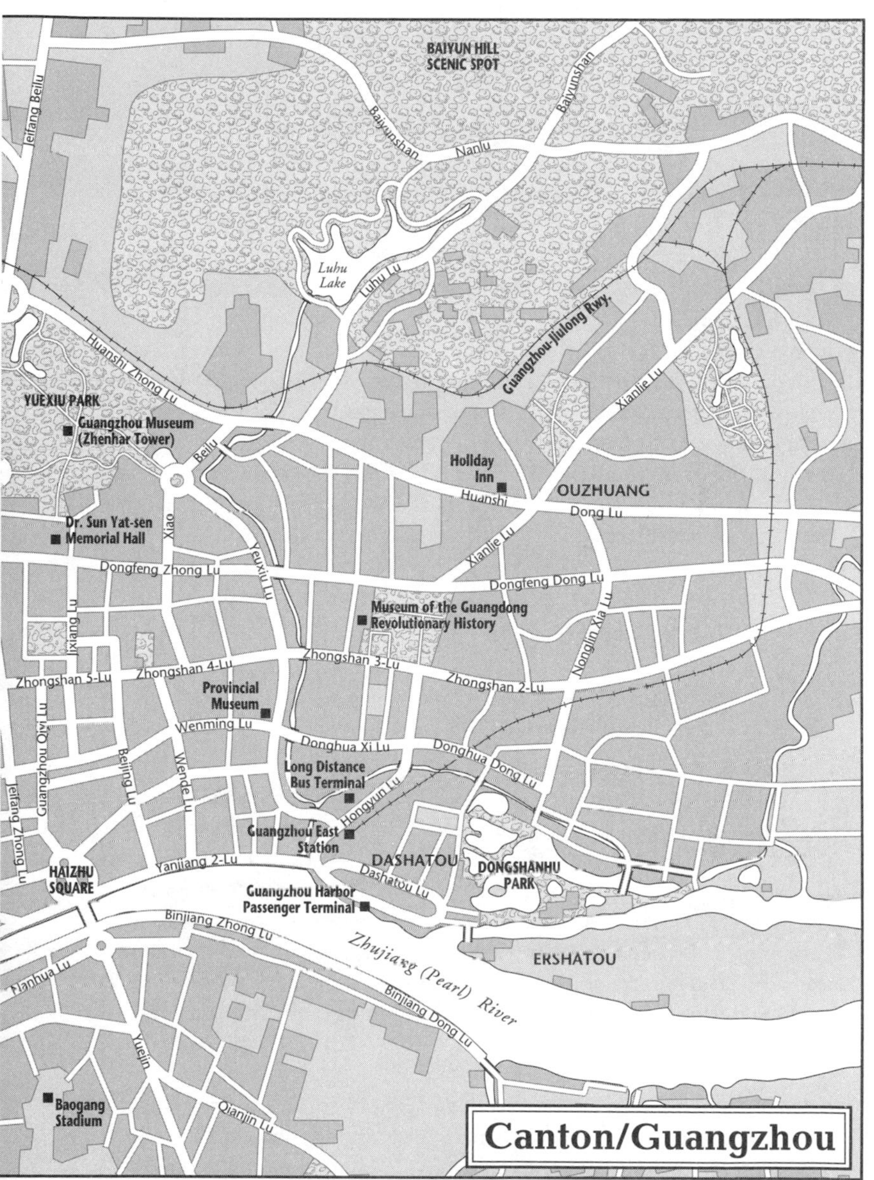

hopelessly overrun and tacky to boot, but again I was surprised. Perched on a raised platform, this statue, made of granite chunks fitted together to form the five impish rams with their coiling horns, is actually an intriguing piece from many angles, and the honeycomb of flowery paths that surround it are explored as much by locals and retirees as by visitors.

Temple of the Six Banyan Trees

One of the most bizarre halls in any Buddhist temple I ever visited in China was at another of Guangzhou's tourist stops, the Temple of the Six Banyan Trees (Liurongsi), open daily from 8am to 5pm (admission RMB 15/$2). Its main attraction is its nine-story **Flower Pagoda (Hua Ta),** first erected in A.D. 537 and situated squarely in the central courtyard. Behind it is a hall with three statues of the Buddha and one of Guanyin, the Goddess of Mercy, who remains throughout China, as in Canton, one of the most popular deities. Several locals bowed low, with incense sticks extended in prayer to the brass goddess. The most arresting sight, however, is not the pagoda or prayer but the death hall. When I entered this hall, immediately to the left of the pagoda, it took me a while to figure out its function. It's a spare chamber, with one monk in attendance. The walls are coated with strips of paper and pictures of the dead. The cost of getting posted in this prayer hall, where your image and spirit are constantly administered to by a government-approved religious worker, is by no means nominal: a stiff RMB 6,000 ($720) per posting.

Qingping Market

A better-known oddity of Guangzhou is fully in keeping with its culinary reputation. **Cantonese cuisine** is China's most complex and varied. The Cantonese tastes are perhaps as wide-ranging and as daring as those of the French. The popular saying in China is that the Cantonese will eat anything on four legs except a chair. To see that this is no exaggeration, browse through Guangzhou's most famous street market, **Qingping**—probably China's most notorious open-air market. You can't escape the lurid reports of exotic and domestic skinned animals nonchalantly hung from hooks at vendors' stands: from tigers to kitty cats, from pandas to dogs.

Qingping Market (open 6am until dark) is a large warren of covered stalls, and animals are indeed one of its offerings. I did walk past cages of dogs and cats and even small deer, all still alive and for sale. There were monkeys, snakes, and bats, too, all highly prized and high-priced fare. But this sideshow of animals is a tiny, tiny segment of Qingping Market, as it always has been. Today, you can roam from herb lane to antique lane to goldfish lane to mushroom lane to fresh flower lane to songbird lane without coming across a gruesome sight. Of course, the lanes are narrow, crowded, and pungent, and the walkways are not the world's cleanest—heaps of atmosphere, in other words.

Island of Sand

Across from the market is Canton's best reason to linger, **Shamian Island,** a quarter-mile-wide, half-mile-long sandbar that became the chief outpost of British, French, and other foreign traders who forced the port to open its doors in 1843. Britain took the lead, backing its merchants in southern Cathay who hungered to unload opium in Canton and return home with tea. It eventually won concessions from China in what became known as the Opium Wars. In 1859, Britain and France were granted territory on Shamian Island. The foreigners moved right in, shored up the embankments with stone, and maintained two bridges to the quays of Canton, shutting the iron gates at 10pm every night to keep the Chinese out. Shamian was soon populated with Western colonial-style administrative headquarters, banks, Christian churches, a Masonic temple, tennis courts, and a yacht club on the Pearl River.

By 1911, the population of Shamian had reached 300, including Americans, Dutch, Germans, and Japanese, as well as the original English and French residents. On June 23, 1925, Chinese demonstrators, fed up with these enterprising invaders, massed on the city shore to attack, and 52 were shot to death by Western armies. Shamian continued as a foreign post until the Communist Revolution in 1949.

The colonial architecture, the lawns and flower gardens, and the great arching banyan trees have endured, and Guangzhou has seized upon this rare legacy, sprucing up the broad avenues, planting garden plots, and slapping bright coats of paint on all the Western facades. Meanwhile, a raft of cafes, craft shops, galleries, and teahouses has moved in. This strange colonial revival has made Shamian into the most pleasant place in Canton and its chief international gathering point. The old Catholic church, **Our Lady of Lourdes** (at the intersection of Yijie and Shamian Dajie), has been reconverted from a printing plant back into a place of worship.

The island is a perfectly shaped oval, great for jogging or strolling, with a view of colonial architecture and modern enterprise within and the surging **Pearl River** beyond. This river is shorter than the Yangzi or the Yellow River but all the more intense, dumping eight times more water into the ocean than the Yellow.

I was strolling the riverbanks, watching the women wash their clothes in the rancid waters on a staircase dipping into the quay, when I was approached by an artist who offered to sell me antique painted scrolls that he kept rolled up in his Shamian apartment. Whether these were antiques or not, I couldn't tell, but I was intrigued by the scrolls he unrolled on his living room floor, and I parted on happy terms with an ink-wash drawing in hand.

The blossoming of Western-style cafes and foreign boutiques in the old buildings on the island is a recent phenomenon. When I first visited Shamian, the architecture was in languid decay and the main new addition was the stunning **White Swan Hotel** (see "Where to Stay," below), which was very nearly the first modern international hotel to spring up in China, appearing in 1982, and among the first three to receive China's official five-star rating. The White Swan remains hale and hearty as it approaches its 20th birthday, its garden waterfall in the high atrium still flowing like a wild cascade. The hotel is a modern monument of China's opening to the West, still a grand place to poke around among the lavish antique shops in the basement. Dozens of tour groups throng its lobby and hundreds of overseas businesspeople retire to the Riverside Apartment complex in its spacious banyan garden on the eastern tip of Shamian, where the traffic of Pearl River is always in full swing. Iced tea and a sandwich in the Riverside Garden Coffee Shop with a view of the waterfall within and the river floating by outside at eye level is still a pleasure, a peaceful haven from the commerce of the streets to which the White Swan has been the beacon for 2 decades.

Cantonese Cuisine

Guangzhou has a final appeal: its food. Cantonese, the great cuisine of China, was born here, and you can still find great Cantonese dining experiences in the city. It is often said, however, and not without justice, that the best Cantonese food is served in Hong Kong, Singapore, Taiwan, New York, San Francisco—in nearly any great capital except Guangzhou. Fortunately, there are some brilliant exceptions. Since I am not a true connoisseur of exotic Cantonese dishes, I leave it to others to try the live snake and monkey brain restaurants for which Guangzhou is notorious. My own choices are far more delicate, depending on fresh seafood and the traditional pungent sauces.

My favorite dining in Canton is at **Bei Yuan** (see "Where to Dine," below), the city's most beautiful garden restaurant. Built in the 1930s, Bei Yuan is segmented into over 40 halls, its tearooms and dining pavilions decorated with carved latticework, covered corridors, and etched window glass. Flowers are the decorative motif. Dim sum, the southern Chinese collection of bite-sized steamed pastries and small delicacies, is served all day, although it's usually taken on at a leisurely tea-drinking brunch that the Cantonese call *yum cha*. The best dinner dishes are the winter melon with green pepper and the mushrooms stuffed with shrimp; the signature dish is a stew of mixed delights, ranging from abalone and pork to chicken and trout.

A second garden restaurant with an outdoor setting is **Ban Xi** (see "Where to Dine," below), along the shores of Li Wan Lake. It, too, is a dragon of dining halls and classic decorations, with black lacquer furniture, gold leaf ceilings, and etched glass from the Qing Dynasty. Dinners run until midnight, and a lake stroll after dark, after a fine dinner, puts one in the mood to dream of a China that has long passed yet is still accessible in the midst of this supercharged metropolis. The dim sum is superb here, too, but extremely crowded all weekend. The Peony shrimp plate is divine. The menu is in English.

My most memorable Cantonese meal, however, occurred not in lake or garden or in some fine hotel but in the restaurant of a third-rate suburban hotel, **Sha He** (see "Where to Dine," below), a half-hour taxi ride northeast of Guangzhou. The Sha He kitchen has been southern China's most famous noodle emporium for 40 years, and nothing would do until I tried it myself. The dining area, on the second floor of the hotel, is dirty on the edges, and the marble tables and stone chairs are a bit cold, but the flat rice noodles *(ho fan)* are hot and succulent. It hardly matters what sauce, vegetable, meat, or sea creature is added. I asked the general manager, Li Yue Cheang, if I could take a peek at the famous kitchen, where 15 chefs and 30 assistants flail away in utter chaos—or rather, in accordance with a 600-year-old recipe. I was allowed to witness the whole process, from sink to wok, in the confines of the hotel's grease-washed dungeons.

The two chief activities of the Cantonese, it seems to me, are business and eating. Excelling at both, they are making Guangzhou the most progressive business city in China and at the same time the tastiest. I know of nothing more divine to do in old Canton than sit down to a Sunday yum cha in a decorated hall with the energy cranked high on all sides and the air crackling with conversation like a thousand lightning rods in a thunderstorm. That's when I drift away like an emperor half asleep, my eyes following the rounds of a dumpling cart loaded with its delicate tidbits: prawns sealed in transparent rice envelopes *(har gau),* shrimp trussed up in pastry shell bags *(shao mai),* and barbecued pork stuffed inside plump steamed buns *(hum bao).* Red tea arcs into my cup, falling from the long neck of a copper pot, snapping me awake. It seems like morning has just begun in distant China.

PRACTICAL INFORMATION

ORIENTATION & WHEN TO GO

Guangzhou is north of the Pearl River Delta, a close cousin of neighboring Macau and Hong Kong, a distant son of Beijing, 1,150 miles to the north. With a population of over two million in the city and another three million in the suburbs, Guangzhou is the economic capital of southeastern China, dominating its region in the way that Shanghai and Beijing dominate the central and northern segments of the eastern seaboard. Guangzhou has been trading with the West for 400 years. It has close ties with modern Hong Kong, and ranks among China's most cosmopolitan and affluent cities. Subtropical Guangzhou has hot, humid summers (lasting from April through September) with plenty of rain. Typhoons can strike in August and September.

Beginning in October and through the winter into early March, the weather is still warm, but the rains diminish, making late fall and winter the best times to visit.

GETTING THERE

By Plane **Baiyun Airport** has flights to cities throughout China, including nearby Hong Kong (25 minutes). Several international airlines also serve Guangzhou, including Thai, Singapore, Garuda, and Malaysian airlines. For airline information, call ☎ 020/8659-6123.

The ride into Guangzhou from the airport requires about 30 minutes. If possible, fax details of your flight arrival to your hotel so that you can be picked up. Otherwise, you may face a protracted battle with the taxi drivers and touts who will waylay you outside. You should insist on a functioning taxi meter and pay no more than RMB 50 ($6.25) for the ride, but you could be hustled into paying three times that much. If you arrive by train, bus, or boat, you could also face some bargaining challenges.

By Train & Bus Trains and buses arrive at stations east and north of downtown. Departures by express buses and trains serving Hong Kong are available all day; the trip takes from 2 to 3 hours and tickets are $20 to $30 each way. Hotels can book air, train, bus, and boat tickets easily. For train information, call ☎ 020/8777-7112.

By Ship Boats to and from Macau, Hong Kong, and Hainan Island arrive at **Zhoutouzui Wharf** on the south side of the Pearl River (for do-it-yourselfers, a 40-minute walk to Shamian Island). A jet-boat catamaran to Hong Kong down the Pearl River takes under 4 hours, while the new Turbo Cat service takes just 2 hours. One-way tickets cost from $30 to $50 each way, depending on class. For ship information in Guangzhou, call ☎ 020/8383-3691 or 020/8382-9933.

GETTING AROUND

Guangzhou is not a joy to walk in, nor to bike in, because of the heavy traffic. So be prepared to hail **taxis** as you go, which is easy downtown. There are plenty of taxis in Guangzhou, and they charge by the size of the vehicle. Every taxi should have a meter. The new **subway** line runs over an 11-mile route with 16 stops, including one near Shamian Island (Huangsha Station); the line links the East Railway Station in the northeast to the Guangzhou Steel Factory in the southeast, following much of Zhongshan Lu cross-town east to west. Tickets cost RMB 2 to RMB 6 (25¢ to 75¢), depending on destination.

TOURS & STRATAGEMS

The main office of **China International Travel Service (CITS)** at 179 Huanshi Lu (☎ 020/8667-7449) can set up tours for individuals, but the hotels have branches and tour desks that do a more efficient job. The tour desks at the **Garden Hotel,** the **China Hotel,** and the **Holiday Inn City Centre** are the best places to arrange tours.

I recently used the ticketing office near the cinema box office in the basement of the Holiday Inn to purchase an air ticket and a city tour. Both requests were handled by an English-speaking clerk in record-setting time. A half-day city tour (RMB 385/$47 for one person; RMB 245/$29 each for two people) gives a cursory but helpful overview of the city and scenic highlights. You can then return to these sights or discover new ones on your own.

American Express maintains an office at 339 Huanshi Donglu, in the lobby of the Guangdong International Hotel (☎ 020/8331-1771), and can arrange tours through the **Guangdong Star International Travel Company,** a branch of CITS, Dong Fang Hotel, 120 Liuhua Lu (☎ 020/8666-2427). The **Tourist Information Center** maintains a hot line at ☎ 020/8669-6882.

WHERE TO STAY

Guangzhou has over a dozen international hotels of good quality. All hotels are subject to a 15% room tax and a 5% subway tax.

In addition to the fancier accommodations below, there's a good budget choice, now called the **Shengli Binguan** but known locally by its former name, the **Victory.** This old colonial-period hotel has a new wing at 53 Shamian Lu (☎ 020/8186-2622; fax 020/8186-1062). Victory is still favored by backpacking visitors who want a clean bed, modest services, and a great location on Shamian Island; but now there are some better double rooms with private bathrooms available at RMB 570 ($70), pricey for what you get, but far below what the upmarket hotels charge. Amenities include a swimming pool, business center, and fitness room—all small—but English isn't always readily understood. There are several inexpensive dining rooms on the premises, and credit cards are accepted.

China Hotel (Zhongguo Dajiudian). *Liuhua Lu (south, across from the Canton Trade Fairgrounds).* ☎ *020/8666-6888. Fax 020/8667-7014. 1,013 units. A/C MINIBAR TV TEL. $200 double. AE, DC, JCB, MC, V.* This 18-story, five-star hotel is deluxe in every way, and is now under the international management of Marriott. Every conceivable service is at hand, from tennis, bowling, and a 25-meter outdoor pool to a coffee bar featuring Starbucks coffee. Many foreign consulates keep offices here. There's an extensive shopping mall, a "food court" in the basement, and a supermarket, not to mention a disco and a deli. This is the kind of hotel you never have to leave, unless you want to see China.

Garden Hotel (Huayuan Jiudian). *368 Huanshi Dong Lu.* ☎ *020/8333-8989. Fax 020/8332-4534. 1,038 units. A/C MINIBAR TV TEL. $180 double. AE, DC, JCB, MC, V.* Another monster hotel with everything, including a 20-lane bowling alley, this 30-story tower has been well maintained since it opened in 1984. It's a spectacular uptown version of the White Swan, with business center, pizzeria, tennis, squash, Jacuzzi, sauna, outdoor pool, and children's playground.

Holiday Inn City Centre Guangzhou (Wenhua Jiari Jiudian). *Huanshi Dong, 28 Guangming Lu. ☎ 800/465-4329 or 020/8776-6999. Fax 020/8775-3126. 431 units. A/C MINIBAR TV TEL. $140 double. AE, DC, JCB, MC, V.* The four-star, 24-story Holiday Inn is considerably cheaper than its five-star stepsisters, but it delivers Cinderellan features: large standard rooms, business center, 24-hour clinic, swimming pool, ticketing office, handicapped-accessible rooms, no-smoking rooms, free shuttle bus service, and more. It's my choice in Guangzhou, because the service is as good and the price is lower than in the bigger luxury hotels. Holiday Inn even has a large movie theater, and it's a short walk from the Friendship Store.

White Swan Hotel (Baitiane Binguan). *1 Shamian Nanjie (on Shamian Island). ☎ 020/8188-6968. Fax 020/8186-1188. 834 units. A/C MINIBAR TV TEL. $210 double. AE, DC, JCB, MC, V.* This was the first of the grand hotels in Canton. Its location on Shamian Island is pretty, and its facilities are dazzling, but it's crowded with tour groups and the service is not as good as in some of the other deluxe hotels. Yet it is a beauty, and it offers all the five-star features: not only tennis and squash but a golf driving range, a jogging track, and two outdoor pools (one a 20-meter lap pool). Its location on charming Shamian Island and its views of the Pearl River are not equaled by any other hotel.

WHERE TO DINE

Guangzhou's two most celebrated garden restaurants are **Bei Yuan Restaurant,** 202 Xiaobei Lu (☎ 020/8333-0087), and **Ban Xi Restaurant,** 151 Longjin Xi Lu (☎ 020/8181-5955). I've tried them both, and they offer superb settings, good Cantonese dishes, and delightful *yum cha* (dim sum buffets).

The single most famous Cantonese restaurant in all of Canton is the **Guangzhou Restaurant.** There are three branches around the city, but the original one, dating back to the 1930s, is at 2 Wenchang Nan Lu (☎ 020/8188-7840). With an atmospheric setting of traditional corridors and courtyards, the Guangzhou serves fairly expensive versions of classic Cantonese cuisine, from dim sum to gold-flaked seafood, as well as dishes from China's other regions.

The best flat noodles in southern China are prepared and served at **Sha He Hotel,** 2/F, 318 Xianlie Dong Lu (☎ 020/8770-5998). It's a 30-minute taxi ride from downtown Guangzhou but worth the experience. Have the hotel desk arrange reservations.

Hotels present some of the best meals in Guangzhou. My favorites for Cantonese dinners are the **Peach Blossom Restaurant** in the Garden Hotel (☎ 020/8333-8989)—decorated in a Three Kingdoms motif, offering a delightful roasted chicken—and **Yuet Fung** in the Holiday Inn (☎ 020/8776-6999)—a bright, rosy place with dim sum, hot pot (pick your own fish from the tank), and "Monk Jumps Over the Wall," a seafood gumbo double boiled for 6 hours. I can also recommend **Chaozhou Garden** in the China Hotel (☎ 020/8666-6888), where hearty dishes in the Chiu Chow style (a regional cuisine of southern China) are beautifully presented. It was here that I sat down to my first restaurant meal inside China, and my first dish was frog's legs. These hotel dinners are all among the most expensive Guangzhou offers; expect to pay big-city, big-hotel prices.

For economical eats, the city is bristling with KFCs and Pizza Huts; there's also a McDonald's. Shamian Island is beginning to offer a number of midpriced sidewalk cafes and small cafes featuring Western and Cantonese dishes—worth taking a chance on. Next door to the White Swan Hotel is **Lucy's** (5 Shamian Yi Lu; ☎ 020/8191-0203), where you can have snacks, tea, and drinks or hamburgers and steaks outside next to the Pearl River. **Kathleen's Café,** 60 Taojin Lu (☎ 020/8359-8045), is a good place for salads, sandwiches, and pizzas. It opens for lunch about 11am and often stays open for drinks until midnight. There's also a **Hard Rock Cafe** at the China Hotel (☎ 020/8666-6888). The best vegetarian restaurant in town is **Caigen Xiang** (167 Zhongshan Liu Lu; ☎ 020/8334-4363), with over 100 non-meat dishes on the Buddhist menu. Credit cards aren't accepted.

Hong Kong: The Dragon of the South

香港

On July 1, 1997, China resumed sovereignty over its richest, most cosmopolitan city, the former Crown Colony of Hong Kong. Britain had claimed the island of Hong Kong in 1841 after defeating China in the First Opium War and later extended its claim to the Kowloon peninsula, but China never recognized Britain's rule. The return of Hong Kong set off massive celebrations on the mainland.

Now known officially as the **Hong Kong Special Administrative Region (SAR),** Hong Kong was assured a high degree of autonomy for 50 years after the handover. Indeed, few changes will be obvious to visitors. Hong Kong is still an international city, vibrant and brash. It is by far the richest, most sophisticated city in China, the one place where East and West meet on confident, familiar footings.

For Westerners, Hong Kong has long been the gateway to China, to its culture as well as to its mainland cities, and it is still the best arrival point for China travelers—a dramatic, fascinating decompression chamber for the journey from the West to the East.

Note that the currency in Hong Kong is still the Hong Kong dollar (HK$), which is pegged to the U.S. dollar. One U.S. dollar equals about HK$7.7.

Diving into Hong Kong

Hong Kong is one of the most beautiful big cities in Asia. The harbor, pinched between Hong Kong Island (officially called Victoria) and the southern peninsula (Kowloon), is the focal point of the city. Day or night, the harbor view is dramatic, and the best view is from the **Waterfront Promenade** that skirts the Kowloon shore (immediately east of the Star Ferry concourse). Head there immediately after arrival to immerse yourself in the city. The skyline of Hong Kong Island, scaling the heights of steep hillsides, is among the most magnificent in the world, rivaled only by that of New York City—and at night, no city in the world can match the skyscraping lights of Hong Kong Island for sheer breathtaking beauty.

The green-and-white **Star Ferry fleet** has been crossing the harbor since 1898, and it constitutes one of the cheapest sightseeing thrills in the world. For HK$2.20 (30¢) you can ride on the upper deck in either direction (daily 6:30am to 11:30pm). Take a seat on a hardwood bench as close to the rail as possible. Hong Kong is among the world's busiest ports, and the Star Ferry cuts across a thicket of vessels calling here day and night. The harbor bristles with the container ships and navy gunboats of the world, with the luxury yachts of Asia's tycoons, and with the skiffs and unpainted junks of Hong Kong's fishermen and boat people.

After walking the harbor and riding the Star Ferry, I recommend diving deeper into Hong Kong by walking its 24-hour streets, from Kowloon's **Nathan Road,** the "Golden Mile" of duty-free shopping, to the uphill vendor alleys of the **Central District** on Hong Kong Island. Then hop one of the historic double-decker electric trams (fare HK$2/25¢) that plow back and forth from Central through the once-notorious **Wan Chai District,** 2 miles to the east, where the world of Suzie Wong once prevailed. The view of the Wan Chai shophouses and massive neon signs, of the people endlessly shopping and eating in the streets, epitomizes the energy, color, and raw pulse of life that rolls through the concrete mazes of Hong Kong like a dragon that never sleeps.

Victoria Peak

The head of the dragon is Victoria Peak, looming 1,817 feet above the harbor on Hong Kong Island. Everyone calls it the Peak, and everyone should take a trip to its summit aboard the historic **Peak Tram.** The panorama unfolds like a vast painted fan at the top. As the extraordinary travel writer Jan Morris once confessed, "For myself there is still no greater pleasure of Hong Kong than the most familiar of all such promenades: the walk around Victoria Peak, crowning massif of Hong Kong Island."

I head up to the Peak whenever I need to escape the crowded, humid, odoriferous streets of the city. From the Peak you can still see Central, Victoria Harbor, Kowloon, and the New Territories beyond, but you see all this from the high, distant remove. The first time I visited the Peak, I had just returned from 6 months of living in a dusty, developing Chinese city, and I was overwhelmed first and foremost by the sweet scent of flowers. The road around the Peak is a botanical paradise, a tropical Eden that soothes the senses which are elsewhere subject to the assault of China's urban environs.

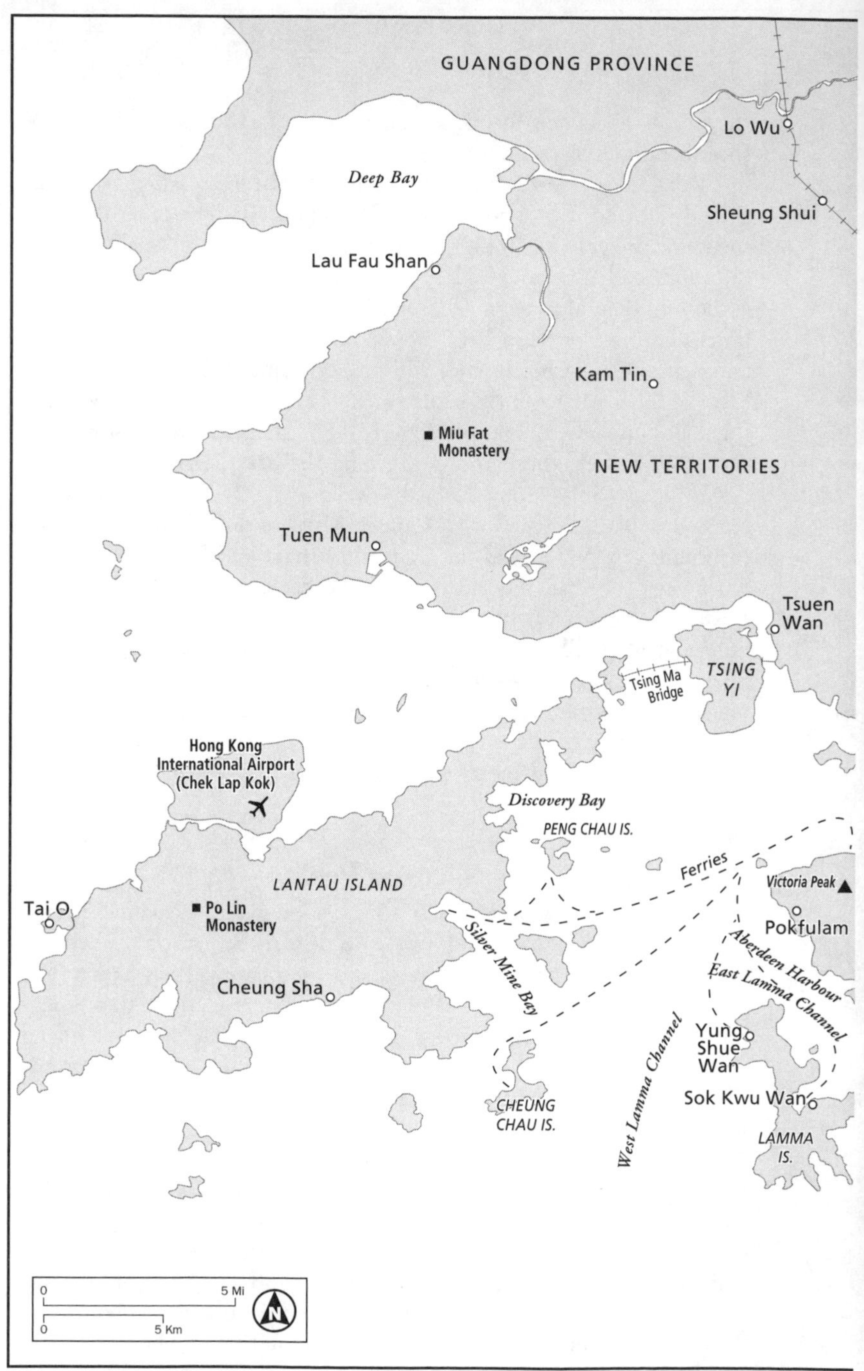
GUANGDONG PROVINCE
Lo Wu
Deep Bay
Sheung Shui
Lau Fau Shan
Kam Tin
Miu Fat Monastery
NEW TERRITORIES
Tuen Mun
Tsuen Wan
Tsing Ma Bridge
TSING YI
Hong Kong International Airport (Chek Lap Kok)
Discovery Bay
PENG CHAU IS.
Ferries
LANTAU ISLAND
Victoria Peak
Tai O
Po Lin Monastery
Pokfulam
Silver Mine Bay
Aberdeen Harbour
East Lamma Channel
Cheung Sha
West Lamma Channel
Yung Shue Wan
Sok Kwu Wan
CHEUNG CHAU IS.
LAMMA IS.
0
5 Mi
0
5 Km
N

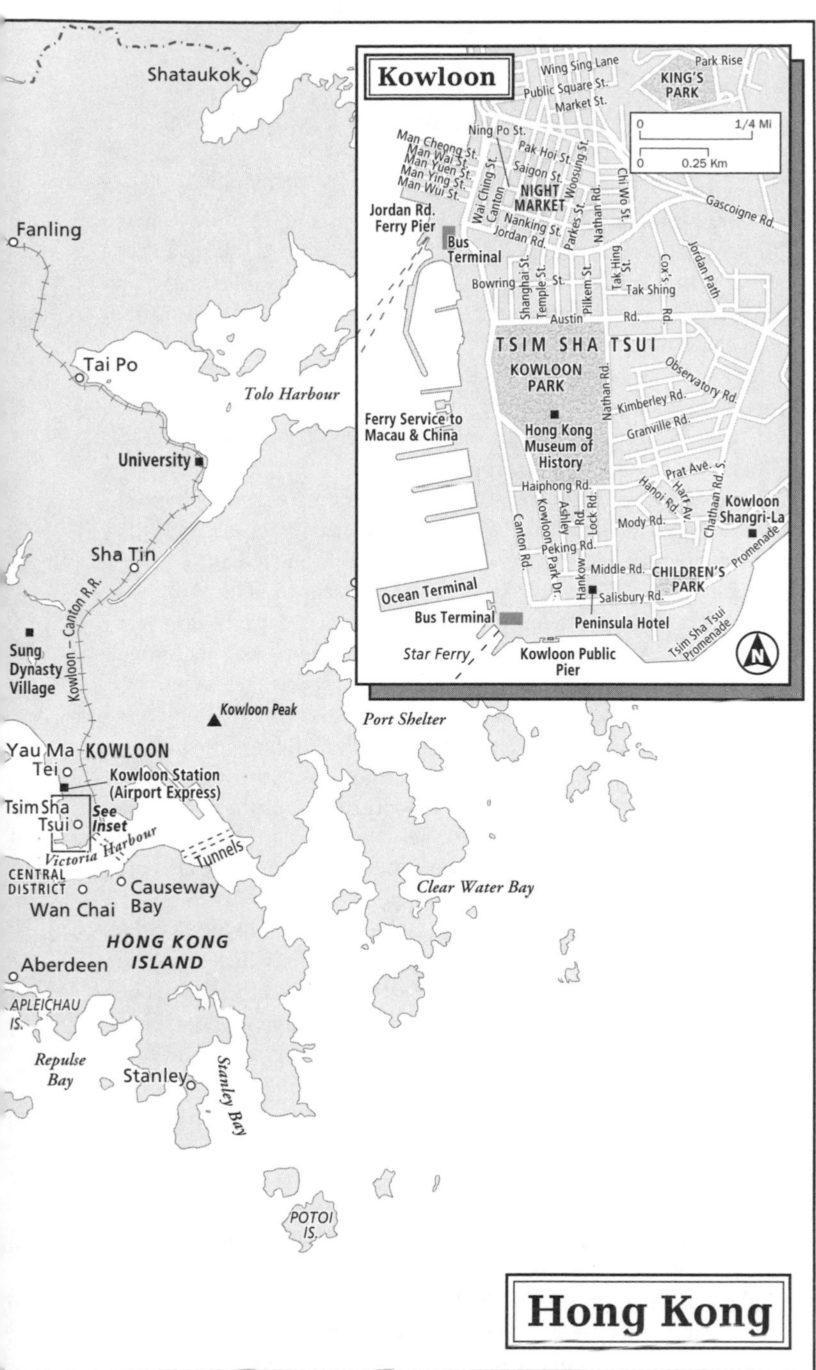
Kowloon
Wing Sing Lane
Park Rise
KING'S PARK
Public Square St.
Market St.
Ning Po St.
Pak Hoi St.
Woosung St.
Saigon St.
Man Cheong St.
Man Wai St.
Man Yuen St.
Man Ying St.
Man Wui St.
Wai Ching St.
Canton
NIGHT MARKET
Parkes St.
Nathan Rd.
Chi Wo St.
Gascoigne Rd.
Jordan Rd. Ferry Pier
Nanking St.
Jordan Rd.
Bus Terminal
Bowring St.
Shanghai St.
Temple St.
Pilkem St.
Tak Hing St.
Tak Shing
Cox's Rd.
Jordan Path
Austin Rd.
TSIM SHA TSUI
KOWLOON PARK
Observatory Rd.
Kimberley Rd.
Granville Rd.
Ferry Service to Macau & China
Hong Kong Museum of History
Haiphong Rd.
Prat Ave.
Hanoi Rd.
Hart Av.
Chatham Rd. S.
Kowloon Shangri-La
Canton Rd.
Kowloon Park Dr.
Ashley Rd.
Lock Rd.
Mody Rd.
Peking Rd.
Hankow Rd.
Middle Rd.
CHILDREN'S PARK
Promenade
Ocean Terminal
Salisbury Rd.
Bus Terminal
Peninsula Hotel
Tsim Sha Tsui Promenade
Star Ferry
Kowloon Public Pier
N
0 1/4 Mi
0 0.25 Km
Shataukok
Fanling
Tai Po
Tolo Harbour
University
Sha Tin
Kowloon – Canton R.R.
Sung Dynasty Village
Kowloon Peak
Port Shelter
Yau Ma Tei
KOWLOON
Kowloon Station (Airport Express)
Tsim Sha Tsui
See Inset
Victoria Harbour
Tunnels
CENTRAL DISTRICT
Causeway Bay
Wan Chai
Clear Water Bay
HONG KONG ISLAND
Aberdeen
APLEICHAU IS.
Repulse Bay
Stanley
Stanley Bay
POTOI IS.
Hong Kong

The easiest way up the Peak is to catch the **free shuttle bus** (the one with the open top deck), located outside the Star Ferry concourse on Hong Kong Island. From 10am to 8pm it runs every few minutes up to the Peak Tram station on Garden Road. This is one of the steepest "train" rides anywhere, reaching a gradient of 55 degrees. Take a seat in the rear car on the right side, if possible. The ride resembles that of a dignified roller-coaster. The tram stops at several stations on the way up, and the scene quickly opens wider, the perspective tilts out of whack, and the city and the harbor fall back downhill as if in a landslide. The tram covers the quarter-mile ascent in 8 minutes, but it seems to take longer. The tram operates 7am to midnight daily. Tickets are HK$18 ($2.25) one-way, HK$28 ($3.75) round-trip.

The lovely polished wooden cars on today's tram are new versions of the cars that began making this curious, neck-breaking climb in 1888, when two gentlemen named Kyrie and Hughes launched the steam-powered High Level Tramway, Asia's first cable railway. The Peak was home to the wealthy and off-limits to others in earlier days. Today there are still mansions on the top of Victoria Peak, but there's also shopping. (You can go nowhere in Hong Kong without the specter of shopping.) The tram loads and unloads inside the **Peak Tower** (1997), which is stuffed with shops, cafes, delis, and even a Ripley's Believe It or Not! "Odditorium." On the noncommercial side, there are also viewing terraces facing Central, the harbor, and Kowloon to the north. When the fog rolls over the edge of the ridge spines, this classic view of Hong Kong, the favorite of a million postcards, takes on a brooding, primordial face.

The **path** running clockwise around the Peak begins across the street from here, at Harlech Road on the left. Harlech, which is closed to motor traffic, flows into Lugard Road partway around the Peak. The walkway is wide, paved, and flat. I usually walk it in under an hour, even with a dozen stops to admire the views. The broad-leafed woodland that coats the hills and ridges in deep greens is a result of deliberate planting. The Peak, like the whole island, was largely barren rock when the British first arrived, but now it's a garden of blooms, hillside waterfalls, butterflies, and black-eared kites streaking from the heights of nature into the creases of the city canyons below. Circling the Peak yields long views over the other side of Hong Kong Island, down the deep jungle valleys that plunge into the blue-water harbors of Aberdeen, Stanley, and Repulse Bay on the south side of the island.

One day I decided to walk down to **Aberdeen** from the Peak. I could see the town—famous for its seafood, its massive floating restaurants, and the boat people who lived on junks sheltered in its harbor—and I had a map showing a walking trail to Aberdeen. I located a signpost on the road by Peak Tower. A hiker's guide suggested that I could reach Aberdeen in 45 minutes. I headed down the path, disappearing into the high bamboo grasses. The walk ended up taking me better than 2 hours, but I did manage to keep from getting lost, always heading southward and downward when the dirt trail split.

The views were lovely, of course, but the human settlements interested me more. I passed through several squatters' villages with their shacks pulled together from construction site discards. I also came across one of the largest Chinese cemeteries I'd ever seen, not far above Aberdeen. The stone chairside graves, to which pictures of the deceased are often attached in bronze frames, were swept clean of leaves here, their urns decorated with fresh flowers. I felt ready for the grave myself, as the humidity was nearing the 100% mark that afternoon, but I managed to walk through the last clearing into Aberdeen. It could have been much more challenging, of course, as I realized when I glanced over my shoulder. A true hill walker would have reversed my course, climbing from Aberdeen back up to the Peak, which from below looked as remote as the summit of a lost world.

Aberdeen

The more conventional way to get to Aberdeen, which lies on the south side of Hong Kong Island, is to catch bus no. 70 at the Exchange Square bus terminal, a few blocks west of the Star Ferry concourse in Central. The HK$4.50 (60¢) trip takes about 25 minutes. On the piers opposite Aberdeen Centre there are numerous sampan ladies who will practically haul you off the seawall to take you on a motorized tour of Aberdeen's waterborne village. If you decide you want a ride with one of the sampan ladies, bargain them down to a decent fare (half of what they're asking).

For a no-hassles tour of the flotilla, look for the **Watertours dock,** where the price is set and the driver speaks some English. A tour gives a close-up look at life on the water and inside the junks, most of which have their own color televisions.

The massive floating restaurants in Aberdeen harbor provide free ferries from their docks. You can poke around the culinary barges and head back without a meal, but if you're hungry try a few dim sum (steamed pastries). **Jumbo** is the largest and best of the floating restaurants, open daily from 7:30am to 11:30pm (☎ 852/2553-9111). Its decor includes garish red-and-gold carved dragons and cranes, with several thousand painted paper lanterns thrown up to the ceiling for good measure. Jumbo's food is rather high priced and not Hong Kong's best, but it's all good enough for one happy meal.

Before leaving Jumbo, check out the seafood tanks on the lower deck, where hundreds of specimens are enjoying their last swims. The last time I checked, the tanks were posted with a warning in English that rather mysteriously read PLEASE DON'T DISTURB THE SEAFOOD.

Shop-Walking in Kowloon

The Kowloon side of Hong Kong on the north side of the harbor is where millions go to shop and eat. They all seem to be here at once. **Nathan Road,** 4 blocks east of the Star Ferry concourse, is the main thoroughfare on the peninsula, a Golden Mile of shops that stretches far more than a mile these days. The streets and alleys parallel to and intersecting Nathan Road house still more tiny duty-free outlets. They all hawk the merchandise Hong Kong is famous for: cameras and jade, clothing and computers, luggage and furs, toys and watches. Even if you're not much of a shopper, you can't escape the bug here. Window-shopping spreads to price-comparing and ends in a purchase you didn't know you were going to make. My own weakness is luggage. If I could travel to Hong Kong without a suitcase or pack, I would do so, because I could pick up three useful pieces here for the price of one overseas.

An absolute delight in **Tsim Sha Tsui** (pronounced "chim-shaw-choy"), the district that covers the southwest Kowloon shopping district, is the landmark **Peninsula Hotel,** one of the old grande dames of Asian accommodations, and after 7 decades still one of the top 10 hotels in the world. The lobby, recently refurbished, defines the word *elegance* in the East. I never pass up a quick walk through the Peninsula. The columns are trimmed in gold, high tea looks grand, and the stringed orchestra seems to play from the mezzanine day and night. If you're in shorts or sandals, don't linger. You'll be politely booted out.

The shopping arcade in the basement of the Peninsula isn't as fussy about dress codes, but its outlets are equally elegant—and the prices soar even higher than high tea upstairs. This is the arcade to seek out if your tastes are for the designer names—Gucci, Tiffany, or Armani.

Kowloon also contains the top location for a celebratory drink—not in the stately Peninsula but down on the harbor promenade in its modern competitor, the Regent Hotel. The lobby lounge, with its wall of glass at water level, frames the Hong Kong skyline like an immense, glittering, ever-changing mural of neon, saltwater, and steel.

The streets of Kowloon are devoted to little else than shopping. One soon becomes familiar with the street stores, the Chinese arts-and-crafts stores, the huge arcades that burrow into high-rises like caves. The **New World Shopping Centre** on the Waterfront Promenade and the **Ocean Galleries** due north of Star Ferry are the most extensive retail malls, good places to go for air-conditioned window-shopping while credit cards heal themselves and revive.

The most sensible way to break this ritual of maniacal "shop-walking" is to make a detour at Kowloon Park.

Kowloon Park

I had been visiting Hong Kong for 10 years before I actually set foot inside this quiet green zone. At 35 acres, Kowloon Park is a fine refuge tucked into the heart of a frantic city. You can enter Kowloon Park at its east gate (on Nathan Road, just north of the Mosque), at its northwest gate (via the Canton Road pedestrian overpass), or at its south gate (on Haiphong Road, a block west of the Mosque, across from the Kangaroo Pub). The grounds contain waterfalls, bird ponds, a flock of pink flamingos, an outdoor sculpture garden, a Chinese classical garden (not the best I've seen), several sculpted outdoor swimming pools (and an Olympic-sized indoor facility), a totem pole from Canada, a kiosk from McDonald's, and a history museum that should not be missed.

The **Hong Kong Museum of History,** 100 Chatham Rd. S. (☎ 852/2724-9042), is housed in the British Army's former Whitfield Barracks. It's open Monday through Thursday 10am to 6pm, Saturday 10am to 6pm, Sunday and holidays 1 to 6pm (closed Fridays); admission is free. It presents a visual history of Hong Kong, arranged chronologically. Hands-on, walk-through displays include a sailing junk, a turn-of-the-century downtown street with offices, an opium den, and a Chinese pharmacy with the original cabinets and instruments in place. Luckily, nothing's for sale in this reconstruction of the past. Otherwise the museum would be as overrun as the streets of Kowloon.

Going Hollywood

Hong Kong Island has its shopping routes, too. The best window-shopping is along **Hollywood Road** and **Cat Street,** where much of China's retail trade in antiques is conducted. From the Star Ferry concourse in Central, walk straight uptown a few blocks and turn right (west) on Queen's Road Central. Keep an eye out on your left (uphill) for **Li Yuen streets** east and west (just past D'Aguilar Street). These are Hong Kong's best-known fabric alleys, narrow lanes that are stuffed on both sides with sheds of bargain silks, cottons, and upholsteries. On one pass through here I noticed that a large number of cats were being kept in the stalls to control the rodents at night. There were many stray cats as well, all of them looking far too thin. I was about to buy some cat food at a corner grocery when I noticed one draper preparing a large communal dinner of fish scraps. She set it down on the sidewalk where the gang of local cats, expecting their daily pay, quickly devoured this pile of leftovers.

If you walk 3 blocks farther west to **Jubilee Street,** you can hook up with the world's longest outdoor escalator and have a free ride uphill. This escalator is worth its own coffee-table book, as it passes over plenty of chaotically compelling intersections while transporting legions of businesspeople and striking characters.

Dismount at **Hollywood Road** and follow it west. Along this twisting street, you'll find junk and antique shops, the latter with show windows that look like museum displays of dynastic treasures, with prices to match. The furniture stores, with their blackwood and rosewood pieces, are particularly tempting, although free shipping to your home is not included.

Man Mo Temple

Keep on Hollywood Road until you reach Man Mo Temple (open daily 7am to 5pm, free admission), at the corner of **Ladder Street** (a stone staircase where the rich were once escalated up and down in sedan chairs on the shoulders of coolies). Man, the god of literature, and Mo, the god of war, preside over this temple, one of the most vibrant in China.

Man Mo Temple is rundown inside and out. It's a working temple of the sort that once held sway over China's daily affairs. Inside, the cramped hall is packed with monks, local worshippers, and the thickest clouds of incense I've ever struggled to part. The wooden chairs on display on one side of the hall were once used to carry the statues of the Man Mo Temple gods in street processions. These were probably the most important gods in town at one time, since Man Mo Temple was for many years Hong Kong's civic and cultural center for the Chinese community.

Incense spirals hang heavily from the ceiling like coiled chandeliers. These fragrant dragons can burn for a month, their pungent smoke petitioning heaven for health and wealth. Whenever I've been here a steady stream of worshippers was crowding inside as well, adding their own burning sticks to the blackening flames. Outside, in the tiny courtyard on Hollywood Road, I've seen old beggar women keeping an eye on the sacks containing their worldly possessions. Man Mo Temple has become their street home.

Immediately below Man Mo is **Cat Street** (Lascar Row), once a notorious strip of brothels, gambling dens, and boardinghouses for seamen. Today it's a flea market, stuffed with fascinating bric-a-brac, from Qing Dynasty coins to opium pipes. It was a few blocks from here, in a small cafe at the top of one of the ladderlike vendors' alleys, that I spotted the actor Jeremy Irons, in town to make a film about Hong Kong's return to China, sitting tall and alone at a simple table, his thoughts far afield.

Temple Street Night Market

Hong Kong's chief night market stretches for better than a mile up Temple Street on the Kowloon side. Take the subway to the Jordan Street stop, walk 4 blocks west from Nathan Road (starting at the Yue Hwa Department Store), and turn right up Temple Street. Every day from dusk to midnight and beyond, Temple Street is an open mall of wall-to-wall vendors offering cut-rate designer jeans and shirts, leather handbags, fake "copy" watches, and whatever's hottest in the toy factories and electronics plants of southern China.

The real action is 5 or 6 blocks up Temple Street, where Chinese opera singers come out and perform popular selections in relaxed but highly spirited performances. It's always interesting to watch the men in the audience, sitting on chairs, smoking and eating and gabbing, singing along, clapping fervently, and passing the hat.

A block north of the opera stalls, in the courtyard of a small temple, there are rows of palm readers and fortune-tellers employing birds, cards, turtle shells, old coins, and other props to divine the future of strangers. The tools of their trade are spread out on the sidewalk or placed on card tables under the light of kerosene lamps. Palm readers analyze palms for HK$154 ($20), discuss a client's fate for HK$231 ($30), and lay out a whole life's story for HK$308 ($40). Fortune-tellers use songbirds from Vietnam and mainland China to answer whatever question you pose. They pass your question on telepathically to the bird, and the bird in turn pops out of its cage and selects a card from a deck. The fortune-teller then interprets what the card says in answer to your question. The performance can cost HK$77 to HK$231 ($10 to $30).

My favorite Temple Street character has long been a streetside dentist who treats toothaches on the spot without benefit of painkillers. I've watched him work for hours hunched down over patients sitting on the dark curbside filling their cavities, attaching stainless steel, ceramic, and gold crowns, and relining false teeth (in 1 hour). He heats his tools over a flame, but he uses no drill to fill cavities. His prices tend to be ten times less than those charged in the West, but then Temple Street is a low overhead operation, small business elevated to the level of performance art.

Stanley

Clear around Hong Kong Island on its southeast side is Stanley, an ancient fishing village once known for its pirates, now known for its designer-clothing market. This is a longstanding tourist stop, so the prices may not be the lowest in Hong Kong, but the selection of name-brand fashions, linens, sports shoes, swimsuits, porcelains, and souvenirs is extensive. Despite its "touristy" reputation, I never fail to enjoy a morning or afternoon in Stanley.

Part of my enjoyment is just in getting there. At **Exchange Square bus terminus,** just west of the Star Ferry concourse in Central, I find the 6A or 6X air-conditioned double-decker bus, drop my HK$8 ($1) fare in the collection box, grab a seat upstairs, and brace myself. This is one of the most thrilling bus rides in China. Everyone drives on the left side, of course, and everyone drives at the fastest speed possible through the narrowest streets imaginable, and there's no bigger vehicle on the road than this tall bus, which seems to be hurtling up and down the tight switchbacks like a heat-seeking missile. The steep, cement-sided hill-sides whiz by, clearing the bus windows by inches. After 30 minutes of this amusement ride, you become fully accustomed to Hong Kong driving, and as the seaside scenery becomes more and more Mediterranean, you soon arrive at the village of Stanley.

The **Stanley market,** which consists of about 200 covered stalls, is across the street from the bus stop and down the hill toward the beach. At the bottom of the hill, the market splits into two sections, running left and right along the shore. I often explore the left side first, then head back to the end of the western section. Beyond there, a block of trendy bars and grills has recently sprung up, with sidewalk drinking and wonderful continental lunches and dinners with a view of Stanley beach and the sea.

As for shopping, I usually return from Stanley with a few cheap "designer-label" polo shirts (under HK$77/$10), a half-dozen "silk" ties (HK$15 to HK$23/$2 to $3 each), sometimes some "hand-embroidered" linen tablecloths, and enough "handmade" souvenirs—that are probably handmade in mainland China—to stuff a few dozen Christmas stockings. Occasionally, I pick up the Christmas stockings at Stanley market as well.

The squatters' village west of the market, where pigs once were slopped in an ingenious pen fed by a labyrinth of pipes, has been leveled to make way for a massive modern apartment, office, and shopping complex. There are still some brightly painted, hand-built fishing boats on Stanley Beach, but the fishermen have been moved south and east into new low-rise row houses.

The future of Stanley will continue to be shopping, it seems, even after a massive edifice from the past is moved into the village. The historic **Murray House,** built in 1844 in downtown Hong Kong and dismantled brick by brick in 1982 to make way for the Bank of China Tower, has already opened in Stanley—not as a museum, of course, but as a shopping gallery composed of a Chinese department store, souvenir shops, coffeehouses, and delis, and a suitably historic pub.

The Walled City

One of the least visited and most fascinating historic sites in Hong Kong is the **Kowloon Walled City Park.** Governed by neither China nor Great Britain, the old Walled City of Kowloon spent most of this century as a lawless no-man's land within walking distance of Hong Kong's Kai Tak International Airport. In 1898, when the Chinese leased the Kowloon peninsula to the British for 99 years, they retained jurisdiction over this tiny 7-acre city-fort, whether by design or through a slip of the map-maker's brush, no one knows. The next year, British soldiers entered the Walled City, ostensibly to quell civil unrest, and evicted the 500 Chinese troops stationed there. But the British never established their authority over the Walled City, nor did the Chinese ever relinquish their claim.

The Walled City became a dark sanctuary, sucking in petty criminals, illegal aliens, opium addicts, prostitutes, fugitives, and the desperately poor. By the time the Japanese occupied Hong Kong in 1941, the Walled City was in shambles. The Japanese pulled down the walls and used them to extend the airstrip along the harbor (at what became Kai Tak Airport).

At the end of World War II, squatters suddenly poured into the remains of the Walled City. By the 1970s, the Walled City consisted of a supertenement, 12 to 14 stories high. It grew organically. Some 350 buildings went up and each one fused with its neighbor, creating a rabbit warren of interlinked hallways.

Inside this tenement fortress, subject to no building regulations or fire codes, illegal enterprises flourished with impunity. Not all the enterprises were nefarious. Dentists, doctors, and lawyers practiced without licenses, charged rock-bottom rates, and built up a large outside clientele. Well through the 1980s much of the dim sum prepared in Hong Kong came from basement kitchens inside the Walled City.

I once did a walking tour of the Walled City after it was finally slated for demolition in the early 1990s. Inside was a dark labyrinth. Electricity, water (artesian wells with water pipes connected to rooftop holding tanks), and sewage (trenches) had all been jury-rigged by private developers who charged tenants for their services. The interconnected hallways were a maze for rats and humans alike. Hundreds of rusted crisscrossed pipes and bare copper wires, supporting in their webs an unspeakable mass of wet garbage, paper wrappings, plastic bags, and rotting food scraps, had been strung overhead in the narrow space between buildings.

Hong Kong conducted an unannounced census of the Walled City on January 14, 1987, turning up 33,000 residents in 8,300 premises. There were nearly 1,000 businesses, primarily food processors, plastic fabricators, and carpentry shops. On the outside perimeter, 150 unlicensed doctors and dentists maintained busy shop fronts. Residents were for the most part very poor, and many were engaged in or were the victims of crime. The Walled City was home for 20 years to an extraordinary Englishwoman named Jackie Pullinger, who lived among the residents, seeking to rehabilitate the drug addicts. Later, she launched assistance programs for residents suffering from AIDS.

The walls of this 7-acre tenement started tumbling down on March 23, 1993, when the first bulldozers arrived. The next year construction of a park and classical garden began on the site. **Kowloon Walled City Park** opened on December 22, 1995, in a ceremony presided over by the last British governor of the colony, the Rt. Hon. Christopher Patten.

This is one of the more interesting, least-visited parks in Hong Kong. Take bus no. 1 (fare HK$4.40/60¢) from the Star Ferry concourse in Kowloon, a 35-minute ride up Nathan Road and east on Boundary Street. Disembark at the second stop on Tung Street, the northern boundary of the park. The park is surrounded by a wall in the style of an earlier fortification built by the Qing government in 1843. The eight complementary landscape sectors inside the walls are also derived from Qing Dynasty models.

The Kowloon Walled City Park should be entered from the old south gate. The foundations of the original south gate and two stone plaques bearing the characters for "South Gate" and "Kowloon Walled City" were discovered here in 1994, in the excavation pit to the right of the entrance. The only historical building still standing is the **Yamen,** a courtyard complex at the center of the park that served as the military command. On exhibit here are old cannons and photographs of the evolution of the old Walled City from fortress to tenement. In one courtyard there is a stone monument honoring Jackie Pullinger for her decades of charitable work.

Frequented by neighborhood Chinese—mostly grandparents and grandchildren spending time together—the Walled City has been transformed yet again, this time into Hong Kong's loveliest classic garden, with graceful pavilions, long covered corridors, garden ponds, and goldfish streams that seem to flow out of an antique century.

The Pink Dolphin

Hong Kong's most beautiful marine animal is also its most endangered—the pink dolphin *(Sousa chinensis).* No more than 150 remain in Hong

Kong waters, and their delicate habitat is growing both ever smaller and more polluted. Pink dolphins were first reported in the waters of southern China in the 7th century during the Tang Dynasty, and they were first sighted by Western travelers in 1637. Without a guide, you'd probably never know that there was a single dolphin pod in these busy waters. This is the most beautiful species of dolphins I've ever seen but also the shyest of the dashing sea animals that Melville called "the lads that always live before the winds."

The dolphins feed over a wide area, some of it concentrated in the new **Sha Chau and Lung Kwu Chau Marine Park,** a 5-square-mile sector of seawater north of the airport. This "dolphin sanctuary" is subject to the drainage of the Pearl River, which carries much of the sewage and industrial waste of southern China. The new airport has also destroyed portions of the pink dolphin's coastline, and even within the new "sanctuary," gill-netting, dredging, and the off-loading of oil tankers go on unabated. The number of pink dolphins is in steady decline as a result, and Hong Kong's commitment to wildlife conservation and environmental protection is notably and traditionally unenthusiastic. Nonetheless, the pink dolphin continues to swim freely in these dangerous waters.

You can still see these rare creatures by booking passage on a **Dolphinwatch cruise,** the best water tour in Hong Kong. Dolphinwatch sails the waters between massive **Lantau Island** (home of the new Chek Lap Kok Airport) and the New Territories (near the ports of Tuen Mun and Castle Peak), an hour northwest of Hong Kong harbor. The scenery is fascinating enough to justify a day's cruise, but the goal is to spot the elusive, shy pink dolphins, usually swimming in groups of half a dozen, breaking the surface and then diving in search of a meal.

The cruises last for 4 hours. A researcher—often founder Bill Leverett—delivers commentary in English and endeavors to find pods of pink dolphins. The dolphins often surface quite close to the craft, making for spectacular sightings and photos. On occasional Sundays, Dolphinwatch also offers a 7-hour cruise on a much larger two-deck ship. Lunch is taken in a local cafe in the quaint town of Tai O during a stopover on Lantau Island. Since Sunday is such an impossibly crowded day to sightsee anywhere in Hong Kong, a Dolphinwatch cruise (whether the half-day or full-day version) is a weekend adventure hard to match.

On my first cruise, after scanning the waters for more than an hour, we spotted a dozen pink dolphins sporting in the waters in front of the Castle Peak Power Station. We spent 2 hours circling the group. Adult dolphins are $3^1/2$ to 8 feet in length. They are a dazzling comic-strip pink, and no one knows why. The infants, who stick close to their parents, are nearly black, the distinctive blush tones emerging only as they mature.

To find out the current schedule, ask at the **Hong Kong Tourist Association (HKTA)** office at the Star Ferry terminal in Kowloon or, better yet, contact **Dolphinwatch** directly (☎ 852/2984-1414; fax 852/2984-7799). Tickets are usually sold in advance at the **Splendid Tours** desk in the lobby of the Sheraton Hotel, 20 Nathan Rd., Kowloon. Tour days and tour lengths vary with the season, but currently 4-hour morning cruises are offered on Wednesday, Friday, and Sunday, for HK$280 ($37) adults, HK$140 ($18) children under 12. Tickets for special 7-hour lunch cruises (when offered) cost HK$400 ($50).

Cheung Chau Island

Three of Hong Kong's 230 outlying islands—Lantau, Lamma, and Cheung Chau—are served by hourly passenger ferries from piers in the Central District. The 60-minute cruise is a delight, and so are the islands, which offer a restorative escape from the big city. The best getaway is Cheung Chau Island, 7 miles west of Hong Kong, an old fishing village without cars, its harbor teeming with sampans and junks.

Cheung Chau is a chapter out of Old China. This 1-square-mile home to seafarers and pirates has an active waterfront, lively markets, a traditional village, and white-sand beaches where the windsurfing is world-class. The ferry from Hong Kong pulls into the western harbor and docks at the **Praya,** the waterfront promenade lined with vibrant pink and blue buildings, their ornate balconies suggesting a Mediterranean port. You can walk directly through the old village and across the island to the eastern beaches in just 10 minutes, but the scenic route first leads north (to your left) along the Praya.

The Praya is filled with cafes and food stalls selling hot noodles and shrimp dumpling (wonton) soups. The harbor is packed with rows of junks. These are the homes of Cheung Chau's water people, who live and fish from their floating houses. About 3,000 of the island's 23,000 people live year-round on the water.

If you walk north and west to the end of the beach road, you come to the **dry docks** where large junks are still being framed and planked by hand, built in the time-honored manner by craftsmen who keep no blueprints but retain entire designs in their memories. They don't mind if you stop in at their tin-roofed sheds to have a look. Even at its birth, a junk is a gorgeous vessel, its horizontal planks curving in golden stripes from a remarkably high stern to a broad bow, each piece of the puzzle shaped and laid in place perfectly, with room left in the seams for the wood to expand as it cures.

About 5 blocks from the pier, you'll see the **Pak Tai Temple** on your right, just past the community basketball court. Pak Tai is the god of the sea, the great protector of seafarers, and still highly revered on Cheung Chau. The temple was built in 1786. It welcomes visitors. Inside, Pak Tai is wearing a golden crown. His reign over the sea is symbolized by the snake and turtle pinned under his feet. An iron sword from the Song Dynasty (A.D. 960–1279) is ensconced beside the temple altar. During the Bun Festival (held every spring on dates determined at the last minute by village elders), Tai Pak and the sword are carried into the courtyard in a century-old sedan chair to preside over the celebrations. The side halls of the small temple are worth inspecting, too. Carvings of the Green Dragon and the White Tiger are enshrined here.

From the temple, cut through the old-fashioned village. The lanes are narrow. The shops and cafes frequently contain bedrooms and offices upstairs. Family clans and trade guilds have survived intact. There are several street shrines to the Earth god, incense always burning on their stone shelves. Many of the island's elders, dressed in long vests and leaning on wooden canes, stop every day to pray. One of the shrine inscriptions reads "If your heart is warm, you will be blessed in old age."

The east side of the island is another world, designed for leisure and water sports. At **Coral Beach (Kwun Yum Wan)** and **Morning Beach (Tung Wan),** a local islander, Lee Lai Shan, perfected her windsurfing skills. She went on to become the first and only Hong Kong citizen to win an Olympic gold medal. Heading down the beach, past the six-story Warwick Hotel, the lower beach road leads out to a **rock carving** from the Bronze Age. These geometric patterns were etched into the sea rocks of Cheung Chau about 3,000 years ago by primitive boat people whose name and fate are lost to history.

If you decide to stay a night or two on Cheung Chau, at either the **Warwick Hotel** (☎ 852/2981-0081; fax 852/2981-9174) or one of the vacation villas the touts on the Praya recommend, you'll have time to explore the more distant temples, cemeteries, and sea rocks on the large southern half of the island. You'll also have time to climb to the viewpoint at the end of the beach road on the northeastern tip of Cheung Chau. HKTA sells a **Cheung Chau Walking Tour** booklet keyed to a useful map of the little island for HK$35 ($5).

From the Warwick Hotel it's a short walk back across the hourglass waist of the island to the Praya. The village of Cheung Chau is densely clogged with old shophouses, fish counters, Chinese pharmacies, bakeries, herbalist stalls, incense shops, bamboo hat stores, mahjong gambling dens, and plenty of curio shops, pubs, and cafes. The fresh shrimp is absolutely superb here. Any cafe will steam up a plateful—you won't even need a sauce.

After staying out on Cheung Chau a few days once, I found it increasingly difficult to return to Hong Kong. The pace of life on this oasis of Old China becomes mesmerizing. As night falls, everyone comes down to the Praya, which is lit by electric lights, lanterns, and candles. The catch of the day sizzles on sidewalk tables. The old women of Cheung Chau, their bare feet up on benches, exchange the day's gossip. Children race by helter-skelter on their bikes. Grandfathers bring their prized songbirds out to show, hanging the bamboo cages on a tree branch or lantern post. Cats and dogs patrol the streets. Cheung Chau is what Hong Kong must have been generations ago before it became a British colony, an international moneymaking machine, and finally China's gateway to the future.

Big Buddha

Hong Kong's largest outlying island, **Lantau Island,** is home to the big airport, but its biggest attraction (at least until 2005, when Asia's second Disneyland opens here) is the big bronze statue of Buddha at the Po Lin Monastery. The statue is worth a look, and Lantau Island is worth exploring, too.

Hong Kong claims a population of 800,000 Buddhist followers. About 40 of them are resident monks and nuns at **Po Lin (Precious Lotus) Monastery,** which is famous for its vegetarian lunches served from noon to 4:30pm daily, at a cost of HK$60 to HK$100 ($8 to $13). The Tian Tan Buddha towers over the prayer halls and shrines on the hill above; a round altar to heaven leads to the steep 260-stair walkway that tethers this Buddha to Earth. This is the second tallest bronze Buddha in the world (the tallest is the one recently created on the shores of Lake Tai on mainland China). Lantau Island's Buddha was actually constructed on the mainland, beginning in 1986. Five years later the 202 bronze pieces (costing about $9 million) were shipped to Hong Kong and assembled.

The hundred-foot-tall Big Buddha is now seated in the lotus position on a lotus flower, right palm serenely raised, atop a three-story exhibition hall. Inside the hall are souvenir stands, a mural depicting events in Buddha's life, signs requesting silence (not observed), and an ancestral hall with electric incense burners and wall plaques naming and picturing the deceased (for which families pay a memorial fee of HK$10,000/$1,300). On the top level of the memorial hall, right under the Buddha, are relics said to be from the real Buddha. Po Lin Monastery claims 18 bone fragments and four teeth of the historical Buddha. In the memorial hall, you can see, if you look very carefully, a tiny fragment of Buddha's bone, like a pearl, on display under a delicate glass cover. The awe-inspiring Buddha statue itself seems to rise above the all-too-human throes of tourism and worship. Buddha's elongated ears, by the way, represent longevity; the swastika-like mark, the Chinese symbol for 10,000, connotes wisdom.

Lantau Island (population 30,000) has its more rural pleasures as well. It is twice the size of Hong Kong Island, but its entire population could be placed in a handful of Hong Kong high-rises. Many Lantau islanders still make a living by fishing or salt-processing. Lantau's peaks are high and remote (many accessible only by hiking trails); the name Lantau means "Broken Hat," a term for something wild and remote. The island's beaches are often deserted. **Cheung Sha (Long Sands),** a 2-mile strand on the south (non–airport) side of the island, does have changing rooms and lifeguards in the summer. Cows often rest on the bluffs here, part of about 300 set free by villagers (who refuse to kill them now, in true Buddhist fashion, because their ancestors worked for the villager's ancestors). The beach is also home to tiger sharks (kept at bay from swimmers by an underwater fence), and the surrounding hills still harbor cobras, green bamboo snakes, and rare barking deer.

The cutest town on Lantau Island is **Tai O,** a 400-year-old port on the west coast that prospered until the 1950s by panning salt. Today its main enterprises are fishing and fish processing. It's a perfect town to stroll. Life is slow, the lanes are narrow, the dogs fall asleep by the steps, fish dry on clotheslines, the shophouses sell medicinal herbs and strange creatures from the sea, and a rope-drawn, flat-bottom ferry, pulled by local Tanka women, crosses the creek that divides the town (although there is now an arched footbridge as well). Tai O is a delight, touristed but somehow undiluted by the modern world.

It's easy to book a **day tour** (see "Tours & Stratagems," below) to see the monastery, Buddha, mountains, and beaches of Lantau Island, with lunch at Tai O, but you can also go on your own, at considerably more leisure, taking a ferry to Lantau and using the local buses or taxis for transport. But there aren't many taxis here. The number of private cars is quite restricted, and by law there are only 50 taxis on the whole island (as opposed to 50 taxis per block in Hong Kong).

PRACTICAL INFORMATION

ORIENTATION & WHEN TO GO

Hong Kong is now a Special Administrative Region (SAR) of the People's Republic of China, but there have been virtually no changes affecting foreign visitors. Most regulations and institutions from the days of British rule remain intact. Visitors from the West will feel more at home in Hong Kong than in any other Chinese city.

The majority of Hong Kong's over seven million citizens speak Cantonese (the southern Chinese dialect), many speak English, and many more are learning Mandarin (*putonghua*, the official spoken language of China). Signs are frequently in English, and shopkeepers and waiters often speak some English. Shopping and eating choices are also manifold for foreigners in Hong Kong. The standard of living is roughly 10 times higher in Hong Kong than on the mainland. While a combination of post-handover blues and the Asian economic downturn of the late 1990s saw Hong Kong tourism plunge, the city's number of annual visitors is once again topping 10 million.

Most of the urban population is collected along the northern shore of Hong Kong Island and across the harbor on the southern tip of Kowloon peninsula. Hotels and shopping are concentrated in Tsim Sha Tsui (TST) on the Kowloon side and in Central, Admiralty, Wan Chai, and Causeway Bay on the island. The island is connected to Kowloon by the Star Ferry system, the underground subway (MTR), and a highway tunnel. Transportation is highly efficient and inexpensive.

Located at the southeast tip of mainland China, Hong Kong is warm year-round. Summer months (June, July, August) are uncomfortably hot and humid, winters a bit cool and cloudy, making April, May, October, and November the prime months to visit.

ENTRY REQUIREMENTS

Americans, Australians, New Zealanders, Canadians, and British citizens are only required to have a valid passport to enter Hong Kong. Upon arrival, the passport for travelers from all these nations is stamped with a Hong Kong visa valid for 3 months. Travel into mainland China requires the purchase of a separate visa, as in the past.

MONEY

Hong Kong maintains its own currency system. Rates are pegged to the American dollar, at about HK$7.7 to US$1 (HK$1 = US13¢). When you arrive, it's useful to convert a few dollars (or RMB) to Hong Kong dollars at the airport banks. Hong Kong has an exchange counter on nearly every corner and in every hotel, but slightly better rates are given by major banks in Kowloon and Central.

GETTING THERE

By Plane Hong Kong is served by most of the world's major airlines. **Cathay Pacific** (☎ 800/233-2742), renowned for its high level of cabin service, is Hong Kong's flagship airline. **United Airlines** (☎ 800/538-2929) also has daily service from North America. **Dragonair** (☎ 800/233-2742) provides the best service between Hong Kong and mainland Chinese cities. Hotels can book tickets on international and domestic airlines (including Chinese airlines) and provide transfers to the airport.

The new airport at **Chek Lap Kok** is on the outlying island of Lantau in the South China Sea. It's immense, but easy to navigate, and its shopping areas offer a good range of souvenir purchases. Airport departure tax for all outbound passengers ages 12 or more is HK$50 ($6.70). Airport flight information is available in English 24 hours a day, ☎ 2181-0000.

There are several options for getting from the airport into the city. The high-speed **Airport Express (AEL)** railway is seamlessly integrated into the airport lobby, where tickets are sold at kiosks and in machines. These trains operate from 6am to 1am daily, taking 12 minutes to reach Tsing Yi Station, 10 minutes to Kowloon Station, and 23 minutes to Hong Kong Station (Central District). Free **shuttle buses** connect passengers to 21 hotels from the Hong Kong and Kowloon AEL stations. Single journey rail tickets (including same-day return journey) cost HK$40 ($5) to Tsing Yi, HK$60 ($8) to Kowloon, and HK$70 ($9.50) to Hong Kong (children ages 3 to 13 about half-price). Round-trip tickets cost HK$70 ($10), HK$100 ($16) and HK$120 ($19) respectively and are valid for 1 month. Credit cards are accepted (AE, DC, JCB, MC, V). Visitors can also catch free shuttle buses from many hotels, complete check-in at many airlines in the Hong Kong or Kowloon AEL stations, and ride the train back to the airport for departure (a procedure that went extremely smoothly when I tried it).

Other options from the airport include the **Airbus,** which has eight routes with stops at all major airports. Check in the arrival hall for schedules and ticket purchase, then follow the Airbus signs outside to the correct stop. The Airbuses to Hong Kong Island (A11, A12) run every 15 minutes between 6am and midnight and cost HK$40 (US$5.30) (A11) and HK$45 (US$6) (A12). To Kowloon hotels and stops, the schedule is as frequent, the price a bit lower: HK$33 ($4.40) (A21) and HK$39 ($5.20) (A22). Fare can be paid upon boarding, too (exact change and HK currency required). Route maps and stop-by-stop recordings (in English) are provided.

Red **taxis** from the airport serve Hong Kong Island and Kowloon; green taxis serve the New Territories; blue taxis serve Lantau Island. To Hong Kong Island, taxis charge HK$325 (US$42) and up; to Kowloon, HK$255 (US$34) and up. Many hotels also provide shuttle bus services by prior arrangement.

The airport also provides a hotel reservation system and HKTA information services (both outlets open daily 6am to midnight), a left-luggage counter, and 12 money exchange outlets.

By Train There are several direct trains daily from **Guangzhou (Canton)** leaving from the Hung Hom Railway Station in East Tsim Sha Tsui (Kowloon). The 3-hour trip costs HK$250 ($32) and tickets can be booked at CTS (see below) or the train station. There is a new luxury 29-hour overnight train from Kowloon Station to **Beijing** (train no. 97 departing from Hong Kong to Beijing, train no. 98 returning from Beijing to Hong Kong), priced at HK$707 to HK$1,192 ($92 to $155), depending on the sleeper class. An equivalent 29-hour overnight service to **Shanghai** (train no. 99 departing from Hong Kong, train no. 100 returning), is priced at HK$623 to HK$1,038 ($81 to $135), depending on sleeper class.

By Ship From the **China Hong Kong ferry terminal** (6 blocks up Canton Road from the Star Ferry concourse in Tsim Sha Tsui, Kowloon), there are many options, including the overnight ship or 2-hour jet boat to **Guangzhou (Canton)** and multiple-night voyages on clean but basic passenger liners to **Xiamen** and **Shanghai,** at about half the ticket price of air flights. Book tickets at the ferry terminal, hotels, or China Travel Service.

GETTING AROUND

By Subway For transportation in Hong Kong, I rely upon the subway system, the **Mass Transit Railway (MTR).** It is clean and fast. All stops are announced in English. The MTR operates throughout Kowloon and Hong Kong Island from 6am to 1am. Purchase ticket cards for each trip at station booths or from machines (price based on distance, HK$4 to HK$26/60¢ to $3.50). I usually buy a stored-value **Octopus Card** (HK$100/$12.50) for convenience in getting through the turnstiles.

By Taxi Taxis are inexpensive, with typical trips around town costing HK$20 to HK$40 ($2.60 to $5.20). Add HK$20 ($2.60) for Cross-Harbour Tunnel, HK$30 ($3.90) for Eastern Harbour Tunnel and Lantau Link, and HK$45 ($5.80) for Western Harbour Tunnel. Not all drivers understand English. Tip with leftover change.

By Ferry/Tram The **Star Ferries,** which operate from 6:30am to 11:30pm and cost HK$2.20 (30¢), are a superb way to cross the harbor. Electric trams, which operate from 6am to 1am and cost HK$1.60 (20¢), are the scenic way to go east or west along the shore of Hong Kong Island.

TOURS & STRATAGEMS

Tours/Information The **Hong Kong Tourist Association (HKTA)** makes touring a breeze. Its offices are staffed with helpful English-speaking personnel. You'll also find a library of sightseeing brochures, and free copies of that indispensable visitors' bible, the monthly *Official Hong Kong Guide,* which covers nearly everything you need to know, from where to shop to where to eat. The HKTA office at the **Star Ferry concourse** on the Kowloon side is open daily 8am to 6pm. The HKTA office downstairs in **The Center,** 99 Queen's Rd. Central, on Hong Kong Island (quite a long walk southwest of the Star Ferry concourse), is also open daily 9am to 6pm. HKTA maintains a multilingual information hot line (☎ 852/2508-1234), a 24-hour fax information line in English (fax 852/900-6977-1128), and a Web site (www.hkta.org).

HKTA operates some of the best specialized **tours** in Hong Kong, including a horse-racing tour, a heritage tour of a walled village, a "family insight tour" focusing on a day in the life of an ordinary Hong Kong resident, a 6-hour "Land Between Tour" of the New Territories north of Kowloon, a twice-weekly "Morning Tea and Tai Ji Tour" (featuring a tai ji exercise lesson, tea drinking, and a dim sum lunch), and a twice-weekly "Healthy Living Tour" (with a qi gong exercise class, a stroll through traditional drug stores, and a "tonic lunch"). Tours cost from

HK$385 to HK$490 ($50 to $65) per person; some include lunch. Book all these tours at either the HKTA office or at your hotel tour desk. HKTA also serves as broker for other approved tour operators that cover Hong Kong, Lantau Island, evening dinner cruises, and the Dolphinwatch cruises.

Mainland China Visits For China travel arrangements, including visa purchase, transportation, hotels, and package tours, I use the state-run **China Travel Service (CTS),** 27–33 Nathan Rd., Kowloon (one floor up in the Alpha House, which is actually a few steps west off Nathan Road, down Peking Road; ☎ 852/2315-7149; fax 852/2721-7757). CTS has always handled my requests efficiently and inexpensively. I've booked air flights, hotel rooms, and visas to China. CTS also provides quick passport/visa photo service.

WHERE TO STAY

Hong Kong has more than a dozen five-star international hotels, representing many of the world's most famous hotel chains. Several of the hotels have achieved legendary status, including the **Peninsula** in Kowloon and the **Mandarin Oriental** in Central. High property values continue to drive hotel rates sky-high, so the rooms in the moderate-to-inexpensive level are quite slummy. Some doubles in the YMCA now cost US$100 a night or more. Room rates posted here can be reduced considerably by travel agents, reservation services, and seasonal specials. All are subject to 13% tax, except the YMCA (10%).

Conrad International Hong Kong. *Pacific Place, 88 Queensway, Central (Admiralty MTR stop).* ☎ *800/445-8667 or 852/2521-3838. Fax 852/2521-3888. 513 units, including 46 suites. A/C MINIBAR TV TEL. $250 double. AE, DC, JCB, MC, V.* Hilton's flagship hotel in China, the recently renovated 61-story Conrad is a deluxe tower with very large rooms (starting at 452 square feet), non-allergenic pillows, in-room safes and fax machines, robes, slippers, Italian marble bathrooms with dual sinks and separate tubs and showers—in a word, sheer luxury, with a service level to match (not to mention a yellow rubber ducky in every bathtub). The hotel is directly connected to the Pacific Place shopping complex.

Amenities: Outdoor heated swimming pool, health and fitness club, Jacuzzi, sauna, large business center, conference rooms, newsstand, 24-hour clinic, concierge, valet, 24-hour room service, same-day dry cleaning and laundry, newspaper delivery, nightly turndown, twice-daily maid service, baby-sitting, express checkout, free downtown shuttle bus.

Holiday Inn Golden Mile Hong Kong. *50 Nathan Rd., Kowloon (across from Tsim Sha Tsui MTR stop).* ☎ *800/465-4329 or 852/2369-3111. Fax 852/2369-8016. 600 units, including 8 suites. A/C MINIBAR TV TEL. $275 double. AE, DC, JCB, MC, V.* This well-situated hotel, in the heart of shopping's Golden Mile, is nearly always full, and for good reason: Its services are superb, fully five-star, even if the hotel facilities are rated a star lower. The public areas, exterior, and restaurants were recently renovated. Rooms all have double or king-size beds, work desks, small sofas, and safes; bathrooms come with marble countertops, hair dryers, and vigorous showers. The lobby is always bustling and the staff knows how to please its Western guests. A special new feature: a complimentary hospitality lounge for guests who arrive early or depart late, complete with sofas, newspapers, telephones, TVs, and changing/shower facilities (a great idea).

Amenities: Rooftop outdoor heated swimming pool, health club, Jacuzzi, sauna, business center, conference rooms, tour desk, beauty salon, newsstand, concierge, valet, 24-hour room service, same-day dry cleaning and laundry, nightly turndown, baby-sitting, shopping arcade, deli, hospitality lounge.

Island Shangri-La. *Pacific Place, Supreme Court Rd., Central (above the Pacific Place Shopping Center at Admiralty MTR stop).* ☎ *800/942-5050 or 852/2877-3838. Fax 852/2521-8742. 565 units, including 34 suites. A/C MINIBAR TV TEL. $310 double. AE, DC, JCB, MC, V.* The tallest hotel in Hong Kong, the Island combines European luxury and design with Asian touches, such as the 18-story atrium draped with a 150-foot 250-panel silk mural of China's classic landscapes. The lobby, restaurants, health club, pool, and ballrooms occupy the podium (levels 5 to 8); the guest rooms are on levels 39 to 55; and the Restaurant Petrus is on the top floor (56). The rooms, the largest on Hong Kong Island, have an old-world elegance, not to mention Austrian crystal chandeliers and marble-top writing desks. The Library (on level 39) is a dream room of classic European design with its own concierge, where you can browse through or borrow books, magazines, and periodicals from the two-story shelves or stick around for high tea (3 to 5:30pm).

Amenities: Large indoor pool, health club, Jacuzzi, sauna, business center, conference rooms, tour desk, beauty salon, florist, shopping arcade, newsstand, 24-hour clinic, concierge, 24-hour room service, same-day dry cleaning and laundry, newspaper delivery, nightly turndown, twice-daily maid service, baby-sitting, express checkout.

Kowloon Shangri-La. *64 Mody Rd., Kowloon (on the harbor, next to East Tsim Sha Tsui high-speed ferry to Central).* ☎ *800/942-5050 or 852/2721-2111. Fax 852/2723-8686. 725 units, including 20 suites. A/C MINIBAR TV TEL. $250 double. AE, DC, JCB, MC, V.* This luxury hotel has one of the best waterfront views in Hong Kong. The restaurants, health club, and business center rate among Hong Kong's very best. The decor features white marble, from the lobby to the bathrooms. All rooms come with safes, coffeemakers, and hair dryers. I like it here because the service is attentive, the view of the harbor uninterrupted, the location quiet, and the local phone calls free.

Amenities: Indoor swimming pool, health club, Jacuzzi, sauna, 24-hour business center, conference rooms, tour desk, beauty salon, florist, shopping arcade, newsstand, 24-hour clinic, concierge, valet, baby-sitting, 24-hour room service, same-day dry cleaning and laundry, newspaper delivery, nightly turndown, twice-daily maid service, express checkout.

The Peninsula Hong Kong. *Salisbury Rd., Kowloon (between the ferry and subway terminals in Tsim Sha Tsui).* ☎ *800/262-9467 or 852/2920-2888. Fax 852/2722-4170. 246 units, including 54 suites. A/C MINIBAR TV TEL. $390 double (original bldg), $460 (new tower), $600 harbor view. AE, DC, JCB, MC, V.* The classic hotel in Hong Kong, perhaps in all Asia, the "Pen" has been a landmark since it opened in 1928. Its facilities are without peer. Its celebrated lobby epitomizes elegance; its high tea, service; and its Rolls-Royce fleet, luxury and history. Service remains impeccable; some staff members have worked here for decades. The five floors of the grand old hotel include 132 original rooms. The 30-story tower added in 1994 features more rooms. All rooms are exceptionally equipped, measure 460 to 500 square feet, and are decorated in a classic European style with Chinese touches. Wicker lounge chairs, laserdisc/CD players, fax machines, and built-in bedside headphones are standard, and all bathrooms come with two washbasins, separate showers and tubs, and a TV set. From high tea in the grand lobby to fusion dishes and drinks at the avant-garde Felix on the rooftop floors, the Peninsula has dining venues to match its rooms and services. Over 130 international designer-label boutiques and shops make up its two stories of shopping.

Amenities: Roman-style indoor/outdoor swimming pool, health club and spa, Jacuzzi, sauna, 24-hour business center, conference rooms, tour desk, beauty salon, florist, shopping arcade, newsstand, concierge, valet, butler service, baby-sitting, 24-hour room service, same-day dry cleaning and laundry, newspaper delivery, nightly turndown, twice-daily maid service, in-house nurse, express checkout.

Salisbury YMCA. *41 Salisbury Rd., Kowloon (next door to the Peninsula Hotel, 3 blocks east of the Star Ferry).* ☎ *852/2369-2211. Fax 852/2739-9315. 365 units, including 62 suites. A/C MINIBAR TV TEL. $95 double, $24 dorm bed. AE, DC, JCB, MC, V.* Superb location and clean, well-appointed rooms with room safes, satellite TV, and coffeemakers—this is one of the world's most deluxe Ys and Hong Kong's best mid-price deal. It is often booked up several months in advance. Guests have access to the Y's two indoor swimming pools, fitness center, squash courts, climbing wall, tour desk, bookshop, and hair salon. There's even a concierge. The Mall Cafe off the lobby is a pleasant bargain cafeteria with fixed-price breakfasts, lunches, and dinners (for under $10). Guests can also order room service from 7am to 11pm. While the service, food, and amenities aren't the equal of those at the nearby luxury hotels, the price is a half or a third (and the room tax is less). The dorm rooms (two bunk beds, separate storage closets) are same-sex, four to a compartment, and far cleaner than hostels and dorms elsewhere in Hong Kong.

Bargain Choices Unfortunately, Hong Kong is the last place to visit if you want to save money on accommodations. There are no decent, cheap lodgings in the city. I recently stayed at the 75-room, air-conditioned **Chungking House,** Block A, fourth and fifth floors (☎ 852/2366-5362; fax 852/2721-3570), in the notorious Chungking Mansion, 40 Nathan Rd., Kowloon. This is the most "deluxe" of the dozens of hostels and guesthouses wedged into this 16-story tenement. The room was spacious but run-down and rife with cockroaches, for whose company I paid nearly $50 a night. The elevator, the back stairs, and the tout-ridden lobby of Chungking Mansion must be negotiated to be believed.

Cleaner rooms are available a block up Nathan Road in Mirador Mansion (56–58 Nathan Rd.) at the **Man Hing Lung Guesthouse** in Flat F2 on the 14th floor (☎ 852/2311-8807; fax 852/2311-6669). The price is about the same. The drawback is room size: These are the smallest doubles imaginable, with narrow bathrooms that become instant stand-up showers. There's no closet. Two friends of mine actually succeeded in doing their laundry in the room's wastebasket. They liked the place, though, finding it clean and economical. There are those who like Chungking Mansion, too.

WHERE TO DINE

In Hong Kong, eating is nearly as important as breathing. Hong Kong residents routinely spend far more of their income on dining than anyone else. The competition this spawns results in some of the best restaurants in the world, ranging from elegant and expensive Chinese seafood emporiums with views of the harbor to single-table street stalls frequented by connoisseurs of regional cuisines. Hong Kong's choice of Western restaurants is also considerable. You could stay a month here without chewing a single bite of Chinese chow.

Hong Kong has about 10,000 registered restaurants; more than half of them are listed and mapped on two on-line services: www.foodeasy.com and www.yp.ht/dining.com/. My listing here is modest in number, but thoroughly field-tested.

Avenue. *50 Nathan Rd., Tsim Sha Tsui (1st floor, Holiday Inn Golden Mile). ☎ 852/2315-1118. Reservations recommended. Fixed-price meals HK$160–HK$200 ($20–$25). AE, DC, JCB, MC, V. Mon–Sat noon–2:30pm, 6pm–midnight. Closed Sun. EUROPEAN.* A fresh, smart, trendy spot with close-up views of busy Nathan Road. The dishes are generally Mediterranean, but they're inventive and not always easy to classify: salsa on melba toast, medallions of chicken on pepper and pumpkin polenta, baked cod and clams, and a fine crème brûlée for dessert. Excellent vegetarian meals are available, too. The interior—white walls, white marble floor, a central oval bar, modern paintings—is as stylish as the service.

California. *30–32 D'Aguilar St., Central (Ground floor, California Tower, Lan Kwai Fong area). ☎ 852/2521-1345. Reservations recommended. Main courses HK$80–HK$160 ($10–$20). AE, DC, JCB, MC, V. Daily noon–2:30pm, 6–10:30pm. AMERICAN.* With the upbeat setting of an upscale West Coast bar, in full keeping with the lively neighborhood, California has been churning out tasty new California dishes for 2 decades. The pizzas, pastas, and hamburgers are tried and true, but this restaurant is known for its more creative concoctions: mu shu pancakes with fried chicken, for example, or shrimp burritos.

East Ocean Seafood Restaurant. *25 Harbour Rd., Wan Chai (3rd floor, Harbour Centre Building). ☎ 852/2827-8887. Reservations recommended. Fixed-price meals HK$77–HK$192 ($10–$25). AE, DC, JCB, MC, V. Mon–Sat 11am–midnight, Sun 10am–midnight. CANTONESE.* This is Cantonese with tasty Western twists. Try the fixed-price meals for some extraordinary mergings of old Cantonese and new California cooking. The entrees are light and fresh, the service stylish, the earth-tone decor upbeat.

Golden Leaf. *88 Queensway, Admiralty (lower lobby, Conrad International Hotel). ☎ 852/2521-3838, ext 8280. Reservations recommended. Main courses HK$110–HK$440 ($14–$58). AE, DC, JCB, MC, V. Daily 11:30am–3pm, 7–11pm. CANTONESE.* Local Chinese come here for the excellent local dishes, which seldom disappoint. The dim sum for lunch is excellent and the dinner dishes are even better. Top choices include the jellyfish appetizers and the braised shark's fin and crispy chicken. The standard dishes here are among the best in China. The dining room has no view, but the high ceilings, formal setting, and uncrowded seating make for a relaxing evening, supported by unobtrusive service.

Green View Noodle Shop. *Basement 1, New World Shopping Centre, Tsim Sha Tsui (east of Star Ferry concourse, between the Waterfront Promenade and Salisbury Rd.).* ☎ *852/2369-0470. No reservations. Main courses HK$35–HK$92 ($4.50–$12). No credit cards. Daily 7:30am–11pm. CHINESE FAST FOOD.* This is the ultimate Hong Kong fast-food cafe, my favorite for almost 10 years now. The food here is fast, filling, cheap, absolutely delicious, the way fast food should be everywhere. The service is quick and precise. You are seated with a glass of hot tea, a saucer of fried peanuts, and a clean set of chopsticks. The decor is McDonald's East: columns tiled in green bamboo, toadstool benches, marble tables. A laughing Buddha of a chef throws together noodle plates behind a wall of glass. The English–Chinese noodle menu is a mile long. The braised e-fu noodles are good, the Singapore-style vermicelli even better.

Indochine 1929. *30–32 D'Aguilar St., Central (2nd floor, California Tower).* ☎ *852/2869-7399. Reservations recommended. Main courses HK$120–HK$250 ($15–$32). AE, DC, JCB, MC, V. Daily noon–2:30pm, 6:30–10:30pm. VIETNAMESE.* The decor is Saigon 1920, cool, elegant, Asian and French. The dishes (with ingredients from Vietnam) are modern Hanoi in style. You might try the light lemongrass fish dishes, the spring rolls (which are flavored with mint), or the spicy soft-shelled crab. Prawn crackers are always at hand. The wine list favors France.

Kung Tak Lam Shanghai Vegetarian Cuisine. *31 Yee Wo St., Causeway Bay (Ground floor, Lok Sing Centre).* ☎ *852/2890-3127. Reservations recommended. Main courses HK$80–HK$170 ($10–$21). AE, DC, JCB, MC, V. Daily 11am–11pm. VEGETARIAN.* The unpretentious and fairly inexpensive spot is the best vegetarian restaurant in town. The dishes are Shanghai-style, meaning they aren't too spicy. The imitation fried "goose" and the cold noodles with seven sauces are crunchy and tasty, and the sweet and sour "pork" is a filling entree. You can also get meatless dim sum (served all day). Portions are large, the place gets noisy, waiters speak little English, and MSG is used, but the menu (in English) and the dishes won't disappoint.

Luk Yu Tea House. *26 Stanley St., Central.* ☎ *852/2523-5464. No reservations. HK$15–HK$46 ($2–$6) per plate. No credit cards. Daily 7am–6pm. CANTONESE (DIM SUM).* More for its history and character than for its food (which is merely above average), this is the place to sample Hong Kong's legendary dim sum. Flag down the metal cases wheeled down the packed rows of diners and point to what you want. The only menus are in Chinese. The setting replicates the original 1925 four-story British teahouse. The ceiling fans, dark wooden booths, stained glass, marble-backed chairs, kettle warmers, and brass spittoons underfoot don't seem terribly Chinese, but the chefs, workers, and tasty pastries are pure Cantonese. Sit back and enjoy the atmosphere, the din, and the delicacies.

Panorama. *22 Salisbury Rd., Tsim Sha Tsui (4th floor, New World Renaissance Hotel).* ☎ *852/2734-6600. Reservations recommended. Main courses HK$150–HK$300 ($19–$38). AE, DC, JCB, MC, V. Daily noon–3pm, 7pm–midnight. EUROPEAN.* This quiet, upscale restaurant serves excellent French and Mediterranean fare at quite reasonable prices.

The elegant setting features a view of the harbor lights. The lobster bisque and beef tenderloin are particularly flavorful and the dessert menu is irresistible, especially the chocolate creations. The wine list is extensive.

Shang Palace. *64 Mody Rd., Tsim Sha Tsui East (Basement 1, Kowloon Shangri-La Hotel). ☎ 852/2733-8754. Main courses HK$124–HK$285 ($16–$38). AE, DC, JCB, MC, V. Mon–Sat noon–3pm and 6:30–11pm, Sun 11am–3pm and 6:30–11pm. CANTONESE.* Shang Palace, with its theatrical setting in imperial red and gilt decor, is grand, gorgeous, and a favorite of gourmets. The entrees cover the entire spectrum of Cantonese classics, from shark's fin to bird's nest to suckling pig and fried rice (which is astonishingly good). The dim sum is light and tasty, too; it's available noon to 3pm Monday through Saturday and 11am to 3pm Sunday (for HK$108/$14).

Western Fast Food The world's busiest **McDonald's** (outside of Moscow) is in the Star Building facing the Star Ferry concourse in Kowloon, and there are literally dozens of other branches nearly everywhere you wander. Given the high price of eating in Hong Kong, McDonald's can be tempting. A good quick lunch chain is **Oliver's Super Sandwiches,** with excellent deli sandwiches assembled to your specifications, as well as a fine selection of baked potatoes. Super Sandwiches has six outlets in Central, four in Tsim Sha Tsui, and many more throughout Hong Kong (☎ 852/2866-8926 for customer services hot line). An excellent taco shop is **Taquer'a La Placita,** Shop D, Houng Sun Building, 45–47 Carnarvon Rd. (corner of Hau Fook Street), Tsim Sha Tsui (☎ 852/2366-9466). This is a step up from Taco Bell. The nine taco types ($2 to $4) are stuffed with everything from beans to seafood. You sit on a stool at the counter.

Central China: Antiquities & Adventures

XI'AN: THE ANCIENT CAPITAL

西安

XI'AN IS CHINA'S CITY OF THE dead—which is to say, China's city of ancient imperial treasures. The First Emperor, Qin Shi Huang (259–210 B.C.), unified China here. Twenty-two centuries later, in 1979, the 7,000 life-sized terra-cotta soldiers buried with him were accidentally unearthed, opening an underground city of the dead that put Xi'an on the world map of tourism. But Xi'an was always China's leading historical site. It served as China's capital over the course of 11 dynasties, reaching its height in the golden age of the Tang Dynasty (A.D. 618–907).

As showcases of China's imperial splendors, Beijing and Xi'an provide interesting contrasts. Beijing was the capital of the last two great dynasties, the Ming (A.D. 1368–1644) and the Qing (A.D. 1644–1911); Xi'an was the capital of the first two great dynasties, the Han (206 B.C. to A.D. 220) and the Tang (A.D. 618–907). Beijing reins in tourists with the Great Wall and the Forbidden City; Xi'an strikes earlier, with the terra-cotta armies of Emperor Qin and the Big Wild Goose Pagoda of the Tang emperors.

Xi'an's historical monuments and sites are even more extensive than Beijing's, stretching from the Banpo Neolithic Village, occupied 6,000 years ago, to the sole surviving city wall of any major city in China, built during the Ming Dynasty. If ancient Chinese history has no attraction for you, then skip Xi'an altogether. But if you're like me, its allure runs deep. I have been revisiting Xi'an ever since I first lived and worked there in 1984, gauging the changes that China has gone through during the last 2 decades, always in relation to the broader and deeper history that is preserved in its streets and walls and courtyards.

The Walls of the City

My first glimpse of the massive city wall of Xi'an transfixed me. This earth and brick structure stands restored to grandeur, 40 feet high, 8 miles round, its old archers' towers still intact. The palaces of the earliest

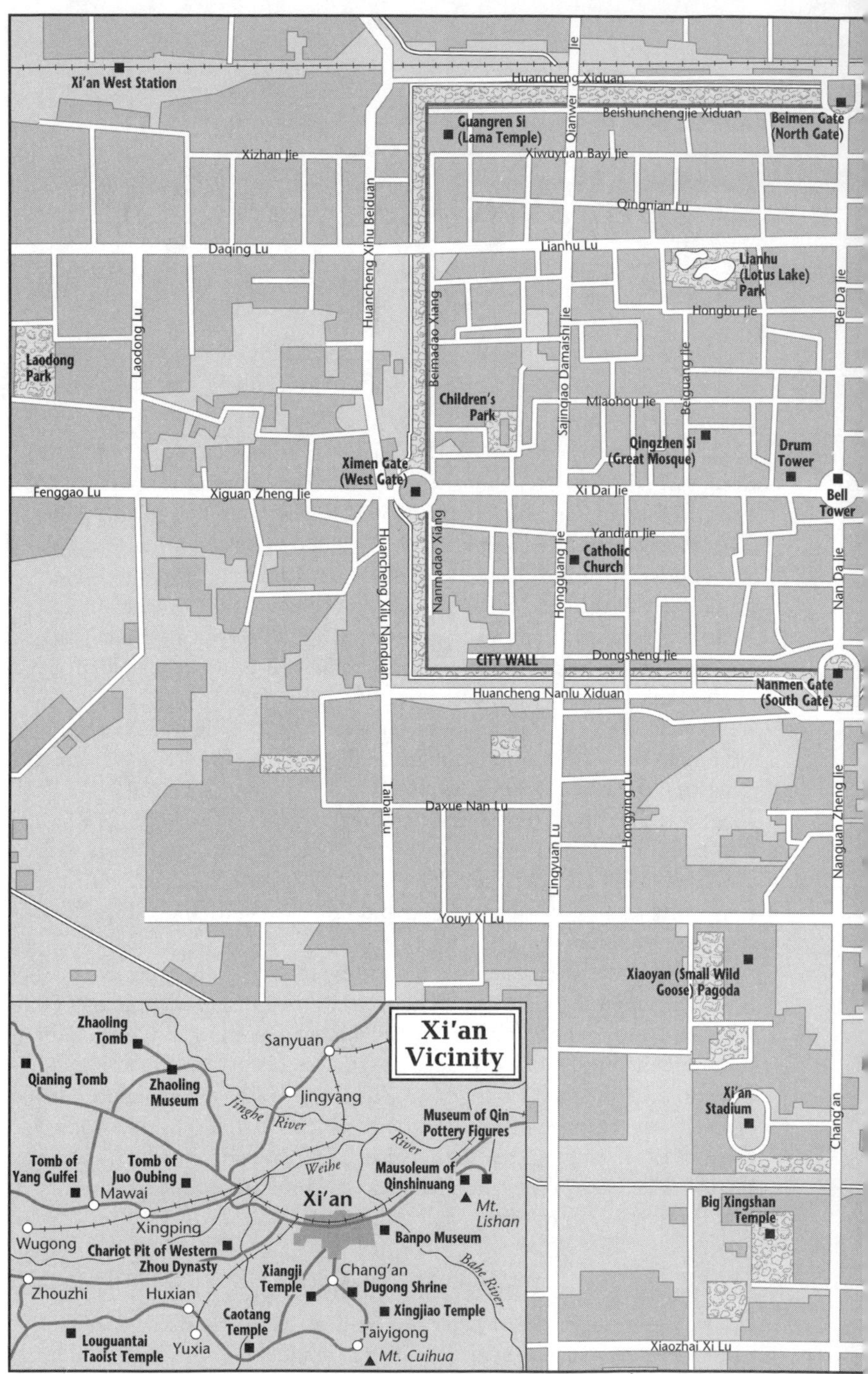
Xi'an West Station
Huancheng Xiduan
Beishunchengjie Xiduan
Beimen Gate (North Gate)
Guangren Si (Lama Temple)
Xiwuyuan Bayi Jie
Xizhan Jie
Qianwei Jie
Qingnian Lu
Daqing Lu
Lianhu Lu
Lianhu (Lotus Lake) Park
Hongbu Jie
Bei Da Jie
Huancheng Xihu Beiduan
Beimadao Xiang
Sajinqiao Damaishi Jie
Beiguang Jie
Laodong Lu
Laodong Park
Children's Park
Miaohou Jie
Qingzhen Si (Great Mosque)
Drum Tower
Ximen Gate (West Gate)
Fenggao Lu
Xiguan Zheng Jie
Xi Dai Jie
Bell Tower
Yandian Jie
Nanmadao Xiang
Huancheng Xilu Nanduan
Catholic Church
Hongguang Jie
Nan Da Jie
CITY WALL
Dongsheng Jie
Huancheng Nanlu Xiduan
Nanmen Gate (South Gate)
Taibai Lu
Daxue Nan Lu
Hongying Lu
Lingyuan Lu
Nanguan Zheng Jie
Youyi Xi Lu
Xiaoyan (Small Wild Goose) Pagoda
Xi'an Stadium
Chang'an
Big Xingshan Temple
Xiaozhai Xi Lu
Xi'an Vicinity
Zhaoling Tomb
Qianing Tomb
Zhaoling Museum
Sanyuan
Jingyang
Jinghe River
Museum of Qin Pottery Figures
Weihe River
Tomb of Yang Guifei
Tomb of Juo Oubing
Mawai
Mausoleum of Qinshinuang
Mt. Lishan
Xi'an
Xingping
Wugong
Chariot Pit of Western Zhou Dynasty
Banpo Museum
Bahe River
Xiangji Temple
Chang'an
Dugong Shrine
Zhouzhi
Huxian
Xingjiao Temple
Caotang Temple
Taiyigong
Louguantai Taoist Temple
Yuxia
Mt. Cuihua

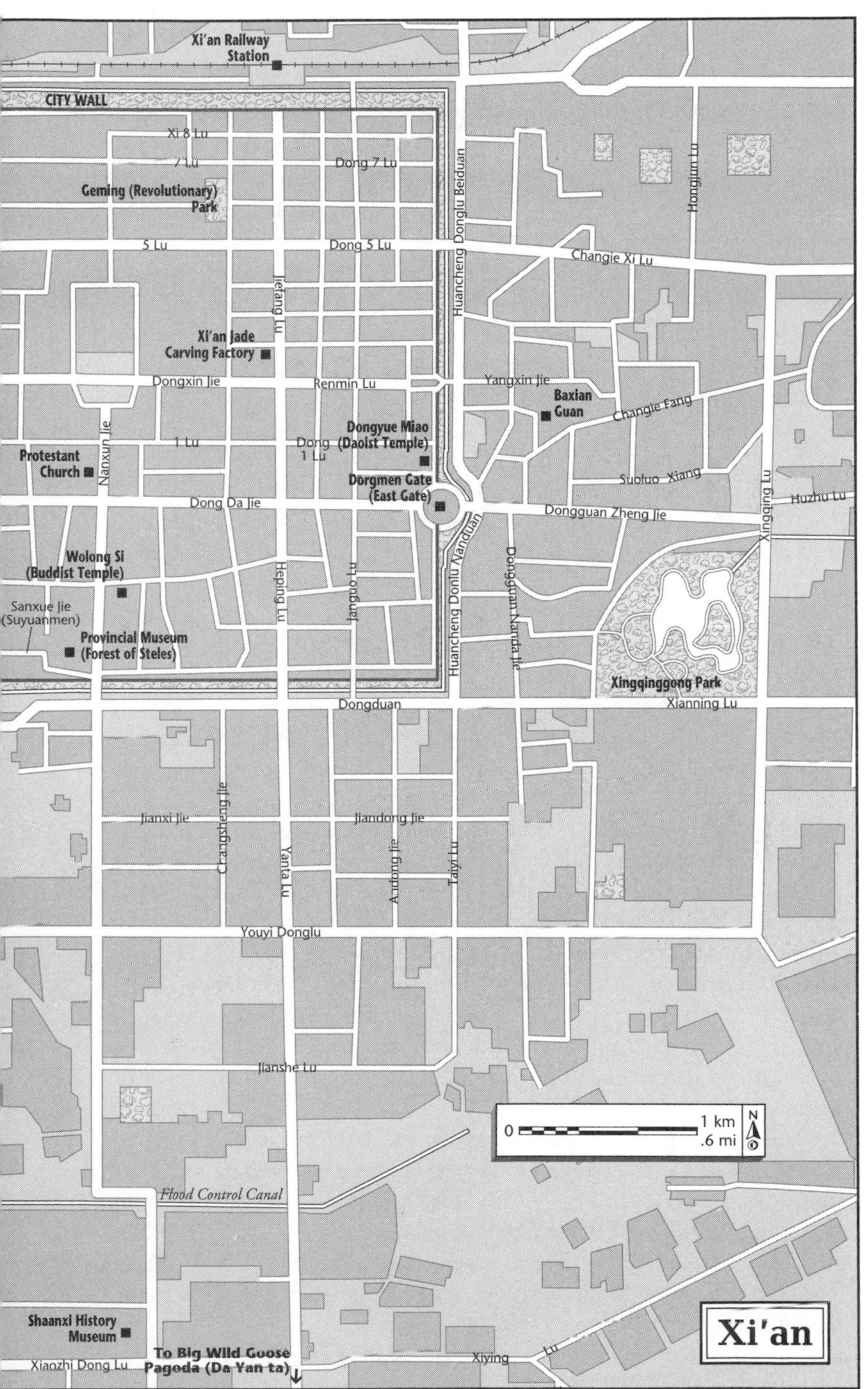
Xi'an Railway Station
CITY WALL
Xi 8 Lu
7 Lu
Dong 7 Lu
Geming (Revolutionary) Park
5 Lu
Dong 5 Lu
Changie Xi Lu
Huancheng Donglu Beiduan
Hongjun Lu
Jiefang Lu
Xi'an Jade Carving Factory
Dongxin Jie
Renmin Lu
Yangxin Jie
Baxian Guan
Changie Fang
Dongyue Miao (Daoist Temple)
1 Lu
Dong 1 Lu
Protestant Church
Nanxun Jie
Dongmen Gate (East Gate)
Suoluo Xiang
Dong Da Jie
Dongguan Zheng Jie
Huzhu Lu
Xingqing Lu
Wolong Si (Buddist Temple)
Sanxue Jie (Suyuanmen)
Provincial Museum (Forest of Steles)
Heping Lu
Jianguo Lu
Huancheng Donlu Nanduan
Dongguan Nanda Jie
Xingqinggong Park
Dongduan
Xianning Lu
Jianxi Jie
Changsheng Jie
Jiandong Jie
Yanta Lu
Aidong Jie
Taiyi Lu
Youyi Donglu
Jianshe Lu
0
1 km
.6 mi
N
Flood Control Canal
Shaanxi History Museum
To Big Wild Goose Pagoda (Da Yan ta)
Xiaozhi Dong Lu
Xiying Lu
Xi'an

emperors and the temples of the first Buddhists and Daoists have vanished from the old capital, but the last incarnation of the wall (built 500 years ago) remains to mark their birthplace. The moat along the south side is filled with water. A greenbelt of parks, trails, and outdoor amusements is gradually wrapping its way around the outside of the city.

You can make an uninterrupted circuit of Xi'an atop the city wall by foot. This is the ideal way to survey Xi'an upon arrival. An admission fee of RMB 10 ($1.20) is collected at entrances inside the wall. The best place to begin is on the southeast, across from the old Provincial Museum. There are entry signs in English.

The path is wide and paved in new stepping stones, and the views over the walls, inside and outside, are always fascinating. From late spring to early fall, the wall is lively with souvenir vendors, tourists, and locals out for a stroll. The entire 8-mile circuit would make a unique annual footrace. There are 18 gates through the wall, the four largest at the north, south, east, and west midpoints, where the traffic now flows in and out. A dozen years ago, much of that traffic was horse and donkey carts, and there wasn't a single taxi. What you see from the wall is a modern city and an old city being shuffled together like two mismatched decks of cards. Solar panels cap the new apartments that rise as high as the wall. At the same time, turn-of-the-century shophouses and old temples hug the foot of the wall for blocks, their roof tiles broken but not destroyed.

From the top of the city wall, the main streets of Xi'an are laid out like a cosmic chessboard. **Nan Dajie** runs straight north, past the big Kentucky Fried Chicken outlet on the left, to the Bell Tower, built in 1384. The **Bell Tower** stands at the center of the city. To its west is the **Muslim quarter,** containing the **Grand Mosque** and the Ming Dynasty **Drum Tower;** to its east is the city's main shopping street, **Dong Dajie.** These areas must be explored on foot, as must the quaint arts-and-crafts lane that stretches from the south gate east along the wall to the museum and its celebrated **Forest of Steles,** the greatest collection of engraved stone tablets in the world.

Looking south from the south gate down Changan Lu, it's possible to see the tips of the chief Tang Dynasty structures still standing in Xi'an's immediate suburbs: the **Big Wild Goose Pagoda,** built in A.D. 652, and nearer to the wall, the **Little Wild Goose Pagoda,** built in A.D. 707–709. For more than 12 centuries these were the tallest structures in Xi'an. Today, as skyscrapers begin to surround the old walled city, spotting pagodas becomes increasingly difficult. Just south of the wall there are new hotels, new offices, and right on the moat a miniature golf course.

I prefer the old world, even in its restored version, and the restoration of the Xi'an city wall is not so perfect as to destroy the spell of ruin, decay, and faded grandeur that evokes a royal past. Looking down and into the city, I'm always eager to discover what has changed, what remains, and what is no more.

In a Forest of Steles

The changed and unchanged, the treasures and the losses, are all to be found in the shadow of the southern city wall. Just east of the big south gate, which has become a flowery, landscaped traffic circle, the sleepy curving lane of **Shuyuanmen Dajie (Sanxue Jie)** has been transformed into a street out of Old Xi'an. A brand-new dragon-carved gate arches over its entrance. (The exquisite little pagoda to one side, Baoqing, dates from A.D. 706, but it is barely noticed now.) Lined with electrified lanterns, bordered by painted banners, festooned with red-and-yellow paper globes, **Shuyuanmen Street** has been remade for tourists. Even the wooden-railed balconies are strung with lights. The wooden shop fronts with their elaborately carved doorways sell every conceivable souvenir. There are several shops with fine artwork (paintings and scrolls) and the crafts for which Xi'an and this province are famous: simple folk paintings from the peasant painters of Huxian county, paper cuts, bright folk-art clothing and cloth ornaments, teapots, chopsticks, porcelain, books, and posters. Several of these Qing Dynasty–style shops sell rubbings made from the priceless stone tablets collected in the city's Forest of Steles nearby, worth picking up later here or outside the Shaanxi Provincial Museum if you spot a tablet you like inside.

The cobblestoned street wanders along the wall for half a mile east to the entrance of the **Shaanxi Provincial Museum,** 18 Wenyi Bei Lu (open daily 8:30am to 5:30pm, admission RMB 20/$2.50). It is located on the spacious garden grounds of the Temple of Confucius, built in A.D. 1374. A number of classical pavilions dot the garden pathways to the heart of the exhibit at the back, the hall of the **Forest of Steles (Bei Lin).** This is my favorite Chinese museum. It has not changed since it became the repository of China's engraved stone in 1952, and its collections reach deep into the world's oldest continuous civilization.

The dullest hall of stone tablets is the first. This large grove consists of a complete edition of the Confucian Classics transcribed on 114 stone slabs, front and back, in the year A.D. 837, becoming the centerpiece of the Forest of Steles collection established in A.D. 1090 under the Song Dynasty. The oldest such surviving transcription, the stone classics constitute the literal bedrock of Chinese ethics and social philosophy.

Other carved tablets in the remaining halls are probably more interesting today. There are pictorial stones of Old China, poems written with characters resembling leaves on a bamboo stem, ancient maps, and the **Nestorian Stele** (on the left, in building 2), carved in A.D. 781 to record the arrival of Christianity in China in A.D. 635. Nestorian Christianity, which traveled over the Silk Road from Persia, found roots in the Tang Dynasty capital and flourished for 2 centuries in Xi'an before its complete eradication. The Nestorian Stele typifies the dimensions of many of these tablets: 9 feet tall, a yard wide, a foot thick—solid limestone weighing in at 2 tons, anchored upright by a turtle-shaped base.

In 1984, I saw several workers making ink rubbings directly from these 1,000 stones, some of them more than 2,000 years old. Each rubbing blackens the stone and takes its toll. A Chinese scholar whom I met on my most recent visit was appalled to see them still making such rubbings in the late 1990s. Metallic models of all the steles have been cast for the creation of commercial rubbings, but as this scholar said, "Money talks," and there are many who will pay for a real rubbing. What I notice is the damage inflicted by more than ink, cloth, and mallet. Almost all these stones have been broken in half or defaced by vandals, possibly by organized vandals at work as recently as the Red Guard movement. I know from talking to many monks who returned to the remains of the temples in Xi'an after 1976 that the destruction of religious and historical pieces was carried out on an unimaginable scale, and much of the damage will never be undone.

Within the halls along both sides of the museum grounds are a number of China's greatest treasures that do survive, few of them protected now from the viewer's touch: unparalleled bronzes and jades from the Zhou Dynasty (1100–212 B.C.), the world's first seismograph (looking rather like a punch bowl set) from the Han Dynasty, tricolored horses and scraps of silk from the days of the Tang, and massive stone animals fashioned 20 centuries ago. I come back to this place often: It defines what a Chinese museum should be—quiet, old, courteous, Confucian, infinitely rich within.

Bell Tower & Drum Tower

In the center of Xi'an, visible everywhere from the surrounding walls, are the city's two Ming Dynasty treasures. Bell and drum towers were at one time as much an ordinary fixture of city life in China as city walls. The bell tower housed a massive bronze bell; the drum tower, a massive drum. Every city and town had these towers, but none are now as famous or grand as those at Xi'an. Now, every day a team of "ancient warriors" accompanied by traditional musicians gathers at the Drum Tower at sunrise to beat the drum 21 times, and returns at sunset to the Bell Tower to sound the bell 21 times.

The two towers are open daily from 9am to 5pm. Both are gorgeous from outside, superb imperial monuments worth viewing and preserving in an increasingly modern city. The Bell Tower is a beacon to all travelers wandering the downtown streets, while the Drum Tower has become the gateway to Xi'an's old Muslim quarter and its historic mosque.

The **Bell Tower** is older (1384) and larger than the Drum Tower. It stands now in the central traffic circle of the inner city; until 1582, it stood 2 blocks west at the center of the old Tang Dynasty capital, near where the Drum Tower is now. The Bell Tower is a stately edifice, its three tiers of green-glazed roof tiles soaring on eaves flaked in gold. Engulfed in Xi'an's most congested traffic center, the Bell Tower long ago clanged its last wake-up ding-dong in downtown Xi'an. The wooden interior feels centuries old, but once inside there's not much to see for the RMB 15 ($1.80) admission beyond sets of chimes and the city traffic and latest construction sites from the balcony. The Bell Tower's great bell has disappeared, as has the Drum Tower's great drum; reproductions have taken up their stations.

The Bell Tower and Drum Tower are tied together now by a sparkling new ultramodern city square, called **Hua Jue Xiang,** looking like some minimalistic expression of public art transported from the West: a wide, flat, open courtyard with benches and Plexiglas lanterns where smoking is not permitted (perhaps a first in outdoor urban China). Along the north side of Xi'an city square are three tiers of a new shopping arcade built in the neo-traditional Chinese style, with bricks and roof tiles. At the west end, on the north side of Xi Dajie (Big West Street), stands the venerable Drum Tower, built in 1370.

The **Drum Tower** also requires an RMB 15 ($1.80) admission, and there is probably even less reason to go in. The entrance is a stairway on the northwest corner. The upper floor contains Qing Dynasty furniture and a drum collection. The original drum is gone, and the Drum Tower no longer beats out the end of the day for Xi'an's residents.

The New Museum

Xi'an's new museum, the **Shaanxi History Museum** is a state-of-the-art facility on a par with the most modern museums of Beijing and Shanghai. Located 2 miles south of the city wall (at 91 Xiaozhi Dong Lu, near Cuihua Lu), it makes an excellent complement to the old Provincial Museum and Forest of Steles inside the wall. It's open daily 9am to 5:30pm; admission is RMB 48 ($5.75). Signs are in English and Chinese, and the lighting is good for a change. More importantly, the historical artifacts are among the best in the Chinese world.

The major exhibit is on the first floor at the rear: 39 Tang Dynasty (618–907 A.D.) frescoes removed from the walls of underground tombs. These murals provide lifelike snapshots of China's golden past, when traders from the West called upon a capital of camel caravans, hunting dogs, and polo tournaments. These scenes of court musicians, dancers, and eunuchs are rendered in pale oranges, reds, and blues, bringing a distant imperial age to life. Although the museum contains an enormous collection of gold, stone, paper, cloth, and jade relics from all the dynasties, the remains of the Tang naturally stand out here. Xi'an was the capital of China when the Silk Road routes to the West were at their richest under 18 successive Tang rulers, and the museum is stuffed with silks, tricolored ceramics, and ladies' fashions of the time.

Upstairs, the Qin Dynasty (770–206 B.C.) contributes five of its famous terra-cotta soldiers. While there are thousands of these clay warriors at the vaults of Emperor Qin's terra-cotta army (see separate chapter) less than 20 miles away, at this museum you can take a close-up, unhurried look. Separated by an inch of glass, you make out the bows on a soldier's square-toed shoes. And you can appreciate the art that went into these figures of royal death. The emperor's men look like flesh and blood buried alive inside skins of clay. Two of their steeds are also on display, neither of them protected by glass.

Pagodas

Xi'an's most monumental relics of the Tang Dynasty are its two pagodas south of the city wall. The **Small Wild Goose Pagoda (Xiaoyanta)** is the smaller and younger of the sisters but also the prettier. It's missing its upper two stories, and its jagged top looks like an earthquake rattled it. In fact, at least one big one did, reducing the Small Wild Goose Pagoda to a 13-story, gracefully tapered blue-brick tower. What's more, it's said that in 1487 an earth tremor split the pagoda in half, head to toe, but in 1556 a second jolt zipped it back together.

Few Tang Dynasty relics remain in the halls of **Jianfu (Commending Happiness) Temple,** surrounding the pagoda, but the pagoda's dark, winding stairs are worth climbing for the view. The temple, its gardens and courtyards, and the old pagoda were built by order of the Tang emperor—the temple in A.D. 684 and the pagoda in A.D. 707—as a safe place to store sutras (holy Buddhist manuscripts). At this time there was need for such storage. Increasingly, monks were setting out from Xi'an and walking west to India, returning after many years with Buddhist texts from the source. The monk Yi Jing was the first to make the journey to India by sea. He left in A.D. 671, returning 24 years later (after some time in Sumatra) with 400 holy works. He translated these sutras up until his death in A.D. 713 at the new Small Wild Goose Pagoda. The Small Wild Goose Pagoda is open daily 8am to 6pm; admission is RMB 10 ($1.25).

The **Big Wild Goose Pagoda (Dayanta),** 2 miles farther south of the city wall, is Xi'an's most famous Tang Dynasty landmark. This seven-story tower, strong and squarish, with large windows from which devotees toss coins for luck, was erected in A.D. 652, again as a fireproof storage silo for Buddhist sutras. It was the first Chinese pagoda I ever saw and the first I studied at length.

This pagoda was built at the behest of China's most famous Buddhist monk, Xuan Zang, who returned to Xi'an in A.D. 652 after 15 years of wandering across the Gobi Desert over the Silk Road to India and Pakistan. Xuan Zang returned with the requisite sutras, carrying all of them in his enormous backpack. His way was lighted by oil lamps affixed to his pack frame. The Forest of Steles contains a famous pictorial stone tablet of this monk on the road, my favorite rubbing. Xuan Zang's journey to the West required 22 years, and the monk's exploits were transcribed into China's most popular epic, usually translated as *The Monkey* or *Journey to the West.* There, Xuan Zang appears as a clever, heroic, mystically empowered monkey who undergoes a series of fantastic adventures on the distant road.

When Xuan Zang returned with his 1,500 manuscripts, he set up a bureau at the Dacien (Great Goodwill) Temple in the southern precincts to translate them from Sanskrit. The Big Wild Goose Pagoda—its name, I suspect, taken from the geese that once landed on its massive eaves—was built on the temple grounds. The whole complex was immense in those days, with 1,000 rooms and 300 monks. Something of a revival is under way in the 1990s. The courtyards have been restored, all the surviving halls cleaned up, and the Big Wild Goose Pagoda is doing big box-office business, second only to the vaults of the terra-cotta warriors. There are vendors galore, a silk carpet factory, a new temple built by local farmers, and oddly enough (but not so unusual for China), a shooting range with machine guns for hire just south of the pagoda entrance.

As for the Big Wild Goose Pagoda, it still manages to look magnificent, perhaps because it can stretch a full, broad, powerful seven stories (200 feet) above the tourist frenzy at its feet. One hundred monks service the grounds, along with hundreds of ticket takers, vendors, tour guides, and hustlers. The temple grounds are open daily from 8am to 5pm, with an entrance fee of RMB 20 ($2.50). The pagoda itself requires another ticket (RMB 25/$3) just for the privilege to climb. Both expenses are worth it.

The Big Wild Goose Pagoda was the highest building in central China for over 1,200 years. What's remarkable about ascending the building today is not just that emperors from the Tang Dynasty stood at the same brick portals admiring the view—it's also the scale of the ancient capital that the view from the top reveals. This pagoda and its temples were once a mile inside the walls of the old city, not 3 miles outside of it. For 1,000 years, from the fall of Rome to the Renaissance, this was the greatest city in the East, but it was as remote from the West as Atlantis and as unreal. The golden age of the Tang Dynasty elevated the city to poetic heights. Xi'an was seven times larger then, the supreme metropolis of the medieval world.

The Great Mosque & The Muslim Quarter

The **Great Mosque (Qingzhen Si)** of Xi'an dates back to A.D. 742, barely a century after the founding of Islam. Although it is often claimed that this is the largest and the oldest mosque in China, I'm skeptical about both claims. What I can say is that this is the most active and serene mosque in China. It used to be even more peaceful and idyllic. Over the last 10 years, it has been renovated extensively (without disturbing its architectural beauties) and added to virtually every guided tour itinerary. The result is that the narrow alleyway connecting the Great Mosque to Beiyuanmen Lu and the Drum Tower has become clogged with vendors. (They do sell some great walking canes.)

The Great Mosque is easy to find. Pass under the Drum Tower and walk north a few blocks. Turn left at the sign to the mosque. Follow the alley (Huajue Xiang) of vendors and shophouses as it curves to the right, and look for the entrance on the left. It's open from 8am to noon and 2 to 6pm daily; admission is RMB 15 ($1.80).

Although the Great Mosque was founded in the Tang Dynasty, its present design is Ming, dating from the same period as the present city wall. In the 1990s, most of the timbers were replaced, fitted, and recarved to mimic exactly the Ming Dynasty model. Some carving and tile work are still going on. The grounds are long and spacious, giving the sense more of a garden than of a temple. Laid out east to west in the Islamic tradition (Chinese temples face south), the four courtyards lead deeper and farther inward to the main prayer hall at the end. Among the treasures of the Great Mosque is a map of the world with a black cube at its center—an Islamic map of the world. Displaced, China lies outside, beyond the western frontier.

In the first courtyard there's a 360-year-old carved wooden archway. Side halls off the arch display Ming and Qing dynasty furniture. The second courtyard contains the wide Five-Room Hall, and through it, carved stone fences and gates, also created during the Ming Dynasty. In the third courtyard is the mosque's most famous and beautiful structure, the triple-eaved **Introspection Tower (Shengxin),** the minaret from which Muslims are called to prayer. On either side are halls containing a Ming Dynasty copy of the Koran and a Qing Dynasty map of Mecca. The One God Pavilion, also called the Phoenix Pavilion, is the final passage to the prayer hall.

The prayer hall is eight bays wide, with a glazed blue tile roof supported by large brackets in the Chinese style. There are stone stairs up to the entrance. Inside, the ceiling is carved in flowery Arabic letters, recounting the scriptures. Pages of the Koran are carved into wooden tablets, half of them in Chinese, half in Arabic. The mihrab (prayer niche) faces Mecca. The floor is covered with prayer rugs. A thousand worshippers can fit inside for a single service. Visitors, after removing their shoes, are often permitted to enter the prayer hall, although when I visited most recently entrance was barred to non-Muslims.

This is an exceptionally active mosque, as the Muslim quarter of Xi'an has at least 100,000 resident believers and an Islamic presence that goes back at least 1,200 years. The Muslims who came from the West put down roots, married, and after centuries of assimilation ceased to resemble Arabs, except in their Islamic practices. They became known as a minority people, the Hui. The Hui of Xi'an live largely in their own quarter, wear white turbans, and practice circumcision. They reject usury, divination, theater, and pork. They maintain their own schools, slaughterhouses, cemeteries, and mosques (at least a dozen in Xi'an). Their neighborhoods are now the oldest and their streets the narrowest and most fragrant with cooking in Xi'an. Their houses are low and conjoined. Some still have packed earth floors and sidewalk water pumps. Vendors tend coal-heated pots in the street, selling lamb on skewers, fried breads, and fresh yogurt—the best yogurt I've ever eaten.

One reason I like to come here is to watch the Muslim Chinese go about their business in the mosque. The other reason is the tranquility. Xi'an, like all Chinese cities, is constantly making noise. But in this quarter, there is almost a silence. The courtyards are like carved wooden screens. Dozens of Hui men shift quietly from station to station toward the prayer hall, bathed and barefooted, their heads covered in thin white turbans, prostrating themselves before Allah, facing Mecca in prayer.

Temples

During its zenith under the Tang Dynasty, Xi'an was the home of China's leading Buddhist temples and Daoist shrines. In the 1980s, I explored a number of these sacred sites inside and outside the city walls. Many were just putting themselves back together after coming under destructive attacks during the Red Guard campaigns of the Cultural

Revolution (1966–76). Some were destroyed so completely they never reopened.

Today at Xi'an there is a **Lama Temple (Guangren Si)** with a library of sutras in the northwest corner of the city, founded in 1705; a **Daoist temple (Dongyue Miao)** to the mountain god of Tai Shan near the eastern gate, founded in 1116; a **Buddhist temple (Wolong Si)** where the Chen (Zen) sect was said to have been founded in China in A.D. 520, located just inside the southern city wall; and several others with long histories and a recent return to worship.

The temple that has fared the best in this era of reconstruction, however, is the ancient **Daoist Temple of the Eight Immortals (Baxian Guan).** Located a mile east of the city wall from Zhongshan Gate (in a poor, crowded, working-class lane on Yongxin Jie), Baxian Guan is the city's most active Daoist sanctuary. Admission is RMB 5 (65¢). Scores of monks and nuns in dark robes, heads shaven, circulate through the small restored temples and courtyards, where there are four sites designated for burning incense and several stone tablets engraved with diagrams of a multilayered divine yin-and-yang cosmos. The chief statue is a large image of a many-armed deity remarkably similar to the Buddhist Guanyin (Goddess of Mercy) reaching out to comfort her petitioners.

On the steps to the main worship hall, I noticed a young woman alone on her knees. She had spread out a piece of paper and placed a set of keys, a hank of hair, and a small bone upon it. When I asked her the purpose of this, she told me that she was praying for the recovery of her ill father.

The best time to come to the Temple of the Eight Immortals is on the first and fifteenth days of each lunar month, at dusk, when a popular festival is held. I first attended a full moon rite here in 1984, when the halls were in ruins. It was a noisy affair. Worshippers were sending burnt offerings to their ancestors and one monk stood at the top of the stairs casting down firecrackers to chase away the demons. The rite had no order I could discern. There was singing, the clanging of wooden sticks, the shouting of prayers, and the chanting of rosaries. It was the din of divine chaos, Daoism as it has been in China for more than 20 centuries.

This was the largest Daoist monastery in Xi'an for a thousand years. New apartments and a machine factory have reduced it to a few blocks of recently restored temples. Across the street, a few other surviving halls have been converted to the city's most interesting flea market, where you can rummage through an odd assortment of old coins, chipped ceramics, and the personal possessions of local families. On Wednesday and Sunday mornings, this temple market expands into a twice-weekly antique market, selling Cultural Revolution posters, Qing Dynasty ceramics, snuff bottles, and opium pipes.

Churches

Christianity was first established in China in A.D. 652, according to the stone tablet in Xi'an's Forest of Steles. The Nestorian version, which traveled out of Persia to the gates of Xi'an in the 7th century, was not quite that of Rome, but the Chinese emperor was satisfied as to the correctness of the "Luminous Religion" (Da Qin) and encouraged its spread. But in A.D. 845, the edict was reversed, "foreign religions" were banned, and Christianity did not reappear in China until Western missionaries started to arrive almost 700 years later. More recently, Christianity in China suffered persecution throughout the Cultural Revolution. Almost all churches were closed, but in the 1980s they began, like the temples and mosques, to reopen their doors.

As is common in Chinese cities, Xi'an has two official "patriotic" Christian churches—one Protestant, one Catholic. Foreigners are welcome to attend Sunday services, though they're not publicized.

The **Protestant Church,** which reopened in 1980, is located north off the main shopping street, Dong Dajie. Go 1 block north up Nanxin Jie (the Friendship store in on the right) and turn left on the first lane. The church is on the north side of the lane, tucked within an unmarked gate, smothered by walls and offices. What is visible from the street is the church's curious tower, part traditional Chinese, part northern European. On Sunday mornings, the worshippers overflow the gate yard, pushing back into the street. If they see you, they'll probably let you through.

The services I've attended at the Protestant church have been ordinary enough. The chapel is unadorned, save for a few scrolls and a gold foil crucifix. A trio of ministers addresses the congregation.

A 30-member robed choir leads in the singing of the hymns, whose melodies may sound familiar to a Western ear. Collection plates are passed. The Lord's Prayer is recited. On your way out, you'll probably be stopped by curious churchgoers, as I have been. Once I was stopped by two old sisters dressed in black, strolling hand in hand. They remembered the Englishmen who had run the church before Liberation (1949). One sister, scrutinizing me matter-of-factly, wondered at last if we were finally coming back.

Xi'an's **Catholic Church** is harder to find. Walk due west on Xi Dajie from the Bell Tower, past the Drum Tower, on for almost 2 miles to Hongguang Jie on your left. Turn south, walk 2 long blocks, first passing Yandian Jie, then turning left on Wuxing Jie. The cathedral is tucked back on your left as you turn east. Again, if you go here on Sunday morning, you can follow the crowds. Christianity is quite popular in Chinese cities these days, among the young as well as the old.

After it was closed down in 1966, the Xi'an cathedral was swallowed up by a candy factory in 1973, which was still running when I first visited in 1984. The priest in those days told me the cathedral was built about 100 years ago by an Italian mission. The style is Romanesque, the material white marble. Inside, there's room for only a few dozen rows of wooden pews. The stained glass is long gone, as is the original furniture, but there are surviving paintings of the stations of the cross hung in gold frames and of St. Francis, a skull at his feet.

The mass is still said in Latin, the confession conducted without benefit of curtain or door. It is Catholicism much as it came to China a century ago, its rituals, its very language, almost forgotten in the West.

Banpo

Xi'an also has an entire chapter from an era of Chinese history that's missing at tourist stops elsewhere: the Stone Age. The **Banpo Museum (Banpo Bowuguan),** 5 miles east of the city, isn't exactly a must-see. It's a strange, ugly exhibit, hardly electrifying—yet oddly unforgettable. It's open daily 9am to 5:30pm; admission is RMB 20 ($2.40).

In 1953, a village of what became known as the Yangshao culture (4500–3700 B.C.) was excavated on the bank of the Chan River. Much of it is preserved under a large auditorium roof. Inside, visitors snake around the edges of the excavation, peering over the rails at the remains of 46 huts (half underground), fire pits, storage cellars, pottery kilns, and 174 grave sites. The ground has been left here in the middle of the auditorium as it was found.

These ancestors of the Chinese not only fashioned stone weapons, but also created striking pottery painted with sharp geometric shapes and the forms of fish and deer (both pottery and tools are on display in the museum). This artwork has a primitive power as potent as that produced by the early dynasties.

The Yangshao society is believed to have been matrilineal. The skeletons and graves are most haunting. Half a dozen of the skeletons can be seen in a corner of the museum under dusty glass in cement cribs. You can almost make out faces on the skulls. Adults were usually buried alone. Children were buried in jars, 73 of them found on this site. At one excavation near the exit, there are eight burial jars standing next to the foundation of a hut. The pattern of the fish on Stone Age pottery, the funeral urns for children, and the gray of this compressed dust—the gray of brain matter, the color of soil after it has utterly died—can stay with you for years. At the very least, Banpo taught me how old the human race really is, and how strange and resilient.

A **Stone Age Theme Park** has opened next door to Banpo, and I haven't found one person who likes it. Even the local tour guides vote thumbs down on this fiberglass village with displays and dancers straight out of a Chinese *Flintstones.*

WHAT TO READ

Digging to China: Down and Out in the Middle Kingdom (Soho Books, 1991, 1994), my own account of living and working in Xi'an, gives a detailed picture of the ancient capital in 1984 and a means to measure how much the city and China have changed since.

PRACTICAL INFORMATION

ORIENTATION & WHEN TO GO

Xi'an is 550 miles west of Beijing in the north-central province of Shaanxi. Xi'an's weather is best in autumn, when it's not as hot and humid as in summer, as cold as in winter, or as dusty as in spring. Xi'an's most important site is the **Museum of Emperor Qin's Terra-Cotta Warriors** (see separate chapter). This ranks as China's most important archaeological discovery of the century; nearly all visitors to Xi'an book a half-day tour to see it.

Xi'an is 2 hours west of the most beautiful of China's Five Sacred Mountains, **Hua Shan** (see separate chapter). Recent improvements in transportation to the mountain and the opening of a cable car mean that Hua Shan can be done as a long day trip from Xi'an. Xi'an, situated at the terminus of an ancient trade route to the West, also serves as the gateway to the **Silk Road** (see the section, "Silk Road China") and the oases of the Gobi Desert.

GETTING THERE

By Plane The new **airport** (☎ 029/870-8450) is quite far from the city, 31 miles to the northwest (at the town of Xianyang). The road is also new and the landscape is interesting because of the number of imperial burial mounds along the way, the unopened tombs of Han and Tang dynasty emperors. The airport is served from Hong Kong daily by **Dragonair,** whose office is located in the Sheraton Hotel lobby, 12 Fenggao Lu (☎ 029/ 426-2988). The flight takes 2½ hours. Chinese regional airlines connect Xi'an to most major cities in China, including Beijing (1½ hours), Chengdu (1 hour 15 minutes), Guilin (2 hours), Hangzhou (1 hour), Kunming (2 hours 15 minutes), and Shanghai (1 hour 40 minutes).

Transfer by taxi from the airport takes an hour and costs at least RMB 200 ($25). There is also an hourly CAAC shuttle bus (RMB 20/$2.50; 5am–5pm) to the airline ticket office in Xi'an (296 Laodong Lu; ☎ 029/870-2299), from which there are city taxis.

By Train The **train station** is located at the north end of Jiefang Lu at the city wall. There are ticket windows on the second floor (☎ 029/727-6076) serving foreigners (open 9am to noon and 2 to 5pm), but it is much easier to buy tickets through hotel tour desks. Direct overnight trains serve Beijing (17 hours), Chengdu (19 hours), Datong (22 hours), Guangzhou (22 hours), and Shanghai (24 hours). Luoyang, site of the Buddhist caves, is 6 hours east by train, and Kaifeng, another ancient capital, is 12 hours east by train.

TOURS & STRATAGEMS

Tours **China International Travel Service (CITS),** 32 Chang'an Bei Lu (☎ 029/526-3841), has its two most effective branches across from the Bell Tower in the **Bell Tower Hotel** (☎ 029/727-9200, ext 2842) and across from the railway station in the **Jiefang Hotel** (☎ 029/743-1023). CITS can book all plane and train tickets and arrange tours of Xi'an's many sights.

Hotel tour desks offer their own day tours. **The Shangri-La Hotel,** for example, offers a 4-hour tour to Banpo and the Terra-Cotta Warriors for RMB 340 ($41) and a 3-hour tour to the Great Mosque, the Bell Tower, the Drum Tower, and the Big Wild Goose Pagoda for RMB 240 ($29).

City Layout Since the days of the Tang Dynasty, Xi'an streets have been laid out on a north–south, east–west grid. Bei Dajie, Nan Dajie, Dong Dajie, and Xi Dajie—Big North Street, Big South Street, Big East Street, and Big West Street—all converge at the Bell Tower traffic circle in the heart of the city. The walled city is 2 miles north to south, 1½ miles east to west. Popular walking areas are the city wall, the Old Town street in front of the Provincial Museum, the Muslim quarter (north of the Drum Tower), and Dong Dajie, the main shopping street. Dong Dajie has recently undergone modernization and now features a covered food mall (Tanshi Jie), a Western fast-food outlet (Bob and Bettey's), an enclosed shopping mall (Xi'an Kai Yuan), Western-label boutiques (Playboy and Crocodile), and a modern international department store (Parkson). It's possible to tour the sights inside the city walls, and the city walls themselves, on foot on your own. Taxis are easy to hail and cost RMB 10 to RMB 20 ($1.20 to $2.50) per trip.

WHERE TO STAY

Bell Tower (Zhonglou Fandian). *Southwest corner of Bell Tower.* ☎ *029/727-9200. Fax 029/727-1217. 321 units. A/C MINIBAR TV TEL. $80 double. AE, DC, JCB, MC, V.* The location of this seven-story hotel right in the very heart of the city helps make it the best mid-priced choice. The view of the Bell Tower is good from the large rooms, which were last renovated in 1994 and 1995 and are showing some wear. There's a disco and a Western restaurant. The service is adequate.

Amenities: Health club, business center, bicycle rental, 24-hour room service, next-day dry cleaning and laundry, tour desk, beauty salon, shopping arcade.

Grand New World Marriott Hotel (Gudu Dajiudian). *48 Lian Hu Lu (near west gate, inside the city wall, corner of Sajinqiao Lu).* ☎ *800/321-2211 or 029/721-6868. Fax 029/721-9754. 480 units, including 36 suites. A/C MINIBAR TV TEL. $110 double. AE, DC, JCB, MC, V.* Recently upgraded, this four-star luxury hotel is now under international management. The rooms are fairly spacious, bright and well-equipped (with desks and safes), and the staff is fairly efficient. A 1,130-seat theater stages traditional performances in the summer. There are Western and Cantonese restaurants and a less expensive "food street" with Cantonese and Xi'an snacks.

Amenities: Large indoor swimming pool, health club, sauna, Jacuzzi, tennis courts, billiards, business center, conference rooms, 24-hour room service, same-day dry cleaning and laundry, concierge, baby-sitting, tour desk, beauty salon, shopping arcade, medical clinic, airport shuttle.

Hyatt Regency (Kaiyue Fandian). *158 Dong Dajie (4 blocks east of Bell Tower). ☎ 800/233-1234 or 029/723-1234. Fax 029/721-6799. 404 units. A/C MINIBAR TV TEL. $150 double. AE, DC, JCB, MC, V.* This 12-story, five-star hotel, located across the street from the new Parkson Department Store, has all the international luxuries. If you're walking to sights in the city, its location tops that of the Golden Flower. If you're taking taxis or tour buses, however, the downtown traffic congestion becomes a drawback. The rooms are small but comfortable, and the service is nearly as high in quality as the Golden Flower's.

Amenities: Indoor swimming pool, health club, sauna, tennis courts, bicycle rental, 24-hour business center, conference rooms, 24-hour room service, same-day dry cleaning and laundry, nightly turndown, concierge, tour desk, beauty salon, shopping arcade.

Shangri-La Golden Flower (Jinghua Fandian). *8 Changle Xi Lu (2 miles east of the city wall). ☎ 800/942-5050 or 029/323-2981. Fax 029/323-5477. 453 units. A/C MINIBAR TV TEL. $150 double. AE, DC, JCB, MC, V.* Since its appearance in 1985, the 11-story recently renovated Golden Flower has been Xi'an's most luxurious and efficient international hotel. Rooms are the largest in Xi'an, and the executive-floor rooms (Horizon Club, floors 9 and 10) are particularly plush, with in-room safes, robes, hair dryers, and free breakfast. There are good street markets and an active night market in front of the hotel, but a 10-minute cab ride is required to reach the city wall.

Amenities: Indoor swimming pool, health club, Jacuzzi, sauna, bicycle rental, 24-hour business center, conference rooms, 24-hour room service, same-day dry cleaning and laundry, nightly turndown, concierge, tour desk, beauty salon, shopping arcade, airport shuttle.

Sheraton Xian (Xilaidun Jiudian). *12 Feng Hao Lu (2 miles west of the city's west wall). ☎ 800/325-3535 or 029/426-1888. Fax 029/426-2188. 438 units. A/C MINIBAR TV TEL. $120 double. AE, DC, JCB, MC, V.* Recently renovated from head to toe, this five-star luxury hotel has fine rooms (with coffeemakers, hair dryers, safe, robe and slippers, and 3 phones), an elegant European restaurant, and a wide range of amenities and services. It's farther from Xi'an's attractions than the other hotels, but it provides exceptional comforts.

Amenities: Indoor swimming pool, health club, Jacuzzi, sauna, massage, billiards, business center, conference rooms, 24-hour room service, same-day dry cleaning and laundry, newspaper delivery, nightly turndown, concierge, tour desk, beauty salon, shopping arcade.

Budget Choices Two of the most popular places to stay among backpackers and budget independent travelers are the **YMCA** (33 Dong Dajie;

☎ 029/723-5479; fax 029/727-5830), located near the Bell Tower; and **Jiefang Hotel** (Jiefang Lu; ☎ 029/721-2368), facing the railway station. Both are basic two-star hotels with tour desks, currency exchange, and Chinese restaurants. Location and low cost are the attractions. Rooms are modern but small, lacking in amenities, and worn. The staff knows little English. Double rooms with private bathrooms are about US$40.

WHERE TO DINE

Ten years ago Xi'an was a culinary wasteland, except for the regional steamed dumpling *(jiaozi)* and shish kabob barbecued by street vendors in the Muslim quarter. Both these items are still available, but dining overall has also improved. The hotels provide some excellent restaurants and there are small cafes with decent fare. Along the main downtown shopping street of Dong Dajie there are many local Chinese restaurants and Western fast-food joints with English menus.

The best of the small cafes catering to budget travelers are **Dad's Home Cooking** and **Mum's Home Cooking,** both located north of the city wall on Fenghe Lu opposite one of the backpacker's favorite lodgings, the Renmin Hotel. These cafes offer low-priced Western entrees, from pancakes to hamburgers, with English-speaking staff and their own tour offices, and they are open from dawn to late in the evening. Other budget choices with English menus include **Bob and Betty's,** 285 Dong Dajie, with jiaozi and pizza, and **John's Café,** 9 Fenghe Lu, which has its own tour agency. **Kentucky Fried Chicken** has a large, clean new outlet on Nan Dajie, 3 blocks north of the city wall's south gate. Along Hua Jue Xiang Square between the Bell and Drum towers there are a number of Chinese cafes with English menus, a **Delifrance** (serving good sandwiches and coffees), and an American family restaurant chain, **Kenny Rogers Roasters.**

De Fa Chang. *Dong Dajie (just east of the Bell Tower downtown).* ☎ *029/721-4065. Reservations required. Dumpling banquet $35. No credit cards. 5–10pm. NORTHERN CHINESE.* Xi'an's most luxurious private restaurant serves Xi'an's most celebrated dish, jiaozi, the steamed wheat dumplings stuffed with a variety of vegetables and meats. There are scores of dumpling choices here (along with noodle and vegetable dishes). Da Fa Chang often fills up with tour groups, so try to reserve a table well ahead.

Shang Palace. *8 Changle Xi Lu (lobby of Shangri-La Golden Flower Hotel).* ☎ *029/323-2981. Fax 029/323-5477. Reservations recommended. Main courses $9–$15. AE, DC, JCB, MC, V. Daily 11:30am–2:30pm and 5–10pm. NORTHERN CHINESE/CANTONESE.* Best of the hotel restaurants for Chinese cuisine, Shang Palace is richly decorated in Qing-style furniture and carved wood wall panels. The steamed dumplings (jiaozi) are the best I've ever had in Xi'an, making for an ideal lunch, and the Chinese dinner menu (in English) is extensive.

Tang Dynasty (Tangle Gong). *39 Chang'an Lu.* ☎ *029/526-1633. Fax 029/526-1619. Reservations required. Dinner and show $50, show only $20. AE, DC, JCB, MC, V. Daily 6:30–9:30pm. CHINESE.* This dinner theater restaurant offers a five-course fixed-price meal of regional and international specialties, prepared and served in efficient fashion. A typical menu consists of seafood pastry, black mushroom consommé, jiaozi, king prawns and walnuts, beef tenderloins and rice, fruit salad with snow fungus, petits fours, and jasmine tea. The 1-hour stage show, starting at 8:30pm, includes performances by an ancient Chinese instrument ensemble, Tang Dynasty dancers, solo singers, and the Emperor's Parade Dance as the finale. Your hotel or CITS can book this package.

THE FIRST EMPEROR'S TERRA-COTTA ARMY

兵马俑

ONE OF THE PRIMARY VISITOR destinations in China is the tomb and the terra-cotta army of China's First Emperor, Qin Shi Huang (259–210 B.C.). The site lies 18 miles east of the old imperial city of Xi'an. Emperor Qin spent more years constructing his tomb than he did building the Chinese capital where he lived and reigned. Capping the tomb is a 125-foot-high grassy mound, making it one of the largest *tumuli* in a region that is clotted with imperial burial mounds. Beneath the mound is a grave the size of a city, its underground walls stretching for miles.

The First Emperor's tomb has not been opened, but 1 mile to the east peasants made an astonishing find while digging for well water in the drought of 1974: the first of three vaults of life-size terra-cotta soldiers, horses, and chariots that had stood guard inside the outer wall of the First Emperor's mausoleum, undisturbed and unremembered for 2,174 years.

The clay army was excavated, painfully reassembled shard by shard, and opened to public display on National Day, October 10, 1980. As a professor in Xi'an once remarked to me, only partly in jest, the local people ought to give Qin Shi Huang the Nobel prize in world tourism. The First Emperor's terra-cotta armies were a sensation. Hailed as the century's most important discovery in Chinese archaeology, the buried warriors catapulted Xi'an into the forefront of Asian tourism. These excavations rival the Great Wall as China's most visited sight.

Is the buried army worth such hyperbole and promotion? Yes—even though increased tourism is doing its best to blunt the full effect and even though the method of displaying the site has never been satisfactory. Housed under ugly, massive shed roofs, the vaults must be viewed from distant catwalks, while what one really longs for is a close-up look, an intimate stroll among the infantrymen, archers, generals, and steeds. That's not permitted, unless you're a visiting head of state; nor is photography allowed. Yet the site is still China's grandest historical spectacle, the field where its first dynasty was buried and came out of the earth

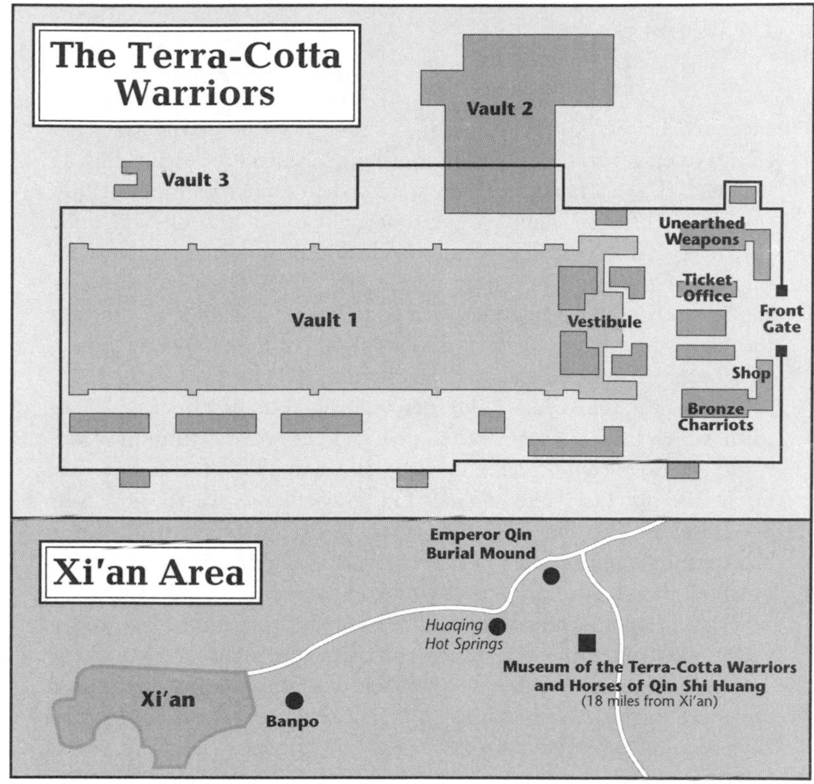

again. Despite the crowds and viewing restrictions, the site's power and monumental beauty pour through.

One aspect I've come to appreciate over the years is the workaday manner in which the vaults are displayed. This is still a work in progress. Teams are often gathered in the pits, sifting, cataloging, and assembling more and more figures as tourists file by. The site is expanding. A second and third vault opened to public view in the 1990s. More excavations will follow. You may not be able to walk up and down the rows where the terra-cotta forces of the First Emperor stand, but you can look over the shoulders of those who have put them back on their feet and opened the vaults after 22 centuries in darkness.

The **Museum of the Terra-Cotta Warriors and Horses of Qin Shi Huang,** as the site is officially designated, has opened three vaults to view. Altogether, they contain about 1,400 items—the soldiers, charioteers, archers, horsemen, and horses of the First Emperor's death guard.

Vault 1

The first vault, the one discovered in 1974, contains 6,000 of the 8,000 horses and soldiers, and this is the place to begin. At first glimpse, this excavated field (203 feet wide, 755 feet long) can be bewildering. The infantrymen are arranged in columns filling 11 corridors, each furrow 15 feet deep. The 38 ranks face east, toward their emperor's tomb. All the soldiers are life-size, standing five-foot-eight to six-foot-one in height. All are remarkably lifelike, with individual faces modeled on the actual soldiers of the emperor's army. They carry real weapons—crossbows, spears, swords, and arrowheads steeped in lethal levels of lead. Probably the most astonishing statistic is that just 1,000 of the 6,000 clay soldiers have been reassembled and stationed here.

In this vault lay China's oldest crossbow and its first brick wall. The paint, which has been scorched, eroded, and peeled away from the terra-cotta figures, once provided a unifying element. The mineral dyes were bright the day they were applied. The gray soldiers we see now were once resplendent—the generals robed in green, the infantry sheathed in black armor—and the ears and nostrils of their horses were painted red as blood, their teeth and hooves white as limestone.

The rear portions of Vault 1 have barely been disturbed, and this is where you'll often get a good view of what the archaeologists are up against: a seemingly hopeless jigsaw puzzle of shattered clay pieces sunken under yet more clay soil, waiting to be put back together. Some workers have been toiling at the pits for 20 years. On a typical day, eight people endeavor to solve the puzzle presented by each figure one piece at a time. Fragments can lay in storage for many years before their place is discovered. Computers are beginning to aid in ending this reassembly nightmare.

As impressive as the restored military forces are, I prefer to look into the pits of the unassembled: the disembodied heads, arms, hooves, and raiments still imprisoned by the dust, floating to the surface like the wreckage of an ancient Atlantis.

Vault 2

The second vault, housed in a more pleasing but still gloomy marble hall, opened on October 10, 1994. It displays an excavation in progress as well, but one that has just begun. Few of its pits are opened. Another 10 years may be required before all the pieces are dug up, and reassembly could take longer. A closed-circuit television system was recently installed so that visitors can watch the excavations on monitors.

Vault 2 contains archers, infantrymen, charioteers, and cavalry. Vault 1 is devoted primarily to foot soldiers, while in this vault the cavalry advances to the fore. One hundred sixteen of the horses are saddled, the earliest evidence in China of such a device. Three hundred fifty-six horses pull 89 war chariots. There are 900 soldiers here, as compared to the 6,000 in Vault 1.

Vault 2 was first detected in 1976 upon the suggestion of a local farmer, test drilled, and covered back up until March 1994 when a formal excavation began. The first step, still under way, was to remove the soil concealing a roof of ancient timbers and mats, and then to remove the roof itself. If you look carefully at the exposed dig, you can see the ancient roof beams used by the original builders. This section of the underground city was built by digging furrows into the ground, paving the floor with bricks, casting the statuary and placing it in precise formation, then covering the furrows with a strong roof that supported a new field of dust, soil, and crops, farmed until the generations forgot what was immediately under their feet.

There is strong evidence that these timbers and ceilings suffered a fire shortly after the death of the First Emperor. Historical accounts indicate that General Xiang Yu looted the royal tomb and torched the underground vaults in 206 B.C. in a failed campaign to succeed to power. (The first emperor of the Han Dynasty soon gained the upper hand.)

Several of the figures unearthed in Vault 2 have been put on special display in glass cases on the visitor mezzanine. The kneeling archer is dynamic, the goateed officer is dashing, and the general is commanding, but I prefer the cavalryman and his horse. The stylized steeds of Qin Shi Huang's army, said to be modeled on the desert horses of Gansu Province, are plump, vivacious, and fluid, just the sort of horse I'd choose for battle—and for beauty.

Vault 3

The third vault is the smallest. It apparently served as the command post. Most of its 68 figures appear to be officers, based on their dress and height. Higher-ranking officers stand taller than those of lower rank. Ordinary soldiers are clad in scaly armor so finely sculpted that the head and stem of each nail are distinct. Generals are clad in war robes, double-tailed caps, and massive square shoes turned up at the toes, like soaring tiled roofs. Their magnificent wooden chariot and its four horses wait in attendance. The figures appear to be in consultation, devising strategies of war, an art that the First Emperor pursued brilliantly and single-mindedly, as he swiftly and often ruthlessly brought all the warlords and kingdoms of China under his rule and molded them into a single Middle Kingdom.

Bronze Chariots

A new two-story **Exhibition Hall** (located to the left of Vault 1 in the entrance courtyard) displays the two bronze chariots found just 20 yards west of the base of the First Emperor's burial mound in a 25-foot-deep pit. Half life-sized, pulled by four bronze horses in gold traces, driven by an intricately rendered driver, each two-wheeled chariot is a decorative piece of extraordinary detail and richness. The windows open, the silver latch on the door of the curved bronze compartment turns, and even the driver's fingerprints are etched in.

These are presumed to be models of the royal chariots of the time. The **High Chariot** is the one with the bronze umbrella and short cart. The **Comfortable Chariot** was designed to carry concealed passengers. The purpose of these models is no longer known—perhaps merely "to keep a drowsy Emperor awake," as the poet Yeats has written.

On the second floor of the Exhibition Hall there are displays of terra-cotta warriors and steeds (for close-up inspection), weapons, and other artifacts from the pits. In the center of the hall are bells, helmets, and other recent finds, including a large solid bronze tripod weighing in at 468 pounds.

Future Digs

The local authorities have always kept their plans for future excavations around Xi'an carefully under wraps. Few of the burial mounds of Han and Tang emperors have been opened for science or tourism, including the most intriguing tumulus of all, the First Emperor's.

Qin Shi Huang's burial mound is a tourist site, but there's nothing to see there except a view of the plain from the top and a closer view of the vendors, antique dealers, and folk artists who line the trail. What's inside the tomb—if Qin's successors or later generations of grave robbers haven't already gotten to it—is an ancient city of treasures. China's Grand Historian, Sima Qian, the Herodotus of the Middle Kingdom, has left a vivid account of what the First Emperor took with him and what his city of endless night looked like. Qin reached the throne at age 13. His buried city consumed the days of 700,000 conscripted laborers over the next 36 years. In life, Qin presided over the unification of China. He regulated the currency, the weights and measures, the span of cart axles, and the writing of the language in his new empire. Qin is also remembered for his pitiless persecution of intellectuals and his burning of ancient books. He is credited with completing the Great Wall. But his greatest surviving artifact is his own tomb and the underground armies that guard it.

The Grand Historian gives this account of the First Emperor's tomb:

> The workers dug through three subterranean streams and poured molten copper for the outer coffin, and the tomb was filled with models of palaces, pavilions, and offices, as

> well as fine vessels, precious stones, and rarities. Artisans were ordered to fix up crossbows so that any thief breaking in would be shot. All the country's rivers, the Yangzi and the Yellow River, were reproduced in quicksilver, and by mechanical means made to flow into a miniature ocean. The heavenly constellations were shown above and the regions of the Earth below. The candles were made of whale oil to insure their burning for the longest time.

We are also told that the emperor's childless concubines and those who worked on the tomb were buried alive. The mausoleum was planted in trees and grass "to make it seem like a hill," as the burial mound does to this day. There is no mention of the buried city walls, of underground palaces, of a vast terra-cotta army standing a mile to the west.

Yet there are tantalizing hints, thanks to recent digs in the area, of what lies buried between the terra-cotta army and the tomb of the old emperor. We know that the burial mound occupies half the area of Qin's underground inner city. Remains of a palace have been detected within the walls of the inner city. An outer city with its own much longer wall, perhaps 3 miles around, encompasses the royal mausoleum. Its contents are largely unknown, although the skeletons of horses and the two priceless bronze chariots were found in these precincts. Outside these walls, more skeletons of horses have been found, indicating that it may be the site of the royal stables, and seven human skeletons have turned up as well, which some think are those of Emperor Qin's own children murdered in a palace intrigue. Ruins of a zoo containing exotic animals and the grave sites of prisoners forced to build the mausoleum have also turned up.

The most recent digs have been centered a few hundred yards east of Emperor Qin's tomb, where since 1998 some 80 gray suits of armor, made of stone flakes strung together with copper wires, and 30 helmets have been recovered. These are the earliest specimens of stone armor ever found in China. The stone armor pit is also the largest pit ever opened in the area, and in one chamber a strange discovery has been made: life-size terra-cotta figures described by officials as "odd," thought to be Qin Dynasty acrobats.

One can envision the day when the entire buried city of China's first imperial dynasty is revealed, although if mass tourism trends continue, Qin's dead capital could become nothing more than an instant theme park. For me, it has always been a dream city anyway. In dreams, I can strip back all the layers of dust and undress the plains of Xi'an; I can stroll among the palaces of jade, the streets of blue brick, the garden walls of stamped brick; and I can tarry in the corridors with a motionless army of kneeling archers, wooden chariots, and vigorous horses, their heads straining, necks glistening, manes forever flying over the grasslands beyond the Great Wall.

PRACTICAL INFORMATION

ORIENTATION & WHEN TO GO

The **Museum of the Terra-Cotta Warriors and Horses of Emperor Qin Shi Huang** (usually called "the Terra-Cotta Warriors," for short) is located 18 miles east of Xi'an. The three vaults under excavation cover about 5 acres and contain 8,000 warriors and horses, as well as 6,000 more artifacts (chariots, bridles, weapons, musical instruments).

There are shops inside all the vault buildings and on the grounds inside the main gate. Outside the gate, where the buses park, a souvenir city flourishes, with everything from postcards to folk-art vests and baby slippers for sale. Bartering is expected outside the gates. The stalls seem calm and well regulated compared to the chaos that used to reign here. Stepping off the bus from Xi'an, visitors used to be rushed by a living terra-cotta army of vendors, all shouting "Yi kuai, yi kuai," which means "One yuan, one yuan" (RMB 1). Today's chant is more likely to be "One dollar, one dollar," a good indication of how inflation has taken off in the more prosperous 1990s.

GETTING THERE

Independent travelers can take bus no. 306 or no. 307 from the Xi'an bus station, located at the northern end of Jiefang Lu (RMB 8/$1). These buses use winding country roads to reach the terra-cotta museum, a slow (1 hour) but absorbing route. The new highway, a toll road opened in 1991, is quicker (30 minutes) and smoother, but you'll see fewer faces of farmers along the way—faces that still closely resemble those of the terra-cotta warriors themselves.

TOURS & STRATEGEMS

Most visitors make the Terra-Cotta Warriors their number one stop when touring Xi'an (see separate chapter), the focus of a half-day or full-day guided tour by bus or car. Two hours at the museum is usually enough for a first visit.

Admissions & Hours The museum is open 8am to 6pm daily, with admission paid at the main gate now set at RMB 80 ($9.65) and rising fast. A separate admission is charged for the hall containing the bronze chariot display (RMB 25/$3).

Tours Tours with English-speaking guides can be booked through hotel tour desks and **China International Travel Service (CITS)** branches in Xi'an (see separate chapter). Hotel tour desks offer their own day tours. The **Shangri-La Hotel,** for example, offers a 4-hour tour to Banpo and the Terra-Cotta Warriors for RMB 340 ($41). Group tours often include other sites as well, particularly **Huaqing Hotsprings,** located a few miles from the Terra-Cotta Warriors at Li Shan (Li Mountain). This used to be an interesting stop, but the old imperial bathhouses are totally remodeled, the massive Nine-Dragon Pool is new, and the surrounding pavilions have received a recent face-lift. Huaqing no longer possesses the atmosphere it once evoked of an ancient summer retreat for Tang emperors and their favorite concubines. It is open daily 8am to 6pm; admission is RMB 30 ($3.60).

Photography Photographs inside the vault buildings are strictly forbidden. You can buy sets of slides, photographs, and picture books at concession stands inside and outside the vaults. Official photographers offer to take a group photo with the terra-cotta warriors in the background for RMB 150 ($21). During my most recent visit, the catwalks were fairly crowded with tourists, and dozens of them (mostly Chinese) were snapping pictures left and right. Several monitors were rushing around the arena screaming at the offenders, but I saw no cameras seized or fines levied (fines run up to $100), and the picture-taking that day continued with little abatement.

KAIFENG: THE FORGOTTEN CAPITAL

开封

KAIFENG IS PERHAPS THE LEAST visited of China's ancient capitals, a walled city south of the Yellow River that served as capital of the Middle Kingdom during seven dynasties, culminating in a 168-year reign that spanned the magnificent Northern Song Dynasty (A.D. 960–1127). The splendors of Kaifeng under the Song emperors are immortalized in an ancient 15-foot-long painted scroll called "Going Up-River for the Festival of Clear Brightness," now located in the Forbidden City (Palace Museum) collection in Beijing. Here we see Kaifeng at its vibrant zenith, with its wide Imperial Way, arched stone bridges, gleaming temples, lively merchant districts, and camel caravans entering its gates. Today, although it remains largely forgotten, Kaifeng is reconstructing itself for visitors as the 12th-century Song Dynasty capital it once was.

I had long dreamed of seeing what treasures remained inside its city walls. One other attraction, an oddity in China, also appealed to me. Kaifeng had nourished a Jewish community for many centuries, and remnants, even descendants of that congregation, were said to still exist there.

It was not difficult to book an overnight train from Shanghai along the Yellow River to Kaifeng, but once there I could find no tour desk or roaming tout to guide me through the city's highlights. I grabbed a taxi into the city, settled into a Chinese hotel, procured a map, and set out to explore Kaifeng on foot. The distances within the crumbling earthen city walls proved to be reasonably short. In a matter of hours I was able to circumambulate the entire city as I searched for two vaunted treasure troves: that of the Song Dynasty capital and that of a Jewish presence in China.

Imperial Way

Striking out from the Dongjing Hotel near the southwest corner of the Kaifeng city walls and walking north along Yingbing Lu, I quickly came

to **Lord Bao Lake (Baogong Hu)** and crossed the bridge that bisects it. I was immediately impressed by the lack of motorized traffic on the wide thoroughfare. I could easily cross the street almost at will, a feat impossible these days in most Chinese cities. Forty minutes later I was standing before the massive gates to the Imperial Way, Kaifeng's recent reconstruction of the Song Dynasty's main avenue. Eight centuries ago, the central passage of the Imperial Way was reserved for China's emperors, and to either side were covered arcades where the leading merchants of the kingdom carried on their trades. Those sidewalks for the common folk were once lined with narrow canals planted in flowering lotuses. Today, the tile-roofed shops hawk local snacks, river fish, antiques, calligraphy, and souvenirs. It's a charming, rather sleepy shopping district running 3 blocks north to the entrance of **Dragon Pavilion (Longting) Park,** once the site of Song Dynasty palaces and imperial gardens. A spacious pleasure park with a central causeway dividing Yangjia and Panjia lakes survives today (admission RMB 15/$1.80). The park's centerpiece is a remarkable raised pavilion constructed atop a tall pyramid base. Dating from 1378, this pavilion was rebuilt during Emperor

Kangxi's rule (1662–1723). Joining its massive main hall are eight hallways, one of which contains 63 life-sized imperial figures in wax. In the Dragon Pavilion's courtyard, dozens of sedan chairs, lavishly covered in red silks, were in the hire of Chinese tourists reenacting royal marriage processions. The park is a pleasant place to stroll, teeming with local families, many of whom rent rowboats for the afternoon. There are several floating restaurants in the form of large dragon boats on the two lakes, and the shore is lined with fishermen, many half asleep, their bamboo poles carefully wedged between rocks.

Up the River

Returning to the park entrance, I walked west along the lakeshore about 30 minutes to the **Stele Forest of the Imperial Academy,** an outdoor collection, recently opened, of 3,500 steles (carved stone tablets), many of which date from the Song Dynasty. The grounds were unfinished and uninviting, however, and the number of steles on display was disappointingly few.

Kaifeng's newest grand tourist attraction, adjacent to the stele collection, opened in 1998. Called **Qingming Park Up the River (Qingming Shanghe Yuan),** this theme park, designed to re-create the city pictured in the famous 12th-century scroll of Kaifeng, hugs the Huanghe River, a tributary of the Yellow River to the north. Its streets, shops, wharves, ships, gardens, teahouses, and pawnshops are supposed to evoke the ancient capital in all its splendor. There is live entertainment, including fortune-telling, acrobatics, and stilt-walking. This Song Dynasty amusement park, open daily 8:30am to 5pm, is located at 5 Longtinxi Lu (☎ 0378/595-5770), and requires an RMB 20 ($2.50) admission.

Iron Pagoda

Having walked the western side of the walled city, I headed northeastward in the afternoon, walking for over an hour before reaching Kaifeng's landmark, the **Iron Tower (Tie Ta),** at 210 Beimen Dajie, where the admission is RMB 20 ($2.50). Erected in 1049, this slender 13-story octagon, 175 feet tall, is actually constructed of brick and covered in glazed tiles that give it a dark metallic sheen. To climb to the top of the pagoda requires a separate admission of RMB 5 (65¢). From its top-story portals, I had a wide view of the walled city, which is almost devoid of high-rises and from afar appears as a Chinese city yet to be modernized, a decade out of date or more. There were no towering skyscrapers, no Western fast-food pavilions, no palaces housing five-star hotels or deluxe department stores.

South of the Iron Pagoda I discovered a section of the Song Dynasty earthen wall that I could mount, but there was little left in the way of archers' towers and watch stations. Weary of walking the dusty backstreets, I returned via taxi, dreaming of the Song Dynasty wonders barely hinted at today.

The Lost Tribe

Kaifeng is a city of many legacies, the most visible ones from the Song Dynasty, but its strangest legacy is that of its **Jewish community,** which written evidence traces back to the late 10th century A.D. The Jews of Kaifeng, thought to have emigrated from Persia over the Silk Road trade routes, have lived in Kaifeng continuously for 1,000 years, establishing their own synagogue here in A.D. 1163. Two pieces of evidence of the Kaifeng Jewish presence can still be seen: the stone tablets recording early Jewish history in China and the grounds of the great synagogue (destroyed for good in the last century). I set out to see both.

The stone tablets are still kept on the third floor of the **Kaifeng Museum,** located on the south bank of Lord Bao Lake (although a new facility is rumored to be opening someday). The museum is a large building graced by upturned eaves but is now falling apart, neglected, its staff openly praying for better days (and more funds). Among its 20,000 relics are some Qing Dynasty writings by Kaifeng Jews and two stone tablets, inscribed in Chinese, to commemorate the rebuilding of the Kaifeng synagogue. These tablets are dated 1489 (with the reverse side composed in 1512) and 1679. Each assigns a different date to the arrival of Jews in China, but they are consistent concerning the Kaifeng synagogue, which has been restored on at least 10 occasions since the 12th century. The 1679 stele at Kaifeng records the rebuilding of the temple after the Great Flood of 1642, when the Yellow River inundated and destroyed much of the town.

Rumors of a Jewish community in China had been circulating since Marco Polo's time but were only confirmed by Westerners after 1605 when Ai Tan, a Kaifeng Jew, met the preeminent Catholic missionary of China, Matteo Ricci. Ai Tan had come to Beijing after reading of the European missionaries and their strange new religion. He suspected that the missionaries were Jews. Ricci, for his part, was thrilled at the chance to meet a genuine Chinese Christian, for Ai Tan announced that he was a fellow believer. Ricci soon realized his mistake, but Ai Tan returned to Kaifeng convinced that Ricci was a fellow Jew from Europe but a bit eccentric in his views. Kaifeng's rabbi later wrote to Ricci, begging him to become his successor and pointing out that odd beliefs were less important than the way a man conducted his life. The good Jesuit's reply to the offer of a rabbinical post in Kaifeng is not known.

The Jewish community continued to worship in Kaifeng until the flood of 1852, which again destroyed the synagogue. The temple was never rebuilt and the Jews remaining in Kaifeng gradually ceased to practice the rituals associated with Judaism. Their place of worship, the Hebrew language, and all ethnic and racial distinctions that set them apart disappeared. As several scholars later pointed out, never before had Jews been so thoroughly assimilated as in China.

According to a Chinese scholar's census, there were 166 descendants of Jews in Kaifeng as of 1980. A number of these people continue to regard themselves as Jewish today. In 1985, Rabbi Joshua Stampfer of Portland, Oregon, hosted one of these descendants, Qu Yi-nan, a 25-year-old reporter for the *People's Daily* in Beijing. She recalled that her family did not eat pork and that her grandfather always wore a blue skullcap. Under the rabbi's tutelage, Ms. Qu quickly became the only Chinese Jew in the world able to read Hebrew and participate in basic Jewish rituals. (She has since married and settled in Los Angeles.)

Curious to see the grounds of Kaifeng's celebrated synagogue, the **Purity and Truth Synagogue (Qing Zhen Si),** I set out for the intersection of Beixing and Pingdeng streets. I knew that the site was near the no. 4 People's Hospital, north of both the Catholic church and the Great Eastern Mosque. (In no other city in China, and few in the world, can one find a Catholic church, an Islamic mosque, a Daoist temple, and the site of a Jewish synagogue within a 4-block walk.) I had determined the synagogue's exact location, at 21 Jiao Jing Lu (west of Cao Shi Jie, east of Bei Tu Jie, north of Nan Jiao Jing Hutong, south of Cai Zhen Dong Jie, to be precise), but I could not find it in the maze of streets and alleys, shops and shanties. Twice I asked for directions.

Ultimately, I stumbled onto a cluttered, nearly vacant, overgrown lot that fit the description. I knew the synagogue had vanished, that pieces of it had been used to build the Great Eastern Daoist Temple; I knew that the Trinity Church had eventually bought the land and rescued some of the relics (including the carved tablets, which until 1912 still stood, in total abandon, in this same yard); and I knew that the no. 4 People's Hospital (at 59 Beitu Jie) had taken over the area occupied for 8 centuries by the solitary synagogue. Local sources said the synagogue had stood on the present site of the hospital's boiler. Before its disappearance, the Kaifeng synagogue would have appeared as a typical Chinese temple of gates, pavilions, courtyards, and ancestral halls, except that its entrance faced east and its worshippers faced west, toward Jerusalem, whereas Chinese temples face south. Here, in Kaifeng, I could not even imagine its existence. Nothing was left but a yard. No trace of gate or foundation. Even the stone of the place of worship had been assimilated into the earth of China.

Kaifeng was missing out on a vital, if small, niche in foreign tourism. Clean up the synagogue grounds, build a small memorial and a museum, employ Jewish descendants as guides, and presto: a unique, exotic travel experience, unlike any other on Earth. Perhaps such a project would make things too easy and misleading. Trying to find traces of the Jewish presence in Kaifeng today certainly gives one a more accurate feel for the ravages of history and the sheer force of cultural absorption.

Temple Market

My last morning in Kaifeng, a Sunday, I set out north again. At the bridge over Lord Bao Lake, a local market was in full swing, its vendors taking over the sidewalks with rather paltry goods. New bras and panties were displayed on clotheslines strung between trees. Belts were custom cut on the spot from wide sheets of leather.

At the north end of the bridge, I turned east into the heart of the city where the old streets were crowded with Sunday shoppers drawn to the open markets near the **Grand Xiangguo Monastery** (admission RMB 15/$1.80) on Ziyou Lu. Founded in A.D. 555, Xiangguo became one of China's most important Buddhist monasteries under the Tang rulers. When Kaifeng became the Song capital, Xiangguo became the number one temple of the empire, as well as the commercial center of the city. The great floods of 1642 completely erased this monastery, but it was rebuilt under Emperor Qianlong in the 18th century. Within the temple, which is replete with monks hawking trinkets and worshippers burning incense and stroking prayer beads, are assorted small treasures: a 12-foot-tall bronze Frost Bell (cast during the Qing Dynasty); a Buddhist figure from Song days; Ming Dynasty porcelains; an umbrella once owned by the Manchu Empress Dowager, Ci Xi; and in its own pavilion, a 1,000-armed statue of Guanyin, Goddess of Mercy, carved from a single tree. Today, the Xiangguo Monastery area is also Kaifeng's leading open-air market, rife with streetside vendors, creating a pungent, gritty, colorful scene. One enterprising vendor was attracting a large throng with his team of three dancing monkeys.

Modern Kaifeng is a city asleep, a city of possibilities, waiting for its past to awaken. There are hints in its temples, parks, and ruins of an imperial grandeur largely lost elsewhere in China, where modernization has erased much of the earthy grime and street life that came to dominate urban areas when the last of the great dynasties was extinguished early in this century. Kaifeng is a forgotten capital, its old treasures and communities reduced to a few glittering, tantalizing tatters. It still awaits the magic wand of China's economic reforms to spiff up its ancient treasures, but one senses that, with its 42 relics under government protection and 167 places designated as historical sites, Kaifeng will one day recast the rich past within its aging walls and be among China's most visited cities, once it completes its return journey upriver to a festival of clear new brightness.

The Jews of China

Information about Kaifeng's Jewish heritage, sometimes including special-interest tours, is available through the **Sino-Judaic Institute,** 232 Lexington Dr., Menlo Park, CA 94205 (☎ 415/725-3436). In Kaifeng, the best contact is Wang Tisha, President, **Judaic Study Society of Kaifeng,** 404 Gongyuan Lu, Building 63, Unit 4, Kaifeng, Henan Province (☎ 0378/595-2374; fax 0378/595-2320).

For background on the Jewish community in Kaifeng, read *East Gate of Kaifeng: A Jewish World Inside China,* edited by M. Patricia Needle (University of Minnesota China Center, 1992). For a portrait of Song Dynasty Kaifeng, see Jacques Gernet, *Daily Life in China on the Eve of the Mongol Invasion 1250–1276* (Stanford University Press, 1970).

PRACTICAL INFORMATION

ORIENTATION & WHEN TO GO

Kaifeng, population about 700,000, lies 6 miles south of the Yellow River in Henan Province on the main railway line between Shanghai and Xi'an. Kaifeng has developed little in the way of hotels or restaurants to appeal to individual foreign travelers. The sights are interesting, but staying is a trial. Autumn brings the most comfortable weather here, warm and not rainy. Winters are cold, with below freezing temperatures. Spring has dust storms, and summers (especially in July and August) are very hot.

It is served by **overnight train** west from Shanghai or east from Xi'an, a 13-hour journey in either direction. There is no airport. **Taxis** are as cheap as you'll find in China, under RMB 10 ($1.20) to most points.

TOURS & STRATEGEMS

The **tourist bureau** located in the Dongjing Hotel can book train tickets, but it does not seem able to help individual tourists with local tours or provide English-speaking guides. The **Kaifeng CITS** head offices, along with the **Kaifeng Tourism Administration,** are located just north of the Dongjing Hotel at 98 Yingbin Lu (☎ 0378/595-5130 or 0378/595-4370; fax 0378/595-5131).

WHERE TO STAY

Only two hotels are of international caliber, but neither is worth writing home about. The **Dongyuan Hotel (Dongyuan Dajiudian),** 1 Xinsong Lu (☎ 0378/291-8888; fax 0378/292-5588), the newer (1992) of the two top-rated hotels, is inconveniently located in east Kaifeng, just outside the city walls near Songmen (Song Gate). It appears somewhat cleaner than its chief rival, the Dongjing Hotel.

The **Dongjing Hotel (Dongjing Dafandian),** 14 Yingbin Lu (☎ 0378/595-8936; fax 0378/595-7705), is owned by the tourism bureau. It contains spacious gardens, and is located in south Kaifeng, inside the city walls, on the main road to the museum, Lord Bao Lake, and the Dragon Pavilion. I stayed at this hotel, which has a three-star rating. One clerk spoke a little bit of English. The tourism bureau consisted of a locked office and service window, closed most of the time. The business center, located behind the reception desk in a labyrinth of hallways, was also closed most hours, although I did manage to send an international fax from there. The rooms are huge but quite run-down, and everything needs a thorough scrubbing. I rented a deluxe room, the size of a junior suite, for RMB 388 ($46) a night, with adequate private bathroom and clean sheets. Standard rooms are RMB 288 ($35). The Dongjing contains large dining halls, karaoke rooms, a gift shop, and a courtyard bonsai garden. Chinese buffet breakfast is included (7:30 to 8:30am only). You must fetch a taxi yourself on the street.

WHERE TO DINE

Finding a decent restaurant in Kaifeng is a miserable task. If you stay at the **Dongjin Hotel,** a breakfast coupon is provided, but the offerings are basic Chinese fare (rice, steamed breads, vegetables, fried pastries, perhaps a boiled egg, tea). The hotel also offers fixed-price Chinese dinners in the large dining room behind the main desk, largely Sichuan-style fare, for RMB 40 ($4.80). Western breakfast and afternoon snacks are available in the lobby of the **Dongyuan Hotel,** east of the city walls.

I tried the noodles at **California Beef Noodles,** located at the corner of Ziyou Lu and Zhongshan Lu, downtown, southwest of the Xiangguo Monastery, and they were hearty fare but not worth trying twice. There was no English menu.

The **Drum Tower Night Market,** at the corner of Sihou Lu and Shudian Lu in the heart of the city, offers a variety of street fare for the daring, including various shish kabobs prepared on the spot over open fires. This was the best dish I found in Kaifeng.

LONGMEN CAVES: STONE GATE OF THE DRAGON

龙门

AFTER CREATING THE MASTERpiece of Buddhist cave art in Datong, the Northern Wei Dynasty moved its capital south to Luoyang in A.D. 494 and began construction of a second sculptural gallery, the Longmen (Dragon's Gate) caves. The project turned out to be even more ambitious. Today, 2,300 caves survive, and 110,000 statues have been catalogued, twice the repository left at the Yungang caves in Datong. The larger scale is explained by the longevity of the project: More than half the carvings at Longmen date from the much later Tang Dynasty period (A.D. 618–907), when Chinese art and sculpture reached its zenith.

The Northern Wei artists set to work at a limestone cliff running a half mile north to south along the west bank of the Yi River (known as the Dragon's Gate), 9 miles south of Luoyang. As at the other great Buddhist caves, Longmen was raided by Western art collectors in the early 20th century. Thousands of the holy figures were desecrated, their heads sawn off, crated up, and shipped abroad. An entire cave tableau is now on display in New York City at the Metropolitan Museum of Art.

Emperors, generals, rich clans, and devoted Buddhist leaders all took a hand at creating these shrines, for political and social purposes. The carvings cover a history of over 500 years. There are no signposts to help foreign visitors, but the caves are laid out in major clusters, reflecting successive periods of construction. The caves are not deep. Centuries of erosion, flooding, and earthquakes have exposed most of the large figures to the sky, the caves receding to large oval niches. Hundreds of small niches pock the cliff face as well. At dawn, when Longmen can be viewed from a distance on the east side of the Dragon's Gate, the rays of the rising sun turn the entire ridge into a golden beehive. The cruder, more rounded figures were carved earliest, in the 5th and 6th centuries.

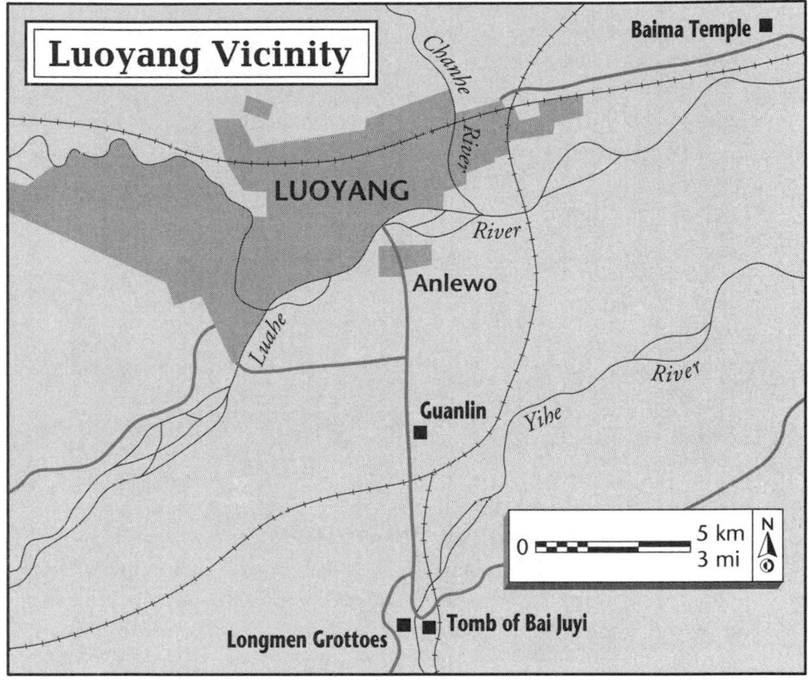

The more complex, ornate, and lively statues date from the 7th and 8th centuries, when Tang art was in flower.

Luoyang

I reached the ancient capital of Luoyang by train, traveling east from another old seat of dynastic power, Xi'an. This is the route that the royal court took in the later days of the Tang Dynasty as its members came to favor Luoyang over the imperial capital of Xi'an as their residence. Luoyang gives almost no impression of its royal past these days. Its landmarks are a tractor factory (China's first), a ball-bearing works, a mining machinery plant. Little is left of the old capital where Daoist founder Lao Zi ran the library 2,500 years ago; where the Han Dynasty Imperial College enrolled 30,000 of the nation's finest scholars in the 1st century A.D.; where the Northern Wei Dynasty opened 1,367 Buddhist temples; where the Sui emperor connected his palace to the Grand Canal so that officials and merchants could sail from the middle of China northeast to Beijing and southeast to Hangzhou in the 6th century; where for 934 years Luoyang was truly the central point of the Chinese imperial compass. Old Luoyang has instead made way for a thousand factories. Its million residents are entering the industrial age. The peonies transported from Xi'an by decree of the Empress Wu in the 7th century are famous here still, but the legendary Seven Sages of the Bamboo Grove, who removed themselves from the political turmoil of the Jin Dynasty (A.D. 265–316) to devote themselves to poetry and music, aren't drinking wine and scribbling in Luoyang anymore. Their bamboo groves have been bulldozed down.

Nevertheless, I came to Luoyang in search of history and beauty, which I hoped to find in the unaltered countryside at the Longmen caves. I checked into the Youyi Binguan, the Friendship Hotel, and ate breakfast in a hall called the Western Dancing Restaurant (its logo, two square dancers in cowboy boots). The booths, covered in orange vinyl, were too low and too deep to be comfortable. Outside, I crossed a public park, filled with trees but not a single blade of grass, and caught the no. 60 bus to the caves.

Bingyang Grottoes

The main entrance to Longmen is at the northern end of the cliff, where the road from Luoyang crosses the river. The bus stopped on the east side of the bridge and I walked back to the ticket booth. Spacious cement-and-stone walkways lead southward along the riverbanks. Railings protect the large caves. Dozens of stone figures tower over the walkway, which has the look of a petrified Macy's Thanksgiving Day parade, with the large floats and balloons turned to stone.

The first cave on the right, **Qianqi Si (Qianqi Temple),** was carved in the early Tang in A.D. 641. Buddha sits on a stone platform, draped in graceful folds. His attendants—bodhisattvas who have reached Nirvana but returned to Earth to show others the path to enlightenment—are elegantly carved female figures.

The next three works, the **Bingyang caves,** are a massive cluster with many Buddhist figures. Bingyang means "Greeting the Sun," as these east-facing monuments do. The first of the three caves is one of the earliest in Longmen, begun around A.D. 500, although many of the figures were not finished until 150 years later. The bare-chested Buddha seated in the middle of the first cave measures 24 feet tall.

The middle Bingyang cave is also among the earliest carved here. An inscription claims that 802,366 craftsmen labored on it for over 20 years. The result is a shrine containing 11 Buddhas. The magnificently robed Buddha seated at the center in the lotus position, one hand raised to Heaven, the other stretched toward the Earth, is 26 feet high. His smiling face is surrounded by a halo. Angelic creatures, the Buddhist angels known as *apsareses,* fly across the half-dome ceiling. In 1935, a large section of this cave with carvings and statues of figures adoring the Buddha was removed and shipped to the United States. Among the missing are the praying figures of the cave's patron, Northern Wei

Emperor Xuan Wu and his wife. The southern Bingyang cave is less richly adorned. It dates from the Northern Wei as well, but the Buddha at its center seems rather tired and sleepy, more weighed down than buoyant.

The Bingyang triptych is followed by the **Jingshan Si (Veneration of Goodness Temple) Cave,** carved out in the 7th century at the beginning of the Tang Dynasty. Guardians of the Buddhist faith, swords raised, are carved in relief, but they did not have the power to keep out Western art collectors who have beheaded many of the figures in this cave. It is difficult after viewing Longmen to innocently enjoy what was taken from it and placed on museum pedestals halfway around the world in the name of preservation.

Cave of Ten Thousand Buddhas

Continuing south, I reached one of Longmen's greatest treasures, **Wanfo Dong,** the aptly named Cave of Ten Thousand Buddhas. In fact, there are 15,000 small Buddhas carved into the walls of this profusely decorated cave. The ceiling itself blooms with a single vast lotus flower, inscribed with the date of its carving, A.D. 680. Each of the 54 lotuses on the back wall erupts with a bodhisattva figure in the middle. Buddha sits at the center on a lotus throne, its panels stamped and carved in the "Ten Thousand Buddha" pattern, with seated musicians below and a dancer in swirling silks. At the entrance is a headless statue of Guanyin, the Goddess of Mercy, vibrant in her pose, sweeping away the flies of life with a swatter and sprinkling the life-giving dew from a bottle. Her statue was carved in A.D. 681, as a commission of the Empress Wu Zetian.

Empress Wu ruled China at the end of the 7th century, subjugating her Tang Dynasty consort Gao Zong and pursuing her devotion to Buddhism by overseeing the construction of thousands of temples and shrines. She is known as a ruthless monarch, the leading figure in many palace intrigues and love affairs. Luoyang became her second capital (after Xi'an) and she spent much of China's treasury supporting Buddhism here, initiating many of the splendid caves and sculptures at Longmen.

Next door to the Cave of Ten Thousand Buddhas is the **Lotus Flower Cave,** which also features a flower on the ceiling. The standing Buddha has been decapitated and the forearms are missing. A fiery halo surrounds the entire body, emphasizing its divine purity. This cave is of earlier origin than its next-door neighbor to the north, having been chiseled out in A.D. 527, when the Northern Wei still held sway.

The Big Cave

The next major cave to the south is **Juxian Cave (Honoring Ancestors),** by far the largest at Longmen. The opening is 100 feet wide. The Buddha inside stands 56 feet tall. This is Empress Wu's grandest creation at Longmen, carved in A.D. 675 and paid for out of her allotment for cosmetics. The celestial guardian who defends the faith, located on the north wall, is a splendid and fierce sculpture. He carries a pagoda in his right hand and tramples a demon under his foot, his left hand defiantly planted on his waist. In her day, Empress Wu entered this shrine through the back of a wooden temple. Never humble, Empress Wu is said to have ordered the sculptor to use her face as the model for that of the colossal Buddha. Art experts consider these figures the best ever sculpted during the Tang Dynasty. They are indeed realistic figures, emanating power, highly decorated, finely detailed, and naturally posed. The large Buddha itself is serene and remote by contrast, elevated by the artist to a higher realm.

Caves of Medicine & Fire

The remaining caves to the south are small. The entrance to the **Medicine Cave (Yao Fang Dong)** is engraved with prescriptions for 120 diseases, ranging from diabetes to madness, from the pharmacies of the mid-6th century. The Buddha and his attendants inside date from several dynasties, including the Northern Wei and the Tang.

The **Guyang Cave** is the oldest cave at Longmen, newly dated at A.D. 478. The Buddha at the center lost his head along the way, but during the last dynasty, the Qing (1644–1911), it was restored. The new head is said to resemble that of the ancient founder of Daoism, Lao Zi, and the cave is locally referred to as Lao Zi's den.

The blackened **Fire-Burnt Cave (Huo Shao Dong)** next door was also carved early, about A.D. 522. It appears to have been struck by lightning. The **Stone Room Temple Cave (Shi Ku Si Dong)** has a fine adoration theme in which a procession of officials in high hats, ladies in long gowns, and court attendants carry umbrellas, fans, and lotus flowers to honor Buddha. In the last cave, Ludong, which has an inscription from A.D. 539, there are wall carvings of the halls and pavilions of the time, used to illustrate Buddha's mortal journey through life as Sakyamuni. The cave is also decorated with carvings in the halo flame design, which burns across the walls of the caves of Longmen like the morning sun.

Several hours of cave-viewing whetted my appetite. I sat down on a low stool in front of a table where two peasant ladies smiled at me as they scooped up a bowl of cold noodles topped with a hot red paste.

They were happy to have me, their only customer at noon, and they didn't even bother to ask where I was from, what I did, or how many children I had—the usual questions asked of lone foreigners. Perhaps they knew nothing of the West. A vendor joined me. A portrait photographer, he tethered his brown horse to the trunk, which contained the imperial costumes in which he decked out his customers. The sun was high and fierce. The golden ridge of Longmen turned a dismal yellow-gray, the lifeless color of the surrounding sands. I walked north to the bridge over the Dragon's Gate River. The fire that ignites this ancient gallery of gigantic Buddhas and lotus flowers has been swallowed by the throats of a thousand silent caves, and even the voice of the most powerful empress in China is drowned in the whisper of the wind that pulls the sands across the long cliff like a curtain.

PRACTICAL INFORMATION

ORIENTATION & WHEN TO GO

The Longmen caves lie 9 miles south of Luoyang, an ancient capital in Henan Province, 200 miles east of Xi'an and 550 miles west of Shanghai. The Yellow River passes about 50 miles to the north. Summers are hot and humid here. Dust storms are common in the spring. Late fall and early winter are the best times to visit.

Song Shan, the Central Mountain of the Five Sacred Mountains of China and home to the celebrated kung-fu temple at Shao Lin, is just 50 miles east of the Longmen caves. If you travel to Luoyang, the Longmen caves and Song Shan (including the Shao Lin Monastery) are musts. See the separate chapter on Song Shan.

GETTING THERE

By Plane The small airport 7 miles north of Luoyang receives several flights each week from Beijing (1 hour 40 minutes), Guangzhou (2 hours 45 minutes), and a few other cities in China. In the summer there are charter flights from Hong Kong (2 hours 20 minutes). The nearest major airport is in **Zhengzhou,** 100 miles west.

By Train Luoyang is well served by trains. Express trains arrive from Beijing (14 hours), Shanghai (18 hours), Xi'an (7 hours), and Zhengzhou (2 hours). The Zhengzhou-to-Xi'an route is served daily by a special double-decker tourist train. Taxis or minibuses from the train station to hotels cost RMB 20 to RMB 50 ($2.40 to $6).

TOURS & STRATAGEMS

The Longmen caves are a day trip from the city of Luoyang.

Admission & Hours The Longmen caves are open 8am to 6pm daily. The admission is RMB 45 ($5.50). By far the best time to view the caves, which face east, is in the morning. Arrive by 8am if possible. The rising sun illuminates the fading paint on the intricate carvings.

Tours **China International Travel Service (CITS)** has helpful branches in the Friendship Hotel, 6 Xiyuan Xi Lu (☎ 0379/491-3701), and the Peony Hotel, 15 Zhong Zhou Xi Lu (☎ 0379/491-3699). They can provide guided tours to the Longmen caves for RMB 240 to RMB 480 ($30 to $60) per person, depending on the size of the group.

On Your Own Public **buses** cover the 9-mile distance from Luoyang to the Longmen caves in 35 to 45 minutes (making many stops on the way). The fare is about RMB 10 ($1.20), depending on the exact departure point. Bus no. 60 stops by the park across from the Friendship Hotel. Bus nos. 53 and 81 also connect Luoyang to Longmen. The return route and bus numbers are the same. **Taxis** can also be hired from hotel desks or in the street. The fare is highly negotiable but should be below RMB 250 ($30) for the round-trip.

WHERE TO STAY

Five-star and four-star hotels of international quality are on the drawing board, but for now you have your pick of two three-star hotels.

Friendship Hotel (Youyi Binguan). *6 Xiyuan Xi Lu (2 miles west of city center). ☎ 0379/491-2780. Fax 0379/491-3808. 325 units. A/C TV TEL. $65 double. AE, JCB, MC, V.* This hotel dates back to the 1950s, when hotels for foreigners in China were built with help from the Russians. The four-story West Building dates from that period and is terribly rundown. Insist on staying in the newer East Building. The rooms are large but still not well maintained. The tub/shower combinations are modern. The hotel has an exercise room, an outdoor pool in the summer, bicycles for rent, and a foreign exchange counter. The uniformed staff will help arrange tours and the hire of private cars.

Peony Hotel (Mudan Dajiudian). *15 Zhong Zhou Xi Lu (1 mile west of city center). ☎ 0379/401-3699. Fax 0379/401-3668. 196 units. A/C MINIBAR TV TEL. $85 double. AE, DC, JCB, MC, V.* The 17-story Peony is more modern, better located, and a bit more luxurious than the Friendship Hotel. The rooms are smaller, but come with satellite TV and safes, and are fairly clean. There's a health club with exercise machines, a business center, a tour desk, a gift shop, and a foreign exchange counter.

Peony Plaza (Mudan Cheng Binguan). *2 Nan Cheng Lu (2 miles west of city center). ☎ 0379/493-1111. Fax 0379/493-2514. 163 units. A/C MINIBAR TV TEL. $100 double. AE, DC, JCB, MC, V.* This 26-story round tower is the flashiest and newest of the city's hotels to date, but its services and maintenance are no better than anywhere else. There are a swimming pool, fitness club, business center, travel desk, and two restaurants (Western and Chinese). The location is good, on one end of Peony Square downtown.

WHERE TO DINE

The **Friendship Hotel** (☎ 0379/491-2780) and the **Peony Hotel** (☎ 0379/401-3699) have good Chinese restaurants with English-language menus. The Peony Hotel's restaurant is more expensive ($20 to $30 per person for dinner). Western food is served at both hotels as well.

Along the main downtown street, Zhong Zhou Zhong Lu, are several restaurants that serve foreigners and provide English-language menus. Two friendly places here are the **HM** restaurant, serving Western dishes, and the **Xuangong** restaurant, serving Chinese dishes. Both charge RMB 35 to RMB 67 ($4 to $8) for main courses. The top restaurant outside of hotels is the **Ya Xiang Lou,** 2nd floor, 4 Anhui Lu, near the Friendship Hotel (☎ 0379/491-1993), with good handmade noodles and chicken dishes. Main courses cost RMB 20 to RMB 40 ($2.50 to $5). No credit cards are accepted outside the hotels. At the Longmen caves, **stalls** sell cold noodle dishes (RMB 5/60¢), soft drinks, bottled water, and tea.

Chongqing: Powerhouse of the Yangzi

重庆

Chongqing, better known to Westerners under its old name, Chungking, is a city of the future. Located well up the Yangzi River, in the steamy southwestern province of Sichuan, Chongqing has not been a favorite of tourists, who have used it mainly as an overnight stop when boarding or disembarking from Yangzi River cruises. That was how I first saw Chongqing, all in one afternoon after cruising up the Yangzi through the Three Gorges, and I did not dream of returning. But return I did, partly to sample some genuine Sichuan cuisine, partly to see the Buddhist carvings at nearby Dazu. Finding myself in the city for a few days rather than a few hours, I discovered that there was much more to Chongqing than a quick glance revealed.

Chongqing is not a romantic city, despite its reputation among Chinese as the "Capital of Mist" and the "City of Mountains." The mist today is liable to be smog; the mountains are simply steep streets winding pell-mell up and down soot-covered hills. Rather, Chongqing is a city of the moment, a city of commerce, industry, and development on a scale seen few other places on the planet. It is in every sense a gargantuan city, brimming with raw power and a thirst for the future. Among its many construction sites is one where the world's tallest building is slated to rise, outstripping recent claimants to that title in Malaysia and Shanghai.

Population & Pollution

Chongqing has a population that corresponds to its gigantic ambitions. On March 14, 1997, Chongqing became a municipality, a designation shared by only three other cities in China (Beijing, Shanghai, and Tianjin). No longer part of Sichuan Province, Chongqing is now free to handle its own affairs and finances, answering to no one but Beijing. The new Chongqing municipality extends over 14 districts, most of them downriver, where 1.3 million people face resettlement before the massive Three Gorges Dam is completed in 2013. The bottom line is that Chongqing's municipal population increased rather dramatically on March 14, 1997—to an unimaginable 30.23 million residents.

The downtown population of Chongqing, those residing in its "Manhattan," a narrowing peninsula bounded by the confluence of the Yangzi and Jialing rivers, was unchanged by redistricting. The city of Chongqing, as opposed to the municipality of Chongqing, numbers a mere three million residents, with the close suburbs north and south of the rivers contributing another 11 million.

Chongqing is also China's most polluted city. To become a beautiful place, as well as a powerful one, Chongqing will need to create environmental cleanup programs on a suitably massive scale. It has already launched a 29-part Green Program designed to reduce acid rain dramatically, and is also committed to building 300 factories to control water pollution, with half these facilities to be placed along the long reservoir created by the Three Gorges Dam. For now, Chongqing is an industrial city, a workhorse of commerce and shipping. But mere ugliness does not exclude it from being an interesting place.

Chongqing is no tourist town, and that's its attraction. If you want to see a real Chinese metropolis, all its raw edges unconcealed and building for the 21st century, this is the place, 1,500 miles upstream from Shanghai. But as much as Chongqing is China's gritty city of the future, it is also a product of its past.

Chongqing received its present name in A.D. 1190 from Emperor Zhao Dun of the Southern Song Dynasty. He had conquered this city on the Yangzi, formerly known as Yuzhou and later Gongzhou, just before he ascended to the dragon throne. Finding himself twice blessed, he named the city that was his stepping stone to power Chongqing, meaning "double celebration" or "twin fortune." That doubling of good fortune is repeating itself today, as this powerhouse of the upper Yangzi fuels the expanding economy of China and at the same time opens a new Gate to the Sky.

Industry

While in Chongqing in 1945, Premier Zhou En-lai wrote a poem beginning, "We are hoping for brightness, ten thousand miles ahead." Half a century later, this new China has begun to arrive in earnest and Chongqing is one of its chief powerhouses. Much of the material that Shanghai converts to wealth at the mouth of the Yangzi River originates upriver at Chongqing. In supplying new China with the basic products of a healthy economy—rice and grain, cotton and silk, coal, iron, and

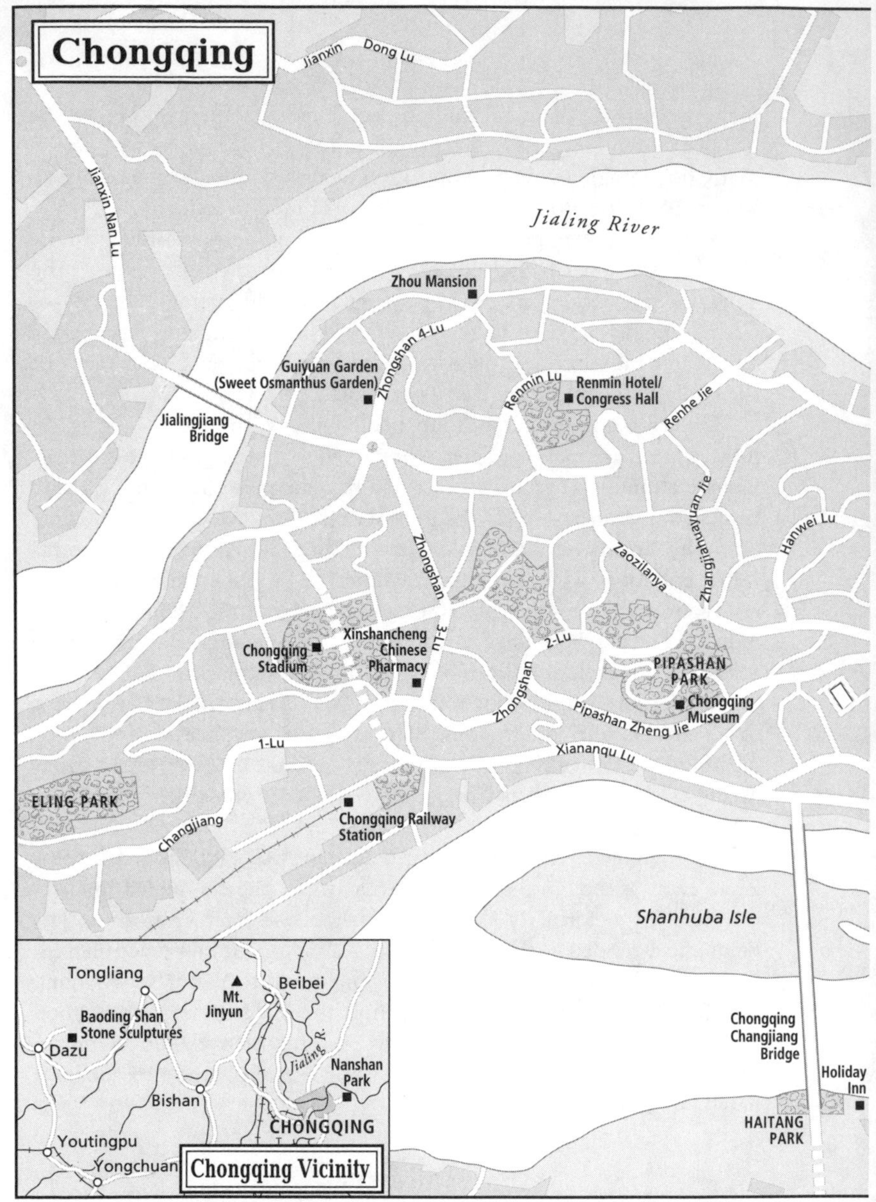

natural gas—Chongqing has become a showcase of modernization and economic development. Opened to direct foreign trade in 1979, Chongqing benefited from early programs that gave its factory managers decision-making power and the freedom to invest in expansion. In the more freewheeling economy of the 1990s, Chongqing has cashed in

on those experiments. Its integrated iron and steel complexes, oil refineries, paper plants, copper smelters, motor vehicle factories, textile mills, and chemical and cement plants are the stuff of progress. Chongqing is fast becoming the Shanghai of western China, the inland colossus of industry and trade.

Chongqing's role will inevitably expand over the next 2 decades, as the Yangzi River is itself transformed. At present, Chongqing's ability to ship its materials and products downstream is limited by the river channel. While shipping is no longer the treacherous business it was in the days of junks and trackers in harness, the Yangzi still permits no ships greater than about 3,000 tons (the size of many pleasure cruisers) to reach Chongqing. With the completion of the Three Gorges Dam (Sanxia) on the Yangzi early in this century, however, a reservoir 600 kilometers long (372 miles) will reach west to Chongqing, enabling the passage of cargo ships of more than three times the current tonnage. Along with the anticipated benefits of flood control and increased hydroelectric power in the Yangzi basin, this massive project should propel Chongqing to even greater prominence as the upper Yangzi's chief manufacturer and trader.

Evidence of Chongqing's mounting wealth is visible in its rapidly changing cityscape. Chongqing is still blanketed in river fog much of the year, its rocky hillsides so steep and numerous that the bicycle—that icon of China—is eerily absent from the streets. In fact, I didn't see a single bicycle during my last visit, not even one being pushed uphill. The alleyways caked with coal dust, the twisting avenues, and the cliffside houses with front doors on the top floors are still part of Chongqing's tough-as-nails cityscape, but shining towers of steel and glass—the skyscraper offices and apartments of a new Chongqing—are shouldering their way through the heart of the city, displacing these grim reminders of the past. Locals say that Chongqing is starting to look like Hong Kong, another hilly city built on manufacture and trade. It's no Hong Kong yet, but it's on its way.

Part of what I find interesting about Chongqing is its roughness. The very foundations of its commerce seem exposed to view, like the skeleton of a skyscraper. The curving avenues, the relentless hills, the endless construction sites, the wide rivers bubbling up with boats and ships and piers and cranes, add to its dynamic feel. Chongqing has long been a city of energy, a city of furnacelike heat in the summer, a city of shipping and freight and industrial haze. I felt its energy every time I walked its streets and steep alleys.

The Gate to Heaven

From **Liberation Monument (Jiefang Bei),** the clock tower at city center, I kept losing my bearings in this metropolis of curves, even as I enjoyed peering into its small shops filled with old scrolls, carved seals, umbrellas, and bambooware, with wool from Tibet and silks from Sichuan that once made Chongqing a port prized by European traders.

Along **Zhongshan Lu** I passed cafes featuring skewers of meat and vegetables awaiting a dunking in hot oil—the sidewalk version of Chongqing's most celebrated dish, hot pot *(huo guo),* which is given more elaborate treatment in the city's best restaurants and hotels. Down **Shangqing Lu** there are outdoor food markets with tea-smoked duck and bite-sized baozi, and after dark, street fairs with still more food and merchandise.

At the eastern tip of the city, where the Yangzi and Jialing rivers converge, I explored the number one urban sight in Chongqing: the **Gate to the Sky (Chaotianmen),** and its docks, linked to the city by black cliffs that run 300 steps up and down. Here the *ban ban jin,* the porters with cargo strapped to their backs or suspended from bamboo poles across their shoulders, hike the 300 cliffside stairs to and from the mudflats and wharves. During World War II, when Chongqing's population swelled as eastern China fell to the Japanese and China's capital moved here, the American General Joseph Stilwell occupied a house high on these flanks above the miserable cantilevered tenements that still survive. Cable cars are strung across both rivers like tourist banners. The northern terminal is a gray cement tower serviced by a wobbly elevator (with an attendant). I rode the dilapidated contraption back and forth (RMB 1.2/14¢ each way), standing up (there were no seats), a bit terrified but awed by the view. It's a cable car ride over a half-mile-wide wilderness of iron and steel, barges and freighters, oil and fire. In a gritty way, this is the essence of Chongqing, the beauty in the marrow of a naked city.

Large bridges connect the downtown peninsula of Chongqing with the north and south shores, and rattling steel ferries, without seats or benches, deliver far more workers than the cable cars ever could.

At the turn of this century, Chongqing was still a backwater, a walled city enclosing barely 250,000 inhabitants. Between 1937 and 1946, when it served as China's wartime capital, the population tripled and new agencies, industries, and educational institutions poured in from throughout China. Chongqing never looked back. The Qing Dynasty city walls came down. An industrial capital took root. Today, a new superhighway runs along the downtown shore and a subway is nearing completion.

Pipashan

The full panorama of this increasingly modern industrial megacity unfolds below **Pipashan Park** on Loquat Hill, at over 1,000 feet the highest point in the city. Weary of more hill walking and doubtful that I could find the way, I hired a taxi to deliver me to the park gate. I still had to walk up a long hill to the summit. There, a teahouse pavilion, or **Hongxing,** rises from garden terraces, a favorite haunt of retired men intent upon card games. There's also a circular monorail, crude and rusting away; its passengers ride the rail on attached bicycles. But it's the view that consumes one's attention. To the north is the Yangzi; to the south, the Jialing—massive rivers, apparent equals from this perspective, meeting at the Chaotianmen docks, the gate to the sky, where the long peninsula of downtown Chongqing tapers to a forked point poised to strike like the head of a fire-breathing dragon.

As it was nearly dusk, I waited for the sunset, which got lost in the smudgy horizon. But I was glad that I waited. After dark, the view from Pipashan Park is far more dramatic. Ignited by the beacons of office, highway, and factory, Chongqing becomes an island winging through the rivers of heaven, an enchanted foundry floating on the arms of two great rivers.

Chongqing Museum

The next morning I headed back downtown. On the south side of Pipashan is the Chongqing Museum (☎ 023/6385-3533), an antiquated repository of artifacts. Chongqing is supposed to be a city without relics or treasures, without refined Chinese legacies, but the museum offers glints of a deeper, richer past. Human history stretches back 3,000 years in Chongqing, to the days of the Ba Kingdom, when nobles were buried in large wooden boats suspended from the river cliffs. Two of these maritime coffins are now suspended in the Chongqing Museum, as is a major collection of Han Dynasty tomb-bricks, their carvings depicting the courtyards and chariots of 2,000 years ago. There's also a dull display of dinosaur eggs and skeletons, as well as a modern art gallery where artists push their works for sale. The museum is a clunky warehouse, poorly lighted and dilapidated. By the time I left, kids on school field trips were at least adding some high-spirited laughter and chatter to its dark, staid chambers. The museum is open daily from 9am to 5:30pm; admission is RMB 5 (65¢).

Luohan Temple

The brightest sight in downtown Chongqing is Luohan Si, a Buddhist temple that dates from A.D. 1000. It is one of the most active temples in China. At the busy intersection outside its entry gate, the sidewalks are filled with Chinese visitors, local Buddhists, and blind fortune-tellers. Inside the gate, a long, narrow entryway is flanked with rock carvings—shrines where dozens of worshippers kneel, burn incense, and pray.

Within the pavilions are modern clay statues of the 500 arhats, Buddhist followers who have reached the first state of enlightenment. Behind a large golden likeness of the Buddha is a mural depicting Siddhartha, the living Buddha, as he cuts his hair to renounce the world. The temple looks far older than it is, having been thoroughly reconstructed after the ravages of World War II, but the sheer activity within gives it an unmistakable air of authenticity. This is no tourist trap; it's an island of Old China, bobbing in an ocean of modern commerce and construction. You can visit the temple every day from dawn to dusk; admission is RMB 10 ($1.25).

PRACTICAL INFORMATION

ORIENTATION

Chongqing is located in southeastern Sichuan Province, far inland on the upper Yangzi River. The chief attraction for sightseers is **Dazu,** an ancient grotto of Buddhist carvings to the west that makes for an excellent day trip (see separate chapter).

GETTING THERE

By Plane The **Jiangbei Airport** (☎ 023/6683-1120), serving many cities in China, is 18 miles from the city center, but allow an hour for the RMB 150 ($18) taxi ride. **Dragonair,** serving Hong Kong, has offices in the Holiday Inn, 15 Nanping Bei Lu (☎ 023/6281-7434). The CAAC airport **shuttle bus** (RMB 15/$1.90) leaves every half-hour from 6am to 6pm; its city terminal is at 161 Zhongshan San Lu (☎ 023/6360-3223.

By Train The railway and bus stations are located on Nanqu Lu in southwestern Chongqing, near the Yangzi River. The train from Shanghai or Beijing can take up to 50 hours; you're better off flying.

By Bus Luxury buses, quite comfortable, now connect Chongqing to Chengdu, Sichuan's capital, 4 hours and 200 miles away via the Chengyu Expressway. The cost is RMB 120 to RMB 200 ($15 to $25). Book through your hotel.

By Ship Many visitors arrive at the wharves of Chongqing after a Yangzi River cruise upriver from Wuhan. From there, it's best to take a taxi to a hotel, although you can reach the city by walking upriver to a local ferry and crossing over to the downtown peninsula. Taxis should cost RMB 15 to RMB 25 ($2 to $3.50).

TOURS & STRATAGEMS

If you are arriving or departing by cruise ship, particularly by **Victoria Cruises,** 3rd floor, 3 Xinhua Lu (☎ 023/6381-5260), its Chongqing office can usually arrange a tour of the city. **China International Travel Service (CITS)** is located inside the Renmin Hotel, 173 Renmin Lu (☎ 023/6385-0188; fax 023/6385-0095). Your best bet if you travel independently is your hotel tour desk.

WHERE TO STAY

A number of international-level hotels have opened in the last few years, with more on the way, including the **Chongqing Marriott,** 77 Qing Nian Lu (☎ 023/6388-8888; fax 023/6388-8777).

Harbour Plaza Chongqing (Hai Yi Fandian). *Wuyi Lu (downtown, east of Liberation Monument). ☎ 023/6370-0888. Fax 023/6370-0778. 390 units. A/C MINIBAR TV TEL. $175 double. AE, DC, JCB, MC, V.* This fairly new (1997) five-star luxury hotel has a great downtown location (next to deluxe shopping on the city's new pedestrian mall) and some of the spiffiest facilities in Chongqing. The two-story marble lobby and wood panel halls lead to large rooms done in bright greens and golds. This is currently Chongqing's most lavish and most expensive hotel. It's managed by a Hong Kong firm.

Amenities: Large indoor swimming pool, fitness club, sauna, Jacuzzi, tennis courts, bowling alley, ice rink, business center, concierge, valet, 24-hour room service, same-day dry cleaning and laundry, nightly turndown, tour desk, beauty salon, shopping arcade, airport shuttle.

Renmin Hotel (Renmin Binguan). *173 Renmin Lu. ☎ 023/6385-1421. Fax 023/6385-2076. 250 units. A/C TV TEL. $75 double. JCB, MC, V.* This landmark hotel, built in the Russian style in 1953, connects directly to the Nationalist Congress Hall, a monumental edifice that resembles the Temple of Heaven in Beijing and is frequently visited by tourists. Its best feature is its downtown location. The rooms are large, but maintenance and service are not up to international levels. The East Wing has modern and fairly clean rooms. The coffee shop serves some Western food and the staff speaks a bit of English.

Wanyou Conifer Hotel (Wanyou Fandian). *77 Changjiang Er Lu (5 miles west of downtown). ☎ 800/528-1234 or 023/6871-888. Fax 023/6871-3333. 379 units. A/C MINIBAR TV TEL. $100 double. AE, DC, JCB, MC, V.* Managed by Best Western and opened in 1998, this 30-story reflective-glass tower has luxurious rooms (with work desks, safes, satellite TV) and good Sichuan, Cantonese, and Western restaurants. The place caters to foreign business travelers. It has the best room-rate specials in town, so inquire through Best Western before booking.

Amenities: Fitness club, sauna, billiards, business center, concierge, valet, 24-hour room service, same-day dry cleaning and laundry, tour desk, beauty salon, newsstand, shuttle bus.

Yangtze Chongqing Holiday Inn (Yangzi Jiang Jia Ri Jiudian). *15 Nanping Bei Lu. ☎ 800/465-4329 or 023/6280-3380. Fax 023/6280-0884. 379 units. A/C MINIBAR TV TEL. $135 double. AE, DC, JCB, MC, V.* Although located well east of downtown, the four-star, 21-story Holiday Inn is the most experienced international-level hotel in town and the best managed. The staff speaks English. The spacious, modern rooms offer 30-channel satellite TV, coffeemakers, robes and slippers, and free local calls. The 16th-floor Executive Club (rooms $160) has its own lounge. The 12th and 13th floors are nonsmoking. Both the Western and Sichuan restaurants offer excellent food. This is the hotel where expatriate businesspeople live and relax in Chongqing.

Amenities: Outdoor swimming pool, fitness club, putting green, sauna, tennis courts, billiards, business center, concierge, valet, baby-sitting, 24-hour room service, same-day dry cleaning and laundry, nightly turndown, tour desk, beauty salon, deli, shopping arcade.

WHERE TO DINE

Sichuan food, spicy and authentic, should not be missed. In Chongqing, it's impossible not to run into a local streetside **hot-pot restaurant;** on every block, there are two or three, and you can't miss them. Ordering is easy. Just ask for "huo guo" (pronounced "hwo gwo"). You'll be served raw vegetables and meats that you cook in a pot of boiling oil at your table.

Golden Sand. *15 Nanping Bei Lu (lobby of Holiday Inn). ☎ 023/6280-3380. Reservations recommended. Main courses $5–$12. AE, DC, JCB, MC, V. Daily 11:30am–2:30pm and 5:30–9:30pm. SICHUAN.* This is among the best Sichuan restaurants in town. The hot-pot items are simmered in a divided pot—one part containing spicier oil than the other. Seating is in private rooms with round tables or in a larger dining area.

Western Choices The Holiday Inn also has an excellent German bistro, the **Bierstube,** open daily 6:30 to 11:30pm, with authentic German food and drinks in an intimate setting; and Western-style barbecues, seafood, and Italian dishes nightly in the **Sunset Grill,** open daily 6:30pm to midnight.

Inexpensive Choices Inside the **Luohan Temple,** there's a vegetarian restaurant with very inexpensive noodles and tofu dishes (open for lunch only, 11:30am to 2pm). And on the streets surrounding the Holiday Inn, there are several Western-style **coffeehouses** with international dishes, such as spaghetti, at reasonable prices.

DAZU CAVES: THE WHEEL OF LIFE

大足

OVER THE CENTURIES BUDDHIST pilgrims who journeyed to the holiest shrines in Western China obeyed a famous dictum: "Go up to Emei Shan, go down to Baoding Shan." Emei Shan is one of Buddhism's four sacred mountains, while Baoding Shan (Precious Mountain) at Dazu is one of China's four great centers of Buddhist sculpture. These sacred carvings are located in Sichuan Province in western China, in Dazu District, about halfway between the cities of Chengdu and Chongqing. Dazu is not a convenient location for the traveler, but its countryside remoteness is part of its attraction. Moreover, for anyone fascinated by the monumental remnants of Old China, of which so few survive, Dazu and its Baoding Shan sculptures are a must.

Baoding Shan possesses the best of the sacred carvings in Dazu, containing about 10,000 of the over 50,000 religious sculptures scattered throughout this highland district. Compared with the three other major rock carvings in China (those at Dunhuang, Louyang, and Datong), the Dazu specimens are of the most recent composition and are arranged in the most compact arena for viewing. This concentration of thousands of carved images within a natural amphitheater enhances the visual intensity of Dazu. Dazu's carvings are also the most realistic of the great holy sculptures, the least abstract and rigid, the most earthy and human, with the broadest social context.

While rock carving began in Dazu during the Tang Dynasty (in the 7th century A.D.) and continued well into the Qing Dynasty (China's last imperial epoch), the sculptures here reached their artistic zenith during the Southern Song Dynasty (1127–1279), when the sculptors turned their attention to creating the unusually unified, compact, and colorful Buddhist grotto at Dazu's Baoding Shan.

Great Buddha Crescent

A friend and I set out for Dazu early one morning from Chongqing. We hired a local taxi for the 70-mile journey, which despite the good roads

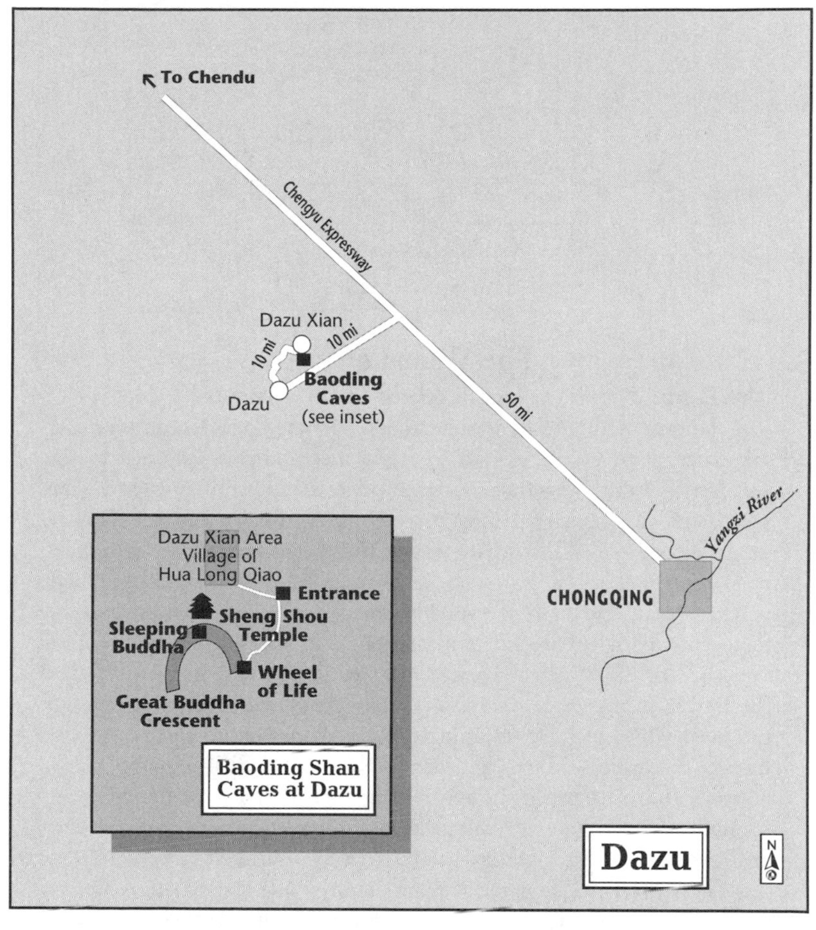

consumed almost 3 hours in either direction. At Dazu Xian, we parked in the village of **Hua Long Qiao (Dragon Flower Bridge)** and walked to the grotto entrance. The main gate and temple are set on a ridge above a stream. On the other side of the gate, worshippers were burning incense while kneeling before small images in rock alcoves. Below us the pathway to the Buddhist grottoes wound downward into a lush river valley.

Zhao Zhifeng, a monk well versed in Tantric (Esoteric) Buddhism, launched this last great venture in outdoor religious sculpture more than 7 centuries ago. The work required 70 years to complete. The setting Zhao Zhifeng selected is dramatic enough: a horse-shaped gully a third of a mile long with sheer cliffs towering up to 90 feet high. Known as the **Great Buddha Crescent (Da Fu Wan),** it is a natural grotto, hidden in the folds of misty mountains and terraced slopes below a sleepy village and above a meandering stream.

As we descended into the Great Buddha Crescent at Dazu, we could see several temples towering overhead. The oldest, **Sheng Shou Si,** was built by Zhao Zhifeng himself in 1179 (and last rebuilt in 1684 during the reign of Qing Emperor Kangxi). This temple is still active, but most visitors are drawn directly down steep stone stairs into the crescent of cliffs where the carvings were completed in 1249.

The Wheel of Life

The Tantric Buddhism long practiced at Dazu is noted for its use of incantations, meditations, and mandalas. Mandalas are diagrams of cosmic forces used by the devout to attain instantaneous union with the Buddha, and these mandalas surge through the crescent as a prominent motif, surfacing most strikingly at **The Wheel of Life,** the exquisite figure in niche no. 3. This ornate wheel of life and death, carved in relief from solid rock, is supported from beneath by tiny human attendants and gripped in the teeth of a superhuman monster, representative of the forces of death in life. The master artisan Zhao Zhifeng occupies the center of the wheel; above him is a pavilion of the Western Paradise, the Buddhist heaven beyond the mortal sphere. The outer two rings of the great wheel teem with animals living, dying, and being born, portraying the cycles of birth and death. Ribbons of divine figures ripple outward from the turning wheel. Altogether, it is a dynamic phantasmagoria on the theme of reincarnation, unlike any other figure I've ever encountered in China, and by itself worth the journey to Dazu.

The Wheel of Life is the starting point on one side of this sculpture garden, a section dominated by carvings of the leading deities of Buddhism. In niche no. 8 (the caves are scrupulously numbered), there is a 1,000-arm **Guanyin (Goddess of Mercy),** an all-seeing eye carved into each of her open palms. The many arms represent Guanyin's almost unlimited capacity to reach out and help others; the many eyes, her ability to see every aspect of life with compassion. Encompassing 88 square yards of the recess, this wheel of mercy is the largest representation of its kind in China.

Sleeping Buddha

The keynote sculpture at Dazu, however, and one of the most famous in China, is the Sleeping Buddha at the midpoint of the crescent. Here, on a grand yet serene scale, the entrance of the historical Buddha, Sakyamuni, into Nirvana is rendered in a dreamscape. The Sleeping Buddha unites the formal devotional aspects that characterize older Buddhist grottoes in China with the more down-to-earth, human elements that set Dazu apart. Here, in the bow of the Great Buddha

Crescent, Prince Sakyamuni reclines on his right side, his back disappearing into stone. The carving measures 96 feet head-to-knees, forming a backdrop for a splendid ensemble of life-sized, lifelike attendants (bodhisattvas and officials in hats) who wade waist-deep through a river of stone in which their prince sleeps the unearthly sleep of the enlightened. The attendants flow gently to and fro before this magnified figure, facing different directions and expressing their individual devotion. They are dwarfed by a divinity so near he can be touched.

The art at Dazu is dynamic and naturalistic, the figures lively and fluid. The niches alternate between acts of devotion and flourishes of storytelling. Not far from the Sleeping Buddha is niche no. 12, **Nine Dragons Bathing the Prince,** depicting the baby Buddha being bathed in a fountain. Water drips into the bathing pool from the mouth of the lowest of nine carved dragons. Farther on are the most populous and lifelike galleries, where thousands of figures adorned in bright colors line tiers on the cliff walls. In **niche no. 15,** the common masses are devoted not to worship but to carrying out the mundane principles of parental care and filial piety. These are among the central themes of native Confucianism. Buddhism, transplanted from India, was clearly having to adapt to Chinese ways.

Heaven, Earth & Hell

The scenes of childbirth, nursing, and nurturing carved in relief at Dazu are unlike any of the representations at the other major Buddhist sculpture shrines in China. At Dazu, these carvings resemble three dimensional comic strips complete with engraved captions. A devoted mother washes her infant's clothes. A father offers a peach to the babe nestled in his arms. Century-old parents watch over their 80-year-old child.

In another colossal comic strip devoted to filial piety in **niche no. 17,** Prince Sakyamuni returns to repay the kindness his parents showed him as a child by now offering his own arm as nourishment. This story is an adaptation of an episode from the Confucian canon's *Twenty-four Examples of Filial Piety,* in which a daughter-in-law is celebrated for her extreme devotion when during a famine she cuts off a finger to feed her elderly parents-in-law. At Dazu, in other words, Buddhism and Confucianism are finally fused.

These family scenes are succeeded by two vast tiered niches whose theme is decidedly more grim: portrayals of the **Final Judgment.** One niche promises elevation from the cycles of death and rebirth to a higher consciousness. **Niche no. 21,** however, illustrates the other side, concentrating on the tortures of the damned. Evil-doers are tormented by monsters, hideous machinery, and an unending waterfall of freezing ice in panels reminiscent of the gruesome visions of Hieronymus Bosch or Aw Boon Haw. Numerous transgressions (more Confucian than Buddhist, perhaps) are dramatized. A drunken husband fails to recognize his wife; a drunken father fails to recognize his son; and a drunken elder sister fails to recognize her younger sister. Even a gentle, beatific farm woman, benignly feeding her chickens, is here consigned to the lower depths, presumably because she will violate Buddhist prohibitions against the slaughter of animals and the eating of meat.

A few of these large stone panels are more formal, peopled with religious figures and worshippers. The tiers of niche no. 22 and the walls of the **Cave of Full Enlightenment,** at niche no. 29, are lined with traditional Buddhist figures, some fierce, some benign. The deep influences of Indian art rise to the surface, reflections of the venerable achievements at the Longmen or Mogao sculpture troves. But it is the new style of the Song masters that distinguishes Dazu. In **niche no. 30,** at the tip of the crescent opposite The Wheel of Life, the themes are worldly and entirely indigenous: oxen-raising and cattle-herding. Farmers, displayed in 10 continuous groupings, lovingly tend their beasts and share a genuine comradeship. These scenes of rural life are translated by the devout as symbolic representations of religious obedience and the taming of one's own animal nature, but for the secular tourist the outstanding elements in these countryside idylls are earthbound and sensuous. In the Song Dynasty, religious sculpture becomes increasingly natural and worldly, more Confucian and more Chinese—hence, the popular saying that at Dazu's Baoding Shan Buddhism becomes "Chinese pure and simple." This type of art—spiritual yet natural, formal yet human—reached its most expansive expression at Baoding Shan.

Nirvana in Stone

After a few hours of viewing the cliffside gallery, we hiked back up to the village and asked our taxi driver to join us for lunch. She selected one of the unnamed indoor-outdoor shanty cafes. The family that owned the business and lived in its back rooms set to work chopping up the vegetables and preparing the trout that we would soon be dipping fresh and raw into a boiling pot of oil—a rural Sichuan hot pot that proved to be hearty and nourishing and (because we were presumed to be wealthy foreigners) undoubtedly overpriced at RMB 50 ($6) per person, including all the tea and local beer we could consume. We didn't mind the price. We were interested in watching the family prepare our meal in the kitchen at the back of the house, which lacked plumbing, and in the life on the village streets where the children ran up and down the hills rolling metal wheels with long pokers. The wheels were seldom wholly round, but several of the children were quite deft at keeping them rolling despite the bumps, holes, and assorted obstacles on the streets.

After lunch we walked the village and took another look down on the Great Buddha Crescent, with its otherworldly art, painted in vibrant reds and blues, and its dreaming Buddha at odds not only with the modern Western world from which we'd come but with the simple, poor village above. Here indeed is the "precious summit" of a monumental Buddhist sculpture that permeated and enriched China for a thousand years and ended at Baoding Shan, where its receding image now sleeps in a Nirvana of stone.

PRACTICAL INFORMATION

ORIENTATION & WHEN TO GO

The Baoding Shan Rock Carvings are located in Dazu County, Sichuan Province, a 3-hour drive from Chongqing via the new Chengyu Expressway that connects Chengdu and Chongqing. Dazu is a day trip from **Chongqing,** which is located in southwest China 650 miles from Beijing, 1,500 miles upstream on the Yangzi River from Shanghai.

Summers are extremely hot and humid in the whole region, making spring and autumn the best seasons to travel. Even winters are not too chilly a time to visit the rock carvings, although the days are short and heavy fog is common.

GETTING THERE

There is no air or rail service to Dazu. Travelling by tour bus or hired car, the turnoff to Dazu is at milepost 257. The Expressway, a four-lane toll road in excellent condition, exacts RMB 40 ($5) per car if you're coming from Chongqing.

TOURS & STRATAGEMS

Guided trips to Baoding Shan can be arranged at the travel desk of the **Yangtze Chongqing Holiday Inn,** 15 Nanping Bei Lu (☎ 023/280-3380), for RMB 500 to RMB 1,500 ($60 to $180) per person, depending on the number of people in your group (from one to six). Prices are roughly the same at the **Chongqing CITS,** 63 Zaozi Lanya Lu (☎ 023/6531-5294).

You can hire a **taxi** for the day for about RMB 800 ($100) total, negotiating the price yourself on the street. The taxi driver will not speak English and will not serve as a guide.

The **admission** at Dazu's Baoding Grottoes is RMB 50 ($6) per person plus RMB 10 ($1.25) to park the car. **Books in English** about the Dazu sculptures can be purchased in the village at the grotto entrance. Books can be most helpful because the signs beside the various sculptures are in Chinese only, although the grotto numbers are rendered in English.

WHERE TO STAY

Dazu is a day trip from **Chongqing.** See the Chongqing chapter for lodging choices there. The best place to stay near Dazu is the **Dazu Guesthouse (Dazu Binguan),** 47 Gong Long Lu, in the town of Longgangzhen, Dazu County (☎ 023/4372-1888; fax 023/4372-2827), which is about 10 miles south of the Baoding Shan site. This small hotel (133 rooms) is not perfectly kept or furnished, but it has modern three-star rooms, a fitness center, a good Chinese restaurant, and the offices of the Dazu CITS (☎ 023/4372-2245). This is a good base from which to explore Dazu's many other Buddhist carving sites, including nearby Bei Shan and Shimen Shan. Doubles cost $30 to $45; no credit cards are accepted.

WHERE TO DINE

If you don't want to risk lunch in a village cafe, be sure to come with your own picnic goodies, purchased the night before in Chongqing. Bottled water, soft drinks, and beer are readily available from street vendors in Dazu.

Chengdu: Home of the Panda

成都

A massive statue of Chairman Mao Zedong still presides over downtown Chengdu, the capital of the southwest province of Sichuan. Such monuments were a fixture in all the cities of China up until the Great Helmsman's death in 1976. With the rise of Deng Xiaoping and the economic reforms that transformed China from egalitarian communism into a kind of capitalistic socialism, Mao's image came down, statue by statue—but not in Chengdu. In Chengdu, Mao still gazes southward to the Jin River from his stairway pedestal at Exhibition Hall, where Renmin (People's) streets North, South, East, and West converge. He has become a traffic landmark, a city center beacon for anyone who navigates the big streets and small lanes of the city, a monument to mapmaking rather than politics.

Renmin Nan Lu (South People's Street), a boulevard of shiny modern hotels, shops, and billboards (one of them, at the bridge, a massive electronic TV screen), runs half a mile from Mao's feet to the Jin (Brocade) River. South of the river on the road to the airport there's an American-style subdivision of villas where there were dusty fields a decade ago. Today, billboards promote it as a middle-class paradise.

Yet Chengdu is still crisscrossed by winding streets of century-old shophouses where the merchandise hasn't changed since the age of emperors. Nor has the fiery Sichuan cuisine, preserved in Chengdu as nowhere else. Chengdu is one of China's most colorful big cities, always a delight to explore. And it is the home, too, of China's most famous animal, the giant panda.

Teahouses & Temples

It's best to begin getting a feel for Chengdu early, by 8am, with a stop at one of the outdoor teahouses on the north bank of the Jin River. Many of China's last great teahouses still operate here, recalling the Three Kingdoms era (A.D. 221–263), when Chengdu was the capital of the Kingdom of Chu and the scholar-officials gathered for conversation,

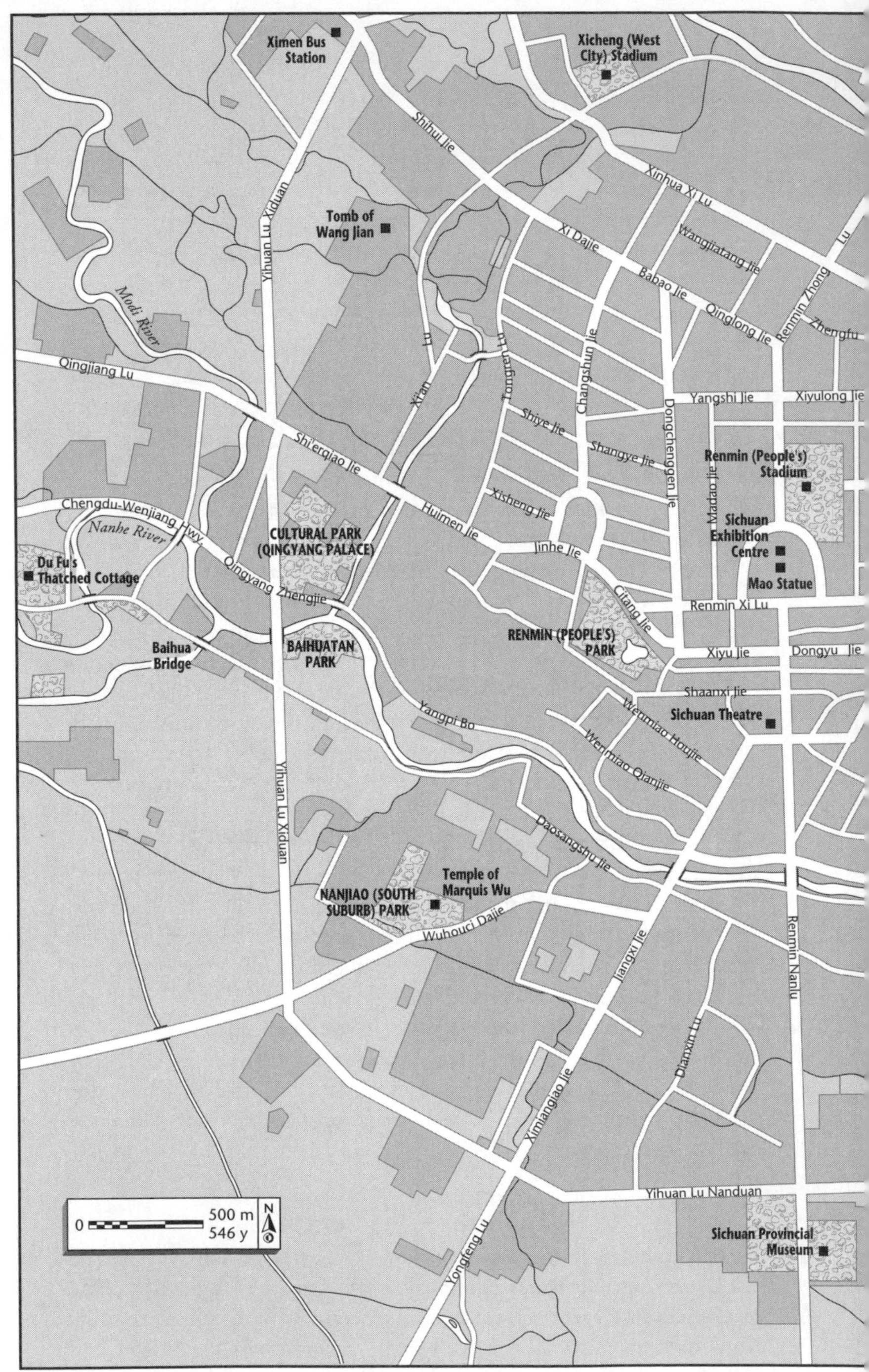
Ximen Bus Station
Xicheng (West City) Stadium
Shihui Jie
Xinhua Xi Lu
Tomb of Wang Jian
Yihuan Lu Xiduan
Xi Dajie
Wangjiatang Jie
Babao Jie
Qinglong Jie
Renmin Zhong
Zhengfu
Modi River
Qingjiang Lu
Xi'an Lu
Tongren Lu
Changshun Jie
Dongchenggen Jie
Yangshi Jie
Xiyulong Jie
Shi'erqiao Jie
Shiye Jie
Shangye Jie
Renmin (People's) Stadium
Madao Jie
Chengdu-Wenjiang Hwy.
Nanhe River
Xisheng Jie
Huimen Jie
Sichuan Exhibition Centre
CULTURAL PARK (QINGYANG PALACE)
Jinhe Jie
Du Fu's Thatched Cottage
Qingyang Zhengjie
Citang Jie
Mao Statue
Renmin Xi Lu
RENMIN (PEOPLE'S) PARK
Baihua Bridge
BAIHUATAN PARK
Xiyu Jie
Dongyu Jie
Shaanxi Jie
Sichuan Theatre
Yangpi Bo
Wenmiao Houjie
Wenmiao Qianjie
Yihuan Lu Xiduan
Daosangshu Jie
Temple of Marquis Wu
NANJIAO (SOUTH SUBURB) PARK
Wuhouci Dajie
Jiangxi Jie
Renmin Nanlu
Dianxin Lu
Ximiangiao Jie
Yihuan Lu Nanduan
0
500 m
546 y
N
Sichuan Provincial Museum
Yongfeng Lu

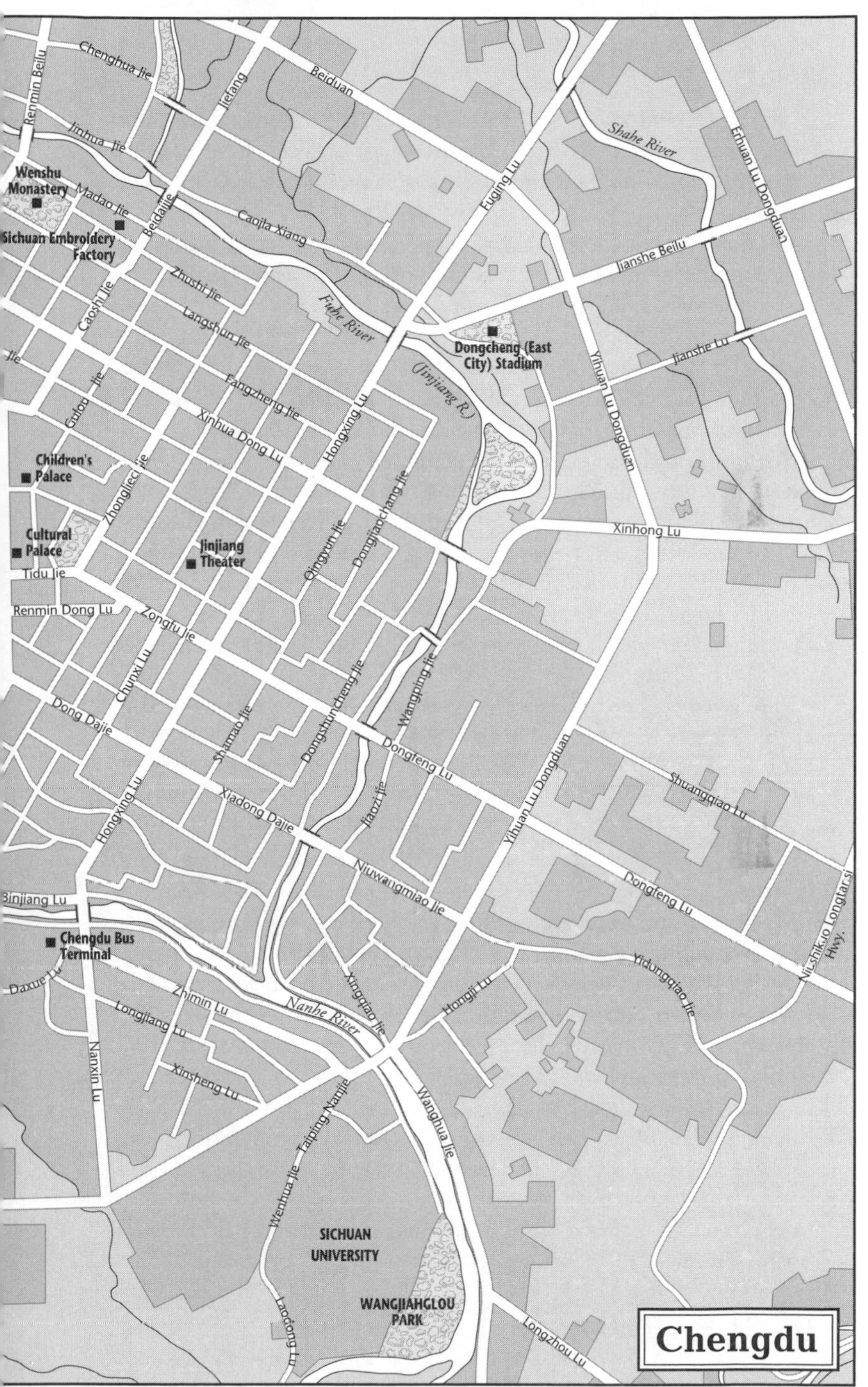
Chengdu
Chenghua Jie
Renmin Beilu
Jiefang
Beiduan
Jinhua Jie
Wenshu Monastery
Madao Jie
Sichuan Embroidery Factory
Beidajie
Caojia Xiang
Zhushi Jie
Langshun Jie
Caoshi Jie
Fuhe River
(Jinjiang R.)
Fuqing Lu
Shahe River
Erhuan Lu Dongduan
Jianshe Beilu
Jianshe Lu
Dongcheng (East City) Stadium
Yihuan Lu Dongduan
Fangzheng Jie
Xinhua Dong Lu
Hongxing Lu
Gulou Jie
Children's Palace
Zhonglieci Jie
Cultural Palace
Jinjiang Theater
Qingyun Jie
Dongjiaochang Jie
Xinhong Lu
Tidu Jie
Renmin Dong Lu
Zongfu Jie
Chunxi Lu
Dongshuncheng Jie
Wangping Jie
Dong Dajie
Shamao Jie
Dongfeng Lu
Shuangqiao Lu
Xiadong Dajie
Jiaozi Jie
Niuwangmiao Jie
Binjiang Lu
Chengdu Bus Terminal
Daxue Lu
Zhimin Lu
Longjiang Lu
Nanhe River
Xingqiao Jie
Hongji Lu
Yidungqiao Jie
Xinsheng Lu
Nanxin Lu
Taiping Nanjie
Wanghua Jie
Wenhua Jie
SICHUAN UNIVERSITY
WANGJIAHGLOU PARK
Laodong Lu
Longzhou Lu
Hwy.

entertainment, and drink at cafes along the river. Perhaps the most famous figure to frequent these cafes of leisure was the Tang poet Du Fu, who composed several hundred poems to the "Brocade City" where he lived in exile.

Du Fu's cottage, his home in Chengdu, has survived as a park and tourist attraction, but unless you are a scholar of Chinese poetry, there's no reason to visit. I did so some years ago and the visit was not memorable. The park did not come into existence until 3 centuries after Du Fu arrived in Chengdu (A.D. 759) and there is nothing belonging to him here, certainly not the rather recently constructed thatched hut. The cottage is open daily from 9am to 5pm; admission is RMB 30 ($3.75).

Wuhou Temple houses the memorial hall of Zhuge Liang, China's greatest military strategist and gentleman-scholar, who lived in Chengdu during the time of the Chu rulers 17 centuries ago. However, a visit here is likewise not worth pursuing, unless of course you happen to be imbued with the literature of the Three Kingdoms and the heroic deeds of Zhuge Liang. Otherwise, keep to the streets of Chengdu, its teahouses and temples. The hall is open daily from 9am to 5pm; admission is RMB 30 ($3.75).

I preferred to start in Chengdu by seating myself in a bamboo armchair at one of the **river teahouses,** chosen at random, where I was quickly served a cup of flower tea. The cup includes a cover to keep the brew hot and an upturned saucer for lifting. To sip tea properly, grip the saucer in thumb and fingers while slipping the lid slightly back with the raised index finger. It takes practice to become a skilled Chengdu tea drinker. For an investment of 50¢, customers can linger for hours.

Vendors drifted through, hawking trinkets and sticks to clean the ears. Ear cleaning is a passion in Chengdu. Downriver, *tai ji quan* masters and other early risers were finishing up their exercises on the mist-laden promenade. Tobacco salesmen were also at work on the sidewalks, selling strong, thick sheaves that are meant to be trimmed and stuffed in the tiny bowls of bamboo-stemmed pipes.

I then stopped for breakfast at the Long Chao Shou Special Restaurant a few blocks north of the river, partaking of the "little eats" (*xiao chi*—dim sum pastries and dumplings) that make up the traditional morning snacks of Sichuan.

After a snack, I waved down a cab on the street and paid a call on **Wenshu Temple,** a mile north of the Mao statue. It's open daily 8am to 5pm; admission is RMB 5 (65¢). Wenshu, the center of Chan (Zen) Buddhism in Chengdu, was founded 13 centuries ago. Today, it is the city's most popular Buddhist retreat, nearly always crammed with families burning incense and bowing to Wenshu (God of Wisdom), Maitreya (Laughing Buddha of the Future), and Guanyin (Goddess of

Mercy). The five great halls are drenched in incense. The carved eaves, doors, columns, and wooden figures are particularly fine work. In fact, the monastery maintains an outdoor courtyard where craftsmen work all day under an awning carving religious statuary for use at the temple and for sale to the public. The wood-carvers don't mind if you watch. Many are young apprentices, happy to practice their English.

Wenshu's oldest hall contains images of 17 generations of abbots, duly worshipped by a large number of monks. This is an extremely active temple. Here I met an 86-year-old man named Nansheng. He became a Buddhist monk at age 16 in Shaanxi Province (the next province north). Wenshu had been his residence since 1966. Now extremely frail, Nansheng spends much of his time sitting on benches, counseling the younger monks, and napping. A number of temple volunteers, mostly older women, tend to his daily needs, fetching his rice bowl and washing his clothing.

Wenshu maintains its own outdoor teahouse in a garden court shaded by ginkgo trees and its own vegetarian restaurant located inside a hall that is always jammed for lunch. The street at the entrance, Wenshu Yuan Jie, is a **temple market** with a medieval look, clotted with stalls selling prayer beads, holy medallions, incense, and firecrackers, not to mention shoe soles, underwear, and bottled water. After looking through the stalls, I crossed town by taxi, stopping a mile west of the Mao statue at Chengdu's most popular Daoist temple.

Qingyang Gong (Green Goat Temple) is as lively a place of worship as the Buddhist shrine. Most Chinese who worship at one of these temples will in fact call on the other, thereby doubling their chances that some god will grant their wish. Qingyang's main temple, the Hall of the Three Purities, is decorated in brightly painted dragons. The bronze statues of the two "good luck" goats at the altar have been showered in coins and rubbed smooth by the hands of hopeful worshippers. Golden statues of the Three Purities—the Jade Emperor of Heaven, the god of the North Pole, and Lao Zi, founder of Daoism—are the focus of continuous bowing and chanting. I walked inside while seven monks and three nuns were conducting a formal service. They were chanting to the sounds of drums and bells. Four very poor peasants in front of me, their clothes turning to rags, were completely prostrate, almost speaking in tongues, echoing every note of the rites fervidly.

Eating Fire

Across the street from Qingyang Gong I decided to try the Sichuan specialties of the **Chen Ma Po Dou Fu Restaurant,** named for the quintessential spicy dish of the region. Fiery *doufu* (bean curd) is at the heart of Sichuan cookery. *Mapo doufu* consists of spicy bean curd, shredded pork, chopped spring onions, and an intense chili sauce pushed to the limits by aromatic vinegar. This particular restaurant claims to occupy the site where mapo doufu was invented during the Qing Dynasty reign of Emperor Tung Chi (1862–75). The story goes that a certain Chengdu chef named Chen Ling Fu was married to a talented *mapo,* which is a woman with a pock-marked face. Her talent was in the kitchen, where she devised a bean curd dish sprinkled with red "pocks" of chili pepper.

The mapo doufu that immortalized this 19th-century "kitchen granny" must be numbingly hot to qualify as authentic; at this namesake restaurant it could not be more authentic or much hotter. Like many restaurants in Chengdu, this one has a ground floor that caters to working-class communal dining, while the floor above is reserved for banqueting and more leisurely dining. I savored my meal on the second floor in a room of darkly stained wood and carved columns, its window shutters thrown wide open to the noisy temple street life across the way.

Here, as elsewhere in Chengdu, I experienced *ma-la* (very hot) dining at its best. I alternated between the hot doufu and a milder fish-flavored doufu, its sauce a deft mixture of vinegar, garlic, ginger, spring onions, and a modicum of hot bean paste. I ordered a third bean curd entree, too, known as drunken doufu, a sweet dish of shredded bean curd in an intoxicating sauce. The hot-and-sour soup *(suanla tang)* subtly complements all three strongly flavored, hotly spiced dishes.

"All Sichuan cooking exists as an excuse to consume hot peppers," a Chengdu local once told me. Perhaps so, but the chili peppers that now seem to define many Sichuan dishes are a relatively late addition—and a foreign one to boot. Chili peppers were introduced to China only in the 16th century, by way of Central America.

Pandas

Eighty percent of the world's 1,000 remaining giant pandas reside in Sichuan Province. In 1978, the **Woolong Nature Preserve** was established 86 miles northwest of Chengdu to protect this animal from extinction and allow scientists to study it in the wild. While there are tours to Woolong from Chengdu, the trip is usually futile if your goal is to see a free-roaming panda. Dedicated researchers often go months without a sighting. The Chengdu Zoo can also be a disappointment. A half-dozen or more pandas reside here (the most of any zoo in the world), but they are displayed only in cages or on one outdoor cement island with a tree and slide, and most afternoons they are asleep.

The best chance to see a giant panda in the near wild, then, is during an early morning tour of the **China Research Base of Giant Panda**

Breeding (Daxiongmao Fanzhi Zhongxin), located 7 miles northeast of city center. The research base hopes to breed both the greater panda and lesser (or red) panda in captivity. But this is not a zoo, at least not an old-fashioned zoo like the Chengdu Zoo 4 miles down the road. Although the pandas are caged at times in breeding houses at the research base, they are also let out to roam across 80 acres of steep hills, forests, and bamboo groves. Visitors follow along on slate walkways, separated by deep moats from a dozen bearlike giant pandas and an equal number of more catlike red pandas who go their own ways, sometimes sitting up a few feet away, other times disappearing into the forest.

I visited in the early morning, leaving at 7am and arriving just after the visitors' gate opened, at 8am. By noon, pandas are usually curled up, out of sight, dead asleep, so morning's the best time to visit. The hills were encased in fog, but before long I spotted a giant panda scratching his back against a stump. He appeared to have just been fed, but he lazily rolled onto all fours, ambled over to a patch of bamboo, sat down, and went to work stripping off shoots. A panda's main occupation is eating bamboo—sometimes up to 18 hours a day are spent this way in the wild (with daily consumption of arrow bamboo averaging over 20 pounds per panda). At the research base, however, more time seems to be spent napping than eating.

The little red pandas are more active. I watched several of them running through the trees, scampering down the steep inner embankments of the moats, and fighting like raccoons over bits of territory.

This was as close to an uncaged panda as I was ever likely to get, so I followed those that I found for about 2 hours. Only a few other tourists were out this early, and the mist still coated the bamboo, blotting out the hilltops. I could pretend for a moment that I was in the unfenced outdoors, that these pandas were free, that I was seeing a sight few humans have ever been allowed to witness.

The research base contains a hospital that is not open for tours and several outdoor panda sculptures. The base hopes to dramatically expand its facilities, acreage, and panda population in the next century, although that depends on finding sources for increased funding. One goal is to release a few captive pandas into the wilds by the year 2005. Recently, two of its pandas, Jiu Jiu and Hua Hua, were sent halfway around the world to take up a 10-year residence in the Atlanta zoo (which paid $4 million for the project).

The research base's **Panda Museum,** unheated when I visited in December, is loaded with stuffed pandas. This motley collection of taxidermy in poorly lit dioramas belongs in a grim socialist museum of the 1950's, which this display too closely resembles. Some of the exhibits seem overly clinical as well, like the jars preserving specimens of panda sexual organs (the penis is short, the vagina long) and the week-old panda baby, 8 inches long. Nearby is a photograph labeled "Get Semen by Electrical Inspiring." For the most part, the Panda Museum is pathetic. The understocked, uninspired gift counter probably doesn't bolster the funding, and the butterfly museum upstairs wasn't even open when I visited.

The giant panda, which was not known to the Western world until 1869, when French priest Pere David purchased a panda skin in Baoxing County, Sichuan, has become a logo for modern China, particularly its wildlife. Conservation of that wildlife is another matter. With proper management and promotion, the panda base in Chengdu could easily become southwest China's largest draw for Western tourists, a source of revenue for China's underfunded wildlife conservation efforts. For now, the panda research base is a step in the right direction—a small step—and despite its drawbacks the only site in the world where so many tourists can see so many pandas in one pleasant preserve. The research base is open daily from 8am to 5pm. The admission of RMB 40 ($4.80) includes the museum.

Chairman Mao Museum

Mr. Tray Lee is a product of the new, more economically liberal China. He is a freelance tour director who works his way through cafes and hotel lobbies where foreigners gather, dishing out his name card, describing his tours, and opening photo albums of the sights to which he can take you. His business card gives his title as "Mr. Lee, Tour Manager" and proclaims "**Lee's Budget Tours Service** (Since 1989). No Risk!!! Use the Service First, Pay Later!!!" He lists his phone, fax, and pager numbers, as well as his home address. Best of all, his tours (to schools, to hospitals, to factories, to kindergartens, to the countryside) are just as Mr. Lee advertises them: fairly priced, efficient, and personal.

Mr. Lee, son of a soccer coach, was born 30-some years ago in Shenyang Province, but he grew up in Chengdu and he knows the older streets well. One afternoon we end up at 23 Wu Fu (Five Happinesses) Street in an older neighborhood. The aging wooden shophouse at this address has been converted into the **Chairman Mao Badge Museum and Research Facility.** The mastermind of this collection of Mao memorabilia is Wang An Ting. He was sitting back on a bamboo lounge when we entered the front room. Wang, a former factory worker, is about 60 years old and very hard of hearing. He was born in this house, and his grandson and wife live in the back room, where they have a bed, table, and a 27-inch color TV. Wang asked me to sign his large guest book, a register that includes the names of visitors from Germany,

France, Japan, Russia, and various cities in China who have come to him to augment their own Mao collections.

The main room and the side room are stuffed—floors, walls, and ceilings—with nothing but Mao: Mao posters, commemorative Mao plates, red flags, ceramic busts, red-and-gold Mao buttons of every size, and Mao's little red book of quotations in its every edition. Corner tables serve as altars to Mao, complete with candles. Coffee tables block the aisles, hundreds of Mao buttons under their sooty glass tops. Red armbands from the Cultural Revolution (1966–76) as well as newspapers from that period of upheaval are pinned to the walls, as are Big Character posters heralding the various social and political movements that tore through the 1950s and 1960s like typhoons.

Chairman Mao is enjoying a nostalgic revival throughout China, perhaps as a symbol of a more orderly time. Many people feel that an image of Mao, like that of a Buddhist or Daoist god, can bring good fortune. Taxi drivers from Beijing to Chengdu have dangled portraits of Mao from their rearview mirrors ever since a rumor spread a few years ago about a cab driver with such an emblem whose life was spared in a traffic accident. Wang himself told us that the life of the former governor of Sichuan was recently saved "by the spirit of Mao."

Mao's ghost is certainly visible enough in this cramped pack-rat museum. Wang told us he had "10 big bags" of Mao items in his collection, and I believed it. His own house has been turned upside down by this passion. Wang is desperately looking for a patron to move his museum to larger, classier quarters. Meanwhile, he spends each day waiting for the next visitor to drop by while he stamps out his own shiny new Mao buttons on a small press. As I departed, Wang An Ting handed me a half-dozen buttons and his bilingual business card on which he is billed as "Head of the Mao Tse-tong's Medals Research Society in China (Preparatory)," "Honorable Member of Shanghai Researchist Coordination Committee," and "Contemporary Cultural Relic of Chief Editor."

Later, outside the Chengdu post office, the enterprising Mr. Lee asked me for one of the newly minted Mao buttons, which he proceeded to pawn off on a not-so-wily street vendor as a "Cultural Revolutionary antique."

That evening, when the sky turned copper red, I was walking back to my hotel, past the saluting statue of Mao, clean and white, when I noticed a street musician setting up his act. He was playing an erhu, a traditional Chinese cello with two strings—except that his was an electric erhu. He had wired its sound box to an amp. He had strapped a microphone to its neck. As he sawed away with his bow, he stomped out a thunderous rhythm with both feet by beating on metal wash pans flipped upside down. He was the Bob Dylan of a new China. This was where the sidewalks of New York started to merge with those of Chengdu, where East and West met head-on in the intersections of the next century. This was an erhu unlike any ever strummed before in all the centuries of teahouses and temples, of calligraphers and emperors. It was a tune to the future, a song Mao never heard.

PRACTICAL INFORMATION

ORIENTATION & WHEN TO GO

Chengdu, a city of over nine million, including its suburbs, is located in the center of Sichuan Province, China's subtropical "rice basket," nearly a thousand miles southwest of Beijing. Summers are hot and rainy (especially July and August) and should be avoided. Winters are cloudy and foggy but mild. Tourist season begins in April and ends in November, with November probably having the best weather.

Chengdu is a few hours north of one of China's greatest outdoor monuments, the Great Buddha at **Leshan** (see separate chapter), which can be visited in one day. Chengdu is also the gateway to **Emei Shan,** the Western Peak of Buddhism (see separate chapter), which requires at least a 2-night stay. Both these sites can be reached from Chengdu by public bus or group tour.

GETTING THERE

By Plane **Shuangliu Airport** is 11 miles south of the city. **Dragonair,** with offices in the Sichuan Hotel, 31 Zongfu Lu (☎ 028/675-5555, ext 6105), has direct flights from Hong Kong (2 hours). Chinese airlines serve Chengdu from most major cities in China (2 hours from Beijing, 2 hours from Guangzhou, 2 hours from Shanghai). Taxis charge at least RMB 65 ($8) for the 30-minute transfer to the city center over a four-lane newly paved highway.

By Train The **train station** is located at the northern end of Renmin Bei Lu, about 5 miles north of the Mao statue in city center. Trains from Beijing (36 hours), Guangzhou (48 hours), and Shanghai (48 hours) are tiring. Flying is a better choice. The overnight trains from Xi'an (16 hours) and Kunming (25 hours) go through scenic mountain terraces and tunnels, and constitute a reasonable alternative to air travel.

By Bus The bus makes sense for destinations within Sichuan Province and for trips to or from Chongqing on the Yangzi River. Express buses, fairly comfortable, with kung-fu movies playing continuously on TV monitors overhead, connect Chengdu and Chongqing via the new 210-mile Chengyu Expressway. This trip takes as little as 4 hours, less than half the time of the train and at lower cost ($12).

GETTING AROUND

To see the city on your own, the key is to purchase a map. Walking the backstreets is fascinating, as is strolling the promenade on the northeast bank of the Jin River. **Taxis** are easily flagged down. The drivers don't speak English, but the map helps. Taxi rides across town cost RMB 10 to RMB 20 ($1.20 to $2.40). **Bicycles** can be rented at the Traffic Hotel, 77 Jinjiang Lu, southeast riverbank, for about $2.50 per day.

TOURS & STRATAGEMS

China International Travel Service (CITS), across the street from the Jin Jiang Hotel at 65 Renmin Nan Lu (☎ 028/665-0780; fax 028/667-2970), can book air, train, and bus tickets and set up tours, with English-speaking guides, to all the major sites. Tour desks in the hotels can do the same. Good guided tours of the sights in Chengdu and beyond are often booked by independent travelers through the **Traffic Travel Service** on the grounds of the Traffic Hotel (77 Jinjiang Lu; ☎ 028/553-1877; fax 028/558-2777).

I also recommend the services of China's best freelance tour operator. **Mr. Lee, Tour Manager,** speaks excellent English, charges competitive rates for all tours and tickets, and gives personalized, reliable service. He often finds foreign tourists at the Traffic Hotel. He can be reached by phone, pager, or fax (☎ 028/555-4250 from 8am to 11pm daily; fax 028/555-4250; pager 028/558-1588, no. 6022; 24-hour telemessage holder 432-3388, no. 8638). Mr. Lee offers excellent countryside tours (his favorite), backstage opera tours, and visits to schools, traditional medicine hospitals, factories, the panda base, and anything else you can dream up. Most tours cost $10 to $20 per person.

WHERE TO STAY

Holiday Inn Crowne Plaza Chengdu (Zhong Fu Huang Gong Jiari Jiudian). *31 Zongfu Lu (4 blocks east of the Mao statue).* ☎ *800/465-4329 or 028/678-6666. Fax 028/678-6599. 433 units. A/C MINIBAR TV TEL. $170 double. AE, DC, JCB, MC, V.* This 33-floor tower, opened in 1997, is Chengdu's most luxurious hotel. The lobby, with its Italian marble floors, gold-trimmed columns, and European murals, is opulent and vast. The rooms, all equipped with writing desks, safes, and coffeemakers, are large, too. Each floor contains three suites with separate showers and bathtubs. There are two "executive floors" (21 and 22), no-smoking rooms, and rooms for the handicapped. The hotel's Rainbow Nightclub is a massive disco with elegant private rooms that include their own bathrooms and steam baths—a facility in China so luxurious that it is nearly impossible for Old China hands to comprehend, as is this hotel.

Amenities: Indoor swimming pool, health club, sauna, tennis courts, 12-lane bowling alley, 24-hour business center, conference rooms, concierge, 24-hour room service, same-day dry cleaning and laundry, nightly turndown, free airport shuttle, tour desk, beauty salon, shopping arcade (new Parkson department store nearby).

Jin Jiang Hotel (Jin Jiang Binguan). *180 Renmin Nan Lu (1 block north of the Jin River).* ☎ *028/558-2222. Fax 028/558-1849. 523 units. A/C MINIBAR TV TEL. $150 double. AE, DC, JCB, MC, V.* For decades, this nine-story landmark was the best (and sometimes the sole) place for foreigners to stay. It is worth strolling through just to see its elegant public areas and massive dining halls, as well as to survey its shops and services. The Jin Jiang has tried to keep up with the times by creating lavish facilities, including a five-star section in the rear wing with two floors of suites. The south wing has excellent standard rooms, while the east wing has some older rooms starting at $100 for a double. The facilities are the most extensive in Chengdu: a full-service post office, film developing, bakery, shopping arcade, medical clinic, dentist on call, gymnasium, outdoor pool, tennis courts, bowling alley. There's also an airport shuttle. But the much newer Holiday Inn Crowne Plaza offers better service.

Traffic Hotel (Jiaotong Fandian). *77 Jinjiang Lu (next to the Xinnanmen bus station, southeast bank of Jin River).* ☎ *028/555-1017. Fax 082/558-2777. 200 units. TV TEL. $25 and $30 double. AE, MC, V.* This is among the best-run budget hotels in China, set up with backpacking foreign travelers in mind. It is suitable for any independent traveler. The front desk staff and the elevator operators are friendly. Standard doubles come with heat and private bathrooms that are clean but worn. The best rooms are the deluxe doubles (just $30), with larger, newer bathrooms. The hotel hallways and lobbies are also well worn, but there are two gift shops, a kiosk with drinks and snacks, a notice board, luggage storage, an exchange desk, two tour offices, a bicycle rental shop (RMB 15/$1.90 per day), and an economy restaurant serving decent Chinese and American dishes at $1 to $3 a plate. Breakfast is included with the room.

WHERE TO DINE

Sichuan is best known around the world for its red-hot cuisine. Its spicy bean curd, aromatic kung pao chicken, tangy dan dan noodles, sweet-and-sour soup, and many other pungent dishes are fixtures on Chinese menus from Los Angeles to London. Sichuan fare has become synonymous with a delightful form of fire-eating, and there's no more inviting way to tour Chengdu, Sichuan's capital, than dish by dish.

Eating in Chengdu is not strictly a journey through fire. Sichuan cuisine has seven traditional flavors. In addition to hot, there are sweet, sour, bitter, peppery, salty, and fragrant. These seven flavors and the "eight methods" of cooking yield some 4,000 separate dishes, which in a Sichuan banquet are alternated to provide a variety of flavors. The *ma-la* ("very hot") dishes of Sichuan ignite the taste buds, but the yin-yang of contrasting, provocative, and piquant flavors is what satisfies the palate. Sichuan is the cuisine of fire, but the flame has many colors.

In addition to serving up some of the best Sichuan dishes on Earth, Chengdu has good local hot-pot cafes in the streets and Cantonese and Western restaurants in its hotels.

Chen Ma Po Dou Fu Restaurant. *113 Xiyihuan Lu (across from Qingyang Temple, 2 miles west of Mao statue). No telephone. Reservations required on weekends. Main courses RMB 16–RMB 67*

($2–$8). No credit cards. Daily 8am–11pm. SICHUAN. Several Chengdu cafes claim the same name and history as the original site where this Sichuan masterpiece, mapo doufu, was first served a century ago. This branch certainly serves the best spicy doufu (bead curd) dishes I've ever sampled. The second-floor tables and carved wooden decor have a lot of character, much nicer than the dirty dining hall below. You can look out on the street through an open window, its shutters thrown back, and enjoy the numbingly complex spices of a number of doufu specialties, including a sweetly flavored drunken doufu. The hot-and-sour soup *(suanla tang)* complements every dish.

Long Chao Shou Special Restaurant (Longchaoshou Canting). *8 Chunxi Nan Lu (at Dong Dajie, north of the Jin River).* ☎ *028/666-6947. No reservations. Sampler RMB 25 ($3). No credit cards. Daily 8am–9pm. SICHUAN.* This is Chengdu's most famous snack restaurant, serving a spectrum of *xiao chi* ("little eats," or dim sum Sichuan style). Dumpling connoisseurs prize these creations for their color, appearance, aroma, and flavor. The dining area is a mess. Order the sampler for RMB 25 ($3) at the window and take a place at one of the crowded tables. You'll be served 14 different snacks, including soup, dumplings, preserved meats, pickled vegetables, cabbage flower cakes, wontons, and sweet *tangyuan* pastries. I liked about half of what I sampled. During breakfast (8–10am) and lunch (noon–2pm), it can be difficult to find a seat. The snack flavors are strong and various, underlining an old Sichuan saying, "A hundred dishes, a hundred flavors" *(Bai cai, bai wei).*

Shu Feng Garden (Shufeng Yuan). *153 Dong Dajie (on corner of Hongxing Lu, southeast of Mao statue).* ☎ *028/665-7629. Reservations required on weekends. Main courses RMB 25–RMB 125 ($3–$15). No credit cards. Daily 11:30am–2:30pm and 5:30–11pm. SICHUAN.* One of Chengdu's newest Sichuan restaurants, this is also one of the finest and most elegant. The third floor is a shrine to the hot pot. Buffet tables hold more than 80 ingredients. Weekends are enlivened by musical revues. The decor is Old European, with white plaster walls, gilded moldings, and sculpted cherubs. Chengdu hot pot begins with a broth made by boiling chicken, beef, or cow bones garnished with hot bean paste from nearby Pi County (renowned for its long-lived population). Peppercorn, spices, and noodles are added. Thin slices of eel, beef, chicken, carp, pig's liver, bean curd, and tender vegetables are boiled to taste at the table. Shu Feng's hot pot is excellent and only costs $4 per person.

On the second floor, setting and cuisine change. The decor is Qing Dynasty "southern bridge" style with bright red columns, silken scrolls, and lacquered rosewood furniture. The best dishes are dan dan noodles laced with pimentos, dry-fried diced pork with bamboo shoots, boiled beef in hot sauce, cauliflower with Sichuan-style bacon, chicken ball soup, sizzling crispy rice with pork and gravy, tea-smoked duck *(zhang cha yazi),* kung pao chicken *(gong bao jiding),* and chrysanthemum cake for dessert.

Sky Lounge. *31 Zong Fu Lu (mezzanine level, Holiday Inn Crowne Plaza).* ☎ *028/678-6666. Reservations required. Main courses $5–$20. AE, DC, JCB, MC, V. Daily 6:30am–11:30pm. INTERNATIONAL.*

If you tire of Sichuan fire in your food, this elegant coffee shop serves all the American and European foods you may have been missing. The breakfast buffet ($10) is excellent, as are the daily high tea buffets ($6.50; from 11:30am to 2:30pm) and the Sunday champagne brunches ($15; from 7am to 2pm).

Other Choices The Jin Jiang Hotel serves international dishes in its two-story atrium off the lobby and excellent Sichuan and Cantonese selections in its elegant **Chinese restaurant** on the ninth floor (☎ 028/558-2222). The Holiday Inn Crowne Plaza has the first American barbecue in Chengdu, the **Mississippi Grill,** on the 25th floor; an expensive Japanese restaurant, **Kiyosato,** with four private rooms, on the 25th floor as well; and a large, lively **Cantonese restaurant** off its lobby (☎ 028/678-6666). Two popular restaurants with independent travelers are the **Highfly Café,** 18 Renmin Nan Lu (☎ 028/550-1572), with inexpensive Western food and e-mail access; and **Paul's,** no. 28, 1 Jinjiang Zhong Lu (☎ 028/672-3074 or 028/667-3074), near the Traffic Hotel, with a cheap international menu and Internet access at just RMB 10 ($1.25) per hour.

LESHAN: AT THE FOOT OF THE GREAT BUDDHA

乐山大佛

AT LESHAN, 100 MILES SOUTH OF Chengdu, the capital of southwest China's Sichuan Province, there's a saying: "The mountain is Buddha, Buddha is the mountain." The words may be poetic, but the meaning is quite literal: There is a mountain here, and the mountain is a Buddha.

China has many great Buddhas, from the statue at Hong Kong to that on lake Tai, but the gigantic image of the Buddha carved into the cliff face of Lingyuan Mountain on the east side of the Min River at Leshan is the greatest. Rising 233 feet straight up from the shore, the **Great Buddha of Leshan (Leshan Dafo)** is one of the few wonders to survive from the Tang Dynasty (A.D. 618–907), and the most monumental.

Building Buddha

The handiwork of a devout, indefatigable monk named Haitong, who set to work with hammer and chisel in A.D. 713, this statue of Maitreya, the Buddha of the Future, is frequently hailed as the largest carved Buddha in the world. Its statistical dimensions befit the superhuman realm. Even seated, hands on knees, the Great Buddha of Leshan rises to the height of 35 men. Buddha's head is 50 feet high. Each eye is 10 feet wide. His extenuated ears are 20 feet long, his shoulders 90 feet broad, and his bare feet, which nearly touch the river, 30 feet across, wide enough to seat 100 sightseers at a time.

The good monk Haitong did not live to see the completion of his sculpture, which was 90 years in the making. It is said that he once plucked out his own eye to impress would-be donors. His mission was to create a guardian presence vast enough to subdue the treacherous waters, to protect the passing boatmen and their cargo, to suppress the river's floods. Today, the waters still teem with commerce and boatmen, many of whom earn a living by ferrying tourists to this singular shrine.

Sailing to Buddha

Although gargantuan, the Great Buddha has a graceful form and benevolent expression. The classic view is straight on from the roiling river Min, where the statue has survived politics and the ravages of wind and erosion for 13 centuries. Unpainted open tour boats, with standing room only, ply the channel for a full frontal view of the Great Buddha. While these boats are not comfortable, they are sturdy and maneuverable. Smaller speedboats and even a few skiffs rowed by hand also look for passengers at the quay near the main entrance to the Great Buddha. The skiffs look rather fragile. The currents are quite severe.

From the river, Buddha appears to be enthroned in a deep recess—sitting in a closet of red sandstone. You can see tourists and pilgrims streaming up and down the stairs carved into the cliff walls on either side of the great image. They dance across Buddha's toes. The riverboats usually swing back and forth in front of Buddha, sometimes slowing to a standoff with the current so that everyone can get a decent picture. On a sunny afternoon, this can make for a spectacular portrait.

Temples, Theme Parks & Graves

The tour boats tie up at an island mountain south of the Great Buddha, where passengers climb the peak to **Dark Green Temple (Wuyou Si),** the major Buddhist shrine on the river. It dates from the same period as the statue, but its four main chambers—the Guardian King, the Maitreya, the Tathagata, and the Mahavira halls—are from more recent dynasties. More recent still are the many kiosks of charms and souvenirs and a teahouse that affords a splendid view of the river and the great holy mountain on the horizon, Emei Shan, gateway to the Western Paradise. It is a steep walk up the temple, and the river view at the top is worth lingering over, especially with a drink from one of the vendors.

A suspension bridge connects the island to Lingyuan Shan, where the Great Buddha is enthroned. At the bridge is the **Oriental Buddha Park (Dongfang Fodu),** a modern collection of Buddhist images from throughout Asia, highlighted by a reclining Buddha 557 feet long—touted as the world's longest. It is also one of the world's tackiest, clearly a quick work in plaster rather than a marble carving. Admission RMB 25 ($3).

Next door is the **Mahao Tomb Museum (Mahao Ya Mu),** with stone coffins and burial relics from the Eastern Han Dynasty (A.D. 25–220). Admission is RMB 15 ($1.85). Along the river are the tiny **cave tombs** where a few images of the Buddha survive from the days when Buddhism first arrived in China almost 2,000 years earlier. These

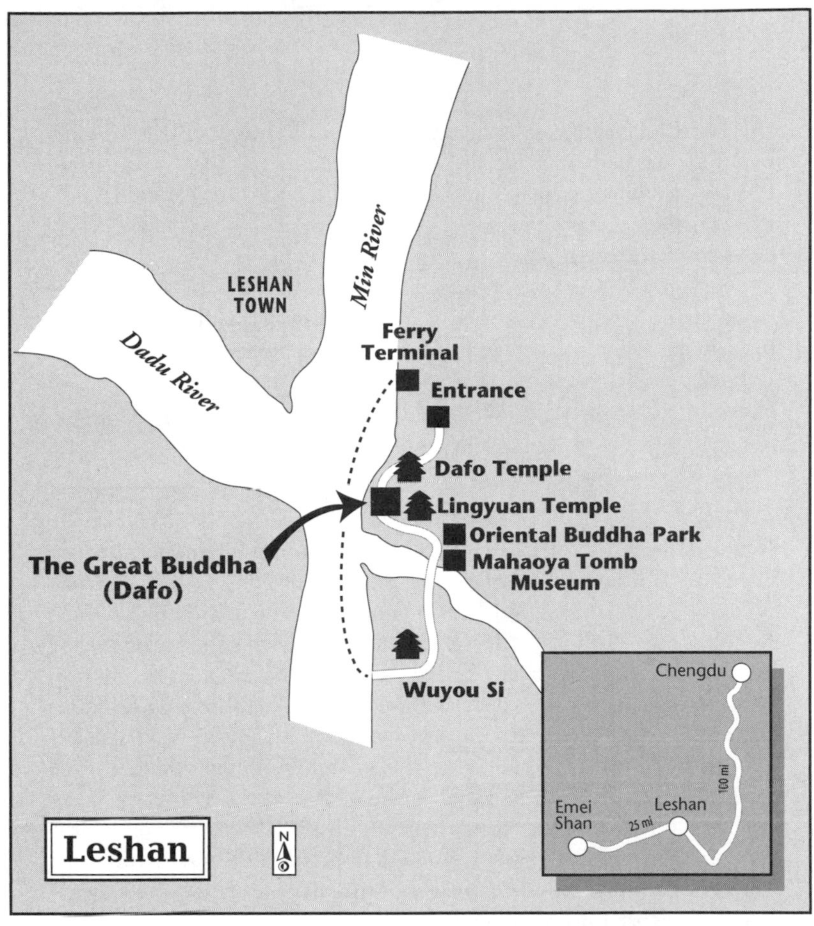

arc off the main path and require persistence to find. Just keep walking along the river, about a quarter of a mile.

Buddha's Feet

Across the bridge, the trail rises again to the heights of Buddha's crown. A labyrinth of steps, the **Stairs of Nine Turnings,** descend to the feet of the statue. These narrow stairs are crowded with onlookers who wind down Buddha's left side.

At the base, children usually make a stone stage of Buddha's colossal feet, acting out songs, dances, and kung-fu routines, while parents and grandparents spread out their picnic lunches on the toenails. Recently, however, park authorities have been putting up signs forbidding people to stand on any part of this "Cultural Relic." I doubt this prohibition will last.

The Buddha's recess is honeycombed with cutout shrines where a multitude of holy statues once resided. Almost all have disappeared because of robbery or rain. On the other side of the Great Buddha, nine more turnings of stairs upward bring climbers level with Buddha's ears. Up close, the forehead in profile is a smooth dome, patched with what looks like concrete. The survival of the statue has had much to do with an ingenious drainage system concealed behind the Great Buddha that empties the rain and hillside runoff into the river below, but a close inspection of Buddha's head makes me think that the rock has been patched and cleaned up over the centuries, too. Otherwise, this statue seems to be in miraculous condition, impervious to the elements and the passage of time.

Buddha's Crown

Buddha's head was once capped by a seven-story pavilion, but this was dismantled during the warfare that erupted at the end of the Yuan Dynasty. Above and behind, there's another temple, **Dafo Si,** the Great Buddha's own. A short road leads down to the north entrance where the buses and river ferries wait. The temple grounds are an ideal spot to linger, to take in the river scenery from the high platforms on Buddha's right side, at one removed from the world of man below.

On Buddha's south side is another temple, **Lingyuan,** dating back to the 7th century but renovated in the 17th century, with yet another laughing Buddha of the Future residing inside. From this side of the carving, there are fine views of Buddha in profile and some statues that most tourists don't get to see, images of the sculptor Haitong, and a cave said to have been his monastic retreat.

In Buddha's temple there is the stone likeness of a celebrated Song Dynasty scholar, Su Dongpo, who lived near Leshan. The pond where Su washed his brushes is still at Buddha's crown. In his most famous poem, Su relinquishes the desire to become a great figure on the world's stage, preferring to "journey about like a wine-laden cloud" among the rivers and hills of Leshan.

Through the centuries, through the ebb and flow of empires—even into this age when mass tourism has replaced pilgrimage and ant-sized gawkers climb from knee to noggin—the Great Buddha maintains its serene countenance, eyes nearly closed, lips in a knowing smile.

PRACTICAL INFORMATION

ORIENTATION & WHEN TO GO

The Great Buddha at Leshan is 100 miles south of Chengdu, the capital of Sichuan. Leshan is a small town. Most visitors to the Great Buddha set out from Chengdu in the early morning, returning in the afternoon. Travelers to the nearby sacred mountain of **Emei Shan** (see separate chapter) often stop at Leshan on their way to or from Chengdu.

Summers are unbearably hot, humid, and rainy here, making early spring (March) and late autumn (November) the most comfortable times to visit.

GETTING THERE

The nearest train station requires a 1-hour minibus to connect to Leshan, and there is no service by air. The easiest way to get to Leshan is by hiring a driver and guide from CITS, a hotel tour desk, or an independent travel operator such as Mr. Lee in Chengdu (see below). Tour buses leave from hotels or from the bus stations in Chengdu, and the journey takes 3 to 4 hours. Public buses take about 5 hours. The new expressway has cut the travel time by 1 hour.

TOURS & STRATAGEMS

Plan to make Leshan a day trip. Even the budget hotels in Chengdu are superior to what's offered in Leshan.

Admissions & Hours Admissions to the Grand Buddha and Lingyun Temple are RMB 40 ($4.80); other temples along the way charge RMB 5 to RMB 10 (65¢ to $1.25). The ferryboats charge RMB 30 to RMB 40 ($3.40 to $4.80). All temples and sites are open from 8am to 6pm.

Tours Day tours to the Great Buddha at Leshan can be booked at Chengdu's **China International Travel Service (CITS),** 65 Renmin Nan Lu (☎ 028/665-0780), or from hotel tour desks. **Mr. Lee** (☎ and fax 028/555-4250) offers a Leshan tour with a private car and himself as guide for about RMB 250 ($30 per person). See the Chengdu chapter. In Leshan, CITS is located at 129 Renmin Nan Lu (☎ 0833/212-4570).

WHERE TO STAY & DINE

Near the Lingyun Temple, the new (1999) **Jifeng Binguan** (☎ 0833/213-0853) has clean double rooms with private bathrooms at about $25, but I haven't tried it. The best place to stay in downtown Leshan itself is the **Jia Zhou Binguan,** 19 Baita Jie (☎ 0833/213-4415; fax 0833/213-3233), a three-star, Chinese-managed hotel with basic modern rooms and a tour desk. Boats to the Leshan Buddha leave from the wharves on the Min River (east Leshan, a long but interesting downtown walk from the Jia Zhou hotel). Near the hotel, at 49 Baita Jie, is a small, inexpensive restaurant, **Yang's,** with Western food and an English menu. The **Great Buddha Temple** has a vegetarian restaurant, and courtyard vendors hawk drinks and snacks, but you would be better off eating an early breakfast and packing your own picnic lunch before leaving Chengdu. Day tours sometimes include lunch at a local restaurant.

Southwest China: Searching for Shangri-La

GUILIN: THE LANDSCAPE OF DREAMS

桂林

THE SCENERY AT GUILIN IS UNLIKE that of any other city on Earth. Its peaks "rise as suddenly from the Earth as trees in a forest," writes one Chinese poet, "surrounding the city like mountains floating in an imaginary sea," claims another. These craggy peaks and pillars of limestone must have been the models for the traditional landscapes painted for centuries on silk scrolls. Until I visited Guilin, I assumed the impossibly contorted, improbably steep, vibrantly swirling mountains of these artists simply did not exist. At Guilin, they do. And they exist inside the city as well as in the countryside.

Guilin possesses "five famous virtues": spectacular caverns, exotic rock promontories, fragrant osmanthus, green hills, and clear waters. It is finally the hills that most beguile me. I would return again and again simply for a view of Guilin's remarkable hills. There are grander mountain peaks, but none so peculiar and so numerous, planted thick as a forest. "Only at Guilin, in a single sweep of the eye, can you see so many peaks spring from the ground like shoots of jade bamboo, jostling one another, some as near as a stone's throw, others faint in the distance," wrote a Song Dynasty (A.D. 960–1280) traveler, Fan Cheng-ta. "For their astonishing strangeness surely the hills of Guilin rank first in the world." And so does its Li River.

The Li River

Guilin's very top attraction is the Li River (Li Jiang), which has posed for more painters and photographers than any other place in China—and for good reason. This is "the best scenery under heaven," as an old saying goes, the best scenery if you like clear rivers, green bamboos, and sheer, twisting limestone pinnacles. Han Yu (A.D. 768–824), a Tang Dynasty poet, composed the classic description of the Li River: "The river is a blue ribbon of silk, The hills are hair pins of jade."

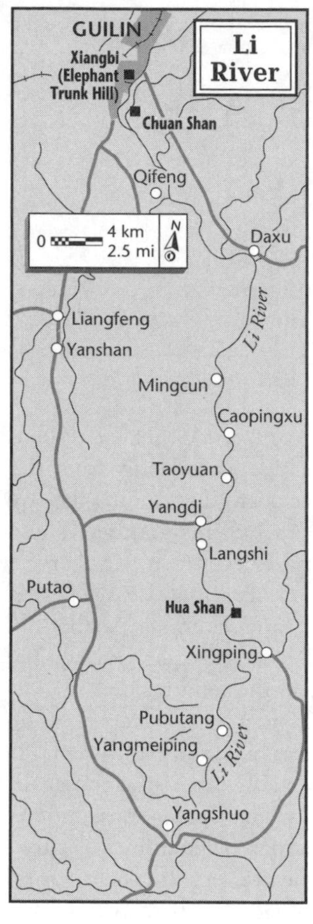

Tour boats by the hundreds make the daily 52-mile journey down the Li River to Yangshuo. My vessel was typical: a flat-bottomed barge, rounded at each end, with seating and tables inside the long cabin and an open observation deck on top. While waiting to depart, I purchased a *pomelo,* a thick-skinned gigantic relative of the grapefruit, from one of the peasant vendors who sailed alongside on a raft of hollow bamboo shafts lashed together like a rural Chinese surfboard.

The first phase of the passage, from Guilin down to the village of Yangdi, is merely a prelude. **Elephant Trunk Hill (Xiangbi),** on the west shore, is one of Guilin's most popular parks and remarkable natural monuments. It clearly resembles an elephant drinking from the Li River. All the great limestone formations in Guilin and down the Li River are said to look like something or someone, but Elephant Hill's resemblance takes little imagination to identify. From the water, I had a perfect view of the hill's trunk, and could see between that trunk and the elephant's legs, **Moon-in-the-Water Cave,** which is said to resemble a silver moon floating on the Li River. Perhaps if the moon is out, it does. Small boats can enter this cave when the water level permits. Jibei Chushi, a Song Dynasty poet, wrote "In Praise of Moonlit Nights" here, a dreamy paradox that reads:

The silver moon is deep below the river.
The silver moon floats upon the river.
The river flows where the moon cannot go.
Where the moon goes, the river cannot flow.

Elephant Trunk Hill is succeeded on the east bank by **Pagoda Hill (Baota Shan),** capped by a Ming Dynasty pagoda that is said to imprison a thousand-legged demon. The hill is also renowned for its maple trees and the red leaves that grace it in the fall. **Pierced Hill (Chuan Shan)** stands next to Pagoda Hill; it is noted for the large round opening in its side, aptly named Moon Cave. There follows on the west bank two craggy towers of note: **Fighting Cock Hill (Douji),** said to resemble roosters at a showdown, with coxcombs prone and wings spread, and **Clean Vase Lying in the River,** both back on the west bank. As I say, this is a mere prelude to the bands of fantastic peaks that lie ahead. At the town of Qifeng (Strange Rock), there's the first hint of the majestic scenery ahead. Here the peaks and hills thicken into a forest.

Three hundred million years ago this region was swallowed by the sea. Two hundred million years ago it reemerged, and the exposed limestone was sculpted by acidic rain, mist, and wind-blown dust. These karst peaks were then sliced apart and honed into immense pillars over the last two million years. The result is a forest of stone shafts and crags that seems to have grown straight up from the banks of the Li, topping out at heights of 200 to 300 feet.

There's a mythic counterpoint to this geological tale of bizarre formations. The story goes that long ago, when the South China Sea threatened to engulf Guilin, the gods decided enough was enough: They would move the northern hills south as a floodgate. The gods transformed the hills into goats in order to herd them south, but a fierce, blasting wind scattered the goats willy-nilly down the Li River, where they changed back into the unruly peaks we see today.

None of the strange hills and cliffs that rise directly from the riverbanks are named for goats these days, but there are hills and pillars named for oxen, islands, a ferry, a lonely lady, an emperor's crown, and a panel of natural embroidery, as intricate as stitched silk. Every hill has a story, but I was content to drift unguided. The river is hushed, well beyond the city streets of Guilin, and the landforms encourage silence. I feasted on each curve of the river, hungering for the next impossible formation. A buffet lunch was served below, a generous one of Chinese dishes, fish, vegetables, and fruits. I saw the foodstuffs cleaned in the river water, but I still decided to eat until I was full. The Li is one of the clearer rivers in China, cleansed by the reaction of carbonic acids with the limestone rocks.

After lunch, I climbed back up on the observation deck to bathe in the scenery. We passed villages of thatched huts. Fishermen were scooping the river bottom for shrimp with funnel-shaped nets. Children were wading and swimming in the sandy bend of the river. Enormous groves of bamboo reached out from the banks, shooting out like green feathery petals. This is a primeval land of extremes: a tropical valley hemmed in by mountains of cold limestone.

From **Yangdi Village,** the midway point of the cruise, it's nearly another hour's float to **Mural Hill (Hua Shan),** probably the river's most famous cluster of razor-sharp peaks. The shadings and fissures on its many faces are said to resemble a fresco of horses bolting, leaping, neighing, rearing, and running. For centuries hopeful would-be officials, scholars on their way upriver to attend the imperial examinations, scoured Mural Hill with desperate eyes: The more horses they discerned, the higher their test scores, it was said. To see nine horses engraved on the flanks of Mural Hill was to secure the highest mark on the exams. I failed to discern a single worthy steed in the hues of this hill, but 800 years ago the poet Chou Hau did better:

How many thousands of years ago
Was this screen carved in stone?
The more it is pelted by rain and winds
The clearer its image.

South of Mural Hill we passed the village of **Xingping** on the east shore. At this ancient county seat, the scenery is unsurpassed. Xingping is an ink-wash landscape fashioned from water and stone. No artist is required. Scores of myths are stored in the odd karst pillars and peaks that resemble scepters, snails, and carp, as well as the followers and fingers of Buddha. Groves of bamboo and willow wave from the banks, which are here spread 300 feet apart as the river's flow becomes almost limpid.

At the end of the river journey, the tour boats pull in at the village of **Yangshuo** (see separate chapter), where the scenery, according to tradition, "exceeds even that of Guilin." The blue hills stretch forever south, west, and east. We tied up at Nanxu Gate under the implacable **Green Lotus Peak (Bi Lian).** The quay swarms with roving vendors. Fishermen pose with cormorants, the birds they've taught to retrieve fish. The tour buses back to Guilin are parked nearby. Above the dock, south along the river, is the eight-sided River Pavilion (Yingjiang Ke), an ideal place for a final view of the river's exquisite landscape.

The buses pull out from the narrow village streets late in the afternoon. The vendors converge on the buses, rapping on the windows, holding up their wares. I first took this road north back to Guilin 14 years ago. At that time, workers were building a new highway beside the old one. They were building it entirely by hand, hauling rock, splitting it to size with mauls, fitting it stone by stone into the roadbed, and paving it over, shovelful by shovelful. The sole heavy equipment on the site was an old steamroller, like a machine out of a childhood storybook. At night the road-building brigades lay down in the roadbed and slept under the stars.

No words or pictures precisely express the spell cast by the uncanny scenery of the Li River. Fan Cheng-ta, who traveled through China during the Song Dynasty (A.D. 960–1280), once complained, "I have often sent pictures which I painted to friends, but few believed what they saw. There is no point," Fan decided, "in arguing with them." Once you've been down the Li River, you'll know what he meant. The reality of the river surpasses the finest print of the camera, the most fantastic simile of the pen, the most extravagant stroke of the ink brush.

The City of Guilin

When I first visited Guilin in 1986, in October, at the peak of tourist season, every hotel authorized to take foreigners was full. I was kicked out of the cavernous Li River Hotel after a single night, without ceremony or apology. Through sheer determination, luck, and door-to-door begging, I ended up in the older wing of the Ronghu Hotel, where I slept under a torn mosquito net, lulled into dreams by the melodic drip of the toilet.

Almost 2 decades later, at least the hotel situation has changed. Holiday Inn, Sheraton, and others have moved into a city that ranks among China's top five tourist attractions. In fact, my complaint about Guilin these days is that the tourist business is ruining what was once a quiet little city in a sublime setting, driving up prices, knocking down old neighborhoods, and fanning the fires of capitalism's darker side: greed. Nevertheless, I was happy to find a hotel that would accept a reservation and not expel me should a large tour group suddenly appear on the scene.

Solitary Beauty Peak

Once ensconced in a reliable hotel, I made plans to revisit the places that had made the deepest impression on me. I set out first for Solitary Beauty Peak (Du Xiu Feng), one of several limestone pillars in downtown Guilin that can be climbed. It's open daily 8am to 5pm; admission is RMB 15 ($1.90). Qing Dynasty poet Yuan Mei described this peak eloquently:

No trace of its origins, no clues to parentage,
Dropped from the sky, a lonely peak.
Strange are the hills of Guilin, nine out of ten,
But Solitary Beauty is the strangest of all.
Three hundred sixty stairs to the top
And the whole of Guilin at its foot.

During the Ming Dynasty (A.D. 1368–1644), the city's ruler, a relative of the emperor, built his mansion at the foot of this peak. Later, it became the regional site for the Imperial Examinations, taken by all those in China who competed for positions in the civil service. Today,

Solitary Beauty Peak is enclosed within the walls of **Guangxi Provincial Teachers' College.** In fact, as I walked north up Zhongshan Lu, I was met by an art student from that college, eager to practice his English. We walked together to the college gate, guarded by two stone lions. Inside the walls, I stared up at the 500-foot-high limestone peak that occupied the center of campus.

At the foot of the stairs to the peak there is a chamber called **Book-Reading Cave;** it resembles the reading room of a marble library, an apt site for the old empire's examinations. Like the other famous crags within the city, Solitary Beauty Peak holds the ruins of temples along its flanks and at its summit an unearthly view of the city and the endless chain of peaks. Alone now, I marched up the tall stone-and-concrete steps, a steep and winding trek. The panorama from the top is quite exceptional. To the north, I had a dazzling view of **Whirlpool Hill (Fubo Shan)** and **Brocade Hill (Diecai Shan),** the two other most famous karst towers in town. To the south, I could trace the Li River as it twisted between **Pierced Hill (Chuan Shan)** and **Elephant Trunk Hill** (**Xiangbi Shan;** see below).

The city itself was undergoing an extensive rebuilding, as nearly every city in China is. Guilin's new buildings were not too high: Most seemed to be under eight stories. A campaign of high-rise construction in Guilin would block its stunning topography, ruining its appeal, but fortunately the horizon was still open. The campus spread out below was particularly attractive because it was more traditional, its soaring tiled roofs and courtyards more in keeping with the landscape. Guilin is not everywhere a beautiful city, but it is enmeshed in a breathtaking natural setting.

Perhaps that's why there are so many art students and art galleries in Guilin. On top of Solitary Beauty Peak these days, some of the art students have taken to selling postcards and sodas to tourists. Guilin is certainly a city pushing to make a buck off its visitors.

I spent an hour savoring the view from the summit. Solitary Beauty Peak is the most dramatic of Guilin's vertical hills and its most central. I've climbed the other city hills in the past, but this one was sufficient for my return. A thousand years ago the poet Chang Ku climbed Solitary Beauty Peak and likened it to a stone pillar holding up the southern sky, "standing aloof between Heaven and Earth." Even earlier, in the 5th century, poet Yan Yanzhi had given this peak its name and noted how, "towering, it floats in the middle of the town" like the mast of a stone ship.

At the foot of Solitary Beauty Peak the student I had met was waiting. We walked down to a local restaurant (named "Local Restaurant") on the east end of Cedar Lake (Shan Hu) near the Li River and feasted

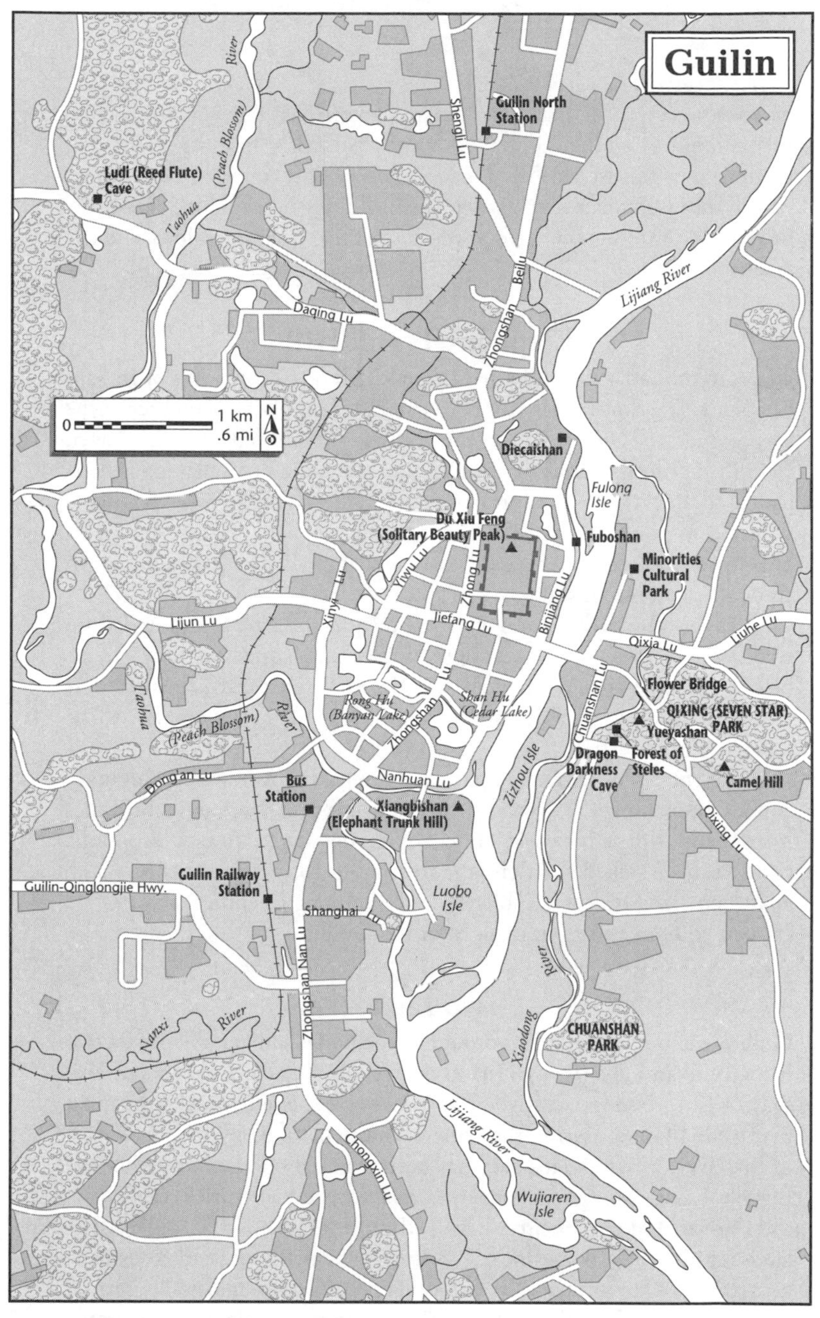

Guilin
Gulin North Station
Ludi (Reed Flute) Cave
Diecaishan
Fulong Isle
Du Xiu Feng (Solitary Beauty Peak)
Fuboshan
Minorities Cultural Park
Flower Bridge
QIXING (SEVEN STAR) PARK
Yueyashan
Dragon Darkness Cave
Forest of Steles
Camel Hill
Bus Station
Xiangbishan (Elephant Trunk Hill)
Guilin Railway Station
Luobo Isle
Zizhou Isle
CHUANSHAN PARK
Wujiaren Isle
Lijiang River
Nanxi River
Xiaodong River
Taohua (Peach Blossom) River
Rong Hu (Banyan Lake)
Shan Hu (Cedar Lake)
Shengli Lu
Zhongshan Beilu
Daqing Lu
Lijun Lu
Jiefang Lu
Xinyi Lu
Yiwu Lu
Zhong Lu
Binjiang Lu
Qixia Lu
Liuhe Lu
Chuanshan Lu
Zhongshan Lu
Nanhuan Lu
Dong'an Lu
Qixing Lu
Shanghai Lu
Zhongshan Nan Lu
Chongxin Lu
Guilin-Qinglongjie Hwy.
0 1 km .6 mi
N

on river shrimp. The plates we ordered cost RMB 85 ($10.50) each—my first indication that Guilin was more than living up to its recent reputation as a tourist rip-off. I had never paid such prices at a street restaurant in China, particularly in a small city where seafood was readily available. At least the seafood was tasty, the owner gregarious, and the lakefront shady.

Elephant Trunk Hill

That afternoon I visited Elephant Trunk Hill on my own. It's open 9am to 6pm daily; admission is RMB 10 ($1.20). This park lies on the southeast corner of Guilin where the Taohua River joins the Li River. I climbed onto the "back of the elephant" where a small pagoda is dedicated to Puxian, an immortal servant of the Buddha who is always depicted as riding on the back of a white elephant. From the top of Elephant Trunk Hill there is a serene view of the Li River running south through a deep karst valley.

Leaving the park, I took a wrong turn in the streets and ended up walking for several miles through unpleasant, congested city streets before I regained my bearings. While the motorized traffic is much less than in many comparable interior cities, it's still heavy enough to be annoying to pedestrians.

And the city is anticipating even more traffic. A new superhighway connects downtown westward to the new airport. The road is lit. Bikes have their own pathway, separated by a wire fence. A new economic zone has been staked out along the freeway, its roads paved, utilities laid, apartments and offices completed, and the foreign-venture factories are starting to hum—just out of sight of old Guilin.

Two Lakes

Guilin's main north–south thoroughfare, Zhongshan Lu, divides its two lakes, **Banyan Lake (Rong Hu)** to the west and **Cedar Lake (Shan Hu)** to the east toward the Li River. These lakes are the remnants of the moat that girded Guilin during the Tang Dynasty (A.D. 618–907). A section of the city's ancient south gate has been restored on the north shore of Banyan Lake, alongside a banyan tree said to be 8 centuries old.

Banyan Lake is encircled by pathways, roads, and a bridge. It is landscaped in willow and peach trees, as well as the occasional osmanthus (cassia) for which the city is named. Guilin means "Forest of Osmanthus," a flowering bush whose blossoms exude a sweet aroma each autumn. At dusk Banyan Lake is fringed in colored lights. Its island pavilions and bridges are lit up, too, making this the ideal place for a romantic stroll. One evening I emerged from the Holiday Inn to take a walk around the lake. As soon as I crossed the street, I was intercepted by a pedicab driver claiming to be a moonlighting student. He offered to sell me a trip around the lake. I declined. He then tried to sell me a massage from a young lady, and finally, the young lady herself.

I walked on, remembering a more innocent time, almost 2 decades ago, when I met another young man at Banyan Lake. He was nearly penniless, I'm sure. He spoke enough English to tell me that he was a "bum," a bum in the old sense, I think. He had been wandering China on his own for months, something thoroughly uncommon in the 1980s—or today, for that matter, when resident permits, difficult to obtain without a job, are required to stay in any city. All he had in his possession was a diary. "I am," he said, "a rolling stone." His dream was to get a job as an English-speaking guide for foreign tourists in Guilin. We rented a rowboat on Banyan Lake and spent the afternoon talking about the world.

Today, the same rowboats with their swan-shaped bows are still for rent on Guilin's lakes. They appear just as heavy in the water, just as difficult to row. But speed is not the objective on these pavilioned lakes. One really wants just to float away. The wanderer I met 10 years ago floated away that afternoon. I'll never know his fate. He despaired of ever landing a government job, since he lacked the right "connections" *(guanxi).* He told me he enjoyed his unusual freedom to the fullest. He never asked me for money, not even money for food.

But today more than ever, in this Forest of Osmanthus, amidst these towering stone pillars, it's money that seems to hold everyone in thrall.

Seven Stars & Cormorants

Seven-Star Park (Qixing Gongyuan) is named for its seven peaks, which resemble the stars of the Big Dipper. This constellation fallen to Earth is a lovely park on the west side of the Li River. I walked to it one morning with my acquaintance from the art school. It's an hour-long walk through the heart of Guilin's busy downtown, across the Li River, and onto **Flower Bridge (Huaqiao),** built of wood in 1456 and rebuilt in stone after the Flood of 1540. Flower Bridge is a graceful arching span encased in a tiled roof gallery over the little Xiaodong River, which borders Seven-Star Park.

Seven-Star Park is for walking, and we walked several miles of its pathways, first turning north in search of the park's chief natural attraction, **Seven-Star Cave.** With its RMB 50 ($6) admission tag (which includes the cave), it's overpriced, but the caves of Guilin are as famous as its limestone hills, so I won't say you shouldn't take an hour's stroll through this brightly lit cavern, one of Guilin's most fascinating and biggest—although **Reed Lute Cave,** west of the city, is more beautiful.

Visitors have left messages carved on the walls of Seven-Star Cave for the last 13 centuries.

On the other side of the cave we had a fine view of **Camel Hill,** which resembles its name. I declined the chance to climb to its summit. The amusement park at its foot was neither inviting nor busy. Its small Ferris wheel, its bumper cars, and even its new water slide seemed to be rusting and cracking into oblivion.

Turning south, we walked downriver along the Xiaodong to Seven-Star Park's primary cultural treasure, its **Forest of Steles,** an overhanging cliff under which calligraphy, poems, and pictures have been carved on thousands of stone tablets over the past 1,600 years. The peak here is called Crescent Moon Hill (Yueya Shan), site of **Dragon Darkness Cave (Longyin Dong),** renowned for its crinkled, scaly walls that resemble the imprint of a departed dragon.

We decided to follow the path up the side of the hill for a view of the river. It was from here that, 10 years earlier, I'd had my first view of cormorant fishing in China. Fishing with these birds is an old tradition, particularly in Guilin. A single cormorant, it is said, can catch enough fish to support an entire family. I'd watched an old fisherman below working with five cormorants. He tied each bird's neck with a ribbon to prevent it from swallowing the fish it snatched. To call his cormorants back to the flat bamboo raft where he stood, the fisherman whacked the river surface sharply with his pole while he jumped up and down fiercely in his bare feet. Whenever a bird returned its catch to his hand, he praised it in a voice that carried to the top of Crescent Moon Hill.

It seems that the cormorant fisherman has moved on, too, since then. The only ones I saw in Guilin this time worked on the river's edge in parks where they charged tourists who wanted their pictures taken with them and their birds.

Minorities, Touts & Discos

The commercialization of Guilin has reached its newest form with the opening of the **Minorities Cultural Park (Feng Qing Yuan),** which is located on the east side of the Li River about a 40-minute walk north from Seven-Star Park, one of the ethnic amusement parks so popular in China and throughout Asia. Guilin's version is open daily from 9am to 11pm, and charges RMB 30 ($3.75) by day, RMB 50 ($6) after dark (perhaps to pay its electric bill). Its grounds are filled with brand-new models of China's minority architecture. The minority people themselves, who perform at each village stop, are authentic enough.

The province, Guangxi Zhuangzu Autonomous Region, consists of over three million members of the Zhuang minority. Many Zhuangs, as well as Miao and Dong people, are thrilled to be spending a summer working in "the big city." While wandering through the village I witnessed performances by gong-and-drum bands, ethnic dancers, and *qi gong* experts. The qi gong demonstration consisted of 10 people in colorful ethnic costume standing on two slabs of marble placed across a young girl's stomach for a period of 1 minute. What this had to do with minority culture in China, I could only wonder, but that's show biz. The one display I did enjoy was a lodge devoted to ancient musical instruments of these ethnicities. I was invited to play several of the gongs, and I obliged, even though as I exited the music hall I was charged RMB 5 (60¢) for the privilege.

Like most minority villages in China, Guilin's version is truly set up only for tour groups. There are no explanatory signs in English for independent foreign travelers, who could better spend their time and money by going to the minority regions directly.

We walked back into town and sat down for lunch in what I took to be a real dive, a seafood cafe that advertised itself with tubs of live delicacies outside—fish, eels, crab—and cages of snakes within. There were tree snakes, water snakes, and five-step snakes available (five steps being the farthest you can get after being bitten by one). I skipped the snakes and went straight to regular Chinese fare. First came a plate of fresh greens, then a plate of hacked-up chicken, its head and claws still in view. The third plate was pork slices in bamboo; the fourth, bamboo shoots in vinegar with rubbery slices of pig stomach. The bill came to slightly more than that of yesterday's lunch. It was time to move back into the international hotel restaurants for my dining.

That evening, I succeeded in convincing the art student into taking me uptown to a very local disco for some cheaper entertainment. The venue was an old school gymnasium, so darkened that the waitresses had to locate tables using flashlights. There was no cover charge. I paid only for the sodas. There were flashing lights around the dance floor, where a few young people danced the disco dances of the 1970s, finishing up the evening with what looked like the bunny hop.

Reed Flute Cave

If you've never ridden a bicycle in China, do so in Guilin. The hotels rent bikes by the hour or day. Bike riding appears more dangerous than it is. Once you're in the flow with other bicycles, it's a relaxing way to travel—just remember to clang your bike bell like a maniac at every intersection. Guilin is compact enough so that you can ride a bicycle into the countryside in a matter of minutes. My favorite destination is Reed Flute Cave (Ludi Yan), 5 miles west of downtown, about an hour's ride. You can also reach the cave by public bus, taxi, or organized city tour. The cave is open daily from 8:30 to 11am and 12:30 to 5pm; admission is RMB 50 ($6).

Setting out from Holiday Inn on the southwest tip of Banyan Lake, I cycled north along Xinyi Lu to Lijun Lu, a major intersection. Turning left, I kept on Xinyi Lu for most of the journey, passing Hua Gai An Temple, Yinshan Hill, Xishan Hill, and Baiyan Hill before the road curved north at Lion Crag and hugged the east bank of the Peach Blossom (Taohua) River. At Daqing Lu, the road abruptly ended, crossing the river over Feiluan Bridge and heading northwest another half mile to the entrance of Reed Flute Cave. The countryside was green, the river clear, the scenery increasingly spectacular. At the cave, there were flat rice paddies with some of Guilin's most dramatic limestone peaks looming in the background. This is the scene that appears on countless travel posters, one of the most beautiful spots for photography in China.

As for Reed Flute Cave, it's worth a half-hour tour. Park your bike in one of the bicycle lots and lock it. This cave once served as an air-raid shelter during World War II when America's Flying Tiger squadron was based in Guilin. Today it is one of China's better-illuminated caves. The quarter-mile-long array of passageways is wet, cool, twisting, and narrow; the stalactites and stalagmites are ornate; and there is one grand chamber, the **Crystal Palace,** where the hero of China's epic novel, *Journey to the West,* is said to have slain the evil Dragon King with a magic needle. The needle, of course, is also in the cave, a garishly lit, harpoon-sized pillar.

I'm not a true spelunker, but it's almost mandatory to take in a cave or two while in Guilin. There are really two Guilins in this karst wonderland. One Guilin is aboveground. The other is below the surface. Poet Yuan Mei compared the two in a graphic verse:

Seeing the blue hills from the outside
Is like touching the exterior of a person.
Seeing the hills from the caves inside
Is like plucking the internal organs.

Reed Flute Cave is probably the single most impressive portion of "underground" Guilin. It's also much too popular. You'll have to shove your way past a hundred vendors and an occasional camel or two towed by aggressive photographers. But for a view of the countryside, its fields and uncanny peaks, it's worth fighting the crowds.

PRACTICAL INFORMATION

ORIENTATION & WHEN TO GO

Guilin, population 700,000, is located in southwest China's Guangxi Province, 1,000 miles from Beijing, 225 miles west of Guangzhou (Canton) and Hong Kong. The main attraction is cruising the Li River from Guilin south to the remarkable village of **Yangshuo** (see separate chapter). To view the minority villages of Guangxi Province north of Guilin, Sanjiang and Longsheng, consult the separate chapter on **Sanjiang.** Southern Guangxi Province is also the location of an unusual town on the sea, **Beihai** (see separate chapter).

The best months for cruising the river are April and May, and September and October, when the river is usually deep enough for a full Guilin–Yangshuo passage. Of course, these months are also the most popular with tourists (up to 3,000 a day), meaning the river can become quite crowded with tour boats. The ideal time to cruise the Li River, then, is early April or late October. In the summer months, the temperature is hot and the humidity high, even on the river. In winter, the temperature and humidity are often at their most pleasant, but the Li River is too low to cruise.

GETTING THERE

By Plane Guilin's new **airport** (☎ 0773/282-3311) is 18 miles west of city center. Air tickets can be booked from hotel tour desks. Flights to Guangzhou (Canton) and Hong Kong take about an hour; to Kunming, 1½ hours; to Shanghai, 2 hours; and to Beijing, 2½ hours. For Hong Kong flights, the **Dragonair office** in Guilin is located on Bingjiang Nan Lu in the Sheraton Hotel on the second floor (☎ 0773/ 282-5588, ext 8895; fax 0773/283-2080).

Upon arrival in Guilin, I took the **CAAC shuttle bus** waiting outside at the curb into downtown (RMB 20/$2.40) and a cab from there to the Holiday Inn (another RMB 20/$2.40). **Airport taxis** charge at least RMB 120 ($14.45) for the complete transfer.

By Train & Bus Mountainous geography has isolated Guilin, making air flights the most practical way to reach the city. There are rail and bus connections, but these methods often require overnight rides (20 hours to Shanghai, 30 hours to Xi'an, 35 hours to Beijing), sometimes with transfers along the route.

GETTING AROUND

After taking an orientation tour from CITS or through your hotel tour desk, it is easy to find your own way to additional sites by foot or bicycle. Guilin is a compact area, and maps are readily available in hotel gift shops or from street vendors. Bicycles can be rented at Holiday Inn, at the Sheraton, and from shops on Zhongshan Lu, the major shopping street, at rates of RMB 25 to RMB 50 ($3 to $6) per day. Bikes are useful for reaching Seven-Star Park (a 2-mile ride) and Reed Flute Cave (a 5-mile ride).

TOURS & STRATAGEMS

The **Guilin tourist hot line** (☎ 0773/282-6533) can be helpful. Be wary of putting your fate in the hands of locals who make your acquaintance on the streets. They will most likely end up costing you more than official CITS guides charge while delivering less information.

Local Tours **China International Travel Service (CITS),** 41 Binjiang Lu, near the Sheraton Hotel (☎ 0773/282-8314; fax 0773/282-7205), arranges city tours with English-speaking guides. **Holiday Inn** (see "Where to Stay," below) offers a half-day city tour with an English-speaking guide for RMB 250 ($30).

Package Tours Many tour operators in Hong Kong, including CITS, offer complete package tours of Guilin, including a Li River cruise. Hotels, meals, airfare, and a local English-speaking guide are included. This is an expensive but popular option, favored by many people who are visiting Hong Kong but want to sample what the mainland offers. See the Hong Kong chapter for a list and description of tour agents and operators.

Li River Cruises The 270-mile-long Li River flows southward through Guilin. Scenic boat cruises on the river are all-day trips from Guilin, where arrangements can be made at hotel tour desks. River trips depart every morning about 8am and arrive in Yangshuo, 52 miles south of Guilin, in the afternoon (after 4 to 6 hours on the river). There's a stop for shopping at the street market in Yangshuo; then, the tour buses make the 2-hour return trip to Guilin, arriving by about 5:30pm. **China International Travel Service (CITS)** sells Li River tours. I booked my Li River tour at the **Holiday Inn Guilin,** 14 Ronghu Nan Lu (☎ 0773/282-3950). The RMB 480 ($58) ticket included an English-speaking guide, a Chinese buffet, and the return bus ride to Guilin. The cruise boat was built for the river, with inside seating, picture windows, a Chinese rest room (not sanitary), and an open-air, stand-up viewing deck with railings on the roof. More deluxe cruise boats (with higher ticket prices) can be booked here during high tourist season, May through October.

The water is always too low in winter to permit boat tours, although it is possible even then to book a short boat tour (2 hours) in Guilin that leaves from Xingping, a village an hour to the south. By April, the water is usually high enough to permit longer boat tours, which often start about 15 miles downriver at Zhujiang (or even farther along, at Yangdi) and end at Yangshuo (a 4-hour trip).

WHERE TO STAY

Hotels are heavily booked in the peak tourist months of May, June, September, and October. Book well ahead. The five-star **Guilin Royal Garden Hotel,** on the east bank of the Li River, caters almost exclusively to tour groups (mostly Japanese) and is not conveniently located for independent travelers. The four-star **Holiday Inn** and the five-star **Sheraton** have the best locations and excellent facilities. Of three-star locally managed hotels, the best of the lot is the **Fubo Hotel.** Guilin hotels tack on 18% in taxes and service charges, one of the highest rates in China.

Fubo Hotel (Fubo San Zhuang). *121 Binjiang Lu (next to Fubo Hill and the Li River in northeast Guilin).* ☎ *0773/ 282-9988. Fax 0773/282-2328. 150 units. A/C MINIBAR TV TEL. $90 double. AE, JCB, MC, V.* This four-story hotel is undergoing a renovation. It has been the best of the "cheaper" inns in Guilin, with fine views. It is locally managed, however, and services are not as efficient as those at the Holiday Inn and Sheraton. English-language communication is not always clear, either. Don't expect turndown service, a swimming pool, or a newsstand. Still, the Fubo has modern rooms that are clean, satellite TV stations, a tour desk, a shopping arcade, laundry service, room service, a rudimentary business center (usually open 8am to 10pm), and a Chinese restaurant, with reasonable prices (for Guilin).

Holiday Inn Guilin (Guilin Binguan). *14 Ronghu Nan Lu (southwest corner of Banyan Lake).* ☎ *800/ 465-4329 or 0773/282-3950. Fax 0773/ 282-2101. 259 units. A/C MINIBAR TV TEL. $120 double. AE, DC, JCB, MC, V.* This is my favorite choice in Guilin: friendly, comfortable. Rooms on all nine floors were recently renovated. The best rooms are on the ninth floor; each possesses cathedral ceilings and balconies with a view of Banyan Lake. Service, rooms, and restaurants are of good international quality.

Amenities: Outdoor swimming pool, health club, Jacuzzi, sauna, rooftop tennis courts, business center, room service (6am–11pm), next-day dry cleaning and laundry, tour desk, beauty salon, shopping arcade.

Sheraton Guilin (Wen Hua Fandian). *9 Binjiang Nan Lu (facing Li River).* ☎ *800/325-3535 or 0773/282-5588. Fax 0773/282-5598. 430 units. A/C MINIBAR TV TEL. $150 double. AE, DC, JCB, MC, V.* The superb atrium lobby and waterfall, the scenic location on the river, and the fine selection of restaurants make this a top choice among foreign travelers and tour groups. Independent travelers and foreign business people tend to favor the less expensive, more intimate Holiday Inn. But the Sheraton has some superior features, including its long (20-meter) swimming pool. The more expensive superior rooms and rooms with balconies are larger than those at the Holiday Inn.

Amenities: Outdoor swimming pool (20 meters), health club, Jacuzzi, sauna, billiard room, 24-hour business center, concierge, 24-hour room service, same-day dry cleaning and laundry, nightly turndown, tour desk, beauty salon, shopping arcade, bicycle rental, airport shuttle (Dragonair flights).

WHERE TO DINE

Local restaurants, which specialize in seafood, snake, and exotic wild animals, present difficulties for foreigners without proficiency in Chinese. There are no menus in English, and sometimes low hygiene standards. Moreover, those local street cafes that do serve foreign visitors often charge three to five times what they should. Stick with hotel restaurants unless you're dining out with a local you trust. An exception is said to be **Yi Yuan Fandian** (106 Nan Huan Lu; ☎ 0773/ 282-0470), which serves spicy Chinese and local dishes for lunch and dinner at reasonable prices (under $5 a plate), but I have not tried it myself. The cafe on the second floor of the big new **Niko Niko Do Department Store (Guilin Wei Xiao Tang),** 187 Zhongshan Zhong Lu (just west of Solitary Beauty Peak), has good Western snacks, sandwiches, soups, and coffees.

The Holiday Inn restaurants include **Sichuan Garden** (☎ 0773/282-3950), a good place for dinner since the chef is Sichuanese, and the **Patio Cafe** in the lobby, which serves a range of international dishes from grilled quail (RMB 45/$5.50) to beef fillet (RMB 95/$12), as well as pastas, nasi goreng, cheeseburgers, and pizza. The lobby bar is unusual in that it produces its own microbrews, usually resembling a mild lager, at RMB 18 ($2) per mug or RMB 60 ($7.25) per pitcher—with tastes that are surprisingly comparable to the microbrews you find in Portland and Seattle.

The Sheraton has a fine **Sichuan restaurant** (☎ 0773/282-5588), a **fast-food outlet** with excellent hamburgers and wontons, and a **Food Street–theme cafe** that serves the local Guilin specialties you find in night markets—river fish, prawns, pigeon eggs, catfish soup—at higher prices (RMB 18 to RMB 42/$2 to $5 per selection) but also at higher standards of preparation and cleanliness.

Yangshuo: The Stone Garden

阳朔

Guilin is reputed to have the best scenery under Heaven, but 50 miles downriver the karst landscape at Yangshuo is even more intriguing. Yangshuo, which means "Bright Moon," is a village laid out in a garden of stone towers, haunting and surreal. Here the swirling, oddly contorted 300-foot limestone pinnacles sprout around every corner and in every empty field. The tour boats that ply the Li River from Guilin end their trips at Yangshuo, and buses transfer passengers back upstream to Guilin, but there's no reason not to linger. Yangshuo is as close to paradise as a traveler gets in southwest China these days. I'd been wanting to explore Yangshuo for a decade, ever since I first set foot in the village, and this time I simply made Yangshuo, rather than Guilin, my base.

A Traveler's Town

Yangshuo's main street, Xi Jie, connects the Li River docks to the Guilin Highway. The street is an anomaly in China, cobblestoned and free enough of traffic to walk in the middle most of the time. Stranger still, it is dotted with small cafes that cater almost exclusively to independent foreign travelers. After checking in at a hotel, I stopped in for lunch at **Minnie Mao's,** which is decorated rather like a crash pad from the 1960s with guitars and posters on the wall. A few tables and rattan chairs line the side walls, and there's a bar at the back. The menu is in English, and many of the dishes are Western. I ordered a plate of noodles, a soda, and for dessert a sundae, which consisted of ice cream sprinkled with bits of apple, banana, and mandarin oranges. The bill came to RMB 14.50 ($1.75), about 10 times less than what an international hotel charges.

Minnie Mao's is a complete service cafe, as are half a dozen others in Yangshuo, meaning it also runs a travel agency—tour prices are posted on the back of the food menu. Other services include cheap faxing, IDD telephones, and even e-mail. It wasn't long before I'd spoken to several backpacking travelers who wandered in. Some of them were staying for weeks.

Yangshuo reminds me of similar towns in Nepal and Thailand, where foreigners can get what they need with ease. Almost none of China's cities have developed along these lines—China started out strictly controlling tourism, favoring well-managed tour groups housed in increasingly expensive and isolated hotels. In Yangshuo, everything is smooth sailing, particularly for outsiders. Prices for tours, hotels, or restaurants are not astronomical. This isn't quite China, perhaps, but it's how China must become if it is ever going to be truly an international crossroads.

My first night in Yangshuo I ended up eating dinner in another Western cafe run by locals. This one happened to be the first foreign cafe set up in Yangshuo, in 1983, even if it has since moved around the corner and changed its name to **Susannah's.** This is the establishment, at any rate, where President Jimmy Carter ate in 1987. The menu is extensive but cheap—nothing over a few bucks. I ordered a plate of mashed potatoes, something I hadn't had for months in China, simple and delicious. The young manager and his "right-hand man" joined me at the table and by the end of the evening we cut a few deals to see some sights together. Yangshuo is the kind of town where it doesn't take long to enter into the daily lives of the people who work with foreigners. Before I left I would know the people from Susannah's Cafe quite well—again, a rare experience elsewhere in China.

Moon Mountain

In the morning, I teamed up with Harold, the manager at Susannah's. We walked down Xi Jie to a row of bikes for rent on the sidewalk, next to the Paradise Hotel where I was staying. I picked out a mountain bike, paid RMB 5 (60¢), and we headed down the highway, turning south along the Li River at the bridge. The countryside is, of course, gorgeous, those celebrated rock peaks soaring straight up like enormous pick-up sticks dropped by the gods on both banks of the river. The air was nippy and my hands were completely frozen to the handlebars after the 40-minute, 6-mile ride to Moon Mountain (Yueliang Shan).

At the entrance there's a shack on a dirt road where I bought tickets (RMB 8/$1) and the woman in charge watched our bikes. It's another 40-minute hike to the top of Moon Mountain, so named because its peak is an enormous stone arch with an opening the shape of the moon. Stone stairways wind through the thick bamboo and brush to the top. Here I could see the Li River at its most spectacular, lazily winding through hundreds of stone towers, squares of vegetables and rice

checkerboarding the flat ground. Harold knew the way from Moon Hill to nearby caves—Black Water Caves, New Water Caves, Dragon Caves, all with underground streams, bats, waterfalls, and swimming pools—but I was content to let the morning run its course from the top of this peak. Why go underground when the most monumental stalagmites on Earth are erupting aboveground under a blue sky beside a river? We spent an hour talking about how much money people make in America and how many cars they own. Harold was frantic to make his fortune in China. He'd just turned 24, with no college, but his grasp of English was sharp enough. He was impatient and impulsive.

Later I warmed up in the **Mei You Cafe,** next door to Minnie Mao's. Mei You is a play on the Chinese phrase familiar to legions of independent travelers—*mei you* meaning "don't have," the constant refrain sounded by the staff in hotels, restaurants, stores, and offices when a request is made that is too bothersome at the moment to fulfill. The Mei You Cafe in Yangshuo, however, has just about everything one needs—good food, tours, help, advice. The dining room contains eight tables with tablecloths. The walls are decorated with the flags of many nations, the straw hats of local peasants, farming implements, and hollow gourds called *hulis,* representing longevity. The bar at the back serves imported drinks. The local beer, Liquan, is flat but cheap, just RMB 4 (50¢) for a quart bottle.

Breakfast at Mei You is RMB 10 ($1.20) for eggs, toast, coffee, and fresh orange juice. The Mei You also serves a special snake dinner for gourmets. You get to eat the snake, drink its blood, and keep the skin—the whole package is only RMB 90 ($11). At the back of the English-language menu is a breakdown of Yangshuo tours, including a demonstration of cormorant fishing after dark for RMB 40 ($4.80). I ordered the trip, not the snake. The woman on duty added some coal pucks to the burner under my table, which warmed me up nicely, then returned to her knitting, a striped wool sweater.

In the afternoon I wandered the cobblestoned street, **Xi Jie (West Street),** northwest of the Li River. The street is lined with old wooden buildings, many of them selling scroll paintings, T-shirts, batiks from nearby Guizhou Province, and carved stones. The stone of this karst region is famous in China, and these trinkets can be expensive.

At the river, where the tour boats from Guilin tie up in the afternoon, there's an extensive outdoor arcade of souvenir and junk dealers, worth combing through. Art students from Guilin display their latest works. Old coins, probably fakes, as well as Mao buttons, Mao's *Little Red Book,* and other recent artifacts of the Cultural Revolution (1966–76) can be picked up here for a dollar or so.

If you spend a week or longer, Yangshuo is the ideal place to take an introductory course in Chinese culture. The **Buckland Foreign Language School** on Xi Jie (it also owns Susannah's Cafe) offers quick instruction in the Chinese language, Yangshuo cooking, classical brush painting, and kung fu and tai ji quan, at about RMB 25 ($3) per session.

In the evenings, the cafes rock with Western pop music, set up laser video screens, or simply sell big bottles of beer to foreigners who congregate inside. I decided instead to go fishing by moonlight.

Cormorant Fishing

Fishing with cormorants is an ancient tradition in many parts of China. I first saw it done on the Li River, where to this day it is an honored enterprise. The birds are outfitted with a noose, tied fairly tightly around their long necks. They then dive in harness for fish, which they capture in their beaks, the knotted string preventing them from swallowing the food. Afterwards, they return to the boat, and their master collects the fish. The boats are flat, narrow rafts consisting of five or six large, round bamboo trunks tied together and upturned at the stem. The fisherman stands on the raft, using a pole to propel the boat. His cormorants perch on his outstretched arms, diving on command. It is said that one good cormorant can feed an entire family.

The **cormorant tours** leave after dark from the Yangshuo docks; they can be booked in many a cafe for RMB 40 to RMB 50 ($4.80 to $6), usually including dinner afterwards. We boarded a large motorized skiff and followed the bamboo rafts as they glided into the river. Lamps on poles illuminated the rafts, their glow luring fish up from the depths. It's a fine adventure to watch on a warm summer's eve, although it was cold as we set out and after an hour on the waters I was relieved to return. In Yangshuo, it is said that the fishermen allow their cormorants to swallow every seventh fish they catch. It keeps everyone content.

Fuli & Xingping

Yangshuo's landscape is stunning enough. The setting of the nearby villages, such as Fuli and Xingping, is even more extraordinary. In the summer, boats take passengers downriver to Fuli or upriver to Xingping. There are even inner tube rentals for those who prefer less formal passage. The weather was too cool and tour groups too scarce for such ventures when I visited in January, so Harold suggested we take the local bus (RMB 5/65¢), which by fits and starts got us first to Fuli and then across the Li River, north to Xingping.

Fuli is a tiny town that holds an outdoor food and crafts market for locals every 3 days. There isn't much for foreigners to buy here, but the peasants who pour in are fascinating to watch. Many are ethnic minorities, and they come to market in their most colorful clothing. I traipsed back and forth among the rows of produce, pots and pans, hoes and rakes and harnesses, without my wallet or bag, since teams of pickpockets are known to work these country markets, and foreigners are an obvious target.

Xingping is a river town that the tour boats pass on the way down from Guilin. It is located in the region's thickest jungle of spiraling karst pinnacles. The streets here are paved in rock, and the houses are made of stone. The port, where dozens of flat-bottomed tour boats dock in the winter, looks like a "Welcome to China" poster, with the sharp peaks standing layer upon layer across the harbor, like a wall of lotus petals. There's a fine, spacious stroll garden on the far edge of this harbor, where an outdoor banquet was in progress. We almost joined in, when Harold realized it was a wake, the meal following a funeral.

Instead, Harold picked out a cafe on the main street of Xingping, run as most of them are by a family. We ordered up a hot pot and some beer. Things were not going well for him at Susannah's Cafe. He quarreled with the women he managed, who were irate that he'd taken the afternoon off to accompany me. His girlfriend, who also worked in the cafe, had just broken up with him and he was crushed, then angry. He said he'd been dreaming of saving enough money to open his own restaurant—but it didn't appear he would last much longer in this job. Harold made less than $100 a month, and his only skill was his English (peppered with a dictionary of slang he picked up from backpackers). If he lost this job he'd have to go back to work with his brother, a local mechanic.

Green Lotus Peak

Everyone who's ever pulled into Yangshuo on a boat down the magnificent Li River has been transfixed by **Green Lotus Peak (Bilian Feng),** which towers over the harbor. The sheer northern face of its little sister peak is often likened to an ancient bronze mirror, and Green Lotus Peak itself is said to resemble an open bloom reflected in the river. A path leads up from the bank to a two-story pavilion, **Yingjiang Ge.** There's a museum nearby with copies of Li River paintings by Xu Beihong, the town's most famous artist, who lived in Yangshuo in the mid-1930s.

Green Lotus Peak is the finest spot in Yangshuo to enjoy a snack on a sunny afternoon, while watching the boats come in off the Li River and snap the harbor market to life. The old fishermen hop down the wharf—pole, baskets, and cormorants in tow—posing for pictures, "10 yuan" a shot (RMB 10/$1.20). The best local snack is the Shatian pomelo, a large grapefruit renowned for its medicinal properties and loaded with vitamin C. Piled in pyramids on roadside stands, it is sold even at night, the displays lighted by fluorescent bulbs.

The river traffic changes minute by minute, the long tour barges giving way to fishing rafts and family junks. There's a legend of the river in which two brothers, Son of the East and Son of the West, compete for the same girl. Her name is Jade. She finally sees both her suitors racing toward her and in a split second she draws a line across the sand with her hairpin, hoping to separate herself from both of them. The Son of the West is swifter. He crosses the line in the nick of time, before it becomes a wide river, and claims Jade. Her line in the sand becomes the jade hairpin to which poets compare the Li River, and the Li River itself carries the meaning of separation.

Yangshuo seems a separate world. Karst castles surround Green Lotus Peak, their names conjuring up a fairy realm of images: Lion Peak and Kitten Hill, Horse Head Ridge and Peach Tower, Dragon Mountain and White Crane Peak. Perhaps this is the landscape the ancients imagined existed elsewhere only on the Moon, a bright garden of limestone parted by a heavenly river with banks of green-waving bamboo. But it is also a place as modern in some ways as the West, a point of international contact as jolting as any in Beijing or Shanghai or Guangzhou.

PRACTICAL INFORMATION

ORIENTATION & WHEN TO GO

Yangshuo is located 50 miles south of **Guilin,** 1,000 miles southwest of Beijing, and 225 miles west of Hong Kong, in Guangxi Zhuang Autonomous Region. The climate is subtropical, with high rains and humidity in the summer.

Winters are usually mild, although a bit chilly. October and April are the best months to visit.

See the separate chapters on four nearby places to visit in the same province: **Guilin** (and the **Li River**), **Beihai,** and **Sanjiang.**

GETTING THERE

Yangshuo is a village without air or rail connections. Guilin, 50 miles north, is the transportation center and gateway to Yangshuo.

By Plane to Guilin Guilin is served by **Dragonair** (☎ 800/233-2080 in the U.S.) from Hong Kong (1 hour) and by Chinese airlines from many other cities, including Beijing (2 hours 15 minutes), Shanghai (2 hours), Kunming (1 hour 20 minutes), and Xi'an (1½ hours). Dragonair's office in Guilin is at the Sheraton Hotel, 2/F, Binjiang Nan Lu (☎ 0773/282-5588, ext 8895; fax 0773/283-2080).

By Train to Guilin Direct trains connect from Kunming (30 hours) and Guangzhou (20 hours).

Guilin to Yangshuo A plethora of **buses** make the 90-minute run from the bus station in Guilin and return from the bus station in Yangshuo. Ask for a bus directly to your destination. The buses leave when full and charge approximately RMB 10 ($1.25).

An alternative is to hire a **taxi** at a hotel desk in Guilin; on the new expressway the ride takes 70 minutes, costing about RMB 250 ($30). In Yangshuo, the cafes can book mini-buses or taxis back to Guilin or direct to the Guilin airport. **Minnie Mao's Cafe** can book taxis to the Guilin Airport (with 1 day's notice), and also air and rail tickets for many destinations in China (with 3 days' notice).

CITY LAYOUT

The **Guilin Highway** (north to Guilin, south down the Li River) takes a jog at Yangshuo, running east and west along the south side of town. The main intersection is at **Xi Jie,** the cobblestoned street that runs northwest through town to the boat docks on the Li River. The **Yangshuo bus station** is 2 blocks west of this intersection (on the north side of the Guilin Highway).

The cafes and hotels are clustered around the main intersection and up Xi Jie toward the docks. Bike rentals are available along Xi Jie.

Foreign currency exchange is handled only at the **Bank of China** (located on the harbor, at 11 Binjiang Lu, north of the entrance to Xi Jie), open daily 9am to noon and 1 to 5pm.

TOURS & STRATAGEMS

Day tours can be booked easily in many of the cafes on Xi Jie. Minnie Mao's Cafe offers fascinating tours of the area. If you spend time in any of the cafes on this street, you'll meet other travelers and can organize a group for almost any kind of tour in the area, including boat trips up and down the Li River.

WHERE TO STAY

You no longer have to rough it to enjoy Yangshuo. A new three-star internationally managed hotel, the Paradise Yangshuo Resort, opened a few years ago.

Paradise Yangshuo Resort. *102 Xi Jie (1 block north of the Guilin Highway on the west side). ☎ 0773/882-2109. Fax 0773/882-2106. 112 units. A/C MINIBAR TV TEL. $100 double. AE, DC, JCB, MC, V.* This two- and three-story courtyard-style resort is situated on its own park grounds with small lakes, arched bridges, and karst pinnacles so close you can almost touch them from your window. The oak floors are as refreshing as they are rare in China. Bathrooms and furnishings in this Malaysian–Chinese joint venture are sparkling clean. Water must be boiled in the electric coffeepot provided. Children under 12 stay free in their parents' room. Larger suites are also available ($150 to $300 per night).

Amenities: Health club, billiards, mahjong, business center, next-day dry cleaning and laundry, shopping arcade.

Inexpensive Choices **The Si Hai Hotel (Xihai Fandian)** on Xi Jie (east side of street, across from the Mei You Cafe; ☎ 0773/882-2013) is right in the thick of things, and the noise of the late-night cafes can be annoying. Dorm rooms and run-down doubles with shared bath are available; doubles with private bath rent for under $25. The **Golden Leaves Hotel** (☎ 0773/882-2860) across from the bus station at 83 Pantao Lu has better (and cleaner) doubles (for $40) and a helpful staff, as does the **Golden Dragon (Jinlong)** (☎ 0773/882-2674) at 34 Die Cui Lu, near the intersection with the Guilin Highway, several blocks west of the bus station. None of these basic hotels offers much beyond towels, soap, air-conditioning, and a small TV.

WHERE TO DINE

The cafes catering to Westerners all offer reasonable prices, Western and local dishes, imported drinks, tour agencies, ticket booking services, plenty of information, a laid-back atmosphere, and English-speaking staff. The best are on the west side of Xi Jie, a block north of the Paradise Hotel. My favorites are **Mei You Cafe** (with its RMB 10/$1.20 Western breakfast and coffee), **Susannah's Cafe** (Yangshuo's original Western restaurant, with its long menu—Jimmy Carter once ate here), **Minnie Mao's** (with its inexpensive noodles and complete travel desk), and **Sunshine Cafe** (with movies in the evenings). All are open from 7:30am to at least midnight daily.

On either side of Xi Jie where it joins the Guilin Highway are the **Green Lotus Restaurant,** with nice outdoor tables and the most elegant Chinese and Western dishes on the street, and **MC Blues Bar,** with plenty of high-energy music, burritos, fried bamboo rats (a type of rat, fried whole and served on a stick), and choose-what-you-dip hot pots. Along the Guilin Highway there are still more choices, including **Planet Yangshuo,** good for a late-night drink, and **Wild Swans,** which has a library of new and used books in many languages.

The **Paradise Hotel,** 102 Xi Jie (☎ 0773/882-2109), has two international-level restaurants, located in a separate new building across from the lobby. The **Xiang Jiang** is a coffeehouse serving breakfast, lunch, and dinner buffets that feature continental, American, and Asian dishes; the cost is RMB 100 to RMB 168 ($12 to $20). The **Xiang Shan** offers Cantonese, Sichuan, and local Yangshuo dishes covering a wide range of prices. Neither was functioning on a regular schedule when I visited in January—spring, summer, and fall are the busy seasons here—but the setting and the cuisine are the best (and by far the most expensive) available in Yangshuo.

SANJIANG: A BRIDGE OF WIND & RAIN

三江

GUILIN, YANGSHUO, AND THE LI River encompass China's most famous scenic landscape, but the province—Guangxi Zhuang Autonomous Region—is elsewhere largely unexplored by tourists. I became curious about some of the villages in the northern region of the province, however, and, teaming up with Klaus, a German I met over dinner in a cafe, I convinced a cafe manager in Yangshuo to act as a guide, something he had done before for other foreign travelers.

I wanted to see the Dong minority village of **Sanjiang** and the rice terraces near **Longsheng.** Neither Sanjiang nor Longsheng are names that come to the top of the list when you talk about places to visit in China, of course—which made them all the more attractive. I wanted to see villages, sights, and peoples that one ordinarily never dreamed existed in the China of Beijing, Shanghai, Xi'an, and Guilin.

Across the Dragon's Spine

We set out from Yangshuo at 9am, taking the local bus up to Guilin, a 90-minute ride. Harold, our guide, was in bad shape. At the Guilin bus station he found a Chinese pharmacy and bought pills for his ailing stomach. The 3-hour trip into northern Guangxi was rough. The rickety buses were uncomfortable to begin with; the seats crammed close together, the suspension nearly nonexistent. We rose and fell with every bump in the potholed road. The bus frequently stopped to take on village passengers, many of them loaded down with sacks of produce destined for market. Most of the passengers were men, and they all smoked furiously.

The scenery became more rugged. The northern region of the province is dominated by spectacular mountain ranges. The passes are marked by nearly endless turns and curves in the road, which the driver

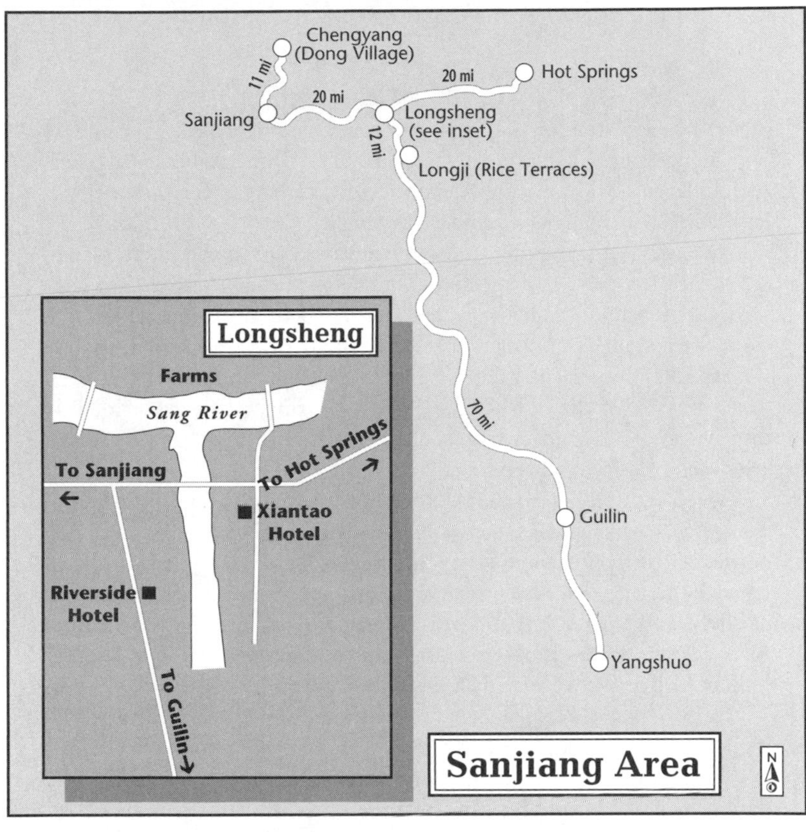

negotiated at the highest speeds possible. We had glimpses of remote farms, their old terraces climbing steep peaks step-by-step, each green platform formed by hand. Cows and water buffalo frequently blocked the road. Slow-moving tractors hauled trailers of logs to town. I had never seen this much logging in China. The forests were thick in the mountains. We passed dozens of roadside mills stacked with lumber, bamboo trunks, and sheets of veneer drying in the sun.

At the village of **Longji** 12 miles south of Longsheng, we got off the bus to see the **Dragon's Spine Rice Terraces (Longji Ti Tian).** Over the centuries the Yao minority people have sculpted 2,000-foot peaks here with terraces that are the most astounding in China. Harold was too woozy to make the climb, but Klaus and I were eager to hike, accompanied by several old Yao ladies who tried to sell us their handicrafts on the way to the top.

The Yao people are not the only minority in the region. The Dong, the Miao, and the Zhuang also call northern Guangxi home. The Zhuang people are China's largest minority group, numbering more than 15 million, most of them concentrated here in their homeland.

Able to assimilate Chinese ways and customs quickly, the Zhuang are largely indistinguishable today from the Han Chinese. Their language, with links to Thai, is distinct, however, and at many of the minority villages spoken Chinese is as obscure as English.

The town of **Longsheng,** where we would spend the night, a busy, ugly urban strip on the Sang River, is the closest thing to a Zhuang capital. Harold found a room with three narrow beds at the Xiantao Hotel, a six-floor walk-up. Klaus and I decided to do some exploring. We walked into the streets. Along a north-running tributary of the Sang River we strolled through the local market, a ripe, odoriferous sidewalk display of bleeding goats freshly slaughtered and dried rats in various sizes ready for frying or boiling.

Mapless, we followed the river west for a mile, crossing a bridge into the terraced farmlands. Cow paths led us through villages of wooden houses and over the boundary walls of dozens of rice plots, fallow in January, but the route was often swallowed up by fields. Farmers greeted us shyly as we made our trek. Fishermen trolling the river sometimes waved to us. By the time we returned to Longsheng, crossing another cement bridge, we were ready for dinner.

In the Xiantao Hotel's main dining room, we feasted on a variety of local dishes and drank beer and glasses of a sweet wine that was warmed in a hot pot. It was dark when I climbed the outside stairs back up to the sixth floor. On the landing outside the restaurant I collided with a goat. At first I thought he was stuffed, but he was still alive, tethered to the railing and waiting his turn to visit the kitchens.

Longsheng is not a town of delicacy and delight. The dark streets were noisy with the sounds of karaoke bars and cinemas. Our room, a cement shell floor to ceiling, was freezing cold. I slept with all my clothes on under two quilts, and I still shivered. There was a shower nozzle on the wall in our bathroom that belched out hot water in the morning. The toilet had no flushing mechanism beyond the pail that stood like a spittoon to one side. Spittoons were stationed at the foot of each bed as well. I began to dream of a Holiday Inn someday reaching even these mountain towns.

The Bridge at Chengyang

We rose early enough to catch the 7am bus to Sanjiang, the center of a rural region where the Dong minority still maintains their traditional villages. The bus was a circus. I know it sounds like a third-world cliche, but part of the way I rode with a bag of live chickens in the aisle wedged against my foot. The engine cover next to the bus driver was piled high with sacks of rice, on which several passengers were seated. The strangest cargo we picked up along the way, however, was 10 large sacks of rocks, which with superhuman effort were loaded by one man, bag by bag, until the aisle was chock-full. Somehow the bus continued under its own power, despite the additional tonnage, completing the trip west to Sanjiang in under 3 hours.

At Sanjiang, Harold hired a minivan for the 40-minute drive on unpaved country roads to the Dong village of Chengyang. The driver was a young woman with whom Harold flirted. When one of the tires was punctured, she pulled over to change it. None of us gentlemen offered her a hand, nor did she need one. She changed it in a snap.

Klaus and I enjoyed the countryside, particularly when we reached the valley of a small river. The riverbank was lined with a series of wooden waterwheels, several of which were still in operation. They are used now as in the past to scoop water from the river to irrigate the fields.

At Chengyang we had our first look at the most famous sight in the region, the **Bridge of Wind and Rain (Fengyu Qiao),** built by the Dong villagers in 1916. Construction took 12 years. It is considered the finest and most beautiful of the 100 wind-and-rain bridges still standing in China. These are superbly crafted covered bridges that not only serve as meeting places where people exchange village gossip, protected from rain and wind, but as the location of religious shrines. Here, five stone piers, one on each bank of the Chengjiang and three erected in the shallow riverbed, provide support for the 210-foot-long 11-foot-wide span. Each support is crowned with an elaborate three-tiered pavilion with layers of soaring eaves. Matching white-trimmed roofs link the five pavilions. The covered bridge is fashioned from cedar. As with the Temple of Heaven in Beijing, this pavilion bridge was constructed without a single nail, secured solely by wooden pegs. From a distance, it resembles a bridge transformed into a long imperial corridor and temple complex.

The Dong village of **Chengyang** on the other side of the river has occupied the lush green valley for 3 centuries. Dozens of traditional wooden-plank houses the size and shape of barns, built atop mud-brick basements where pigs are penned, surround the village pond and a placid stream, called the Pingtan. The upper two stories of a typical house are lined with spacious balconies, supported by peeled timber columns that also support the tiled roofs. A local English-speaking villager invited us inside a house. The living areas are entered by wooden stairs or ladders. Inside, there are simple, dark, unadorned rooms with bare wooden walls. An open hearth on the floor serves as a stove. We were invited to sample the Dong tea, made from bricks of tea leaves that steep for 20 minutes. It was a deeply flavorful brew.

The village was electrified, but few cars or trucks traveled the unpaved streets. Hand-pushed wooden carts and bicycles were the principal machines. The women, most of them dressed in gray pants and black coats, with white cotton scarves covering their heads, were washing buckets of laundry in the stream. The hillsides and valley floor were terraced in plots of vegetables, grains, and rice. Lumber, stone, and straw seemed to be the other principal commodities. There didn't seem to be any power tools about, even in the tiny mills. Everything was done by hand.

A small shop selling snacks and village crafts stood by the entrance to the bridge. I bought several carved wooden decorations and a bottle of spring water. As we headed back across the Wind and Rain Bridge, we were intercepted by a gaggle of local women in black and indigo quilted jackets armed with baskets and knit bags of crafts and trinkets. They accompanied us across. All down the river the waterwheels turned slowly like ancient bamboo Ferris wheels.

Longsheng Hot Springs

The next morning we caught another bus out of Longsheng going the other direction, east down the Sang River. This trip was only an hour, but mostly uphill, past stunning mountain rice terraces and wooden villages. The Yao minorities dominated the countryside in this direction. Higher up, between forested peaks, we arrived at the local hot spring, **Wen Quan.**

The hot spring is currently undergoing a massive hotel and resort development. We walked the road to the pool at the top, about a mile. The road is lined with dozens of restaurants and crude inns. Harold explained that as well as those who came to take the waters, this place was also the haunt of businessmen and officials who came to take pleasures of another order—about 200 prostitutes work the resort. I decided not to indulge in a massage (RMB 50/$6) and headed instead for the outdoor mineral pool (RMB 40/$5), a large, steaming cement basin surrounded by tiled bathhouses, mountain peaks, and the statue of a goddess. Klaus and I enjoyed a 20-minute soak in the moderately hot spa waters.

A clear stream tumbles out of the mountains by the hot springs. If you cross it via a ragtag suspension bridge, you can hike into the forested hills, where there are wild monkeys, according to the locals. We chose to take lunch instead at one of the sidewalk cafes specializing in two dishes: sticky rice cooked in bamboo shoots and dried strands of pork.

The road back to Longsheng and then south over the winding mountain that passes down into the karst plateau of Guilin and

Yangshuo was like a return from a medieval wilderness to modern Chinese civilization. Harold would find he was without job or girlfriend when he got home, but he seemed unconcerned. He'd made contact with the bus conductress and rode next to her up front on the engine cover.

At the edge of the mountain roads I kept seeing the villagers, men and women, trekking up and down the terraced slopes. They had machetes holstered to their sashes for slashing tree limbs. The limbs were bundled and driven to town where they became charcoal sticks for heating stoves. Occasionally we passed hunters, their rifles essentially handguns equipped with long pipes for barrels. From a distance, they looked like blunderbusses. Klaus fell asleep. He didn't seem to know a word of Chinese, or English either, but he had been on the road in China for 55 days straight, roughing it on buses like this one, alone, visiting villages and waterfalls every bit as remote as the Bridge of Wind and Rain. I began to doze, too, as we came down out of the mountains, descending as if from a lost world where cedar barn houses loom like dinosaurs and bamboo waterwheels spin like ancient banners that the passing centuries forgot to tear down.

PRACTICAL INFORMATION

ORIENTATION & WHEN TO GO

Sanjiang and Longsheng are located on the mountainous northern border of the Guangxi Zhuang Autonomous Region, about 70 miles northwest of Guilin, 1,000 miles southwest of Beijing, and 225 miles west of Hong Kong. This remote, hilly region is dominated by minority groups, chiefly the Dong, Yao, Miao, and Zhuang, who pursue terrace farming, hunting, and logging. Longsheng is on the main highway to Guilin. Sanjiang is west of Longsheng.

Normally, spring and late autumn are the best times to visit this hot and humid region, but in these mountainous regions, late summer is better. Skies are clear and temperatures are warm. As winter nears, the thermometer drops sharply. Heavy rains are common from February through May.

GETTING THERE

Frequent **buses** make the 3½-hour trip to Longsheng daily from Guilin. The fare is RMB 20 ($2.40). Longsheng is connected by frequent daily buses to Sanjiang; the trip takes 2½ hours and costs RMB 8 ($1). The nearest **air and rail** service is in **Guilin** (see the Guilin chapter for details).

TOURS & STRATAGEMS

Formal and informal guided tours can be arranged in **Yangshuo** (see the Yangshuo chapter). The cafes on Xi Jie in Yangshuo abound with tour options to Sanjiang and Longsheng. I arranged my tour with a person who worked at

Susannah's Cafe in Yangshuo, although nearby Minnie Mao's Cafe and the Mei You Cafe offer more formal tours of the region.

The two of us paid our Yangshuo guide RMB 350 each ($42), which covered transportation, admissions, and lodging for 2 nights in Longsheng, with visits to the Wind and Rain Bridge and Dong minority village near Sanjiang and the mountain hot spa east of Longsheng.

In Longsheng, travel information is available at the **Riverside Hotel** (see below); in Sanjiang, at the **Wind and Rain Bridge Travel Service** (☎ 0772/861-3369).

WHERE TO STAY

If you hire a guide, he or she can make the decision about where to stay. If you're on your own, the best place to stay and eat is not at Longsheng but at Chengyang Wind and Rain Bridge, 11 miles north of Sanjiang, in the **Chengyang Bridge National Hostel** (☎ 0772/861-1444). This is a newer wood building built in the Dong style, with dorm rooms and small doubles (shared bathrooms). The friendly staff speaks some English. As you might expect, this hotel, like all the others in the region, offers no frills whatsoever. Otherwise, at Longsheng, head for the **Riverside Hotel (Kaikai Lushe)** (☎ 0773/751-1335) at 5 Guilong Lu, downhill toward the bridge from the bus station on Guilong Lu. An English teacher runs this dormitory/hostel and she's an unbeatable source of information. There are no frills, no private bathrooms, and rates are levied per bed. The price is RMB 20 to RMB 40 ($2.40 to $4.80). I stayed at the **Xiantao Hotel** (no phone) on Xinglong Zhong Lu, 1 block south of the bridge into downtown. A room with three beds and a private bath with shower, in run-down condition, cost RMB 90 ($11). The power frequently failed and there is no elevator. This seems to be the best hotel in town (there are others like it), but it would be difficult to get a room here unless you speak Chinese. Again, there are absolutely no frills, except for a tiny black-and-white TV.

WHERE TO DINE

A guide will make life easier in Longsheng and Sanjiang. Few of the hotel or street restaurants cater to foreigners in any way, except the Riverside Hotel in Longsheng (see above), which has very inexpensive food with an English menu. If you don't speak Chinese, try the **food stalls** (point-and-eat) around the downtown bridge on Xinglong Xi Lu, or the **floating barge restaurants** on the riverbank, which sell hot-pot lunches and dinners for about RMB 60 ($7.25) per person. The best place to eat near Sanjiang is at the **Chengyang Bridge National Hostel** (see above); the staff serves Chinese dinners (costing $3 to $5) on the balcony.

Beihai: Sandworms & Pearls

北海

Until the 1990s, Beihai was an obscure coastal port on Beibu Bay in the South China Sea facing Vietnam. The emperors favored Beihai for its pearls, still a thriving industry in this sunny town 275 miles due south of Guilin. But the pearl city also has Silver Beach, pronounced the best beach in China, and as the big cities on China's eastern seaboard began to boom, so did Beihai, as a tropical resort. The resort boom has already quieted down, leaving Beihai still largely undiscovered. Few Westerners pass through.

Just 340 miles west of Hong Kong, a short hop by air, Beihai sounded like an ideal getaway. My interest was piqued by stories I heard. Beihai had served as a treaty port a century ago, opening to Western traders in 1876, and the European legacy could still be seen in the architecture of its main street. The harbor was said to be crowded with fishing junks, colorful enough to be favored by movie directors filming historical novels about Old China, and the seafood was judged to be exquisite, particularly the shrimp and a local delicacy, the sandworm. And far out in the bay were volcanic islands, virtually untouched by modernization, where Catholic cathedrals were still standing, the islanders predominantly Catholic. I decided I would take a look at this countryside seaport and its silver beaches before it was overrun by yet another resort boom.

Old Town

The four-lane 9-mile expressway from the Beihai Airport was flat, straight, new, and nearly empty when I arrived. Green fields in red soil stretched toward rolling hills on either side. Water buffalo grazed the median strip, cows crossed the highway, and bicycles rolled along the inside lanes, often heading against traffic. Barefoot peasants in straw hats marched up the off-ramp to the town. They had piled the grain on the pavement to dry. There's plenty of room for country life on the wide expressway.

The entrance to my hotel was lined with massive palm trees. The lobby floors were marble, trimmed in teak. Two-story glass panels framed a picture of the sea. Like most of the resort hotels, this one faced the northern shore of the Beihai peninsula. Silver Beach was across town, on the southern shore. I hired a guide at the hotel to show me around Beihai. She was from Beijing. She said she loves the slow, friendly pace of life in Beihai, so far from that of the capital.

Beihai's fishing industry is concentrated in **Di Jia Town** in a protected inlet on the northwest tip of the peninsula. Every morning, the large fishing junks tie up at the pier on Haijiao Lu and the middlemen meet them. The catch is examined, bartered over, and carted away to markets and cafes in large baskets. The junks and wooden houses along Beihai's north shore have barely changed over the centuries. Many of the hundreds of junks anchored here are owned by the families who live in the houses on the shore, but they have prospered in the 1990s and no longer man the boats themselves, hiring the captains and crews for the dangerous business at sea. Many of the boats docked here house the more than 10,000 boat people in Beihai, ethnic Chinese expelled from Vietnam in the late 1970s.

Much of the day's catch ends up in the fish market on Yunnan Lu, south of the harbor. A new building has been constructed for the vendors there, but the atmosphere is traditional enough. Under a spacious covered concrete concourse, open on all sides and supported by dozens of square columns, the women of the fishing villages squat or sit on the wet pavement beside their plastic pans filled with live seafood. There are no tables or platforms. The women are mostly minorities, including the Zhuang who have occupied the southern reaches of Guangxi Province for several thousand years, and the Jing, Vietnamese who have lived on the islands off Beihai for the past 4 centuries. They weigh each purchase with the traditional handheld scale, consisting of a bamboo stick gripped at its midpoint, a weight dangling from one end, the purchase from the other. Dried seafood specialties capture the big prices here.

At the heart of Beihai, a mile east of the fishing harbor and market, is **Zhongshan Lu,** the "Old Street" district of European embassies. The British, French, German, and Dutch all set up consulates here as soon as the Qing Dynasty signed the Yantai Trading Agreement of 1876. Foreigners set up their own offices, schools, and churches, and Zhongshan Lu is still lined with these European-designed edifices, most now occupied by grocery stores, pearl shops, Chinese offices, and apartments.

The buildings the Europeans left behind are not as grand as those on Shanghai's Bund, but they are striking. They're built of brick, plaster, and concrete. Their fronts are faced with immense wooden doors, and

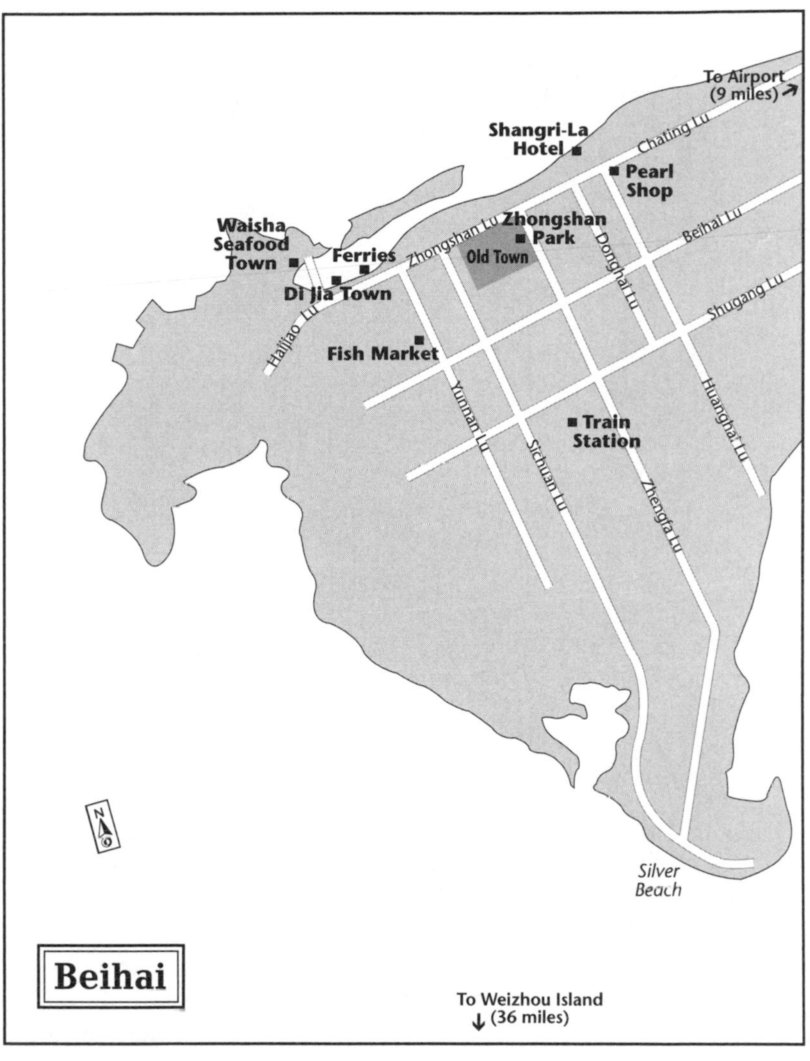

their upper stories extend into the street, supported by columns and arches, giving the sidewalk the cool, shady aspect of an arcade. The facades of the taller buildings, usually just three stories, have some decorative flourishes at their peaks, but the overall effect is plain and massive. Pedestrians tunnel through the sidewalk arcades, shopping and running their daily errands. There's a curious absence of motorized traffic along Old Street these days.

Walking in those streets, I happened to look up and spot a cross. Below it was a sign, in English: "Beihai Christ church." The windows had arched panes of clear glass, but they could easily have been filled with stained glass a century ago. Since it was Sunday, I suggested we drop in. We were directed upstairs. Inside a large, plain room a service was under way. A place for us was cleared at once. We sat on a back pew. A psalm was being sung and the church was full. I stayed only a few minutes, feeling like an intruder, no matter how welcome I may have been. They say there are many Christians in Beihai, my guide remarked. It was her first look inside a Christian church.

She did know where the **former British Embassy** was, just off Zhongshan Lu, near Zhongshan Park, which the locals like for its hill of monkeys. The two-story embassy is a stately building in the same style as the Old Street facades, an arched arcade supporting the upper floor. Not only is it not open, it is empty and unused. The embassy grounds contain a half-dozen colonial brick-and-plaster bungalows, all unoccupied. It should be a museum, a park, a tourist attraction. Of course, with so few Western visitors here, the beach and nightclubs are the prime attractions, not some graceful but empty monument of the days of imperialism. It is surprising enough that these foreign embassies still stand at all, here at the southwestern end of China.

We hitched a ride on a pedicab, heading back to the north shore, east along Chating Lu. There was a large pearl shop on the way. I'd been admiring the pearls for sale on the streets of Beihai. They were cheap, about RMB 100 ($12) for a necklace of hundreds of tiny pearls, but my guide said the quality was poor. The pearl stores and the hotel shops sell the best of Beihai's "southern pearls." The Japanese buy the raw pearls here; the settings are done abroad. Twenty-five miles east of Beihai are the ruins of the **Bailong Pearl City,** where emperors as early as the Han Dynasty (206 B.C. to A.D. 220) sent their emissaries in search of the finest pearls.

Sandworms

Waisha seafood town, located on a woebegone flat strip of sand near the fishing harbor, is the place to eat in Beihai. Connected to Beihai by a small bridge, Waisha is a neighborhood village where the fishermen have been cooking their catch at home and serving it on the spot for years. A reputation for freshness, family recipes, and low prices made Waisha the gourmet's choice for seafood. In 1996, the Beihai government opened a "town" of Waisha restaurants, 72 of them placed side-by-side in two long wings. The buildings aren't much: They look like row shacks without fronts. But the seafood inside is superb.

Selecting a **cafe** from the six dozen nearly identical storefronts seems impossible. They are not numbered or named, but they seem to all have local followings. Customers window-shop the tanks and plastic pails until some display of live seafood hooks them. The cafe I selected was superb. It was also the only one with a big fat pussycat out front. Long-haired, white and reddish yellow, with yellow eyes, she was tethered by a jeweled collar and beaded leash to a folding wooden chair. I knew I'd found the right place.

Four enormous rectangular tiled tanks the size of bathtubs, each with a pump, were the living menu. The cafe cat's leash couldn't quite reach the tanks. The restaurant had five round tables, each with a cloth, and a floor of beach sand. We ordered seven seafood dishes, including a fresh clam soup for two. The RMB 140 ($17) tab included beer, tea, and a plate of noodles. The clams and the snails were excellent. The shrimp, some enormous in size, were divine. They must be peeled at the table. A small plate of regional celery refreshed the palate. Snails were next. I dug them out with a toothpick. The last dish was the best: two dozen plump, freshly boiled sandworms, which look as hideous as their name. Four to six inches long, segmented, wriggling, and pink, they were dug up from these very sands in which my chair was sitting. They were chopped up and cooked to a divine sweetness.

The cafe cat had her lunch as well. She snapped up fish bones tossed to the sand, took them under a chair, and shredded them over her rice bowl.

If you come here in the evening, my guide confided, you see quite a spectacle, like no other in China. Every night, a procession of luxury cars pulls in and lines up at their owners' favorite cafes. There are dozens of such exotic cars—we're not talking just the ordinary Cadillac, Lexus, or Mercedes. A Ferrari, for starters. A Rolls Royce or two. The more expensive and exotic, the better. The real estate boom made a few overnight millionaires in Beihai, but their motorized toys arrived illegally via Vietnam and other ports, snatched from the streets of Hong Kong, Tokyo, Los Angeles, and New York, and bought for a song in Beihai. The police turn a blind eye here. In the rest of China, however, these racing machines remain contraband. Their owners can drive them around and around, back and forth to their heart's content, but only in Beihai. They are high-priced adult kiddy cars, and at dusk they all line up so that their owners can feed on the best fresh seafood in Southeast China.

The Dancing Maidens of Silver Beach

Silver Beach is 7 miles south of the fish market and downtown Beihai. Ranked as "the first beach in China" by tourism officials, it is a 14-mile stretch of white sand with gentle waves and a notable absence of sharks. In the summer, the Chinese flock to Silver Beach for sandcastle contests, volleyball, wading, sunbathing and, in the evenings, tent camping on the beach. In the winter when I visited the beach it was nearly deserted, although the sun was out and the temperature mild. A cleanup crew, lying down in the sand, jumped into action when they saw us approach.

One of the oddest things about Silver Beach is the new architecture surrounding it. Dozens of fantasy resorts, white and red villas with turrets and towers, vaguely European, now empty, line the highway to Silver Beach, along with Swiss chalets and garish theme parks. During Beihai's early 1990s boom, developers and overseas investors moved in, erecting scores of seaside palaces for the expected onslaught of free-spending tourists. Tourists do come to Silver Beach—which really does look like one of China's finest beaches—but not in the large numbers once dreamt of by landowners and resort operators.

I walked the long, flat beach in January, trying to imagine how it looked in the summer, filled with vacationers like a beach in Thailand or Miami. The wide brick promenade, planted with palms, runs to a horizon punctuated with red turrets. There is almost nothing anywhere that indicates this beach is in China—certainly no temple roofs or tiled pavilions with golden finials. The centerpiece is a curious modern sculpture and **musical fountain:** an immense hollow globe sheathed in writhing copper panels, a massive southern pearl set on a marble pedestal, its equator encircled with eight beautiful maidens. These maidens of the pearl, linked in a circle by garlands held loosely in their hands, are vibrant sculptures twice life-sized. They are also completely unclothed and frightfully well endowed. They are classical nudes borrowed from the Western tradition, as are the other fanciful monuments that populate Silver Beach.

When the fountain is operating in the summer, the dancing maidens no doubt appear more chaste. Local boosters hail this musical fountain as the world's largest, its jets spraying more than 220 feet into the air. On festival days, including the Spring Festival (Chinese New Year), the Lantern Festival (in February or March), the China Orchid Fair (in late February), the International Sand Sculpture Contest (in August), and the Beihai International Pearl Festival (in October), the fountain square holds exhibits, performances, and nightly fireworks.

A final incongruity is the **camel.** Even before the fantasy resorts encompassed Silver Beach, a local entrepreneur had been trying to drum up business by enticing visitors to take a ride and pose for snapshots on the ocean sands aboard his two-humped business partner, who would probably have been more at home in the deserts of the distant Silk Road. The venture has been successful. Not only is the camel a summer fixture in Silver Beach, he has company: Other camels walk the sands, too.

An Island of Catholics

Due south of Beihai, 36 miles by sea, 90 miles east of Vietnam, **Weizhou Island** is a tropical Eden of lava and coral. It is also where Christians from Beihai fled persecution and where a century-old Catholic cathedral stands in the center of a Chinese island village.

I arrived just as the ferry was about to depart. The hotel thought departure from Beihai was at 9am, which it was when the fast boat was running, but Monday was a slow boat day and the departure was at 8:30am. The cab driver knew. When I told him my destination, he began to drive like a maniac, swerving in and out of traffic, nearly driving on the sidewalk. He kept opening the glove compartment to consult his imitation gold Rolex watch, shouting "Ba dian ban" (8:30) and shifting up another gear. I kept looking through the back window, thinking we were in a movie chase scene. I made it to the ferry landing with 5 minutes to spare, purchased a ticket, and scurried aboard.

The slow boat to Weizhou took 3 hours on this particular morning. The seating area reminded me of a bus. There were 50 seats. All faced the TV monitor, which played two complete kung-fu action movies. It was a relief to pull into Weizhou harbor. It's a small island, 10 or 12 miles across in any direction, and a low island—no soaring peaks, just a rolling plateau a hundred feet above the water. In the port, several dozen large fishing junks were at anchor. Our ferry tied up at the main wharf. There were low, ugly cement buildings along the shoreline, against the banded sandstone cliffs of the plateau; and to the right, a new town commercial center with white-tiled walls housing village cafes, shops, and fish markets.

I had no idea what to do on this island—no map, no guidebook. A friendly tout motioned me off the wharf to a bus. I looked inside. There were a few people already seated. I shrugged. There wasn't much option. The bus filled up and departed. The driver gave a tour in Chinese. He drove down shore, then up to the plateau. Here a dirt road cut across banana plantations. With the exception of a few buses and a stray taxi, the road was dominated by ox carts. We descended to the beach again, to a much more beautiful stretch, utterly pristine, with dramatic outcroppings of rock.

We took a walk on the beach. What I noticed first were the innumerable shells underfoot, unbroken and brightly colored. Next, I was entranced by the strange sea rocks that rimmed the shore, draped in trees and ferns. They consisted of hundreds of narrow, flat, uniform layers of sand and lava. Several children dressed in red and orange had anticipated our arrival. They were skipping along the sands carrying strings of pearls and baskets of shells for sale. Orange starfish clung to boulders embedded in the beach. There were fishing junks scattered up and down the shore, waiting for the tide to take them out.

Our ultimate destination was the **French cathedral** in a small village in the middle of the island. We followed the red dirt road inward through large sugarcane fields, past a People's Liberation Army outpost, into the village. Many of the houses were built of stone and had dark tiled roofs. Cacti grew beside them, low to the ground. Our bus stopped at the town square. There, like a tropical mirage, rose a three-story, stone-and-brick, century-old cathedral, dwarfing the tiny village of mud streets, stonecutting yards, and ox carts loaded down with cane, rocks, and tree limbs.

The cathedral was built shortly after the Yantai Trading Agreement of 1876. It seats about 300 under a high arched ceiling. Framed portraits of Christ with Chinese captions are affixed to the walls. To one side of the raised altar there is a forest of candles; to the other, a sculptured rock cave. The missionaries to Beihai seem to have been unusually successful. Hundreds of Christian converts fled to Weizhou Island during times of persecution, finding refuge in this church. Its priest lives in Beihai now, and there are services on the island only on important religious occasions, such as Christmas and Easter, despite the fact that at least 80% of Weizhou's population is Catholic.

From the village cathedral, this Chinese tour headed over to the island lighthouse, a modern construction. There, on a paved path that leads by a series of switchbacks down the cliff face, we reached a volcanic shoreline, all lava, rife with small sea caves and blowholes. The layered cliffs and volcanic outcroppings were covered in small cactus plants—not at all the kind of beach one associates with China. But this is southern China, nearly as far south as the Middle Kingdom stretches, nearer the equator than Hong Kong or Macao.

The coral island of Weizhou, like the pearl city of Beihai, is a simple seaside paradise with a curious Western legacy. In a nation teeming with Industrial Age cities and tourist-clogged imperial treasures, both Weizhou and Beihai are quiet, unhurried, and undiscovered.

PRACTICAL INFORMATION

ORIENTATION & WHEN TO GO

Beihai is a port on the South China Sea, 340 miles west of Hong Kong, less than 100 miles east of Vietnam, in the southern province of Guangxi. It lies 275 miles south of **Guilin, Yangshuo,** and the **Li River** (see separate chapters). The weather is tropical, warm year-round. High season for Chinese tourists is during the humid months of July and August. In September, rains and an occasional typhoon can strike. March, April, and May are pleasant months to visit, although Silver Beach, rated the best beach in China, really doesn't start operations until June.

GETTING THERE

By Plane The Beihai Airport, 9 miles east of downtown, can be reached from 11 cities in China, including Beijing (3 hours), Shanghai (2 hours), Kunming (1½ hours), Guilin (45 minutes), and Hong Kong (1 hour). Few of these flights are daily; some, like the flights to and from Hong Kong, are rather expensive charters. The nearest city with extensive and frequent air connections is Nanning.

By Train Beihai is connected to China's rail network via **Nanning,** a 3-hour trip. From Nanning, a major terminal, the train lines run northwest to Chengdu (26 hours); northeast to Guilin (10 hours), Beijing (41 hours), and Shanghai (46 hours); east to Guangzhou and Hong Kong (36 hours); and southeast to Pingxiang (4 hours) on the Vietnamese border.

By Bus By bus from **Nanning** is a 5-hour trip.

By Ship There is a daily 10-hour ferry from Haikou on China's **Hainan Island.**

GETTING AROUND

Transportation around town is inexpensive. **Taxis** and **pedicabs** cost about RMB 13 ($1.60). Bicycles can be rented at the hotels for less than $1 per hour.

The slow **ferryboats,** known as Feiyao vessels, leave for Weizhou Island from Beihai's northwest pier on Haijiao Lu at 8:30am daily. Tickets are RMB 50 ($6) each way. The voyage takes 2 to 3 hours. The return trip leaves Weizhou at 2:30pm. The Freida ferry is a faster alternative (75 to 90 minutes), but it doesn't run every day. Freida tickets cost RMB 150 ($18) round-trip. The tour bus meeting passengers on the Weizhou Island dock charges RMB 20 ($2.50) for the 2-hour tour. Seafood lunch at a cafe (no English menus) in the new civic building near the dock costs RMB 30 to RMB 40 per person ($3.60 to $4.80).

TOURS & STRATAGEMS

China International Travel Service (CITS), 6 Beibuwan Lu (☎ 0779/303-3038; fax 0779/305-4477), provides tours of Beihai, plane tickets, and maps. Hotels can also assist with booking tickets and day tours.

WHERE TO STAY

Shangri-La Hotel (Xiangge-Lila Fandian). *33 Chating Lu (on the north shore).* ☎ *800/942-5050 or 0779/206-2288. Fax 0779/205-0085. 364 units. A/C MINIBAR TV TEL. $100 double. AE, DC, JCB, MC, V.* This 17-story four-star resort hotel is the only place to be if a typhoon strikes—its rooms don't flood and there's an auxiliary power system. Despite being the best hotel in Beihai, the Shangri-La is not expensive. The rooms are large, and they include a writing desk, coffeemaker, and hair dryer. There are two executive floors (Horizon Club, 13th and 14th floors) with concierge services and two handicapped-accessible rooms (one twin, one king). Specify a seaside room for the view. Service and amenities are first-rate.

Amenities: Outdoor swimming pool (separate children's pool with water slide), health club, Jacuzzi, sauna, two outdoor tennis courts, business center, conference rooms, room service (6am–midnight), next-day dry cleaning and laundry, nightly turndown, CITS tour desk, beauty salon, shopping arcade, free airport shuttle.

WHERE TO DINE

The best seafood (shrimp, snail, sandworm) is at **Waisha,** a fishing town across a bridge from the town harbor (off Haijiao Lu in northwest Beihai). There are 72 "no-name" cafes here, most run by local fishing families. Look for the one with the cat on a leash. Expect to pay RMB 70 to RMB 100 ($8.45 to $12) per person for a six- to eight-course dinner.

Western, Asian, and Chinese breakfast buffets, fixed-price lunches, and weekend dinner buffets are served in the Shangri-La Hotel's **Coffee Garden,** 33 Chating Lu (☎ 0779/206-2288), open daily 6am to midnight. This is an elegant coffee shop, with rattan furniture, teak-paneled walls, and a picture-window view of the bay and sculptured swimming pool. The set breakfast (pot of coffee, orange juice, rolls, toast, omelet with ham and cheese, potatoes, bacon, sausage, rice crispies, hot and cold milk) costs RMB 44 ($5.40), including tax.

Shang Palace. *33 Chating Lu (second floor, Shangri-La Hotel).* ☎ *0779/206-2288. Dinner reservations recommended. Main courses RMB 30–RMB 300 ($3.75–$37.50). AE, DC, JCB, MC, V. Daily 7–11am, 11:30am–2pm, and 5:30–10pm. CANTONESE.* This elegant sea-view restaurant with nine private dining rooms employs chefs from Beijing and Hong Kong. The dim sum menu for breakfast or lunch has 22 choices priced at RMB 6 to RMB 8 (75¢ to 95¢) per plate. Cooks prepare the day's live seafood of your choice in nine ways (steamed, fried, stewed, stir-fried, as sashimi, etc.). The seven vegetarian dishes, such as panfried lotus root with pickled olives and black fungus, are the best deal in the house at about RMB 32 ($4).

KUNMING: CITY OF ETERNAL SPRING

昆明

SITUATED ON A HIGH, LUSH PLATEAU in the Yunnan Province, bordering Vietnam, Kunming was long regarded by the Chinese as untamed and remote—in fact, as barely civilized. Officials fallen from favor in the imperial capital were routinely banished to these backwaters of the Middle Kingdom, where tribal peoples were constantly in rebellion. Even today, over a quarter of Yunnan's 35 million people are minorities, members of 24 groups that have retained their non-Chinese customs and dress.

This preponderance of racial minorities imparts a splash of color and diversity to Kunming that is missing in most other cities of China, where the crushingly homogeneous Han Chinese, nearly 99% of the population, hold sway. Kunming even maintains an Institute for Nationalities, a university of over 20,000 minority students.

This said, I have found upon several recent returns to Kunming that even here China's rapid modernization is altering the cityscape. The pace of life in Kunming can no longer be described as that of a village. General Claire Chennault, who stationed the legendary Flying Tigers and the Fourteenth U.S. Air Force here during World War II, described Kunming as a "sleepy backwoods Oriental town" where "water buffalo, cattle, and herds of fat pigs were not uncommon sights." They are uncommon enough now. The streets are paved and jammed with new cars, buses, and trucks, like any street in the West, and lined with ever-taller offices and department-store towers. Ten years ago, Kunming bore few outward signs of an American presence. Today, the Americans have returned to Kunming—not in person, for there are few foreign faces in this city, but as models for Kunming's future. The architecture, the automobiles, the department stores, the clothing—it's all in the American mode.

The old Kunming is slipping into the backstreets and curling up in a few parks and temples. That's precisely where one has to go these days to find the remains of what has long been one of China's most exotic cities. Fortunately, a search can still turn up strange treasures.

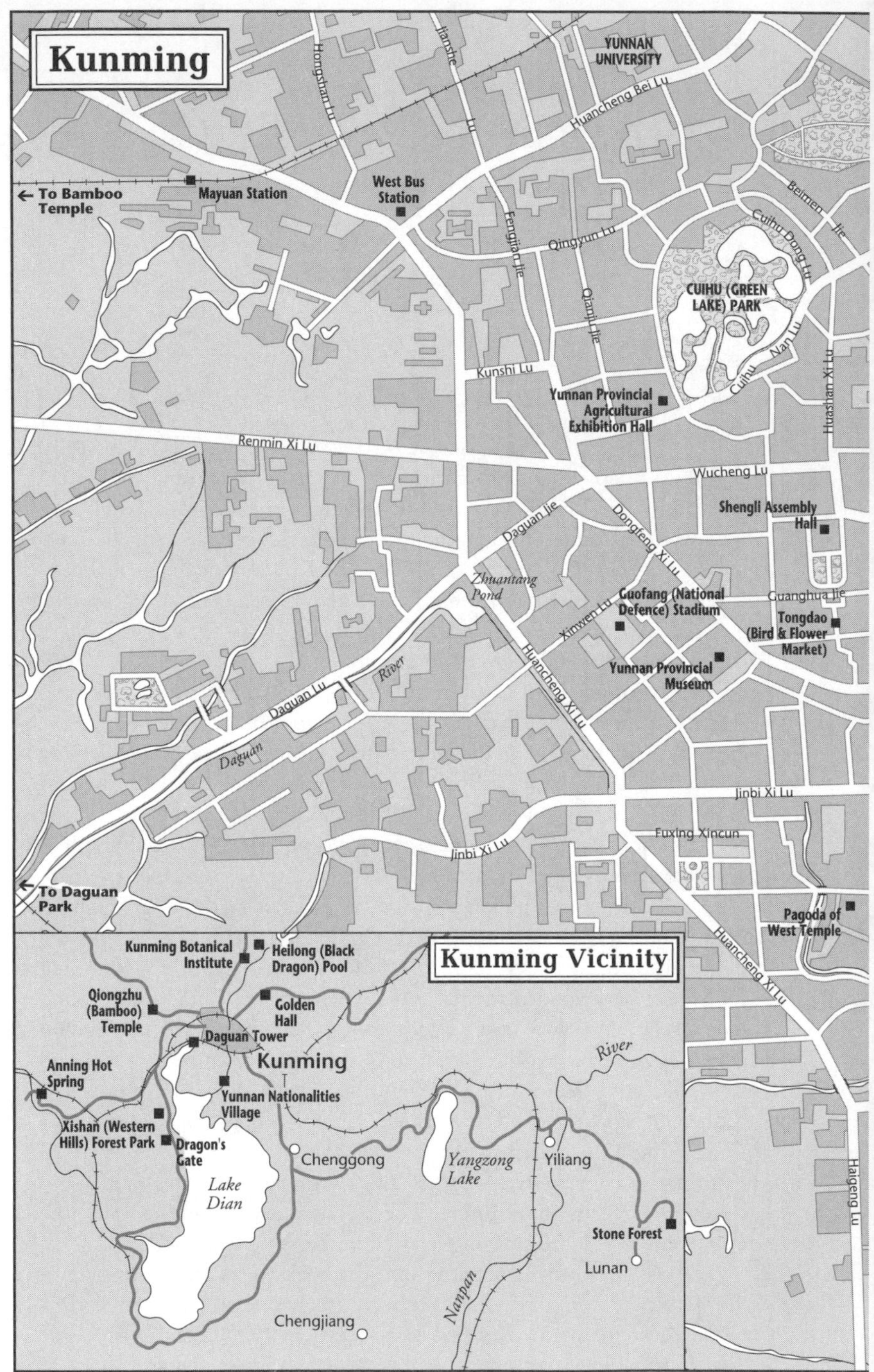
Kunming
YUNNAN UNIVERSITY
Hongshan Lu
Jianshe Lu
Huancheng Bei Lu
← To Bamboo Temple
Mayuan Station
West Bus Station
Beimen Jie
Cuihu Dong Lu
Qingyun Lu
Fengjian Jie
Qianju Jie
CUIHU (GREEN LAKE) PARK
Cuihu Nan Lu
Huashan Xi Lu
Kunshi Lu
Yunnan Provincial Agricultural Exhibition Hall
Renmin Xi Lu
Wucheng Lu
Shengli Assembly Hall
Daguan Jie
Dongfeng Xi Lu
Zhuantang Pond
Guofang (National Defence) Stadium
Guanghua Jie
Xinwen Lu
Tongdao (Bird & Flower Market)
Huancheng Xi Lu
Yunnan Provincial Museum
River
Daguan Lu
Daguan
Jinbi Xi Lu
Fuxing Xincun
← To Daguan Park
Pagoda of West Temple
Haigeng Lu
Kunming Vicinity
Kunming Botanical Institute
Heilong (Black Dragon) Pool
Qiongzhu (Bamboo) Temple
Golden Hall
Daguan Tower
Kunming
Anning Hot Spring
Yunnan Nationalities Village
River
Xishan (Western Hills) Forest Park
Dragon's Gate
Chenggong
Yangzong Lake
Yiliang
Lake Dian
Stone Forest
Lunan
Nanpan
Chengjiang

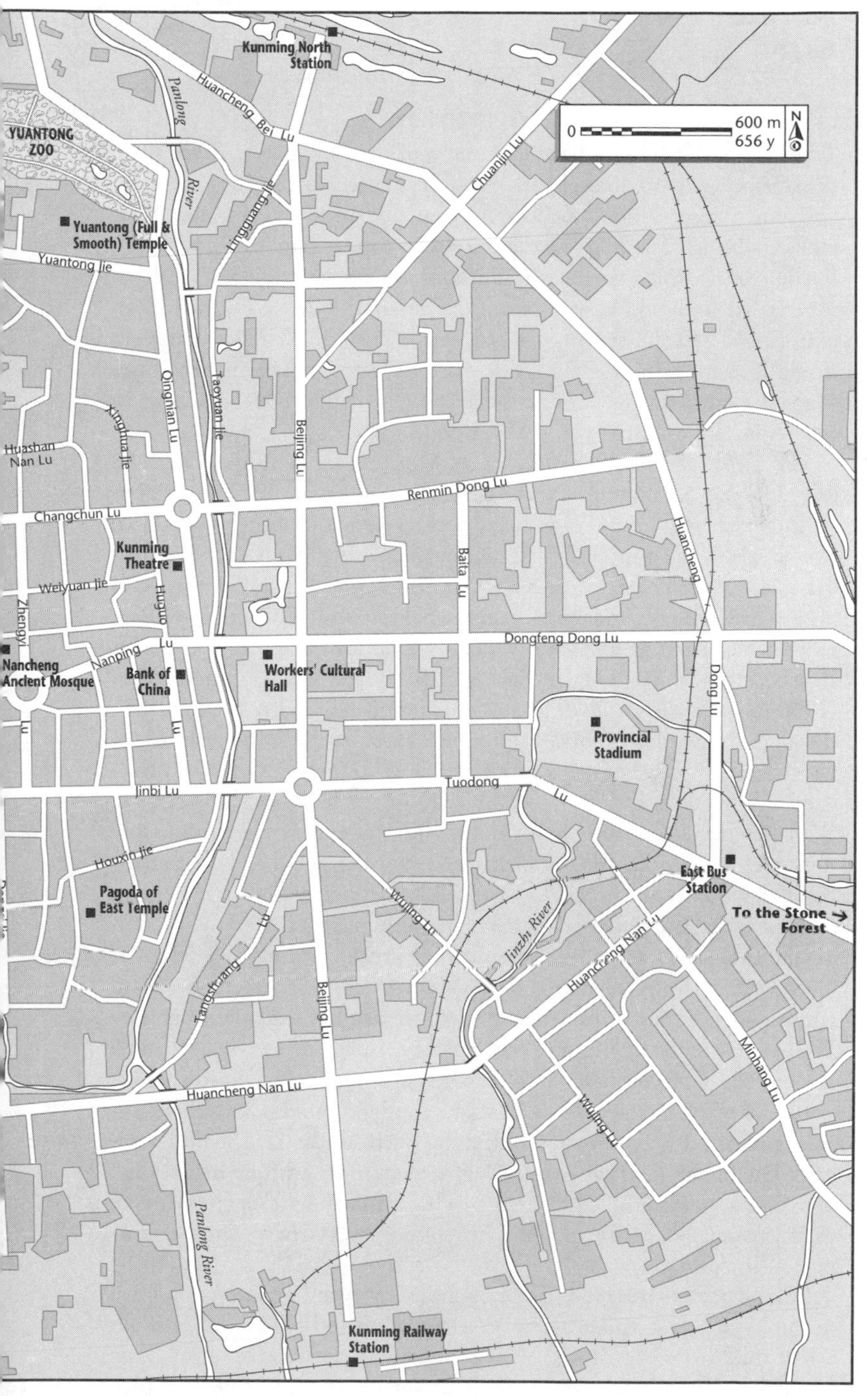
Kunming North Station
Huancheng Bei Lu
Panlong River
YUANTONG ZOO
0
600 m
656 y
N
Chuanjin Lu
Lingguang Jie
Yuantong (Full & Smooth) Temple
Yuantong Jie
Qingnian Lu
Taoyuan Jie
Beijing Lu
Xinghua Jie
Huashan Nan Lu
Renmin Dong Lu
Changchun Lu
Kunming Theatre
Baita Lu
Huancheng
Weiyuan Jie
Huguo Lu
Zhengyi Lu
Dongfeng Dong Lu
Nanping Lu
Nancheng Ancient Mosque
Bank of China
Workers' Cultural Hall
Dong Lu
Provincial Stadium
Jinbi Lu
Tuodong Lu
Houxin Jie
East Bus Station
Pagoda of East Temple
Wujing Lu
Jinzhi River
To the Stone Forest →
Huancheng Nan Lu
Tangshuang Lu
Minhang Lu
Huancheng Nan Lu
Panlong River
Kunming Railway Station

Downtown

The streets of Kunming have lost much of their old exotic flavor since the economic boom of the late 1990s. The department store at the main downtown intersection of Nanping Lu and Zhengyi Lu has been replaced by a glistening new **super store** (open 9am to 9pm daily). Inside, the marble stairs with spittoons on every landing have been superseded by brand-new escalators. The staff is decked out in clean uniforms. The counters are stocked with heaps of cosmetics and electronic appliances from abroad. There are still enough local commodities to make a quick swing through the aisles worthwhile, but the poorly lit, cavernous emporium of the 1980s is gone.

So too is the **Nancheng Ancient Mosque,** for centuries located a few blocks up Zhengyi Lu (at the corner of Chongyun Jie), but replaced recently there by a new mosque. The Hui people (Chinese Muslims) have made it into a more formal tourist site, with trinkets and postcards for sale outside. After removing your shoes, you can enter the plain prayer hall upstairs and have a quiet look around. The mosque, even rebuilt, has fared better than a nearby Buddhist temple, which was smashed by the Red Guards during Mao's Great Cultural Revolution (1966–76). Left in a pile of glazed green roof tiles and red bricks, with its stone temple lion toppled onto the sidewalk, this temple has now been replaced by a high-rise office building, four stories of blank concrete and whitewash.

While the backstreets in downtown Kunming are beginning to lose their rough appeal, I still saw plenty of **street markets** northwest of the main downtown traffic circle, their stalls stocked with fresh flowers, tropical fruits, and pork bellies. Itinerant quilt makers thread their looms on the sidewalks. Seamstresses tend their treadle sewing machines. A block west of the mosque on the north side of Jingxing Jie, the **Bird and Flower Market** has outgrown its alley (Tongdao Jie), still identifiable by overhanging signs in Chinese and English. Along the side streets you'll find caged songbirds, fish of marvelous shapes and colors, lizards, monkeys, and other creatures from Yunnan's southern jungles, as well as pets such as small dogs and cats. Continuing north to the next main boulevard, Guanghua Jie, I crossed through an **open-air antique market** full of prayer rugs and ethnic handicrafts. This is still an "old" neighborhood, with wooden two-story shophouses looming everywhere, but modernization is closing in.

Some of the street life has been chased eastward from Nanping Lu to the huge public square at the **Workers' Cultural Hall.** This is about a half mile from downtown, where Nanping Lu turns into Dongfeng Dong Lu, Kunming's prime east–west boulevard. The square, which occupies both sides of the street, fills up before 8am with Kunming's exercisers—dancers, *tai ji quan* groups, and badminton players. After 8am it becomes congested with shoppers, idlers, and vendors offering foods I couldn't identify. One entire row of vendors sits behind small tables with hand-painted signs advertising their services. These are the blind masseurs of Kunming, who for a pittance ($1) will deliver a crushing back massage right on the square or on platforms set up in nearby patches of a city park. Dozens of other masseurs ply their trade from head to foot (reflexology), each dressed like a doctor in a white smock. There are also fortune-tellers, ice-cream hawkers, batik vendors, and a large portion of Kunming's floating population milling around—unemployed peasants from the countryside.

These days, the farther you move from the heart of the city, the more country people you see trying to make their way in from the fringes, selling rural crafts, produce, and their skills on the streets. Many of them are dressed in minority clothing, knowing that for today's Chinese visitors, as well as for foreign tourists, an exotic costume gives a sales edge. The longer I wander the streets of Kunming, the clearer becomes the split between the rural life of the past and the urban rush of the present. Mending that split will take decades more. In Kunming, the urbanization of China's vast rural population is at its inception—where it stood in America more than a century ago.

Green Lake

Northwest of city center, a 40-minute stroll up Dongfeng Xi Lu, then a right on Cuihu Nan Lu, is Kunming's answer to Central Park, Green Lake (Cuihu). Some of the neighborhoods here are still populated with the two-story wooden-shuttered houses that characterized city life in Kunming a century ago, but most are being torn down.

At the eastern entrance to Green Lake Park, vendors conduct games of ring toss on the sidewalks. The prizes are cheap ceramic figurines. Stalls sell intricately sliced curlicues of fresh pineapple on a stick. Lined with willows, the lake is gorgeous, crisscrossed by small arched bridges in imitation of Hangzhou's more famous West Lake. The best time to come is on Sunday, when the pathways are crowded with families on their weekly outings, and the best season is winter, when days are warm and sunny and the large flocks of black-headed "laughing gulls" with their cackling cries arrive from breeding grounds in Siberia, as they have been doing for the last 10 years. The gulls enjoy not only the legendary "eternal spring" weather of Kunming but also the crumbs of steamed bread, sold in plastic bags by vendors, that visitors toss them.

Green Lake Road, running south of the park entrance back toward downtown, was developing into a trendy "international" avenue of small cafes in the late 1990s, but as the 21st century begins it has become dominated by a row of scores of small shops selling batiks, carvings, scrolls, and the traditional clothing of the Bai people. The French Parasol Restaurant and the Cafe De Jack, backpacker bistros, are gone. All that's left here of those easygoing hangouts is the Blue Bird Café, its open-air wooden porch nudging the crowded sidewalk.

The Best 500 Arhats in China

The temples of Kunming are numerous, and today they can put one more directly in touch with the ancient past. Most tourists bent on seeing a temple at Kunming first head east from Green Lake to **Yuantong Si,** a thousand-year-old Buddhist complex with a new statue of Sakyamuni in white marble, a gift from the king of Thailand. A more interesting religious shrine, however, is the **Bamboo Temple (Qiongzhu Si),** 8 miles northwest of city center. A taxi is the easiest way to get there; the cost is around RMB 20 ($2.40).

The Bamboo Temple dates back to the Tang Dynasty (A.D. 618–907), but the present halls were rebuilt in the 1880s when the amazing sculptor Li Guangxiu arrived on the scene. Molding clay over wooden skeletons, Li composed the most demented congregation in China, perhaps in the world. Had Goya and Dali collaborated as sculptors, their work would have resembled the 500 arhats of the Bamboo Temple.

The 500 arhats (or 500 luohans) are a fixture in major Chinese monasteries. They are the 500 followers of Buddha who achieved their own salvation. Concerned only with personal redemption, they practice deliverance from the mortal world in bizarre, often grotesque ways. In Li's version, the 500 figures perch tier upon tier, filling two halls. Their faces twist and erupt in wild contortions, creating a vivid three-dimensional mural of exaggerated emotions from joy to despair to madness. Devotees ride oceanic crests on the backs of animals, mythic and natural. Eyebrows 2 feet long sprout from perplexed foreheads. An arm streaks 10 feet across the room, its finger shattering a ceiling of clouds like a thunderbolt. This is the ultimate mixture of surrealism and expressionism, Buddhism and dementia. Li Guangxiu is said to have parodied the faces of his contemporaries in Kunming, who criticized his art not for its extreme exoticism and depiction of horrors but for its realism. For sheer inventiveness, these 500 arhats put even modern Western comic book illustrators to shame.

Golden Temple

Another temple that repays a visit to the outskirts of Kunming is the Golden Temple (Jin Dian), located atop **Ming Hill (Mingfeng),** 7 miles to the northeast. At the northern entrance (admission RMB 15/$1.90) one must scale a formidable forested hillside via a wide stairway, passing through the first and second gates of heaven (Yi Tian, Er Tian) before making the final push straight up. Near the third gate are two rather odd attractions, a camel waiting for tourists to pose with it for portraits (RMB 10/$1.25) and the "Golden Temple Alpine Coaster," the third longest "tublose-rail" alpine coaster in the world, with two-thirds of a mile of track up and down the sacred slopes (RMB 30/$3.70 per ride).

The main attraction, however, resides still higher, beyond yet another gate (Lingxingmen), not to mention an upper parking lot favored by tour buses: the Golden Temple itself (also called Taihe Palace). The Golden Temple is surprisingly small, but exquisite. It was first built in 1602 and moved to this hill in 1637, though the present form was cast in 1671. Weighing in at 250 tons, this is the largest bronze work of architecture in China. Double-tiered, 25 feet wide, 21 feet high, ensconced on two platforms of marble, the Golden Temple has a dark patina and looks its age. Inside, its altar is dominated by the statue of the Zhengwu Emperor, with a Gold Boy and Gold Girl on either side, the altar guarded by images of a fierce tortoise and snake. In the "Chinese Golden Temple Expo Garden" to one side of the temple is the Zhengwu Emperor's own legendary "seven-star" double-edged sword.

The Golden Temple is surrounded by old steles (engraved stone tablets), including in the wall one on the far side of the temple with the image of Lao Zi, ancient founder of China's major indigenous religion, Daoism. Chinese visitors here (I was the only foreigner, in fact) often face this engraved image, cover their eyes with one hand, and march forward with an arm outstretched, attempting in a kind of blind-man's-bluff to strike the venerated figure (a successful blow ensures longevity).

Beyond the Golden Temple, in the upper folds of the hills, at the park's true summit (elevation 6,752 feet), is the **Bell Tower.** There are signposts in English and Chinese along the way. This three-story tower with its 36 flying eaves, decorated with singing phoenixes, soars to over 90 feet, and it looks old, but in fact it was built here in 1984. The ancient treasure hangs inside, a 10-foot tall, 14-ton **bronze bell** cast in 1423. It once hung in the south gate of the old city walls of Kunming.

To one side of the Bell Tower is the **Golden Temple Camellia Garden,** particularly glorious in the spring, when its 15,000 flowers (200 varieties) are in bloom. I was hardly surprised to learn that it was billed as the largest camellia garden in China (25 acres).

Rather than retracing one's steps the rather hefty distance back down the hill and searching there for a taxi, one can follow the signs to the **Jinbo Cable Car,** which connects the Golden Temple park to the International Horticultural Exposition Park below. On my way to the cable car I spotted an old man lying at the side of the road who immediately sprung to life as I neared. He turned out to be an itinerant fortune-teller who could not be dissuaded from reading my palm, my ears, and my head. He cast my fate on the basis of the small metal slats I happened to draw, despite my protests, as I couldn't understand a word of his dialect, nor he of mine. I paid him off and proceeded on. Traveling alone, one is frequently a victim of such colorful inconveniences in China.

The Jinbo Cable Car, over a half-mile in length, opened in January 1999, expressly to connect the Golden Temple with the grounds where the last world exposition of the 20th century was held. Each cable car holds just two persons, a loudspeaker on each post blasts out Chinese pop music, but the view is spectacular, including a glimpse of the city of Kunming and its skyscrapers in the far distance. The Jinbo Cable Car operates from 9am to 6pm daily, and costs RMB 15 ($1.90) one-way, RMB 25 ($3) round-trip.

International Horticultural Exposition Park

The international horticultural fair (dubbed Expo 99) is over, but the vast expo grounds (more than a mile across, covering 538 acres) are still worth the stroll. The park has kept the special exhibition gardens of bamboo, bonsai, herbs, trees, fruits, and teas. Five large exhibition halls also remain, foremost the large circular courtyard **Green House.** Its chief display is a miniature Yunnan alpine landscape of native plants that thrive on the high plateau above 9,000 feet. The expo grounds are stuffed with other attractions, too, from a butterfly house (admission RMB 15/$1.90) and food plazas to viewing towers and an amusement park.

The International Horticultural Exposition Park, about 4 miles northeast of Kunming (southwest of Golden Temple Park), is open daily 8am to 7pm. Admission is RMB 30 ($3.75). Taxis take 20 to 30 minutes from downtown locations, and charge RMB 20 to RMB 30 ($2.50 to $3.75).

Grand View Park

Kunming is a horticultural Shangri-La. The new expo gardens are large, but the city's most famous flower gardens are located at an older site, **Daguan Gongyuan (Grand View Park),** 2 miles southwest of city center, a 150-acre botanical paradise on the shores of expansive Lake Dian

(Dianchi). The walkways, arched bridges, courtyards, and ponds here are interspersed with luxuriant flower gardens. The queen of England, on the first visit to China by an English monarch in history, planted rose bushes in this park on the afternoon of October 17, 1986. I know because I was caught in Kunming's first major traffic jam that day, the result of streets suddenly closed off in anticipation of the queen's entourage passing by. I visited Daguan Park the next day but couldn't find the queen's roses.

Returning more than a decade later, I still found no one to direct me to the royal plantings. Daguan Park has become a playground for Kunming's youth, full of snack stalls and carnival games, but it has its ancient sites. **Daguan Pavilion (Tower of the Magnificent View)** contains poems in fine calligraphy extolling the beauties of the park, including a nostalgic 118-character rhyming couplet, the longest in China, etched upon the gateposts by Sun Ranweng in the early 18th century (and recarved there in 1888 after Muslim rebels destroyed the original).

Daguan Pavilion was built 300 years ago and rebuilt in 1869 after a fire. Emperor Kangxi saw to construction of the original tower in 1690. He used it to enhance his view across Lake Dian to the Western Hills. In profile, these hills outline the figure of a woman reclining, her long hair rippling into the lake. Locals call the range "Sleeping Beauty Hills." Its steep flanks, connected by ferries from Daguan Park, are honeycombed with carved stone shrines and temples, capped at the peak by Grand Dragon's Gate.

Grand Dragon's Gate

The **Western Hills (Xi Shan),** a band of sheer cliff faces, rise 2,000 feet above the shore of Lake Dian (elevation 6,200 feet) in the flat farmlands 10 miles southwest of Kunming. A series of paths, stairways, and tunnels—linking a succession of stone temples, seemingly perched in thin air—has been carved into the face of the cliff, spiraling ever upward to Dragon's Gate at the summit. For the fit hiker, the entire 5-mile journey from the bottom, starting at the town of Gaoyao, takes nearly 4 hours, particularly if the way is crowded, as it usually is, with hundreds of fearless Chinese sightseers.

Most of the effect and the best vistas can be had by starting farther up. I hired a taxi from Kunming (RMB 210/$25 for the afternoon) and was driven most of the way up the Western Hills to **Sanqingge (Pavilion of Three Purities),** a Daoist temple complex on nine terraces. Once a 13th-century imperial villa, Sanqingge is nowadays a parking lot and tourist trap of restaurants and souvenir stands, a 2-mile walk below Dragon's Gate. Less than a mile from here, the **cliffside grottoes**—originally cut out of the sheer stone walls by Wu Laiqing and his band of daring monks over a 54-year-period starting in 1781—begin in earnest. This is not a walk for those with even a faint touch of vertigo. The caves and niches along the way contain statues trimmed from rock, serving as shrines to Guanyin (Goddess of Mercy) and other Daoist deities.

Grand Dragon's Gate overlooks Lake Dian straight below. In the far distance eastward, the new high-rises of Kunming are also visible. Lake Dian, 30 miles across north to south—the sixth largest lake in China—is divided by a causeway. The waters in the northern section were dammed a few years ago to serve as a massive sewage treatment facility.

In fact, the entire lake is so poisoned by pollutants that few fishermen can make a living anymore. Many families have been given permits to pursue a new profession, becoming vendors along the cliff paths and temples of the Western Hills. Their stalls and tables, selling everything from bottled water to polished rock images of the gods, now line the pathway to Dragon's Gate from bottom to top. A new **cable car** stretches from the far side of Lake Dian to Dragon's Gate, too. It is the second cable car built in the Western Hills during the 1990s. Another connects Dragon's Gate to **Taihua Temple,** 3 miles lower down on the Western Hills. The cable car charge is RMB 20 ($2.50) one-way, RMB 30 ($3.75) round-trip. Dragon's Gate Park is open dawn to dusk daily and charges RMB 15 ($1.90) admission.

The best route remains the 2-mile walk from Sanqingge to Dragon's Gate and back. There are fewer vendors, more overlooks, and plenty of recessed shrines here. The cave walls are scorched black with burning incense. At the top, where you can lean out over the stone railings and glimpse the stone path you've just edged up, is one of the grander views in all of China—the view a Daoist immortal might have taken, perhaps, in which all human perspectives dissolve: Cities, farms, lakes, and roads become mere lines on a cosmic map, and the mind floats free of all its past moorings, buoyant as a cloud.

The Big Plaza

A sign of modern Kunming is the new Yunnan Golden Horse and Green Rooster Tourism and Commercial Plaza, a long-winded title for the shopping and entertainment complex that has just opened on Jinbu Li, a block south of the downtown center. **Jinbi Square,** as it's popularly known, is something of a theme park for shoppers, harkening back to Yunnan's traditions. There are three plazas, three main streets, two crossroads, and two open courtyards, all lined by two-story shophouses modeled on the old architecture of Kunming and constructed of blue stone and roof tiles. This is Yunnan's largest tourism commodities center, built at a cost of US$78.45 million. There's even an underground plaza, served by 24 elevators and several open-air escalators. The streets and squares are carless, cobblestone avenues.

The center contains four craft workshops, two traditional (reconstructed) buildings (the Deyiju House and the Jianshui County Guild), a 90,000-square-foot Jewelry Plaza (the largest in China), and plenty of small cafes featuring local snacks and dishes (from Weishan long noodles and Dali casserole fish to Cross-the-Bridge Rice Noodles). Food fairs and ethnic performances are often staged in the courtyards. A Kentucky Fried Chicken outlet is rumored to be on the way, but that would be a true first. Alone of all major Chinese cities and provinces, Kunming and Yunnan have resisted the tide of Western fast foods. No McDonald's, no Burger King, no Pizza Hut—it's the law here, so far.

East & West Pagodas

Oddly enough, you can still walk a few blocks from city center and the new Jinbi shopping plaza and find monuments to Kunming's recent and distant past—sacred monuments. At 418 Beijing Lu (just north of the Tuodong Lu intersection), for example, I came across an active **Catholic church,** a compact two-story structure of cement and marble with a statue of Jesus above its altar. A high-lift crane dangling a wrecking ball on the end of its cable stood ominously close in the rear alleyway. Then, walking west toward Jinbi Square, I happened upon another church, at 61 Jinbi Lu, this one with new blue-framed windows. An old man sat smoking a small pipe on the steps. I asked if it was all right to go in. He nodded. Inside it was a plain church with brown pews seating a few hundred. There was a balcony and an altar with a gold-colored cross, but very little decoration. It turned out to be a **Protestant church,** again quite active, with YMCA-sponsored meetings.

My destination on this morning ramble, however, was toward a different religious tradition represented by two pagodas, a west pagoda and an east pagoda mirror images separated by a few blocks. They stood just south of city center and Jinbi Square. Once the tallest structures in Kunming—probably the tallest towers for a thousand miles—they were now swamped by the wake of high-rise construction that was sweeping through the city. In fact, I wouldn't have set out to find the two pagodas if I hadn't noticed them from the window of the new hotel tower and been overcome with curiosity.

The **West Pagoda** (Xi Ta) is located down a narrow alley off Dongsi Lu. I could see it as I walked down the street, through an old neighborhood that was fast meeting the wrecking ball; I soon spotted an alley entrance and took it. This pagoda was built between 824 and 895 during the Tang Dynasty, then restored in 1499 during the Ming Dynasty. The pagoda temple grounds carry an admission charge of 5 mao (6¢). The four-sided pagoda has 13 stories (although I could only count 11), with Buddhist statues in the niches of each story. The pagoda cannot be entered, but there is a picturesque, decaying two-story courtyard hall surrounding it, where a few monks live, and a small cafe—quite a setting for a cup of tea, with the pagoda almost within touching distance of your table.

The West Pagoda's twin, the **East Pagoda** (Dong Si Ta) is located on the next major street to the east, at 61 Dongsi Lu. It is newly landscaped and newly opened. Admission is also 5 mao (6¢). Built during those same years (824 to 895, during the Tang Dynasty) and last thoroughly renovated in 1883, the 13-story East Pagoda stands 132 feet tall, has most of its statues in the outer niches, and seems to be leaning slightly to the west. There's an attached pavilion and garden to the east. Across the street, between the ancient East and West Pagodas (largely forgotten, submerged in an armada of modern steel and glass pagodas), I passed by a children's hospital. I could see into the hospital room windows as I passed, and the hospital entrance and courtyard were lined with parents and toy vendors.

Later, returning back down Beijing Lu, the remote old China reached out to touch me. An old peasant woman came up to my side as we waited at a busy intersection. She looked up at me, raised her hand, and with one finger lightly stroked the red hairs on my arm. I told her, yes, the hair of the foreign devil is indeed strange, but she didn't understand me. I smiled, but she was transfixed. She raised her hand again, this time to lightly stroke my curling beard with the same extended finger. The light changed, we crossed, and we were separated.

Yunnan Nationalities Village

In 1992, Kunming opened its version of an ethnic theme park, an attraction that is sweeping China and other Asian countries. The Yunnan Nationalities Village is 7 miles west of downtown on the shores of Lake Dian. It is linked to Kunming by a wide expressway and to the top of the Western hills by that new cable car.

I've visited several of these parks in China, and Kunming's is the best, or at least the most extensive, with two dozen exhibits of ethnic village architecture, crafts, costumes, and—if you're there when a big tour group happens through—song and dance performances. A motorized shuttle train links the exhibits. Horses can be rented as well. The park is open daily from 9am to 5pm. Admission is RMB 28 ($3.40).

Some of the minority people, all in village costume, speak enough English to explain a bit about their cultures, and there are snapshot opportunities, but the experience is not one I find worth repeating. Better to see the minorities in their actual villages in **Yunnan** (in the Stone Forest, a popular day trip from Kunming), or in the towns of **Dali** and **Lijiang,** farther to the west.

Stone Forest (Shi Lin)

Kunming's most celebrated attraction is a geological wonder, the limestone pillars clustered in the Stone Forest, 50 miles to the east. There's a new highway to the **Sani minority village** of Five-Tree in Lunan County at the park entrance. A decade ago the highway followed a more circuitous route, usually broken by a stop midway at the Nut House, on the shores of Lake Yangzhong where the American Air Force partook of R&R during World War II. It constituted a pleasant stop in the 1980s. Tea in a glass and walnuts in the shell were served up in the lobby of the Nut House, which looked like a stately 1940's inn.

As this new century begins, the highway to the Stone Forest is becoming overrun with roadside attractions, amusement parks, burgeoning towns, and a raft of gift shops. Many of the Stone Forest tour buses that leave from Kunming's hotels every morning stop at the San He Yuan restaurant, a modern "minorities" cafe where one sits on short benches on a straw floor. Behind the restaurant there's a shooting range, where visitors can rent everything from a military rifle to a machine gun. And even placid Lake Yangzhong has received a face-lift. A large resort village has gone up on its shores, along with a golf course and a factory with a tall belching smokestack.

Yet the countryside here still ranks among the most beautiful in China. The ride to the Stone Forest can be as interesting as the site itself. Roadside factories are busy carving up figures of lions from white stone. Ducks are cooked in small brick furnaces outside cafes, much as lobsters are steamed outdoors in Maine. We passed several horse carts serving as local buses, 10 people standing on each trailer. Trucks haul massive piles of brick and stone. The Yunnan countryside is a vast quarry. Herds of goats block the side roads. Ponies and water buffalo work the green fields.

At the end of the road, now just a 90-minute ride from Kunming (it used to take nearly 4 hours), the Stone Forest erupts like a primordial dream. Acres of vertical limestone shafts, exposed 270 million years ago when the ocean receded from southwest China, sprout like an immense grove of bamboo. Wind and rain have drilled creases and fissures into

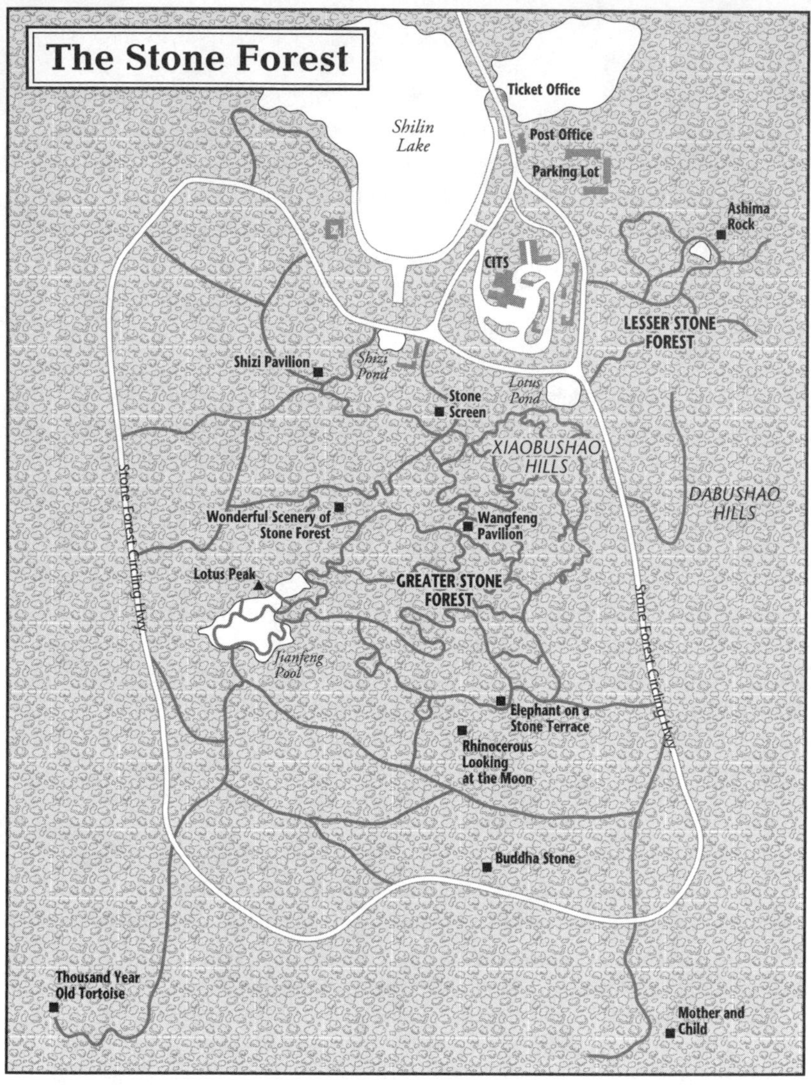

each tall pillar. The Stone Forest is like a cavern raised above the ground, its dome lopped off, open to the blue sky.

Miles of pathways twist through the karst landscape, edging along reflecting pools and rising on stone steps to pavilions perched on the limestone summits. It is a maze of massive stone pickup sticks, dropped by a playful deity. Sani women in full ethnic dress stand at every turn, offering to be guides or directing visitors to kiosks.

In the late 1990s the park painted red signs on the sides of the rocks in English as well as in Chinese. BETTER TO REST HERE FOR A WHILE, one reads. Other signs identify the chief formations: THOUSAND-YEAR-OLD

TORTOISE, ELEPHANT ON A PLATFORM. New stones pave the trails and a new section with a broad green lawn has been opened for visitors.

The park admission was up to RMB 55 ($6.90) on my most recent visit. I traipsed for several hours through the Stone Forest maze, ending up at **Sword Peak Pond,** where buildings have been erected selling trinkets and fast food. Photographers for hire dress up tourists in ethnic outfits for vacation portraits. The Stone Forest doesn't fully emit its grandeur until the tourists disappear in the late afternoon. Then you can take a solitary stroll through this microcosmic version of the uncanny peaks of Guilin, reduced to a thick grove of 100-foot-tall stone columns. It resembles a petrified forest left standing in the wake of geologic time, a thicket of gigantic exclamation points, a geologist's field of dreams.

This is why it's best to stay the night at the Stone Forest. There are several guesthouses at the park entrance and in Five-Tree Village across the bridge on the other side of Stone Forest Lake. Just before dusk you can enjoy the sights and the people at a slower pace, perhaps even make a purchase of Sani batiks, which are lovely. The people are friendly, once the heat of the sales day wears off. On many nights, there are performances of Sani dances at the inns or in the park, enthusiastic affairs where the audience is encouraged to join in. And **Stone Forest Lake,** between the park entrance and the bridge to the village, is stunning at sunset, the pillars sprouting from its waters like castle turrets in the fading light. The air is fragrant and the sky is choked with stars.

The ride back across the high Yunnan plateau is unforgettable. The villages are built of the red clay. Long red peppers and yellow ears of corn dangle from gray-tiled roof eaves, curing in the sunlight. The Sani farmers till their fields, dressed in embroidered clothing—bright reds and golds. The shoulders of the road are coated with rice spread out to dry. Along the wide riverbanks, the oval kilns of brickmakers are clustered one after the other like the tents of nomadic tribes. This is the Chinese Connemara, possessed solely by the sharpest elemental colors: the red of the soil, the green of the hillsides, the white of the limestone, the blue of the sky.

But the road from Kunming is turning into one long resort strip, and Kunming is losing its remote and exotic flavors. The past is nearing obliteration.

PRACTICAL INFORMATION

ORIENTATION & WHEN TO GO

Kunming, with a population of one million, is the capital of Yunnan Province in southwest China. Its subtropical location and high elevation (6,213 feet) make it a lovely place to visit, even in winter. May and June are peak months for foreign travelers, but the Chinese tourists favor December. October is the most beautiful month of all.

Kunming is the gateway to the fascinating Bai minority village of **Dali** and the Naxi town of **Lijiang** (see separate chapters), an hour's flight or a day's bus ride on the Burma Road, west from Kunming.

GETTING THERE

By Plane The new **airport** (☎ 0871/313-3216) is 5 miles south of city center, a quick RMB 30 ($4) 20-minute taxi ride via a six-lane expressway. Kunming is served by **Dragonair,** 157 Beijing Lu (☎ 0871/356-2828), with a daily flight to Hong Kong (3 hours). Several Chinese airlines provide connections to and from cities in China, including Beijing (2½ hours), Chengdu (1 hour), Guilin (1½ hours), and Shanghai (2½ hours). Purchase tickets at hotel tour desks.

By Train There is a long-distance train to Chengdu (overnight, 24 hours) that travels through glorious mountain scenery. Shanghai, Beijing, and Guangzhou are also connected by rail to Kunming, but because of the mountainous geography these trips can require several days and nights (up to 60 hours). Flying is a more efficient, if costlier, option.

GETTING AROUND

With a map, you can tour downtown sites on foot. It takes about 90 minutes to walk across town east to west from the Holiday Inn to Green Lake. Exploring by taxi costs RMB 15 to RMB 30 (about $2 to $4) per trip. Outlying sites, such as Dragon's Gate, can be reached by taxi or tour bus (or by rented bicycle or public bus, if you are more adventurous).

TOURS & STRATAGEMS

Visiting the Stone Forest To reach the Stone Forest, ask the hotel to book a taxi or catch an early morning bus at the **Western Bus Station** on Renmin Xi Lu or a minibus leaving from near the **King World Hotel** (Huancheng Nan Lu/Beijing Lu intersection). The last buses return to Kunming from the Stone Forest entrance at 3pm. You can stay overnight at the two-star **Stone Forest Hotel (Shi Lin Binguan)** in front of the main gate to the Stone Forest Park entrance (☎ 0871/771-1405). The rooms, with private bathrooms, are worn but clean ($35 to $60 double), and the hotel has a restaurant.

Tours The two most useful branches of the **China International Travel Service (CITS)** are on the grounds of the **King World Hotel,** 28 Beijing Nan Lu (☎ 0871/313-8888), and in the **Holiday Inn** (☎ 0871/316-5888). They offer day tours of Kunming and the Stone Forest with English-speaking guides, but it is easier just to book tours (and plane tickets) directly from the hotel tour desks. The **Camellia Hotel** also has a very useful and friendly tour desk. A day tour of the Stone Forest, including lunch, costs RMB 210 ($26); a tour of the Western Hills costs RMB 180 ($22), lunch included.

WHERE TO STAY

Camellia Hotel (Chahua Binguan). *154 Dongfeng Dong Lu (2 miles east of city center). ☎ 0871/316-3000. Fax 0871/314-7033. 279 units. TV TEL. $30–$40 double. No credit cards.* Still the favorite of independent budget travelers, this 13-story hotel has three levels of accommodation in its three wings: standard two-star doubles with private bathroom; budget one-star doubles, also with private bathroom, but smaller and more rundown; and no-star dorms with shared showers that are in high demand. The Camellia offers few luxuries, but for backpacking travelers it provides a message board, luggage storage, tour desk, foreign exchange counter, and bicycle rental (across the street). The staff speaks some English and tries to be helpful when pressed. A new, more luxurious Camellia tower is currently under construction.

Harbour Plaza Kunming (Hai Yi Fandian). *20 Hong Hua Qiao (northeast shore of Green Lake). ☎ 0871/538-6688. Fax 0871/538-1189. 321 units. A/C MINIBAR TV TEL. $125 double. AE, DC, JCB, MC, V.* This beautiful new (1999) hotel with its undulating wall of windows is the place to stay on Green Lake. The rooms are well appointed with work desks and satellite TV; the earth tones and light wood trim create a cheery feel; and the bathrooms are bright and clean. There are three executive floors and three restaurants (Western, Japanese, and Chinese). Public areas are elegant; dining alfresco near the lakeshore is particularly appealing.

Amenities: Outdoor swimming pool, health club, sauna, 24-hour business center, conference rooms, 24-hour room service, same-day dry cleaning and laundry, nightly turndown, tour desk, beauty salon, shopping arcade, free airport shuttle.

Holiday Inn Kunming (Yinghua Jiari Jiudian). *25 Dongfeng Dong Lu (1 mile east of city center). ☎ 800/465-4329 or 0871/316-5888. Fax 0871/313-5189. 243 units, including 9 suites. A/C MINIBAR TV TEL. $135 double. AE, DC, JCB, MC, V.* This 18-story, four-star Holiday Inn offers the most efficient service in Kunming. Rooms are large, clean, and modern. Executive floors 15, 16, and 17 offer more luxury and their own lounge (at $172). There are also no-smoking rooms and rooms with handicapped access. The Babalu Disco is a popular nightspot (open 8pm to midnight) and the full-service tour desk offers a complete range of tours and tickets.

Amenities: Indoor swimming pool, health club, sauna, 16-lane bowling alley, 24-hour business center, conference rooms, 24-hour room service, same-day dry cleaning and laundry, nightly turndown, tour desk, air ticket counter, beauty salon, shopping arcade, medical clinic, free airport shuttle.

Westin Kunming (Wei Si Ting Jiu Hua Jiudian). *157 Beijing Lu (1 mile south of city center). ☎ 800/937-8461 or 0871/356-2828. Fax 0871/356-1818. 554 units, including 134 suites. A/C MINIBAR TV TEL. $140 double. AE, DC, JCB, MC, V.* This 37-story tower with its vast high-tech atrium at the entrance is Kunming's first attempt at a grand modern five-star international hotel (once the five floors of new shops and the pool and health club on the sixth floor are finished). Few hotel guest rooms cause one to gasp happily upon entrance, but these are gorgeous, with wooden floors and walls of window glass, glass-top work tables, data ports, safes, plush decorations, and plenty of elbow room (not to mention a non-smoking floor, handicapped facilities, and six executive floors). All bathrooms come with separate showers and baths, and with Kohler fixtures. These are quite the best rooms in Kunming. The service is good, though the Holiday Inn is more experienced. Nevertheless, the Assistant Manager desk in the spacious lobby can take care of any problem.

Amenities: Indoor swimming pool, health club, sauna, Jacuzzi, squash court, business center, conference rooms, 24-hour room service, same-day dry cleaning and laundry, nightly turndown, valet, tour desk, beauty salon, shopping arcade, medical clinic, free airport shuttle.

WHERE TO DINE

Yunnan cuisine has a number of distinct dishes. The most famous is **Crossing-the-Bridge Noodles,** a hot pot consisting of steaming chicken broth to which you add rice noodles, vegetables, mushrooms, and meats, seasoned with chili peppers. The oil on top keeps the food swimming below warm. The dish was invented a century ago, according to legend, by the wife of a scholar who carried the pot across the bridge to her husband's study, where he enjoyed the dish hot despite the long trip from the kitchen.

Fried goat cheese and french fries are also local favorites. Yunnan sweet ham, Yunnan coffee, and Yunnan mushrooms are highly regarded throughout Asia. The mushrooms are considered medicinal by those in the know. Hundreds of Japanese travel to Kunming primarily to consume special varieties of locally gathered fungi, paying small fortunes for a plate of the rarer specimens. The Ji Zong mushrooms, long and stringy, are treasured for their ginseng-like properties. Many Yunnan dishes are laden with an allegedly healthful, fat-reducing pharmacopoeia of herbs and spices. Chicken stewed with medicinal herbs in an earthen dish *(qiguoji)* is another specialty that is quite delicious.

The **Kunming Hotel,** 52 Dongfeng Dong Lu (☎ 0871/316-2172), across from the Holiday Inn, serves the best Yunnan dishes, including Crossing-the-Bridge Noodles, steam-pot chicken, and as a special order, an entire banquet prepared from a single goat. The dining room is plush and so are the prices, up to $50 a person for the goat banquet.

Cheaper versions of Yunnan dishes, including fried goat cheese patties, french fries, steamed chicken, and Crossing-the-Bridge Noodles, are available just off Dongfeng Dong Lu up Baita Lu (across from the Holiday Inn) at the **Yunnan Typical Local Food Restaurant.** The service is not friendly nor is the decor appealing, but the cafe has an English menu, low prices (RMB 18 to RMB 34/$2 to $4), and well-prepared local fare.

Among new restaurants in Kunming is the **Thai Kitchen,** 5 Dongfeng Dong Lu (next to the Kunming Hotel). It's open 11:30am to 2am daily and has an inexpensive menu (in English, with pictures) of Thai and Chinese dishes, including curries, shish kabobs, clay-pot dishes, and noodles with spring grass. Most dishes are RMB 15 to RMB 30 ($1.90 to $3.80); frog legs are $10. There are dozens of pleasant window tables with settings on bamboo mats and a microbrewery on the premises. Where else can you see a

Chinese waitress in a green Thai costume skipping by with a fly swatter in one hand and a big orange can of insect repellent in the other?

Holiday Inn features some of the best Western food in town. **El Dorado's** on the 18th floor (☎ 0871/ 316-5888, ext 6576; open daily 3pm to 1:30am) has American favorites from hamburger to pizza for $5 to $10 per entree. The **Marco Polo Restaurant** on the second floor is a coffee shop with breakfast, lunch, and dinner buffets ($9 to $23), offering a choice of international dishes, from Chinese to Italian. **Charlie's Bar and Beer Garden** in the lobby is a crowded pub with live music nightly until 1am. The **Westin Kunming's** third-floor cafe also has fine Western buffets for breakfast, lunch, and dinner. Outside of the international hotels, there's the venerable **Mr. Ball's,** 172 Beijing Lu (☎ 0871/ 355-0703), which has inexpensive steaks, as well as Chinese dishes, prepared under the watchful eye of Mr. Ball himself, a local with 50 years' experience.

The **Moon Star Tea House (Xing Yue Cha Lou),** 5 Cuihu Nan Lu (☎ 0871/517-9598), facing Green Lake, not only offers tea and snacks amidst the crafts shopping, but also a once-a-week "English corner" in which local professionals, professors, students, and others congregate with foreigners to practice their spoken English. These gatherings meet every Sunday from 10am to 1pm; the teahouse levies an RMB 2 (25¢) charge.

The most vibrant restaurant on the Green Lake strip is the **Blue Bird Café,** 69 Dongfeng Xi Lu (☎ 0871/ 531-4071), open until the wee hours. It's a relaxing place, with blue tablecloths and little white flowers on its benches, Bob Marley posters, drum parties on Thursdays (starting at 10pm), and an inexpensive Chinese and Western menu (pizzas for $5, sandwiches for $3, fresh mango juice for $1.25).

One of the more interesting ethnic spots for food and entertainment is the **Wankelong Islamic Wedding Palace,** 99 Rongle Lu (☎ 0871/ 462-4757), a spacious two-floor emporium with Hui minority specialties. Beef shish kabobs are just RMB 4 (50¢) a skewer; cold rice noodles are nicely seasoned; chickens come fresh from local farms; the ox-tail with brown sauce (RMB 32/$4) is simmered for hours; and the fried rose leaves with lemon juice and honey are unusual, to say the least.

DALI: THE FAR KINGDOM
大理

DALI IS LOCATED AT THE CROSSroads to Burma and Tibet, in the western province of Yunnan. This is a small town with an exquisite setting, pinched in a narrow band between a long lake and a high mountain range. West of Dali are the shores of Lake Erhai, 3 miles across and stretching 25 miles north; east are the snowcapped Cangshan Mountains, whose highest peak is over 13,500 feet. In the past, Dali was the capital of an indigenous minority kingdom, for centuries independent of Chinese control. Today Dali is an antique village, home to the Bai minority.

One of the loveliest places in all of China, Dali is also the friendliest; the Bai people, the warmest. What's more, Dali's weather is even more pleasant than that of Yunnan's capital, Kunming, the renowned City of Eternal Spring. If I could choose only one place to spend my days in the Middle Kingdom, it would be here.

Cafe Life

My return to Dali after my first visit 3 years earlier was not entirely auspicious. The taxi from the airport was held up by a police roadblock; my taxi driver was delayed for 30 minutes while she worked out a permit dispute with the highway patrol; but eventually I was delivered into the center of the old village, to the doorstep of my hotel.

Dali at the dawn of the 21st century has not been leveled by the tide of modernization that swept the big east coast cities of China leading up to the nation's 50th anniversary party in late 1999. Its main shopping streets and monuments received something of a scouring, but the feel of a remote Shangri-La persists. Some of the familiar faces and places have vanished, but the quaintness of its streets has not been erased. This medieval village is still a place to linger. Cafes and hotels still cater to foreign travelers who have made it to the southwestern edge of China.

There are two main streets catering to travelers: **Huguo Lu,** running east and west, and **Bo'ai Lu,** running north and south. Parallel to Bo'ai Lu is **Fuxing Lu,** the main shopping street, which connects the north and south gates of the old city. After a few minutes I remastered the layout.

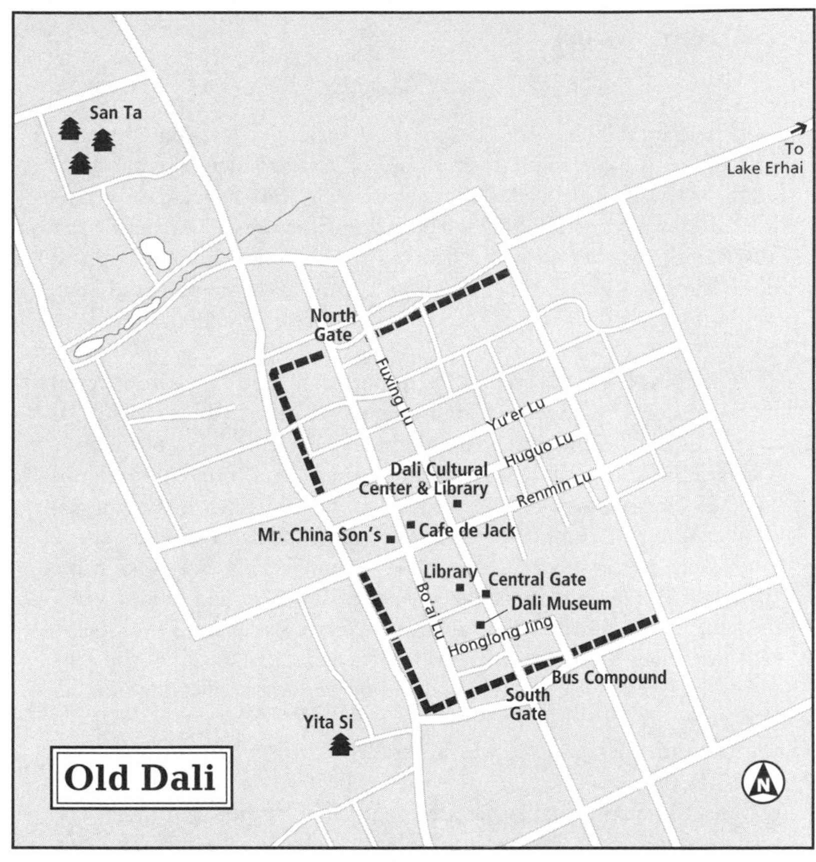

The guesthouses along Huguo Lu have their painted wall murals advertising various amenities (usually hot water) in English. Souvenir shops double as full-service tour agencies. The tiny cafes in wooden buildings, their front walls paneled in glass, provide Western and Chinese foods at rock-bottom prices.

Inside **Cafe de Jack** on Bo'ai Lu, with its down-and-out feel of a coffeehouse in Greenwich Village, circa 1967, I pulled up a rattan chair at a small table under an India bedspread tacked to the ceiling, ordered eggs, toast, and strong coffee for RMB 10 ($1.20), and watched the world go by on horse-drawn carts. This is Old China—a remote China as well. Many of the Bai people heading for work were dressed traditionally, which is to say colorfully, in bright tunics sashed at the waist, dazzling headdresses, and black cotton shoes trimmed in crimson ribbons. The Bai, who are a branch of the Yi minority, differ from the Han Chinese in at least one fundamental way: They place as high a value on friendship as kinship. Certainly they have made Dali as friendly a city to outsiders as any in China.

There are still plenty of cafes for those seeking a slow, contemplative pace of life. A block south down Bo'ai Lu, past two bicycle rental shops on the sidewalk, I had coffee at a table outside **Jim's Peace Café,** a typical run-down two-story dwelling with a small restaurant just inside and a warren of basic dorms and rooms (all sharing one bathroom) up and down the side stairs. Tibetan medicine and massage are practiced here, as Jim himself is half-Tibetan, and a good storyteller and local guide to boot.

Back past Jack's and around the corner, on Huguo Lu, there are even more choices. The **Tibetan Café** is one of the oldest ("Since 1990"). It has the usual blue-and-white tablecloths, rattan chairs, local tour service, Western breakfasts, sandwiches, steaks, desserts, and coffees (most items \$1 to \$3), as well as a Tibetan menu. Another old-timer is the Yunnan Café, at the east end of Huguo Lu, an unremodeled two-story shophouse open to the street. It has a menu spanning East and West. More than once I've devoured tortilla chips with salsa here, and followed that up with a bean burrito. The cafe also maintains a lending library and sells a number of books in English. Upstairs, Dr. Mu Qing Yun performs facial massages, acupuncture, and *qi gong* (the application of inner vital energy force to heal and enhance vitality).

On both these streets, which parallel or cross the main shopping street (Fuxing Lu), there are new cafes where others stood in previous seasons, with names like Sisters Cafe, the Old Café, the Sunshine Café, Claire's Café, Star Café, the Old Wooden House, and the Yak Cafe. They may or may not be here on the next visit, but their immediate descendants will be, expertly run by young Bai folks. The cafe I miss most is Leah's Place, across the street from Cafe de Jack's. Leah, a 22-year-old Bai woman who spoke fluent English and cooked like a dream, had just opened it when I first came to Dali. I still remember her eggplant *gonghao,* a stir-fry with ginger, green pepper, and soy sauce, from a recipe she'd acquired from a foreign guest; I remember, too, the smoothies, consisting of banana, yogurt, cinnamon, and ice cream, the dark Yunnan coffee, and the snow tea brewed from white leaves grown on nearby Cangshan Mountain.

It was at Leah's Place that I met an Englishman named Eric. Dressed in heavy hiking boots and a Guatemalan poncho, carrying a guitar case, and sporting his straight red hair at shoulder length, he'd just arrived from Hong Kong to propose marriage to a local Bai girl. Eric needed the approval of his intended's parents, who lived in a Bai village on the other side of Lake Erhai. He was 40, she 18. He knew a smidgen of Chinese; she knew almost no English. He was a club musician in Hong Kong; she, a hostel maid. I won't say it was a marriage made in heaven, but several of the women in the village had married Westerners.

The Bai people seemed to accept such arrangements. Several of Dali's cafes are owned by foreigners who have married locals.

By the time we parted 3 years ago, Eric had struck an agreement, brokered by a local cafe owner and author, Uncle Li: Eric was to finance his betrothed's college education starting in the spring, and she was to see no one else in the meantime. Now returning, I found no trace of Leah or of her cafe, but Uncle Li was still in town, and I was able to complete the soap opera I'd been a part of: Eric indeed ended up marrying the girl from Dali, finally taking her back with him to Hong Kong. Meanwhile, Leah herself enrolled in a university in Kunming.

Old Shopping Street (Fuxing Lu)

The Dali for sightseers—and there are more each day—is encamped along the 2-mile pedestrian street of Fuxing Lu which runs from the north gate to the south gate of the old city. It turns out that this is where the tourism dollars have been funneled to spiff up the old shop fronts, to open scores of new souvenir and minority craft stores, and to line the pavement with cast-iron lanterns—even to add a brand-new "ancient" central gate. Dali is still a pretty village of old two-story wooden houses, their double-tiered tiled roofs dividing the upper and lower floors. The fronts are planked and faced with folding doors, carved windowpanes, and wooden railings stained a dark red. A typical Bai house has a courtyard, usually decorated in flowers and shrubs, particularly camellia and bougainvillea. In Dali, the Bai women are known as "Golden Flowers."

And touches remain in the alleys of Yunnan's rural life: markets with raw meat, lads manning watch repair booths, a small battalion of young soldiers marching south with straw brooms on their shoulders. But there are plenty of modern touches. The old shopping street is dominated now by boutiques and galleries selling the slabs of polished marble, by banks with ATMs, by tiny shops advertising e-mail access.

Between Huguo Lu, at the heart of downtown, and Renmin Lu, the next major cross street heading south, is the **Dali Cultural Center and Library,** a large public courtyard and park with stone tables where the local people gather for mahjong games and tai ji exercises. Old men bring their caged birds here for an outing. It's a good place to mix with the people of Dali.

The new **central gate** further south on Fuxing Lu is built in the ancient style of the original north and south gates. Surrounded by new shopping arcades built in the same old Dali style, the central gate offers a few of its own outlets, as well as evening Bai cultural performances (starting at 8pm) upstairs in its tower. A block further south, at 200 Fuxing Lu, is the **Dali Museum** (daily 9am–5pm, admission RMB 5/65¢), recently refurbished and expanded. Its halls contain a mishmash of relics from a dozen dynasties: Tang mirrors, a 3rd-century clay vase, a horse with saddle dated at A.D. 289, even some tools from the stone age. In a separate new museum hall there's a bronze bell under a pavilion, a row of headless men and horses, and two courtyards filled with steles (engraved stone tablets) bearing dates from the 12th to the 19th centuries. So far, there are no signs in English.

The **south gate** to the old city is a two-story pavilion with soaring eaves set on top of a remnant of the 30-foot-high battlements that once ringed the city. The city wall has very recently been restored and extended, part of the great 1998 project to gentrify old Dali. From the heights of the south gate tower there's a complete view of the town, the near mountains, and the long lake heading north. South of the lovely, flower-laden courtyard outside the wall, Fuxing Lu begins to revert to its pre-tourist, pre-modernization days. The shops are rough and plain; the stores carry necessities rather than trinkets; and the shophouses are often workshops where laborers saw and carve wooden furniture by hand and work with the slabs of local marble. The tower over the south gate requires an RMB 2 (25¢) admission, but it's a good place for snapshots and inside there's a Bai tea house featuring snow tea.

The **north gate** of old Dali is a few blocks beyond Huguo Lu (one of the two main cafe streets). The shops on this segment of Fuxing Lu haven't been restored recently; older, humbler businesses quickly take over, and the cafes, unscrubbed and undecorated, no longer cater to foreign visitors. Nearing the north gate there are two new tenants, the Dali Old City Christianity Reading Room and, next door, the Dali Church of Christ, a building fashioned with stones, uncapped by any cross. The north gate charges an RMB 2 (25¢) admission, has a shrine to the town god in its upper story, and contains a very friendly teahouse in its lower story.

On my way back from the north gate, I once came upon a large funeral in the cobbled streets. It was a simple, happy procession. The mourners of Dali wield brightly colored banners, and the coffin, carried by hand, is draped in a long, white sheet. As one life ends in Dali, a new century is set to begin.

The Three Pagodas

On my first visit to Dali I became so embroiled in the daily cafe life that I ceased to be a tourist, but you should endeavor to make at least one pilgrimage to the nearest sights. Just a mile north of town on the old main highway is Dali's most famous historic landmark, the **Temple of the Three Pagodas (San Ta Si).** These three towers are situated at the very foot of the 10th peak in the massive Cangshan range. Founded in A.D. 825, the temple was later destroyed, but the three pagodas survive. They are the oldest such monuments in the region. The four-sided, 16-story middle pagoda, **Qiantun Ta,** is the tallest, at 226 feet; its two eight-sided, 10-story sisters are shorter, at 138 feet each. They are a graceful trio from a distance, finely tapered in the style of the Little Wild Goose Pagoda in Xi'an. The pagoda builders of Dali, in fact, were said to have come from Xi'an, which was then the Tang Dynasty capital.

The temple on the grounds is for the worship of Guanyin, Goddess of Mercy. Locals tell the tale of how a monk was working on a bronze statue of the goddess at this site when he ran out of bronze. Suddenly, bronze balls rained down from the heavens. The people melted down the bronze raindrops and the statue was finished.

There isn't much to do here but admire the beauty of the brick towers and their setting against the snowcapped peaks. The towers are sealed up. The grounds are ringed by hundreds of vendor's stalls, many of them selling slabs of the local marble, their grains resembling mountain peaks. The temples are open daily from 8am to 5pm (8pm in summer), and charge an admission of RMB 20 ($2.50).

A more invigorating excursion is provided free of charge by the slopes of **Congshan (Green Mountains).** These 19 peaks, 10,000 to 13,500 feet high, form a screen of stone and snow paralleling the city walls of Dali and the shores of mile-high Erhai Lake. Unpaved roads and trails run straight up the mountain from downtown Dali. With a local map in hand, you can easily walk out of Dali and into the walls of the stately **Yita Temple** on some nearby slopes. It's easy going, and the 10th-century pagoda within the temple walls is uncanny, silent as the lake below, sealed up and utterly deserted. It looks about a million years old.

Mr. China's Son

The most remarkable person in Dali, and one of the most remarkable men in China, is Uncle Li. His full name is He Liyi. He was born in a Bai village in 1930. Eventually, he became the first Bai in history to go abroad. He is home now, proprietor of **Mr. China's Son Cultural Exchange Cafe,** on Bo'ai Lu. When I first wandered in 3 years ago, he immediately made me feel at home. His English, Uncle Li's third language after Chinese and Bai, was marvelous. He had learned it from BBC broadcasts after selling a pig to buy a short-wave radio. Upon my return, it was Uncle Li who had changed the least, his cafe barely altered by the accelerated stream of time all of China seems to be swept up in.

Uncle Li's life story is the stuff of 30 novels. In fact, he has published that story in English. *Mr. China's Son: A Villager's Life* appeared in 1993 (Westview Press). His autobiography received excellent reviews in America, but, alas, few copies were sold—a pity, since there are no first-person accounts of 20th-century life in rural China to rival it. Uncle Li has been able to reprint a few copies for sale only in Yunnan, which he keeps on hand at his cafe. He opened the cafe on June 22, 1995, having reached the age of retirement. I bought a copy of his book. Uncle Li wrote a long, generous dedication on its title page, puffing away on his long-stemmed pipe.

His story is direct, personal, and extremely frank. In the late 1950s he spent years in a labor camp. After his release, he made his living by fetching night soil from public toilets for use as fertilizer. He divorced and remarried. He experienced what he calls "years of unspeakable humiliation and suffering," but he is not a bitter man today. After returning from a summer in England in the late 1980s, he settled into village life, opened his cafe, and now hosts foreigners who chance his way.

I signed Uncle Li's guest book once again, and I asked after his son, He Lujiang, a teacher in the English section of the Dali Medical College in nearby Xiaguan. I remembered how I had once helped Uncle Li with a sign he was writing announcing in English that patrons of Dali's new "plush toilet" were obliged to pay the attendant 5 mao (about 6¢) per flush. In fact, the sign had needed no correction. The very next day I saw it posted on the wall when I paid a visit to the RMB 200,000 ($25,000) public lavatory at the west end of Huguo Lu. It was then and it is now the only public toilet in all of Dali that could be described as plush, although there wasn't and isn't a piece of tissue paper to be had in the place.

Now, after catching up on the Dali news, drinking a coffee, having a sandwich for lunch, and reading what was posted from all over the world on the cafe walls, I found that Uncle Li was spending much of his day behind the small counter typing on a manual typewriter the manuscript of a new book, a memoir of village life that takes up and is intertwined with his own continuing life story. I reviewed an episode and came up with a few suggestions. He is always in search of the pungent phrase, which he savors as though words were truly edible.

By late afternoon, the sunshine had moved across the street and I followed it, basking at an outdoor table at another cafe. After long travels, I was content to let the sun rise and set on Dali. Leaning back, conversing, eating and drinking, I let the world do the traveling for a change.

Erhai Lake

One morning I decided to take a stroll from Dali to the shore of Erhai Lake. Dali is a tiny town, and walking from one end to the other takes only a few minutes. I headed east down Huguo Lu, south down Fuxing Lu, then east on Renmin Lu, the next big street. When Renmin Lu dead-ended, I jogged south half a block, then continued east toward the lake again on a winding dirt road that starts at a sign in stone reading DA YUANZI.

The dirt road wove through fields to a village named **Caicun** along the lakeshore. It was an hour's walk. The wall of mountains behind me took up half the sky. Ahead, Erhai Lake—its name means ear-shaped—was a narrow blue band lined with more fierce mountains. The sun shines brightly here almost year-round. Twice I was passed by horse carts ferrying people between the villages, and they stopped for me each time, but I preferred to walk.

The village on the lakefront was a maze of tiny corridors. It's easy to get lost, and I did. Paths branched off to the lake where fishermen dried their nets and cormorants their outstretched wings. Double-ended junks were tied up to stone jetties, and large black-and-white cows wandered the fields. Kids stood in the courtyards of clay and wooden houses setting off firecrackers. Parents were lighting the crackers for the smaller tykes, who were in the throes of exquisite delight.

Eventually I hailed a horse cart and rode back to Dali, promising myself I would return and sail across the lake to one of the distant village markets on the other side. The next day I did just that.

Wasa Market

The top day excursion from Dali is a visit to the market at Wasa, a tiny village on the other side of Erhai Lake. Markets are held there every 5 days or so (usually on the 5th, 10th, 15th, 20th, 25th, and 30th of the month). I booked a ticket the day before at Café de Jack's for RMB 20 ($2.50), which included everything but lunch and a guide. Plenty of independent travelers do the same from their guesthouses and at other cafes. The bus left the cafe at 9:30am, and rumbled through town to the lakeshore, where a small local ferry was waiting. There was room for about 20 aboard, with benches in the cabin and room to sit on the deck or stand at the rails. It was a superbly peaceful ride of 1 hour 10 minutes on a sunny, glass-smooth lake rimmed by snowcapped peaks. You can see other local ferries and small fishing boats rowed by hand, the ends of their oars nothing, it appears, but flat squares of wood like crude Ping-Pong paddles.

At Wasa we disembarked from the high pointed bow via a 6-inch-wide plank and walked straight into the market square, which was filled with the rural people of this remote kingdom, who still keep their own language and colorful dress quite apart from that of the Chinese. Many bring their wares to market on donkeys and horses, and what wares they are, from spices to squash, from chestnuts to rice. I even came upon areas devoted to horse-trading. Several hours slipped by as I strolled through the square and up and down the narrow lanes of the village. There are stalls selling the fantastic woven fabrics of the Bai people; stalls selling basic household goods; stalls selling tea, dried fish, live chickens; stalls selling odds and ends from an attic-cleaning. This is a real market: not an item in sight for a tourist or a foreigner.

Most merchants have no stalls at all, only the woven baskets filled with their wares, and the unpaved lanes are littered with merchandise. The market square has a cluster of large white umbrellas to provide shade. In cement stalls at the rear the meat sellers are hacking away, and beyond there's an open yard of live pigs and chickens. Pigs in fact are strolling amongst the buyers and traders and visitors. It's a sweet, unpretentious rural Chinese market that has not surrendered to the needs of tourists, Chinese or foreign. Here is the serious business of the countryside in full swing.

In the afternoon, at about 2:30pm, I returned to the wharf, and as I waited for our ferry to disembark, I watched a fearless fisherman strip down to his shorts, dive in, and resurface. He held up what turned out to be a television in his arms; but the submerged treasure was broken and he tossed it back, swimming out and swimming back, shouting and laughing with his companions on shore.

Shaping Market

North of Dali, the village of **Shaping** is also famous for its market, which usually convenes on Mondays. Cafes and tour agencies in Dali sell bus tickets, costing RMB 11 ($1.30), for the round-trip, leaving at 9am and returning about noon. The road edge is planted in mature eucalyptus trees, a legacy of the French influences that once penetrated this part of China from the colonial capitals of Vietnam and Indochina.

The Shaping market spreads across a dusty hillside near the highway. When I arrived, the alley into the market was so clogged with vendors on carts and trucks that I had to wait before I could begin to squeeze through. Shaping is a marketplace packed with Bai vendors hawking housewares, batiks, vegetables, spices, paintings, silver jewelry, and cut-and-polished stone. Dali is well known for its marble, and on the road to Shaping we'd passed many rock-cutting yards with crude machinery designed to slice the quarried boulders into neat slabs. Dali marble, with its grains suggesting classical landscapes, has ended up decorating the

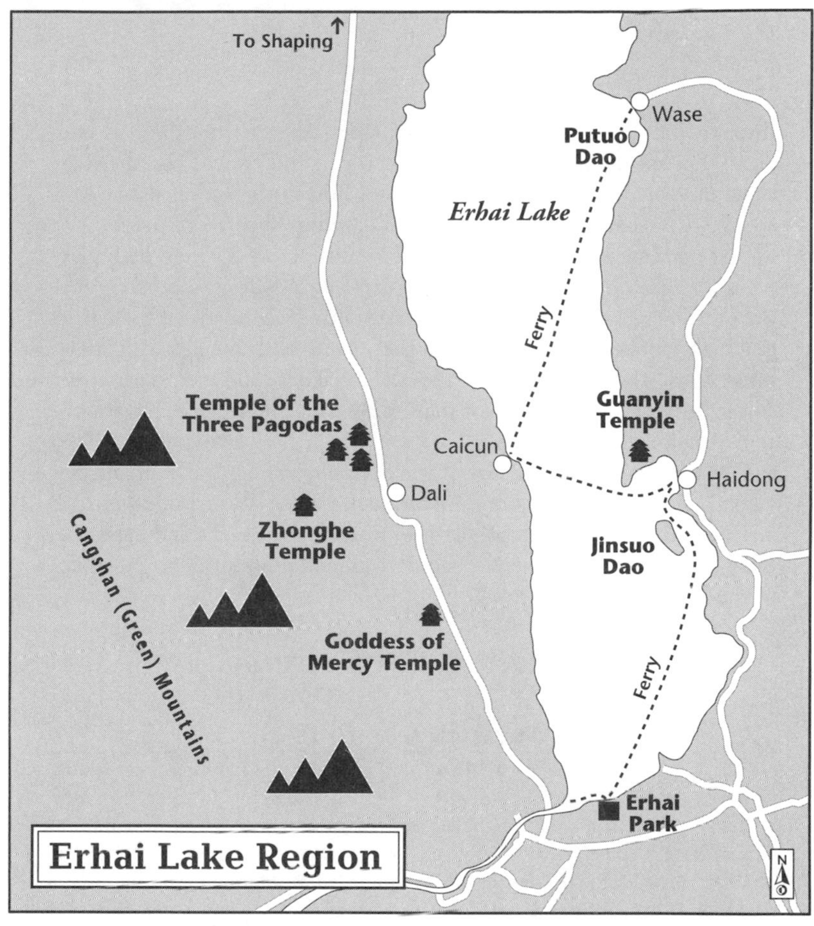

chairbacks and tables of the Summer Palace at Beijing and the walls of the private gardens of Suzhou.

I spent several hours culling the market stalls. Whole sections of the hillside are devoted to woven baskets, the vendors pitching umbrellas and sitting down in the dust next to their goods. Yards of dark blue batiks hang from clotheslines. Posters of smiling girls are pinned to a wall of dried mud bricks. Down in a hollow below a cluster of earthen brick kilns, locals corral dozens of horses, some for trade, most as a means to get home.

The countryside women dress to the nines for the market, many of them topping off their red, white, and blue jackets and long quilted tunics with plumed caps trimmed in bands of sequins. They carry their babies as they do their long fluted baskets, lashed to their backs. I watched two old women in matching red vests and long blue skirts shopping for spices, sampling the wares from open sacks. Farmers rush through the crowded lanes with bright pink piglets squealing in their arms. There's hardly a Han Chinese face in the crowd, but there are thousands of Bai faces and the faces of China's other minorities everywhere, sunburnt black, their clothing a dazzling rainbow of dyes.

At one intersection in the market I came across a young man playing one of the oldest confidence games on Earth. Adroitly shuffling cups over seeds on a newspaper in the dust, he took in loads of cash from gullible onlookers. He worked the shell game with a shill, who sometimes wins, while the innocents always lose. These con men scurry from corner to corner, setting down then folding up their game, always one step ahead of the authorities.

The main road in and out of the Shaping market was still jammed when I tried to leave. Vendors and buyers from the countryside were still arriving, standing on the open beds of trailers, their sacks and baskets at their feet. Their smiles were broad. It was market day, the brightest day of the week.

PRACTICAL INFORMATION

ORIENTATION & WHEN TO GO

Dali is 160 miles northwest of **Kunming,** the capital of southwestern Yunnan Province. Kunming (the subject of a separate chapter) is 900 miles west of Hong Kong. Yunnan Province borders Laos, Burma, and Tibet. Dali is also a 3-hour minibus ride south of **Lijiang** (see separate chapter), another Yunnan Shangri-La, via the new expressway that runs along Erhai Lake. Over 80% of China's Bai minority, numbering 1.1 million, live in Dali and the surrounding villages and countryside, an area known officially as the Bai Autonomous Prefecture.

Dali is located in a mountain valley at an elevation of 6,496 feet. Its climate is pleasant and sunny year-round, although winter nights can be nippy. Perhaps the most interesting time to visit Dali is during the annual **Sanyuejie (Third Moon Festival),** which starts on the 15th day of the third lunar month (April 8 in 2001, April 28 in 2002). For 6 days and nights the Bai people of Dali and minorities from elsewhere in Yunnan gather in the foothills of the Green Mountains to sing, dance, and attend a large market. The problem is that accommodations are extremely scarce then, as they also are in June and July, the months of the high tourist season.

GETTING THERE

By Plane The new **Dali Airport** at Xiaguan (10 miles south of Dali) has daily flights to and from Kunming, the gateway to Dali. On my 35-minute flight, the Yunnan Airlines flight attendants started serving refreshments 9 minutes before landing and handed out T-shirts. There is an airport shuttle bus that meets all incoming flights at the Dali Airport, but don't take it unless you want to go to Xiaguan (10 miles south of old Dali). Hire a taxi instead, and share it if possible. The transfer takes about an hour and can cost up to RMB 80 ($10) for a taxi.

By Bus For a full dose of Yunnan scenery, passengers have a choice of a number of buses that travel the **Burma Road** for 257 miles between Kunming and Dali. It is a long, not always comfortable 10-hour trip over a mostly paved, winding road that served as a vital supply link between Rangoon and Kunming during World War II. There is now, however, a new expressway that many buses take, far quicker (4 to 5 hours) and not as colorful or historic. The **bus station** at Dali is just inside the south gate of the city on Fuxing Lu. Bus tickets can be purchased from any of a dozen travel agencies and cafes located in downtown Dali on Huguo Lu and Bo'ai Lu.

Work on a rail link connecting Xiaguan and Dali to Kunming is under way, despite the steep terrain.

TOURS & STRATAGEMS

The small storefront **travel agencies** on Huguo Lu, with signboards advertising their prices out front, are all surprisingly efficient and reliable. They provide day tours, taxi rentals, and air and bus tickets, and can direct you to bicycle rental stands. Many of the Dali cafes provide similar services, and in fact the cafe managers often serve as guides for foreign travelers and tour groups. The **Dali CITS** has a branch at 73 Bo'ai Lu (☎ 0872/267-7416).

A typical cafe travel agency will provide a variety of tours, including a boat trip on Erhai Lake, which costs RMB 20 to RMB 40 ($2.50 to $5) per person, depending on group size; horseback riding to a mountain monastery or local Bai village, for about RMB 80 ($10) per person; and cormorant fishing on the lake in a fisherman's boat, for about RMB 180 ($22) for six people. Local English-speaking guides can be hired through cafes at RMB 30 to RMB 50 ($3.75 to $6) per hour, RMB 200 ($25) per day.

Asian Pacific Adventures in Los Angeles has specialized for many years in group tours of southwest China, in particular of Yunnan Province, including Dali (☎ 800/825-1680 or 213/935-3156).

WHERE TO STAY

There are a half-dozen guesthouses in downtown Dali offering basic dormitory-style accommodations. Favored by backpacking independent travelers, they offer beds and shared bathrooms and showers for as low as RMB 10 ($1.25) per night, with some doubles as well. The **No. 2 Guesthouse** (☎ 0872/267-0423; fax 0872/267-0309), also known as the Red Camellia Hotel, located on the western end of Huguo Lu, off Bo'ai Lu, is the old standby, the first guesthouse to open to foreigners in Dali (in 1984); it has a few doubles with private bathroom for $25. The **Old Dali Inn** (☎ 0872/267-0382; fax 0872/267-5360), also known as the No. 5 Guesthouse, at 51 Bo'ai Lu (south of Renmin Lu), has two wings of two-story wooden Bai buildings, a courtyard, and a cafe, and offers basic dorm rooms, rooms with shared bathrooms, and a few doubles with private bathrooms for $17.

The **Dali Hotel,** 245 Fuxing Lu, south of Renmin Lu (☎ 0872/267-0387; fax 0872/267-0551), has some newer standard doubles for about $30 and many basic doubles at RMB 100 ($12.50) with private bathroom that look out on a picturesque courtyard garden, hemmed in by the tiled-roof wings of the hotel. Everything here is in romantic decay: the bed, the shower, the carpets, the courtyard balconies. The Chinese-speaking staff is fairly efficient, and the mute masseur who has an office in one wing is always in the lobby to help guests. The **MCA Guesthouse** (☎ 0872/267-3666; fax 0872/267-1999), well south of town at 7000 Wenxiang Lu (a continuation of Fuxing Lu), is the pick of the hostels, with beautiful grounds, dorms, rooms with shared bathrooms, a few doubles with shared bathrooms ($16), laundry service, bicycle rental, a tour desk, a cafe, Internet access, and even a beautiful outdoor swimming pool.

There is one upscale hotel, 1 mile south of Dali on the old main highway—not an easy walk from town. The **Asia Star Hotel** (☎ 0872/267-1699; fax 0872/267-2299), a China–Taiwan joint venture, is a four-star international-class luxury hotel with clean, well-appointed double rooms starting at RMB 750 ($91). The staff is friendly, but they spoke no English the night I stayed there.

Tour groups and some budget travelers favor the two-star **Jinhua Binguan,** at the corner of Huguo Lu and Fuxing Lu (☎ 0872/267-3343; fax 0872/267-3846), in the heart of Dali. It offers double rooms with private bathrooms and showers for RMB 200 ($25), and "deluxe" versions of the same for RMB 300 ($38). I stayed here on my last trip to Dali. Its guest rooms, cramped and rundown, are furnished with a surprising number of amenities, from a hair dryer to slippers, towels, and shampoo. The bath tubs are tarnished, but the water is hot. There's next-day laundry service, a hot-water thermos and tea bags, even a pencil, ruler, and scissors on the desk—not to mention a free (terrible) breakfast served in the dining room (one runny egg, dense toast, instant coffee). Inside my door a warning in English was posted: PLEASE BUTTON UP THE STEAL DEFENCE!

WHERE TO DINE

The traveler's life revolves around the cafe scene in Dali. The foreigners' cafes are located along Huguo Lu and Bo'ai Lu. The meals are inexpensive but good, the staff—mostly young Bai—unusually friendly and helpful. Cafes come and go each year. They open about 7:30am and close around midnight or later, if they are doing any business then.

Cafe de Jack, 82 Bo'ai Lu (☎ 0872/267-1572), is a popular hangout, renowned for its pizzas. It offers outdoor seating, perfect for sunbathing in the late afternoon, and a good tour agency. **Jim's Peace Café,** on the opposite side and south down Bo'ai Lu, has drinks during the day and dinners at night. It's small, but Jim himself is often on hand to tell hair-raising stories of his adventures in China, Korea, and Tibet, and to serve his "famous" grilled steaks, huge slabs laden with fries and vegetables.

Also popular for food and drink are the **Tibetan Cafe** and the **Sunshine Cafe,** on opposite sides of Huguo Lu (the other main cafe street which crosses Bo'ai Lu). Further east down Huguo Lu, at no. 15, past the big Fuxing Lu intersection, is the **Yunnan Café** (☎ 0872/267-0083), with Mexican and Italian specialties, a lending library, traditional Chinese massage upstairs, and an interesting view across the street of a storefront carpenter at work.

By all means drop in at **Mr. China's Son Cultural Exchange Cafe,** 67–5 Bo'ai Lu (west side, between Huguo Lu and Renmin Lu). Proprietor He Liyi sells autographed copies of his riveting autobiography (in English), cooks up Western and Bai dishes, helps with practical problems that foreign travelers need solved, and even makes up early morning (6:30am) breakfasts if you order in advance. Uncle Li can also help with tours and bus and airline tickets, and he now has an Internet-engaged PC for rent.

LIJIANG: CHINA'S SHANGRI-LA

ACCOUNTS BY EARLY TRAVELERS all agree: Lijiang, located in the remote northwest sector of Yunnan Province where it touches Tibet, is China's Shangri-La. For centuries Lijiang served as the capital for the mountain kingdom of the Naxi, an indigenous people whose origin is a mystery, whose language and way of life are unique, whose rulers are women rather than men. Untouched by any civilization, East or West, Asian or Caucasian, Lijiang was the equivalent on Earth of the Western Paradise evoked in Buddhist scriptures. Its face lies in a veil of snowy peaks beyond the gates to the Middle Kingdom. The 300,000 Naxi people today live here and in the borderlands of Tibet and Sichuan to the north.

Lijiang was previously the domain solely of adventurers, explorers, and eccentrics from the West, and then the haunt of hardy backpackers; but it has recently opened to the world and become the destination of small tour groups and independent travelers from China, Asia, Europe, and North America. A new highway from Dali and a new airport with 1-hour service to Kunming have put this Shangri-La on the doorstep of modern tourism. The monstrous earthquake of 1996 that leveled much of Lijiang but spared the quaint old town and its Naxi architecture ironically prompted a flood of tourists. Lijiang joined the UNESCO World Heritage list, development funds poured in, and the legendary village, while still remote and picturesque, surrounded itself with new hotels for visitors and new town sites for residents. I recently joined the rush of visitors to see what was left of China's Shangri-La, following at a considerable distance those earlier explorers who had written Lijiang into the world book of romantic travels, from Joseph Rock, who introduced readers of *National Geographic* to the wonders of "the ancient Nakhi Kingdom of Southwest China" in the 1920s, to Bruce Chatwin, the travel writer who ventured here with some of the first foreign backpackers in the 1980s.

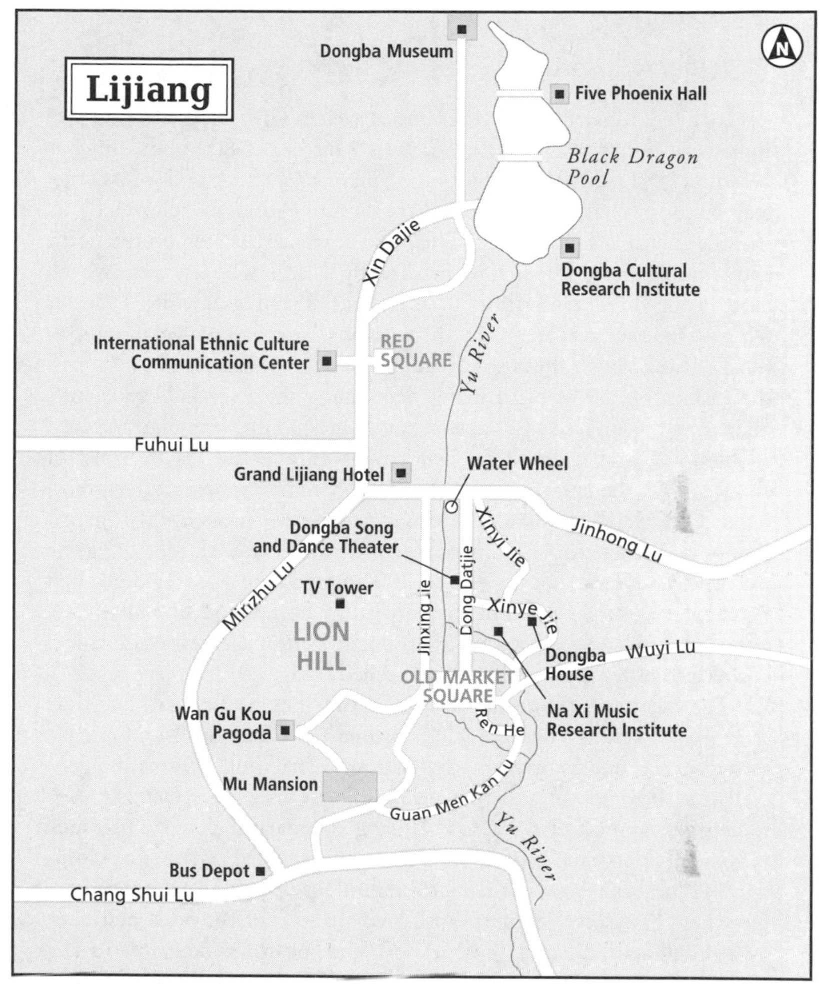

Old Town (Dayan)

Lijiang is situated more than a hundred miles north of Dali, beyond the Armor Mountains (Tiejia Shan) which divide the Bai Kingdom to the south from the Naxi Kingdom, itself isolated by even higher ranges to the north. The town is located in a valley sheltered by rugged ridges, right at the foot of the Jade Dragon Snow mountain range, whose peaks tower well over 18,000 feet. (Lijiang itself is at 7,800 feet.) On the west side of Lion Hill is modern Lijiang; on the eastern flanks is old Lijiang, a warren of traditional Naxi shophouses, market squares, cobbled lanes, canals, and arched bridges.

It is old Lijiang that invites the traveler. This antiquated district consists of over 6,000 households, with a history of 800 years. Since it became a UNESCO World Heritage Site in 1997, thousands of its original buildings have been preserved, its stone bridges renovated, its streams and canals cleaned up. The main entrance (located on the north end along Jinhong Lu) is now marked by a large wooden waterwheel, part of the 1998 renovation of this district and a favorite spot for Chinese tourists to snap group photographs. The waterwheel is spun by the Yu River, which flows south along the edge of Lion Hill and forms the eastern border of old Lijiang. Paralleling the river is old Lijiang's main street, Dong Da Jie, newly paved in smooth, irregularly-spaced cobblestones and reserved for pedestrians only. Dong Da Jie runs for about a mile, the length of the old Lijiang shopping district, terminating at Old Market Square. The other major lane through old Lijiang's shopping district, Xinyi Jie, begins near the waterwheel, too, alongside the new Giordano boutique, and it also runs south to Old Market Square, but it does so in a highly serpentine fashion. Several alleys and waterways crisscross these two main north-south passageways, forming a labyrinth of traditional shops and arched bridges.

The old town **shopping district** is tiny, but its twisting lanes are crowded and nearly unchartable. Fortunately, Lion's Hill and its TV tower serve as one compass mark (east); the canals and streams run generally north to south; and the meshing lanes do have street names—sometimes even street signs. Old Lijiang is a marvelous maze in which to wander. Every lane is filled with shops selling local crafts, Naxi clothing, and local snacks, and there are several dozen small cafes catering to foreigners that serve Western and Naxi dishes, coffees, teas, and beer, owned and staffed largely by Naxi people. The stone-bed streams and canals are crossed by stone bridges where the men sit, swap tales, and admire the falcons that the hunters carry.

It is the people of Lijiang that make old town the dream that it is, particularly the women, young and old, who cling to the traditional dress (smocks with aprons and cross-banded capes in dark blues and whites) and do most of the business even today, carrying their wares, and sometimes babies, from home to shop on their backs in large wicker baskets. The Naxi cape is remarkable, its upper back the dark blue of night, its lower back the white of day, this cosmology divided by a sash embroidered with the seven stars of the heavens. Very old women still wear an image of the sun on one shoulder, the moon on the other. The locals are largely oblivious to modern visitors. They go about their tasks, laughing and stopping to chat with their neighbors on the street, or taking the day's wash down to the stream for a beating on the stones and a rinse.

Black cats sit or pace at shop entrances, tethered by strings to their jobs: the elimination of mice.

The southern tip of old Lijiang's shopping district is distinguished by the **Old Market Square (Si Fang Jie),** a wide expanse of cobblestones surrounded by shops and bridges. Every day is market day here, with the vendors setting up shop under awnings. Beyond the endless tables of crafts and trinkets are large displays of bright copper pots, plates, and pans, all hammered out by hand. From the Old Market, it's possible to head southeast up Lion Hill or west and south to Mu Mansion via the narrow Ren He Courtyard alley, but to get one's bearings, it is wise to stick first with the main shopping district.

Wise, too, to pull off to the side at one of the **cafes** for a drink or a snack. The waitresses are usually willing to converse and answer questions. My first cafe in Lijiang happened to be the Sunroom Café, where salads were less than a dollar, all pizzas (including Hawaiian) went for $1.25, and spaghetti was priced at under $2 a plate. The Chinese menu had nothing above $2: *jiaozi* (potstickers) were 50¢ each, and the Sunroom's famous apple pie (with ice cream) cost me just $1.10.

As in Dali, there are plenty of street cafes to sample, all of them cozy and inexpensive. The Blue Page has an extensive vegetarian menu; the Well Bistro, a pleasant coffeehouse atmosphere; the Zhongdian Tibet Café, Tibetan toast and a fascinating corner for people-watching; and Mama Fu's, the best outside dining of all, located on a curving waterway. There are several strictly Naxi restaurants, too, as well as an assortment of small guesthouses and a growing number of theaters devoted to ethnic music and dance.

It doesn't take long to become swept up in the life of the old town. A day or two of wandering unravels the maze of alleys, winding streets, and twisting waterways. It helps to sit still against the flow, to take a seat on the stone ledge at the southeast end of Old Market Square, get one's bearings, and watch the people. Chinese visitors outnumber Westerners thirteen to one, according to one waitress I spoke with. In the square there are Naxi in bright costume waiting to ferry tourists in sedan chairs around town or up Lion Hill; while idle, they joke among themselves and wear their hats upside down. It was while watching the sedan chair carriers that I got a jolt one early afternoon when a traditional funeral procession came marching down from Lion Hill and along the east side of the square, heading north through old town. Every mourner wore white, and the first mourners were littering the path with white confetti. I moved closer to take a picture, but was immediately shamed into proper respect: many of the marchers were weeping.

From Old Market Square, **Jinxing Jie** runs north, parallel to Dong Da Jie, the big new main street that one usually takes down into the market. Jinxing Jie is a bit higher up the slopes of Lion Hill, and it's worth a stroll since the tour groups usually don't have time for it. Its shops, which look decidedly poorer, specialize in Naxi and Tibetan antiques, wood and stone carvings, and jewelry. It was on Jinxing Jie one morning that I saw a woman shopkeeper knitting in the doorway, her ball of yarn in a basket. As I neared, she suddenly rose from her bench, strode across the lane, her knitting in hand and the yarn ball anchored to the basket, the knitting stretched across the road like a wool umbilical cord; at the riverbank she spit with fervor into the roaring stream and returned to the bench in her shop by the time I passed.

Naxi Music

The chief entertainment at night in old Lijiang, apart from coffee and dessert or beer and pizza in the local inns, is traditional music. There are now at least four theaters devoted to nightly performances, all of them quite atmospheric, with wooden stages for the musicians and wooden chairs or benches for the audience. The largest new venue, the **Dongba Song and Dance Theater,** is on Dong Da Jie (☎ 0888/518-1598). It has a colorful stage and a dining area, as well as memorabilia and photographs of Austrian-American explorer Joseph Rock, who lived in Lijiang for 2 decades, beginning in 1922, and was the first Westerner to document in detail Naxi customs. Performances start at 8pm nightly; tickets are sold at the entrance during the day, for RMB 40 ($5).

Perhaps the most authentic musical renditions are given at the **Na Xi Music Research Institute,** nightly at 8pm. Admission is RMB 30 ($3.75). This theater is located across from Mama Fu's and Dong-Ba Garden on the curving lane connecting Dong Da Jie (the main street) to Wuyi Lu (which runs east from Market Square), just north of the Old Market Square. Under the direction of narrator Xuan Ke, a renowned local expert, the musicians perform many of the two dozen ancient songs that have survived on Naxi instruments that resemble lutes, banjos, gongs, cymbals, flutes, and drums. Xuan Ke provides information in English. Purchase tickets at the theater as far ahead of time as possible, as the shows often sell out hours before 8pm. Even if you can't attend, drop by during the day to take a look inside the theater, which is intimate and colorful.

Black Dragon Pool (Hei Long Tan)

Directly north of old Lijiang, within walking distance, Black Dragon Pool Park rewards a visit. Its vistas, particularly of the nearby Jade

Dragon Snow range, are superb. There's a trail along the east bank of the Yu River, which flows into old town from Black Dragon Pool, but it doesn't go all the way to the park. The usual stroll is north along busy Xin Dajie. On the west side of this avenue, past the "Sexual Health Thing Shop" on the first corner, is the new space-age International Ethnic Culture Communication Center, where conventions and exhibitions are staged. On the east side of the street is Red Square, with its monumental white statue of Chairman Mao. Peter's Café, with its log-cabin facade, is on the north side of Red Square, and within a block is the Ali Baba Café, down an alley with a produce and meat market. If you continue east and north along this alley, it leads to the park entrance, and it's a fascinating winding residential lane, with plenty of courtyard homes. As I was walking it, two kids jumped out, shook my hand, said "Hello," and ran back into their house laughing.

Black Dragon Pool Park is open daily dawn to dusk; admission is RMB 20 ($2.50). At the gated entrance, turn right (south) and follow the pathway counterclockwise around the lovely lake. Where the Yu River cascades out of Black Dragon Pool, there's a fine pavilion and arched bridge; beyond it, there's a log cabin where an armless artist, brush in mouth, is at work painting and selling calligraphic works. Further up, on Elephant Hill, which forms the eastern boundary of the park, is the **Dongba Cultural Research Institute (Dongba Wenhua Wanjiushi),** a collection on halls and Naxi architecture, as well as a library where local scholars are collecting and studying the ancient Naxi culture. In this compound there's a small gift shop next to a fine specimen of a traditional Naxi log house. *Dongba* is the term for the Naxi shaman, authors of the small booklets in Naxi language that are studied here. There are currently more than twenty Dongbas living in Lijiang.

Black Dragon Pool is divided into three portions by stone bridges. The longest bridge, Belt Bridge, is capped by **Moon Pavilion (De Yue Lou),** dating from the Ming Dynasty but reconstructed in 1964 after a local official and his lover, it is said, ignited the old structure in a fiery double-suicide. At the northeast end of the lake is **Five Phoenix Hall (Wu Feng Lou),** a 400-year-old Tibetan hall with extravagant eaves that once stood in a major Lama temple complex (Fu Guo Si) 20 miles away. It was under renovation when I visited recently, but in the past it has held a display of Dongba artifacts, from headdresses and charms to prayer wheels and scrolls.

The west side of Black Dragon Pool is highlighted by a long row of Naxi vendor stalls selling local crafts and souvenirs.

Dongba Museum

At the pool's northwest entrance is a new museum that should not be missed. The **Lijiang Dongba Museum** (☎ 0888/512-8383), a 25-minute walk from old town Lijiang, is open daily 9am to 5pm, and costs RMB 5 (65¢). This institution holds a remarkable collection of Naxi relics and cultural displays. The Naxi people, who have their own Tibeto-Burman language and pictographic writings, were a northern tribe driven southward into remote Lijiang a thousand years ago or more. Their creation myth begins with a common ancestor, *Tabu,* who hatched the tribe from a magic egg. The Dongbas have recorded the Naxi history and its elaborate rituals in a series of small booklets, many of which are collected in the new museum. One remarkable characteristic of Naxi culture is the powerful role of women, who rule the society (and do much of the work). A sort of "walk-in" marriage is still practiced by many Naxi people today, in which young women choose their partners periodically and invite them into their homes. Partners can change, according to a woman's desire; the children remain with the mother in her home; former husbands return to live with their mothers when a relationship is over.

The museum has interesting displays of Naxi dress, their wooden homes, their pictographic booklets (5,000 of the 30,000 still in existence), and their rituals, over 80 of which are still practiced in nearby villages (including the sacrifices of pig and sheep). Each of the four buildings in the courtyard-style museum explores a different theme, including one devoted to the Western myth of Shangri-La propagated by 20th-century explorers such as Joseph Rock and Peter Goullart. The artifacts include an inflated sheepskin (used by the Naxi to ford streams and rivers), and a tombstone from Wutai engraved with the names of eight members of the 20th Bomber Command of the American Air Force killed in World War II, dated July 1944.

Mu Mansion

Lijiang was ruled by the Mu Shi clan from the time of Kublai Khan to the end of the last Chinese dynasty in the early 20th century. The first patriarch was Celestial King Mu (Mu Tian Wang), who came to power as a child in 1598, defended China's western borders, and built a series of Tibetan Buddhist temples (Karmapa sect). The Mu Mansion (Mu Fu), a garden estate from which the clan ruled Lijiang for nearly 500 years, has recently been restored on the road south of old Lijiang's shopping district, at the southern foot of Lion Hill.

To reach Mu Mansion, follow Guan Men Kan Lu, the lane at the very southeast edge of Old Market Square (or Ren He alley, which connects to

Guan Men Kan Lu). It's a 10-minute walk. The road undulates along the river, then turns and passes through a traditional archway to a lane crowded with vendors and sedan chair carriers. Mu Mansion is on the right. It's open daily 10am to 5pm; admission is RMB 35 ($4.25).

After the great Lijiang earthquake of 1996, a World Bank loan financed a 3-year renovation. The grounds, which stretch for a quarter of a mile, are impressive and expansive, facing east to meet the rising sun. The large halls are separated by white stone courtyards that resemble those of the Forbidden City in Beijing. In fact, during the Ming Dynasty, Mu Mansion was said to rival in splendor the Imperial Gardens of the distant Chinese capital. Many of the original halls were destroyed during the later Qing Dynasty and its stone archways by Red Guards during the Cultural Revolution (1966–1976). The main gate, consisting of a tripartite stone archway with a tile roof, bears the inscription "Da Yu Liu Fang" (a homophone in the Naxi language for "Let Us Read").

There are six main buildings, which ascend up Lion Hill a short way. The main meeting hall, where the clan chiefs met, is first, followed by a library (Wan Juan) of Dongba writings and paintings and the Back Hall (Hu Fu) where the family held its own meetings. The fourth building (Guang Bi) was dedicated to the gardens; the fifth (Yu Yin) for singing and dancing; and the last hall (San Qing) for Daoist rites. The halls are rather empty, but there are some treasures, especially in the main building near the entrance, where the Mu throne and a tiger skin are on display.

Mu Mansion gives visitors a sense of the grandeur of the Mu Kingdom of the Naxi during its semi-autonomous golden days centuries ago. The courtyards sometimes fill with local Naxi ladies performing circle dances and with musicians, mostly older men, playing traditional instruments. The back gardens and covered corridors are beautifully re-created, and there are steps at the rear that lead steeply up Lion Hill to a hidden back entrance, where ancient Naxi rites are performed to this day.

Lion Hill

The formidable hill that forms the western backbone of old Lijiang and the eastern edge of new Lijiang, Lion Hill, can be climbed from many points, including the rear of Mu Mansion. I approached it first, however, from Old Market Square, where a cobblestone lane leads up its flanks from the southwest corner. There are signs reading **Wan Gu Lou,** which is the name of a new pagoda at the summit of Lion Hill built expressly for sightseeing. I followed the signs as I wound uphill, past tiny shops, local cafes, courtyard dwellings, and two or three estates that had been converted into dorms and cafes, asking the way to Wan Gu Lou when no more signposts appeared. The slopes of Lion Hill are covered with old Naxi houses; the neighborhood, known as Huangshan, is one of the region's oldest.

When the lane finally petered out, I followed a worn trail through the thick woods, finally coming out at a formal stone stairway that seemed to rise forever. I could just make out the square wooden pagoda at the top. Wan Gu Lou is billed here as the tallest wooden tower in all of China. It was built of old local timbers, which serve as its 16 massive pillars, each 72 feet tall. Its 13 upward curving eaves represent the 13 peaks of the Jade Dragon Snow range. Altogether there are over 2,300 Dongba designs, such as the moon and stars, carved by Naxi craftspeople into this structure, and 9,999 motifs, including the grand jade dragon of the snows, etched into its ceiling. The tower was completed in 1998. It stands 108 feet tall (33 meters, each meter meant to represent 1,000 of Lijiang's 330,000 people). Surrounded by a wall, Wan Gu Lou is open from dawn to dusk and costs RMB 15 ($1.90) to enter.

The walk up to the observation deck covers five large stories. The deck has windows on all four sides, affording a most exceptional view of Lijiang, old and new, and the grand Jade Dragon Snow Range to the north. It also has two free telescopes turned on the Jade Dragon Snow peaks. This range is extremely steep and sheer, cutting deep gorges into the upper Yangzi River. The highest peak is the glaciated Shanzidou (also known as Mount Satseto), at 18,360 feet; its summit remained unconquered until 1963. The tower is the best place to view the mountains, which are about 20 miles from Lijiang, although the range does attract its share of rolling and obscuring cloud banks. This is also the place for a bird's-eye view of old Lijiang, a lava bed of tightly packed, black tile roofs, and the new town areas that are being built all around it on the high plateau.

The Latest Shangri-La

Old Lijiang is beguiling, but it is also surrounded by irresistible wonders. Many travelers spend little time in the village that earlier visitors hailed as Shangri-La and push ever farther into the remoter villages, mountains, and river valleys in search of the "real" Shangri-La.

These excursions, many requiring a day, some a night or more away from Lijiang, can be booked in town at the tourist offices or through the hostels and cafes that cater to independent foreign travelers. Popular day trips include the one to Dragon Spruce Meadow, 10 miles north of Lijiang on the slopes of Jade Dragon Snow mountain, where a chairlift

travels to an altitude of nearly 15,000 feet; Baisha, a small Naxi village 7 miles north of Lijiang, with a temple built during the reign of Kublai Khan and some beautiful frescoes; and Nguluko, a small Naxi village containing the home of anthropologist and adventurer Joseph Rock, who lived here for nearly 30 years, beginning in 1922.

More remote destinations include Baoshan Stone City, a tiny town carved from stone cliffs, perched above the Upper Yangzi River; Shigu, the village at the "First Bend of the Yangzi River"; and the celebrated Tiger Leaping Gorge (Hutiao Xia), one of the world's deepest (over 12,000 feet), an upper Yangzi destination renowned for its rugged hiking and extreme conditions. All these places are within a few hours' drive of Lijiang. Lugu Lake, on the Sichuan border, still plied by native minorities using dugout canoes, requires an overnight stay. Still farther from Lijiang (but now a journey of a day rather than of days) is Zhongdian, the gateway to Tibet, an old border town that is undergoing a fierce modernization. There are other small villages and remote mountains to explore in northwest Yunnan, where mass tourism has so far feared to tread; these Shangri-Las are still awaiting discovery.

Of course, it is we, the travelers and modern tourists, who have erased one Shangri-La by our very presence and rewritten it into ever more remote mountain valleys. The notion that if a tourist like me can reach Shangri-La, then it can't be Shangri-La anymore, is the catch-22 of modern travel. As for the native residents of this fabled valley, most will tell you without hesitation that Shangri-La is indeed still located in Lijiang—not in the old town, mind you, with its cisterns and dirt floors; not in the distant villages of stone and poor TV reception, absolutely not; but in the new town apartment blocks of Lijiang, where there's hot running water, central heat, flush toilets, and satellite TV. The real Shangri-La, according to its own residents, is just over the mountain, in Levittown East. This may be, but as a traveler from the already quite modern West, I prefer old Lijiang to a thousand new towns, whether they be in China or Timbuktu.

PRACTICAL INFORMATION

ORIENTATION & WHEN TO GO

Lijiang is about 200 miles northwest of **Kunming,** the capital of southwestern Yunnan Province. Kunming (the subject of a separate chapter) is 900 miles west of Hong Kong. Yunnan Province borders Laos, Burma, and Tibet. Lijiang is also a 3-hour minibus ride north of **Dali** (see separate chapter), another Yunnan Shangri-La, via the new (1998) expressway.

Lijiang is located in a gorgeous mountain valley at an elevation of 7,800 feet. Its climate is pleasant year-round, although there are rainy days in the fall, and winter nights can be nippy. June and July bring the most Chinese tourists, making spring and autumn better times to visit.

Many of China's Naxi minority live in Lijiang and the surrounding villages and countryside; the old town area of 6,000 households preserves something of the culture of the people, who have their own language, dress, and customs.

GETTING THERE

By Plane The new **Lijiang Airport** is 15 miles southwest of the city, a 30-minute taxi ride away (RMB 80 to RMB 100/$10 to $12.50, including an RMB 10/$1.25 toll road charge). Across from the terminal is a small canteen and a branch of the **Yunnan Lijiang CITS** (☎ 0888/512-3416 or 512/5999). There are several daily flights to and from Kunming; they take about 50 minutes and cost about RMB 450 ($56) one-way.

By Bus Passengers have a choice of a number of comfortable minibuses that travel the new highway south to Dali, a 3-hour mountainous journey that costs RMB 30 to RMB 60 ($3.75 to $7.50), depending on the bus. The bus to Kunming (10 hours) costs RMB 120 to RMB 150 ($15 to $18). Bus tickets can be purchased from travel agencies, hotels, and cafes in Lijiang. The main **bus station** is located on the southwest side of Lion Hill, on Minzhu Lu

(☎ 0888/512-5953), a 30-minute walk uphill to old Lijiang hotels (or an RMB 10/$1.25 taxi ride).

TOURS & STRATAGEMS

Many of the cafes and hostels in old Lijiang have travel agencies that provide day tours, air and bus tickets, and bicycle rentals. The **Lijiang CITS** has a branch on Xin Dajie (☎ 0888/518-2599 or 512-5991), just north of Red Square, that caters to independent travelers, offering day trips that include Lijiang, Dragon Spruce Meadows, and Baishan; overnight trips to Tiger Leaping Gorge; and a 3-day trip to Lugu Lake. **Asian Pacific Adventures** (☎ 800/825-1680 or 213/935-3156) in Los Angeles has specialized for many years in group tours of southwest China, in particular of Yunnan Province, including Lijiang.

WHERE TO STAY

There are many one- and two-star guesthouses in the old town shopping district of Lijiang. They offer basic dormitory-style and double-room accommodations (some with private bath). These are friendly places, favored by independent travelers and backpackers. The **Dongba House** (formerly called the MCA Guesthouse) on Xinyi Jie (☎ 0888/517-5431; fax 0888/517-5431), connected to the Zhongdian Tibet Café, offers a travel desk, Internet access, bicycle rental (RMB 15/$1.90 per day), and Naxi courtyard rooms for RMB 20 to RMB 50 ($2.50 to $6). The **Sanhe Hotel** at 4 Xinyi Lie has doubles with private bathroom for RMB 280 ($35). The **First Bend Inn** at 43 Mishi, off Xinyi Jie (☎ 0888/518-1688) charges RMB 100 ($12.50) for twin rooms with a shared bathroom.

Grand Lijiang Hotel (Gelan Da Jiudian). *Xinyi Lu (on Yu River, north entrance of old town Lijiang). ☎ 0888/512-8888. Fax 0888/512-7878. 127 units. A/C MINIBAR TV TEL. $60 double, $80 deluxe, children under 12 free. AE, DC, JCB, MC, V.* This is the best choice among Lijiang's upscale hotels, and one of the finest three-star international hotels I've come across in China. The facilities are clean and modern, as are the rooms, fitted with twin beds, table, chairs, desk, pants presser, robes, slippers, safe, and 12-channel satellite TV (CNN, CNBC, free in-house American movies). Bathrooms have clean marble floors and counters, tile walls, hair dryers, telephones, and a good range of amenities. The service is good, with many of the staff speaking some English. The location is superb and the view of the Jade Dragon Snow range is simply grand.

Amenities: Business center, conference rooms, 24-hour room service, same-day dry cleaning and laundry, shopping arcade, bar, restaurants, good Western buffet breakfast free to guests.

WHERE TO DINE

The old town shopping district of Lijiang is full of excellent, friendly cafes catering to foreign travelers, with Western and Naxi menus (in English), at very inexpensive rates. It's fun to shop the cafes and try as many as possible.

The **Sunroom Café** on the twisting Xinyi Jie lane through old town has salads, pizzas, pastas, thick Naxi breads, Chinese dishes, and an excellent apple pie with ice cream, all for under $2. Upstairs there's a separate dining room; downstairs, more seating and an Internet computer for hire. The **Zhongdian Tibet Café,** located on an excellent people-watching bend of Xinyi lane, has indoor and outdoor dining, Daoist toast, pizza for under $2, and cans of Coke for 50¢. You can watch the Naxi vendors in the courtyard selling amulets and silver jewelry over a good latte here. The **Old Place Café** on the same lane, next to the San He Guest House, is cozy, with a wide-ranging Western menu and Internet access upstairs.

One of the in-spots these days is the **Well Bistro,** a large, pleasant coffeehouse with windows on Xinyi lane. It has six long wooden tables with wicker chairs, lots of information (tacked to the walls) of interest to independent travelers, and a menu that includes Dutch coffee and Hawaiian pizza. Nearby is the **Blue Page,** with half a dozen tables by the windows and an extensive vegetarian menu of soups, salads, rices, and Chinese and Mexican entrees priced under $3. This is a serene little cafe for dinner or dessert.

On the west side of the Old Market Square, there are two choices with superb views of the river, stone bridge, and market: the **Old Market Restaurant** and the **Tower Café.** Just north of the market square, on the big lane running southeast off Dong Dajie, is **Mama Fu's,** with its extensive outdoor courtyard seating on the Yu River. It's often packed with foreign travelers.

More upscale dining, featuring Naxi dishes, is available at the dining room overlooking the Yu River in a separate building of the **Grand Lijiang Hotel** and in the spacious **Naxi Family Café** and the **House of Lamu's,** located across the street from each other just south of the main north entrance to old town on Xinyi Jie. Old Lijiang is an excellent place to drop in on these and other small, locally owned and staffed restaurants with their rock-bottom prices on simple but tasty Western, Chinese, and Naxi dishes. McDonald's, Pizza Huts, and Starbucks seem a million miles away from this little Shangri-La of cafes.

Silk Road China: Cities of Sand

EAST AND WEST FIRST MET MORE than 2,000 years ago on the fabled Silk Road, for centuries China's only major connection to the outside world. The Silk Road was a trade route that crossed the Gobi Desert from China into Central Asia, where Persian and other merchants transferred fine Chinese silks into the courts of imperial Rome. In return, China received strange new commodities from the West. The most lasting import, however, was cultural, artistic, and religious—the introduction of Buddhism from India.

Buddhism altered the face of China, shaping its temple architecture and religious arts. Buddhist missionaries found a tolerant home in the Chinese capital, Chang'an (now Xi'an) during the Tang Dynasty (A.D. 618–907), when the silk trade reached its zenith and long caravans of up to 1,000 camels routinely arrived at the western gates after crossing the desert frontier. This is the way Marco Polo is said to have reached China from Italy in the 13th century, centuries after the fall of Rome and the disintegration of the mighty Han and Tang dynasties.

In the last few years, for the first time in history, a trickle of tourists has entered northwest China, retracing the route of the Silk Road. From Xi'an, 550 miles southwest of Beijing in north central China, modern travelers are now crossing the remote provinces of Gansu and Xinjiang. They are stopping at the legendary oasis towns and rummaging through the medieval marketplaces of Urumqi and Kashgar. Along the way they pass the ruins of desert cities, the caves of splendid Buddhist sculptures, the last outposts of the Great Wall, and lakes and mountain passes clinging to the fringes of imagined heavens. The Silk Road spaces through which they move are vast and empty, populated by nomads and wild camels. The towns between are remote, marked by mosques rather than temples, occupied by Uighur Muslims rather than Han Chinese. The Silk Road winds through a lost world, an alien landscape of howling sand dunes and silent snowy peaks. It is a China few visitors have seen.

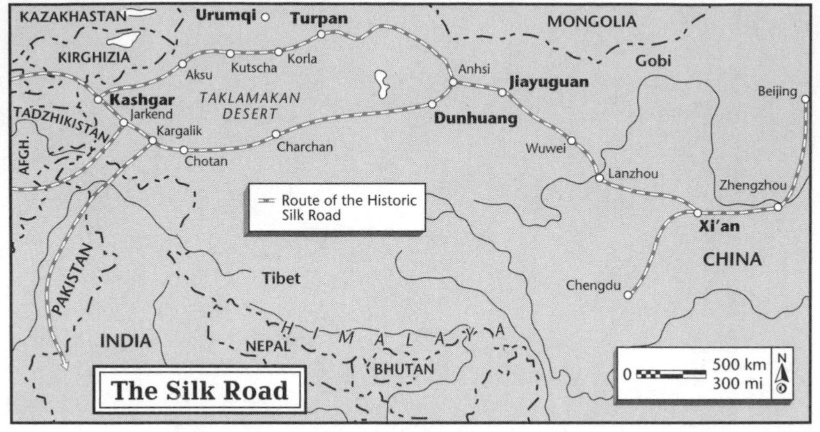

The Explorers

The first official Chinese mission on the Silk Road set out in 138 B.C. from the capital at Xi'an. Emperor Wudi of the Han Dynasty (206 B.C. to A.D. 220) charged General Zhang Qian and his 100-man caravan to make contact with the desert tribes of the west and to forge an alliance against the Huns (the Xiongnu), who were raiding China with impunity. The Chinese general made it all the way to Persia. He didn't return from the Silk Road for 13 years. At his death, Zhang was awarded the imperial title of "Grand Traveler."

Other grand travelers followed, mostly caravans of traders and monks rather than diplomats and soldiers. By the 1st century A.D., silk garments were such a rage in Rome they were considered a drain on the treasury. Oasis towns sprang up to replenish the Silk Road caravans that sometimes perished in the fierce Taklamakan Desert, whose very name means "enter and do not return."

As trade flourished, Buddhist monks and pilgrims set out from India to China, spreading their art and religion. In the oasis towns of China, wealthy local merchants were soon sponsoring the creation of large shrines in nearby sandstone caves, where Buddhist statues and frescoes were sculpted as divine petitions for the safe passage of the caravans. At Dunhuang, where the main north and south routes from the West merged, the greatest repository of Buddhist manuscripts, paintings, and statuary outside of India was fashioned at the Mogao caves.

Silk Road pilgrimages became a two-way street. The Chinese monk Fa Xi'an (A.D. 337–422) set out from Xi'an in 399, passed through Dunhuang, and crossed over the Himalayas into India. He returned to China by sea 15 years later. China's most renowned religious pilgrim, Xuan Zang (A.D. 600–664), traveling at night on foot and by horseback, set out on the Silk Road in 629, studied in Indian monasteries for 14 years, and returned to Xi'an in 645 with over 500 sutras (Buddhist scriptures) and relics. The Big Wild Goose Pagoda, which still stands in

Xi'an, housed his souvenirs, and the 16th-century comic epic, *Journey to the West,* also known as *Monkey,* has immortalized his journey for Chinese readers ever since.

Marco Polo (1254–1324) became the first Western explorer to compose a popular and lasting account of the Silk Road. Many scholars regard his travels as fictional—an account cobbled together from the anecdotes and adventures of many traders—but Marco Polo's observations of the trade route across China often ring true.

In the early 20th century, the Silk Road beckoned to foreign explorers as never before. In a rush to empty the newly rediscovered Buddhist caves and ruined cities of their ancient treasures, Sven Hedin of Sweden, Baron Otani of Japan, Paul Pelliot of France, Von le Coq of Germany, Langdon Warner of America, and above all Sir Marc Aurel Stein of Britain made difficult and dangerous forays on behalf of major museums in the West. Thousands of manuscripts, relics, frescoes, and statues ended up in overseas collections by the time this race was over.

Fortunately, not everything was pilfered in the name of history, scholarship, and nationalism. The Silk Road retains many of its relics and much of its remoteness. Today, for the first time, organized tourism is making inroads, and the Silk Road's exotic treasure house is opening to outsiders.

What to Read

The most complete guide, tailor-made for the China portion of the Silk Road, is Judy Bonavia's *The Silk Road: From Xi'an to Kashgar* (Passport Books, 1993). Vikram Seth's *From Heaven Lake* (Vintage, 1987) is a fine travel narrative through the region. Peter Hopkirk's *Foreign Devils on the Silk Road* (Oxford University Press, 1986) is a lively history of the gold rush by foreign explorers for the cave treasures of Dunhuang and elsewhere earlier in this century.

PRACTICAL INFORMATION

ORIENTATION & WHEN TO GO

Starting from Xi'an, the Silk Road sweeps northwesterly up through the Hexi Corridor of Gansu Province. Anyone heading to the west on the road passes through this 750-mile-long channel, 125 miles at its widest, with the Qilan mountains to the south and a series of bone-dry deserts and mountain ranges to the north. The most impressive sight in the Hexi Corridor is **Jiayuguan Pass,** where the Silk Road narrows to a bottleneck and the western terminus of the Great Wall served as China's frontier outpost. This area is known as Yumen, the Jade Gate, and to most Chinese minds it was truly the end of the civilized world.

Beyond the **Jade Gate,** the Silk Road divides at Dunhuang, site of the magnificent Mogao Buddhist grottoes. The north and south routes through the **Taklamakan Desert (the Tarim Basin)** reunite at **Kashgar.** The desert is the central feature of Xinjiang, a province the size of Alaska, making up one-sixth of China. Kashgar is nearly as far west as you can go in China. The borders of Kyrgyzstan, Tajikistan, Afghanistan, and India are close at hand, and so is Pakistan via the Karakoram Highway. From Kashgar, the Silk Road enters the high mountain passes, reemerging at Samarkand in Central Asia.

The majority of the 23 million people of Gansu are Han Chinese. Mongols, Tibetans, Kazaks, and Huis (Islamic Chinese) make up a considerable minority population as well. In Xinjiang, the distribution changes remarkably. The Turkish-speaking Muslim minority Uighurs make up a majority in many places, such as Kashgar, while the Han Chinese, bolstered by recent "economic transplants" from eastern China, hold sway in other towns, such as Urumqi. Kazaks, many still leading a nomadic life, often dominate in rural areas. With a population of just 15 million, the gigantic Xinjiang Uighur Autonomous Region feels uninhabited through most of its stretches. The Silk Road becomes increasingly desolate, increasingly Islamic, and increasingly remote as the traveler moves west. By the time one reaches the present Chinese border near Kashgar, it again seems as if one is about to step off the edge of the modern inhabited world.

Climate along the long Silk Road varies. For information on the best times to travel, see the individual chapters below.

TOURS & STRATAGEMS

There are three possible ways to tour the Silk Road.

Group Tours The most popular and comfortable method of touring the Silk Road is by group tour. Groups follow much the same routes and often stay in the same hotels and eat in the same places as independent travelers, but they do so faster and in the hands of guides, local and foreign, who are charged with keeping everything running like clockwork (tickets, tour buses, meal times, nightly entertainment where available, site lectures when needed). The tours I've observed seem well run. Hotel and restaurant conditions are often below international standards (generally worse than is found in other regions of China), and transport by bus or train can sometimes be a hardship, but for anyone in reasonably good health and with the right frame of mind, Silk Road group tours are not strenuous or stressful. Just remember that the Silk Road is an adventure in a remote region of the world, rather than a luxury cruise.

Many adventure tour operators offer 16- to 30-day group tours (with usually 12 to 20 people per group) that include sectors of the Silk Road both in and out of China, often with such destinations as Islamabad (Pakistan), Lahore (India), and Hunza (Jammu/Kashmir). Tours of Xi'an and Beijing are often included. Cost, including airfare, runs about $6,000 to $12,000 per person—not bad considering the immense distances covered. These extended trips on the Silk Road usually depart in May and June and in September and October. Some of the best operators include **Geographic Expeditions** (☎ 800/777-8183), **Abercrombie & Kent** (☎ 800/323-7308), **Asian Pacific Adventures** (☎ 800/825-1680), **Wilderness Travel** (☎ 800/368-2794), **Overseas Adventure Travel** (☎ 800/221-0814), **Travcoa** (☎ 800/992-2003), and **Mountain Travel/Sobek** (☎ 800/227-2384). **Independent Tours** Another option is to set up an independent tour through a Chinese tour operator. Traveling alone, I decided to book ahead so that I had a local guide in each place I visited, hotel reservations, meals, and all transportation (plane, train, private car). I negotiated for the best lodgings and methods of transport available at each juncture.

My individual Silk Road tour was put together in 2 days by China Travel Service (CTS) in Xi'an. Based on my proposed itinerary, Susan Su (Su Yan Hua), the CTS business manager, made the arrangements by phone and fax from Xi'an and procured the air tickets. The cost was higher than I expected, in part because I was traveling alone, in part because I needed all the bookings done quickly, and in part because the only cheaper way to put together a Silk Road tour is on your own. Everything promised for my tour was delivered as advertised (with the exception of an RMB 200/$24 fee levied on me by the local travel officials in Urumqi when their booking of my hotel fell through).

My 8-day Silk Road tour for one began in Xi'an and included Jiayuguan (and the end of the Great Wall), Dunhuang (and the Mogao grottoes), Turpan (and the ancient cities, tombs, and wells), Urumqi, Tianchi (Lake of Heaven), and Kashgar (and the Sunday market), with the return to Xi'an after a second night in Urumqi. The all-inclusive price was $2,650, payable in cash (RMB). CITS in Beijing or Hong Kong can make similar arrangements. In Xi'an, contact Susan Su, **China Travel Service (CTS),** 3rd Floor, 63 Changan Rd., Xi'an (☎ 029/523-0257, or mobile phone 029/909-0136; fax 029/526-1821).

On Your Own If you are an intrepid, resourceful backpacker or a bit of a China hand experienced with backroads travel, you can do the Silk Road on your own. Train tickets, bus tickets, and flights can be purchased, local hotels booked, restaurants patronized, and regional CITS offices, city buses, or taxis hired to get to the historic sites. For the determined who wish to be free of guides, daily deadlines, and other "hindrances," independent travel is rough but ready.

JIAYUGUAN: END OF THE GREAT WALL

嘉峪关

ACCORDING TO A POPULAR MYTH, the Great Wall ends at the Jade Pass (Yamen) near Jiayuguan, a town far up the Hexi Corridor in the northwestern province of Gansu. When the First Emperor, Qin Shi Huang (259–210 B.C.), unified ancient sections of the wall in 211 B.C., Jiayuguan did mark the end of the Great Wall, but during the subsequent Han Dynasty (206 B.C. to A.D. 220) the wall was extended farther west, with beacon towers stretching deep into the desert. These extensions were eventually swallowed up by the desert sands. When the Great Wall achieved its final form under the Ming Dynasty (1368–1644), including those segments visited today near Beijing, Jiayuguan again became the garrison on the final frontier.

In 1372, General Feng Shang drove the Mongols out and built a fort at the end of the Great Wall. It became known as "The Greatest Pass Under Heaven," and it remains standing today in Jiayuguan. West of here, the vast Gobi Desert opens its threatening jaws. Every traveler setting out from Jiayuguan Pass followed the same custom, hurling a stone at the western wall. If the stone bounced back, it meant the traveler would come back to China. If not, there would be no return.

Wei-Jin Tombs

The flight from Xi'an to Jiayuguan, 800 miles, takes nearly 3 hours, and the winds over Gansu Province are bumpy. I was the only Westerner aboard, but there were 75 Japanese tourists, too. The Japanese are great fans of the Silk Road and its Buddhist treasures. Inside the China Northwest Airlines jet prop plane, it smelled like old socks. An hour into the flight, I could see an endless pink-and-cream-colored desert below and a few white oasis towns with small fields and blue reservoirs connected by a thin string of roads. As we set down in Jiayuguan, I spotted the snowcapped Qilian mountain range to the south, the unbroken wall of the Hexi Corridor.

I was met by a local guide, Martin Yuan, who briefed me on the town. Jiayuguan has a population of 120,000, of whom 8% work in a single Russian-built steel factory, the largest in northwest China.

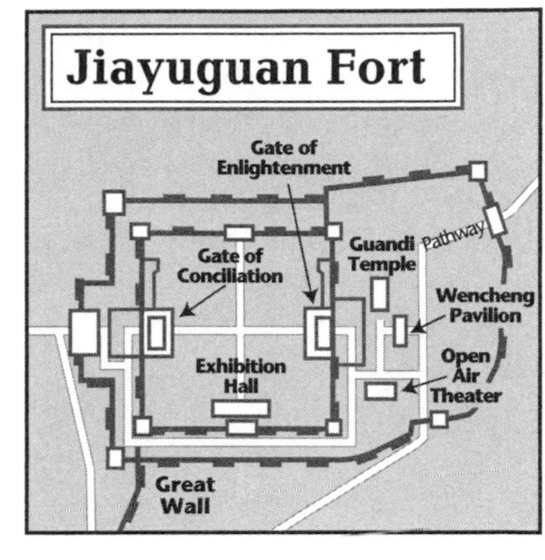

We set out first not for the garrison at the end of the Great Wall but for a site less dramatic, although quite ancient: the Wei-Jin Tombs. Thirteen tombs were built 12 miles northeast of town during the Northern Wei (A.D. 220–265) and Western Jin (A.D. 265–316) dynasties. This cluster consists of rounded mounds about 6 feet high, heaps of sandy soil scooped up from the desert flatlands—as desolate a graveyard as I have ever seen. Driving the 12 miles out to the Wei-Jin tombs, we passed many fields of such mounds. Some 14,000 tombs of officials have been counted in the area. The 13 Wei-Jin tombs open to visitors were discovered in 1972. They're open 8am to 10pm; admission is RMB 10 ($1.25). The burial chambers are several stories under the ground—the mounds are merely markers.

We strolled down the stairs into **Tomb 6,** which like many others has been looted by grave robbers in the past but still retains its chief treasure: the brick paintings depicting daily life. This tomb consists of three burial chambers, representing the three courtyards of the official and his wife who are buried here.

The walls of this first small underground chamber are constructed of 1,700-year-old bricks laid without mortar. The bricks are brightly painted with scenes of animal husbandry—the herding of goats and the tilling of fields by oxen in this oasis, fed by subterranean rivers originating in the distant mountains. In the second chamber, connected by a low archway, the walls depict the journey this official and his wife made to the Chinese capital, Luoyang, an immense overland trip of more than a thousand miles—the trip of a lifetime. There are scenes of rich banquets, processions, and entertainments enjoyed at the capital. In the final burial chamber, the picture bricks record the official's worldly wealth, his boxes of jewels and shelves of silks, the treasures traded on the Silk Road. These brick paintings are simple renditions outlined in black, with red the most enduring color. The coffins are also here, on the floor against the final wall.

The Fort

Jiayuguan Fort, the single most stunning sight along the Silk Road, is 4 miles from town (☎ 0937/622-5518). It's open 8:30am to 12:30pm and 2:30 to 6pm; admission is RMB 20 ($2.40). This garrison at Jiayuguan Pass is magnificent. It rises from the desert sands and is composed of the same earth. The walls are 35 feet high, the outer fortifications 3,400 feet around. The outer wall has turrets for the archers and several pavilions at the corners, watchtowers for the troops stationed here during the Ming Dynasty.

It is easy to see why the wall ended here and how the fort could control the traffic of the Silk Road. The Hexi Corridor is pinched between the high Qilian Mountains and the Black Mountains of the Mazong (Horse Mane) range to the north. Across this pass, earthen walls extend like raised arms east and west, forming a long fence.

Inside the outer wall is an inner wall surrounding the barracks where the general and his troops were stationed. The inner eastern gate, crowned with a 50-foot-high tower built in 1506, guards a courtyard running to the outer wall where caravans could be held for questioning before continuing into China. The western gate has a similar double-walled courtyard that served as the departure station for those crossing the desert out of China.

Climbing the wall, walking from turret to turret, blockhouse to blockhouse, I looked west from the pass into the desert. China's first official mission over the Silk Road, headed by General Zhang Qian, went out through here in 138 B.C. and returned 13 years later with just two survivors. Believers say that even earlier, Lao Zi, founder of Daoism, passed through Jiayuguan and the Jade Gate (Yamen) on his way to the Western Paradise.

The fort at Jiayuguan could not be in a more dramatic desert setting, nor could it look at once more imposing and more forlorn. The present fortification is partly reconstructed with brick, with improvements made as recently as 1988, but the original Ming Dynasty earthen walls are fully exposed and the old watchtowers are still in place. Within the inner walls there is an ornate, tiled-roof opera **theater,** built during the Qing Dynasty (1644–1911) for entertaining the Great Wall troops, its empty open stage sheltered by soaring eaves. A single camel and a saddled horse are tethered in the inner courtyard, their master and his portrait camera waiting for customers.

My guide took me down into the empty yard of the fort and told me some local stories. According to one, the emperor charged a local man with procuring the bricks necessary to build the fort. If his count was off, even by a single brick, he would pay with his life (the ancient answer to cost overruns). The man predicted that 100,000 bricks would be required for the project, and he confidently placed the order. As it turned out, only 99,999 bricks were needed, but he was able to conceal the left-over brick when the royal inspector arrived by placing it unmortared along the inner wall. The unmortared brick is still somewhere on the wall, according to my local guide.

Entering the western courtyard between the inner and outer walls of the fort, he told me another story. Once there were two sparrows, very much in love. One became shut inside the fort; the other escaped into the desert. The trapped bird waited and waited, singing out until it pined away. Today, when you hurl a rock at the inner wall, you can still hear its cry. I picked up a stone, and like thousands of travelers who stood here on the Silk Road, I hurled it against the wall, sanded smooth by the desert winds.

PRACTICAL INFORMATION

ORIENTATION & WHEN TO GO

Jiayuguan, a trading post and oasis during the Han Dynasty, served as the fort protecting the western entrance to China from the Silk Road during the Ming Dynasty. Today it is an industrial town deep in Gansu Province, 1,300 miles west of Beijing. Because of its elevation (above 4,000 feet), Jiayuguan is usually not scorching hot in the summer. Early spring and late fall are known for fierce dust storms, however, and winters for extreme cold temperatures.

GETTING THERE

By Plane China Northwest Airlines has one flight daily to Jiayuguan from Xi'an, a 2½-hour trip.

By Train The train station is about 2 miles south of the city center. It's served by buses (labeled no. 1) and taxis. Jiayuguan is 30 hours from Xi'an, 51 hours from Beijing. There are four trains daily. Tickets can be booked at hotel travel desks.

TOURS & STRATAGEMS

Visitor Information The **Jiayuguan International Travel Service,** 2 Shengli Bei Lu (☎ 0937/622-6598; fax 0937/622-6931), can provide English-language guides and tours of Jiayuguan, Dunhuang, and other points along the Silk Road.

Jiayuguan has a **Great Wall Museum** (☎ 0937/622-5881), open 8:30 to 11:30am and 2:30 to 6pm; admission is RMB 20 ($2.40). However, it's not impressive. There are photographs and maps, very few relics (and some are copies), and a model showing how the Great Wall was built (pounded earth at the core, sun-dried mud brick or granite exterior). A gift shop and an old war plane are stationed in the courtyard.

There are plans to develop Jiayuguan into a larger tourist attraction, with the re-creation of an ancient marketplace and residence district, a fish and bird garden, an amusement park, horse stables, an archery field, and a complex of "holiday villas."

WHERE TO STAY

Great Wall Hotel (Chang Cheng Binguan). *9 Jianshe Xi Lu (between train station and downtown). ☎ 0937/622-5200. Fax 0937/622-6016. 160 units. TV TEL. $65 double. AE, JCB, MC, V.* This five-story three-star modern hotel, built in the shape of a fort, is the best in town. Rumpled, unmaintained carpets line the long hallways. The rooms are spacious and dusty. The private bathrooms (tub showers) are new and clean. Towels, linens, and bathroom amenities are provided daily. Long-distance international calls can be made from the rooms, but they go through the hotel switchboard. Off the lobby there's a large gift shop with local crafts, and beyond that, in a separate building, a dining hall that serves meals to tour groups. From the hotel's "faux-ramparts" there is a fine view of a local minaret and the Qilian mountain range, towering over 20,000 feet to the south. This is a modern hotel, adequate for cleaning up and sleeping, but with few luxuries beyond a fitness center, a small swimming pool, a tour desk, and bicycle rental. There's no air-conditioning.

WHERE TO DINE

Jiayuguan is too small and remote to provide Western-style restaurants. I had a Chinese dinner (mutton as the main course) at the clean new restaurant run by the local tourist office, the **CITS Tourism Restaurant** (☎ 0937/622-6470) on Shengli Bei Lu.

But the best meal I ate in Jiayuguan was downtown at the local **outdoor market.** Martin Yuan, my local guide, took me in hand. Skewered mutton is cooked over open coals—20 skewers are braised at a time. You sit on a long bench inches away from the coals. The cook hands you a batch of five or six, and you strip the mutton off the metal skewer with your teeth. As you eat, the cook's daughter slices more mutton from the carcass of a sheep hanging from the stall (about 2 feet from where you sit) and dices and spices the mutton strips. Each emptied skewer is tossed into a box to one side. The meat is extremely spicy and delicious. A dozen skewers cost about RMB 10 ($1.20). The town is relatively prosperous, thanks to the big steel mill, and local ironworkers are said to eat 200 mutton shish kabobs at a sitting, washing them down with cheap local beer.

DUNHUANG: CRESCENT MOON LAKE & THE SINGING SANDS

敦煌

TWO THOUSAND YEARS AGO, DUNhuang (Blazing Beacon) was a vital and flourishing caravan stop, the westernmost oasis under Chinese control. Three major trading routes from the West merged here, making Dunhuang a major supply center.

The history of this outpost reflects the changing political winds that have swept across the Silk Road over the centuries. Tibetans ruled Dunhuang for almost 2 centuries before a Chinese warlord drove them out in A.D. 851. After the Tang Dynasty fell, the Uighur people swept in and established the Kingdom of Shachow in 911. Mongols took over in 1227, as Genghis Khan stormed in from the Gobi. Muslim forces cleared out the region in the 16th century. The Chinese resettled Dunhuang once again in 1760.

The most crucial event in Dunhuang's history unfolded early on, in the 4th century A.D., when work began on the Buddhist sculpture and murals in the Mogao caves. As the importance of the Silk Road diminished at the end of the Tang Dynasty (A.D. 618–907), Dunhuang languished for centuries, but in the 20th century these ancient grottoes made Dunhuang an important desert town once again and a major stopover for travelers.

Of course, modern travelers no longer arrive on sand-dune marching camels. Tourism has replaced trade as the source of Dunhuang's new wealth, and the Mogao caves are the chief attraction for Chinese, Asian, and the few Western travelers retracing the Silk Road route.

My immediate goal at Dunhuang, however, was to get on a camel and cross a few dunes myself. The great Mogao caves would wait for another chapter of travels (see the next chapter). I wanted to see a still more ancient phenomenon at Dunhuang, what Marco Polo called the "rumbling sands" of Crescent Moon Lake.

The Road to Dunhuang

The Silk Road across the desert sands from Jiayuguan northwest up the **Hexi Corridor** to Dunhuang used to require 3 weeks by camel caravan. Today there is a 240-mile blacktop highway connecting the two oases. The **Qilian Mountains** to the south are oil rich. China's first oil field was opened west of Jiayuguan in the Qilian foothills in 1936. The train cars barreling down the Hexi Corridor are loaded with black oil cars. There's a large nuclear plant as well. Gansu is a very poor province, but it is supplying much of the raw energy for the rest of China.

After a 2-hour drive, the southern mountains fade into the flat horizon. Sand and sand bluffs dominate the severe landscape. Thorn bushes are the only vegetation, except at rare villages where earthen houses are clustered around a green oasis and the domes of small mosques rise toward the clear skies. Goat herders dressed in tatters move across the sandy fields of the Gobi with their small flocks.

Deep into the desert we reached the ruins of **Qiaowan,** the dream city where Qing Dynasty emperor Kangxi (1654–1722) ordered a palace built. He became obsessed with a dream he had that was set on the Silk Road. In the dream he saw a palace located on a river with two enormous trees, one shaped like a crown, the other like a sash. He dispatched two officials to locate the place and finance the dream temple. The officials built a humble walled dwelling instead, pocketing most of the construction funds. When Kangxi discovered their deceit, he had the officials slain, using the skins of the wrongdoers to cover the heads of the palace drums. Only ruins remain at Qiaowan now.

The drive to Dunhuang consumes 4½ hours, even on a paved road. Drivers here learn to fight the monotony of interminably straight, flat stretches and the frequent eruption of massive potholes, entire unpaved strips, and barely passable detours that appear unannounced. There are road crews—men and women with nothing but shovels and bicycle carts—patching the roadway every 2 or 3 miles, and traffic must slow to a stop to negotiate what the elements have torn to bits. At noon we reached Dunhuang, a long, green oasis lined by trees for many miles where a river, the Danghe, cuts through the sands, exposing stone bluffs. Here tractors pull carts of crushed stone into town, and hardened, sunburnt men, taking a break from hauling tree limbs to market, nap on their trailers under shade trees.

The Singing Sands

Three miles south of downtown Dunhuang there are enormous white sand dunes, part of the Singing Sand Mountains (Mingsha Shan). The dunes look like a poster of the Sahara. In their deep folds they trap

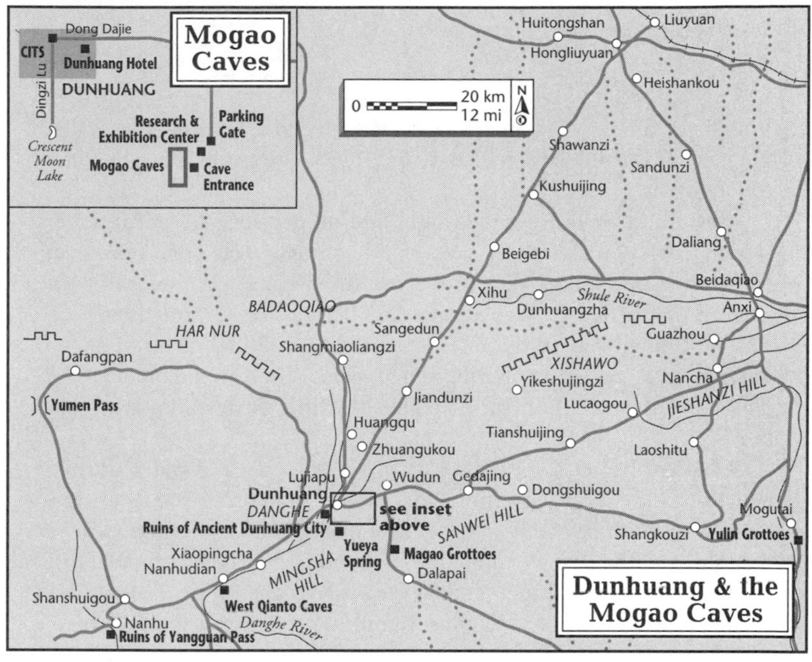

underground springs, creating **Crescent Moon Lake (Yueya Quan),** a celebrated pool where Silk Road travelers, including Marco Polo, paused to drink.

The afternoon sun was blisteringly hot when Martin Yuan, my local guide from Jiayuguan, and I set out to cross the fine sands for Crescent Moon Lake. The site is open from dawn to sunset and after; admission is RMB 20 ($2.50). Donning a straw hat, plastered in sunscreen, I was already sweating after the first few steps. My feet sank several inches into the crunching sands. It was like crossing a beach, a thousand miles from the nearest sea. Under awnings a hundred camels and their drivers waited for riders. Heated by the sun, slowed by the Gobi sands, I hired us each a camel (RMB 30/$3.60 each) for the 15-minute trek each way—to avoid the long, hot walk. Obviously, I would have dropped dead in my tracks if I'd been one of the early traders trying to cross these dunes.

The two-humped Bactrian camel has inhabited the Silk Road for 2,000 years. They roam wild over the Gobi to this day. Single-humped camels could carry as heavy a load, but they lacked the stamina and speed of their two-humped cousins. These enormous creatures are fairly docile under their masters' watch. My camel knelt on his front legs, then his back legs, and I climbed aboard between his two humps. The humps, parted by a heavy blanket, proved to be a most comfortable saddle. Tethered to the driver's camel in a caravan of three, we loped across the sands at a steady pace, gently rising and falling with the camels' walk.

We skirted a large oval concrete pool on our right, used to store water. On our left was the largest of the sand dunes, towering over a hundred feet above us.

Beyond the pool we turned right and headed for a beautiful three-storied pavilion with soaring eaves that had been erected on the edge of Crescent Moon Lake. Martin told me the original pavilion had been savaged by the Red Guards during the Cultural Revolution (1966–76). The restoration was remarkable: The pavilion still had its air of antiquity, and its upper balconies proved marvelous observation points for the dunes and the lake. Our driver halted the little caravan, lowering our camels.

Crescent Moon Lake these days is a narrow slash of water situated between the pavilion and a formidable wall of sand rising 600 feet nearly straight up from its northern bank. Dunhuang had been experiencing a drought, and the lake was quite low, but still pretty, a reed-studded belt of blue in a bowl of white mounds. We ordered cups of tea and sat on a veranda, the remains of a Buddhist temple where incense is still lighted. The lake received its name from its crescent-moon shape. The local people attach a story to the lake. It is a story like many of the Silk Road, of parting and grief. Here in Dunhuang a young girl parted with her lover, who set out to cross the desert. The caravan was lost, and he never returned. She died in mourning, with one eye forever opened in the shape of a crescent, watching the desert for the return of her lover.

Returning by camel, we dismounted and climbed the largest mound, **Mingsha Dune,** 820 feet high, a veritable mountain of sand that seemed an endless task to scale. Sand sleds and para-gliders can be hired here, but I preferred to hike. I removed my shoes, soaked in the fine sands. At its summit, the view of the oasis was superb, a long, green island in the midst of a sea of sand, and to the west, whipped-cream dunes that stretch for 80 miles into the empty horizon. We sat atop the dune until the sun became too fierce, then descended like children, seated, "sand sliding" to the bottom, trying to make the sands sing as they have for eons here, although I could hear only a whisper of their legendary music.

On our way out Martin told me about a party of 70 foreigners who'd visited the singing sands a few years back and formed a long caravan indeed. The group was led by one of my famous American compatriots, he said, a chap named Bill Gates, founder of Microsoft—one of the richest "traders," I pointed out, who'd ever ridden a camel on the Silk Road.

Then the wind came up, stirring the sands to a fine powder. The sound was a low rumble, often likened to a drumroll by Chinese poets. A Dunhuang legend tells of a Chinese army camped here that was surrounded by the enemy once darkness fell. The Chinese army beat its war drums, and its call to arms was answered by the gods, who dispatched a sandstorm across the desert, burying both armies alive at Crescent Lake. To this day, people claim to hear the buried armies wailing and beating on their drums when the winds roll in.

"Man made the Buddhist caves," according to a local adage, "but the gods made Crescent Moon Lake," and these desert gods, it seems, can unmake caves, lakes, and even whole armies in the wink of an eye.

PRACTICAL INFORMATION

ORIENTATION & WHEN TO GO

Dunhuang is a desert oasis in northwest Gansu Province near the border with Xinjiang Province, about 1,500 miles west of Beijing. Summers are very hot; May and October are the mildest months to visit. In July and August, the town fills up with thousands of tourists from China, Japan, and other parts of Asia, with a smattering of Westerners. While the oasis population is over 150,000, the downtown section is small and compact, with about 15,000 urban residents.

The major attraction for visitors to Dunhuang are the ancient Buddhist murals and sculptures at the **Mogao caves** (see separate chapter on Dunhuang). **Crescent Moon Lake (Yueya Shan)** and **Singing Sands Mountain (Mingsha Shan)** have the best sand dunes on the Silk Road.

GETTING THERE

By Plane With the opening of a new **airport** at Dunhuang, flights from Xi'an (3 hours), Beijing (4 hours), and other cities in China are becoming more frequent.

By Train The main train line through Gansu Province stops well north of Dunhuang at the small town of **Liuyuan.** From Liuyuan, frequent buses make the 80-mile connection to Dunhuang (about a 3-hour trip). From Liuyuan, it is a 6-hour train ride east to Jiayuguan, 36 hours to Xi'an, and 57 hours to Beijing. Heading west, the train to Turpan is 13 hours, to Urumqi 16 hours.

By Car & Bus The paved road from Jiayuguan (240 miles) is served by hired cars (5 hours) and buses (8 hours).

TOURS & STRATAGEMS

This was my second stop on an 8-day independent tour of the Silk Road arranged by China Travel Service (CTS) in Xi'an. The site I visited is located 3 miles south of city center at the end of Dingzi Lu. During high season (July and August), try to come here as early in the morning as possible (by 8am) or near dusk (after 6pm) to avoid the intense heat.

Visitor Information The **Dunhuang China International Tourist Service (CITS)** (☎ 0937/ 882-2494) has a branch at 1 Dong Dajie (2 blocks west of the Dunhuang Hotel, downtown). There are also two branches on

Mingshan Lu. They can each provide local guides, but the tour desk at the **Dunhuang Hotel,** 14 Yangguan Dong Lu (☎ 0937/882-2538 or 882-2008), is more experienced with Westerners.

WHERE TO STAY

Dunhuang is prospering as tourism flourishes, spurred by an increase in domestic travelers from inside China, and several new four-star hotels are under construction. At present, the Dunhuang Hotel provides the most experienced services for Westerners.

Dunhuang Hotel (Dunhuang Binguan). *14 Yangguan Dong Lu (4 blocks east of city center off Dong Dajie). ☎ 0937/882-2538 or 0937/882-2415. Fax 0937/882-2195 or 0937/882-2309. 171 units. A/C MINIBAR TV TEL. $75 double. AE, JCB, MC, V.*

This three-star three-building compound is where China's state leaders spend the night (present leader Jiang Zemin and late paramount leader Deng Xiaoping stayed here). The VIP Building is not usually open to tourists, so the new North Building—strikingly clean and modern—is the best section to stay in. It has its own lobby (with white plaster statues and colored ceiling lights) and staff, and an attached dining room that serves excellent Western and Chinese fixed-price meals (up to 12 dishes, including spaghetti). The staff speaks little English but tries to be helpful. The South Building (across the street) contains the shopping arcade, gym, and most of the 15 dining halls.

Amenities: Health club, sauna, business center, next-day dry cleaning and laundry, beauty salon, shopping arcade, tour desk.

WHERE TO DINE

If you are in Dunhuang on tour, your guide will set up meal times and restaurants. The **Dunhuang Hotel,** 14 Yangguan Dong Lu (☎ 0937/882-2415), has excellent Chinese and some Mongolian dishes in its restaurants (RMB 42 to RMB 125/$5 to $15). The Terrace Cafe in the lobby has drinks and Western-style snacks (sandwiches, cakes).

Near the bus station on Dingxi Lu (the southern portion of Mingshan Lu) there are a number of small **cafes** with cheap Western dishes catering to independent foreign travelers. Their names (Shirley's, Charley Johng's, John's) and their menus are in English.

Two blocks from the Dunhuang Hotel (west on Dong Dajie toward the city center traffic circle), there's a large **night market.** Entrance is on the south side of the street through a gate; look for the lights, food stalls, and outdoor billiard tables. Local food, including excellent spicy mutton on skewers, is cooked by sidewalk vendors. Sweet melons, grapes, and other regional fruits are also sold in the streets.

The Caves of Mogao
莫高石窟

Of the top four Buddhist grottoes in China, the Mogao caves at Dunhuang are considered supreme. Nevertheless, visitors are often disappointed. The caves containing the priceless wall paintings and sculptures created at this ancient oasis on the Silk Road, honeycombing a sheer cliff face, are all sealed by locked doors. The guides must constantly search for the person with the key. You must view Mogao cave by cave, piece by piece: In a morning or afternoon, you can see only a tiny portion of these treasures locked in stone. At the other three major grottoes—the Yungang caves at Datong, the Longmen caves at Luoyang, and the Buddha Crescent at Dazu—visitors can freely wander in front of magnificent sculptures, open to wide and dramatic views.

Nevertheless, the treasures at Dunhuang—those not shipped abroad by Western explorers at the turn of the 20th century, that is—are the benchmarks of Buddhist art in China, and I was glad to have seen them for myself. Several days' viewing here is more rewarding than a few quick hours, and it helps to arrange the caves in rough chronological order in one's mind. The styles and themes change over the centuries, and with a little background, the history of Buddhism and the Silk Road itself unfolds at Dunhuang like chapters in a stone picture book.

The Cave Builders

China's richest treasure house of Buddhist paintings, statues, and manuscripts lies 16 miles southeast of Dunhuang in the Mogao caves. These magnificent caves were created over a thousand-year period stretching from the 4th century to the 14th century A.D. Nine dynasties rose and fell during this time, and the artists of each period contributed.

The grottoes had as much to do with business and politics as religion. The rich merchant families and the rulers of Dunhuang sponsored the carving and painting of many of them. Such acts, no doubt, cast them in a favorable light to Buddhist believers who ran the rich caravan trade. The first cave was hewn in A.D. 366 by Lie Zun, a Buddhist monk who was inspired by the golden rays of the sun illuminating the cliff face. Lie Zun commissioned a fellow pilgrim to paint the walls with holy images, decorating a shrine where he could pray for his safe passage over the Silk Road. Thus, the purpose of this desert gallery was set from the first—a divine insurance policy for the caravans of the Silk Road. The grottoes functioned as shrines where traders and pilgrims could pray, but above all as a place where Silk Road travelers and merchants could petition for divine protection of their caravans, which faced daunting obstacles in crossing the deserts that loomed east and west of Dunhuang.

Over the centuries, the repute of Dunhuang increased. New dynasties often sent their best artists there to construct and decorate new grottoes to commemorate their rules and cement their commitment to the religious community. Over 45,000 murals and 2,000 statues, fashioned from stucco rather than the loose sandstone of the cliff, have survived, housed in almost 500 caves. The desert air has preserved the art for 15 centuries.

The chief dynasties represented are the Northern Wei (A.D. 386–534), the Western Wei (A.D. 535–557), the Sui (A.D. 581–618), the Tang (A.D. 618–917), and the Five Dynasties (A.D. 907–960). The styles vary with the dynasties. The themes were all derived from the various schools of Buddhism as they arrived and were adapted in China.

The earlier figures of Buddha and his attendants retain a strong Indian influence, rendered in rigid, geometric poses, but the Chinese gradually added movement and realism to these figures. They reached their zenith with the Tang artists, who created 213 of the 492 caves that survive. The backgrounds painted on the cave walls flow with cloud scrolls, floral patterns, fantastic landscapes, and architecture that almost from the first came from Chinese models. The main themes are derived from the life of Sakyamuni as he journeys to enlightenment and from the holy manuscripts *(sutras)* that preach the cosmic doctrines of karma and reincarnation and portray the mortal world as one of vanity, illusion, and suffering.

To heighten depictions of these themes, the Dunhuang painters plastered the walls and ceilings with mixtures of mud, dung, straw, animal hair, and a smooth coating of clay, to which they applied tempera (water-based) pigments of vivid blues, yellows, greens, reds, cinnabar vermilions, fleshy pinks, and powdered gold leaf. The statues are made either with plaster over wooden frames or with plaster over figures cut from cave rock. The caves are squarish, often with a large figure of Buddha on a dais at the back and attendants on both sides. The large chambers measure about 30 feet wide and deep and 16 feet high, while the smallest caves are barely the size of a tiny bedroom, with ceilings as low as 54 inches. The ceilings may be sharply pitched, lantern shaped, or domed in a series of tapering, concentric squares.

For the casual observer, the main technical point to note is the evolution of the art from the rigid, narrow, representational figures in the early caves to the rounded, realistically rendered, more human figures portrayed in the later Sui and Tang Dynasty caves, as the gulf between the divine and the earthly all but disappears.

Guardian Angels & Foreign Devils

The history of Buddhist art in China contained in the gallery of caves at Dunhuang is part of the larger political history of the Silk Road. As the Tang Dynasty declined, the Silk Road was subject to invasions from Tibetans and groups spreading a new religion, Islam. The Xi Xia Kingdom (1038–1368) gained the upper hand, chasing Buddhists out of Dunhuang. The Mogao caves were abandoned. Monks sealed their documents and sutras in a single cave and fled the invaders. The Dunhuang grottoes remained unused and undiscovered for at least 800 years. Near the beginning of the 20th century, a Daoist monk named Wang Yuanlu, seeking refuge from the famines in Hubei Province, arrived at Dunhuang, and, clearing out a cave, discovered a door leading to a dark inner chamber filled with thousands of manuscripts and paintings. The Chinese government, unable to finance the removal of the treasures, ordered Wang to reseal the inner storehouse, but Wang, intent on raising funds to restore the Mogao grottoes, began to sell the treasures to the highest bidders.

It was Westerners who recognized the worth of the newly discovered manuscripts and who came across the Silk Road to snap them up for museums. Sir Aurel Stein arrived first, in 1907. He purchased silk painted banners, 7,000 scrolls, 500 paintings, and other relics, which he crated up and transferred to the British Library, where they still reside. Paul Pelliot came the next year, selecting paintings and 5,000 scrolls for the Bibliotheque Nationale in Paris. Japanese, Russians, and more Western collectors quickly followed, including Langdon Warner, who removed sculptures and wall paintings and shipped them from Dunhuang to the Fogg Museum at Harvard in 1924.

In the end, Dunhuang was left with virtually no manuscripts. A sutra copied onto paper and dated A.D. 406, and a paper scroll of the Diamond Sutra dated A.D. 868, considered the world's first printed book, are now in England. Fortunately, most of the wall paintings and much of the statuary remains where it was created, in the desert caves of Dunhuang, beyond the reach of foreign specialists, who are seen by some as the heroic preservers of a Chinese history that would otherwise have been lost and by others as modern-day raiders of the Silk Road.

Inside the Grottoes

I visited the **Mogao caves** (☎ 0937/886-9060), 15 miles southwest of Dunhuang, on a bright spring morning. They're open daily from 8:30 to 11:30am and 2 to 5pm. The admission of RMB 80 ($9.65) included a local guide, an English-speaking student attending the Dunhuang Research Academy, which is devoted to the study of the caves. I rented a flashlight at the ticket booth (RMB 3/35¢ with a deposit of RMB 10/$1.20)—the caves are unlighted—and crossed a wooden bridge over the Da River to the sandstone cliff.

All the caves are numbered, although not in any discernible order. The oldest are in the central portion of the mile-long cliff. Four tiers of cement walkways with railings, replacing the wooden ladders and catwalks in the 1950s, connect the grottoes.

Roughly 30 of the 492 chambers are usually available to tourists, with the guide deciding which ones to visit. Some caves can be visited only by special advanced permission and payment of extra fees; photography inside is forbidden except by special arrangements and fees. Since even the caves open for visitation are often locked and there are no signposts, a guide is useful, although one can crisscross the platforms on one's own, dropping in at open doors and latching onto various guided groups. There are many interesting caves that are off-limits to ordinary visitors, including Caves 462 and 465, containing figures engaged in sexual union. This particular representation of divine enlightenment is a frequent theme of Tantric Buddhism, which was popular during the Yuan Dynasty (1271–1368), when this cave was painted.

The most dramatic sculpture is behind a nine-story wooden pagoda. Decorated with paintings of the zodiac and erected a century ago, the tower of soaring eaves rises to the summit of the sandstone ridge. Inside **Cave 96** is a 113-foot-tall Buddha, carved from the sandstone cliffs during the high Tang Dynasty (A.D. 705–781). Seated, wearing the robes of an emperor, this *Maitreya Buddha* (Happy Buddha of the Future) is the fourth largest in the world and the largest single clay sculpture at Dunhuang. It was repainted in the 19th century and its left hand was repaired a decade ago.

Among the caves I was shown, these are of particular note:

Cave 16 is where Wang Yuanlu stumbled onto the treasures of Dunhuang at the beginning of the 20th century. The nine figures on the platform are a recent addition (Qing Dynasty, 1644–1911), but the tile floor is probably from the late Tang (848–906). The west wall is a Five Dynasties (907–960) mural depicting the holy mountain of Wutai Shan, its temples labeled, and the east wall contains portraits of a ruling family of the region from the same period, who sponsored the cave art. The ceiling is decorated in the *Ten Thousand Buddha* motif, the repeated pattern achieved by the use of block stamps or stencils that were painted in. The lotuses decorating the walls date from the 11th century. It was usual for artists of later dynasties to add to or even paint over existing shrines, as space for new caves was eventually exhausted.

Cave 17, linked to the passageway to Cave 16, is where Wang Yuanlu found the trove of scrolls, sutras, and paintings that Sir Aurel Stein and other Westerners bought and shipped to museums abroad, starting in 1907. Known as the Canjing Ku, this cave is where the oldest book in the world (A.D. 868), the Diamond Sutra, was discovered.

Caves 61, 62, and **63** date from the Yuan Dynasty (1271–1368), when the Mongols seized control of China. The statues, presumably posed in the sexual positions favored by Tantric Buddhism at the time, were demolished by Moslems. The 40-foot-long wall mural of the holy mountain of Wutai Shan, its scores of temples labeled, is splendid and dates from the Northern Song (960–1127), when Dunhuang's ruling family opened a painting academy devoted solely to artwork in the Mogao grottoes.

Cave 98 is from the Five Dynasties (907–960). The ceiling is funnel shaped. The Cao Yi Jin family, high officials of the period at Dunhuang, sponsored this and several other caves, notably Cave 427. The wall portraits are of the ruling family of Khotan, a city on the Silk Road. The king wears a beaded hat. There are also lively scenes of female musicians and a royal hunting party.

Cave 130 contains a magnificent Buddha, 86 feet high, carved during the high Tang period (705–781). The platform and statue are original, except for the Buddha's right hand, which broke and was replaced during the Northern Song (960–1279). The murals on the side walls are also from the Northern Song. This is the second tallest statue at Dunhuang, and it can be appreciated from the ground or from the two upper galleries. The head measures 22 feet high, the ears 6 feet.

Cave 148 contains the 53-foot-long, golden-faced *Sleeping Buddha of Dunhuang.* It was carved in 755 to portray Buddha about to enter Nirvana. Seventy-two disciples are in attendance. The east wall contains a painting of the Western Paradise, the Buddhist "heaven."

Cave 152 features a passageway with tiles and ceiling paintings from the Northern Song (960–1127), with two Daoist figures in the back chamber.

Cave 237 has a statue of Guanyin, Goddess of Mercy, in its center, with Manjusri, God of War, riding a lion, and Pusan, God of Compassion, atop the holy mountain of Emei Shan. These figures were added during the Qing (1644–1911) in a cave whose wall paintings of the Buddha and the Western Paradise were placed here in the middle Tang (781–848).

Cave 257, with a pillar in the center, contains unretouched paintings from the Northern Wei (A.D. 386–534), some of the oldest art at Dunhuang. The figures are dressed in Indian clothing, and the facial features are not Chinese. The mural on the west wall portrays the story of a drowning man rescued by the Deer King, a representation of Buddha.

Cave 259, said to contain the oldest artwork at Dunhuang, holds several statues of Buddha carved during the Northern Wei (A.D. 386–534). The figures are stiff, the heads squarish, the nose hooked, the lips curled (into a smile often compared to that of the *Mona Lisa*)—all characteristics of the Buddhist sculpture in India at the time.

Cave 427 was a gift from the Cao family, high officials at Dunhuang during the Northern Song (960–1279) who controlled the Silk Road routes for 120 years. Husband, wife, and family are portrayed on the front passage walls. A pillar holds up the gabled roof over the chamber at the back, which contains nine stately, long-bodied statues of Buddha, sculpted during the Sui Dynasty (A.D. 581–618). The three figures in the middle are "Buddhas of the Present"; the three on the left, "Buddhas of the Past"; and the three on the right, "Buddhas of the Future."

Cave 428 has a lotus and peacock ceiling and stamped clay figures of the *Ten Thousand Buddhas* on the walls, but its attraction is the picture of court life given in the Northern Zhou Dynasty (A.D. 557–581), a brief period linking the Wei and Sui dynasties from which little survives. Over 4,000 royal contributors to the cave art are pictured on the east wall, along with the halls and pavilions of the time. There is also a panel depicting the story of three brothers who hunt a tiger. One brother unselfishly gives his life to the tiger so that she can feed her cubs, and he is reborn as Buddha. My guide told me that in 1922 Russians fleeing the revolution bivouacked in this and other caves, which they blackened with fires, damaged with bullets, and stripped of gold leaf.

Morning or afternoon tours generally take in just a dozen of these and other caves, hardly enough to gain a full appreciation of what exists at Dunhuang. Spend a second day, if possible, and by all means visit the museum at the entrance to the site, a joint venture between China and Japan. The **Research and Exhibition Center** (☎ 0937/882-1981) is open daily 9am to 5pm; admission is RMB 20 ($2.40). It contains lighted replicas of seven caves, copies of the missing manuscripts, and relics from the caves. A tour of the center helps put the intricate and complex desert gallery into perspective.

I once covered 17 grottoes in 2 hours with a local guide, but this proved too rapid to enjoy and study the paintings, particularly the details in the murals. At Dunhuang, it is the paintings that dominate. At other grottoes, it is the sculpture, much of it on a grander and more prolific scale than at Dunhuang. But the painted miniatures of Mogao, in hundreds of caves, record thousands of stories and scenes from the days of the Silk Road that are otherwise lost. Inspired by the sutras carried across mountains and desert into China on the backs of early pilgrims, artists for 9 centuries painted their best work on the walls of these caves. The holiest shrines of the Silk Road are also its supreme works of art.

PRACTICAL INFORMATION

ORIENTATION & WHEN TO GO

The Mogao caves (Mogao Ku) are located 15 miles southeast of Dunhuang, a desert oasis in northwest Gansu Province on the Silk Road, 1,500 miles west of Beijing. Summers are quite hot, but July and August are high season for tourists, mainly those from China, Japan, and other parts of Asia. May and October are more pleasant and less crowded months to visit.

GETTING THERE

For information on how to get to Dunhuang, see the previous chapter. Once in the city, any minibus or taxi driver hailed in the streets knows the way to the Mogao caves. They should charge a fare of no more than RMB 20 ($2.50).

TOURS & STRATAGEMS

Most Westerners reach Dunhuang and the Mogao caves on group tours of the Silk Road. I booked an independent tour of the Silk Road from China Travel Service (CTS) in Xi'an. See the introduction to the Silk Road chapters for details.

Tours At the caves, English-speaking guides are assigned to visitors at the main ticket booth. For information on tour operators in Dunhuang, see the previous chapter.

Visitor Information Photography in the caves is strictly prohibited. Cameras and all bags, including purses, must be checked at the ticket booth. An RMB 2 (25¢) deposit is required.

WHERE TO STAY & DINE

If you are staying the full day at the Mogao caves, either pack a lunch or try one of the cafes or stands near the ticket booth. For information on where to stay and dine in Dunhuang, see the previous chapter.

Turpan: Lost Cities

吐鲁番

The first thing that strikes outsiders traveling west from Gansu Province into Xinjiang Province is that they are no longer quite in China. This vast northwestern region—China's Alaska—is divided into northern grasslands and southern deserts by the Heavenly Mountains (Tian Shan). The dramatic, arid landscape is a sharp break from what's found in the rest of China, but Xinjiang's ethnic makeup is an even more striking departure. Kazakh nomads predominate in the northern pastures; Uighur farmers are a majority in the southern desert basin; and most of the Han Chinese, a distinct minority, are recent arrivals.

Xinjiang is foremost the land of the Uighurs, who account for almost half of the province's 13 million people. They are Turkic-speaking, fiercely Islamic, and decidedly non–Han Chinese. They look and dress like Central Asian people of Turkish descent. Here, the Silk Road passes through a middle ground of history and race like no other land on earth, an Islamic culture under Chinese rule in a land of irrigated oases and bone-white heat.

A Uighur empire rose up in the Tarim Basin in the 8th century. Uighurs controlled the Silk Road routes through Xinjiang. They first adopted Buddhism, then Islam as their faith. During the Qing Dynasty, they were swept up in the 1862 Muslim rebellion led by Yakub Beg. The Chinese did not regain control over Xinjiang, which had become known as Chinese Turkestan, until 1877. In this century, there has been an uneasy truce between the Chinese and Uighurs, sometimes broken by protests, even by violence.

At Turpan, in the heart of Xinjiang, the northern route of the Silk Road steps down into the second deepest continental basin on Earth (next to the Dead Sea). Turpan is 260 feet below sea level, while nearby Moon Lake (Aiding Hu) is 505 feet below sea level. This low lake is encrusted in salt, freezing in winter, melting in summer. Two-thousand-year-old beacon towers still guard the lakeshore, where some of the salt factory workers, sent from coastal cities to labor here during the Cultural Revolution (1966–76), have never returned to their homes.

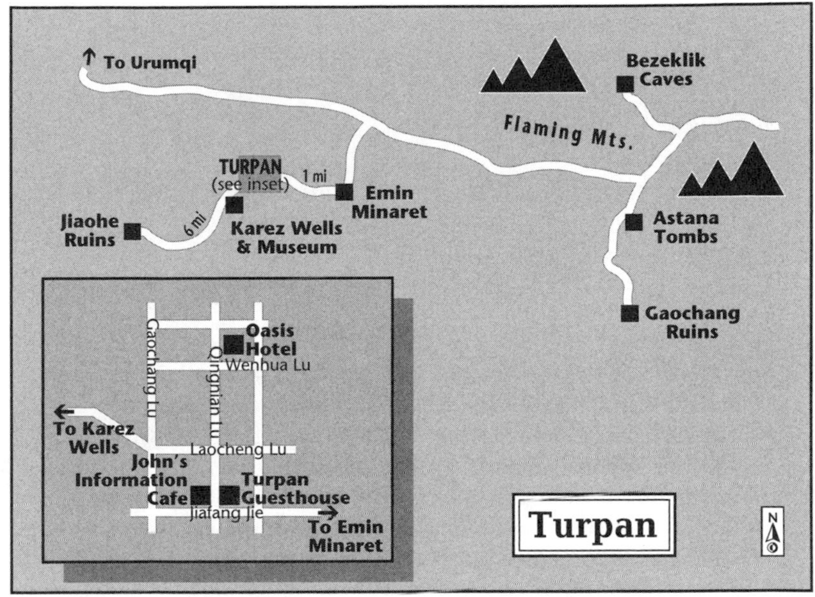

Turpan, just 34 miles from Moon Lake, is far more hospitable. In fact, it is a model Silk Road oasis, a sleepy desert town shaded by poplar trees and grape arbors, peopled by Uighurs in traditional dress and irrigated by a vast system of hand-dug underground channels that funnel the melting snows of the Heavenly Mountains into Turpan. This 2,000-year-old irrigation system has kept Turpan alive while other desert boomtowns have withered up and died. Two of those ancient cities, empty and returned to the sands with which they were built, still remain on Turpan's doorstep, two of the most impressive imperial ruins anywhere on the Silk Road.

Bezeklik Thousand Buddha Caves

Turpan is China's hottest city, its "Land of Fire," with summer temperatures routinely reaching a roasty 104°F (40°C). I arrived on the first of May and the temperature was already 2 degrees above that. I had been doing nothing but traveling for hours. The day before I was driven for 3 hours from Dunhuang north to Liuyuan, past the earthen ruins of the Han Dynasty Great Wall, past a group of five wild camels, and over the Horse Mane Hills, where the sand disappeared and the exposed rock, shattered into bits the size of fingertips, coated everything in lunar gravel. At Liuyuan I boarded an overnight train stuffed with happy Japanese tourists. I arrived at Turpan at 4am, where my local guide, Christina, and a driver met me in the dark. They suggested I nap a few hours in my room in the Oasis Hotel (a fourth-floor walk-up), but of course I couldn't. I was eager to see the sights of Turpan, its old mosques and graves, its fabulous wells, its ruined cities, the Flaming Mountains, and Bezeklik.

The **Flaming Mountains** line the northern rim of the Turpan Depression. Consisting of barren red limestone, the 60-mile-long bluff resembles a tableau of fiery tongues when ignited by the afternoon sun. It is a sight familiar to Chinese readers of the novel *Journey to the West,* an allegorical version of Buddhist monk Xuan Zang's historic journey by foot from China to India over the Silk Road in the 7th century. The trip from Dunhuang west to Turpan, which took me less than 24 hours by car and train, would have taken Xuan Zang or any other pilgrim or caravan trader at least 3 weeks—3 terrible weeks in the desert. Xuan Zang got lost here. Running out of water, he wanted to turn back but instead wandered on, half dead. He made it, of course, to Turpan—or rather, to the city of Gaochang, now in ruins near the site of the Bezeklik caves—where he taught for several months.

The caves in the heart of these mountains, 35 miles northeast of Turpan, are a major Buddhist site. Beginning in the Southern and Northern dynasties (A.D. 420–589), caves were hewn into the cliffside, and large murals, like those at Dunhuang, were painted on the walls and ceilings. The site is now known as the **Bezeklik Thousand Buddha Caves.** It's open daily 9am to 5pm; admission is RMB 20 ($2.50). In Uighur, *bezeklik* means simply "place of paintings."

Bezeklik is situated in absolutely stunning surroundings, high up a cliff in the Murtuk River gorge. From a distance, the caves cut into the ridge, and the brick temples, as well as the smooth mosque domes, look like a holy city chiseled out of a vertical mountainside. But close up, Bezeklik is nearly empty—worse, it has been looted and defaced. The painted walls of its 83 grottoes with their arched ceilings have nearly all been erased or stolen. The Buddhist statuary is also missing. It is a superb Buddhist grotto emptied as if by desert winds or stone-eating monsters.

In fact, Bezeklik has been emptied by men. The Uighurs themselves, having converted to Islam in the 10th century, did not look favorably upon the Buddhist images in their midst. They defaced some murals, beheaded statues, sealed up the caves in sand, and built domed mosques in place of the brick temples. Much of this took place in the 1870s, when Turpan and most of Xinjiang Province broke away from Chinese control and became Chinese Turkestan.

Greater destruction came from the West. The German Albert von Le Coq arrived in Turpan in 1902; he departed with 2 tons of treasures and relics. Two years later, he returned for more. Other expeditions from Europe arrived, crating off whatever remained. At Bezeklik, the German experts found Turpan's treasure house: 1,000-year-old murals in perfect condition with bright portraits of Buddha over the centuries, yellow-robed monks from India, and even a red-haired traveler from the West. The best frescoes were removed and shipped to the Museum for Indian Art in Berlin for safekeeping—beyond the reach of Uighur farmers and Islamic fanatics, it was argued at the time. Later, World War II bombing raids destroyed the Bezeklik wall murals in Berlin, where only fragments remain on display.

A man with a key opened the doors to several caves. There are 83 grottoes here; about 40 retain frescoes, all in poor condition. The few defaced murals I saw give strong hints of the vibrant reds that dominate the art here and of the glowing greens and blues the painters employed as trim. On one arched ceiling, I could make out a familiar motif, the Thousand Buddhas in meditation, row after identical row, unrestored and crumbling.

Ancient Cities

South of the Thousand Buddha Caves (about 25 miles southeast of Turpan) are the ruins of **Gaochang (Kharakhoja),** an ancient desert capital founded in the 2nd century B.C. as a garrison on the Silk Road. It served as the capital of Xinjiang (the Western Territories) during the Tang Dynasty, starting in A.D. 640. From 840 to 1209, Gaochang became the Uighur capital. It was destroyed in 1275 and has stood unoccupied ever since.

The dry air and lack of rain have preserved the outlines of Gaochang's adobe outer walls (3 miles in circumference) and inner buildings—its bell tower and a few of its many Buddhist temples.

At the entrance (RMB 20/$2.50), we hired a young Uighur driver and hopped aboard his flatbed donkey cart for an hour's ride (an extra RMB 15/$2) inside the ancient walls. The pace was slow and the donkey driver relaxed—this was the proper speed at which to drive through a ghost town on the Silk Road. At the center of this city of sand, which is nearly a mile across, there is a large temple, its platform and shrine still evident, and close by a two-story circular pavilion surrounded by a square wall where the pilgrim Xuan Zang preached in A.D. 630 on his way to India.

The city is empty of human remains, of course, but the royal graveyard, a few miles away, is now receiving visitors. The **Astana Tombs** are open daily 9am to 5pm; admission is RMB 20 ($2.50). They have been blessed with centuries of dry weather, meaning that the corpses, their silk wrappings, and even the foods buried with them have survived in fine fettle. The earliest of the 500 graves is dated A.D. 273; the latest, A.D. 782. The burial chambers are 16 feet below the earth. Wall murals depict the pleasures of family life and the beauties of nature, particularly of birds. Among the 10,000 relics excavated at Astana is a pair of woven linen shoes and a fossilized *jiaozi* (steamed dumpling), both specimens from the Tang Dynasty.

Coburial of husband and wife was common. Inside the last of the three chambers open to the public, the mummies of a man and a woman lie next to each other, under glass, on a rough mat. Their hair has grown long in death and so have their fingernails. They have barely begun to disintegrate with the passage of 12 centuries, but they look dry, very dry. If a splash of water stirred them to life now—it looks as if it could—what a strange world would greet their imperial gazes. My foreign face perhaps would be the most terrifying image of all.

On the opposite side of modern Turpan, 6 miles to the west, is a second ruined city, **Jiaohe (Yarkhoto),** perched on a leaf-shaped 100-foot-high plateau between two rivers. A mile long and a quarter mile wide, it's nearly the size of Gaochang, but in better shape. UNESCO has contributed to its preservation. The outlines of many of its buildings are sharper, and there are some signposts in English. The city is open daily 9am to 5pm; admission is RMB 30 ($3.75).

Jiaohe, like so many Silk Road towns, began as a garrison during the Han Dynasty. It reached its peak under Uighur control in the 9th century during the Tang Dynasty. It has been abandoned for more than 5 centuries, but it has preserved its ancient cityscape in sand and brick. A Buddhist temple stands at city center, with Buddhas (heads now missing) carved into its niches. Streets and the courtyards of houses were dug into the ground. Jiaohe looks like a life-sized model of a Tang Dynasty city, sculpted from a high sandstone column standing between river gorges, or like an oasis stripped by a miraculous wind of every piece and particle that was not composed of sand or brick.

A Minaret & the Karez Wells

Turpan is 80% Uighur. Christina, my guide, was a local Han Chinese, meaning she probably went to a Chinese school and was not taught the Uighur language. Uighurs attend their own schools, in which Chinese is studied as a second language. Each side coexists sweetly, it seems. Christina had a dream of visiting America. She wanted to see the west—the Wild West of cowboys that she knew from the movies. I told her that today Turpan is the Wild West. She had another dream she wanted to make a reality in America: She wanted to listen to jazz in a jazz bar, together with her friends. So pervasive are these media images of America that they penetrate even the remotest oasis on the Silk Road, shaping the images of a generation.

In the morning, we visited **Emin Minaret,** a mile east of the city, the prettiest tower on the Silk Road. It's open daily dawn to dusk; admission is RMB 20 ($2.50). Also called Sugong Tower, the minaret was built of blue brick and completed in 1778. The bricks of the circular, smoothly tapered tower are laid in various patterns: waves, pyramids, and flower petals. The architect was a Uighur named Ibrahim. Attached to the 144-foot minaret is a white stone mosque, the largest in the region. Its interior is plain. The roof is of woven mats. The floor is covered in prayer rugs. The Iman's seat is a humble, straw-woven chair.

The Emin Minaret is surrounded by grape arbors. Grape vines came into China on the Silk Road 2,000 years ago and residents of Turpan planted them immediately. At the western base of the Flaming Mountains, there's an entire valley called Grape Gorge (Putao Guo), a park of vineyards and fruit groves with trellised walkways and courtyard picnic tables. The grapes are dried in hundreds of ingenious outbuildings ventilated by the open brickwork of their walls, creating the sweet raisins for which Turpan is renowned.

The *sine qua non* for grapes—for all of life along the Silk Road—is water. Turpan's source is locked up in the snows and glaciers of the Heavenly Mountains to the south. For the last 20 centuries the mountain waters have reached Turpan through a massive underground network of tunnels, an irrigation system known as the **karez.** Wells are dug to tap the subterranean streams that originate at the foot of the mountain. Tunnels are hollowed out and elevated so that gravity pushes the well water across the desert to the canals of Turpan. More than 1,000 miles of tunnels have been dug under the desert floor at Turpan, some stretching as far as 25 miles. The karez system suffers from continual clogging. To maintain it, a man must frequently be lowered down a shaft into a tunnel. By the use of pulleys, his horse hauls up buckets of mud tethered to a rope until the passage is clear.

One karez well site has opened at an exhibition center in Turpan, complete with a museum (admission RMB 15/$1.90) offering displays and pictures. Visitors descend into several hand-dug tunnels for a look at the irrigating waters. The tunnels are spacious enough to stand up in, and they are cool, the coolest spots in town. Working in them must be like digging in a mine. The local people regard the karez wells as one of China's three greatest ancient works, the other two being the Great Wall and the Grand Canal.

Falling Down the Well

Turpan is a pleasant town to walk before the sun rises too high or after it sets. The flat roofs of the mud-brick Uighur homes are coated with grains and seeds for drying. Every backyard seems to have its clay bread-baking oven and lattice-roofed patio. In the poplar-lined streets, silk rugs hang for sale and donkey-cart taxi drivers cruise the traffic circles looking for riders. Chinese and Westerners are vastly outnumbered here. The sidewalks belong to the Uighurs and the white-capped Huis (Islamic Chinese).

Grape trellises are everywhere, sometimes shading entire city blocks. It's a good thing. The summer sun is scorching. This is *heat,* sucking every ounce of moisture to the surface of the skin like a karez well; heat that makes coffins unnecessary at funerals; an embalming heat that shrivels grapes and turns out mummies guaranteed to last a millennium, no other treatment required. My room's air conditioner was on the fritz and the temperature was pushing 106° Fahrenheit, but at least I didn't have to fear what foreign travelers reported 60 years ago. There were no large scorpions lodged under sleeping mats, hidden in shoes, or parachuting on me from the roof beams while I napped, no jumping spiders "as large as a pigeon's egg" grinding their jaws over their prey, and no 2-inch-long Turpan cockroaches with hairy feelers and red eyes.

On my last evening in Turpan I walked down to the **Turpan Guesthouse** to enjoy an evening performance of Uighur song and dance. The costumes were flashy and the master of ceremonies was proficient in the three languages Xinjiang employs: Uighur, Chinese, and English. A sheepskin tambourine, played with vigor, kept the swirling dancers on track. I walked back through the pitch dark. At the traffic circle I was in mid-sentence with Christina when I disappeared into the third-world traveler's worst nightmare: an open manhole.

This is, fortunately, not a cartoon. Rather than vanishing, my momentum tipped me forward when I stepped into open space. I fell to the pavement on one knee and an elbow, scraping my shin against the manhole rim. Only my lead foot plunged into the dark well and I pulled it out and stood up. Not such a nightmare after all. One foot hurt, my left buttock ached, I was scraped here and there, and my shoes—I hated to think what at least one of them had stepped in. Nevertheless I could walk, as I must. I was barely halfway across the Silk Road.

PRACTICAL INFORMATION

ORIENTATION & WHEN TO GO

Turpan (called Tulufan by the Chinese) is a desert oasis on the northern Silk Road in central Xinjiang Uighur Autonomous Region, 1,900 miles west of Beijing. It is located in the **Tarim Basin,** 260 feet below sea level, in the "oven" of China, the hottest city in the country, where summer temperatures routinely soar well above 100° Fahrenheit. The **Heavenly Mountains (Tian Shan)** lie to the south; their glaciers and snows feed the underground streams and springs that have been tapped by the karez well system, an ancient engineering feat on a par with construction of the Great Wall and Grand Canal. Nearly 70% of the 200,000 people in Turpan county are Uighur, a Turkish minority, formerly nomadic, that originated south of Lake Baikal. Here public signs are written in Arabic first, Chinese second. Qingnian Lu is the main north–south street in town, where the hotels and cafes catering to foreign travelers are located. In late August there is a vibrant **Grape Festival.** May and October are the coolest months to visit; winters are freezing cold.

GETTING THERE

By Plane The nearest airport is at **Urumqi,** 114 miles northwest, a 4-hour journey over a paved highway by car or bus from Turpan.

By Train The nearest train station is at **Daheyan,** 35 miles north of Turpan. Eastbound, the train to Liuguan (Dunhuang) takes 13 hours (overnight), 49 hours to Xi'an, and 70 hours to Beijing. Westbound, the train to Urumqi takes 3 hours. From Turpan to the train station at Daheyan, a bus or hired car takes an hour. Make onward travel arrangements in Turpan at the Oasis Hotel (see "Where to Stay," below).

GETTING AROUND

Downtown Turpan is small, quiet, and shaded by poplar trees and grape trellises. Donkey carts are the main form of transportation, and many of them offer 1-hour trips to the tourist sites for RMB 24 to RMB 40 ($3 to $5). Bicycles can be rented at hotels and cafes for RMB 20 to RMB 30 ($2.40 to $3.60) per day.

TOURS & STRATAGEMS

This was my third stop on an 8-day independent tour of the Silk Road booked through China Travel Service (CTS) in Xi'an (see introduction to this section for details). **China International Travel Service (CITS)** in Turpan is located in the Oasis Hotel, 41 Qingnian Lu (☎ 0995/852-1352 or 852/2907). CITS can provide guided tours of Turpan, train tickets (with transfers to the Daheyan train station), and plane tickets (for flights from Urumqi).

WHERE TO STAY

Oasis Hotel (Liuzhou Binguan). *41 Qingnian Lu. ☎ 0995/852-2478. Fax 0995/852-3348. A/C TV TEL. $50 double. No credit cards.* This two-star, six-floor hotel is as good as it gets in Turpan, so there's no reason to look further. The rooms are modern and large but shabby—the wall-to-wall carpets are a hazard, as they've never been attached to the floor. The elevators work most of the time, as does the air-conditioning. The lobby has a tour desk run by the local CITS. There's also a gift shop, post office, beauty shop, and bicycle rental.

WHERE TO DINE

The **Turpan Guesthouse (Tulufan Binguan)** (☎ 0995/852-2301), 3 blocks south of the Oasis Hotel at 2 Qingnian Lu, has an outdoor cafe in the back with an English-language menu, Chinese and Uighur foods, and cold beer. The **Oasis Hotel** itself has several Chinese restaurants of good quality where some English is spoken. **John's Information Cafe** (☎ 0995/852-4237), across the street from the Turpan Guesthouse, offers inexpensive choices (Western and Chinese) and an English menu; it is open all day and well into the night, with Internet hook-ups available. John's also has branches in Kashgar and Urumqi, with their own in-house travel agencies catering to independent foreign travelers.

URUMQI: THE LAKE OF HEAVEN

乌鲁木齐

NO CITY IN THE WORLD IS MORE distant from the sea than Urumqi, which lies 1,397 miles away from the nearest ocean. The city's name means "beautiful pastures" in Mongolian, but Urumqi, capital of the Xinjiang Uighur Autonomous Region, is a modern industrial metropolis with a population of 1½ million, and all its beautiful meadows lie well outside the city limits.

Urumqi is the most Chinese of the Silk Road cities. Nearly 80% of its residents are Han Chinese, recent "economic immigrants" who were induced to move west, attracted by the higher wages and better opportunities available on the frontier. The Uighurs, the nomadic Kazakhs, and other minorities dominate the surrounding lands. Muslim rebels have ruled the city at times, both before and after Urumqi was declared the capital of China's Western Territories (Xinjiang) in 1884. At the beginning of the 20th century, the city maintained separate Muslim, Chinese, and Russian quarters. The influence of the three groups remains strong today, but the Han Chinese are firmly in control of Urumqi's administration and factories.

The overriding truth about Urumqi, however, is that it is an ugly industrial monster set in one of the least appealing spots on the Silk Road—little more than a slag heap on which to heap more slag. On the other hand, the new Chinese workers and investors are planting greenways and replacing slums, making Urumqi the most modern city on the old Silk Road, a new crossroads for traders from China, Russia, and Central Asia. For travelers, the chief attraction of Urumqi is not trade or industry, of course, but the "beautiful pastures" hinted at in Urumqi's name, and those places are within reach. In the southern pastures of the Heavenly Mountains and at Heavenly Lake, where the Kazakhs roam on horseback, the alpine beauty of the Silk Road is at its grandest.

The Road to Urumqi

The highway northwest from Turpan to Urumqi has no center line and it is under constant repair. The land is flat, bordered on the north by the Heavenly Mountains (Tian Shan) and dotted by shrub brush and oil rigs. It took us 4 hours to drive 114 miles. We passed a new wind farm, the propellers still in a light breeze. At the town of **Dabancheng,** the second largest salt lake in China lies in a basin, its shores ringed by a scum of salt like a dirty bathtub. The road winds up out of the Turpan Depression and crosses a blackened plain into Urumqi at 3,000 feet altitude.

Downtown Urumqi's avenues are tree-lined. Modern construction is underway everywhere. There also are Russian-style buildings left over from the 1950s, their iron roofs painted green and their bright porticoes giving the gray cityscape a splash of color, and there are over a hundred mosques, many of them new. Covered Uighur markets throughout the city also break the monotony of modern industrialization.

A touch of Old China is supplied by two parks on the banks of the Urumqi River, which flows along the western edge of the city. In **Hong Shan Park** (admission RMB 20/$2.50), the nine-story Zhenglong Pagoda ("Pagoda to Suppress Dragons") atop Red Hill (Hong Shan) towers over Urumqi. It was erected on the "dragon's head" in 1788 to prevent floods, and the hills became a Buddhist center until warlords burned down the pavilions and temples. The Qing armies pastured their horses on Red Hill a century ago. Nearby **People's Park,** on the west bank of the river, has a lake and hall modeled after the Forbidden City in Beijing, both built in the early 20th century by one of the ruling warlords. This park is popular with locals, particularly on Sunday.

We stopped for lunch at a downtown hotel, the **Liuguan.** The lobby was chock-full of businessmen from nearby countries: Russia, Pakistan, India, and Mongolia. Rail links to Kazakhstan have brought a steady stream of traders from Central Asia and beyond into Urumqi since 1992. The Russian presence is strong. Next door to the hotel there is a busy Aeroflot office. More than any other city on the Silk Road, Urumqi has reverted to its glorious past: It is a major crossroads for East–West trade.

Southern Pastures

Every spring and summer, the Kazakhs ride into the **White Poplar Valley** and up into the **Southern Mountains (Nan Shan),** an extension of the Heavenly Mountains. They pack up their families and their tents, called yurts, and make the move on horseback. The attraction is the pastures, where they graze their sheep herds. Farther up the mountain is a 65-foot waterfall.

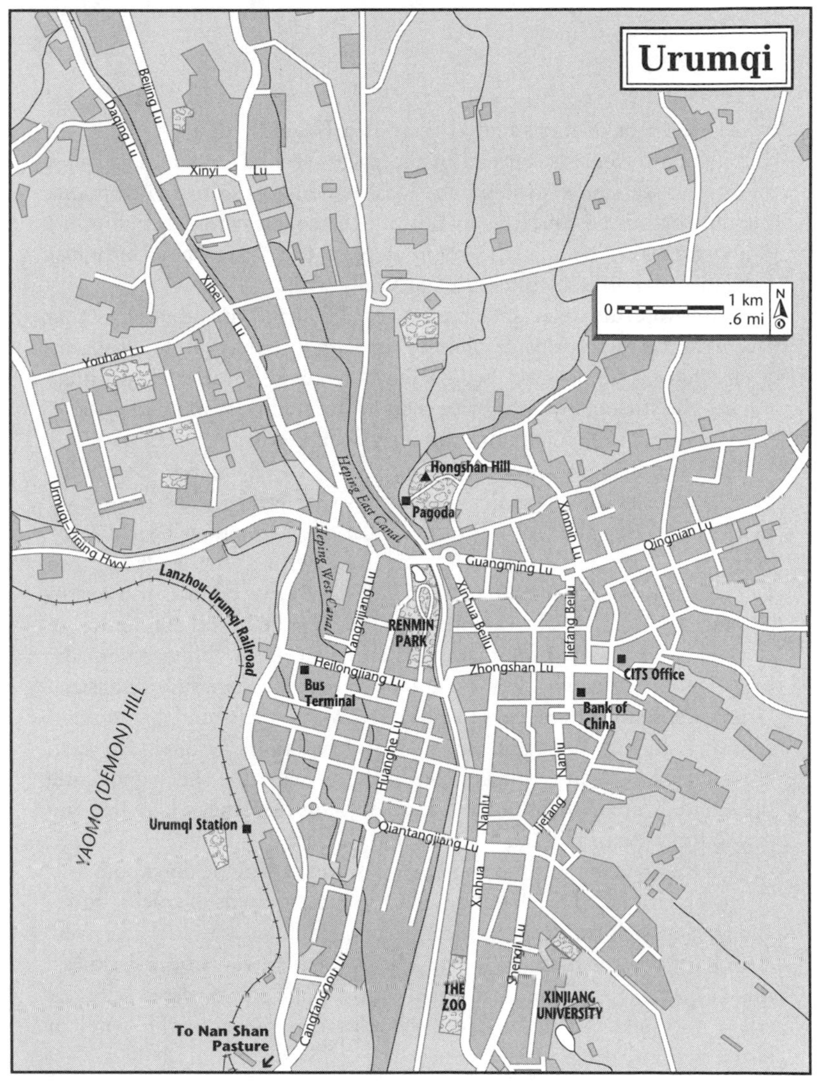

The highway winds up the valley 46 miles south from Urumqi. It is a relief to leave the city. The suburbs are filled with shacks and small mosques. Huis (Chinese Muslims), Uighurs, and Kazakhs wander through the unpaved lanes, donkey carts in tow. On the southern outskirts of Urumqi is the largest chemical factory I have seen in China. Smoke blots the landscape for miles. But the southern meadows are another world entirely. The mountain peaks are steep and green with tall spruces and pines. The river is clear and swift, tumbling by remote mud huts on the hillsides. We slowed for sheep in the road, lovely sheep, black, brown, and white.

At the foot of the waterfall there is a **Kazakh village** of huts and yurts, open to tourists. Several of the yurts serve as cafes and souvenir shops. One vendor tried to sell me local handicrafts from a yurt, pointing out that his brother lives in Boston. In the late summer, traditional riding games are held on the grassy steppes. Girls court boys in horseback races. Those they catch they playfully whip.

The **waterfall** is at an elevation of 7,000 feet in mountains that resemble the Swiss Alps. It plunges through a narrow chute, dropping 90 feet into a stony streambed. A rainbow-colored steel arched bridge crosses the stream, but otherwise there is little mark of modernity here. Kazakhs search the mountainsides for ginseng roots.

The Kazakhs—known as the Cossacks by the Russians—descended from the Turkic-speaking Wusun nomads who were pushed southward by the Huns into the foothills of the Heavenly Mountains nearly 2,000 years ago. Excellent horsemen, they rode with Genghis Khan and Kublai Khan as the Yuan Dynasty (1271–1368) swept north and east to conquer China. In 1958, the Chinese established pastoral communes in this region of Xinjiang, but many Kazakhs continue to follow a nomadic life in the grasslands and mountain valleys surrounding industrial Urumqi, sustained these days by revenues from tourism and government subsidies. In July, they gather for a 6-day **nadam,** a summer fair with horse racing, wrestling, and competitions involving the sheep and cattle they herd. More than a million Kazakhs live in Xinjiang, where they are now outnumbered by Han Chinese and Uighurs.

By the time we left the southern pastures, a violent downpour was cleansing Urumqi. The cloudburst had halted hundreds of trucks, buses, and taxis in their tracks, particularly at flooded intersections. The drivers abandoned their vehicles in the middle of the highway. In the darkness, there were no lights to mark the breakdowns. The police passed by, powerless it seems. We ran a dark, wet obstacle course to the hotel in Urumqi from where even the nearby pagoda on Red Hill had been snuffed out by spring rains.

Heavenly Lake

East of Urumqi, on the way to Heavenly Lake, two wild camels loitered on the roadside. We pulled off and they scattered. Later, rising into the foothills of the Heavenly Mountains, I saw another camel munching on tree leaves. We entered valleys where sheep and goats blocked the road, where village huts are sometimes made of stone—round huts in the shape of yurts. Horsemen ride across the hilltops. The countryside belongs to the Kazakh herdsmen.

The road, which did not exist until 1958, winds up the **Stone Gorge (Shi Xia),** a hillside of white boulders, to a broad, green embankment a quarter of a mile wide. At the end of the embankment, high up under snowy peaks, 75 miles from Urumqi and at twice its elevation, Heavenly Lake (Tian Chi) is encased like an Alpine jewel. My first glimpse of it was magnificent. No mountain lake is prettier. It reminded me of Canada's Lake Louise, but Heavenly Lake is surrounded by horse trails and yurts. It is 2 miles long, a mile wide, 300 feet deep. Sheep graze on its rocky banks. Tied to a wharf on a green lip of the lake are covered launches and small speedboats for tourists. Several white ponies stand on the shore, their Kazakh masters ready with traditional costumes—red jackets, white lace robes, gold-trimmed caps—to outfit visitors who want a picture taken on horseback, the divine lake and mountains as a backdrop. In the parking lot, a family was pitching a large yurt, swiftly erecting the wooden accordion that is its skeleton.

According to one legend, 3,000 years ago Han Emperor Wudi was invited by Xi Wang Mu, the immortal Queen Mother of the West, to a banquet at Heavenly Lake. The peach tree of immortality was served. The emperor saved the pits to plant, but Xi Wang Mu told him the soil of China could not sustain them, that fruit appeared but once every 3,000 years.

There are two smaller pools east and west of Heavenly Lake, where Xi Wang Mu washed her feet. She bathed her face in the big lake, which mirrors the solid blue sky and steep mountain peaks that frame it. The two small pools were nearly dry when I visited in the spring. They are located on steep ledges. Christina, my guide, told me that last year one of her colleagues ventured off the path, slipped, and fell to her death beside one pool. Her body had not yet been found. She told me another local legend: Heavenly Lake was created from the tears Xi Wang Mu shed when her lover departed for the East.

It is possible to hike around the lake and into the mountains. **Bogda Peak** is the highest mountain, at 17,864 feet, 11,000 feet above Heavenly Lake. Kazakhs hire out their horses for mountain treks and act as guides; the cost is RMB 100 ($12.50) for an 8-hour tour. Higher up where the snows remain even through summer, there are yurts that take in travelers. I would have loved to make such a trek, but my time was spoken for.

I contented myself with a walk up into a nearby pasture, where a dozen yurts were pitched. A Kazakh woman bid me inside. The inside of her yurt was dazzling. The floor was covered in carpets, woven with wools dyed vibrant blues, reds, and greens. The felt walls were hung with rich embroideries and quilts. A baby was sleeping on a quilt on the floor, mindless of foreign intruders. Children here are named on the second day after birth. The mother leaves the tent and fixes on the first thing that comes into her mind. That becomes her child's name. The mother told me I could stay the night if I wished, but I had to decline. She offered me a chunk of thick baked bread, known as *nan*, which I saw diligently through, washing it down with Kazakh tea, a brew of mare's milk and the snow lotus that grows in the dragon spruce forests of Heavenly Lake. If I could stay anywhere on the Silk Road it would be here, in the high mountains beside a blue sapphire lake, in the carpeted tents of nomads who roll up their homes as the seasons change and ride across these stream-fed pastures.

PRACTICAL INFORMATION

ORIENTATION & WHEN TO GO

Urumqi, which the Chinese call Wulumuqi, is the capital of Xinjiang Uighur Autonomous Region, China's northwesternmost province. It is 2,050 miles from Beijing, just north of the most northern route of the ancient Silk Road. The city is large and highly industrialized. The majority of the residents are Han Chinese who come from other parts of China. Uighurs (30%) and Kazakhs (10%) make up the city's largest minorities. Russian businessmen constitute the most noticeable group of visitors. Urumqi is the largest city in Xinjiang and the most modern, although compared to China's other large cities it is a rugged frontier outpost. Winters are extremely cold. April and October are the most pleasant months to visit, although industrial pollution and dust storms are constant threats.

GETTING THERE

By Plane **Urumqi's airport,** 10 miles from city center, has international connections to Moscow, Karachi, Islamabad, and Tashkent. Over 30 cities in China are served, including Hong Kong (5 hours), Shanghai (4½ hours), Beijing (3½ hours), Xi'an (3 hours 45 minutes), and Kashgar (1 hour 20 minutes). Taxis charge about RMB 100 ($12.50) for the 30-minute airport transfer.

By Train The express train from Beijing requires 64 hours, the longest ride in China. The daily express to Xi'an is nearly as grueling: 50 hours. Trains to other places on the Silk Road are shorter: 3 hours to Daheyan (Turpan), 18 hours to Liuyuan (Dunhuang), and 24 hours to Jiayuguan. There is no train yet to Kashgar, the last stop in China on the Silk Road, but a new line there should be opening soon. As it stands now, the bus takes 3 days, making an air flight to Kashgar almost mandatory.

TOURS & STRATAGEMS

This was my fourth stop on an 8-day independent tour of the Silk Road booked through **China Travel Service (CTS)** in Xi'an (see introduction to this section for details).

China International Travel Service (CITS) in Urumqi is located at 51 Xinhua Bei Lu, south of the Holiday Inn in the Luyou Hotel (☎ 0991/282-5794; fax 0991/281-0689). The best places to book air tickets and to set up city tours and trips to the Southern Pastures (Nan Shan) and Heavenly Lake are the travel desk in the **Holiday Inn Urumqi,** 168 Xinhua Bei Lu (☎ 0991/281-8788), and **John's Information Café** on Guangming Lu, between Hong Shan Park and People's Park (☎ 0991/231-0191).

WHERE TO STAY

Hoi Tak Hotel (Hoi Tak Binguan). *1 Dong Feng Lu. ☎ 0991/232-2828. Fax 0991/232-1818. 318 units. A/C MINIBAR TV TEL. $115 double. AE, DC, JCB, MC, V.* Urumqi's first five-star hotel, this 32-story silver and green tower has all the services and luxuries, but not the international experience, of the Holiday Inn. There's a Muslim restaurant, the Village Inn Chinese Restaurant, a Western dining room, a coffee shop, and a food court for snacks. The clean rooms have views either of the city or the Tian Shan mountain range.

Amenities: Indoor swimming pool, health club, Jacuzzi, sauna, snooker, eight-lane bowling alley, business center, 24-hour room service, same-day dry cleaning and laundry, tour desk.

Holiday Inn Urumqi (Xinjiang Jiari Dajiudian). *168 Xinhua Bei Lu. ☎ 800/465-4329 or 0991/281-8788. Fax 0991/281-7422. 383 units, including 22 suites. A/C MINIBAR TV TEL. $125 double. AE, DC, JCB, MC, V.* This 24-story four-star international hotel is legendary in China, one of the most remote Holiday Inns in the world, but with all the luxuries—and good service to boot. No other hotel in Urumqi comes close. The rooms and bathrooms are clean. There are executive floors, no-smoking floors, and handicapped-accessible rooms, as well as a disco, a deli, and a 24-hour Western restaurant.

Amenities: Health club, Jacuzzi, sauna, tennis courts, snooker, business center, 24-hour room service, same-day dry cleaning and laundry, tour desk, beauty salon, shopping arcade, free airport shuttle.

Hongshan Hotel (Hongshan Binguan). *108 Xinhua Bei Lu. ☎ 0991/282-4973. 204 units. $30 double. No credit cards.* The choice of backpackers and independent budget travelers, the Hongshan offers run-down, no-frills doubles and cheap dormitory rooms with communal showers. The location is good (a block from the Holiday Inn) and there are travel agents and freelance tour guides in abundance.

WHERE TO DINE

Downtown hotels and cafes near the Holiday Inn serve Uighur dishes, such as noodles *(lamian)*, flat breads *(nan)*, and mutton shish kabob, but a local guide is necessary to interpret the menu and negotiate prices.

Two of the city's best restaurants are in the Holiday Inn itself. Also, **John's Information Café** (☎ 0991/231-0191), across the intersection from the Hongshan Hotel (2 blocks north of Holiday Inn toward the Red Hill Pagoda on Xinhua Lu), caters to foreign backpackers with inexpensive Western dishes and Chinese food.

Caravan. *168 Xinhua Bei Lu (ground floor, Holiday Inn). ☎ 0991/281-8788. Main courses $5–$12. AE, DC, JCB, MC, V. Daily 24 hours. WESTERN/CHINESE.* This place serves the best Western food in town. Breakfast buffets are RMB 100 ($12). Buffets are provided at lunch (noon to 3pm) and dinner (7 to 11pm) as well.

Kashgari's. *168 Xinhua Bei Lu (ground floor, Holiday Inn). ☎ 0991/281-8788. Reservations recommended. Main courses $7–$18. AE, DC, JCB, MC, V. Daily 12:30–3:15pm and 7–10:30pm (closed for lunch on Sun). MUSLIM.* Uighur, Kazakh, and Muslim specialties are served here in an elegant atmosphere. Three private function rooms can be reserved for Muslim banquets.

KASHGAR: THE GATE TO CENTRAL ASIA

喀什

THE OASIS OF KASHGAR IS LOCATED at a great junction in the Silk Road. Heading east, traders swapped horses and yaks for camels to cross the vast deserts of China. Heading west, they readied their pack animals to brave the high mountain passes into Central Asia. From Kashgar, the camel caravans trekked eastward from oasis to oasis to reach the ancient capital of China, while teams of packhorses trudged westward through India and Persia to Rome. Marco Polo heralded Kashgar in the 13th century as the "starting point from which many merchants set out to market their wares to the world."

The westernmost city in China, Kashgar is the place no one traveling the Silk Road today should miss, if only to see its Sunday market, said by some to be the largest on Earth. The oasis is overwhelmingly Islamic. More than 90% of its residents are Uighurs. The streets are crammed with mud-brick houses, sidewalk bazaars, and mosques. There are more horse carts than cars. Chairman Mao's statue presides over People's Park, but Kashgar is a city from another time and place, a medieval village where women shop the streets covered in long brown veils.

Kashgar first came under Chinese sovereignty during the Han Dynasty in the 1st century A.D. Under Tang rule, Chinese troops fortified the oasis, but Tibetans and later Turkish tribes often held sway. Kashgar was just too remote for China to hold tightly. From the 16th through the 19th centuries, various Islamic leaders ruled the Kashgari kingdom, with the Chinese mounting periodic assaults to regain control over the region. In the 1930s, an Islamic movement based in Kashgar declared the formation of the Republic of Eastern Turkestan, but the city fell again to the Chinese (assisted by Russian troops from Urumqi) in 1933. It was not until the Communists established the People's Republic of China in 1949 that Kashgar came firmly into Chinese hands. Before that, Kashgar was a pawn in the "Great Game" played by other major powers in the region, including Britain, which maintained a consulate there, and Russia, whose embassy, opened in 1882, is now the Seman Hotel—where I, like many a modern traveler, began my stay in Kashgar.

Abakh Hoja Tomb

A dust storm was whipping across the airstrip at Kashgar as my flight from Urumqi neared. My plane was an old Russian prop jet, owned by Air Volga, with a small notice on the fuselage stating that it had been rented by Xinjiang Air. The cabin was like the inside of a ruined bus. The seats were the most uncomfortable in the sky, but the bag of green raisins handed out for a snack was delicious. The dust thickened as we descended over Kashgar. The plane hit the ground sharply.

I was the first to complete the walk across the tarmac to the waiting lounge. The Japanese tourists lingered, snapping photos of each other disembarking through the blowing dust. Sadik, a local guide, met me. At the Seman Hotel, the century-old former Russian compound, I was also met by dancing girls in Uighur gowns and a band of horns and pipes. The doorman handed me a steaming face towel. It was the most gracious entrance I'd made in China—if this was China. It looked more like eastern Turkey, and I'd yet to see a single Chinese face.

The first place on the tourist route was the holiest site in the entire province of Xinjiang, the Abakh Hoja Tomb, in the northeast suburbs of the oasis. This is more than just a tomb: It is a monumental hall, finished in 1640, with a large dome of dazzling glazed green tiles. The **Tomb Hall** reminded me of a small Taj Mahal. Inside, the entire tiled floor is covered in 58 rounded sarcophagi, also beautifully tiled, which contain the remains of five generations of the Islamic prophet and Kashgar ruler Abakh Hoja, who died in 1639. Two of the tombs under the domed ceiling are draped in green: that of Abakh Hoja and the one reputed to contain the remains of his granddaughter, Iparhan, who is known to Chinese history as Xiang Fei, the Fragrant Concubine.

Xiang Fei was captured by the Qing army in the mid-18th century and sent from Kashgar all the way across China to the Forbidden City in Beijing. There she was presented to Emperor Qianlong. For the next 25 years, she lived in the capital, serving the emperor as his "Fragrant Concubine"; it was said that her natural scent was as sweet as the bloom of a flower. She wept for her desert home and rejected the emperor's advances. Obsessed with winning her affections, he built her a Turkish bath and a tower turned toward Kashgar, but she did not give in. Finally, the emperor's mother, fearing that the Fragrant Concubine

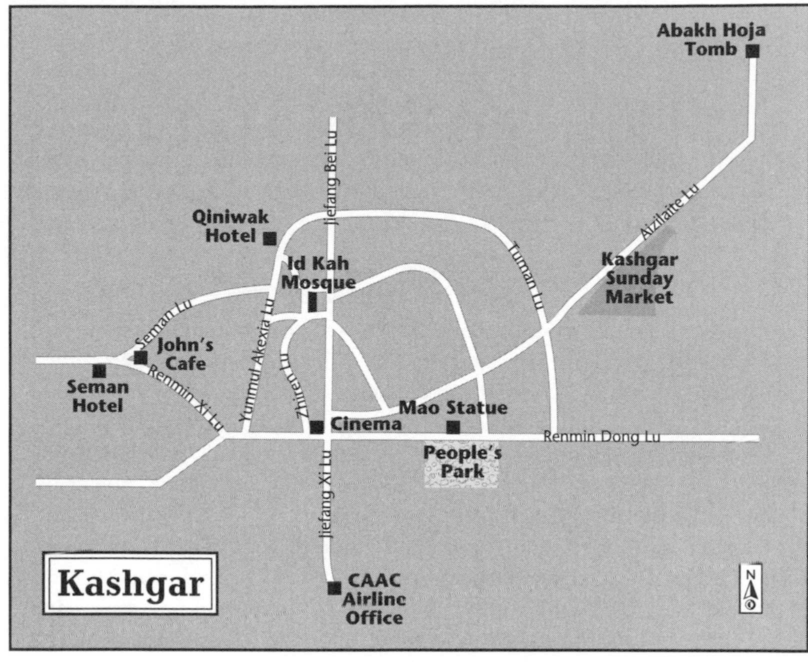

would murder her son or become the rallying point for a palace coup, ordered Xiang Fei to kill herself with her own bare hands in 1761. The coffin of the Fragrant Concubine was wheeled back to Kashgar, in a journey that consumed 3 years.

The story of the Fragrant Concubine is perhaps more fiction than fact, but Chinese and Uighur alike insist on its veracity. The cart that supposedly carried her back over the Silk Road stands near the railing inside the Tomb Hall, although it is clearly too new and too undamaged to be anything but a reproduction. I have read reports that the Fragrant Concubine's remains have been removed to Hebei Province, but of course here is the proper location for her tomb, the perfect ending to her story.

To the right of the Tomb Hall there is a large walled graveyard with thousands more of the coffin-shaped tombs. These are not tiled; they are the color of sand. Some are pierced so that the soul can escape to travel. A **Teaching Hall** and a **Prayer Hall** are also open to view at Abakh Hoja.

The grounds of the complex are entered through a magnificent turreted square gate three stories tall, faced in swirling blue tiles. Abakh Hoja Tomb is open daily from 8am to 5:30pm; admission is RMB 10 ($1.20). There's also a new RMB 2 (25¢) surcharge for those wishing to take pictures. As we explored the area, my guide just shook his head. He was quite upset. The government was nearing the end of a 3-year project to restore and replace the tilework on the main Tomb Hall and he said they were going about it all wrong. They should have left it alone, he felt, expressing the common feeling here among the Uighur majority that the Chinese Han administrators don't have the slightest idea how to run things.

Sunday Market

Every cart and camel on the Silk Road seems to pour into Kashgar on Sunday for one of the largest open-air markets in Asia. It's open daily, but Sundays it is in full swing and the horse traders come into town. The Uighurs call it the **Yekshenba Bazaar (Sunday Bazaar),** and the Chinese, although not many are in attendance, call it Zhongxiya Shichang (Western Central Asia Market). By any name, it has no equal in China. By dawn, the donkey carts start arriving from the desert and the mountains, converging on Aizilaiti Lu on the east side of the Tuman River. The larger carts and trucks carry upward of 20 people standing on their belongings. Herds of sheep, goats, cows, and horses make their way through the city to separate trading compounds. The market radiates out for a dozen blocks and is packed with Muslim farmers, merchants, and traders, as well as whatever foreign tourists and business travelers happen to be in town. The crowds are immense. I've seen estimates ranging from 50,000 to 150,000 people, all converging at the Sunday Bazaar.

I entered the market from the east, shouldering my way past the carts and animals, past large lumberyards and lovely Uighur homes with ornate columned balconies and shuttered windows lining the upper floors. Sidewalk merchants line the highway for a half mile down to the river. There are straw mats unrolled on the dusty shoulder of the street next to tables of pots and pans pounded out of sheet metal and tin. There are knives and jeweled scimitars, high sheepskin boots and long scarves, and table after table of fresh oasis melons and bagel-shaped breads. There are woven carpets, embroideries, tapestries, and clothing such as the people themselves wear: hats, scarves, veils, jackets, coats, dresses, all dyed in rainbow colors in an endless arabesque of geometric and floral patterns. Several roadside alcoves are filled with hundreds of straw brooms, hand-woven and tied. There are shoemakers stitching without machines, and barbers in belted black tunics and black wool caps trimmed in white fur at work in the shade of white umbrellas, their customers bolt-upright on plain wooden chairs waiting nervously for a close shave.

In the formal market grounds by the river, corrals hold livestock. Sheep, horses, cattle, and donkeys have their own yards. Within each arena, families or clans rope off their animals from those of competitors.

Animals and people crowd together, bartering and jostling and braying and neighing, while on the periphery of these delightfully pungent pens vendors serve up hot noodles, flat breads, goat soups, milky teas, jars of yogurt, and ice cream. The ice cream is served on sticks or in bowls, kept chilled by enormous blocks of ice wrapped in cloth and delivered by pushcarts to the stands.

Surrounding the animal yards are awnings, tents, and long alleyway arcades. Wooden baby cradles with lathe-turned fences, the knobs painted glossy reds, greens, and blacks, occupy one cobblestoned lane. Down another, red-draped stalls sell bolts of dyed silk and cotton. Another arcade sells nothing but hats—the hats of all the tribes of the Silk Road, cotton and fur, peaked and flat, white and sequined.

On the fringes of the market there are streets devoted to vegetables, hauled in from the farms in gunny sacks; to debarked, unmilled shanks of lumber, shining white; to saddles, bridles, and harnesses; to sheepskins and felt carpets draped over donkey carts; to baskets woven from red twigs; to songbirds in cages. In the shadow of a new gallery of empty shops built by the Han Chinese government—which the Uighur merchants have shunned since the day it opened—there is a street of used clothing, of worn shoes and patched coats, of discards that belong in the dump. There is also a square where dogfights were once held and where occasional cockfights still break out when officials are looking the other way.

This market has met in Kashgar for 1,500 years. Walking the streets, squares, and alley arcades, I constantly brushed up against donkeys, sheep, horses, and wooden carts. The sun through the dust gives the market an ancient patina. There are con men squatting low, playing a shell game. There are old men in black, experts in horseflesh, puffing on long, thin pipes. Across the river, above the market swirl, I could see the old town of Kashgar on a hillside, its square huts and houses packed together like crates, a city of unpainted mud and brick, the single color of desert sand, with no hint of the modern world east of the desert or west of the mountain snows.

The Largest Mosque in China

The busiest, and some say the biggest, mosque in China, **Id Kah Mosque,** occupies the central square of Kashgar, where it has stood since 1442. On Friday afternoon, upwards of 20,000 men pack the courtyards and prayer hall inside. My guide, Sadik, took me in on a Sunday. The grounds were filled with worshippers even then, old men and young dressed in long, striped cotton coats (chapans) and high leather boots. The prayer hall, holding up to 5,000, is plainly decorated, with 140 carved wooden columns. The carpets on the floor are a gift from Iran. The Iman leads prayers from a simple chair and microphone. Sadik told me there is a mosque for every 20 households in Kashgar, but Id Kah is the grandest. The women and children wait outside the large rectangular yellow-tiled gate with its massive blue doors. Two tall minarets, banded in decorative blue and red tiles, flank the wide facade, shielding the large dome of the prayer hall inside.

The streets running east and west from the mosque constitute a permanent bazaar that is in some ways more interesting than the Sunday Market. Shops on Zhiren Street (to the west) specialize in a variety of goods: skull caps, fur-trimmed hats, prayer caps, and even the simple Mao caps once favored by Chinese workers; large tin dowry chests, ornately decorated; pots and pans hammered into shape on the street in front of tiny factories. There are even musical instrument shops with miniature two- and five-stringed Uighur guitars (*dutahs* and *rawupus*) hanging above the counters. These small instruments (built of inlaid woods, including apricot) are for decoration, but behind the counter there is often a musician playing the real thing.

Most fascinating are the narrow **jewelry shops.** Gold is the metal of choice in Kashgar. I was told that you can buy an ounce for less than $15 here. I was also surprised to find that many of the jewelers are children. They work at benches inside on raised platforms behind the display counters, shaping gold into pendants, pins, rings, and necklaces.

East of Id Kah Mosque are streets devoted to the sale of **carpets:** felts of rolled wool, rough hand-tied carpets with dyed geometric designs, and sometimes Kashgar kilims, the handiwork of nomads. Many of the carpet outlets are located inside wooden-shuttered shophouses, their front courtyards shaded by second-story balconies supported by finely turned pillars.

South of the mosque, on Jiefang Bei Lu, there are larger stores and offices, but even here the street looks more like those of Islamabad than Beijing. On the corner of Jiefang and Renmin streets, a former cinema, built in 1954, its second-floor shuttered windows and small balconies typical of Uighur architecture, has a Chinese red star emblazoned on its peak. East down Renmin Dong Lu is Kashgar's **People's Park,** a fixture in every Chinese city. A 59-foot bone-white statue of Chairman Mao looking south faces the park, which is little more than an open, scrubby field. Elsewhere in China, such statues have often come down during the years of economic reform, but I have a feeling Mao is here to stay in Kashgar, where the Uighurs feel very much under the thumb of the Han Chinese.

I waited for dusk to fall over Kashgar at an outdoor table under a large canvas awning at **John's Information Café,** a favorite hangout of foreign backpackers. The cafe is situated a short walk from the compounds of the former British and Russian consulates, now the main hotels of Kashgar. Fierce winds began to shake the awning, and desert sands swept across the city. Uighur women drew their brown veils tight around the necks and hastened home from the bazaars. John's Café advertises itself in a sign in English reading A LITTLE BIT OF HOME, but it's difficult to imagine being farther from home than Kashgar, sipping a soda at the end of the Silk Road.

PRACTICAL INFORMATION

ORIENTATION & WHEN TO GO

Kashgar, with a population of 120,000, is an oasis in far western Xinjiang Province, more than 2,400 miles inland from Beijing. The vast **Taklamakan Desert** stretches eastward into China and the snowcapped Pamir Mountains form a wall to the west. The **Karakoram Highway** leads to Pakistan (300 miles), and there are long, difficult overland routes to India and Tibet. Urumqi is over 600 miles to the northeast. April and October are the most pleasant months to visit, although the middle of summer, when it becomes increasingly hot, is high tourist season.

GETTING THERE

A train line connecting remote Kashgar to Urumqi was to open with the new century, but has been delayed.

By Plane Currently the only efficient medium of travel is by air, on the once-daily flights between Kashgar and Urumqi (1½ hours). This flight can be canceled by sandstorms. The airport is just 7 miles from city center, but taxi drivers often ask foreigners to pay RMB 100 ($12) for the transfer. There is also an airport bus (RMB 5/60¢) that makes the run between the airport and the CAAC airline station (☎ 0998/22-2113) downtown on Jiefang Nan Lu (3 blocks south of the main downtown intersection of Jiefang and Renmin streets).

By Bus Buses take 3 days to make the journey from Urumqi, although there is one 36-hour sleeper bus on this route.

TOURS & STRATAGEMS

This was my fifth and final stop on an 8-day independent tour of the Silk Road. See the introduction to this section for more information.

Kashgar, like all the cities of China, is officially on Beijing time, despite the fact that it should be several time zones west of the capital. Local Kashgar time is 2 hours earlier. Thus, don't expect anything to open until about 10:30am. Breakfast usually begins at about 9:30am, lunch at 1:30pm, and dinner at 7:30pm.

Dress in a manner appropriate to a Muslim society. That is, cover the body—no shorts, tank tops, and other fashions that might be considered immodest. Arms and legs should be fully covered when entering mosques, with shoes removed when entering prayer halls.

Tours **China International Travel Service (CITS)** in Kashgar is located at the Qiniwak Hotel, 93 Seman Lu (☎ 0998/282-3156; fax 0998/282-3087). It's open 10am to 1:30pm and 3:30 to 7:30pm, and has English-speaking guides for hire. More helpful is the tour desk at the **Seman Hotel,** 170 Seman Lu (☎ 0998/282-2129), located in the old no. 2 building, which arranges 1- and 2-day city tours, as well as longer excursions into the desert and the mountains. It also books air tickets to Urumqi. **John's Information Café** near the Seman Hotel (☎ 0998/255-1186) offers comprehensive English-language tours and ticket-booking services.

WHERE TO STAY

The two main hotels for foreign travelers are both adequate but not up to international standards. The Qiniwak is favored by Pakistani traders and travelers. I stayed at the Seman Hotel.

Qiniwak Hotel (Qiniwake Binguan). *93 Seman Lu (at Yunmulakexia Lu, 5 blocks northwest of Id Kah Mosque).* ☎ *0998/282-2103. Fax 0998/282-3842. 140 units. A/C TV TEL. $40 double. No credit cards.* The five-story two-star round tower, built in 1990, offers slightly more modern rooms than the Seman Hotel provides. The British Consulate (built in 1890) stands on the grounds, and it once played host to early 20th-century Silk Road adventurers and explorers, including Sir Aurel Stein, Sven Hedin, and Albert von Le Coq. If you are a member of a tour group, this is an adequate place to stay, but independent travelers, male and female, have reported instances of unwanted attention paid by persistent fellow guests.

Seman Hotel (Seman Binguan). *170 Seman Lu (1 mile west of city center).* ☎ *0998/282-2129. 212 units. A/C TV TEL. $35 double. No credit cards.* Occupying the picturesque grounds of the former Russian Embassy (built 1882), the Seman's Building 1 is more modern than Building 2 (which has cheaper dormitory-style accommodations). The service is extremely gracious and friendly. The room card proclaims that "many people have ranked it as one of the top 10 hotels in the world based on service and facilities," but this ranking must have been drawn up 100 years ago. The rooms, with gold curtains, are rundown. Unenclosed showers flood the blue-tiled bathrooms. There are a small gift shop and foreign exchange counter but no elevator. The grounds include a pleasant park and Russian outbuildings, several converted to restaurants. Building 2 contains a full-service tour desk and bicycle rentals.

WHERE TO DINE

The **Seman Hotel,** 170 Seman Lu (☎ 0998/282-2129), has the best restaurants in town. The Chinese restaurant on the second floor has set breakfasts (RMB 12/$1.50), lunches (RMB 20/$2.40), and dinners (RMB 28/$3.50). The **Uighur restaurant** in a charming building on the Seman Hotel grounds has even better meals for the same price.

John's Information Café (☎ 0998/282-4186), east of the Seman Hotel toward city center (at the intersection of Seman Lu and Xiamalibagh Lu), has Western food (pancakes, sandwiches) and Chinese dishes for under $3. Coffee, cold soda, and beer are also available, as are courtyard tables. This cafe is the favorite meeting spot of foreign independent travelers seeking to hook up with local guides and to book adventure tours and overland bus tickets.

Mountain China: Pinnacles & Sacred Peaks

THE CHINESE, PERHAPS MORE than any other people, have long been enraptured by mountain peaks. For over 2,000 years, they conducted pilgrimages to sacred summits, in particular to the Five Sacred Mountains staked out by the native Daoist priests and to the Four Famous Peaks established later by the Buddhists. People walked to the top of these great mountains by the thousands, even by the hundreds of thousands. Emperors joined them, performing imperial rites in the temples that lined the slopes. At the summits, pilgrims knelt before the high altars of the mountain gods and prayed. "Thousands of men and women who wish for a good harvest, health, heirs, or longevity ascend lofty mountains," writes an 18th-century man of letters, "climbing like monkeys and following each other like ants."

China's emperors often ascended the sacred peaks to pray for an end to a devastating drought. In the past most Chinese seemed to believe that certain mountains were divine beings with considerable powers. These peaks were treated as massive stone gods who could be swayed by sacrifice or prayer. They linked Heaven and Earth and gathered the clouds unto their heights to deliver timely rains to parched lands.

These nine sacred summits still exist in China, although the great pilgrimages came to a standstill in this century. The Sacred Five and the Famous Four once formed the cosmic compasses of Old China. Each mountain anchored one of the Four Directions—north, south, east, and west—to which the Daoists added a mountain in the center. Today, despite decades of neglect and destruction, these peaks retain dozens of venerable temples, miles of stone stairs for modern pilgrims (mostly Chinese sightseers) to ascend, and summits with the most spectacular views in the Middle Kingdom.

It is at these nine mountains that Old China still exists within New China. They have always been, for me, the most fascinating sites in the Middle Kingdom, combining history, religion, and natural grandeur. On the other hand, these remote peaks at the four corners of the Middle Kingdom are modernizing. Most have cable cars in place to take the drudgery (along with the adventure and tradition) out of mountain pilgrimage. A few have decent hotels in nearby villages. Vendors line the mountain stairs, selling snacks and plastic souvenirs. Temples are being renovated rather than razed.

Altogether, the sacred mountains, fusing past and present, present some of the most exhilarating experiences in all of China. But to make your own sightseeing pilgrimage to these peaks is still not an easy undertaking. Some require that you rough it with a long bus or train ride from a major city. The climb to the summit can be arduous, often requiring a 4- or 5-hour ascent on steep stairways and narrow paths. Accommodations and food services are often crude. Yet the undertaking produces unforgettable moments, unlike any others in China.

Mountain (Shan)	Direction	Religion	Elevation	Province
Emei Shan	West	Buddhist	10,095 ft	Sichuan
Heng Shan Bei	North	Daoist	6,617 ft	Shanxi
Heng Shan Nan	South	Daoist	4,232 ft	Hunan
Hua Shan	West	Daoist	6,552 ft	Shanxi
Jiuhua Shan	South	Buddhist	4,340 ft	Anhui
Putuo Shan	East	Buddhist	932 ft	Zhejiang
Song Shan	Center	Daoist	4,900 ft	Henan
Tai Shan	East	Daoist	5,069 ft	Shandong
Wutai Shan	North	Buddhist	10,003 ft	Shanxi

Hua Shan is the most stunning of the Nine, Tai Shan the most interesting and venerated. To these ancient peaks I have added three other spots: **Huang Shan,** simply the single most beautiful mountain in China; **Wulingyuan,** known to the Chinese as Zhangjiajie, the remote Yellowstone Park of China; and **Lu Shan,** a delightful mountain retreat, for centuries a getaway for China's rich and famous.

WHAT TO READ

Edwin Bernbaum, *Sacred Mountains of the World.* San Francisco: Sierra Club Books, 1990.

William Geil, *The Sacred 5 of China.* Boston: Houghton Mifflin, 1926.

Hedda Morrison, *Travels of a Photographer in China,* 1933–1946. Hong Kong: Oxford University Press, 1987.

Mary Augusta Mullikin and Anna M. Hotchkis, *The Nine Sacred Mountains of China: An Illustrated Record of Pilgrimages Made in the Years 1935–1936.* Hong Kong: Vetch and Lee, 1973.

Susan Naquin and Chun-fang Yu, editors, *Pilgrims and Sacred Sites in China.* Berkeley: University of California Press, 1992.

Huang Shan: The Summit of Beauty

黄山

Huang Shan (Yellow Mountain) is the supreme example of Chinese mountain scenery and prime model for classic landscape paintings, as the poets and painters of Old China amply testify. From the Tang Dynasty (618–907) to the Qing (1644–1911), Huang Shan was celebrated in no fewer than 20,000 poems. Li Bai, the Tang's great poet, compared the cluster of peaks at Huang Shan to a golden hibiscus. Twelve centuries later, the modern poet Guo Moruo echoed that sentiment, naming Huang Shan's vistas "the most spectacular under Heaven."

Skeptical of this high-flown hyperbole, I was eager to see the mountain and to draw my own comparisons. My opportunity came more by chance than design. I was descending a nearby mountain when I was befriended by four young lads from Wuhan who were on their way the very next morning for a whirlwind tour of the fabled Yellow Mountain. I couldn't help but tag along. Although I could see the Huang Shan range from where we set out at dawn, the bus required 6 bone-rattling hours to reach it. On the way, we were stopped cold by a broad placid lake, where the bus had to board a ferry.

It was just after noon by the time we reached the village of Tangkuo, at the southern tip of the park. A minibus transported us another hour up the eastern flanks of Huang Shan to Yungu Temple. From there, a cable car ferried visitors to the peak in 8 minutes (today there are two more cable cars), but my four comrades were not about to waste money on a route they could climb for free. There was plenty of time, they said, to reach the summit via the stone staircase cut into the mountain, a mere 3-hour hike—5 miles up, with a mere 20,000 stairs between us and the final peak.

Seeing Is Believing

Huang Shan, according to tradition, consists of 72 peaks. In fact, there are many more. At least 77 of these stone pillars, formed 100 million years ago, exceed 3,200 feet elevation, the base of the mountain lying at 2,000 feet. It's a fierce ascent. The highest point, Lotus Flower Peak, rises to 6,115 feet. The network of footpaths, mostly stone steps, makes a circuit exceeding 30 miles. The eastern path to the summit is 5 miles, if no detours up and down individual pinnacles are taken. The western route, by which we descended, is longer and more scenic; it runs for 9 miles, requiring 6 hours to complete.

The cable car is strung parallel to the eastern route, which rises up a deep declivity forested with granite pillars. I was exhausted after the first 20 minutes of the climb, but there was no choice but to keep walking. More than one emperor has ascended Huang Shan by this same route, albeit in the comfort of a sedan chair propelled on the shoulders of powerful runners. Such chairs are still for hire, at about $100 for the round-trip.

So far, I could see that the peaks of Huang Shan are towering and exquisite, indeed, granite rivals of the famous limestone karst pillars of Guilin, but I was like a dead man, hauling my own corpse up an endless flight of stairs. It wasn't until we were almost at the central summit, Beihai Peak, that I found a new resource of strength and began to appreciate the grandeur. We struck out on a northern detour to **Seeing Is Believing Peak (Shixin Feng).** This 5,472-foot promontory has its own wicked set of steep stairs. At the top, I was in a cluster of jagged rock spires. Mist was blowing in and out of the twisted pinnacles. At times, I had glimpses of what's below: pine forests, cascading streams, narrow gorges. There's a legend of an ancient skeptic who denied Huang Shan's unique beauty until he reached this viewpoint. I seemed to be following in his footsteps. Any doubts I had about the Yellow Mountain's claim to the most dramatic mountain scenery in China were erased here.

Seeing Is Believing Peak is connected by a bridge of stone, **Duxian Qiao,** known as the Bridge to Heaven. By the bridge stands one of Huang Shan's celebrated pines, **Duxian Song,** which appears to be bowing to welcome travelers. Many of these bare swirling granite pinnacles have a pine tree or two sprouting from their joints, pointing like green umbrellas not only vertically but horizontally into misty space. The Huangshan pine grows in poor soil and on rocky crags. Its roots secrete an acid that erodes rock, allowing roots to burrow into crevices for nutrients and moisture. The roots are often several times the length of the trunks, enabling the pines to withstand fierce mountain gales. Several of these sturdy mountain pines are believed to be over a thousand years old.

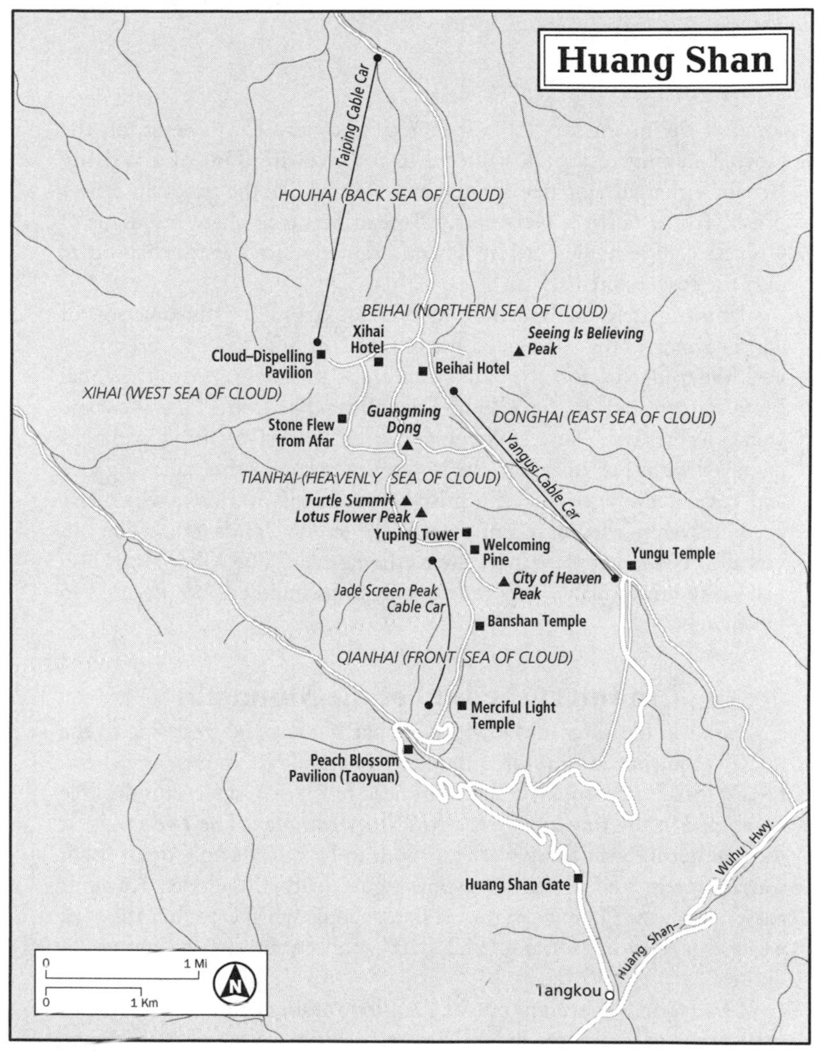

Nevertheless, on my most recent visit to Huang Shan, locals told me that one of the immortal pines capping a crag had been obliterated by a storm; it is said to have been replaced by unknown hands with a plastic stand-in.

Sea of Clouds

The twin summits, **Beihai and Xihai**—the Northern Sea of Clouds and the Western Sea of Clouds—are the prime gathering points for watching sunrise and sunset. I was hoping to stay the night at Beihai, in a modern hotel, and wake early to join the crowds at sunrise. Beihai has some of the mountain's most spectacular scenery. To the east, on the tapered summit of a peak named **Flower Growing Out of a Writing Brush,** a gnarled pine tree sprouts heavenward like the tip of an artist's brush. To the north is **Refreshing Breeze Terrace,** where hundreds of Chinese congregate just before dawn in rented quilt coats to rhapsodize over the rose-colored sky.

Unfortunately, the Beihai Hotel was booked solid with some sort of convention, and the corrugated metal Quonset huts nearby were full as well. We trudged across the cloud summit 30 minutes more to the Xihai Hotel and rested at the **Cloud-Dispelling Pavilion.** This is where young lovers also pause, following the custom of securing padlocks engraved with their initials to the iron fence to pledge their undying love and tossing the keys into the misty gorge. This overlook, which has become overcrowded in recent years, dispelled no clouds today. The sun was absorbed long before it set fire to the horizon. The Xihai Hotel also had no rooms available. My four companions huddled. We decided to move on.

An Inn at the End of the Mountain

The sun was bleeding into dusk. We tacked across the west side of the range, inquiring at several unmarked hostels. No rooms anywhere. Huang Shan was booked. Full darkness fell like a stage curtain. We encamped in the tiny lobby of a dormitory complex. The two clerks at the counter insisted there wasn't a room to be had, but plenty of other travelers were joining us. Everyone argued with the clerks. An hour passed this way. There were rooms here, people whispered, but the staff was too lazy to open them. The staff withdrew from the counter for dinner.

I waited in a courtyard outside. A group from Beijing, consisting of three German foreigners and a Chinese, joined me. One of the German women was traveling with her Chinese boyfriend, and she, speaking good Mandarin, went inside to try her luck at negotiations. "She's completely ruthless," the other Germans assured me. "Whatever it takes, even a bribe, she will get it done." One of them, Wolf, told me they had been on the road a week. Nothing quite this bad had befallen them until now, he said. He wondered how I came to be with four Chinese, who meanwhile were talking with some Huang Shan locals about renting a cottage for the night.

We joked about sleeping on the open trail tonight. About midnight there was a breakthrough. Places to sleep suddenly materialized. Two bunkhouses up the hill inexplicably opened their doors. We climbed a score of stairs in the pitch dark. Our bunkhouse contained beds for eight. There was nothing more inside, not even a basin of water. The problem was that there were already people sleeping here, and with us joining them, there weren't enough beds. Eventually one of the lads, probably by bribe rather than argument, convinced some of these surplus sleepers to seek other accommodations—this, after we'd already paid twice the going price for the "inconvenience" of needing a place to sleep after dark.

Two of the guys from Wuhan slipped out into the dark in search of supper, returning with loaves of bread so heavy I could barely swallow them and with some hideously pale lunch meat processed into finger-shaped wieners.

There was no water to drink or wash up with. I lay down in my bunk. I'd been up since six. Right then I never wanted to see another stone step on another mountain again.

Cloud Ladders

It is twice as far down the west side of Huang Shan, nearly 9 miles. This is where the great peaks reside, every one of them a stupendous detour by carved stairway. We scaled each and every prong. The climbs are extraordinarily severe, up hundreds of irregular stone steps that end in a singular panorama, followed by a shock-absorber descent, and a few minutes later by another looming precipice.

We began at the **Stone That Flew from Afar (Feilai Feng),** a 30-foot-tall rock perched on the top of a stone tower, looking as though it just sailed in on a cloud. Just to the east is Huang Shan's second highest peak, **Guangming Ding,** at 6,040 feet. It has its own strange crown: a modern weather station.

Turtle Summit (Aoyu Feng), slightly lower at 5,840 feet, requires a scramble through a cave whose stairs lead like a ladder to the slim summit. Next stop on this so-called descent was the highest peak in the range, **Lotus Flower (Lianhua Feng),** elevation 6,115 feet. It's a climb of 800 steps seemingly straight up—in fact, at an 80-degree incline in some places. Nonetheless, the overlook on the top has become very popular.

The earliest recorded climb of Lotus Flower Peak was in 1268. The party required 3 days to complete the ascent. Of course, there were no cable cars, guesthouses, trails, or stone stairways at Huang Shan in those days. The first stairways seem to have been cut into the mountain about 1606, when monks began to connect the many temples. During the Yuan Dynasty alone (1271–1368), 64 temples were added to Huang Shan's slopes. Today, hardly half a dozen remain. It is not a sacred mountain, but it is sublime.

At the foot of Lotus Flower Peak is the site of **Yuping Lou (Jade Screen Pavilion)**—a famous Buddhist temple until it burned down in 1952 and was reconstructed as a guesthouse and restaurant. The Jade Screen Pavilion is the midpoint on the western route, a fine place for a cup of tea. And here, too, is the most photographed panorama of Huang Shan, featuring a thousand rising peaks and spires and a single, stately pine tree, its boughs outstretched. Known as the **Welcoming Pine of Huang Shan (Huang Ke Song),** it is believed to be over a thousand years old. Its likeness has been painted on a wall in the Great Hall of the People in Beijing.

Just south of the Jade Screen Pavilion is Huang Shan's second-highest granite tower, **Tiandu Feng (City of Heaven Peak),** elevation 5,938 feet. It was the last peak I could possibly climb. I was ready to crawl.

City of Heaven Peak is formidable. It's an hour's detour to the top, a 2-mile-long ladder through the clouds ending in an unnerving and narrow 30-foot span, lined with a slack chain-link railing and sheer drop-offs on both sides. This lovely single-file passage of terror is called **Carp's Backbone Ridge (Jiyu Bei).** From it I could see all at once the four elements the Chinese traditionally demand of a perfect mountain landscape: soaring spires, grotesque pines, clear-running mountain streams, and seas of mist and cloud. Everything except sanity and safety. At least I had satisfied the ancient dictum: "Without reaching Jade Screen Pavilion, you cannot see the mountain; without climbing the City of Heaven Peak, your trip is in vain."

Peach Blossom Springs

After squeezing through a region of boulders and narrow fissures known as the **House of Clouds,** we paused for lunch near Banshan Temple at a restaurant that, oddly enough, doubled as a brick factory. Porters filed back and forth past our table, bundles of fresh bricks tethered to their poles. The bricks were piled in the back of the cafe, near the mouths of the kilns. The lads from Wuhan ordered beer, and feeling euphoric after their successful descent of Huang Shan, tore off the bottle tops with their teeth. Sheepishly, I fetched a bottle opener from my backpack. Meanwhile, the porters came and went, brickload by brickload, staring at me as I slurped down a bowl of red-peppered noodles.

It was only 2,000 more stone steps down to the bamboo groves and hot springs of **Merciful Light Temple (Ciguang Ge),** a favorite of the Ming Emperor Wanli, who visited here about the time the pilgrims landed on Plymouth Rock. All I wanted to land in was a hot tub of water and a comfortable bed.

At **Taoyuan (Peach Blossom) Hot Springs,** I parted ways with my four tireless companions from Wuhan. They took cheap rooms next to a public bathhouse; I retreated to the slightly more modern Taoyuan Guest House. I'd now felt how the Chinese travel on their holidays—quickly and cheaply—and I must conclude that they are far tougher travelers than I ever was, and in a much madder rush. My tendency is to dwell for hours at a site, for days on a peak, but they chew up entire mountain ranges as if they could hear the tick of each minute on a hand-wound 1-day clock.

One more mountain like this and I was finished. It's important to find your pace and stick with it. I meant to linger in this small village with its hot springs, waterfalls, forested peaks, and pavilions before I moved on. The hot mineral waters of Cinnabar Springs along the Peach Blossom Stream are said to heal those who climb the peaks.

Huang Shan is the most picture-perfect of Chinese mountains, so rife with bizarre rock forms, sword-point peaks, and deep fissures that it resembles a giant's game of pick-up sticks. Surmounting its 77 peaks requires days of climbing the stairs up the steep sides of immense granite pillars and the crossing of stone ladders floating on an everglade of clouds. As the Tang poet Li Bai proclaimed 12 centuries ago, the first ancients to scale these flowery peaks must have been astounded to find that they could look down upon the sky.

PRACTICAL INFORMATION

ORIENTATION & WHEN TO GO

Huang Shan (Yellow Mountain), China's most famous mountain for scenic beauty, is located in Anhui Province, 125 miles west of Hangzhou, 250 miles southwest of Shanghai, and about 40 miles from Tunxi, which is often called Huangshan Shi and is the nearest big town to the mountain. It is from **Tunxi** that many travelers begin their assault on the mountain, since this is the major air and rail link, has better hotels, and provides useful travel agencies for the mountain.

The mountain's history has not changed. Known as Yi Shan, its name was officially changed to Huang Shan by Emperor Tang Xuanzong in A.D. 747. Today it is a park, managed by the Huang Shan Municipality (established in 1987). Farming, wood gathering, hunting, mining, and construction are prohibited. The major threats to the environment are fire and water pollution, brought on in part by increasing tourism.

The large number of visitors (more than 500,000 a year) has strained the resources of the park administration; it has also fueled the development of the major summit points, with new restaurants and vendors setting up shop. From May through October, the trails are packed with hikers, making April an ideal time to visit Huang Shan. Rainfall, humidity, and temperature peak in July. Snow coats the peaks 158 days a year.

Fog and mist, essentials in the eyes of Huang Shan's artists, occur 256 days a year. Temperatures, even in summer, are subject to sudden changes with the altitude and winds. Carry layers of clothing: sweaters and rain jackets as well as T-shirts. Hats and umbrellas are also useful.

Most of the forests are pine. There are also alpine juniper, oak, beech, and ginkgo. Due to the large crowds, little of the indigenous wildlife is seen, but the parklands are home to 300 species, including macaque, black bear, wild dog, civet, sika deer, pangolin, oriental white stork, and clouded leopard. Huang Shan was inscribed on the UNESCO World Heritage List in 1990 in an effort to recognize and preserve its natural and cultural treasures.

GETTING THERE

By Plane **China East Airlines** has introduced daily direct flights from Shanghai (1 hour) to the new airport at Tunxi (also called Huang Shan Shi). There are flights as well from Beijing (2 hours), Guangzhou (1 hour 45 minutes), and Hong Kong (2 hours).

By Train A new daily express train connects Tunxi to Shanghai (12 hours). **From Tunxi to Huang Shan** Tunxi, the main transportation hub for Huang Shan, is 35 miles from the town of Tangkou, which in turn is still a few miles south of the mountain entrance. From the air, rail, and bus terminals in Tunxi, minibuses and taxis make the 2-hour trip to Tangkou. From Tangkou, it is necessary to continue to the east gate at Yungu (1 hour by minibus or taxi) if you want to use the cable car or the eastern mountain trail (recommended). From the Peach Blossom Hot Springs area and the start of the western mountain trail, it is a 30-minute walk down to the Tangkou bus station.

TOURS & STRATAGEMS

Visitor Information Tunxi has a helpful branch of **China International Travel Service (CITS)** at 12 Jingyuan Bei Lu (☎ 0559/251-5231 or 0559/251-5303; fax 0559/251-4014). It can provide English-speaking guides and private cars.

Exploring the Mountain The park entrance fee is RMB 90 ($11), payable at the start of the western or eastern trails. The Yungusi cable car (running 8am to 4pm) costs RMB 75 ($9.10) round-trip, RMB 55 ($6.90) one-way, and the waiting line for the 8-minute ascent can be 1 to 2 hours. Hiring a sedan chair can cost $100 for a 2-day round-trip; the price is always highly negotiable. A second cable car, the Yuping Cableway, runs from the Taoyuan Hot Springs area on the western trail up to the Jade Screen Pavilion; it costs RMB 55 ($6.90) each way. The third cable car comes in from the north side of the mountain, beginning near the town of Taiping and terminating west of the main summit at Pine Forest Peak near the Cloud-Dispelling Pavilion, a 4,000-foot rise; it costs RMB 55 ($6.90) each way.

WHERE TO STAY & DINE

There are hotels in Tunxi, but the town is 1 to 2 hours from Huang Shan's hiking trails. Closer accommodations are in Tangkou Village at the south entrance to the mountain and inside the park where the western trail begins at Peach Blossom Hot Springs. Plan on spending a night at a hotel on top of the mountain. Phone ahead for reservations, particularly from May through October.

There are plenty of stalls and a few hole-in-the-wall cafes on the mountain trails. Bagged snacks and boiled eggs might be hygienic enough to risk eating, but as much as possible stick to the good (and hygienic) Chinese and Western restaurants in the hotels listed below.

In Tunxi, the best hotel is the three-star **Huang Shan International Hotel** on Xiao Huashan Lu (☎ 0559/252-6999; fax 0559/251-2087). A double costs $85, credit cards are accepted, and there's a good tour desk.

At Tangkou, nearer the Huang Shan entrance, there are dorm rooms and crude doubles at the **Free and Unfettered Inn (Xiaoyao Binguan)** (☎ 0559/556-2571), which is almost worth staying at just for the name. Don't expect any frills. Doubles with private bathrooms cost RMB 300 ($36). The staff speaks some English.

At **Peach Blossom Hot Springs,** where the western trail begins, the inn of choice is the **Peach Blossom Hotel (Taoyuan Binguan),** 3 Yanan Lu (☎ 0559/556-2666; fax 0559/556-2888). It carries a three-star rating, but don't expect luxuries even when you pay up to $100 a night for a double. Rooms and bathrooms are quite small but modern, and American Express, MasterCard, and Visa are accepted.

At **Yungu Temple,** where the east trail begins, there's another three-star choice, the **Cloud Valley Villa Hotel (Yungu Binguan)** (☎ 0559/556-2466; fax 0559/556-2346), which charges $75 for a double (American Express, MasterCard, and Visa are accepted). The rooms are small but modern, and the staff is helpful. There's even a shopping arcade.

On the summit of the mountain, there are two decent choices. The **Northern Sea Hotel (Beihai Binguan)** (☎ 0559/556-2555; fax 0559/556-2708), rated at three stars, has a heavy Russian-style appearance (it was built in 1958) and could benefit from a thorough renovation. Doubles are $75, hot water flow is irregular, and no credit cards are accepted. A nicer, and much more expensive, choice is the Swiss-designed **Western Sea Hotel (Xihai Fandian)** (☎ 0559/ 556-2818; fax 0559/556-2988). The large, modern doubles cost up to $150. The hotel does have hot water on demand and accepts American Express, MasterCard, Visa, and Japan Credit Bank cards.

WULINGYUAN: CHINA'S YELLOWSTONE

武陵源

THE CHINA OF VAST, CROWDED cities—and even the China of endless farming communities and terraced fields—occupies but a fraction of the Middle Kingdom's geography. Most of China is rugged and remote, dominated by nearly uninhabitable mountainous terrain. Yet there are few parks devoted strictly to the outdoors, to nature as the supreme destination. The most notable exception I've run across is a park located in western Hunan Province, not near anything at all, known locally as **Zhangjiajie** but officially as the much easier-to-pronounce Wulingyuan Scenic and Historic Interest Area, a vast nature reserve that UNESCO designated as a World Heritage Site in 1992. Local boosters have proclaimed Wulingyuan "China's first Yellowstone-type national park," but it's just beginning to be developed for visitors from the outside world. I recommend it only to the hearty, although it could become a major attraction if it's made more accessible. The opening of a new airport has helped.

For the Chinese, Wuling is synonymous with the remote and the inaccessible. Small mountain villages, some reachable only by ropes, have clung to these slopes since the Ming Dynasty (1368–1644). There are stories of a certain Han Dynasty lord named Zhangliang who lived here as a hermit 2,000 years ago. A Tang Dynasty (A.D. 618–906) writer, Liuzhongyuan, praised its wild scenery. Otherwise, a history of the region is nearly nonexistent.

At present, Wuling Park is a wilderness paradise, an unpolished gem. It already possesses a superb system of paved walkways and stone stairs. But Wulingyuan dreams of placing itself at the forefront of Chinese tourism, improving its facilities in order to pamper as well as delight outdoor vacationers. If the local administrative power moves ahead with its ambitious programs of afforestation, conservation, and personnel training, and if the paving of the roads and upgrading of accommodations continue, Wulingyuan could indeed become a Chinese Yellowstone.

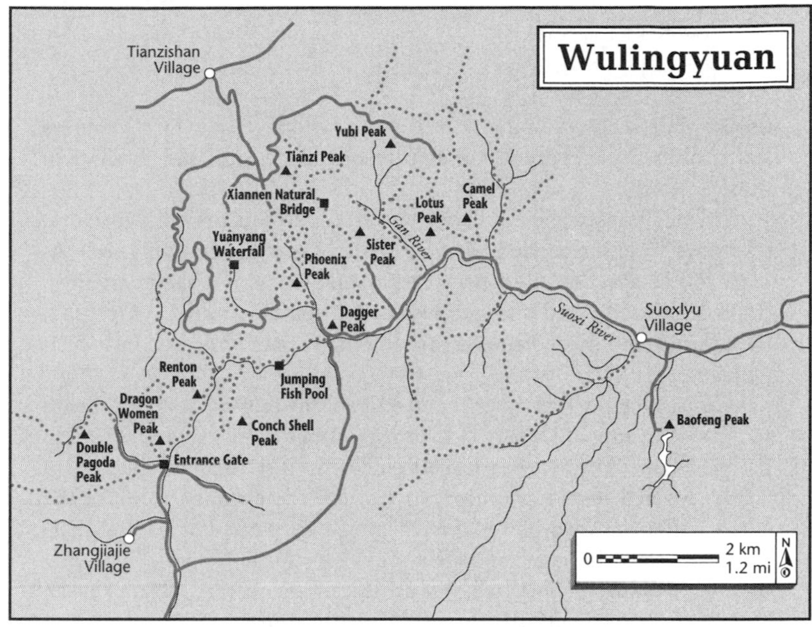

On my first visit to the area, I was fortunate. I'd met a local who insisted that Wulingyuan was the most beautiful place in China, and when I challenged him on this point he agreed to take me there. It can sometimes be tough to travel with a local Chinese in the difficult way that Chinese travel. From Changsha, we took a bouncing overnight bus, equipped with narrow bunk beds and quilts, 250 miles west to Zhangjiajie City (Dayong). The beds weren't long enough, the roads were uniformly unrepaired, and when we arrived 8 hours later at dawn, I'd hardly slept a wink. We ate breakfast on the street, were besieged by touts, and eventually found a minibus that delivered us to the park entrance at Zhangjiajie Village. To attempt this on your own seems to me insane at best, no matter how gorgeous the scenery, but some hearty travelers do.

Dragon Woman's Peak

Wulingyuan has been divided by the local park administration into a 65,208-acre core area and a 31,320-acre buffer zone. The park core is a deep basin of peaks and pillars, streams and limestone caves, drained by the Suoxi River. A web of hiking trails and steep stone stairways is connected to a rudimentary road system in the buffer zone. There are hillside farms populated by several of China's national minorities. What makes Wulingyuan distinctive, however, is its array of majestic quartz sandstone pillars, erupting from the valley floor and piercing the constant mist. These strange pinnacles resemble those found at better-known tourist sites such as Guilin and Yunnan's Stone Forest, but Wuling's stone columns tower over those in Yunnan and are more statuesque than those at Guilin.

I first glimpsed these pillars a few steps beyond the park entrance, where we were surrounded by stone sentinels on a gargantuan scale, as high and as sheer as any I have ever seen. It is as if a thousand steep peaks have been sliced into narrow, vertical shafts hundreds of feet tall, then turned and shaped on nature's lathe by eons of wind and mist, heat and ice.

Consulting the trail maps engraved on stone tablets, we found a path to the summit of Dragon Woman's Peak and beyond that to Huangshizhai. Porters tried to persuade us to hire their bamboo sedan chairs, covered in red awnings, but we were determined to make the climb under our own power. Several times we paused at natural platforms on the winding stone stairway where local vendors, emptying their bamboo packs, hawk tea, soft drinks, and handicrafts. It took us an hour to draw even with the tips of the quartz spires.

Even the sharpest, most inaccessible of these shafts is wreathed in trees and bushes. There are about 3,100 of these strange pillars in the park. Eighty-five have been given fanciful names, such as Double Pagoda, Conch Shell, and Rabbit Watching the Moon (Tianzi Shan), which at 4,149 feet is one of the highest points in Wulingyuan.

As we enjoyed the scenery, a troupe of minority dancers entertained us. Their children overtook us on our ascent, skipping effortlessly uphill, leaving behind the echoes of their "mountain songs" as we gasped for oxygen. The national minorities add a cultural dimension to Wulingyuan. The Tujia and Bai minorities predominate, with a scattering of Miao people. The minority farming villages are mostly in the buffer zone. Ten mountain strongholds *(shanzhai)*, built in the Ming and Qing dynasties and often reachable only by ropes, remain in the park but are no longer occupied. Today, some of the minorities are engaged in performing their songs and dances, selling native crafts, carrying sedan chairs, and running inns and restaurants.

Descending the west face of Dragon Woman's Peak, we encountered lines of porters hauling heavy sacks on shoulder poles—sacks of concrete for the latest construction project, a cable car to whisk sightseers to the top of nearby 3,438-foot Huangshizhai. It's now in operation; the round-trip costs RMB 70 ($8.75).

A Village on the Rim

When we reached the valley floor, **Zhangjiajie Village** was clogged with travelers, many dressed in their finest clothes, as if they'd arrived for a wedding reception rather than a backpacking adventure. Wulingyuan receives over 500,000 visitors yearly, nearly all of them from within China. Some come for a casual stroll, some for a serious trek, some even for a honeymoon, as my friend did last year.

Having allotted just 2 days to cover the high points of Wulingyuan, we could not tarry. If I ever return here, I'll stay an extra day, to slow the pace if nothing else. We followed the stream running through Zhangjiajie Village into a valley forest of oak, maple, and Chinese plum, and crossed a flat wooden bridge. There we located another steep stairway rising into the creases of massive stone slivers. Halfway up, a fine mist enveloped us. Wulingyuan is often under clouds, and rain is a constant feature all summer. Farther up, we broke through the clouds.

The trail continued to rise, whipping back and forth a dozen times. Eventually, we headed away from the river valley toward the top of a wide, level ridge, stopping at a hillside village of terraced rice paddies for a simple lunch. An unpaved road runs through the village, and we were able to hail a bus grinding its way east along the northern rim of the basin. An hour later, we stopped at a roadside inn on the ridge and rented a room for the night.

The **inns** inside the park are new, locally built, and a disaster. Since they're new, they're still somewhat clean, but they're very spartan. You get a bed with a quilt and a bathroom that may not have its plumbing in working order. Meals come from one or two cafes down the street—extremely basic fare: noodles, vegetables, and meat in unimaginative variations from bowl to bowl. Not a soul here speaks English; even standard Chinese *(putonghua)* is almost a novelty.

At dusk we enjoyed a superb view of the basin below. The canyon walls make a sheer drop. The valley teems with thousands of wrinkled spires that could have served the ink-brush artists of old as the supreme model for their uncanny landscapes. On the horizon are layers of blue-and-gray mountains, softly rounded. I felt as if I were standing atop a roofless cavern where a sea had receded, leaving exposed a chamber of lances and spears, thrust into the earth by a regiment of giants.

The Bridge Across the Sky

The next morning we continued on foot along the northern rim of the park toward **Tianzishan Village,** pausing at several overlooks to view some of the 239 natural scenic spots identified in the core area. At Tianzishan, one vista point has been developed into a wayside commemorating a local military hero. The stone formations below are said to resemble a cavalry division massed for inspection by a general.

Starting at a partially completed visitors center in the style of a pagoda, we descended a stone stairway into the heart of the basin, weaving among Wulingyuan's largest columns. The trail branched off, enabling us to climb up and down several sharp peaks before rejoining the main path. At a stone archway known as **The Bridge of the Immortals (Xianrenqiao),** we came upon a Chinese tour group decked out in yellow baseball caps. They were being entertained by a vendor with a monkey on a chain, the only specimen of the park's wildlife I'd seen. Wulingyuan is a preserve for nine rare and three vulnerable species of plants, as well as a number of threatened mammals, including the Asiatic black bear, the Chinese water deer, and the clouded leopard. No clouded leopards have actually been seen in the park, but there are signs that a few inhabit the area.

Perhaps the single most spectacular rock formation appeared halfway down the basin trail. **Tianqiaoshengkong (The Bridge Across the Sky)** is an archway joining two massive vertical columns. We eased out to a platform with a metal railing constructed to give a close-up view of the stone bridge, which visitors can also cross if they dare. Under this 130-foot-long stone span, the canyon walls drop straight into an abyss 1,171 feet deep. A survey by UNESCO suggests that it "may be the highest natural bridge in the world." Trees clinging to the arch lend it the appearance of a floating forest spread like a banner between two stone towers.

Yellow Dragon Cave

We reached the valley floor at the vacation town of **Suoxiyu.** Suoxiyu contains several large, modern hotels, opened a few years ago to capture an anticipated increase in overseas travelers, a boom yet to materialize. This is the place to stay for some luxury and comfort, a good base for day trips whether you come on your own or on a tour. In Suoxiyu we hired a motorized cart and rode 12 miles into the countryside to **Yellow Dragon (Huanglong) Cave**—touted as the largest cave in Asia. About a third of Wulingyuan consists of limestone caves and underground streams. Of the 40 caverns, Yellow Dragon is the most spectacular. About 7 miles long, it features a chamber with a 150-foot waterfall and ferryboat rides on its subterranean river. It's open daily dawn to dusk, and costs RMB 50 ($6) to enter. The cavern is fully developed for tourists, complete with English-speaking guides, photographers for hire, and an avenue of vendors lining the lane outside its pavilion entrance—a hint of what Wuling Park will become in the future.

Wulingyuan remains difficult to reach and difficult to travel through—it's still an emblem of the remote and the inaccessible.

Whether Wulingyuan is truly the most beautiful place in China, as my friend from the same province insisted, is a matter of taste, but its ranks of stone spears brushing the vaults of heaven in a valley of forests, rivers, and caves form a natural tapestry unsurpassed elsewhere in China.

PRACTICAL INFORMATION

ORIENTATION & WHEN TO GO

Wulingyuan (better known to the Chinese as Zhangjiajie) is located in a remote northwest section of Hunan Province, about 700 miles west of Shanghai and 500 miles north of Hong Kong. Wulingyuan became China's first National Forest Park in 1983. In 1992, it was listed as a UNESCO World Heritage Site, and ambitious conservation programs, including limits on tourism, were announced. The nearest major city is **Changsha,** Hunan's capital, 160 miles northwest by air, 250 miles by rail or road.

Spring and fall are mild but rainy, winter is cold, and summer—when hundreds of thousands of Chinese visit the park—is hot and humid.

GETTING THERE

Changsha, capital of Hunan Province, is the transportation hub of the region. Unfortunately, it is 8 to 10 hours' travel by road or rail from Wulingyuan. **Zhangjiajie City** (formerly called Dayong) is about 20 miles south of the park entrance. It contains a rail station and airport. At the park entrance, there is a small town called (to confuse matters) **Zhangjiajie Village.** The bus, rail, and airport terminals are connected to the village and park entrance by roving minibuses that make the 1-hour transfer for RMB 20 ($2.40) per person.

By Plane **Hehua Airport,** 3 miles from Zhangjiajie City and 18 miles from the park entrance, has newly opened air routes to 22 cities in China, including Beijing (2 hours), Shanghai (3 hours), and Guangzhou (4 hours). It can handle 700,000 passengers annually. In 1999, it began air service from Hong Kong and Macao, dramatically increasing the number of tourists. **Changsha,** a hard 1-day (or overnight) trip from Zhangjiajie, has a major airport with connections to many Chinese cities.

By Train The **Zhangjiajie Train Station** is 6 miles south of town. There are now overnight express trains to and from Beijing and Guangzhou and a daylight express train to Changsha (8 hours). An overnight express train to connect with Shanghai is being planned.

By Bus Buses to and from Changsha require at least 8 hours to cover the 250-mile route. From Zhangjiajie City, it is another hour by bus to the main park entrance at Zhangjiajie Village.

GETTING AROUND

Transportation inside the park is sketchy. You can hike the trails or hail local buses that circle the rim as they stop at villages. A local bus connects

Suoxiyu Village and Zhangjiajie City, a spectacular 3-hour trip over the mountains on the southern edge of the park. Suoxiyu Village, located at the southeast entrance to the park, is also a good base for hiking into the park, viewing the nearby Yellow Dragon Cave, and booking a white-water raft trip (summers only) on the Suoxi River.

TOURS & STRATAGEMS

Admission to the park is RMB 62 ($7.65).

Visitor Information Since 1988, the park has been managed by the **Wulingyuan Administration Bureau,** based in Zhangjiajie City (☎ 0744/822-8010). **China International Travel Service (CITS)** has a branch in the Zhangjiajie Hotel in Zhangjiajie Village, near the park entrance (☎ 0744/871-2718). In Zhangjiajie City, CITS has a useful office at 34 Jiefang Lu (☎ 0744/822-7718 or 0744/822-3968) and nearby at the Dragon International Hotel (see below). The travel desk in the **Jinbianyan Hotel** (☎ 0744/271-2096) at the park entrance is also helpful; it offers guides for park and cave tours.

WHERE TO STAY

In Zhangjiajie City, the best hotel is the **Dragon International Hotel (Xianglong Guoji Dajiudian),** 46 Jiefang Lu (☎ 0744/822-6888; fax 0744/822-2935). Double rooms are $75. The tour desk here can arrange guided tours of Wulingyuan. The Dragon does not quite reach international standards in service and its facilities are limited, but the rooms are clean and modern. This is the most deluxe place in town.

In Zhangjiajie Village, at the park entrance, the **Zhangjiajie Binguan** (☎ 0744/571-2718 or 0744/571-2388) offers modern double rooms in its new wing (RMB 290/$35) but is otherwise quite basic. Better facilities are offered just inside the park by the **Pipaxi Guesthouse (Pipaxi Binguan)** (☎ 0744/571-8888; fax 0744/571-2257), renovated in 1999, which offers nice doubles for $60, complete with international satellite TV. Pipaxi accepts major credit cards.

Hikers inside the park must rely on **local inns,** which charge RMB 85 to RMB 168 ($10 to $20) per night. I stayed in an inn south of Tianzishan Village on the canyon rim, newly built and run by local minority farmers. The bedroom contained two single beds with quilts (no sheets), a TV set, and a tiny bureau. The bathroom had a Chinese-style toilet, a sink that drained directly onto the floor, and a shower nozzle fastened to the wall. The water was steaming hot, once we alerted the staff across the street that we wanted to shower.

WHERE TO DINE

Zhangjiajie (both city and village), **Tianzishan,** and **Suoxiyu** have inexpensive restaurants featuring spicy Hunanese dishes, but the cuisine is not outstanding, nor are English-language menus available. The hotels have restaurants that are more accessible to foreign travelers.

LU SHAN: HILL STATION OF THE RICH & FAMOUS

LU SHAN IS CHINA'S ANSWER TO the hill stations and highlands of Southeast Asia, notably of Malaysia, complete with tea plantations, villa resorts of the colonial era, misty mountain peaks, and rich green forests. For the Chinese, it is the epitome of nature in its pristine beauty, engraved in tradition by countless landscape artists and classic poets. In recent centuries, Lu Shan became the private retreat first of European traders and missionaries, then of powerful Chinese landowners and political scions, from Chiang Kai-shek to Chairman Mao. Today, it is a favorite cool mountain resort for thousands of ordinary Chinese vacationers, affording an ideal combination of outdoor scenery and culture. All summer it is jam-packed with tour groups, while the rest of the year it can be sacked with cold mists, blowing rains, and freezing snows. By official estimates, at least 190 days of the year Lu Shan is clouded with "vapors," the layers of fog that rise from numerous lakes, rivers, and waterfalls.

Journey to Guling

Situated between the mighty Yangzi River to the north and the great lake of Boyang to the southeast, Lu Shan covers an area about 15 miles long by 6 miles wide, rising suddenly in a cluster of over 90 peaks with elevations of 4,000 to 5,000 feet. The gateway is the city of Jiujiang (Nine Rivers) on the south shore of the Yangzi River, 20 miles to the northwest. Known to Westerners as Kiukiang, Jiujiang became a Treaty Port in 1861, open to foreigners who made the town a major shipping center for tea and porcelain. In the heat of summer, Lu Shan became a hillside retreat for the colonials, who made the steep journey from Jiujiang on the arms, shoulders, and feet of porters—whole families were carried in sedan chairs. Today, the buses from Jiujiang to Lu Shan retrace the old route up a series of switchbacks known locally as the "Four

Hundred Turns," reportedly because Chairman Mao's driver kept a tally of them using 400 match sticks. However many they may be, the twists are numerous and sometimes wrenching. Inside Lu Shan Park there is a charming small tourist town, Guling, inundated now with shops on its main street—an excellent place to buy pouches or canisters of Lu Shan's most famous product, Cloud Tea (Yunwu Cha).

Guling contains scores of European villas and mansions from the colonial days, when wealthy foreign traders and many Christian missionaries sought it out as a cool summer retreat from the intense heat of the lowland Yangzi valley. Westerners called the town Kuling, creating a fortunate pun on the word "cooling," which accurately describes the climatic allure of Lu Shan in the days before air-conditioning. Formally established as a summer resort in 1895 by E. L. Little, an English investor, Guling more than a century later retains its original architecture—a residential version of the Bund's commercial row in Shanghai. Here are the surviving homes and guesthouses of a foreign summer community that numbered nearly 2,000 by 1917, as well as the villas, training centers, and meeting halls of Chiang Kai-shek's Nationalist government and finally Chairman Mao's inner circle of communist bigwigs.

Meilu Villa

The most interesting of the colonial mansions to visit these days was built in 1903 and donated by its owner, Mrs. Hallett, wife of a rich Western physician, to the Chinese leader, Chiang Kai-shek, in the 1930s. The house became his personal summer home. Meilu Villa (Meilu Bieshu) was named for Chiang's wife, Song Mei-ling. The Song sisters are legendary in China. One married the founder of the modern Chinese republic, Sun Yat-sen, and stayed active in communist politics after the revolution in 1949; the other, Song Mei-ling, married China's president, Chiang Kai-shek (Mao's foe), and fled with him to Taiwan after the Nationalists' defeat in 1949.

Strangely enough, communist China did not see fit to raze the Lu Shan villa of Mao's most bitter enemy; instead, Mao himself simply moved in when the mood to escape the summer heat seized him. Today, the crumbling villa and its gardens are the number one cultural attraction on the mountain. It is not a grand house. Its yellow-walled rooms and stone fireplaces are in disrepair and its overstuffed furniture is worn, but there are plenty of historic relics, such as a large bathroom fitted with Chinese and Western facilities, paintings by Song Mei-ling herself, Song's lavish bedroom, photographs of Chiang and Song, and even an original kerosene-powered Electrolux refrigerator in the kitchen. There's

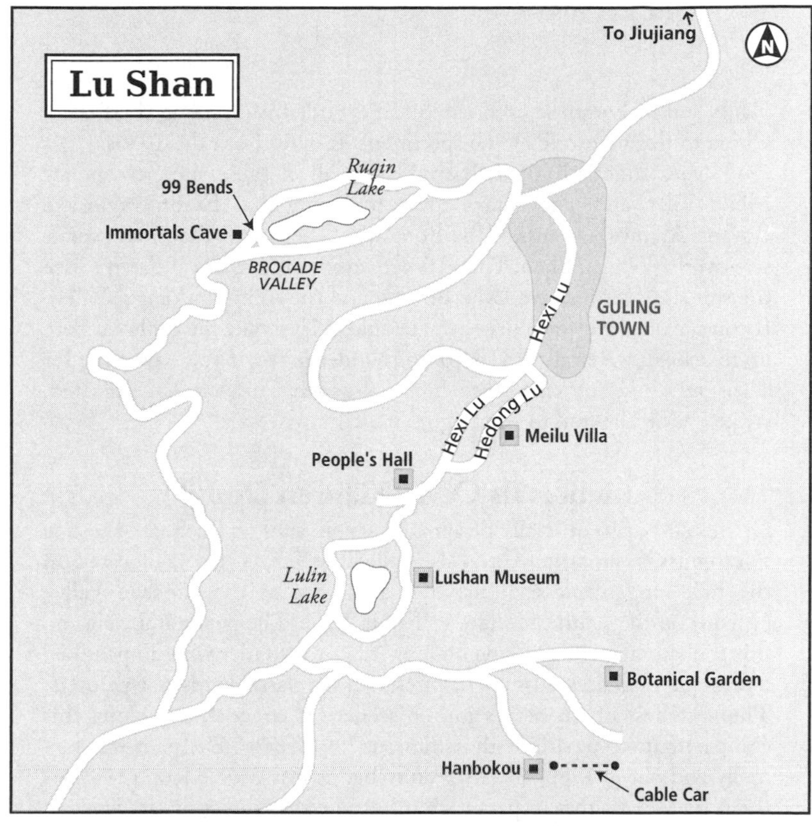

also a photo of Chairman Mao in a wicker chair; it was snapped by his wife, Jiang Qing, who was later convicted of crimes as the leader of the Cultural Revolution's Gang of Four.

Meilu Villa, which is usually swamped with tourists, is open from 8am to 8pm; admission is RMB 10 ($1.25). It's located about a quarter-mile southwest of central Guling, down the main sightseeing road of Hexi Lu on Hedong Lu. Another half-mile farther down the main road at 504 Hexi Lu is People's Hall (Renmin Juyuan), which has the same hours and admission charge. This was the conference hall where two major meetings chaired by Mao in 1959 and 1970 changed the course of modern communist China; it is now a rather uninteresting museum of the political history of Lu Shan. Still farther down the same road is the more entertaining Lushan Museum (Lu Shan Bowuguan), which has displays of the mountain's political history too, but also exhibits on local religious culture and natural beauty. This museum gives a nice overview of what the park has to offer. A half-mile east of the museum is the Botanical Garden (Zhiwuyuan), open daily from 8am to 5pm; admission is RMB 10 ($1.25). Famous for its 3,000 native highland plants and its hothouse cacti exhibit, the garden was among the first in China to feature exotic alpine specimens. It dates from the 1930s.

If your time is limited, I would skip all of these sites, except for Meilu Villa, and take a taxi down to Hanbokou (Embracing Lake Boyang Archway), south of the Botanical Garden, for the most expansive overlook in Lu Shan. This is where everyone gathers at dawn to see the sun rise over massive Lake Boyang and the southern Yangzi Valley. If you can't make it for sunrise, you should at least take the cable car here up to a small waterfall (RMB 50/$6 round-trip) or, if you have time for a leisurely hike into the steep hills for which Lu Shan is celebrated, strike out on the trail to your right.

Immortals Cave (Xianren Dong)

Of the 200 or so officially designated scenic sites at Lu Shan, the one not to miss is Immortals Cave, also called the Fairy Cave. It's located on the mile-long scenic trail in what is known as the Brocade Valley (Jinxiu) on the southeast shore of Ruqin Lake. The peaks and vistas on this trail are magnificent; one no longer has to wonder what impossible, uncanny mountain landscape inspired China's classic landscape painters. The very best of Lu Shan's mystic scenery is concentrated along this compact but steep path, with its famous "99 Bends." The path was formally laid out in 1980, and its granite bed is just wide enough to allow the hordes of visitors to pass each other in either direction. Its viewing platforms, most without even a cursory railing, are studies in vertigo.

Aside from the overlooks, sheer peaks, ribbons of fog, and deep ravines, one comes across several unexpected monuments. The first is a large plaque carved into stone like an ancient stele, except that this is a modern engraving in both English and Chinese. Its carved gold lettering reads exactly as follows: "THE NIGOCIATION PLATFORM From July to September, 1946 Five-Star General G.C. Marshall, the special envoy of the president of the United States came to Mt. Lushan eight times to mediate the negociation between the Communist Party of China and the Kuomingtang. This is the place where General Marshall and Chiang Kaishek met."

The Immortals Cave itself is a rock chamber on the edge of a precipice, hollowed out in part by a deep spring inside, which still flows. The altars and carvings of Daoist priests have occupied the chamber for many centuries, creating a remote cave temple. It was here that Lu Dongbin, one of the Eight Immortals of Daoism, was given a sword by a fire-breathing dragon. With this sorcerer's sword, Lu was able to fly through the Middle Kingdom, walking on clouds and slaying all the demons in his path. Lu also became the patron saint of China's ink-makers, and the cave of his origin is as inky black and mysterious as ever. It is fronted on the outside by enormous pines, and occupied inside by a large stone shrine and stone railings. Locals say the cave has the shape of Buddha's hand, the five stone fingers held upward like a lotus flower. Monks in white robes, their black hair pinned into buns, preside over the cave temple, selling incense to visitors.

Lu Shan is the lotus flower of Chinese scenery. Over 2,000 years ago, it was mentioned by Sima Qian, the Grand Historian to the First Emperor of unified China, Qin Shi Huang Di (B.C. 259–210). Sima told the tale of seven brothers who lived in the mountains here, giving the area the name Lu Shan, which means Cottage Mountain. During the Eastern Han Dynasty (A.D. 25–220), it became the center of Buddhism in China, with hundreds of temple buildings (Lu Shan is not regarded as a sacred mountain, however). The major surviving temple is Donglin Si (Temple of Eastern Grove), where Hui Yin founded the Pure Land Sect in the 4th century, a form of Buddhism that was to be imported to Japan (where it still flourishes) by Japanese monks who visited Lu Shan.

Lu Shan's two most influential promoters were the Tang Dynasty poets Bai Juyi (A.D. 701–762) and Li Bai (A.D. 701–762). Bai Juyi concluded in one of his poems that Lu Shan was unrivaled in its beauty anywhere in China; Li Bai compared the peaks of Lu Shan to "golden lotus sculpted in the transparent sky." Whether one stays a few hours or a few days, you'll see that Lu Shan contains exactly the kind of scenery that strikes at the core of a Chinese sense of beauty—serene yet wild, spiritual yet natural, mystical yet human. In 1996, Lu Shan was inscribed by UNESCO as a World Heritage Site because of its prominence "as a cultural landscape of outstanding aesthetic value and its powerful associations with Chinese spiritual and cultural life."

PRACTICAL INFORMATION

ORIENTATION & WHEN TO GO

Lu Shan (Cottage Mountain) is the most famous mountain resort in China. It is located just south of the Yangzi River and just west of Boyang Lake in Jiangxi Province, 370 miles southwest of Shanghai. The nearest city is **Jiujiang,** on the south shore of the Yangzi River, about 20 miles away. Lu Shan is a raised plateau with a cluster of steep peaks, rivers, waterfalls, forests, and the remains of a late 19th century foreign enclave of resort villas. Summers are cool; spring and autumn bring the threat of dense fog and rain; and winters are cold, with frequent snows. Many Chinese tourists come here from June through September.

GETTING THERE

The nearest major **airport** is 20 miles south of Nanchang, which itself lies 50 miles south of Lu Shan. The airport provides connections to major cities throughout China. The Yangzi River town of Jiujiang, which is the gateway to Lu Shan, now has its own airport, but it has just a few flights a week to a handful of Chinese cities (including Shanghai and Guangzhou). Jiujiang and Nanchang are about 2 hours apart via bus or taxi on a new expressway. Jiujiang is also connected by **train** with Nanchang and to cities along the Yangzi by **cruise ship.** From Jiujiang, visitors to Lu Shan must take either a bus or taxi to enter the park (a mountain ride with lots of turns, taking about 30 minutes). Buses to Lu Shan cost about RMB 10 to RMB 20 ($1.25 to $2.50); they depart Jiujiang from the large Yangzi River ferry terminal and the long-distance bus station.

TOURS & STRATAGEMS

The admission to the mountain park area, approachable by road from Jiujiang, is RMB 50 ($6).

Visitor Information Within Lu Shan, the town of Guling has an array of tourist services. The Lu Shan office of the **China International Travel Service (CITS)** is located near the Lushan Hotel and Meilu Villa at 443 Hexi Lu (☎ 0792/828-2497; fax 0792/828-2428). This CITS office is open daily and has a good reputation for assisting foreign visitors. It can book accommodations, bus tickets, group tours, and English-speaking guides. CITS offices in Jiujiang (28 Nanhu Lu; ☎ 0792/822-3390) and Nanchang (78 Bayi Dadao, Jiangxi Hotel; ☎ 0791/628-4345) can arrange transportation to Lu Shan.

Exploring the Mountain The tourist town of Guling is located on the northeast edge of the park. Its main shopping street is Guling Jie, but the sights, hotels, and CITS are to the southwest along Hexi Lu (most within a mile or less). It is possible to walk the roads and trails in the park to see all the major sights, but taxis are an inexpensive time-saver—they cost RMB 10 to RMB 20 ($1.25 to $2.50).

WHERE TO STAY

The best accommodations are at the three-star, 60-room **Lushan Hotel (Lu Shan Binguan),** 446 Hexi Lu (☎ 0792/828-2060; fax 0792/828-2843), an inn that once served colonial traders. It is situated on the main road about a half-mile southwest of central Guling. There are overseas investors and staff involved in the hotel; service is adequate and some of the staff speaks some English. Modern double rooms with private bathrooms start at RMB 400 ($48), as do the villas tucked far uphill in the woods. The nearby two-star **Lushan Villa Hotel,** 179 Hedong Lu (☎ 0792/828-2927; fax 0792/828-2275) has less expensive villas, as does the **Mei Ling Villa (Mei Ling Shanzhuang),** 5 Hedong Lu (☎ 0792/ 828-1268; fax 0792/ 828-1638). So far, credit cards are not accepted at any of Lu Shan's hotels.

WHERE TO DINE

The best restaurant is at the **Lushan Hotel** (☎ 0792/282-2060), where a full Chinese dinner, featuring a plate of local alpine mushrooms, costs under $20. The other hotels listed above also have reasonably good dining in their restaurants. An interesting local spot to try is the **Sanhe Fandian,** located across from People's Hall on Hexi Lu; the menu has plenty of familiar Chinese dishes on it, all under $5 a plate.

WUTAI SHAN: BUDDHIST PEAK OF THE NORTH

五台山

WHEN THE ZEN MASTER XU YUN made his pilgrimage to Wutai Shan (Five Terraces Mountain) in 1882, it took him 2 years to walk the 900 miles from Shanghai, in part because he insisted on bowing down and bumping his head on the ground every third step of the way. My own 100-mile journey north from Tiayuan by car took just 4 hours, but it was bumpy, too. Once we left the main highway and rose into the foothills of Wutai Shan, we encountered one of the worst strips of road I've ever traveled: a bed of dirt and rock being dug up and rebuilt by hand. We averaged 5 miles per hour, tops. I counted hundreds of workers with shovels and picks along the way, spread out for miles in small teams. We frequently had to stop for them, and when an oncoming truck asserted its right of way, we had to squeeze over on the shoulder of the lane-and-a-half of plowed furrow that called itself a highway.

When we reached the top of the high ridge after 90 minutes of lurching, I could see across the roof of northern China under a bright blue sky. This could have been Tibet, and in fact many Tibetans, as well as Mongolians, have congregated at Wutai Shan ever since the 13th century, when Lama Buddhism spread to China's borderlands. The founder of the Yellow Hat sect of Lama Buddhism lived here. The exiled Dalai Lama is his divine descendant.

We dropped into a broad crater, encompassed by the Northern, Southern, Eastern, and Western Terraces—peaks in a cluster that make up Wutai Shan. In the center of this compass is the Central Terrace, site of a temple village, Taihuai, clotted with more temples than any other city in the Middle Kingdom.

I checked into a new hotel a mile south of the temple village. The desk staff couldn't find me a map of the temples or peaks. They told me it was impossible to walk to the highest peak, the Northern Terrace,

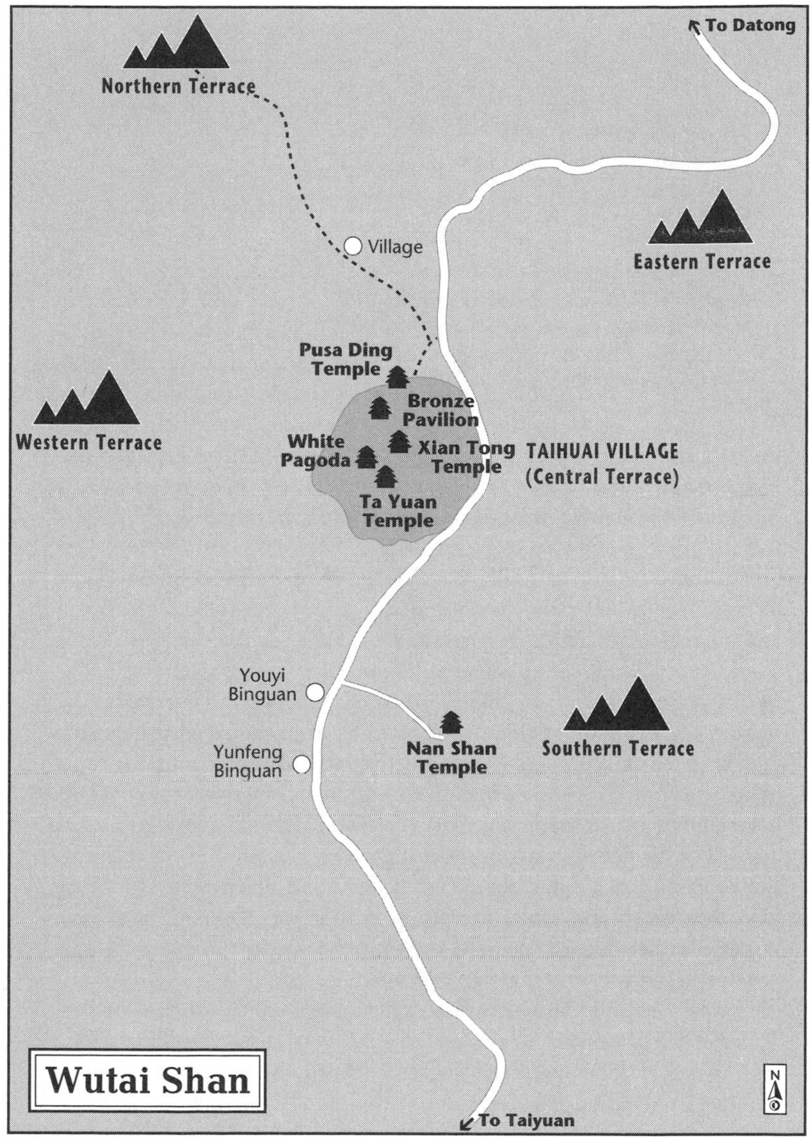

because the summit was under snow. Then they issued me a special permit, stamped with a red seal that read "aliens' travel permit."

So branded, I set out on a sunny morning for the temple village and the top of the snowy terrace beyond. On the way to town horsemen twice passed by. They tried to persuade me to hire their steeds. I was tempted. Such fine horses, the horses of Wutai Shan: tall, sleek, brown bodies, black manes and tails, fitted with ornate red saddles and red bridles. But I resisted. I meant to keep walking through the temple village to the top of Wutai Shan's Northern Peak, regardless of a scarcity of maps and an abundance of snow.

The Temple Village

The Temple Village of Taihuai at Wutai Shan, in the crater of the terraced valley, is extensive, as beautiful and active as any I've seen in China. That's not to say the temples of Wutai Shan are what they once were. A century ago, there were over 300 holy shrines here; 50 years ago, travelers counted 100 monasteries and temples, of which 30 were devoted to Lamaism. Today, the census is down to a few dozen. But the heart of the village is still as it was, a little city of temples crowded one into the next, uphill and downhill, with streets and walls running every direction—enough temples flowing into temples to get lost in, like a maze.

In the center of the village is Wutai Shan's landmark, the **Great White Tibetan Pagoda,** often called a *stupa* or *dagoba,* a *sarira* or *chorten,* meaning a reliquary, a monument for a relic said to have come from the real Buddha—a fingernail or a thigh bone, for instance. The White Pagoda of Wutai Shan is shaped like a monumental wine decanter tapering to a golden spire, with an exquisite finial that resembles a folded umbrella. It stands 150 feet tall, and was constructed of brick and lime 5 centuries ago. Two hundred fifty-two bronze windbells dangle like lanterns from the fringes of its finial, chiming in the wind. The devout pilgrims from Mongolia once circled this monument hundreds of times a day, touching the scripture doors around its base with their foreheads. Now, the White Pagoda was deserted, or at least not easily accessible; the nearer I got to it, the deeper the maze of walls, courtyards, and shrines that surrounded it.

I made my way through temple streets, clogged with dozens of vendors offering thousands of trinkets, drinks, snacks, hats, walking sticks, and souvenirs. The stairs and streets between the temples were lined with beggars and cripples, more than you usually see these days in one place in China.

Passing under a large towered gate, I followed a back road along a wall. There were six young men squatting down along that wall, gambling with cards, all of them dressed in the black sports coats favored by taxi drivers and pickpockets. I entered the door to the **Fine Thread Penetration Temple (Xiantong Si),** which consists of over 400 buildings. Inside, I walked through several darkened rooms into one that was even darker: a bare brick room with a ceiling high enough to accommodate a slender golden bronze pagoda 13 stories tall, said to house a lock of hair from Wan Shu himself, the Buddhist god of Wutai Shan.

Surprisingly, this unlit chamber is connected to a shrine of more recent vintage, a shrine to Chairman Mao Zedong, whose white plaster bust is set upon an altar and draped in a bright red-and-gold shawl—a most modern Buddha, the revolutionary god of China. Mao must have slept here. His bedroom is preserved next door to his shrine, complete with a dozen photographs of the chairman pasted above a spacious *kang,* a heated bed of bricks, covered in wicker mats. Worshippers have tossed offerings onto his bed: small coins, mostly, and cigarettes. Strange shrine, one of hundreds at Wutai Shan.

The Mouth of the Dragon

I walked out into another courtyard, heading north for the top of **Central Terrace,** the hill that rises at the far end of the Temple Village. I could see more stupas and bronze pagodas ahead and dozens of fine glazed-tile roofs. Most splendid of all is the **Bronze Pavilion,** cast in the Ming Dynasty. It resembles a miniature metal temple, barely tall enough to admit human worshippers, coated inside with thousands of tiny bronze Buddhas. Its form is intricate, as if a thin layer of hot bronze were meticulously poured over timbers, columns, tiles, and carved wooden figures and allowed to cool.

Ascending Central Terrace, I entered the mouth of the dragon, the dragon being the **Pusa Ding Temple,** Wutai Shan's most famous shrine. Its undulating walls and many pavilions are coiled on the top of the hill, 108 stone steps above the many temples and lamaseries below. The faithful once left locks of their hair on each step to the entrance gate, offerings to Wen Shu in hopes he would grant them rebirth. One modern-day beggar raised his half leg to me as I passed him on the stairs.

Two Qing emperors of China made Pusa Ding Temple their residence during official pilgrimages to Wutai Shan. Wen Shu himself is believed to live in this temple. Wen Shu is the Buddhist bodhisattva of Pure Wisdom, known in India as Manjusri. Born of a ray of light from the crown of the Buddha, he had no earthly parents and was born free of sin. He introduced Buddhism to Nepal, then, by Chinese accounts, made his home on the Central Terrace of the five terraces of Wutai Shan. He sits on a lion, a book in one hand, a sword raised in the other.

Wen Shu's temple home is encircled today by innumerable vendors. Monks charge admission at his gates. Five thousand lamas lived here a century ago, and some still remain, plodding back and forth in brown robes and caps, yellow sashes, and padded shoes. There are butter lamps, prayer banners, and small brass prayer wheels spinning in the courtyards, and inside one small shrine I spotted some of the old musical instruments from the days when Lamaists gathered here to watch the spirited

Devil Dances: two immense demon-mouthed trumpets, as long and heavy as alpenhorns. The yellow roof tiles of Pusa Ding Temple, donated by the Qing Emperor Kangxi almost 3 centuries ago, gleam in the sun, and the red columns are freshly painted, but the dragon temple seems gutted, barren as the hills that were deforested at the command of that same emperor when he called upon the people to settle the wilds of Wutai Shan.

From Pusa Ding Temple there is a fine view of the temple village below, as well as the White Pagoda and the river valley. Most of the buildings at Wutai Shan are really no older than a century or two, rebuilt countless times after each destructive turn, human or natural. The curious thing is that these days almost no tourist or pilgrim comes to Wutai Shan to climb its peaks. The temples are enough to occupy their curiosity. But to my uninformed mind, these temples are just husks—pretty to look at, a bit strange in form, but nothing much inside for me, whether it be Mao or Wen Shu with book, sword, and lion.

The Northern Terrace

It was before noon when I began to climb the highest peak, the Northern Terrace, its summit topping 10,000 feet. I was already at 6,000 feet, and the route to the summit didn't look steep or impossibly far. I skirted the dragon wall of the Central Terrace and found a road up the northern valley. I didn't meet a soul until I came to the end of the pavement and struck up the mountain valley on a dirt road. At the intersection, there was a poor peasant woman, threadbare. She opened both empty hands to me, and I could see that she was the sort of peasant who really has nothing.

The dirt road goes straight up the valley and ends in a farming village. Three children spotted me. They dashed out for a look, but they were afraid to come too close, even though they called out to me. I walked around the village walls, keeping the stream on my left. The houses are fashioned from mud, not brick. There's electricity but no cement.

There's no road, either—only a series of paths that farmers use to tend their plots, walled in with piles of rock. The ground is too rocky for easy agriculture. The peasants work the plots with oxen hitched to plows. I felt like an intruder, wandering amongst their fields, but they paid me little attention. The hills that fold into the river valley are denuded of trees: hard scrabble up to the peak, a bit of grass and brush for grazing. Black hawks, wings tipped white, sailed across the empty span. I could see the Northern Peak ahead. There were several wide patches of snow near the top, looking like leftover glaciers, but they were too thin to be barriers.

An hour above the village I could no longer see the temples in the valley. There were snatches of green alpine grasses and tiny wildflowers in the brown stubble. The high slopes were crisscrossed with sheep paths. Shepherds guided their flocks to thin pastures on the flanks.

Near the summit I found remnants of a stone platform but still no trail. I bushwhacked up the final untracked rise, cutting between snow crusts, crossing a field of buttercups. At the summit, a chilly wind swept over the Northern Terrace southward into China. Here was a forlorn panorama of white stone and soft green meadow grasses with patches of snow and yellow buttercups. I was alone, except for a few hawks, a squirrel by the stream, two golden quail I scared up, and in the distance a lone fox sprinting up the slopes.

The bald terraces of Wutai Shan are not dramatic, perhaps, but they are severe—the softly colored hills of a broad, high desert. A receptacle for solitude. Other peaks, crowded with temples and tourists, allow no time for meditation, no time for ease. On Wutai Shan the wind is cold and unbroken; it blows without obstacle. As I walked back down the Northern Terrace, the farmers called out to me, resting their arms on the backs of their black oxen.

The Southern Terrace

The sun held court for another day and I spent it at the **Southern Terrace in Nan Shan Si,** the Southern Peak Temple of Wutai Shan. At the river the horsemen tethered their steeds, hoping to sell rides up the steep hillside, but there were no takers. I admired their horses, showy in their imperial outfits. Their owners were the only annoyance pursuing me.

I took a back trail up the Southern Terrace. The Nan Shan temple complex was built during the Yuan Dynasty (1271–1368), when the Mongols ruled China. Rewi Alley, the Australian journalist and traveler, who saw extensive stonework being done on these buildings in 1935, wrote, "This huge temple reminds one of some Norman Castle, for inside are winding stairs through great thick stone walls to towers and pavilions." This morning it was almost deserted. The formal entrance consists of 108 wide cement stairs, fronted by a shadow gate to block the straight lines along which evil beings travel. Its 108 steps are symbolic of the 108 passions, the 108 earthly delusions, and the 108 rosary beads a devout Buddhist clutches. At the top of the stairs, I was stunned to discover a vendor with a pellet rifle, set up for visitors who might want to partake of a bit of target practice before entering the temple.

There are three main temples here; they were joined together for the first time in this century. Although the oldest of the three dates back to the time of the Great Khans, to 1296, all were restored in the Qing Dynasty and are being redone today. Inside is pretty much whatever one dreams of finding in a Chinese temple: 18 lohans (Buddha's followers) carved during the Ming Dynasty, a six-armed statue of Guanyin, and a fresco called **Journey to the West,** celebrating a Buddhist monk's adventures in the 7th century. This celebrated fresco, painted on three walls of a pavilion, is crude; worse still, a fourth panel, a modern one, has been added, and it's even more amateurish. Far more striking is a brightly painted version of a **Thousand Buddha Hall** with its multiple carved images of Buddha. The twisting forms and bold colors give a decidedly fantastical, Lamaistic air to their rarefied subjects.

As I climbed from station to station, I was waylaid by monks who begged me to go inside and have a look at what was on display, usually a statue or carving I could barely decipher in the darkness. With one monk I engaged in a short chat. He was pleased I'm an American and refrained from cajoling me into making a donation.

In the center of one deep courtyard I found a stupa that seemed to be an exact reproduction of the Great White Pagoda located in the center of the Wutai Shan temple village. Here, its proportions no longer seemed monstrous. What relics it housed, I couldn't determine.

After reaching the top of the Southern Terrace, I immediately descended through a maze of marble walls and moon gates, stairways and frescoes, stone courtyards and temples with finely carved wooden doors and porches. I descended in a light breeze and kept moving. The sound of wind cracking stone on the mountain's back drove me down the terrace and up the cold stream into the valley of the temple village.

PRACTICAL INFORMATION

ORIENTATION & WHEN TO GO

Wutai Shan (Five Terrace Mountain), the most northerly of the four sacred peaks of Buddhism, is 200 miles southwest of Beijing in Shanxi Province, about 100 miles north of the provincial capital, Taiyuan. Four peaks, reaching 10,000 feet in elevation, cluster about the central terrace and temple village of Taihuai, at an elevation of 6,000 feet. The temperatures are generally cold at these elevations, but July and August are crowded with Chinese tourists; the times to come are June or September. A recent change is the development of **Dailou Peak,** directly east of the village, which affords a nice viewpoint from its temple on the summit for those willing to ascend the 1,080 steps or pay for a cable car ride (RMB 15/$1.90 each way).

Not far to the north, in the same province, is the holy Daoist mountain of **Heng Shan Bei** and the city of **Datong,** with its Buddhist grottoes of Yungang (see separate chapters).

GETTING THERE

Wutai Shan is located in a remote, mountainous region. The nearest airport connections are at Taiyuan to the south and Datong to the north.

To Taiyuan & Datong Taiyuan has plane connections to many cities in China, including Beijing (1 hour), Shanghai (2 hours), Xi'an (2 hours 20 minutes), and Hong Kong (3 hours). Trains to Taiyuan originate from Beijing (13 hours), Xi'an (14 hours), and Zhengzhou (13 hours).

Datong has train connections with Beijing (7 hours), Taiyuan (7 hours), and Xi'an (20 hours).

To Wutai Shan To reach the mountain, there are daily buses from Taiyuan, now about a 5-hour trip (RMB 45/$5.50), and from Datong, about a 6-hour trip (RMB 65/$8). For bus tickets and car hires, contact hotel desks in Taiyuan or Datong. I hired a car in Taiyuan from the travel desk in the **Shanxi Grand Hotel,** 5 Xin Jian Nan Lu (☎ 0351/404-3901), which reduced the journey to 4 hours but cost $100. Cars can also be hired from CITS offices and hotel desks in Datong (see the chapter on Datong for more information). The roads from the north and south to Wutai Shan have been improved over the last 5 years. Park gates have also been added to these highways, at which an admission fee of RMB 50 ($6) is extracted from each visitor.

TOURS & STRATAGEMS

There are no group tours to Wutai Shan, although the **China International Travel Service (CITS)** office in Datong, located at the train station (☎ 0352/502-2265), can assist with bus tickets and might even be persuaded to let you hire one of its English-speaking guides. CITS also has an office at Wutai Shan just south of the village at 18 Mingqing Jie (☎ 0352/654-2142) and another in the Yunfeng Binguan, 2 miles south of town, where maps, information, and tours are available.

WHERE TO STAY & DINE

The Friendship Hotel (Youyi Binguan), a mile south of the temple village (☎ 0352/654-2678), and the **Yunfeng Hotel (Yunfeng Binguan),** 2 miles south of the temple village (☎ 0352/654-2566), are both three-star hotels with modern rooms and private bathrooms. The Friendship Hotel charges $70 for a comfortable double; the Yunfeng charges $50 for similar rooms. No credit cards are accepted at either hotel. The Youyi Binguan has slightly nicer facilities and is closer to the main temples. The Yunfeng Binguan has a tour desk and the more helpful staff.

Wutai Shan has no restaurants catering to foreigners. The Youyi Binguan and the Yunfeng Binguan both have good restaurants that serve fixed-price Chinese meals that cost RMB 34 to RMB 85 ($4 to $10).

HENG SHAN BEI: SACRED MOUNTAIN OF THE NORTH

衡山北

HENG SHAN BEI, THE LONG Mountain of the North, is situated between two sections of the Great Wall of China. For many centuries it stood as the final barrier against China's ancient enemies, the barbarians from the north. The Han Dynasty Emperor Wu Di traveled to Heng Shan Bei with China's greatest historian, Sima Qian, in 100 B.C. Nine centuries later, in A.D. 746, a Tang emperor gave the mountain its highest title, "King, Pacifier of Heaven."

But despite its symbolism and history, the northern mountain proved to be less than an insurmountable barrier. Eventually the Khans and other outsiders swept down, subdued China, and set up their own dynasties. In response, this sacred mountain of the north was moved to the south. Heng Shan Bei was "relocated" for centuries, its title bestowed on another peak, to prevent direct contamination by the invading hordes. Only in the Ming Dynasty, when the Han Chinese again ruled the Middle Kingdom, was Heng Shan Bei reestablished on the slopes and peaks where thousands of years earlier it ruled over the mind and spirit of the empire.

Heng Shan Bei is not only Old China's northern defender. It is also the Water Mountain, its god long believed to possess the power to bring rain. As superintendent of rivers and streams, the god of Heng Shan Bei is sought out by farmers seeking his benediction to ensure the health of their livestock and the fertility of their fields. Certain royal ceremonies performed at Heng Shan Bei up until the time of the modern republic (1911) involved the slaughter of an ox in the cold before the dawn—the ox's blood offered in a bowl on the altar of the highest temple. The hope was to bring the spring rains to China. As recently as half a century ago these cliff temples were shining symbols of mountain spirits that both guarded the edges of an empire and delivered the nation from droughts.

When I first saw Heng Shan Bei myself, a massive rampart of stone rising like a natural Great Wall in the midst of a high desert plateau, I understood how the mountain itself could personify these qualities. Nowhere else in this vast region of dryness did the clouds seem to gather, giving visible shape to the thirst for rains that must have gripped generations of northern Chinese, who repeatedly faced starvation. Times have changed, of course, but this northern mountain of water still holds reminders of its former functions and grandeur, despite a remote, even obscure, site in an isolated part of modern China.

The Road to the Long Mountain

Heng Shan Bei is about 50 miles southeast of the northern coal city of Datong. The country road from Datong to the mountain is paved most of the way to Hunyuan, the sacred village at the foot of Heng Shan Bei. The terrain is a terraced plateau of sandstone, coal, and soda ash. Between sandy bluffs and pinnacles are cave towns, every dwelling sculpted of dry mud. These villages resemble remote oases. The camel caravans of the past have been replaced by rows of electric power lines and ranks of buses and coal trucks.

Snaking through the crowded streets of **Hunyuan** in a taxi hired in Datong, I could see Heng Shan Bei ahead—more a wall of exposed limestone than a mountain, a high ridge of stone on a plain of gray sand and rock. From this village—once containing 200 temples and surrounded by an eight-sided city wall—we rose through the Mouth of the Golden Dragon, a valley of exposed limestone that parts to empty a river. This narrow gorge was widened for travel in A.D. 397 by a Wei Dynasty emperor and his 10,000 men. On the west wall of the gorge is the Temple Suspended Over the Void (see the chapter on Datong for a complete description of this marvel).

At the south end of the gorge a steel-and-concrete dam (187 feet high, 338 feet wide) was completed in 1958, creating the vast Heng Shan Reservoir. The surrounding barren plateau, useful only for its low-grade coal, was long known for its killer droughts. Today, however, it has achieved what incense and pilgrimage failed to secure: a regular supply of water from the mountain, thanks to the gods of science and technology.

The Mountain Gate

We drove up the Magnet Gorge in a flurry, through a tunnel on the west wall of Heng Shan Bei, around an edge of the long reservoir, then east and north to the parking lot on the south side of the peak. A traditional three-arched gate with red columns and golden eaves, guarded by two stone lions, marks the entrance to the 30 mountain temples and shrines that rise up the slopes of what the ancients called the "Grand Column of the North."

Heng Shan Bei is a mountain of cliff faces and bluffs. The temples perch on ledges, spread out across terraces, and climb section by section up steep stone walls. A trail from the south entrance saunters up the mountain, threading together the overlooks and shrines, leading to the high peaks and pavilions and finally the summit, **Tian Ling Feng,** at 6,617 feet.

Hall of the Pure Sun

It took me less than 20 minutes to reach the mountain's first large temple, the **Hall of the Pure Sun (Zhong Yuan Kong).** The inscription at the entrance thanks the mountain god for bountiful harvests. On a clear day, pilgrims can see from here all the way across the barren plains to the sacred mountain of Wutai Shan, 50 miles to the south. Today, the air was filthy with fine particles and I couldn't see the outlines of distant peaks with any precision.

I forged on, pausing only to buy tea from a vendor at the **Traveler's Greeting Pine,** a lonely umbrella of a tree near a pavilion with a famous overlook known as **Gu Sao Cliff.** The sheer drop-off is considerable. A local story tells of a widow named Gu who refused to remarry, despite her family's insistence. Gu threw herself from the mountain at this spot. Her brother's wife, Sao, understanding her sadness, followed her into the abyss. Both were transformed by the mountain god into larks who forever chase after each other across the mountain spaces, crying.

Temples of the Ming

After another hour's climb, I reached a cluster of cliff temples and pavilions not far below the summit. The most important shrine here, **Heng Zong Monastery,** dates from the Ming Dynasty (1368–1644), when Heng Shan Bei reclaimed its importance as a major pilgrimage site for Daoists. The halls have been restored recently, although the red brick exteriors that rise on stone terraces up a white cliff face look both ancient and Tibetan. Bell and drum towers stand at the bottom. One hundred three stairs lead to the highest hall, in which there is a bearded statue of the supreme mountain god of Heng Shan Bei and an inscription over the shrine entrance written by Emperor Kangxi during a 17th-century visit.

Kangxi, a Manchurian, inherited the Qing Dynasty his grandfather established. Even if his own ancestors were barbarians from the north, Kangxi came to Heng Shan Bei as a strictly Chinese monarch, paying homage to China's native religion (Daoism) and legitimizing his rule over the Han Chinese nation by honoring its traditional sites.

On terraces below and west of the Heng Zong Monastery are many halls I barely had time to take in: the **Chun Yuang Palace,** which has a statue of Lu Dongbin, one of the Eight Immortals in the Daoist tradition who has triumphed over death and rides with the clouds; and the **Jiu Tian Palace,** where pilgrims pray to the goddess Xie Nu for male offspring. The latter is still one of the most active shrines on Heng Shan Bei. These temples are small, humble, gritty abodes, each with a monk or nun in attendance, and they all have an authentic feel that larger, more tourist-laden shrines lack.

The westernmost temple on the mountain is devoted to **Gui Xing, the North Star God.** The statue of this god is portrayed as keeping one foot planted on a sea monster while supporting the Pole Star constellation, which Chinese astronomers picture as a bushel (rather than as a bear or water dipper). Gui Xing is a god of the harvest—therefore a favorite of farmers wishing for bushels of good crops each year. The North Star god was also once a favorite of China's students, as he was said to light the way to knowledge. Those hoping to pass the national civil service examinations used to troop up the mountain to this shrine by the thousands. Today, the temple to the North Star is virtually empty.

Other ledge and cliff temples here have their tiny treasures, mainly tablets inscribed by Qing Dynasty emperors who traced their lineage north to the Mongolian steppes. I stopped at one more shrine, the **Palace of the Immortals,** which has images of 72 minor Daoist immortals, eight cave-dwelling angels, and three other gods—dispensers of wealth, happiness, and long life, gifts even science and technology can't always bestow.

A Summit in Space

Anxious to reach the summit, I climbed above the last of the big temples and wound up the cliff past several pavilions to the **Slab of Qin and Qi,** a natural stage of solid rock. The backdrop is a smooth cliff face, inscribed with large Chinese characters painted red. As with much of the mountain, this formation refers to another fantastical story in the Daoist tradition, this one concerning two immortals who performed on a cosmic stage before vanishing into the heavens.

The rough trail to the summit brought me to an elevation of 6,617 feet, a rise of 1,200 feet gained over a leisurely 2½-hour climb. Southward, the plains on the margins of China simmered with dust, smoking like shaken coal flakes. I looked across an infinity without depth, without exact horizon, with no final line of definition, no known boundary, as if I was standing on the edge of space.

The sacred mountain on the northern frontier is almost forgotten today, but its slopes still hum with some of the temples of old, and the barren vistas are impressive. The summit where I stood is empty but altogether formidable and massive—pure space and dust, as elemental as China gets. This is where the mountain god of the north was worshipped for centuries by commoner and emperor alike as defender against barbarians and herald of rain, as harbinger of good harvests, as protector of farm animals, and as controller of tigers, leopards, reptiles, and worms. His powers may have been usurped by modern science, but his ramparts remain as striking as ever. Even the silence is as vast as any I've experienced, broken only by the song of larks.

Practical Information

ORIENTATION & WHEN TO GO

Heng Shan Bei (Long Mountain of the North), the most northerly of the Five Sacred Mountains of Daoism, is 200 miles southwest of Beijing in Shanxi Province, about 50 miles southeast of the city of Datong. The summit is at an elevation of 6,617 feet. Winters are long and cold, making the summer months the best time to visit.

Datong, the gateway to the mountain, is worth visiting for its own attractions, which include the Buddhist grottoes of Yungang and the Temple Suspended Over the Void (see the Datong chapter). South of Datong and Heng Shan Bei, in the same province, is the holy Buddhist peak of **Wutai Shan** (see separate chapter).

GETTING THERE

By Train to Datong The nearest rail terminal is located at Datong. Datong has convenient daily railroad connections with Beijing (7 hours) and Xi'an (20 hours).

To Heng Shan Bei To reach Heng Shan Bei from Datong, hire a **taxi** for the day (about RMB 600/$72) or make arrangements with **CITS** (see below). It is also possible to take a **public bus** from Datong to the village of Hunyuan. From Hunyuan, there are minibuses that cover the remaining 10 miles to the mountain. Public transportation is cheap (RMB 20/$2.50 each way) but time-consuming and difficult for those without skill in the language or China travel experience.

TOURS & STRATAGEMS

Check with the **China International Travel Service (CITS) offices** in Datong (☎ 0352/502-2265) about tours and transportation to Heng Shan Bei. CITS maintains offices at the Datong train station and in the Yungang Hotel, 21 Yingbin Dong Lu. You can hire an English-speaking guide and a car for the day, if they are available. CITS also offers convenient tours to the Temple Suspended Over the Void, which is very near Heng Shan Bei, but the mountain and its temples are not included on these tours.

The mountain is a day trip from Datong. Be sure to depart from Datong early. The trail to the summit is about 4 miles, and hiking up and back takes 4 to 5 hours. Admission tickets are sold at the entrance gate to Heng Shan Bei (RMB 20/$2.50).

WHERE TO STAY & DINE

Heng Shan Bei has no accommodations. The nearby village of Hunyuan has only the most basic inns. Plan on making the mountain a day trip, returning to your hotel in Datong in the evening. See the chapter on Datong for hotel information.

If you hire a CITS guide, your guide will select a local restaurant in the village of Hunyuan. Otherwise, if you're on your own, pack a day's worth of food in Datong and take it along. The vendors on the mountain path sell bottled water and drinks as well as simple local dishes such as noodles and hot sauce.

Jiuhua Shan: Buddhist Peak of the South

九华山

Jiuhua Shan, Nine Lotus Mountain, is the supreme dwelling place of Dizang, God of the Underworld. Pilgrims used to come to Jiuhua Shan to seek this god's intercession in ending the torments their ancestors and family members suffered after being cast into the Buddhist inferno. Getting to this mountain gave me a taste of what the bus system in hell must be like.

I boarded the long-distance bus from Hangzhou to Jiuhua Shan at 6:45am, stuffing my backpack into the corner of the bench seat next to the rear window. Several groups of old women boarded. They were wearing the knit caps and Buddhist rosary beads of Old China's pilgrims. The bus finally lurched out of its slip at 7am. The conductor, sitting across the engine cover from the driver, smoked up a storm; so did many of the passengers.

Our mastodon of a bus, with its petrified suspension, soon struck enough unpatched cracks in the road to make me wish I'd not drunk that second cup of coffee. The seats were spaced so that I barely had room for my lower legs; my knees received a steady pounding. I tried to steel myself against this nasty parody of motion, with little success.

A Chinese bus is not only slow and cramped; it's dangerous. Passing is an adventure. Since a bus is one of the larger vehicles on the narrow open road, whenever it swings out to pass, the rest of the traffic, including those vehicles coming straight at it, shift to the shoulder, scattering bicycles, rototillers, and pedestrians. The bus horn blasts constantly, but most of the way even brute passing is impossible. The highways are just too full. And the villages are so crammed that our bus often had to brake to a complete halt. Top speed between settlements is about 40 miles per hour; average speed, 20 miles per hour.

The fields were full of graves, rock-faced mounds capped with fresh white flags. The farming villages were a swelter of pigs, water buffalo,

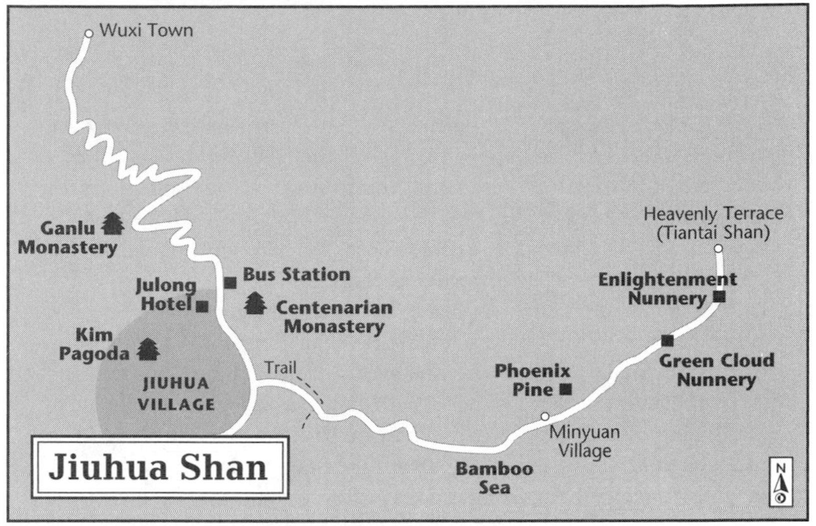

and pods of ducks and ducklings. Not until midafternoon, 8 hours after departure, did a range of mountains, encrusted in haze, break through the horizon. Our final ascent was via a hairpin road that wound upward between steep green bamboo slopes. The old women slid open every window for a view, but the unpaved road muddied the pure mountain air, lacing it with road dust. We were on the flanks of the holy mountain, and we couldn't see or breathe.

In Buddha's Navel

We corkscrewed halfway up the legendary 99 peaks of Jiuhua Shan on a new unpaved road from Wuxi Town. The old pilgrim route, which the devout walked up until the late 20th century, still exists, but almost no one climbs it anymore. Not far from the top of this spiral highway I saw the magnificent **Sweet Dew Monastery (Ganlu),** its white walls five stories high, chiseled into a declivity in 1667. Sweet Dew Monastery was destroyed by the Taiping rebels and rebuilt about 1875, but it still looks as ancient as the bamboo rain forest. From the road, I caught only a glimpse of its white walls, enveloped in dust as if in mist. A dozen more turns upward, beyond the Second Gate of Heaven, the bus slumped into Jiuhua Terminal and collapsed like a beaten hound.

I had reached what locals call the navel of the pot-bellied Buddha, the very village of monks and tourists, monasteries and souvenir stands, hotels and cinemas, where 1,700 years ago, after days of hard climbing, solitary monks and nuns pitched their thatched huts in the heart of "Lotus Buddha Land" and meditated upon the mountain void.

The void has been filled in and brought up to date, although it's not exactly midtown Manhattan. Hawkers line Jiuhua Street, but this is a small, faraway place and the hurricane of entrepreneurs has not arrived with full force. True, as soon as I came off the bus I was led uphill by a woman to the street's newest hotel, the **Julong,** but she was no pushy vendor on commission. Besides, the Julong Hotel was where I would have stayed had I known it existed. I'd come here with practically no information, except a few historical accounts.

The hotel isn't exactly a palace, but it does have a lobby—even if there's nothing in the lobby, not a single chair. There are no brochures or maps in English, either—no one speaks English here—but the staff is exceptionally cordial. I've dealt with much worse hosts in Shanghai and Beijing. After 11 hours of mechanical chiropractic in the bus, I had just enough flexibility left to walk from the hotel to the end of the road, which is crammed with shops and tiny cafes for 6 blocks. An occasional large temple has been left standing for atmosphere.

Then, at precisely 6:59pm, electricity to the little town blew its central fuse. I could barely see my way back, although a number of stalls were firing up candles and lanterns as I staggered back to the hotel in the dark.

Temples & Mummies

Jiuhua Shan was immortalized in Chinese tradition by two contemporaries who met each other on these very slopes. The best known is Li Bai, the magnificent Tang Dynasty poet, who lived in a secluded cottage on Jiuhua Shan from A.D. 746 to 747. He penned the lines that not only named the mountain but gave final definition to its castellated crags:

Looking far beyond this village wall
I see the peaks of the Southern Mountain
Emerging from the River of Heaven
As nine magnificent lotus blossoms.

The other famous resident was Kim Kiao Kak, a monk from Korea, who made a pilgrimage to Jiuhua Shan in A.D. 719 and founded a temple to Dizang, the God of the Mountain, known in India as Ksitigarbha. As the Earth–Womb bodhisattva, Dizang wades into the bowels of Hell to aid the damned. To put it more gently, Dizang sets free those who are unhappy—those undergoing the agonies of Hell—and points them to a higher, purer level once they have tasted the pains of the underworld.

Dizang is therefore a god of salvation. Like Guanyin, the Goddess of Mercy, he changed sex during a long translation into Chinese Buddhism. He was taken up in China readily enough, changing to a man and becoming the intercessor before the 10 judges who mete out the 10 punishments for earthly sin.

Prince Kim prayed to Dizang for 75 years here, and upon his death he became the incarnation of the mountain god. At age 99, he gathered his disciples around him. The Earth split open and into its cleft the monk sank to his death. His disciples buried him on the spot but opened his coffin every 3 years. The corpse refused to age. A pagoda was erected on the tomb; a temple was built around the pagoda; and inside this temple-pagoda resided the undecayed body of the transformed pilgrim-prince, Dizang made flesh.

This monk from Korea became the flesh body that has sanctified Jiuhua Shan. ("Flesh bodies" are the mummified remains of devout Buddhist monks and patriarchs.) Flesh bodies on the holy mountains of China—and there are scores of them—serve a simple purpose: They sanctify a mountain, demonstrating that it is indeed a place of miracles, of Heaven-infused Earth. When the flesh body was that of a Buddhist, it converted the mountain to Buddhism as well.

Jiuhua Street still contains the **temple of Kim/Dizang's earthly remains** and his indoor seven-story pagoda, reached on a stone stairway of nine-times-nine steps. Branching off this thoroughfare are short paths to a bell tower, an incense hall, and a handful of old monasteries with singularly evocative names: Sandalwood, Illusion City, Centenarian. **Centenarian Monastery,** consisting of 99½ prayer halls and monks' rooms (to be exact), was first called Star-Plucking Temple but was renamed to honor Wu Xia, a wandering monk who died here in the 16th century, reportedly at the age of 126. The 350-year-old flesh body of Wu Xia is now on display in this monastery, his legs crossed in lotus position and arms folded in space—a seated mummy of skull and bones lacquered in gold. Like Prince Kim, Wu Xia achieved bodhisattvahood, a complete identity with Dizang. His transcription of the *Sutra of the Adornment of Buddha* in 81 volumes, a work over which he labored for 24 years, is also contained in this monastery. What sets this opus of copywork apart is that he brushed every character of it in his own blood after mixing it with gold.

Crossing the Bamboo Sea

Despite all these ancient attractions, the temples and halls of Jiuhua Shan, my mind was on the mountaintops. A Chinese guidebook sums it up thus: "Those who have already ascended to Jiuhua Street always think of climbing atop Heavenly Terrace Peak to fulfill their wish of reaching the summit and gazing into infinity." Yes: to gaze into infinity—that would do nicely.

Heavenly Terrace (Tiantai Shan), at 4,340 feet, is the chief peak of the traditional 99 peaks of Jiuhua Shan, and the march to its ramparts is

5 miles of trails and stone stairs. In fact, according to the official census, Jiuhua Shan contains 250,000 stone steps, cut and laid by hand.

I set out at 8:30am, following a path of stone slabs east off Jiuhua Street. It led me past a stunning public lavatory, a spacious white building with a lofty tiled roof that I would have mistaken for a temple were it not for the characters for man and woman hand-painted on either side. A canal cascaded down from this outhouse, marking the mountain trail.

The old pilgrim women from my bus were not far ahead. Perhaps they'd come with a real purpose: to petition Dizang for the release of family members from the prison cells of the afterlife. Most of the people ascending the trail were not so devout. They were sightseers dressed in jeans, V-necked sweaters, blue-jean jackets, and white running shoes. They did not burn joss sticks at every station along the route.

From where I started, I could barely make out Heavenly Terrace, one of the distant jagged peaks in a broad fortress, separated by a deep valley. After surmounting the ridge that rises above Jiuhua Street, I descended into that intervening valley.

The stair trail was clean at first, bordered by fields of bamboo, pink blossoms, and tea rows. Vendors had pitched their canvas-topped stalls every so often, and my first stop after an hour's stroll was to buy a bottle of water. Spring water in plastic bottles has flooded the Chinese marketplace. Visitors to Jiuhua Shan gulp water and cast the empties into the green margins. At the base of the valley is a village, **Minyuan,** its buildings washed white. Whitewashed nunneries dot the enfolded hillsides. I don't remember ever seeing so many monasteries and nunneries in one place in China. They face Zhuhai, the Bamboo Sea, great repository of those plastic bottles.

The Circles of Hell

Crossing a vibrant stream, I left the valley behind and ascended more stairs to the **Phoenix Pine (Fenghuang Song),** said to have been greeting pilgrims with its wide arms for a thousand years. The pine had been encircled recently with a marble wall. Beside it, visitors gathered to rest and gossip. Some, mounted on brown ponies and costumed in long black robes with matching Stetsons, paid a roving photographer for their portraits. Everyone paused at the pine, including the sedan chair porters. I counted at least 20 carriers. Their chairs are of bamboo and wicker, squarish, straight-backed, with matted headrests. Their long carrying poles are bamboo as well. It's exceedingly tough work for two men: The stairs are steep enough to make me sweat.

The trail beyond the Phoenix Pine meanders from temple to temple, and even right through the heart of a temple, where I brushed past nuns tending open fires of incense. I came across more old women, two of whom are munching on sugarcane, tearing off mouthful after mouthful. They had their sticks of incense, and sheaves of paper money filled their shan bags. They'd come well stocked with offerings to burn for those in the underworld who are short of cash. These notes from the Bank of Hell, written in monstrous sums, are used by the dead to bribe their way through the Ten Courts of the Underworld, said to be located under this very mountain.

The Chinese circles of Hell are courts of punishment that grow more severe with depth. The second court, for example, is a great frozen lake for general torture. The third is populated by unfilial sons and disobedient state officials. The fourth is for those who committed fraud and those who let their animals disturb others. Other courts are tailored to the punishment of other sins, and most of the sins are more Confucian than Daoist or Buddhist, concerned with violations of the family hierarchy in all its manifestations. There is a deep court reserved for the most heinous criminals, for murderers who must sweat it out until their victims are reincarnated.

Buddha's Bunny

Walking from temple to temple, I came upon a vendor who had vacated his low chair in front of a shop and left tethered to it a fat rabbit—probably more meal than pet or talisman. When Buddha took a stroll in the forest, so one story goes, all the animals showered him with the foodstuffs they had gathered, except for the rabbit, who is not a gatherer. Still, moved to an act of transcendence, the rabbit hurled itself into the flames of the campfire to serve as a meal, and by the time Buddha could rescue it the rabbit was roasted through. Buddha immortalized the creature by granting it dominion over the lunar orb, and ever after, just as we look for the man in the moon, the Chinese look for the rabbit.

Today, Jiuhua Shan is neither lunar nor infernal. If this be hell, it is an absolutely pleasant one. The fires seem confined to incense burners, a few of which, placed in the middle of the road, are towering: 12 feet high and tiered like iron pagodas, bells swinging from their pitch-black eaves.

Green Cloud Nunnery

The rock cliffs that make up the summit are perfectly vertical. The stairs coil tediously around and about. I passed through one small temple filled with fire and smoke, its low walls black as a cave. Then came a stretch of yet steeper stairs with a stone railing, called the **Heavenly Staircase,** which ended high above in the **Green Cloud Nunnery.** Green Cloud is fronted by a narrow gallery affording a splendid view of the valley floor at the bottom of a vast ravine from which I had just climbed. Just below me, on a spur trail, dozens of old women paraded before a small stone incense burner. They collapsed to their knees and elbows to pray. Several were nuns, dressed head to foot in black silk gowns and caps.

Above me, the rock outcroppings tapered into the sky, resembling uplifted sword blades. I inched upward on the steep stairs. Just ahead was **Enlightenment Nunnery,** a five-story edifice capping a dramatic drop-off. This nunnery is an impregnable fortress pinioned to a perch under the final peak like a palace for eagles. Here I had reached the subrealm of Guanyin, the Goddess of Mercy, and she had endowed the way to the Heavenly Terrace with her own image, transformed into a single slender rock. It is a startling likeness of the goddess, life-sized, with flowing long hair and a meditative posture. Yet it appears to be a natural rock form poised in space, surveying the deep valley I crossed an hour ago. Someone had draped her in a red cape to keep her warm. She's surrounded by other formations, fissured and weathered into suggestive shapes, the candles and censers of a mountain altar. Above this monument to mercy, the mountain belongs to Dizang and the Ten Judges of Hell.

Heavenly Terrace

The trail twisted up to Heavenly Terrace Peak, Dizang's high throne, with its **Temple of Ten Thousand Buddhas** and the **Sun-Holding Pavilion.** I reached this supreme summit with a determined grunt, well before noon. This high platform of Jiuhua Shan is nearly bare, paved in large white square blocks. White, not black, is the Chinese color of death, which perhaps explains the white walls of all the nunneries, monasteries, and temples. Pilgrims, even many of the young Chinese tourists, were busy here tossing incense sticks into two round three-legged black pots. A hundred steps below me, vendors did a brisk business in joss and charms.

Beyond this platform, the throng spread out on a narrow spine for views in every direction as far as the Yangzi River. For once, the claim of 99 peaks was not a poetic exaggeration: There are hundreds of peaks. I walked along the narrow spine of the summit, sat down in a niche, and took in the view.

The Jiuhua Shan I found today may not be the Jiuhua Shan of yesteryear. But no matter that there are but half as many temples, nunneries, and monasteries as travelers found a century ago. No matter that the 7,000 pilgrims a day who visited here at the end of the last dynasty have dwindled to a few hundred tourists, a few score believers. I could feel that the old connections were waiting to be seized and plugged in, if only one could recommend how. At the summit of this mountain paradise is the ancient gate to Hell. The line is thin but sublime.

PRACTICAL INFORMATION

ORIENTATION & WHEN TO GO

Jiuhua Shan (Nine Lotus Mountain) is located in southern Anhui Province, 140 miles west of Hangzhou, 260 miles southwest of Shanghai, and 40 miles northwest of Huang Shan (Yellow Mountain), a 4-hour bus drive on mountain roads. Subject to heat, humidity, and rain in midsummer, Jiuhua Shan is ideal to visit in May and October. The annual temple fair usually runs from mid-August to mid-September, during which 100,000 tourists visit. Jiuhua Village, halfway up the mountain range (9 miles from Wuxi Town), is where the 5-mile trek to the 4,340-foot summit begins.

GETTING THERE

By Bus There is no rail service or airport near Jiuhua Shan, making a bus trip necessary. If you visit **Huang Shan** (see separate chapter), there is daily bus service from there to Jiuhua Shan (4 hours) on a new highway. Otherwise, the most convenient bus connection is to and from **Hangzhou,** a 7- to 11-hour trip. Bus tickets to Jiuhua Shan (about $7 one-way) can be purchased in Hangzhou from the **Shangri-La Hotel,** 78 Beishan Lu (☎ 0571/797-7951). In Jiuhua Shan, bus tickets to Hangzhou and Huang Shan are sold at the ticket office of the bus station, which is to your left at the entrance to Jiuhua Village.

TOURS & STRATAGEMS

Visitor Information There is a **China International Travel Service (CITS)** office on Jiuhua Street in the village (☎ 0566/501-1318; fax 0566/501-1202). It offers information and maps.

Exploring the Mountain At the entrance to the village you are required to buy a ticket for the mountain for RMB 50 ($6). At Phoenix Pine (Fenghuang Song) on the trail to the summit there is a new **cable car** (RMB 30/$3.75 each way) that runs nearly to the top. Taxis and some minibuses at the village gate go to the cable car terminal. If you want to see the sunrise from the summit, catch the cable car, since its terminal at Phoenix Pine is less than an hour's quick walk from the village.

WHERE TO STAY

The best choice is the **Julong Hotel (Julong Dajiudian)** (☎ 0566/501-1368; fax 0566/501-1022). Located on the right-hand side of the street a block uphill from the bus station in Jiuhua Village, the Julong carries a two-star rating, which is generous. The rooms and baths are modern but a bit rundown. No credit cards are accepted. The closest thing to a pool is the fountain outside the entrance, where guns for target practice can be rented. Doubles cost $50.

WHERE TO DINE

Jiuhua Shan has no restaurants of note, certainly none with English-language menus. The **Julong Hotel** (☎ 0556/501-1368) has a large Chinese restaurant where foreigners are served fixed-price breakfasts, lunches, and dinners for RMB 42 to RMB 100 ($5 to $12). If you continue up the main street through the village, you pass dozens of small cafes and food stalls. The mountain trail to the summit also has many vendors selling snacks, drinks, and hot meals (usually noodles with hot sauce), and there are local cafes at Phoenix Pine.

Heng Shan Nan: Sacred Mountain of the South

衡山南

Heng Shan Nan is the southern peak on the Daoist compass of China's Five Sacred Mountains. According to an ancient record, "The Heng Mountain rules the Southern Land by the virtue of Fire." The fire god lives on the highest of Heng Shan Nan's peaks, Zhurong Feng, elevation 4,232 feet. To see what remained on the highest peak of the sacred mountain of the south, I set out in the morning on a bus from Changsha, the capital of Hunan Province, finally reaching the village of Nan Yue and the gate to Heng Shan Nan 3 hours late, owing mostly to the bus driver running out of gas in the countryside.

Heng Shan Nan is commonly called Nan Yue, which means "Southern Peak," but knowing its local name didn't help me much. I had no local map, just a rudimentary sense of direction. I walked a mile up an unpaved road to the village at the foot of the mountain. At the end of the village, the road forks up a steep hill. I found a parked bus aimed up the mountain.

I drew a crowd when I inquired if this was the bus to Ban Shan Ting, a region of the mountain where I wanted to lodge for the night. People gave me smiling stares and motioned me aboard. I took a seat, opened my pack, and dug out the lunch I packed in Changsha. It was approaching 3pm, and having skipped breakfast, this was the first food I'd tasted today: crackers that could have used a touch more salt.

The bus was parked in front of **Nanyue Miao,** the Temple of the Southern Mountain. This is one of the three most famous Buddhist temples in China. It is also the largest Buddhist complex anywhere on the Five Sacred Mountains. Nanyue Miao was built in A.D. 725 but leveled many times, most recently in the 19th century by the Taiping Rebels, their leader a rabidly anti–Western Hunanese who fancied himself the brother of Jesus Christ. The present set of buildings, with their yellow-glazed tiles, dates back but to 1882. When the final emperor of China assumed the throne in 1911, an ox was sacrificed at this temple, but aside from its largest hall, supported by 72 pillars, each 72 feet high in honor of the 72 peaks of Heng Shan Nan, the temple did not attract me. The mountain did.

The character of the mountain is confusing, or perhaps it is just Daoist. Red is its symbolic color, fire its primordial element, but the mountain has a history shaped by legendary Emperor Yu in his epic struggle against floods 3,000 years ago. Yu is credited with subduing the rising waters that besieged the lower Yangzi River basin by constructing nine abatement channels. Heng Shan Nan is just south of the Yangzi. It has a long history of attracting officials and even emperors to its altars, where they prayed for deliverance from the floods. Perhaps it takes a mountain god of fire to subdue the floods of China's mightiest river.

Mr. Ma Gu

The bus rolled out as I finished lunch. The highway up the mountain crisscrossed the stone steps of the old pilgrim path. There has been a paved road to the top for many decades. It was resurfaced in 1933 by order of the governor of Hunan, who maintained his own elaborate summer house partway up the sacred peak, as did many officials and merchants. I could see why they made this their retreat. The scenery is pleasing. In the gentle mist, I had a romantic view of rice terraces along the Nanyue Reservoir. Passing a 1942 memorial to those who died when the Japanese invaded here in 1937, we began a steep rise. I disembarked at Ban Shan Ting.

Ban Shan Ting was once the site of a Daoist guesthouse, a midway pavilion built in 1878 as a resting place for pilgrims. Today, not a single pilgrim was in sight. In fact, there were no travelers of any description. The rain was pounding down. I opened my umbrella. The road was dotted with a few concession booths, all closed. I struck out up the road. I didn't know what else to do and I didn't know where I was going.

I came to a billboard with a map. An arrow was aimed at a hotel. A boy stopped beside me, staring too at the sign. I asked him if he knew the way to a hotel. He nodded. We came to an intersection. I wanted to go right, since that was the way up the mountain, but he motioned me left. He guided me to a modern guesthouse on a bluff. Inside, the lobby was empty, save for a single clerk fetched by my companion. I was led to the rear and outside, up two flights of stairs to a balcony. I could look over the bright green tiles of the lower roofs and across the valley to a crowded screen of distant peaks.

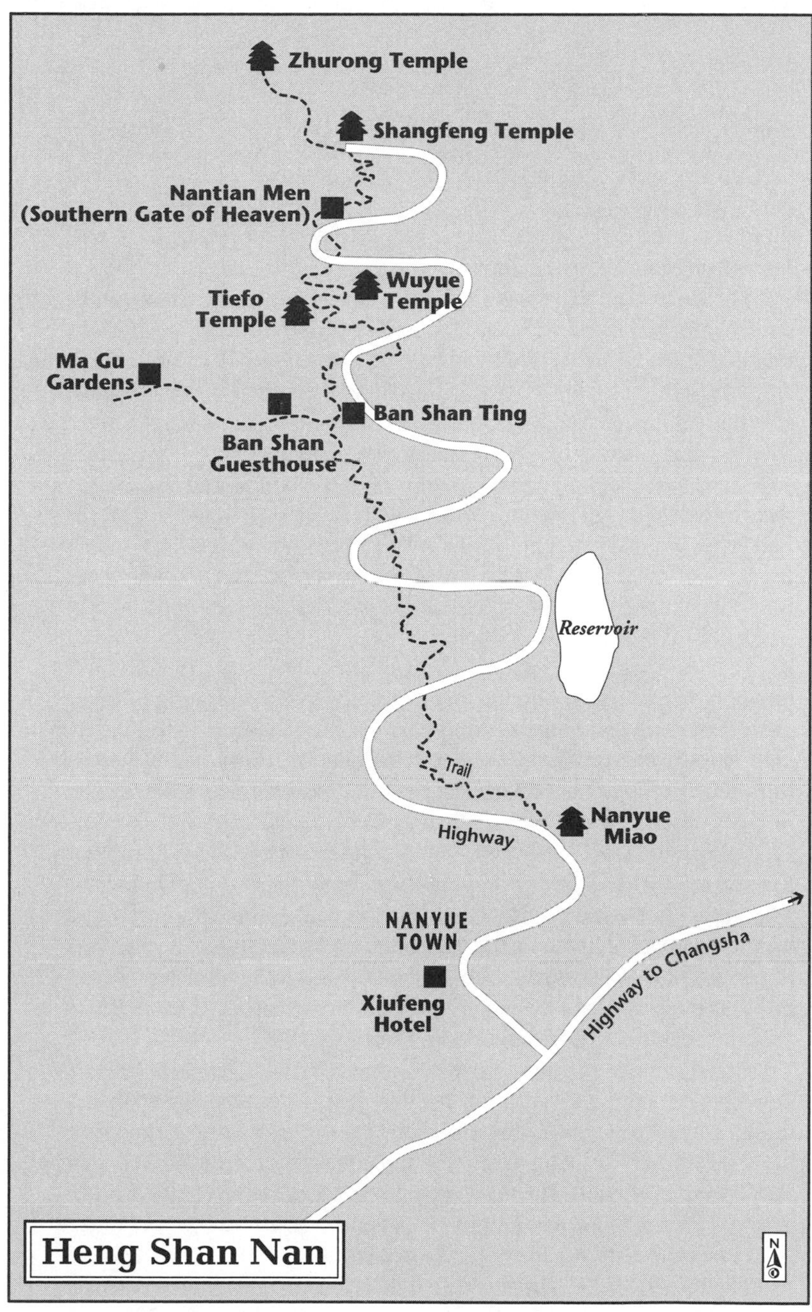
Zhurong Temple
Shangfeng Temple
Nantian Men
(Southern Gate of Heaven)
Wuyue
Temple
Tiefo
Temple
Ma Gu
Gardens
Ban Shan Ting
Ban Shan
Guesthouse
Reservoir
Trail
Nanyue
Miao
Highway
NANYUE
TOWN
Xiufeng
Hotel
Highway to Changsha
Heng Shan Nan
N

The accommodations resembled those of an extremely shabby summer resort. I paid for a night in room 307, a room with a splendid view. In a photograph, my immediate surroundings would resemble a misty mountain paradise, dotted with remote monasteries, temples, and old summer homes. Fifty years ago, China's Republican officials were selling housing lots left and right up here for summer homes.

The room was spacious with plenty of wooden furniture: a wardrobe with a mirror, a night table, a desk, and two overstuffed chairs, plus a thermos bottle of boiled water and two tea cups and my own spittoon on the floor. The tiny color television on the desk received one station: the government channel from Beijing. There were no toilet paper or towels. The Western toilet with its black seat was gurgling—not a good sign. The bed was made up Chinese style, with a blanket and a quilt, no sheets. I waited a few minutes, then headed out to see something of the Ban Shan Ting settlement, but I didn't make it out of the lobby unaccompanied. The hotel boy latched onto me again. We headed somewhere west along a mountain terrace. He escorted me on a quick tour of a fanciful **hillside garden,** complete with pools, stone stairways, carved boulders, and white marble statues of maidens and stags. We climbed terrace to terrace. I couldn't figure out what we were visiting: perhaps a sort of fairyland amusement park. The grounds are dedicated to Ma Gu. The fantastical Mr. Ma Gu was a celebrated herbalist and alchemist from the dim Daoist past. My teenaged guide scaled the garden terraces in rapid order; I persuaded him that I'd had enough.

Back in the hotel I requested dinner. The staff flew into action. They handed me a menu containing four items, including soup and chicken. I nodded. They asked me to sit in the lobby while dinner was prepared. The lobby was unlighted in the dark rainy weather, furnished with rows of rattan chairs stacked one in front of another—all the furniture seemed to be in transition, like that of a resort between seasons. The staff was understandably idle: I was their only guest.

A girl sauntered over. She spoke a few words of English. She sat down beside me and asked if she could look at the notebook I was writing in. I handed it to her. She proceeded to read every page of my intimate travel diary. When she was done, I asked if she understood what I'd written. Not really, she answered. Good thing, I thought. I sat like this for an hour. China has taught me patience. An enormous water beetle crossed the dirty marble floor. No one else paid it the least attention. The insect wobbled all the way to the door and wriggled outside. After a few minutes I went out on the porch to see if I could find it. No trace. The rain kept falling like a curse.

I was summoned into a back dining room and seated at a large table. The hotel boy joined me for an enormous dinner, complete with bottles of beer. He ate through every plate in rapid-fire fashion. The dinner cost a fortune by ordinary Chinese standards, nearly $10. Heading back to my room, I noticed a spittoon positioned outside every door. A small bar of soap and some brown paper towels had been delivered. All night the fire god of Heng Shan Nan delivered buckets of fragrant rain.

Stepping into the Clouds

Forgoing Sunday breakfast at the inn, I sneaked through the lobby and popped out the door before 7am, the hotel boy nowhere in sight. I skipped down the road and inquired of a local the way to **Zhurong Feng,** the highest peak of Heng Shan Nan. My morning climb should cover about 3 miles with a 2,000-foot rise from Ban Shan Ting. Once off the highway, I kept to the trail of slab stairs that rises in straight segments, bisecting the curving highway the buses take to the summit.

There was a heavy blanket of fog on the slopes. Nan Yue is renowned for its storms. I could see only a hundred feet ahead, sometimes half that much. I passed a few inns and cafes, a handful of temples, and several simple tables of souvenirs and foodstuffs. The low visibility, the tea plants, the bamboo forests baffled the sounds of the outside world. The mountain was silent.

The bamboo forests are impressive, the bamboo stocks as large as water pipes and probably as strong. I saw no wildlife at all—too civilized, given the paved highway to the top. There weren't many other people on the trail, although the slopes were littered with plastic wrappers and containers. Perhaps this weekend's tourists had already ridden a bus to the summit.

I savored the slow pace, the quiet, the solitude. I saw a small herd of black cows, unattended, near a cave temple dedicated to Guanyin. The Goddess of Mercy seems to be on every mountain, Daoist as well as Buddhist. On this Daoist peak of the south, scores of pilgrims are said to have once leaped from **Guanyin's Cliff** to their deaths, rapt with divine ecstasy and the hope of breaking through to a better world. That merciful cliff never pierces the fog, which filled in all gaps this morning.

After an hour's walk, a tiny, worn temple parted the fog a hundred stairs above. I could hear chanting within, whispers becoming soft voices as I neared. Cloaked in mist, the temple itself seemed to be speaking. But upon arriving at the door of this enchanted temple, I was hurled back to solid earth: Two novice monks were manning a card table at the entrance, selling admission tickets to the performance within.

I pushed on, catching up with a peasant boy shouldering a shovel. He kept pace with me. The trail merged with the road and a confusing terrain of buildings. We arrived at a construction site. I could see higher peaks ahead. The boy joined other laborers at an excavation, but he pointed me the right way to the top.

This paved highway certainly robs the mountain of its centuries of romance and remoteness, although in inclement weather, especially in the mist, the intrusion is veiled. Otherwise, Heng Shan Nan would be little short of a Chinese version of Yosemite Park. I scarcely realized that I was passing through more than a construction site; passing through, in fact, the **Southern Gate of Heaven (Nantian Men)**—a three-legged stone gate *(pailou)* engraved with this inscription, painted bright red:

Here is South Heaven.
Look down at the hills and the five rivers
One by one etched in the scene.
Meandering and winding up ascending stairs,
Step into the clouds.

The Peak of Fire & Rain

I had in fact stepped into the clouds. I was now one slope from the summit, outside the long walls of **Shangfeng Si,** a large temple. The fog was melting, flying off in long streamers. First I could see the high steel girders of a transmission tower behind the temple, then a garden of radar or microwave dishes—a modern communications center that has nothing to do with Daoism. Before me was the final rise, a newly restored path of granite and concrete, with stone benches for resting along the way. I was not surprised to find a ticket seller charging RMB 1 (12¢) for the final hike.

I could see that the path is well worth following, not only for the panorama it affords but for the high altar on the top, **the Temple of the Fire God (Zhurong Dian).** Built in the 16th century and restored in the 19th, it was apparently completely rebuilt in the 1930s after a bone-crunching storm. In the near distance, in the banners of fog, it looks much older, like a ravaged remnant of primordial China, an ancient outcropping of mountain worship, the abode of an angry fire god who has not left so much as his own altar unscorched.

I seated myself on the wall of this temple's courtyard, one little stairway below the Fire Temple, waiting for the last wisps of fog to be torn away. The courtyard teemed with sightseers, mostly young people, brightly dressed. Several had donned the yellow robes of high officials and ancient royalty to have their portraits snapped on the summit. Groups of students found me out—as they always do—once I was motionless and visible on a mountain peak. They seated themselves next to me, one by one, while their friends snapped away with their cameras.

I was more a sight than any mountaintop or temple. Some practiced a smattering of English, but I was quite surprised when a young woman introduced herself to me in fluent English. She turned out to be one of a half-dozen college students climbing the mountain with their teacher, who was an American, too, I was informed, and more than that, she was a minority. Her students were quite excited about that fact: It made their teacher that much more exotic.

When she arrived with the other students, I learned that she was an anthropologist interested in the struggles of the minority peoples in rural China. She taught English at the university in Xiangtan, a small city between Heng Shan Nan and Changsha. As for her minority status, she was Jewish.

I linked up with her entourage. Together we ascended to the Temple of the Fire God. The entrance consists of many folding doors, painted red. A fire extinguisher is posted at one door on the right side, and above it, quite out of place, a huge round clock with white face, black hands, and Arabic numerals. The walls are square cement blocks; the roof is metal tile. The interior of the shrine is an unlit, humble affair, its dark walls furnished in simple posters. The bust of Emperor Yu—standing in for the fire god—is ensconced in a curtained recess behind the altar. Bedecked in long strands of black beard, hands crossed just below his neck, shoulders draped in a red silk robe, the god of Heng Shan Nan is framed by a wall of frescoes in red paint and gold leaf. Candles and long sticks of incense sputter in iron holders welded to the altar table.

Two long risers before the altar contain several dozen dirty patchwork cushions on which a surprising number of young tourists knelt, clutching lighted incense between their hands. One of the Xiangtan students was pushed by her classmates into buying joss sticks from the monks. She took her turn in beseeching the god. As she knelt, she giggled self-consciously; her girlfriends took flash pictures. She bowed her head, whispered, and rose with a smile.

Outside, behind the temple, we had fine views of the many peaks of Heng Shan Nan. Clouds line the deep bowls of the valleys. This is where Hugh Farley, a journalist, spent a night in 1935, a night he wouldn't soon forget, when the Temple of the Fire God was too new, too untempered by the elements to possess any romantic appeal. "It was not a very satisfactory reward for the steep climb," he reported, "as it had been rebuilt last year, and its newness and lack of distinction were rather disappointing. Perhaps I was unduly prejudiced by the masses of ugly stinkbugs that covered its floors, walls, pillars and ceilings with a squirming horde, three or four deep in some places." Farley did not blame the monks for the neglect; they were forbidden by their vows to destroy any form of life, no matter how creepy. "Magnificent, on the other hand, was the view," Farley wrote, "for the temple stands on a pinnacle of rock with unobstructed vision in all directions . . . Never before in China have I so fully appreciated the proximity or contrast of fertility and barrenness, of water and of drought, of living greenness like the sea and stark brownness like the desert."

In the decades since, this vista has endured, although I would not term it spectacular; the Temple of the Fire God has improved with age, however, and is the perfect monument for the highest platform of any holy mountain: decrepit, dark, humble, naked, cold, and forbidding.

The New South

I ate lunch with the five students and their teacher outside the temple, at the rear. The student who first approached me was particularly precocious. She was majoring in linguistics; she had mastered a smooth, slangy English. She asked me about Noam Chomsky, then quizzed me on minute details about the American presidency and international events. She told me that she had just been accepted for graduate studies in Wuhan, but she hadn't decided whether to accept. The great temptation for college students, especially the most brilliant undergraduates, is "to go south" to Guangdong Province, where the Chinese economy is boiling hot and a student who speaks English can get a job on the spot as a company clerk or a hotel receptionist and make a fortune overnight. Such a job pays ten times what a teacher, even a professor, can expect to pull down. Money is the temptation. I tried to talk her out of going south, although in her place nothing but pure idealism would have held me back, either, from Canton or Shenzhen.

We descended Heng Shan Nan in the sun, everyone sweating. I thought of the story of the Daoist pilgrim with a stiff leg of iron who climbed 6 miles of stairs to this peak and woke to see the sunrise. Looking up, he proclaimed, "The sea of cloud washes my heart clean." I felt cleansed, too, and removed from the world, oddly enough—unattracted by the wealth of the south, purged of all particular desires—as I stepped down the mountain, its bamboo forest soaked in the low clouds like a long ink-brushed scroll.

"What did your schoolmate pray for in the temple?" I asked. I was unable to imagine what people today would pray for at the top of this mountain, where fire and flood once reigned. She prayed for a good job, I was told: for prosperity. Last year, two of her classmates came to the top of Heng Shan Nan and prayed to find high-paying work in the south; their wishes granted, they planned to return this summer, a year later as prescribed, to thank the god of the mountain for his blessing.

So, if the sacred mountains have lost their original powers, they have not lost a certain metaphysical presence. They still act as receivers of personal petitions.

One student draped me in a necklace of brown wooden beads, the pilgrim's rosary. We caught a bus down to the village, where we had lunch in town. Several buses later—nothing according to schedule—we were in Xiangtan, an hour from Changsha, just before dark. With the students' help, I flagged down a bus to Changsha. I sat by an open window. Pure darkness rushed in. Poor workers and peasants jumped on and off at the stops. They pressed against me, sharing the same seat, hip to hip, elbow to elbow, not knowing in the dark what strange creature they were rubbing against.

I was thinking my own thoughts, unrelated to theirs. I was thinking that a new constellation of gods had risen from the grave of Maoist-Marxism to serve as Deng Xiaoping's divine dispensers of cash; that the sacred compass of China had been realigned, its cardinal points marked with dollar signs; and that today's pilgrims are parading to these mountain altars like contestants in a *Wheel of Fortune* game show, petitioning the gods of rain and fire for high-paying jobs.

PRACTICAL INFORMATION

ORIENTATION & WHEN TO GO

Heng Shan Nan, also called Nan Yue, the sacred southern mountain in the Daoist tradition, is located 370 miles northwest of Hong Kong, 600 miles southwest of Shanghai, and 70 miles south of Changsha, the capital of Hunan Province. Springs here bring heavy rainfall, summers are hot and muggy, and winters are cold, making autumn the best time to visit.

GETTING THERE

By Plane There are daily flights to Changsha from Beijing (1½ hours), Guangzhou (2 hours), Shanghai (2 hours), Xi'an (1 hour 40 minutes), and Hong Kong (2 hours 10 minutes). A taxi from the airport costs about RMB 100 ($12.50).

By Train There are overnight trains to Changsha from Guangzhou (15 hours), Shanghai (20 hours), and Hangzhou (16 hours).

By Bus to the Mountain Changsha is the urban gateway to Heng Shan Nan and the village of Nan Yue at its base. Morning buses make the 3-hour trip south from Changsha to the mountain (RMB 20/$2.40 each way). Bus tickets can be purchased at hotels in Changsha. A less convenient alternative is to take the train from Changsha (3 hours) south to the town of Heng Shan and then a 30-minute minibus from the Heng Shan train station to the mountain (7 miles to the west).

TOURS & STRATAGEMS

Visitor Information A branch of **China International Travel Service (CITS)** in the Lotus Hotel (☎ 0731/443-3355) dispenses information and books air, bus, and train tickets, as does the main CITS office on the 11th floor of Xiaoyuan Mansion, Wuyi Dong Lu (☎ 0731/228-0439). The **Dragonair** office, for tickets to Hong Kong, is at 298 Fu Rong Nan Lu in the Grand Sun City Hotel (☎ 0731/521-8888, ext 3111).

Exploring the Mountain Heng Shan Nan has no tour operators or travel agents. In Changsha, there are no tours available to the mountain. You are on your own. It is possible to make this a day trip from Changsha if you ride the bus to the peak and return the same way, but this gives you only a few hours for enjoying the mountain, which has wonderful trails through the bamboo forests and many temples scattered across its slopes.

The mountain park entrance is at **Nanyue Temple,** on the north side of the village, along the road leading up the mountain. Admission is RMB 30 ($3.75), which includes a map in English and Chinese of Heng Shan Nan. The buses to the summit, which depart often from the park entrance, cost RMB 10 ($1.20). A new mile-long cable car system also operates from the Xuan Dao Temple, partway up the mountain, to near the summit. The footpath from bottom to top is 9 miles long.

WHERE TO STAY

There are several inns at Ban Shan Ting halfway up the mountain, and at Shangfeng Temple just below the summit, with very basic doubles for about RMB 250 ($30). At the entrance to Nan Yue village at the base of the mountain is a newer hotel, **Xiufeng Binguan** (☎ 0734/66-6111), which charges more ($40 for a modern double) but offers no amenities or services of note. There is also a two-star hotel, **Yinyuan Binguan,** 70 Zhu Rong Lu (☎ 0731/566-1329), near the new cable car terminal.

In Changsha, most of the international-caliber hotels are on Wuyi Lu, near the bus and train stations. The most convenient choice is the three-star 15-story **Lotus Hotel (Furong Binguan),** 8 Wuyi Dong Lu (☎ 0731/440-1888; fax 0731/446-5175). Its 265 rooms are modern, with plenty of amenities. When I stayed there, major credit cards were accepted, but only during banking hours (9am to 5pm). Doubles cost $50 and $75, with the best rooms on the upper floors.

WHERE TO DINE

The village of **Nan Yue** has plenty of local restaurants that welcome foreign guests. None have English menus, however, so if you try one (the touts will usher you in) be sure to set a price per person for the entire meal. The trail to the top has vendors' stalls with snacks and hot plates of noodles. Try to pack as much food for the journey as you can when setting out from Changsha.

PUTUO SHAN: BUDDHIST PEAK OF THE EAST

普陀山

PUTUO SHAN, WHICH MEANS "White Flower Mountain," is an island in the East China Sea, east of Hangzhou and south of Shanghai. In the Chinese tradition it is the supreme dwelling place of Guanyin, Goddess of Mercy. For many centuries pilgrims have worshipped Guanyin, touched by her compassion. She became the most popular divinity in China. She still is. Pilgrims petition her for the birth of male children and the return of mariners safely to shore. This island mountain remains her home.

I reached Putuo Shan by a circuitous route: a train from Hangzhou to Ningbo; the wrong ferry from Ningbo, which dumped me at a nearby island; a pedicab across the island to a wharf; and finally a fishing boat to Putuo Shan. The boat was an unpainted motorized skiff. The fisherman placed me down in its hold. A quilt was spread out on the floor. I lay down on it. Beside me was a young monk, head shaven. He was dressed in a golden robe and golden slippers. He sat up, cross-legged; I reclined.

We set out on this final passage to Putuo Shan together, wordless before the roar of the engine. I closed my eyes. The boat rocked like a cradle. The monk sat up straight, eyes cast down, as if in meditation. It was nearly noon, but dark in the hold. Above was the gray sky; on the edges, the spray of rough seas. The diesel cracked like an unoiled clock, its fumes wafting in the wind. The monk seemed to be presiding over me. A patch of faint light swayed overhead. I stared at the monk's white leggings, banded at the calves. I was very nearly rocked to sleep. Then the engine stopped. We drifted.

I peered out from the hold. I could see the huge ornate gate to Putuo Shan, ancient in the fog, resembling a hairy three-legged mammoth turned to stone, mounted on an outcropping of rounded boulders on the southern tip of the island. The romance of its appearance at that moment, at our angle of approach, lent it a rich cloak, one it seems to have worn since the beginning of Chinese time, its three portals capped by soaring tile roofs. Here is the Southern Gate of Heaven, the pilgrim's entrance to the holy mountain in the sea. For a moment I felt I had truly crossed into an ancient world, divided from 20th-century China by iron mist.

Of Incense & Emperors

Putuo Shan has an intense history of worship. In 1638, a gentleman named Chang Tai visited here aboard a pilgrim's boat. Once landed, he accompanied other 17th-century pilgrims through the three great temples on the island to the peak known as Buddha's Head. The devout making this trek had to bow every three steps, shouting the name of the Goddess of Mercy, Guanyin. Spending the night on Putuo Shan in the Great Hall, clogged with incense smoke as thick as fog, these pilgrims of the past waited for a divine manifestation. Chang Tai set the old scene thus: "Thousands of men and women sit in rows like packed fish . . . not one inch of space is unoccupied. During the night many nuns burn incense on their heads or burn their arms and fingers. Women from good families imitate them. They recite scriptures and try not to show signs of pain."

The pilgrims came then and for centuries more to see Guanyin float across this seascape of pines and camphors, tea plantations, engraved stones and "powdered gold" beaches, "fine as silk." Guanyin is still the bodhisattva in residence, one of 33 enlightened ones dedicated to saving the living. Known in Buddhist India as the god Avalokitesvara, Guanyin changed sex in China, becoming a goddess sought out by those petitioning for the birth of a male child. Over the centuries, her worship spread across China, west to east, culminating at Putuo Shan, the living *Potalaka* (Little White Flower) mentioned in the sutras, the holy mountain wrapped in a sea of water lilies.

In the highest temple on the island, the second emperor of the Qing Dynasty, Kangxi (1661–1722), inscribed in stone this homage to Putuo Shan:

Coming to this island, the moaning of the waves and the chanting of prayers can be heard, the deep purple temples can be seen, and peace can be had as expansive as the wide sea . . . This renowned island has become a kingdom of the gods. It is like a ship of mercy upon the great sea; hills blue as the fleecy sky, and high as the heavens of Brahma; upon this lucky clean place the waves dash up to bathe the sun. Its reputation stands as a pillar, supporting the sky. From its summit, all places are connected.

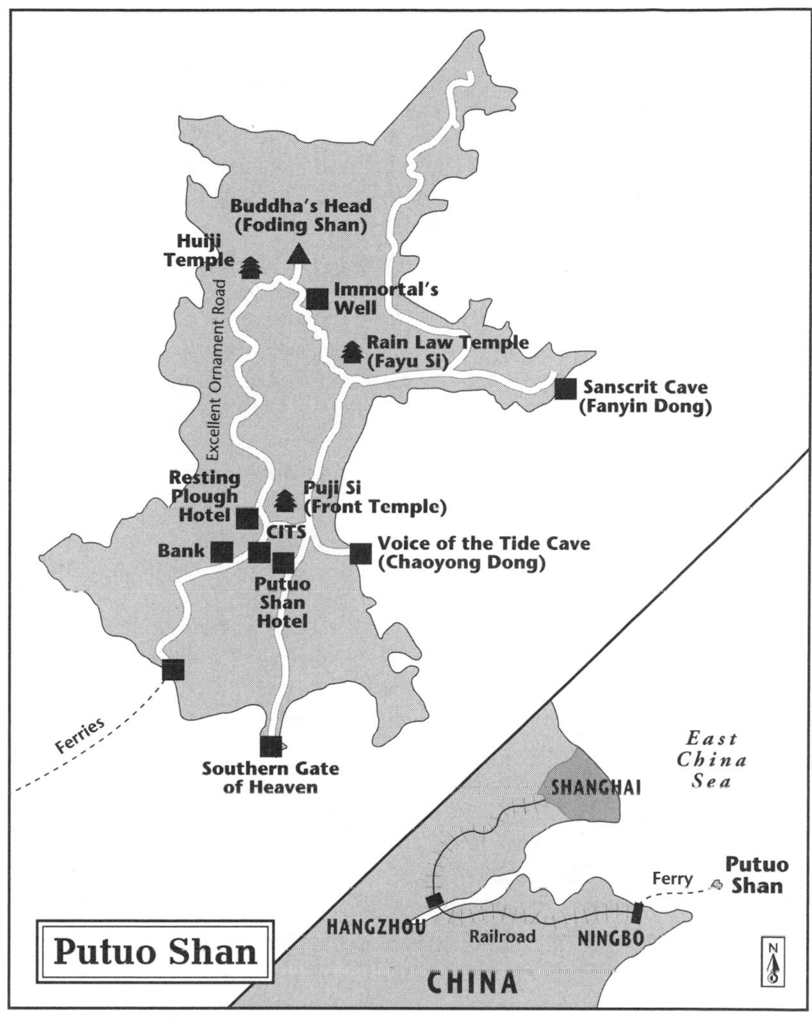

High praise and imperial promise—enough to spur me to reach Putuo Shan as quickly as possible, even to the point of boarding a latter-day "pilgrim's" boat. Little had changed: I crossed a sea of iron-pronged water lilies using such conveyances as lay in my path.

Front Temple

I checked in at the Resting Plough Hotel and took a stroll around through the village on the southern tip of the island. Putuo Shan is a sort of summer resort, an island getaway these days, but it has its charms. The old rock formations are trimmed in tea terraces; the large temples are enlivened with bright paint. Near my hotel is a winding cobblestone path with a fine stone wall on either side. And there's the **Universal Salvation Temple Complex (Puji Si)**—also known as the Front Temple—the oldest and most elaborate on the island, its halls and pavilions fronted by an immense lotus pond.

This pond, rather rundown and devoid of its lotus flowers, is crossed by several arched bridges and presided over by a five-story pagoda (Duobao), built in the 14th century. Putuo Shan has been subjected to many cycles of decay and rebirth, fully in keeping with a Buddhist holy place. On one of the imperial tablets stored in this temple, Emperor Kangxi recounts how before the Qing Dynasty (1644–1911) "the island was overthrown by pirates, and all the temples were destroyed by fire. After the 22nd year of my reign, peace and order were established. Priests returned from the mainland, looked upon the old foundations, cleaned away the weeds and debris, and began to build anew . . . and I myself prayed, saying, 'May the temples forever keep the sea in subjection.'"

The temples are not eternal, however—not in a literal sense. They decay, are soon looted or razed, and are finally rebuilt, often from the ground up. Their lineage may go back 9 centuries and more, but they themselves are more youthful incarnations. Only their natural setting resists the wear and tear of regimes, if not the pummeling of salted waves, cold winds, and hard rains.

Some of the pilgrims here today had resisted politics and erosion. I ran across groups of old women, yellow shan bags slung over their shoulders and tied about their waists. For centuries, pilgrims stopped at each temple on this island, burned incense, and for a small donation had the temple monks affix a red ink seal to their mountain purses. The old women were outnumbered today, however, by young sailors; they were everywhere on the island, giving it the feel of a military base.

On the narrow street rising north of the Front Temple grounds there are dozens of hole-in-the-wall cafes with live seafood swarming in plastic pans of water; and plenty of beauty salons, too, mere shacks, doors wide open, hair blowers ablaze, posters of Western pop stars and celebrities pasted to the walls. There are farmers in the fields, oblivious to tourism and pilgrimage alike. Tour buses park at the lotus pond, but not a single foreigner had I yet seen. I received a hail of friendly greetings when I walked the southern arc of the island. On my way from the fishing boat to the Resting Plough Hotel, I passed a dog lying on the centerline of the highway to the village, legs folded under. There were plenty of people walking the shoulder, but no one stopped to examine the dog.

This is no longer an island of mercy—an irony, since as one of the four centers of Buddhism in China and the grand mansion of the

Goddess of Mercy herself, one expects all life to be held sacred: horses, dogs, bedbugs. Somewhere on Putuo Shan there is a stele engraved with this holy admonition: "All that has life should not intentionally be killed. In the classic it is also said, 'The winter months breed lice; take them and put them into a bamboo joint; keep them warm with cotton, and give them oily food to eat lest they might freeze or starve.' Such is the doctrine of the Goddess of Mercy." But this and other doctrines of its ilk are temporarily out of service in the new, unsuperstitious China.

Tonight I fell asleep quickly, and during that steep descent into oblivion I experienced a strange disturbance: An image of Guanyin, the Lady in White, printed itself like a cameo on the darkness, flooding my eyes for a few moments, startling me awake.

The View from Buddha's Head

At dawn, when I set out for **Buddha's Head Peak (Foding Shan),** which rises less than a thousand feet above the level sea, I was inspired by one of the many simple inscriptions in the rocks of Putuo Shan: "Ascend and enter the region of formlessness."

From the Front Monastery, I struck out northward on Excellent Ornament Road, hoping it would dwindle into a forest path long before I reached Buddha's Head. It didn't. The scenery up the western side is fine, and were it not for the asphalt of the curving highway and an occasional Chinese tour bus grinding by, I would have been alone in remote pine forests tumbling steeply down to the sea below. Along the shoulder of the highway, I came across tiny shrines cut out into the smooth moss-covered cliffs. Stone figures of Guanyin are ensconced inside. I followed the paved road toward Buddha's Head, rising above the salt pans and tea plantations, the nunneries and temples, the beaches and fishing junks.

After a several-mile climb, I reached Putuo Shan's second great temple, **Huiji Si, the Enlightenment Temple.** Buddha's Head looms above. I strolled through a tour bus parking lot. The halls to one side were stocked with souvenirs, snacks, and drinks. I bought two boiled eggs and a glass of Buddha tea. The summit was immediately above me, connected to the parking lot by stairs. An elderly ticket vendor squatted behind a long table, reading a rented book. He was wrapped in a full-length green army coat, its collar trimmed in brown fur. I bought a ticket from him and started the final ascent. A hundred steps later I stood on Buddha's Head atop Putuo Shan.

Or almost atop. The summit is actually fenced off. Its gate is locked. A sign on the gate reads NO VISITORS. Inside the fence is a brick building without windows. Perhaps it's a weather station or a communications outpost—certainly a government installation. Near the gate is a coin-operated telescope. Truly, I had reached a state of pure formlessness unique to our century: unimperial and technological. Buddha's Peak is closed to modern pilgrims—a military outpost. Putuo Shan is merciless in its emptiness. Yet the view from Buddha's Forehead is sweeping. The hills are layered into the hem of the sea and scores of islands radiate outward all the way to the clouds on the horizon.

Rain & Drought

I descended Buddha's Head Peak by the eastern route: a thousand stonecut stairs inscribed with lotus petals. This is the path where the faithful were said to touch their heads every third or fifth step. Few such pilgrims were here today, but the grungy Immortal's Well was doing a brisk business hawking incense sticks and magic spring water by the glass in the cleft of a massive rock. Here, a hermit of the Eastern Jin Dynasty (A.D. 317–420) discovered a source of spring water that never dried up and never turned salty.

This spring was once an emblem to Imperial China of a sacred cure for drought. Emperors petitioned Putuo Shan on several occasions for rain, and indeed just a few hundred steep steps below this cave is the third great monastery of the island mountain, **Rain Law Temple (Fayu Si).** Rain Law Temple was rebuilt a few years back. It rises in tiers up the hillside of Buddha's Head Peak. One of its halls was shipped here from Nanjing by Emperor Kangxi. Its central image is a statue of Guanyin.

Bridge of Great Being

I paid a visit to the **Voice of the Tide Cave** along the eastern shore, where for at least 900 years pilgrims have reported seeing manifestations of Guanyin, serene, bathed in purplish golden light. In 1209, an abbot ordered the building of the **Bridge of Great Being** from which the faithful could look into the cave for an appearance of Guanyin as she is described in the Chinese classic *Journey to the West:* in her "white silk robe bathed in holy light." Late in the Ming Dynasty, pilgrims and monks would kneel and kowtow all the way to the tidal cave, arriving blood-soaked. Many threw themselves into the sea at the first appearance of a rainbow in the pinched, sunstruck spray—so many that monks once routinely scoured the waters with baskets, trolling for bones to be cremated.

No such suicidal hopefuls gather here anymore. All that's left to contemplate are a pile of rocks, an old bridge, a pretty jetty, and some dazzling waves. The most hardened devotees of all used to come here to set their fingers afire, to burn them out of existence. A gazetteer for the year 1361 notes that in A.D. 848 "a foreign monk came to the Voice of the Tide Cave. He burned his ten fingers in front of the cave. When the fingers were burned off, he saw the Great Being who preached *dharma* to him and gave him a seven-hued precious stone."

Ten living sticks of incense . . . . I stood on the Bridge of the Great Being looking into the womb of the goddess, trying to imagine how anyone could withstand such pain. From peak to cave, Putuo Shan is exactly as it was in ancient China, but its transfiguration into the island home of the merciful goddess seems to have disappeared from the minds of the people.

Pilgrims & Submarines

On my way to the ferry dock on the southern tip of the island, I met four retired Americans who were teaching in Hangzhou, accompanied on their tour by a student. With a native guide, everything had gone like clockwork for them. I tagged along, relaxed for the first time on my journey.

We boarded a direct ferry back to **Ningbo** and spread out in the soft-seat lounge up front. The island mountain faded away into the morning mist as it has for centuries. For a moment it was as if nothing had changed. Then I noticed a battered old submarine break the surface, heading for its holy port. Putuo Shan has slipped the reins of emperors, pirates, and abbots, and is now ridden by the Chinese Navy.

I suppose it doesn't matter, this displacement of the spiritual. For the most part visitors these days are sightseers, more concerned with prices and wages than with visions. But on the rear observation deck, packed shoulder to shoulder with standing passengers, I did come across a handful of true pilgrims: tiny old women with shan bags, rosary beads, and knitted wool watch caps, every one of them smiling. They thought I was quite the strangest sight in the world and they started to giggle. I didn't mind entertaining them.

Is this the same place as the old Putuo Shan where the Song poet Wang An-shih stood a thousand years ago, calling it the mountain that overpowers the sea, the island where "the sun and moon shine before anywhere else"? Everywhere the landscape of this island was once fabulously transfigured, its stones into saints, its ledges into pulpits, its caves into eyes, its springs into elixirs, the very rain into the law of Buddha—and finally the rainbowed sunlight of the sea spray into the halo of the Goddess of Mercy. Today, a familiar disfiguration has assumed control. Vendors offer tapes of chanting monks. Rats dart through the streets. Sailors in blue uniforms stroll in twos and threes. A peasant herds pigs from town to temple. The golden sand beaches are deserted, and so are the long spits of rock where the fishing junks tie up.

Perhaps the Island Mountain retains its ancient power, for those who know how to summon it. Perhaps it is still Guanyin's home, for those who know how to see it. But for now the tide is out—the tide of ancient empires—and with it the old petals of compassion, carried far and drowned in the wide, wide ocean of China.

PRACTICAL INFORMATION

ORIENTATION & WHEN TO GO

Putuo Shan is a small island (4 miles long, 1 mile wide) in the East China Sea, 100 miles south of Shanghai, 100 miles east of Hangzhou, and 50 miles east of Ningbo, the nearest city. A small village, located on the south end of the island, serves as Putuo Shan's port. The **Front Temple,** just north of the village, is surrounded by a large central square with many shops and cafes. Buddha's Head Peak, in the center of the island, is the highest point (elevation 1,000 feet). Summer is high season for tourists. In the first week of April, thousands of pilgrims throng the island for the goddess Guanyin's birthday.

Admission to the island is currently RMB 40 ($4.90); most temples and sacred sites charge RMB 5 to RMB 15 (65¢ to $1.90). The newest attraction is called **South Sea Guanyin** (Nanhia Guanyin), a towering statue of the goddess, placed atop a two-story exhibition hall; this big, new but rather serene Guanyin is located on a peak southeast of the Puyi Temple (you won't have trouble finding her).

GETTING THERE

Putuo Shan can be reached only by **ferry,** although there is an **airport** on the nearby island of Zhujiajian (30 minutes away by ferry). There are also plans to construct a bridge to the mainland from Zhujiajian. (Zhujiajian, which is being promoted as an Oriental Hawaii, holds an annual International Sand Sculpture Festival from September 26 to October 28 and now receives four million visitors a year). There is a direct ferry daily to Putuo Shan from Ningbo (5 hours) and one every 2 days from Shanghai (11 hours). On weekends, there is a catamaran from Shanghai (5 hours).

Ferry tickets for Shanghai and Ningbo can be purchased in Putuo Shan at the dockside office on the south edge of the village. Shanghai–Putuo Shan ferry tickets can be purchased in **Shanghai** at most hotels or from the ticket office located on **Jinling Dong Lu,** opposite the Bund. Tickets cost RMB 150 to RMB 200 ($20 to $26) for small, fast boats (4 hours) one-way; RMB 60 to RMB 600 ($7.50 to $75) for large, slow ships (12 hours) one-way, depending on cabin class. In **Ningbo,** ferry tickets to Putuo Shan can be purchased at the **Passenger Ferry Terminal,** located 3 blocks north of the Yongjiang Bridge along the Yong River. Tickets cost RMB 50 to RMB 80 ($6 to $10) each way; the voyage takes about 3 hours.

TOURS & STRATAGEMS

On Putuo Shan there is an office of **China International Travel Service (CITS),** ☎ 0580/609-1183, across from the Bank of China at 112 Meicen Lu, the main road connecting the village to the Front Temple (Puji Si). CITS can provide guides, though with a map in hand a guide is scarcely necessary. Taxis and pedicabs charge RMB 5 to RMB 15 (65¢ to $1.90) per ride, but the island is small enough to explore on foot.

WHERE TO STAY

I stayed several nights at the **Resting Plough Hotel (Xilai Xiaozhuang)** (☎ 0580/609-1644 or 0580/609-1522; fax 0580/609-1023), located on Meicen Lu, the main road north of the ferry terminal near the Front Temple. It provides large doubles (modern but rundown), room service, and daily turndown. No credit cards are accepted. The staff is helpful, speaking some English. Doubles cost $55. The price is the same at the three-star **Putuo Shan Zhuang** (☎ 0580/609-1666; fax 0580/609-1667). Although located a long walk southeast of the Front Temple, this hotel is one of the newest and most modern on the island. Still, it has no more services than the Resting Plough Hotel.

In **Ningbo,** the best choice is the new **East Seaport Hotel,** 52 Caihong Bei Lu (☎ 0574/737-3188; fax 0574/733-3646). This 14-story four-star hotel, located near downtown stores, has plenty of international-level luxuries: pool, gym, business center, room service, and its own row of shops. Rooms are clean, modern, and spacious ($125 double). The first-floor Chinese restaurant is excellent.

WHERE TO DINE

The **Resting Plough Hotel** (☎ 0580/609-1644), southwest of the Front Temple and central square, has a good restaurant with an English menu. It's open daily 7am to 10pm. The dishes are Chinese and Shanghainese, heavy on the seafood. Dinners cost RMB 60 to RMB 168 ($7 to $20) and up, depending on whether you order exotic seafoods. Many small local restaurants line the enormous square around the **Front Temple.** I didn't try any of these (although several workers inside waved as I passed). I did buy snacks (boiled eggs, fried breads) from sidewalk vendors.

Tai Shan: Sacred Mountain of the East

泰山

Tai Shan is said to be the most-climbed mountain in the world, although it is virtually unknown to the West. Situated at the midpoint between Beijing and Shanghai, Tai Shan has been the most celebrated of the Five Sacred Peaks of China for the last 2,000 years, the highest altar in the Middle Kingdom for countless pilgrims and a great many emperors, including China's first. The first recorded temple on the mountain was built in 351 B.C. By the Ming Dynasty (1368–1644), pilgrims numbering over 200,000 annually made the trek to the top of the mountain. Today the numbers are even more imperial: four million visitors annually (including 500,000 foreigners). From this summit, Confucius (Kong Zi) once proclaimed the world small and later Chairman Mao pronounced the East Red. But in post-Mao China, the world view from Tai Shan is altered once again, as I would find when I made my own ascent.

Dai Temple

I began my modern sightseer's pilgrimage in the old way, at the temple at the foot of the mountain, in the town of Tai'an. The Dai Temple (Dai Miao) is a large walled fortress, a town within a town, of restored halls and pavilions housing ancient relics. Everyone from pickpockets to the imperial family used to set out from this shrine. One visitor described the temple grounds in 1628 as "a motley collection of stalls and stands" inhabited not only by pilgrims but by "cock-fighters, ball players, equestrians, and story-tellers." I didn't see anyone kicking a football around this morning, but I did come across scores of vendors encamped within the 30-foot walls.

The temple grounds are populated with carved stone tablets, one recording the mountain's appointment as "Emperor of China" by the

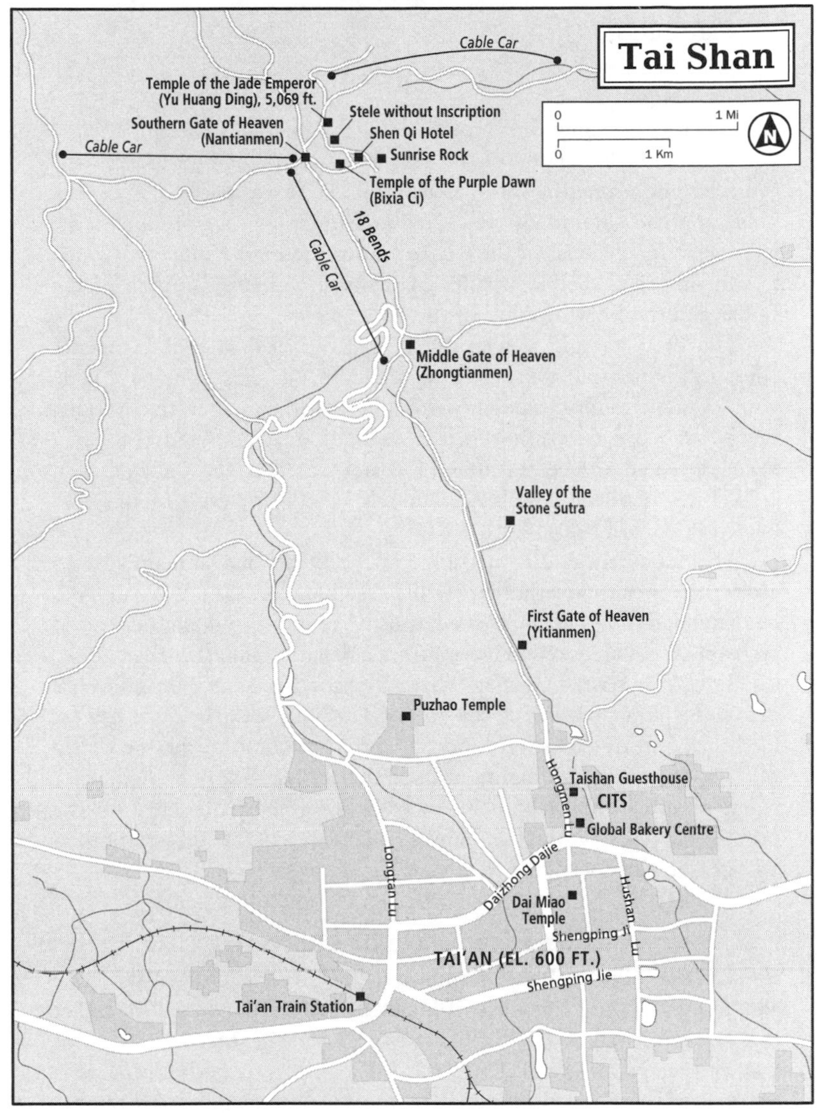

Song emperor in A.D. 1011. Every city and town in China once had a flourishing Eastern Mountain Temple of its own, part of the massive Tai Shan cult that died only with the Communist Liberation in 1949. Dai Mao also contains one of China's oldest steles, the **Qin Tablet,** thought to have been carved in 209 B.C., when China's First Emperor, Qin Shi Huang Di, climbed Tai Shan. This inscribed monument stood on the summit until devoured by fire in 1740. A fragment with nine characters is now preserved outside the red stone hall where many an emperor once rested before his climb. It is mounted under a plate of glass. Sima Qian, China's ancient historian, was present when Emperor Qin ordered the full inscription "praising his own virtues," and it was partly Qin's act of hubris on the summit of this Dragon Mountain that prompted the Confucian intellectuals of the day to censor the First Emperor—which in turn impelled their new ruler to retaliate with the Burning of the Books and the Burying Alive of the 480 Scholars.

The main temple at Dai Miao, called the **Palace of Heavenly Blessing,** is palatial in every sense, including its size: nine bays wide with a double roof of imperial yellow tiles. Within its massive wooden cavity, stained a dark crimson, the God of the Mountain, Tai Shan Wang, is seated on a central altar. His black-bearded face is enameled in gold. Five sacrificial vessels surround him, one for each of the Five Sacred Peaks of Daoism.

This mountain god is the Judge of the Dead, but he maintains no abode on the summit. Rather, it's his daughter, the Jade Woman, who has ascended to the heights. She has usurped her forbidding father and reigns supreme on the supreme summit, a deity of life rather than death.

Since this base temple is where the good pilgrim burns incense before the climb, presenting the god of Tai Shan with the favor nearest his heart, I made my petition, too. I wished to climb to the top of Tai Shan today, spend the night, and see the sunrise from the same spot where everyone from Confucius to Mao has greeted the dawn for the past 2,500 years. From the temple gate I could see that summit—a jagged, notched cliff face some 6,293 steps away.

The First Gate of Heaven

Pan Lu, the Pilgrim's Road, begins at the north edge of town, at a stone arch known as the **First Gate of Heaven.** Here, I purchased my ticket to Tai Shan (RMB 30/$3.75). The way up is broad, with spacious ramps and massive granite steps. From the First Gate to the Middle Gate is about 3 miles. From the middle to the top is under 2 miles but far steeper. There are more than 250 temples and monuments along the way, and every rock and cranny, ravine and stream, wears a poetic name or invokes a romantic tale or two out of China's past. Above all there's the sacred graffiti. Hundreds of flat-faced rocks are etched in calligraphy, some of the finest specimens in the world. There are other signs of the past, too—living signs: beggars, working each rung of the stone stairway, and porters, dozens of them, hoisting their loads on wooden poles, the "bamboo tigers" of New China, as of old.

Many of Tai Shan's holy pavilions have been converted into snack bars and souvenir stands. At one cafe, I found the staff and patrons sitting outside, watching television. At another, there was a computer monitor, a vendor rattling its keyboard like an abacus. The screen radiated with a green glow, matching the overarching canopy of trees, a canopy pierced by thick electrical lines running up the mountain. The lower half of the sacred mountain has been modernized, electrified, even computerized, although the stone stairs, tall pines, steep cliffs, and embroidery of carved characters manage to shine through. The gaily dressed, money-spending tourists of New China are everywhere, far outnumbering a few old pilgrims, wiry porters, and the beggars who cling for life to their single step on the route.

Tiring of the stairs, I made a detour into the **Valley of the Stone Sutra,** where 6th-century Buddhists engraved the 2,500-character Diamond Sutra on the exposed banks of an extinct stream bed. The stone banks are wide, flat, and smooth, forming a stone scroll unrolled by nature, but rain and wind have washed over the text, erasing much of it.

The Middle Gate of Heaven

After a 3-hour steady march, I reached the **Middle Gate of Heaven (Zhongtianmen),** and it was a nightmare, clotted with a thousand vendors and pocked by a gigantic parking lot for tour buses ferrying "climbers" up from the bottom. To top it off, this is where one can catch China's first large-scale **cable car** and thereby reach the holy summit in 8 minutes flat.

Keeping to my regimen, however, I struck out on foot, heading for the **Eighteen Bends,** a gargantuan stone ladder to the Southern Gate of Heaven, still far above. I hoped to leave behind this modern Pilgrim's Way that has been transformed into a high emporium of carnival shooting galleries, cheap charms on chains, shacks serving Coca-Cola, and roving photographers for hire.

The next landmarks belong to China's first emperor: a pavilion where Qin Shi Huang took shelter from a storm as he descended in 209 B.C.; a pine tree awarded the fifth military rank when it sheltered Emperor Qin from the rain; a rock in the first emperor's calligraphy with characters cut so large it's known as "Stele a Hundred Thousand Feet High." Then there's a stone arch named "Rise to Immortality," and finally 2,000 ruthless stairs to the top.

I paused on every intervening ramp. So did the porters, resting their bundles and bamboo carrying poles on the stairs. I followed one porter typical of those on Tai Shan, his skin burned auburn, head shaved, blue cotton pants rolled up to his knees, back drenched in sweat, feet shod in black cotton shoes. Dangling from the thick rope on one end of his carrying pole were three heavy gunny sacks; on the other end were two red roosters, suspended by their claws upside down, both still alive. The average porter shoulders 110 pounds on the carrying poles, makes two roundtrips a day, and is paid about RMB 16 ($2) for a hard day's hauling.

In the middle of one flight of stairs I stepped around a dilapidated cardboard box, presided over by a tiny plaster figure of Buddha painted gold. It was a beggar's collection box, unattended, but there was a beggar on the next flight, both his legs shorn off at the thigh.

The walls of the ravine closed in on me. This is where the Tai Shan gazetteer mentions that a bully was crushed by a falling rock "so that the fat of his body polished the stairs," we're told. "Nothing was left. His family could retrieve only one of his fingers." I'm amazed. Here is a mountain where villains are actually punished.

A Milky Way of supplicants still flows up and down this stairway, but now, if indeed people burn incense in the high temples at all, they are probably requesting cash, trunks of it. But even in greed, Tai Shan follows tradition. When Han Dynasty Emperor Wu arrived at Tai Shan, the local officials lined both sides of the road on their knees; dispensing with offerings of fruit, they piled cash along the roadside, imploring the imperial blessing.

The Southern Gate of Heaven is a square red tower at the top of this long, long mountain staircase. Its hollow understory dates from 1264. Its upper story is known as **The Pavilion That Touches the Sky**—Heaven was once reckoned to be precisely 17 inches above the roof peak.

The Southern Gate of Heaven

Reaching the Southern Gate of Heaven (Nantianmen), I squeezed through the Pavilion That Touches the Sky—and then I realized that I was still not at the summit of Tai Shan. Beyond here was a mile of vendors, coin telescopes, rock carvings, temples, and still more stone stairs. But it was not so steep now. I quickly wound my way to the Shen Qi Hotel, where I checked in.

There are plenty of monuments and temples on this broad summit, more than on any of China's other holy peaks. First there are the **Tang Dynasty Rock Inscriptions (Mo Ya Bei),** the most ostentatious in outdoor China, the ultimate in cliff calligraphy. In A.D. 726, Emperor Xuan Zong ordered that an account of his own imperial pilgrimage to Tai Shan be carved here—and it was carved large, in huge characters, 996 of them, each measuring a good 7 inches square and gilded in gold foil. The page of rock chosen for the imperial inscription faces south; the golden text is 43 feet high and 16 feet wide.

Then, on the very tiptop of Tai Shan, there's the Summit of the Celestial Pillar, where the **Temple of the Jade Emperor** (Yu Huang

Ding) stands. In its courtyard is a marker stone recording the metric elevation of Tai Shan (1,545 meters, a mere 5,069 feet). And in the lower courtyard is the **Stele Without Inscription (Wu Zi Bei),** one of China's most celebrated tablets, long believed to have been placed here by First Emperor Qin during his visit in 219 B.C. Everyone who comes this far must touch this wordless stone tablet. The Chinese say it is the most touched stone on Earth, which is perhaps why it is completely blank. Twenty feet high, 5 feet square, the tablet is a true counterweight to the extravagantly wordy cliff carving just down the hill.

Finally, immediately below my hotel is **Bixia Ci,** the **Temple of the Purple Dawn,** where the Jade Woman (Bixia Yuan Jun) resides. She's the pilgrims' favorite, the Daoist equivalent of Guanyin, Goddess of Mercy. Over the centuries, as more and more sought her out on Tai Shan in preference to her father, Tai Shan Wang, the Jade Woman assumed two special powers: She could cure blindness and bless a petitioner with children. She became the great midwife of China.

As I wandered across the summit I saw more worship on Tai Shan than I expected, more incense burning at the shrines, more money tossed into the altar boxes, often by parents with young children. And there were forms of worship here I didn't understand at all.

Just below the Temple of the Purple Clouds is a large incense burner: It's an entire building, as big as a pavilion, and was well attended this afternoon. There was an offering box in front of its fiery mouth. Alongside were many flowering bushes that had hundreds of stones caught in their limbs and branches—whether by design or nature, I couldn't tell—but dozens of people were down there tying red ribbons to the limbs. I wasn't sure for what they were praying: children, money, health—surely some such universal desire, practical rather than what the West regards as spiritual. One doesn't climb all this way to engage in abstract reasoning.

While the temples on top of Tai Shan are among the most magical in China, there's also a communications complex with a weather station here rising higher than any temple and piercing the floorboards of Heaven. Pagoda of the Great Transmitter, Stupa of the Satellite Dish, these modern shrines of jade become electric.

Sunrise

At 4am the next morning, there was a knock on my door. Rise and shine for the ultimate ritual of Tai Shan: the sunrise. Light is born in the east each day, and Tai Shan, as the Eastern Mountain, presides over all origins, over life itself.

Outside, it was very dark. The winds chewed at my flesh. I joined a stream of sightseers flowing east across the summit. Many had rented full-length padded army coats, green with fur collars. One traveler even carried a large suitcase. A few had flashlights. I was the only Westerner this morning.

At the eastern edge of Old China, we settled into the rock ledges and waited for the sun to rise out of the East China Sea. The stars faded out. At 5:07am, the sun chipped through the cloud bank. The crowd gasped. Everyone pointed toward the sun.

From Confucius to Mao and beyond, we had all gathered here for the dawn of a new day. The sun was a feeble disk of yellow light, barely strong enough to penetrate the gray clouds, the vast haze of industrial progress steamrolling its way through China. Despite Mao, the East is no longer red; it's toxic gray. For the next hour, we watched the rising sun slice through the purple clouds of dawn like pinking shears, trimming away the raiment of the Jade Woman.

Back in Beijing, Chairman Mao's corpse, that of an emperor out of season, is encased in a slab of black granite from Tai Shan. But the imperial age and the age of the great beliefs—Daoism, Buddhism, Confucianism, and lately even Communism—is passing away. From Tai Shan, one must descend into the modern underworld. At Heaven's highest gate today, a vendor stands. He offers paintings brushed on black velvet: of tigers and dragons, eagles and cute kittens. The colors on these fuzzy, sofa-sized canvases are bright as neon, ideal for tourist and pilgrim alike. They roll up like scrolls. The cable car, and below that, the air-conditioned buses, await. The world no longer seems so small, even if it is fast approaching a commercial uniformity. The world is bigger than a dynasty, bigger than the Middle Kingdom, bigger than the circumference of China's sacred mountains.

PRACTICAL INFORMATION

ORIENTATION & WHEN TO GO

Tai Shan (Great Mountain) is the most famous sacred peak in China. It's located midway between Beijing and Shanghai in Shandong Province, facing the East China Sea. Its base, in the town of Tai'an, is at 492 feet elevation; its summit is at 5,069 feet. The best months for visiting are April to October. Winter months are icy and rainy.

Tai Shan was inscribed on the UNESCO World Heritage List in 1987. Guo Moruo, a modern Chinese writer, described Tai Shan as a "microcosm of Chinese culture." There are presently 819 carved stone tablets and 1,018 cliff-face inscriptions on Tai Shan, as well as 22 active temples.

GETTING THERE

By Plane The nearest major airport to Tai Shan is at **Ji'nan,** a large city 40 miles north. Ji'nan has flights to Beijing (1 hour), Shanghai (1 hour 40 minutes), and Hong Kong (2½ hours). From Ji'nan, a traveler must then book a train (75 minutes) or bus (90 minutes) to Tai'an.

By Train There are several trains daily from Beijing to Tai'an, at the base of Tai Shan. My train from Beijing was scheduled to take 8 hours but took 11. Conditions aboard were cramped, but the passengers were interesting, including those who disposed of their emptied beer bottles by tossing them out the open windows. Tickets for "soft-seat" class cost RMB 58 ($7) one-way. There are also daily trains to Tai'an from Shanghai and other major cities in China.

TOURS & STRATAGEMS

Visitor Information **The Tai'an Tourism Bureau,** 45 Hongmen Lu (☎ 0538/822-4451) can be helpful to independent foreign travelers. So can the **China International Travel Service (CITS),** 22 Daizong Archway, Hongmen Lu (☎ 0538/822-3259; fax 0538/833-2240), which offers guided tours of Tai Shan for RMB 100 ($12) per person. The CITS branch office in the Taishan Guesthouse (see below) also arranges tours, and it is especially helpful in booking train tickets.

Exploring the Mountain The mountain is visible from Tai'an. The entrance gate Is straight north up Hongmen Lu. Dai Temple (Dai Miao) is straight south down Hongmen Lu. The temple is open daily from 7am to 7pm and charges RMB 15 ($1.90) admission. Admission to the mountain itself is RMB 50 ($6). A journey to Tai Shan would be incomplete without viewing sunrise from the summit. Plan to spend the night at the top. Take warm clothing and a flashlight.

The trail to the summit, which consists mainly of stairs, is 5 miles, the last 2 miles being particularly steep. The rise in elevation is about 4,500 feet. There are two trails to the midway point (at Zhongtianmen, the Middle Gate of Heaven). The eastern trail is more interesting; the western trail is more rural and often deserted.

It is possible to reduce the hike considerably. Buses and taxis make the run from Tai'an to Zhongtianmen. From this midway point it is an 8-minute ride on a 25-passenger **cable car** to the summit (RMB 45/$5.50 up, RMB 40/$4.90 down). It is a half-mile walk along the shop-lined, stone-railed Tian Jie (Heavenly Lane) to the main temples and sights on the summit.

Recently two other cableways (equipped with four-person gondolas) have been added. One runs between the summit and **Peach Blossom Ravine (Taohuayuan)** on the west side of the mountain, costing RMB 30 ($3.75) one-way, and connects via National Highway 104 with Ji'nan and Tai'an. Another new cableway on the backside of the mountain (northeast side) lets visitors explore two less-crowded wilderness areas of Tai Shan: **Rear Rock Basin** and the **Tianzhu Peaks.** The fare is RMB 30 ($3.75) one-way. The Tianzhu Peaks are near the seldom-used east gate of Tai Shan, 3 miles from the Rear Rock Basin Cableway terminal.

WHERE TO STAY

The most convenient hotel in Tai'an is the five-story three-star **Taishan Guesthouse (Taishan Binguan),** 26 Hongmen Lu (☎ 0538/822-4678; fax 0538/822-1432). It is situated on the road to the main gate to the mountain, which is also about 3 miles from the train station (via taxi or no. 3 city bus). Double rooms start at RMB 420 ($51) and come with private bathroom, as well as green plastic fly swatters and hard pillows. The hotel contains a small bar, some good Chinese restaurants, a good tour desk, a small fitness center, and a poorly lit lobby.

Farther from the mountain, but closer to the Tai Shan Temple (Dai Miao) and railway station, is the newer, more luxurious, four-star, 19-story **Taishan Overseas Chinese Hotel (Huaqiao Dasha),** located on Dongyue Zhong Lu (☎ 0538/822-8112; fax 0538/822-8171). Its double rooms start at $100; most major credit cards are accepted. It offers Italian food and Western dining, not to mention swimming, bowling (six lanes), business center, beauty salon, English-language TV stations, and other international offerings. China Travel Service (CTS) has a tour desk in the hotel (☎ 0538/822-8371).

The hotel at the summit of Tai Shan, now called the **Shen Qi Binguan** (formerly the Daiding Binguan), is located at 10 Tian Lu (☎ 0538/822-3866; fax 0538/833-3150). The CITS office, on the fifth floor of Taishan Guesthouse, can make reservations at the Shen Qi Binguan if you plan to spend the night on the top of Tai Shan. It offers TVs (that seem to receive no stations) and private bathrooms (but no hot water). The 102 rooms are modern but stark, with doubles commanding up to RMB 700 ($87) per night. The staff speaks only Chinese, but they make sure you're up long before sunrise.

WHERE TO DINE

No restaurants stand out in Tai'an, along the mountain trail, or in the "village" on the summit. Trailside vendors offer ice cream, bottled drinks, and hot noodle dishes. In Tai'an, the **Global Bakery Centre,** 7 Hongmen Lu, sells pastries and snacks for the long hike. The **Taishan Binguan** (☎ 0538/822-4678) has a restaurant in a separate building that provides set Western breakfasts ($3) and set Chinese lunches and dinners ($5 to $10). On the summit, the **Shen Qi Binguan** also offers fixed-price Chinese meals in its restaurant ($10 to $20). The pricey **Taishan Overseas Chinese Hotel** (☎ 0538/822-8112) has the best Western food in town in its cafe and Italian restaurant, as well as good Cantonese and Shandong dishes in its Chinese outlets.

Emei Shan: Buddhist Peak of the West

峨眉山

"No spot in the world could be found more aptly to emphasize and accentuate the lofty ideals and mystic dogmas of Buddhism," Julius Eigner wrote after his visit to Emei Shan (Eyebrow Mountain) in 1935. "Leopards, even snow leopards, are not infrequent," he claimed. He also spoke of a lost Chinese world:

> Sometimes an old white-haired monk, leaning on a long staff, will slowly descend the steps, looking like an ancient Chinese sage come to life again. Or a water buffalo will peacefully browse along the banks of a rivulet, with a small boy sitting on his back blowing determinedly on a wooden flute. Is it not a picture a Westerner would associate with those pastoral times which reigned in this country in some dim past age, when the gods came down to earth to visit the daughters of man?

Arriving 7 decades later, at a time when the whole country seems to be stretching out toward a technological future, I still harbored the hope of finding such a China of dreams on the slopes of Emei Shan. If I could take this holy peak at my own pace, lose myself in its folds, and disappear along its lazy trailsides under ink-brushed cliffs, then by the time I stood on its golden summit perhaps I would be blessed with an ancient vision: a halo in the clouds, framing my shadow for an instant before the sun melted everything down into steel and concrete.

Shrine of Limpid Waters

I boarded a morning bus in Chengdu, the capital of Sichuan Province. Emei Shan is less than 90 miles to the southwest. I'd joined a Chinese group tour, a no-frills tour to be sure. I was curious to see how the

Chinese toured the mountain. By the time we reached the foothills of the mountain, darkness filled the hot sky. I got just one glimpse of Emei Shan, its massive triple summit rising like a wall over the low plains, the forests, the mountain streams. At 10,167 feet, its summit (Wanfoding, Peak of the Ten Thousand Buddhas) is the highest of any of the nine sacred mountains of China.

At 8pm we stopped partway up the mountain at **Jin Shui,** the **Shrine of Limpid Waters,** where hotel rooms awaited us. I filled out the registration papers at a counter smack-dab in the middle of a cafeteria and ended up in the one wing that accepts foreigners. My room contained its own bathroom, three beds, and a local tour guide. This guide attached himself to me the moment I entered the hotel and he wouldn't let go. We sat down on bed no. 2 and hammered out tomorrow's itinerary. He spoke not a single word of English. Tomorrow morning we would catch a predawn minibus to see the sunrise from the summit, then come down the mountain on foot. My self-appointed guide would knock at my door at 4:30am.

After he left, I examined my accommodations. The bathroom sink emptied directly onto the floor. I pulled back the quilt on each bed, finding all the bedding, down to the mattresses, equally damp. It would be like sleeping in the tub.

The Bus to Sunrise

I slept a few moist hours before dressing, then greeted my guide at 4:30am. Outside, it was still pitch-black under a crown of stars, but the humidity was high. Emei Shan was a steam bath. I was eager to see the sunrise from Emei Shan's **Golden Peak (Jinding).** It's there that worshippers have gathered over the centuries to pay their respects to the mountain god and to look over the edge of a massive precipice. "Emei is lofty, piercing heaven," writes a Ming Dynasty poet, "A hundred miles of mist, built in the void."

The minibus was late, however—quite late. By the time we drove up the back side of Emei Shan to the last parking lot under the peak, it was 7am and the sun had been up a good while. So many vehicles were racing to the top this morning that there were several traffic jams. We saved a bit of time by taking the new cable car up the last steep slope, although we had to wait another hour in line. Of the 300,000 who visit the summit each year, 200,000 arrive by cable car.

The summit of Emei Shan is imposing—a vast, nearly vacant plain of rock and sand. To the east, there's a sheer cascade of limestone, a 2,000-foot drop; to the west, on a sunny morning like this one, a splendid view of the even more formidable Gong Ga Shan (Kunlun) range,

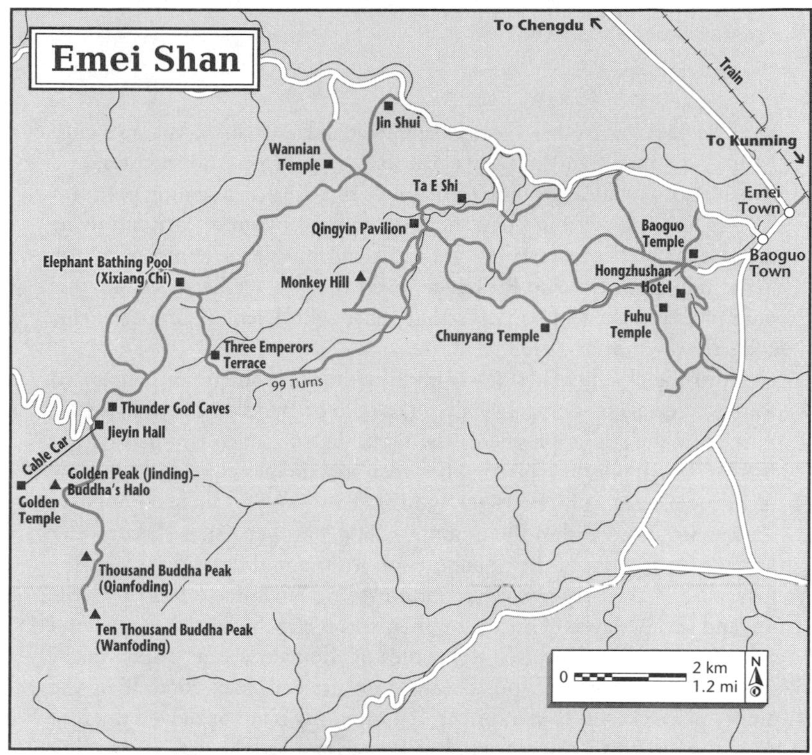

the final horizon of the Middle Kingdom. To the Chinese Buddhist of the past, this chain of eternally snowy peaks was the ever-remote location of the Western Paradise. A Ming Dynasty traveler called them "the Snowy Mountains, running athwart like a long city wall, and looking like festoons of white silk."

Buddha's Halo

Emei Shan is the final gate to a Nirvana that here assumes physical as well as spiritual definition. To reach the Western Paradise requires the help of the god of Emei Shan, Puxian, the bodhisattva of wisdom. He alone can give the faithful pilgrim the final nudge up this last rung on Heaven's ladder.

Puxian came from India in the 3rd century on the back of a white elephant. He is the Sun God of Chinese Buddhism, his mountain shrine forever associated with the heat of the southwest and the element of fire. Puxian was once the bridge between the ancient worship of nature and the new religion of the Buddha, which arrived in China just 2,000 years ago. Whoever made it to the summit of the Western Peak could then petition Puxian to escort them across a river of clouds to the divine shore.

The shortcut to this Western Paradise is Emei Shan's massive cliff. Every holy mountain in China has its legacy of ecstatic suicides, and Emei Shan provides not only the highest but the most inviting platform for the leap. Below this ledge there is often an ocean of soft and wondrous clouds. There certainly was this morning as I approached the metal railing on **Suicide Precipice,** even though overhead the sky was pure blue and the sun so fierce that those who'd rented Chinese army coats for the morning chill shed them.

Into the cloudy sea beneath my feet the sun sometimes penetrated so as to create a magnificent halo—the halo of Buddha. These halos are formed as the sun impregnates the water-laden clouds. Framed within this halo, each pilgrim, standing between sun and cloud, sees the shadow of his own head as he bows to Buddha. I was not fortunate enough to see my own head within the mountain halo, but many an earlier traveler had left an account of the phenomenon. In the middle of the 11th century, a Song Dynasty traveler reported seeing "an aureole of mixed colors and several layers. Out of the mist was a clearly defined image of a god astride an elephant." In the center of the halo was a "bright space, serenely clear. Each person looking saw the image of himself in the empty place exactly as in a mirror. If I lifted my hand or moved my foot the image followed the motion, but I could not see the person standing by my side."

When Reverend Hart, spreading the word of the Gospel throughout remote western China, reached this terrace in the summer of 1887, he seems to have seen something of Buddha's glory himself, for he found that as he stretched forth his arms, his giant shadow did likewise. He dismissed it all as a natural phenomenon but admitted, "I also found myself when the aureole was brightest making insensible advances toward the image in it."

Autumn is the prime season for halos and suicides—in April I was out of sync with the seasons. I contented myself by swaying a moment or two on the terrace, surveying the wide bowl of layered clouds. It was easy to see how a circular rainbow could form here. The air was filled with a million droplets of prismatic water, awaiting the visionary torch of the sun.

Golden Temple

I can report one phenomenon from Emei Shan's summit that earlier travelers did not: The wide face of the cliff is coated in tons of trailside garbage—primarily plastic bags and containers—cast from the terrace by a million modern tourists. The eyebrows of Emei Shan are desperately in need of a divine scouring of wind and rain, snow and lightning.

The summit is flat and empty. Acid rain has devoured entire forests here. To one side there is a communications tower and a dismal two-story hostel of cement and sheet metal, complete with a medical clinic and restaurant. There are plenty of itinerant vendors, including a few peasants with small monkeys on leashes perched on their shoulders. Emei Shan is nearly as famous for its bands of robber monkeys as for Buddha's halo. Now the monkeys have become cogs in the moneymaking machine that's bulldozing the mountain into a convenient national park of cable cars and tour buses.

There's still a shrine on top of Emei Shan, the **Golden Temple,** to house Puxian. This was the last stop for the incense-burning pilgrim—once, according to the 19th-century missionary, Reverend Hart, the place "most exalted in the empire," where for "hundreds of years the stream of religious humanity . . . flowed and ebbed without diminution." The Golden Temple has been rebuilt continuously since the Han Dynasty. Today's stand-in is but a decade old, rebuilt on the site of a fire that gutted its previous incarnation (a fitting disaster, since Puxian is a fire god himself). The new temple is small, set on its own high platform, and while not cast entirely in bronze, the golden tiles of its flying eaves blaze in the sun. Inside, the image of Puxian is painted gold.

I took one last glance over the edge of the Golden Summit, hoping to discover my own shadow swaying in the clouds below, but my prayer was unanswered. I witnessed nothing more than a wide cliff drawn closed like a curtain by the clouds, waiting to be parted by the sun on its daily march across the heavens to the snows of Paradise.

Temple of Ten Thousand Years

Leaving the summit, I persuaded my impatient guide to forgo the cable car. We labored downhill on stone steps for 90 minutes. According to a Chinese gazetteer of Emei Shan compiled in 1887, there are 5,728 steps down the zigzag slope back to Jieyin Hall, where the cable car begins. At this point we caught a bus to the hotel, ate lunch, and then set out together back up the mountain on foot.

We were climbing the ancient path of the pilgrims at last, no buses nearby, no cable strands. Emei Shan is a long, intricate mountain of 90,000 stone stairs; trails wind for 50 miles from the golden summit to the base town of Emei. I began this afternoon above the halfway point, and in 4 or 5 hours I was able to encircle the main great temples on the body of the mountain. On my own, I could easily spend a week walking this mountain, temple by temple, each concealed within its own green hallowed fold of forest, stream, and terrace. A Chinese tour, however, is measured out in minutes and hours, not days and weeks, and like it or not I had locked myself into mass tourism, Chinese style. My bus back to Chengdu would leave tomorrow.

My walk on Emei Shan began at a monastery converted to an elementary school for children who live on the mountain. There is a resident population of about 2,000 scattered across these slopes. This schoolyard is of packed dirt, a basketball hoop with a tattered net at either end; the yard was empty after lunch except for a half-dozen chickens. Vendors were showing their wares under awnings roofed in galvanized sheet metal. I watched a grandfather and his tiny grandson hire a sedan chair for the climb. The boy sat on his grandfather's lap. Off they dashed together; on either end of the sedan chair poles, the two porters were stripped down to T-shirts, their pants legs hiked up.

We followed after them into the hazy green hills under a bleeding sun, sweating all the way. According to the old book I had in hand, *Omei Illustrated Guide Book* (1891), it is some 1,258 steps up to the first great monastery, **Wannian Si,** the **Temple of Ten Thousand Years.** I felt every single stair tread in the heat. Somewhere along here, 4,000 years ago, the legendary yellow emperor paused to inquire of a Daoist wanderer the way to the summit, and later the Tang Dynasty poet Li Bai stopped to pen some evocative lines about these temple-infested terraces:

Bearing the Emerald Tapestry Lute,
A Sichuan monk descended the grand western peak.
With a brush of his hands on the strings
He made me hear a sound like the rushing
of pines in deep caverns.
My heart was cleansed by the flowing waters;
The lute's quaver mingled with the knell
of a temple bell in frost.

Uncleansed by any magic lute, I reached Wannian Si, founded 17 centuries ago, the oldest temple on the mountain. Although this temple complex is beautiful and in a luxuriant natural setting, most of its great halls, save the one housing Puxian and his elephant, burned down in 1946. Wannian Si is at 3,000 feet elevation, just above the jungle belt, thick with camphor and banyan, mulberry and banana. I could feel the steam rise and swirl into these highlands, a 15-mile walk below the Golden Summit where I stood this morning, staring into a mirror of blank fog.

The building that has survived the longest on Emei Shan, the mountain's holiest shrine, is at Wannian Si: a squat hall of brick, 50 feet square. Inside, under a beamless vault, is Puxian's white elephant, cast in bronze in A.D. 980, now plastered over with painted stucco. Puxian, eldest son of Buddha, rides on top, his saddle a golden lotus. Modern pilgrims burn long sticks of incense outside the main doors. I took a gander at elephant and mountain god, then followed my silent guide up and down the 2,436 twisting steps to **Qingyin Pavilion.**

Golden Monkeys

Of the Emei Shan staircase, an imperial inspector, Shou P'u, once wrote, "When descending the hill, travelers go crab-fashion, with one man's feet on another man's shoulders. When ascending, they go like ants stuck onto each other, with one holding another's foot in his mouth." The trail is everywhere as crowded with trailside vendors as with visitors, the slopes green with bamboo and a few straggly tea plantations. Along this path the Ancient Forest of the Virtuous One once stood, planted by a devout monk in the Ming Dynasty. He was said to have planted 69,770 trees, one for each character of the Lotus Sutra, but not a single one has survived.

At the pavilions of Qingyin, we turned west toward the **Hill of the Monkey (Hou Wang Po),** pausing to bathe ourselves in the White Dragon stream. I was drenched in sweat, so it felt good to stop for a splash. I was determined to keep going upstream for a glimpse of Emei Shan's celebrated monkeys. Most of the animals that frequented Emei Shan in its remoter days, a century or less ago, have fled to more impenetrable Western paradises.

The trail twisted through a narrow river canyon over a series of bridges and planks, with bends so tight only one or two people could pass at a time. The canyon was dark, even on this bright afternoon. The sun must seldom, if ever, sound its depths. The monkeys lay in wait. The Chinese have their own way of dealing with the monkeys. I sighted the first of these golden creatures on the iron railing of a bridge. They were being taunted by the sedan chair carriers and a crowd of visitors. By the time I reached the railing, the monkeys had scurried up a sandy bank of ferns and bamboo. The crowd tossed them scraps; the monkeys sauntered down to accept the offerings. Several of the Chinese started to tease the monkeys again, luring them down the slope with outstretched palms, then hissing or opening an empty hand and laughing. One monkey suddenly leveled a swipe at the back of a little girl's head. A moment later another monkey, a mother carrying her baby, bit a woman's extended hand.

This band of monkeys was outnumbered by the hordes of tourists. For the most part, the passing crowds forced them to higher ground. No longer can they block the road like toll collectors. We are making the world a safer place for tourists, if not for the creatures the tourists come to see. On Emei Shan the golden monkeys have been subdued. Every temple, every parking lot, now has a handful of portrait photographers bearing monkeys on their shoulders. Many of these captives are dressed in silk; all are chained. For RMB 1 (12¢), the handlers allow tourists to pose with a monkey balanced on its hind legs in their hand; pictures are snapped; prints are mailed to purchasers. It's another way to turn a profit in the wilds—rural enterprise, blessed by God and Party, with conservation postponed until the next century.

After watching the crowd taunt a few more monkeys, I turned back. I'd seen enough for today of mountain and temple, bronze elephant and golden monkey.

Pure Sound Pavilion

I rested up at the **Qingyin (Pure Sound) Pavilion,** so named for the melodious meeting of the White and Black Dragon streams. According to an Emei Shan gazetteer, "Clear sounds are heard near the lofty pavilion, as if Buddhist spirits were playing musical instruments." I splashed myself with a few wet notes scooped from the chilly stream. With its narrow waterfalls, swift white rapids and cascades, arched bridges, tile-roofed kiosks, and viewing halls perched on ledges and terraces in a rain forest of bamboo, Pure Sound Pavilion is a postcard of the past, before cable cars, buses, and bottled water vendors lined the 90,000 stone stairs, before the tigers were caged or shot or driven to Tibet, before the golden monkeys were chained.

Below two arched bridges, known as the **Twin Flying Bridges,** the limestone canyon of the river dragon deepens into what a Chinese mountain guide of 1844 describes as the place "with pure sounds of music, where the waters wash the heart of an ox into a Buddha." This is where the White and Black rivers merge—the Ox-Heart Stone beneath the Flying Bridges. I followed my guide downhill. The sun was falling behind the forehead of the mountain.

Thunder Gods

We passed **Ta E Shi,** the Great Stone of Emei, on which a Ming Dynasty minister of education carved a message, "Heaven of the Holy Mystery." I was too beat to entertain more mysteries. We emerged at a small village and waited for bus connections. I bought two boiled eggs from an old woman. She charged me the paltry Chinese price for eggs—a fine, honest woman. Meanwhile, peasant photographers were displaying their leashed monkeys, and a farm girl strolled by, her water buffalo tethered to a rope.

Back in my hotel room at Jin Shui, I fell into bed before dusk. Emei Shan was where I imagined I would spend a week or two wandering from temple inn to temple inn, but now all I could do was sleep. Just past midnight, however, the mountain was socked by an electrical storm, a boisterous one. Crack after crack of lightning woke me. Puxian, the mountain god, was speaking. Or perhaps the ancient thunder gods still dwell in the hidden recesses beneath the summit. Less than a century ago, pilgrims and officials gathered on a platform to the thunder gods at the top of Emei Shan to pray for an end to drought. "First one drops some incense and money down," explains the mountain gazetteer of 1891. "If rain does not come, then one drops in a dead pig and women's clothes. Then the thunder and rain will surely come."

Tonight the thunder and rains had come. I'd hoped to follow in the footsteps of Chung-yo, an artist who a hundred years ago roamed Emei Shan for months. "So taking my brush along in its bag," he wrote, "I went, combing my hair with the wind and washing my hair with the rain, let down by ropes through dangerous places, and penetrating secluded spots."

I'm no true mountain dweller, I suppose. Sixty years ago, Sheng Chin, abbot of Qingyin, described my dream in the simplest manner: "Formerly I constructed a thatched hut in the mountains, and passed several summers and winters there, subduing my passions and destroying desire." I'd built no mountain hut, subdued no passions. I was ready to return to Chengdu. This was too big a mountain for me.

Emei Shan's signature is its immensity. Layer after layer of terrace, stream, and pinnacle are peeled back as a traveler rises to the summit. And on the summit, on the wide eyebrows of limestone, the boundary between empire and paradise becomes visible. Halos dance on a sea of clouds. The shrunken cities are 1,000 miles to the east and the Western Paradise but one fatal step away.

PRACTICAL INFORMATION

ORIENTATION & WHEN TO GO

Emei Shan (also written as Omei Shan) is 87 miles south of **Chengdu,** the capital of Sichuan Province in southwestern China. The mountain is far inland, about 1,100 miles southwest of Beijing, 1,200 miles west of Shanghai. The nearest towns, both to the east, are **Emei,** where there is a railway station, and **Baoguo,** which is inside the mountain entrance gates. Emei Shan occupies a large territory. The slopes contain 50 miles of trails and about 30 active Buddhist temples. Minibuses link major temples along the way with the base and summit. Nearby places to visit are **Leshan,** 25 miles east of Emei Shan, and **Chengdu,** with a myriad of attractions.

Emei Shan was inscribed as a natural and cultural World Heritage site by UNESCO in 1996. It has designated protection zones for plants (including 29 species of rhododendron) and landscapes. Ten percent of China's plant species grow here. Threatened animal species include the red panda, Asiatic black bear, Asiatic golden cat, and Tibetan macaque.

The climate ranges from subtropical to cold-alpine, depending on altitude and season. The base of the mountain is at about 1,500 feet elevation, while the summit is over 10,000 feet. Winters are cold and snowy, making climbing dangerous. Summers are rainy and hot. Early spring and late autumn are the mildest periods to visit.

GETTING THERE

Chengdu, the gateway to Emei Shan, can be reached by train or air from all over China. See the Chengdu chapter for details.

By Train from Chengdu to Emei Shan There are several trains daily serving Emei Town from Chengdu. This is a 2- to 3-hour trip. Minibuses and taxis connect the Emei Train Station (which is 2 miles east of town) to the mountain entrance at Baoguo (20 minutes, RMB 10/$1.20 fare).

By Bus from Chengdu to Emei Shan Buses leave for Emei Shan all morning from the North Railway Station in Chengdu, pulling in at either Emei Town or Baoguo Town. Baoguo is the best terminal, since this is where the mountain trails begin. Emei Town is connected to Baoguo Town by minibuses (20 minutes; RMB 10/$1.20 fare). The bus from Chengdu costs RMB 30 to RMB 50 ($3.60 to $6) each way and takes 4 to 6 hours.

Many of these buses to Emei Shan are actually group tours (RMB 50/$6) that stop at Meishan, a town on the way, and at the Leshan Great Buddha. I don't advise taking a Chinese tour bus, since they spend only 2 nights on the mountain and restrict the time you can spend there. Try to book a bus that goes just to Baoguo from Chengdu. From Baoguo, which is a one-street town, it is easy to book a ticket back to Chengdu at any time.

TOURS & STRATAGEMS

Emei Shan is a large, confusing mountain park. Base yourself either in Baoguo at the entrance, or 7 miles by road up the mountain at Jin Shui. Baoguo has the best hotels and restaurants, while Jin Shui puts travelers closer to the major temples and sites. Emei Shan tickets are sold at the entrance near the Baoguo Temple and cost RMB 50 ($6). The temples on the mountain charge nominal entrance fees, usually RMB 4 (50¢).

Visitor Information The mountain hotels and temples are not good sources of information, with the exception of the **Red Spider Mountain Hotel (Hongzhushan Binguan)** in Baoguo Town (see below). Freelance tour guides, often speaking little if any English, abound in the hotel lobbies, temple courtyards, and village streets. They're probably worth hiring, and a guide can be handy when it comes to ordering food in a temple, cafe, or trailside stall.

Exploring the Mountain Reaching the upper peak at Jinding (Golden Summit) for the sunrise is a problem.

It's too far to hike, especially in darkness. You can stay overnight at Jinding in the temple (see below) or take a predawn bus from Baoguo (2 hours) or Jin Shui (1 hour). Below the summit, at Jieyan Hall, a cable car runs up to the Golden Summit (RMB 70/$8.65 round-trip) from the last parking lot, but the lines in the early morning are very long for the 20-minute trip.

From the Golden Summit, there are trails to the highest peak (Wanfoding), a 30-minute walk, or back down to Jieyin Pavilion, a 2-hour trek. Six to 8 hours later (or more) brings one back to Jin Shui, halfway down the mountain. A new cableway now connects Wannian Temple to Jin Shui.

The mountain has two main parallel trails. The northern and southern trails rise westward to the summit from Baoguo, coming together at Qingyin Ge (Clear Sound Pavilion), then splitting. The northern trail proceeds through Wannian Temple, with a branch trail (or cableway line) north to Jin Shui. The southern trail continues up from Qingyin Ge through Monkey Hill. The two trails merge again and fuse below Xixiang Chi (Elephant Bathing Pool), beyond which there are more packs of monkeys and ultimately the cable car and summit.

To see all the temples and explore the trails and vistas fully takes many days. Temples provide very basic sleeping quarters and meals (vegetarian). Weather can change quickly, so layers of warm (and cool) clothing are required, as are reliable hiking shoes and rain gear.

WHERE TO STAY

The monasteries and temples offer extremely basic accommodations (basic room with dormitory-style beds, quilts, washbasins, and little else) for about RMB 60 ($7.25) a night. At **Jieyin Pavilion,** near the cable-car terminus, at Jin Shui, and in Baoguo Town, there are also some modest guesthouses that have run-down, moldy doubles with run-down, moldy private bathrooms and not much else. Doubles cost RMB 180 to RMB 250 ($21.75 to $30). The only hotel of note is in Baoguo Town.

Red Spider Mountain Hotel (Hongzhushan Binguan). *Baoguo Town (on a side road running south off the highway connecting the town and the temple). ☎ 0833/552-5888. Fax 0833/552-5666. 180 units. A/C TV TEL. $40 double. JCB, MC, V.* Among its dozen wings and buildings, this villa-style hotel has a three-star section (no. 5) with modern doubles, opened in 1998. It offers currency exchange, overnight laundry, and most importantly, a tour desk. This is the place to get maps of the mountain trails and travel advice. The hotel also books train and bus tickets, and it accepts credit cards.

WHERE TO DINE

The major temples all have vegetarian restaurants. The food is cheap—RMB 18 to RMB 25 ($2 to $3) a meal—and bland. Trailside stands serve up noodles and soup at even cheaper rates, as well as bottled water and canned sodas.

In Baoguo Town, the **Teddy Bear Cafe** (on the main road, ☎ 0833/559-0135) has an English-language menu and some inexpensive Western and spicy Chinese dishes. Best of all, this is the place to get practical information on Emei Shan—where to stay, where to eat, where to book train or bus tickets. The owner speaks English, and English-speaking local guides often turn up here.

Hua Shan: Sacred Mountain of the West

华山

THE MOST ANCIENT GODS OF Chinese civilization once dwelt upon Hua Shan, a mountain strong enough to bend the Yellow River to the sea. The first emperor and his successors performed the spring and autumn rites here for a thousand years, praying to the mountain god to open Heaven to Earth. Daoist hermits, alchemists, and sorcerers retreated to Hua Shan where they became the immortals of Chinese tradition. And countless pilgrims, scaling the almost impossible heights, sought a glimpse of Heaven, a taste of immortality in the open hand of Buddha—in the crown of five peaks at the summit of Hua Shan, the Flowery Mountain.

I first climbed this mountain in 1984, an altogether remarkable event, and again in 1993. I returned to see if the changes that are transforming China at the dawn of the 21st century have reached all the way to this holy mountain of the West.

At the Gate to the Mountain

At the Xi'an long-distance bus depot, Eddie Han bought us cheap tickets to Hua Shan. Eddie was a young English teacher I'd met a day earlier. When he heard I was returning to the sacred mountain, he offered to accompany me. I knew that with a local Chinese along, the journey would be smoother. The bus depot was infested with beggars, entire families in rags. Eddie said they were lazy, but he gave money to the children.

Every seat on the bus to Hua Shan was taken. Because two passengers refused to pay two extra mao (about 4¢), the bus did not use the new four-lane toll road. After 3 hours of the usual delays and discomforts, a mountain range erupted to the south, dwarfing the mud villages. We reached Hua Yin Village at the foot of Hua Shan an hour later. Touts hit us like an updraft of gnats.

This village was a wide spot in the road in the 1980s and 1990s, when I stayed in a one-dollar room, but today Hua Yin is another tourist trap. The tourists are Chinese; I didn't see a single foreigner. The strip to the mountain gate was glutted with pedestrians, shops, and vendors. A new hotel, half-finished, boasted an amusement arcade in the shape of a fiberglass dragon that swallows families whole. I really didn't recognize the street or the village now, but change in China is always sudden.

Three old women hounded us, selling incense. We were on the grounds of **Jade Spring Temple,** "picturesquely situated at the start of the ascent to the mountain," as Hedda Morrison wrote. The adventurous Mrs. Morrison photographed Hua Shan in the summer of 1935. In her book of photographs, she writes that the "importance of Hua Shan lay partly in its proximity to the early centers of Chinese civilization, and partly in its being a supreme example of the type of landscape so appreciated by Chinese artists." The "spectacular mountain forms" and "solitary, cloud-capped peaks" of Hua Shan captivated her, captivated the great Song Dynasty painters, and first captivated me in the 1980s. In 1935, one could spend a night in the Jade Spring Temple and enjoy a hearty vegetarian meal prepared by monks. Today, the temple has been demolished; the meals, served from a hundred stalls, are neither Daoist nor Buddhist; and Eddie and I were forced to buy tickets just to cross the temple's foundations. At the mountain gate, we were detained again. I was required to buy a special permit for foreigners. Altogether, I forked over RMB 48 ($5.75) before I could hit the trail.

River Gorge of 18 Bends

It was the same mountain, yet nothing was the same. The trail up the mountain river had been widened, smoothed over, and filled in with solid granite curbstones. A power line runs along the bank. New gates arch over the path, and small vendor-towns, roofed with cloth awnings, crop up every quarter mile. The sheer white cliffs on the other side of the river are altered, too. They once served religious hermits as remote refuges. Carving a few ladder rungs up the cliffside, those ancient ascetics disappeared for months into high, unapproachable caves. Today, several "hermit caves" have been carved out and opened to visitors.

I still saw some Daoist monks on the trail, but the essence of the mountain—wild, distant, fierce, holy—has disappeared from the lower flanks. The dreams that accompanied me on my first trek up Hua Shan dissolved into fresh pavement, souvenir stands, and sedan chairs with green bamboo poles, their carriers for hire. At the mountain gate there are even tennis shoes for rent.

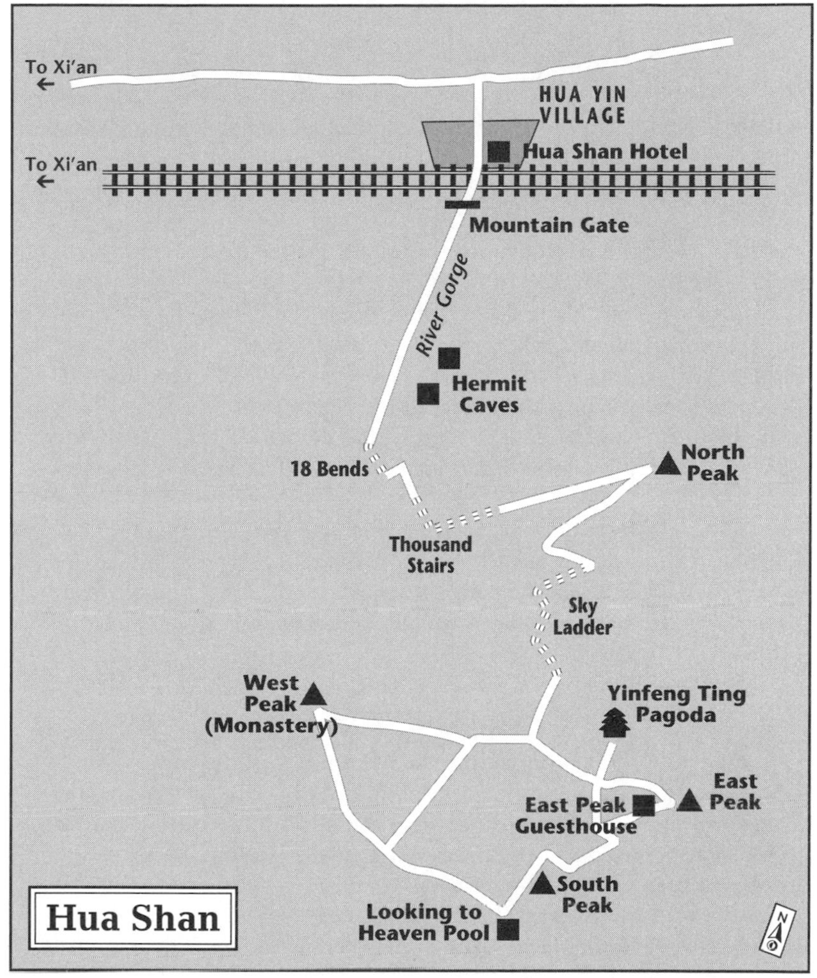

The Thousand Stairs

The second phase of the journey, however, where we left the river canyon for the stone spires of the peak, was not without its terrors, even in this modern age. People still die on Hua Shan every year, falling from its edges. Even the sedan chair carriers drop back here, 2 steep miles from the top. "In places the track led up almost perpendicular rock faces in which steps had been hewn and iron chains of uncertain reliability set in the rock to provide hand-holds," Mrs. Morrison wrote in 1935. "Some of the sheer stretches were for one-way traffic only, and when we reached them we would call out so as to ensure that we did not meet some descending pilgrim half way."

Little had changed here. I knew these stairs well; they are something one never forgets. I once saw a porter lose his load on this stone ladder, these "Thousand Stairs." Today, this chimney, which actually consists of two long streamers, has been rehewn and widened, but the chains are still in place. It is just as steep as ever, although there are now separate staircases up and down, and the small temple at the top of the stairs, which once had an iron trapdoor to seal off the mountain from intruders, is long gone.

Other temples along the way have been rebuilt since I visited, but they seemed empty. Those on the North Peak—the thumb of the five-fingered Hua Shan cluster—straddle a narrow spine of stone, dramatic from a distance. Eddie and I reached the North Peak in our third hour of quick climbing. We ordered a roadside dinner, a horrible one, and overpriced. Eddie confided that as soon as vendors see me, the prices double.

Hedda Morrison once tarried for days at the **North Peak Monastery,** where she met five Daoist priests and a boy sent to them for his health by anxious parents in Shanghai. Later she would meet a pilgrim who had traveled to the top of Hua Shan by foot, all the way from Beijing.

The Sky Ladder

The North Peak is connected to the other peaks of the compass by "a hair-raising track . . . known as the Sky Ladder" with a sheer drop-off on both sides—the stone web between thumb and fingers. Beyond that lies an even more terrifying traverse, the Azure Dragon's Ledge, which has now been removed from the trail entirely.

A Tang Dynasty poet, Po Chu-i (A.D. 772–846), described the ledge succinctly: "The chasm beneath me, ten thousand feet; The ground I stood on, only one foot wide."

By the time Eddie and I crossed this final bridge to the peaks of the immortals—where the white fungus of wisdom grows and beans said to satisfy one's hunger for 49 days sprout—the sky had darkened, the wind had chilled. We mounted the East Peak, then traversed the hand of the mountain to the West Peak. I was hoping the old monastery where I spent nights on earlier climbs remained, that it had not been redone, that I could say of it, "You're no Holiday Inn."

West Peak Monastery

I was not disappointed: The monastery on West Peak had not been spruced up or made over one iota, save that the outdoor toilet once cantilevered over the cliff edge had been swept away. The rooms were unrepentantly crude. Only the price had kept up with the times: We had to pay RMB 25 ($3) apiece (as much as Eddie pays for a modern guesthouse in Xi'an) plus an RMB 15 ($1.80) surcharge for my not being Chinese. Our suite was a cubicle on the top floor with two hard cots, each with a dirty quilt. The foot of Eddie's bed collapsed every time he sat on it.

A bare electric bulb dangled from the ceiling. When it quit, a monk arrived with a kerosene lantern. We secured the door with a brick. There was no bathroom down the hall and no water, neither a thermos nor a basin; we couldn't even wash up. I liked it. The room hadn't improved with the decades. The lattice ceiling was stuffed with bamboo matting and newspaper. A few sections of white butcher paper were tacked up here and there. The wooden floorboards were rotting away. The paper walls and loose windowpanes rattled in the night wind, sounding like a scurrying army of rats.

This monastery would leak and creak all night. I lay back on the hard pillow, zipped up my windbreaker and pulled on my stocking cap, and crawled under the quilt to warm up. I was haunted by a fine photograph that Hedda Morrison composed in 1935 of two Daoist monks in ceremonial combat, one armed with a sword, the other with a fly swatter. "The fly whisk, made from a yak's tail and known as a cloud sweeper," Mrs. Morrison explained, "is thought to impart the ability to ride the clouds."

I felt too heavy in limb and bone to levitate on this edge of the void. There would be no visions of holy peaks and Daoist immortals to sugarplum my sleep tonight—just hard facts, hard as the pallet upon which I fell to rest.

In Buddha's Palm

We woke on the mountain at dawn, left the monastery, and circled the peaks—the five petals of the stone lotus. We stopped beside an empty crater, the **Looking to Heaven Pool.** In 1932, when the Australian maverick, Rewi Alley, accompanied by R. Lapwood, arrived at the summit of Hua Shan after an "ascent that surpassed all our expectations," he discovered the same pool filled with rainwater. "Here farmers still prayed to the Black Dragon for rain," he wrote. Here Alley met a monk who claimed to be 120 years old. He was said to have gone sleepless for 20 years running, tending his herb gardens both by sun and moon.

The mountain was once pregnant with fantastical stories of hermits who became immortals endowed with the power of flight. Ancient kings are said to have paid homage at Hua Shan as early as 1766 B.C. Qin Shi Huang Di, the first emperor of unified China, is believed to have reached the summit in his search for the white fungus. The first emperor of the Ming Dynasty dreamed of his ascent up this pillar of Heaven. Lao Zi, the ancient founder of Daoism, left his iron plough here, although no one's seen it lately. Guanyin, Goddess of Mercy, once had her likeness carved in a valley between peaks at the Holy Stove Temple, where she shared the altar with Lao Zi and his cow.

The Jade Maiden of Chinese myth was celebrated on Hua Shan, too—she arrived on the back of an ethereal dragon. The whole mountain is in the shape of a dragon, some say. The true god of this mountain may well be the dragon, once synonymous with China itself. There is Chinese legend that a dragon coiled itself over these slopes and deposited its skeleton on the outside, forming the dramatic ridges. The steep cliffs are antediluvian.

What struck Eddie about the rock walls of Hua Shan, however, was their color: white, bone white. Indeed, the presiding God of the Mountain is the White Spirit. According to Reverend Geil, who left an exhaustive trove of stories about Hua Shan after his visit in the 1920s, the White Spirit resides on the very same West Peak where I spent last night. Wearing white robes and a top hat, the White Spirit could open and close the doorway to Heaven. He rode a white dragon in a procession of 4,100 fairies.

I took a final glance at Hua Shan's **West Peak,** its supreme summit, the edge of the void, with a view of the Yellow River valley, the cradle of Chinese civilization, where Xi'an stands. One can see why emperors came to this peak to validate their reigns. It is nature at its grandest. Indeed, in 1383, Wang-Li composed his classic album of Chinese travel pictures here, some 40 landscapes that forever defined nature in China. The scenes survive today in the Palace Museum at Beijing and in the Shanghai Museum, but the original persists in nature, little altered by humans. One can still feel how Hua Shan became the ultimate refuge not only for hermits but for exiles of all stripes, politicians out of favor, disinherited children, criminals and saints. Hua Shan's beauty is wild, belonging more to the clouds than the streams and the earth. It is as if we can see the very mold of nature at the instant it was pulled away into the stars, the rock not quite cooled.

Hua Shan's dome is a summit worthy of the word, composed of bare rounded white granite, with the cleaver mark of a hero of the old myths on its skull, its flanks as sheer and long as any in the Middle Kingdom, seeming to roll straight down to the plains of dust where China was born. This was once the cliff of divine suicides, where pilgrims threw themselves into undifferentiated space, high above all worldly shapes, praying for the heavens to open and swallow them up. But the dragon in stone is today repaved and reinterpreted, its temples transformed into cafes and souvenir sheds, its immortals into faint clouds, its scales into the stuff of a traveler's fantasy.

Back to the Future

We descended Hua Shan rapidly, stopping only once for plastic bottles of mineral water and a repast of boiled eggs, greasy donuts, and millet gruel. There were mothers and fathers coming up the mountain with babies in their arms, but I encountered few of the devout old women, feet bound, who took on Hua Shan the first time I did. There were plenty of couples on outdoor adventures. They purchase padlocks to secure to the chain-link rails near the summit, a way of commemorating their love, and toss the keys into the abyss.

As for China's mythic past, most of that has been looted and dispersed. The essence of the new Hua Shan is a mad rush, a commercial opportunity, a street of touts that runs from Xi'an to this remote summit once believed to hold up the heavens. Years ago Hua Shan touched and changed me; now, in a harder age, I come and go like a shadow.

Practical Information

ORIENTATION & WHEN TO GO

Hua Shan (Flowery Mountain), the most beautiful and steep of the nine sacred mountains, is located 75 miles east of the historic city of Xi'an in Shanxi Province, 500 miles southwest of Beijing in central China near the Yellow River. The village of **Hua Yin** is at the foot of the mountain, which reaches an elevation of 6,552 feet. With the area's cold winters and hot summers, spring and autumn are the best seasons to visit. **Xi'an** serves as the travelers' gateway to the mountain.

GETTING THERE

By Plane & Train to Xi'an Xi'an can be reached by air from Hong Kong (2½ hours), Beijing (1½ hours), Shanghai (1 hour 40 minutes), and many other Chinese cities. There are also overnight trains from Beijing (17 hours), Chengdu (19 hours), and Shanghai (24 hours).

From Xi'an to the Mountain From Xi'an, there are direct **trains** in the morning (2½ hours). The train station at Hua Shan Town is a 20-minute walk east from Hua Yin Village at the foot of the mountain, although there is now a small train terminal (West Hua Shan Station) at Hua Yin with a few trains connecting to Xi'an. **Buses** leave daily (3 to 4 hours). The faster buses use the new four-lane expressway. Train and bus tickets may be purchased at hotels in Xi'an or from the terminals, which are located at the northern end of Jiefang Lu, just inside the Xi'an city wall. Buses gather in front of the Huashan Jinrong Binguan, a new hotel on the main street of Hua Yin village at the foot of the mountain.

TOURS & STRATAGEMS

Visitor Information **China International Travel Service (CITS)** in Xi'an, 32 Chang'an Bei Lu (☎ 029/526-3841), with branches at the Bell Tower Hotel (☎ 029/727-9200, ext 2842) and the Jiefang Hotel (☎ 029/743-1023), can arrange bus and train tickets to Hua Shan. CITS can also provide English-speaking guides and hired cars. Hotel tour desks in Xi'an might also be able to provide assistance.

Exploring the Mountain Entrance admissions, collected at several points at the base of the mountain, will total about RMB 55 ($6.75).

It is now possible to tour Hua Shan as a day trip from Xi'an, thanks to a new cable car that makes the ascent to the North Peak. It costs RMB 80 ($10) round-trip. The cable car's lower terminus is well east of the base village, an RMB 10 ($1.25), 30-minute taxi ride away. Buses return from Hua Yin Village to Xi'an as late as 8pm.

The full mountain experience, however, demands an ascent on foot. The trail is about 9 miles from base to summit, requiring 6 to 8 hours. The last 2 miles of the ascent are steep and narrow. This is the most dangerous of the nine sacred mountains to climb, with vertical stone steps, chain-link rails, and deep drop-offs along the way.

If you base yourself in a guesthouse at Hua Yin Village, you can climb up and down in one long day. You can also stay overnight on the West Peak in a monastery, thereby being on the summit to watch the sunrise. The vista from the West Peak is quite dramatic.

WHERE TO STAY

The **Hua Shan Binguan,** west on Jianshe Lu 2 blocks from the mountain entrance gate (☎ 0913/436-2836), is the most convenient place to stay in Hua Yin Village. Basic doubles with private bathrooms cost RMB 350 ($42). You don't get much in the way of amenities or services (and no credit cards are accepted), but the views from the rooms at the rear are superb. The **Huashan Jinrong Binguan** (☎ 0913/436-3119) has slightly nicer double rooms for RMB 450 ($55). Ignore the guesthouse touts who work the main road to the mountain gate; the accommodations they are hawking are neither clean nor comfortable.

On the summit of Hua Shan, rooms are available in the **Daoist monastery** on West Peak. These are like run-down barracks, with two narrow beds and no private bathrooms or even sinks—just a place to sleep under a quilt, with no heat or air-conditioning. Doubles are about RMB 85 ($10). On the East Peak, there is a small modern hotel, the **East Peak Guesthouse (Dong Feng Fandian).** Doubles with private bathrooms are overpriced at RMB 500 ($62), but it's the best hotel on Hua Shan and is a superb viewpoint at sunrise.

WHERE TO DINE

If Hua Shan is a day trip, try to carry with you all your food and snacks. Water and drinks can be purchased on the trail. The trailside vendors and village cafes are expensive—RMB 85 to RMB 168 ($10 to $20)—and the food is nothing special. The best restaurants are in the hotels and guesthouses, where the dishes are basic Chinese combinations of vegetables, noodles, and meats.

Song Shan/Shao Lin: Sacred Mountain of the Center

嵩山

Song shan (high mountain) is the Daoist peak at the center of China. According to a Chinese mountain guide, the people "thought that Song Shan lay directly under the heart of heaven and on the liver of the Earth," and they called it the "pearl in the cradle of ancient Chinese civilization." Of its many temples, the two most famous still exist: **Zhong Yue,** China's oldest Daoist temple, and **Shao Lin,** world center of the martial arts and birthplace of Zen Buddhism.

The 72 peaks of Song Shan are situated in Henan Province between two ancient capitals, Luoyang to the west and Zhengzhou to the east. I approached the mythic middle of the Middle Kingdom from Luoyang, turning east at Shao Lin Monastery for the holy city of Dengfeng at the southern foot of Song Shan.

Dengfeng is an ugly strip, once glorious. It was the capital of the early Xia civilization, then hometown of the holy Central Mountain. It received its present name in the 7th century when Empress Wu of the Tang Dynasty—one of the most notorious figures in all of Chinese history—built her summer home in the foothills. Dengfeng means "Ascend to Bestow Honors."

I checked into a modern but already aging and decrepit hotel. The electric lights didn't work, no water ran in the tub, and the door to my room didn't lock. Still, it was spacious and I had a view of the peaks of Song Shan to the north. The Central Mountain is a formidable wall of bare white rock peaks, once described by Wang Wei, a Tang Dynasty poet, as "towering aloft in the skies and piercing halfway to Heaven."

Imperial Academy

My aim this afternoon was not to climb to the top but to visit a few of the famous sites on the lower flanks of Song Shan. I had no map, but I could see the range to the north. I set out in that direction, looking for a likely road out of town. After an hour of bad guesses and detours, I discovered a path into the hills. It quickly led me to **Song Yang Academy.**

When China's capital was at Xi'an and later Luoyang, the intelligentsia enjoyed the coolness of summers at Dengfeng, and there they established this academy, one of China's four great centers of Confucian learning. Song Yang began as a Daoist temple. The Han emperor, Wu Di (140–87 B.C.), pausing here on his way to perform the spring rites on Song Shan, planted three cypress trees, the **Three Generals,** two of which survive, or so it's believed. They certainly look like antiquities, gnarled and grand, venerable enough to stake a claim to a birthday 2,000 years ago.

Tang Emperor Gaozhong made this site his residence for a short while in A.D. 683. It became an imperial academy as early as A.D. 951 and served as a Confucian college for 9 centuries, reaching its zenith under Emperor Kangxi in China's final dynasty. In 1936, General Chiang Kai-shek, who lost the civil war to Mao, celebrated his 50th birthday at the academy and ordered the digging of a well, which still works.

Plenty of history here—but now Song Yang Academy is just a few tiled-roof buildings inside a low wall with a ticket taker at a table and some soft drink vendors on the doorstep. The interior is a museum, its 60 rooms all renovated within the last 100 years. The academy's most impressive monument is in the front courtyard, a massive 8th-century stele (carved stone tablet) 30 feet tall, crowned with an elaborate sculpture of two lions clasping a ball in their raised paws. Its inscription reports that in A.D. 744 Emperor Xuanzong, age 61, took a beautiful young concubine, Yang Kuei-fei, and promptly ordered the Daoist alchemists at the Song Yang Academy to hand over the elixir of eternal youth. Apparently, the transaction went awry, as emperor and concubine achieved immortality only in story and myth.

The Oldest Pagoda in China

From the academy I struck northward through wheat fields, in search of the oldest brick pagoda in China. The land is hard and dry, filled with white stones. There are dirt caves under the green terraces where farmers store seed and cuttings, even machinery. I followed a streambed uphill until I caught sight of a brick pagoda. I cut across a field of brush, scaled a hillside, and forded a rock-terraced stream. Teams of stonecutters, sun-darkened men in black topcoats hauling sizable sledgehammers, were working up and down the streambed.

On the other side of the stream I found a highway. After walking along it for an hour, I finally reached **Song Yue (High Peak) Temple** and the old pagoda. The grounds are in a sorry state. There's some rehabilitation in progress, but the temple walls have caved in. The uncut

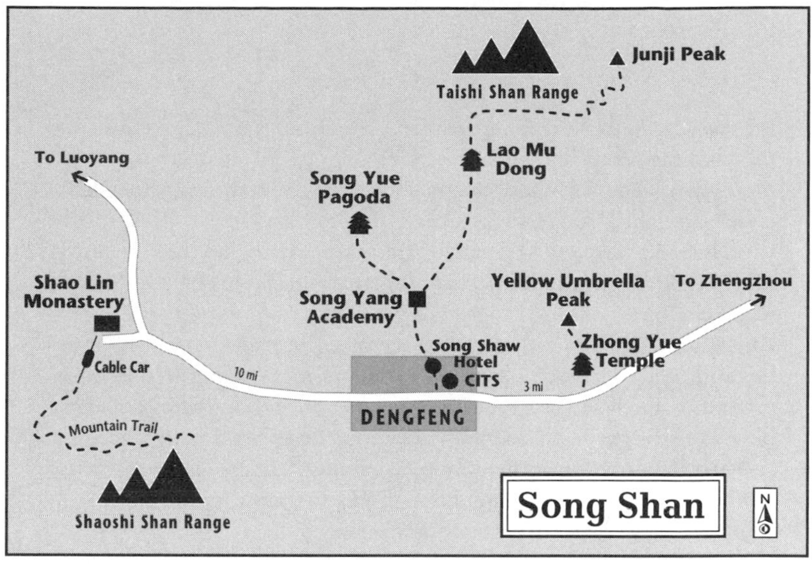

courtyard grasses, green and yellow, nipped at my thighs. Several halls and pavilions are tumbling down. And the complex is deserted. At its heart is China's oldest brick pagoda, 12-sided like the zodiac, 15 stories and 123 feet high, damaged but still solid. It's in the shape of a pine cone growing skyward. The pagoda's tip is carved into an inverted lotus leaf that serves as the platform for the Buddhist wheel of life. There are 500 doors and windows in its walls, many fitted with carved figures, including 40 lions.

It's the sole pagoda of this style in China, piled high with small black bricks mortared into a 12-sided cosmic wheel spinning into the heart of Heaven. Empress Wu Zetian stayed the night here in A.D. 696. The pagoda was already a relic then—nearly 2 centuries old. It dates from A.D. 520. The temple was founded even earlier, in 509, to serve as a portable shrine-away-from-home for the Northern Wei royals. It still looks as if it were in some kind of catastrophic transit.

I climbed back down the white stone hills. The sky above the distant shafts of Song Shan was blue. The riverbed of the mountain was being paved in stone. Work crews were breaking, ferrying, and laying rock. The water that pours down from Song Shan has a long tradition of purity and curative powers. Recent reports claim that no one living within 3 miles of the river has ever suffered a single case of cancer.

First Mountain of the World

The sky was a sharp and even blue when I set out for the central peak of the Central Mountain just after dawn. My destination was **Junji Feng,** elevation 4,900 feet. It required 30 minutes to retrace my steps up the river basin to Song Yang Academy. I skirted the academy wall and followed the power lines up a steep embankment to a gravel road. A few more twists and I was above the final foothill. The summit of Song Shan lay straight ahead, one among a pack of 36 peaks.

The road gave way to a path of stone steps rising up the river basin. A temple hung on the last terrace below the cliffs. In the river basin I heard the pings of chisels against stone. The temple on the terrace is named **Lao Mu Dong.** I knew nothing of its heritage, but someone was investing money in its restoration. Vendors had congregated upon its grounds. I purchased two boiled eggs and a can of soda. Behind the temple was a stairway to the summit, fashioned from hewn blocks, each the size and shape of a small stele. I'd spent almost 2 hours just to reach this temple. It would take me another 2 hours to gain the top, all of it by stairs that looked like they would never level out.

I passed through another temple that is on no map I've ever come across. It too was being restored. It was already active with monks dressed in long black robes. Several worshippers had black beards, a rare sight in most parts of China.

Against the wall of a massive peak, the trail bent east. I stopped at a shrine, a single building at the back of a ledge. A young man came out on the porch. I couldn't tell if he was monk or merchant. I could tell he was very poor. He also had no hands and no wrists. He smiled at me. He knew one English phrase: "Okay." "Okay," he laughed. "Okay."

Carved into a cliff across the way were characters announcing that Song Shan is the First Mountain of the World. Ahead was a staircase of a hundred steps or so, and beyond that more staircases switching back and forth up the sheer face of the peak. A steel railing had been installed. I could see a figure or two on the pinnacles above, and I met two or three groups of hikers on the stairs. Otherwise, the trail was deserted. The last vendor I came across had pitched his cart on a narrow ledge between staircases. I bought a can of soda.

This high up, I could survey the entire Dengfeng Valley to the south, hazy in the dust. To the west, I could see a second mountain range—the western half of Song Shan, known as Shao Shi Shan, the junior range, with Shao Lin Monastery at its foot. I was scaling the Tai Shi Shan half of Song Shan, the eastern half, the "great" side. These were the same peaks that once attracted emperors and pilgrims, although they now attract almost no one.

Summitry

Each flight of stairs became more tedious. The sun was fierce. It seemed to take me hours to surmount the last ladder of steps. The top of Junji

Peak was farther still. Three women gathering plants and herbs motioned for me to sit down beside them on a green patch. They proceed to eat their lunch. They weren't in the least disturbed that we spoke few words in common. I sat down with them and finished my drink.

At noon I reached a construction site marked with red-and-white flags. The summit was a few steps more. And on this summit, this central summit of the Central Kingdom, halfway between the midpoints of Heaven and Earth, what is there? Nothing. No temple, no altar, no marker, no ruin. Not even a vendor. There is only nature: a slope of green grass and white stone.

In December of A.D. 696, Empress Wu stood here, on this summit, paid homage to the earth, and appointed Song Shan emperor of Middle Heaven. Wu entered royal life as a concubine for one Tang Dynasty emperor, became the consort of his successor, and succeeded them both as supreme ruler and China's first great empress in A.D. 684. Hoping to establish an immortal dynasty of her own, she made Song Shan her sacred residence. The mountain was given an imperial title. Her prayer to the God of Song Shan, engraved on a tablet of gold weighing 280 grams, was unearthed in 1982 on the summit.

The view on a cloudless day from the top of Song Shan was a fine one. For the first time I saw why the ancients maintained that the sky was round and the earth square.

A Tall, Dark Stranger

An hour passed at the summit. I turned back. As I passed the new buildings, a very dark man with a dark beard, dressed in black patches, stopped me. He raised both hands and touched his fingertips, forming a pyramid at the base of his neck. I mirrored his greeting. He reached out a hand. We shook. He invited me to accompany him inside; I declined. He stood aside; I walked down the mountain.

Mao Ch'i-ling (1623–1716), on his second attempt to scale Song Shan, met a stranger, too: one who revealed to him the secrets of true Confucian wisdom, transforming his life. Me, I just keep walking up and down in China. It took me 3 hours to descend, each mile slower than the last, until I was amazed I could move at all. I saw almost no one on the way back. The herb gatherers had disappeared, the stonecutters vanished.

Zhong Yue Temple

China's modern travelers do not come to Song Shan to climb peaks. They come to visit the temples—either Zhong Yue, the Daoist temple to the Central Mountain, or Shao Lin, the Buddhist temple to Zen and the martial arts. Zhong Yue lies 3 miles to the east of Dengfeng; Shao Lin, 10 miles in the opposite direction. Both are on the main highway; neither requires a climb.

Twelve centuries ago, Zhong Yue Miao, the Central Peak Temple, was one of the three greatest Daoist temples in China, consisting of nearly a thousand halls and pavilions. The God of the Central Mountain lived here. Since Han times he had presided over quite an assortment of geographies and beings: over rivers and valleys, mountains and fields, sheep and oxen, fruits and food—over nearly everything, animate and inanimate.

It is thought that the temple was visited by Han Emperor Wu Di in 110 B.C. and that it was founded in the time of the first dynasty, the Qin (221–207 B.C.). Today, of course, Zhong Yue is shrunken—what hasn't of ancient China under the press of the new centuries?—and the buildings aren't old, dating back only a century or two to when the Qing emperors visited and sacrificed oxen in the spring on the platform of the main hall. Then there were still 11 courtyards and plenty of gnarled trees, as many as 1,000, 300 of them said to have been planted over 1,000 years ago.

A few courtyards deep, I found the famous **Four Iron Guards,** statues 10 feet tall, fierce in their armor, modeled after the soldiers of the time and cast in A.D. 1064. Some children swung from their iron fists. Daoist monks sat at tables nearby, dressed in dark blue robes, white leggings, and straw hats, selling incense. The courtyards were full of worldly vendors, too. One photographer posed customers on the back of a stuffed tiger. Another sold shots in a pellet gun aimed at a wall of balloons—strange entertainment at a temple.

The stele I most wanted to find is known as **The True Map of the Five Mountains.** It was carved in 1604. A magic symbol for each mountain—Heng Shan Nan to the south and Hua Shan to the west, Heng Shan Bei to the north and Tai Shan to the east—is placed on its compass point, with Song Shan, where I now stood, in the center. I found the Five Mountains tablet out in the open, exposed to the elements. It's a bit worn these days, its rounded topstone washed smooth, but the five mysterious characters for the Sacred Five are still clear 500 years after they were carved.

Outside the last hall is the path up **Yellow Umbrella Peak (Huangtai Feng),** where Han emperor Wu Di noticed a big patch of yellow cloud as he made his ascent of Song Shan. There's an ornate little pavilion now, and those who want a quick holy climb wander up in droves. Admission to the temple complex is RMB 10 ($1.25).

The Fighting Wooden Monks of Shao Lin

I returned to the highway and caught a bus back through Dengfeng and on to **Shao Lin Monastery,** 9 miles farther west. Shao Lin is a monument to mass tourism Chinese style. Open daily from 8am to 6pm, it's a commercial maze of souvenir vendors inside and outside the temple complex, always crowded. Even the People's Republic of China is doing kung-fu films that glorify the fighting monks of Shao Lin, and they're filming them right here, on the actual site. This is China's Universal City Studios of Flying Fists, the spiritual and commercial world center of the martial arts.

I was here to see history and culture, and I suppose that's what I was seeing. This is the center of the modern Chinese centrifuge—in brute contrast with the quiet old peak I reached yesterday, virtually alone.

Certainly Shao Lin Monastery has plenty of Old China attached to it, too. Shao Lin was founded in A.D. 495 by Emperor Xiao Wen Di of the Northern Wei Dynasty and expanded and enriched by the second Tang Dynasty emperor in 625 in gratitude to the monks who helped him wage war against a rival. In between, in 527, Da Mo, also known as Bodhidharma, the 28th incarnation of the Buddha, arrived from India, crossing the Yangzi River on a reed. At Shao Lin, he spent 9 years in solitary meditation staring at the wall of a cave. The cave is still here: Even the shadow he left on the cave's wall is still here, or so it's said. When Da Mo emerged from 9 years of "wall-contemplation," he founded a new sect of Buddhism, known as Chan in China, as Zen in Japan.

Da Mo also picked up credit for formulating the Chinese style of hand-to-hand combat known as *wu shu* or more popularly *kung fu*. Unconcerned about shifting from religion to religion, it seems, good Zen Buddhist patriarch Da Mo is also said to have written Daoist classics on the cultivation of the muscles and the purification of the marrow.

The martial arts, not Zen, are what bring the tourists in these days. In the 15th and 16th centuries, the fighting monks of Shao Lin were taking on the pesky Japanese pirates off China's coast. During the 1920s, when China was in civil turmoil and local warlords held sway, the Shao Lin Temple was a haven for runaway soldiers who terrorized the local population. In 1928, one of the most famous of these warlords, Feng Yuxiang (Shi Yousan), the "Christian general," routed the monks and set fire to the monastery. Shao Lin burned for 40 days.

I elbowed my way through the late morning crowds to see **Thousand Buddha Hall,** built in 1588, with its fading fresco of monks going all out in martial arts battle—it would make a dandy movie poster—and the single most famous temple floor in China, roped off now and unlighted, where the monks practiced their stompings and leaps so diligently that the heavy stone floor became indented. Even cursory inspection suggested to me that the water table was high or the subsoil unstable under this floor, and that here and there it simply sank. I have a concrete driveway that looks about the same, and it was poured long after the 16th century.

To stretch the imagination further, I lined up for a peek at the **Shadow Stone,** removed from Da Mo's cave. A Chinese traveler described it this way in 1623: "I saw the shadow stone of Da Mo. Less than 3 feet high, it was white with the black traces of a vivid standing picture of the foreign patriarch." What I saw was a slab of rock, burned or discolored, with the vaguest outlines of a human figure in meditation.

Shao Lin also contains a magnificent **Forest of Stupas,** the largest collection in China of these small brick pagodas that hold holy relics and the remains of great monks, abbots, and even their followers. From what were once 500 stupas, 227 of these grave markers remain. They span 1,000 years of burial, from the Tang to the Qing dynasties. The oldest of the stupas is that of Ching-tsang (A.D. 675–746), built in the year of his death—the oldest stupa in China.

More vibrant, and more in keeping with the holy amusement park atmosphere of modern Shao Lin, is a courtyard surrounded on three sides by open-air displays of wooden, life-sized monks in dramatic fighting poses. They look like old carvings, but they may be merely dusty. Some are armed with swords or poles and locked in fierce combat. These mannequins of the martial arts are used as models for monks in training. These days Shao Lin does a hefty business running scores of martial arts schools for everyone from schoolchildren in China to visiting kung-fu clubs from Japan, America, and Europe.

The Far Side of Song Shan

Visiting Shao Lin Monastery in 1965, Australian journalist Rewi Alley was told about "some temples up on the hills, where in times of trouble the monks had gone." There is now a gondola that ferries visitors up the 36 peaks that make up Song Shan's western range—a mirror image of the main cluster of 36 Song Shan peaks that make up the Sacred Mountain proper.

I decided to take a look. From the rising gondola, I could see the Shao Lin Monastery and the tourist road that outlined it like a noose. The crowds and tour buses were brushed out of the picture of the tile roofs, brick walls, and green hills rising to the north. I could see Da Mo's Cave, where he emptied his mind so thoroughly that his shadow stuck to the wall.

At the cable-car terminal on the peak, I followed a trail into the woods. It took me to a world far removed from the Shao Lin circus.

Threading my way up towering cliffs, eventually I came out on the southern side of the range. The stone walls that line the back of the western Song Shan are 1,000 feet straight up. The trail sliced across the cliff face. Sections of the trail were cantilevered out from the rock, forming catwalks over empty chasms, which I treaded across gingerly.

The far side of Song Shan is dazzling. Some parts of the path are wide enough only for single-file passage—hardly a problem, as I met almost no one coming or going. I zigzagged along this natural stone wall for an hour from declivity to declivity. There were a few temples and pavilions in recesses and ledges, but I knew nothing about them, not even their names. They were deserted.

Eventually I came to a house perched on a small rock terrace. An old man and his wife invited me inside. The house had a dirt floor, almost no furnishings, and a shrine in a nook with incense burning. The two didn't seem to want to sell me anything. In fact, they seemed out of touch with the world, or mad. I asked them how to get back to Dengfeng Town. They pointed straight down, and they were serious.

The long slabs of rock that tumbled down the cliff from their house contained remnants of a railing, enough of it still pinned to the rock to point the way down. After an hour's steady crawl, I reached a long formal stairway of stone that took me down to ground zero. At the bottom of the mountain I was able to hire a motorcycle-driven cart back to Dengfeng. The dirt road rolled across the "liver of the Earth" under the shadow of the 72 peaks that once pierced "the heart of Heaven." Silent, nearly forgotten, Song Shan, in the middle of the Middle Kingdom, has been reclaimed by nature.

PRACTICAL INFORMATION

ORIENTATION

Song Shan is located south of the Yellow River in Henan Province, 420 miles south of Beijing and 550 miles west of Shanghai. The town at the base of the main Song Shan mountain range, Dengfeng, is midway between the cities of Luoyang (50 miles to the west) and Zhengzhou (45 miles to the east).

Shao Lin Monastery is 9 miles west of Dengfeng, at the base of the western (lesser) range of the Song Shan mountains. **Zhong Yue Temple,** the most important Daoist shrine to the Central Mountain, is 3 miles east of Dengfeng. From Dengfeng, it is a 4-hour climb north to the top of Song Shan. The oldest brick pagoda in China, **Song Yue Pagoda,** is 3 miles northwest of Dengfeng in the Song Shan foothills.

Other important attractions in the immediate region include the ancient capital of **Kaifeng** and the Buddhist grottoes of **Longmen** near Luoyang.

GETTING THERE

There is no airport or train station at Dengfeng. Zhengzhou is the nearest major transportation hub, with plane connections to major cities in China, including Beijing (1 hour 20 minutes), Guangzhou (2 hours 20 minutes), Hong Kong (2½ hours), and Shanghai (1 hour 20 minutes). Trains serve Zhengzhou from Luoyang (2 hours), Xi'an (10 hours), Beijing (12 hours), Shanghai (14 hours), and Guangzhou (36 hours).

Minibuses connect Dengfeng and the mountain to Luoyang and Zhengzhou, a 2- to 3-hour trip that costs RMB 20 ($2.40). Taxis and hired cars make the trip a little faster and provide more comfort, at a cost of $50 or more, depending on how negotiations go with the driver.

TOURS & STRATAGEMS

Visitor Information The Dengfeng branch of **China International Travel Service (CITS)** is located in the Song Shan Binguan, 48 Zhong Yue Lu (☎ 0371/287-2137). The staff speaks English and can give helpful information. There are no guided hiking tours to the mountain peaks of Song Shan. The CITS offices in Luoyang, at the Peony Hotel, 15 Zhongzhou Zhong Lu (☎ 0379/491-3699), and in Zhengzhou, at the Novotel Hotel, 114 Jinshui Lu (☎ 0371/595-2072), sometimes provide bus tours of Shao Lin Monastery and Zhong Yue Temple.

The **Shaolin Martial Arts Training Center (Wu Shu Guan)** near the Shao Lin Monastery (☎ 0379/274-9120) is the only public kung fu training school in Shao Lin. It has a basic hostel for guests and students and an inexpensive restaurant.

Hours of Operation & Entrance Fees No ticket is required to climb Song Shan from Dengfeng. Entrance fees are charged at Zhong Yue Temple (RMB 10/$1.25; open daily 8am to 6pm), Shao Lin Monastery (RMB 60/$7.25; open daily 8am to 6pm), and Song Yue Pagoda (RMB 4/50¢; open daily 8am to 5pm). The gondola from Shao Lin Monastery to the western range of Song Shan is RMB 25 ($3) one-way.

WHERE TO STAY

In Dengfeng, the only hotel taking foreigners is the **Song Shan Binguan,** 48 Zhong Yue Lu (☎ 0371/287-2755), at the east edge of town. This is an aging complex with run-down modern rooms and private bathrooms. I had little hot water and my door did not lock. Doubles are $30. The restaurant out back offers quite good (and large) fixed-price Chinese meals for $3 to $5. CITS has their offices in a separate building in the front courtyard (☎ 0371/287-2137). No credit cards are accepted at this hotel, and the services and amenities are extremely limited, but the staff is friendly and helpful.

Zhengzhou has the best accommodations for hundreds of miles in all directions at the new **Holiday Inn Crowne Plaza,** 115 Jinshui Lu (☎ 800/465-4329 or 0371/595-0055; fax 0371/599-0770). This five-star, five-floor, 222-room, deluxe international hotel has virtually every amenity and service, and takes credit cards (AE, DC, JCB, MC, V). Doubles start at $133 (plus 20% surcharge).

WHERE TO DINE

The **Song Shan Binguan,** at the east end of town on the main highway (☎ 0371/287-2755), has the only decent restaurant in Dengfeng. There's no English menu or English speakers on the staff, but foreigners are served hearty fixed-price Chinese breakfasts, lunches, and dinners for RMB 25 to RMB 42 ($3 to $5). It's open daily from 7am to 10pm.

CHINA BY RIVER: UP & DOWN THE YANGZI

长江

A CRUISE UPON ASIA'S MOST fabled river, the Yangzi (or "Changjiang" in China), has been the dream and somctimes the nightmare of millions of merchants and boatmen, farmers and poets, emperors and outlaws, since Chinese civilization began. Unchanged for centuries, the scenery is various, earthy, and spellbinding, particularly at the **Three Gorges,** where the third longest river on Earth is forcibly contained (as a Song Dynasty poet wrote) like "a thousand seas poured into one cup." Of pressing concern for all travelers are the plans to block this scenic heart of the river—from the Three Gorges all the way upstream to Chongqing. This dramatic section will eventually be drowned by the Sanxia Dam, the world's largest construction project, scheduled to be completed around the year 2009. Thus, the rush is on to see the Long River before it changes forever.

The Yangzi is *The Romance of the Three Kingdoms* made visible, each bend in the river a passage from that classic Chinese novel of history, adventure, and lore. Although most foreigners are not familiar with this book, all Chinese are. The Yangzi River has mythic, as well as natural, qualities.

Intrepid independent travelers have been cruising up and down the Yangzi River for decades, purchasing tickets at river ports and using Chinese cruise ships. Since the early 1990s, however, there has been a more luxurious alternative: **Victoria Cruises,** an American-managed line that now has six fine ships on the river. I favor Victoria Cruises because of its good management and Western cruise directors, who make all the difference and enhance the experience of the river for foreign travelers. The longest of Victoria's several options is a 10 day/ 9 night cruise upriver from Shanghai to Chongqing, which slowly takes in virtually the entire navigable length of China's greatest river.

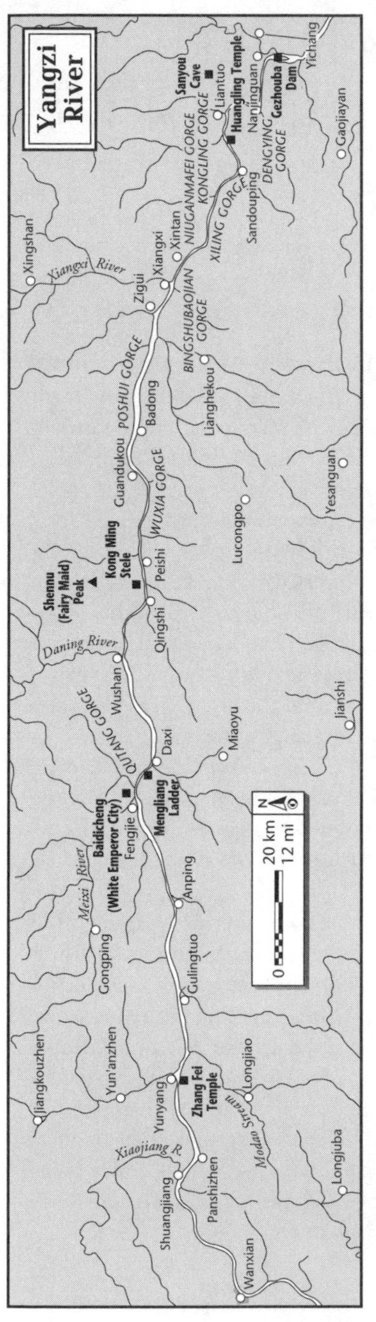

Shanghai (Day 1)

I boarded the M.S. *Yangtze Princess* in Shanghai at Shiliupu Pier, located at the southern end of the Bund, in the early evening, settled into my stateroom, had a buffet supper in the dining hall, and came out on deck for a spectacular departure. The Huangpu River was lighted up on both sides now, with the monumental European architecture of colonial days illuminated on the western shore and the new Shanghai of Pudong's skyscrapers ablaze on the eastern shore. I was setting out on my voyage into the remote interior of China by passing through a tableau of recent Chinese history, the past on one side, the future on the other—a light show one can not easily forget.

Yangzhou/Nanjing (Day 2)

After an early breakfast (7am) the next morning, our ship docked at Yangzhou for the first of many shore excursions. The Yangzi River between Shanghai and Wuhan meanders through vast, flat deltas, its scenery hardly dramatic, but even here the river passes near some of China's greatest sights. Buses on the docks, manned by local English-speaking guides, whisked us past downtown Yangzhou for a walk through the grounds of **Tian Ning Temple,** a 1,500-year-old Buddhist complex, where Emperor

Qianlong resided during his southern tour of the Grand Canal in the 18th century. The Yangzhou guides then escorted us down the road along a moat for a brief look at **Slender West Lake (Shouxi Hu),** said to resemble the more famous West Lake in Hangzhou. There we strolled the garden shores of the narrow, scenic waterway with its celebrated triple-arched bridge (Wutang Qiao), constructed in 1757, about the time Emperor Qianlong came to town to try his luck at fishing. The emperor's fishing platform is still in place here. On our way back to the ship, we passed a funeral procession marching alongside the freeway. The mourners were setting off firecrackers; two of them were pushing their motorcycles.

After lunch back aboard the ship and an introductory lecture on the Yangzi River, we sailed upriver to Nanjing, a city with a substantial political history in the 20th century, when it served as China's capital under the Nationalist regime. On our city tour, the bus crossed China's most famous modern bridge over the Yangzi River, the 2 mile-long **Nanjing Yangzi River Bridge,** opened in 1968, which served to create the first rail link between Shanghai and Beijing in history. The tour concluded with the chance to walk the 300 wide stairs up to the **Sun Yat-sen Mausoleum (Zhongshan Ling),** an imperial-sized tomb built for the founder of the first Chinese republic. Sun died in 1925; his Nanjing tomb began to be built a year later. Today it is one of the main stops on any Chinese's political pilgrimage, as Sun Yat-sen is venerated by both communists and nationalists as the father of modern China.

The evening concluded in high cruise-ship style with a captain's cocktail party (complete with Chinese champagne), dinner in the Dynasty Dining Room, and the Victoria Fashion Show in which members of the 118-strong Chinese crew modeled costumes from the major dynasties on the disco floor.

Huang Shan (Day 3)

During the night, our ship moved upriver another 130 miles to the tiny port of **Guichi,** where buses on shore took us another 110 miles to the foot of China's most beautiful peak, **Huang Shan (Yellow Mountain).** At the Taiping Cable Station, where itinerant beekeepers were encamped, we rode the ropeway 15 minutes to the summit, rising over 3,000 feet through the parting mists. There, we received a brief but splendid introduction to the sheer rock formations, gnarled pines, and terrifying overlooks for which the Yellow Mountain is so famous. Armed with wooden walking sticks and cameras, our group enjoyed lunch at the top and spent 2 leisurely hours exploring the trails and nearby peaks. Descending in the afternoon, we napped on the 3-hour bus trip back to the ship, dined, and then slept soundly as our ship again used the night to traverse another 150 miles.

Lu Shan (Day 4)

We docked in the former Treaty Port of **Jiujiang.** This day's excursion took us to another mountain, **Lu Shan,** the fabled hill station where foreign colonials and later a gallery of China's 20th-century political leaders established a summer resort. Despite the fog and light rain, we were able to tour Meilu Villa, the summer home of both Chiang Kai-shek and his bitter foe, Mao Zedong, and then hiked a serene mountain trail in the Brocade Valley (Jinxiu) to Lu Cave, a temple carved out of the overhanging rock by nature. The village of Guling at Lu Shan presented excellent afternoon shopping, particularly for the locally grown Cloud Tea.

Wuhan (Day 5)

Arriving at the large city of Wuhan the next morning, we anchored here all day, awaiting those passengers who would join us the next day for the standard Wuhan-to-Chongqing Yangzi River Cruise. In the meantime, we could explore the waterfront on our own. The streets are well worth wandering; you can explore the old European architecture on the shoreline (highlighted by an old clock tower), the lanes of small Chinese shops, and the new eight-story Galaxy Plaza shopping complex on Zhongshan Da Dao, with its boutiques, its KFC, and its two McDonald's.

The afternoon was devoted to touring two exceptional cultural sights. The new **Hubei Provincial Museum (Hubei Sheng Bowuguan),** opened in 1999, is one of China's premier exhibition centers, nicely lighted, signed in English and Chinese, and tastefully carpeted. It's the repository of over 15,000 relics unearthed from a Warring States Period (B.C. 475–221) tomb of Duke Yi of Zeng located 40 feet underground. Among the coffins removed were those of his 21 concubines, ages 13 to 26, who were poisoned upon their master's death, and another for his dog. The duke's own inner and outer painted wooden coffins, weighing some 400 pounds each, are displayed in the museum, as are chariot pieces, gold cups, bamboo strips with ancient writings, jade wine glasses, a large bronze wine cooler, and a large bronze barbecue. There is also an exquisite bronze statue of a crane with a long, long neck and deer's antlers (as both the crane and the deer are symbols of good fortune).

The centerpiece of the museum, literally displayed at its heart, is the **Chime Bells of Duke Yi of Zeng.** There are 65 bronze bells, suspended in three tiers on a wooden frame. The bells are decorated with 3,755 inscriptions and their collective weight is over 5 tons. These ancient bells, the only complete set in the world, are tuned to five-, six-, and seven-note scales. Although the original music of the chimes has been lost, scholars have reconstructed songs from other ancient scores. Four times a day in a special museum auditorium these songs are played by a local concert group (which now periodically tours the world) on a replica of the ancient chimes, accompanied by zithers, drums, flutes, and an English-speaking narrator. These performances are included in the museum admission of RMB 20 ($2.50). The museum is open daily 9 to 11:30am and 1:30 to 4:30pm.

The second cultural site on our tour drew from modern history, that of Chairman Mao, for whom an elaborate estate was maintained on scenic East Lake in Wuhan. Recently opened to the public, **Chairman Mao's Villa (Mao Zedong Bieshu)** is a 1950s Western-style mansion with high ceilings, peeling wallpaper, and stained carpets—strangely enough, it's been unrenovated since the heydays of Maoist Thought. Here Mao visited some 20 times, swimming in the Yangzi River on nearly every visit. His private Olympic-size indoor swimming pool is still in place on the estate, as is his huge bed. Guests these days who are willing to shell out RMB 25,000 ($3,000) per night can have the run of the entire Cold War compound, which comes complete with an elaborate air-raid shelter in its basements (they can be seen in all their creepy dampness today by any visitor for RMB 2/25¢ extra).

Wuhan (Day 6)

After a night at anchor in Wuhan, we enjoyed yet another shore excursion. Wuhan is an industrial port that serves as the main eastern terminus for most Yangzi River cruises, and it's usually ignored by tourists, but as we'd seen the day before in its streets, at the Hubei Provincial Museum, and in Mao Zedong's Villa, it has some cultural treats. The city actually consists of what once were three cities: Wuchang, Hankou, and Hanyang. Hankou, Wuhan's city center, where we have anchored, contains the architectural stamp of British, German, French, and Japanese colonials. In Hanyang, adjacent to Hankou, we toured the 300-year-old **Guiyuan Temple (Guiyuan Si),** one of the largest along the Yangzi, where locals actively light incense and pray for prosperity and health at shrines to the golden Buddha and Guanyin, the Goddess of Mercy. The main attraction is a cluster of the 500 arhats (followers of Buddha), molded from clay in the early 1800s by a father and son into lively, comic poses, painted with gold powder, and placed on benches to face each other.

Across the Yangzi in the Wuchang district, up a steep hill (known as Snake Mountain), and past the inkstone of poet Li Bai, is the **Yellow**

Crane Tower (Huang He Lou), a high pagoda that dates from the 3rd century A.D. Rebuilt countless times (most recently in 1985, in Qing Dynasty style), it has been renowned through the ages because of its vistas of the Yangzi River and also because of a moving poem by Tang Dynasty master Li Bai. Today its 144 stairs to the top can be overcome by a new elevator (admission RMB 1/12¢ each way). Li Bai's poem can be translated thus: "At Yellow Crane Tower I bid farewell to Meng Haoran and watch his sail go farther, ever farther, until it vanishes under blue sky; but my heart runs with the Yangzi waters, flowing, ever flowing." Our excursion up and down the tower was rewarded with a tea ceremony conducted in a pavilion at the base of Snake Mountain.

For those who boarded at Wuhan, as most passengers did, it was the first day of a 6-day, 5-night cruise upriver to Chongqing that traverses 841 miles of the Yangzi (which is barely a fifth of its east-to-west 3,906-mile length). As we pushed out from Wuhan, the river darkened. All I could see from the railing were lights, some passing, some receding, and overhead the stars that never seem to move, even over China's longest river.

Yueyang (Day 7)

At dawn, after joining the ship's doctor for his daily tai ji exercise class, I took a look at the Yangzi above Wuhan. The placid waters were wide, dotted with small whirlpools but devoid of rapids. Long, rusty barges heaped with coal, rice, and other products of the interior chugged downstream toward Shanghai, the sailors calling out and whistling as we passed. Sheaves of grain are unloaded along the way and stacked on shore in piles the size and shape of barns. Logs are carried from shore by hand.

Even here the Yangzi is etched with the history of the Three Kingdoms period (A.D. 220–280), when the Wei, Shu, and Wu kingdoms contended for control of China along the Yangzi. At **Red Cliff (Chibi)**—scorched that color, it is said, by the flames that engulfed the Wu and Shu armadas in their celebrated battle with the Kingdom of Wei in A.D. 208—pavilions and a museum of weaponry commemorate this critical confrontation. Zhuge Liang, China's most respected military strategist and political advisor, was present at the battle, in which the Wei army, led by the villainous Duke Cao, met defeat due to his brilliant stratagems.

Our ship made a port of call at **Dongting,** China's second largest freshwater lake. Massive accumulations of silt have reduced the size of what was China's largest lake, but its beauty and history are unaffected. On the east side is **Yueyang Tower,** where admirals of the Three Kingdoms period once reviewed naval maneuvers. The tower dates from the 8th century. It was most recently rebuilt in Song Dynasty style in 1985, complete with the Thrice Drunken Pavilion where Daoist Immortal Lu Dongbin engaged in revelries. Unfortunately, this is my least favorite site along the river. There's little to see or do, and the weather is usually miserably wet. I suggest you skip it altogether, stay aboard, and learn to play mahjong (as I did).

From the mouth of Dongting Lake upriver, the land is flat, girded by the 111-mile-long Jingjiang Dike that originated 16 centuries ago. This bulwark against flooding ends at Sashi, 334 miles from Wuhan. Sashi is the gateway to the **Jingzhou,** whose city walls—10 miles long, 30 feet high, last rebuilt in A.D. 1646—were fashioned, according to local legend, by Three Kingdoms hero Guan Yu, later deified as a Chinese god of war. Jingzhou has a **museum** that contains the remains of a Han Dynasty county governor, Mr. Sui, who died in 167 B.C. at age 60 of a stomachache. Preserved in water and mercury sulfide within a tripartite cedar coffin and buried 30 feet deep, the mummy was unearthed in 1975. After 2,142 years, the corpse proved to be perfectly preserved, with arm and leg joints still flexible. Some cruise ships stop to see the walled city of Jingzhou, although Victoria Cruises has recently dropped it from the itinerary.

Three Gorges Dam/Yichang (Day 8)

The upriver gateway to the Three Gorges is at **Yichang,** once a foreign treaty port and the great transshipment point for Yangzi traffic. Here China's largest dam to date, Gezhouba, was completed in 1986. Boats and ships must pass through its hydraulic locks. Gezhouba has raised the level of the Yangzi some 65 feet behind its walls. The ship's crew ran an informal lottery with the passengers here. Whoever came closest to predicting the time we passed out of the locks was the winner.

Above Gezhouba, I spotted the M.S. *Kunlun* at anchor. Once Chairman Mao's state boat, it later served as a luxury cruiser for wealthy tourists. Neglected now, it seems to be quietly rusting away. A new generation of cruisers has usurped its place on the river, led by the six *Victoria* vessels designed solely for navigating the Yangzi safely, with shallow drafts and double-bottom hulls.

Our next destination was the **Three Gorges Dam,** located at Sandouping Village, 27 miles above the Gezhouba Dam. When fully operational in 2009, it will raise the Yangzi to almost unimaginable heights. More than 20,000 workers and 3,000 engineers are on site, and both shores teem with heavy construction. Situated on a ribbon of granite that crosses the more fragile limestone basin of the Yangzi, the Three Gorges Dam span will be 6,600 feet (1.23 miles) wide and 607 feet high, dwarfing all other dams ever built. The final cost could easily exceed $30 billion.

This cement barrier will create a reservoir 370 miles long, transforming the wild Yangzi into a calm lake that will submerge 13 cities, 140 towns, 1,352 villages, 657 factories, and 75,000 acres of cultivated land, necessitating the relocation of at least 1.3 million people. The deep, narrow Three Gorges themselves will be reduced to a few floating islands. First proposed by Sun Yat-sen in 1919 and seconded by Chairman Mao in 1958, this project is slated to provide as much as 15% of China's electricity, reduce the severity of flooding, and facilitate passage of considerably larger ships through the Three Gorges to and from Chongqing in Sichuan, China's rice bowl. Our *Victoria* cruise ship, at 3,000 tons, was currently the heaviest ship able to navigate the Yangzi; after the great dam is completed, ships more than three times its size will link Sichuan to Shanghai.

At present, the channel flow of the Yangzi is being redirected so that the dam itself can be poured. We followed a diversion channel on the east side, anchoring at **Moping** and boarding buses there for a trip to see the dam construction close-up. The sky seemed to be filled—and will be filled for years—with a fine dust. On our way to the Three Gorges Dam Observation Tower, the road through the center of Moping village was jammed. Traffic stopped completely and didn't seem likely to restart. Apparently there were no detours. Our local guide, who had adopted the Western name Hamlet, was at his first day on the job and seemed immobilized. I wasn't. I left the tour bus and walked down the street, finally finding the bottleneck a few blocks around the bend. It was a sign of new times in China: an impromptu strike by local taxi drivers led them to block the thoroughfare with their abandoned taxis. In the course of the next 20 minutes I heard at least five versions of what prompted this daring strike. The most likely story was that a policeman stopped a woman taxi driver, demanded her permit, and struck her when she refused, leading to a sympathetic strike. After an hour, a settlement was negotiated and the traffic rolled.

We traveled through portions of the new town being built for the 100,000 local residents who will lose their old town to the dam, then crossed a new bridge, the tenth over the Yangzi, opened in 1997. We could see the sides of the Three Gorges Dam in place on either side of the river now, columns of concrete 600 feet high, the right and left margins of the span yet to be poured. The Observation Tower lies atop a hill, a round building encircled by a fresco commemorating heroic workers; below it is a hall displaying models of the great project. On one side is the Yangzi, soon to be spanned; on the other, parallel to the Yangzi, is a new empty river, the cement bed of a massive shiplock system to raise and lower all vessels.

Returning to the ship, we continued through the first of the three gorges this dam will drown, **Xiling Gorge.** From here on, the scenery improves rapidly. Mountains rise abruptly from the banks of the Yangzi, eventually forming a massive wall on both sides, pinching and speeding the river flow. These gorges were created 70 million years ago as an inland sea withdrew to the east, its waters slicing into the limestone faults and creases where two large mountain systems had been smashed together. This primordial geology is written on the steep cliffsides that threaten to eclipse the sun.

Xiling, the longest of the three at 47 miles, actually consists of a number of gorges named for legends of the Three Kingdoms or the resemblance of their formations to other objects. The **Sword and the Book of the Art of War** is the gorge where Zhuge Liang stored grain for his troops and hid his book of military strategy. Other gorges within Xiling include the **Oxen Liver and Horse Lung Gorge** and the **Gorge of Shadowplay.**

Xiling Gorge was once one of the most hazardous regions on the Yangzi, rife with rapids and whirlpools. A pile of human bones once resided on its banks, heaped in the shape of a white pagoda, as a reminder to navigators of the dangers here. Seventy years ago a British naval commander described the Three Gorges' "boiling, seething infernos of tumbling, tossing water, whirlpools, eddies, backwaters and sudden vertical 'boils.'" One in 10 junks was stranded in the gorges; one in 20, lost forever.

Xiling Gorge is still not easy to navigate, but more than a hundred shoals and reefs have been dynamited in recent times, and the river is now lined with several thousand navigational buoys with all-weather beacons. These buoys, which resemble small dinghies, must be relocated every 2 weeks, since the channel changes that often as waters rise and fall and silt is carried from bank to bank.

The gorges are in some places cloven with steep ravines where hillside farms produce wheat, rice, maize, legumes, rapeseed, and tangerines. For some of these severely isolated farms, junks and small barges provide the main link to the outside world. In the next century, these farms will be underwater.

At **Zigui,** just past the small stream of Xiang Xi, home to Han Dynasty heroine Wang Zhaojun, we passed out of Xiling Gorge. Cruise ships often spend the night here, entertained on the wharf by local peasant singers and dancers. Zigui is the home of poet Qu Yuan, whose Ming Dynasty statue resides at a memorial hall. When his advice went unheeded by the king of Chu, Qu Yuan drowned himself in Dongting Lake. Ever since, he has been commemorated by China's annual dragon boat races (on the fifth day of the fifth lunar month) and by the eating of *zongzi,* a packet of sweet steamed rice tied in leaves that villagers originally tossed into the sea to lure fish away from Qu Yuan's body.

For centuries, the Yangzi served as the graveyard for those too poor to afford a land burial. Even today, one can spot corpses. Our American tour director counted 23 corpses on her 40 trips last year, including six in a single gruesome day. The river people call them "floaters." The ship's captain reported seeing Yangzi corpses every day. People fall in and can't swim, he said with a smile. I kept my eyes on the river the whole way, but all I saw were the rowboat channel markers like caskets in a treacherous river.

We tied up at the village of **Badong.** The night was black, but warm. I spent a few hours on deck, enthralled by the town's brilliant lights, spilling down the banks like a cascade of Christmas bulbs.

Greater & Lesser Gorges (Day 9)

This was the most intense day for sightseeing along the river. We entered the middle gorge, **Wuxia (Witches Gorge)** in the morning. Wu Gorge contains the most dramatic mountain peaks on the Yangzi, crowned by **Goddess Peak,** which has a likeness in stone of Yao Ji, youngest of the 12 daughters of the queen mother of the East. These 12 sisters stole away to Earth and met Yu the Great, tamer of floods, who was fighting the 12 dragons of the floodwaters. The sisters slayed the dragons and were eventually immortalized as the 12 peaks that assisted mariners in navigating Wu Gorge. In the midst of this gorge is **Gathered Immortals Peak** and the **Kong Ming Tablet,** supposed to have been inscribed by Zhuge Liang himself when he served as prime minister of the Shu Kingdom. In a Tang Dynasty poem written here, Li Bai (A.D. 701–762) recalled how his boat tried for 3 days to surmount a single set of rapids. "But for all this time the peak remains beside us," he wrote. "I wonder how many of my hairs turned gray."

Wu Gorge ends at the **Golden Helmet and Shining Armor Valley,** where the gray walls of enfolded limestone resemble ancient armor and the rounded mountaintop shines like a golden helmet. We docked at the town of Wushan, home to legendary Emperor Yu, who created the Three Gorges. Wushan marks the end of the middle gorge and is the gateway to excursions on the **Daning River,** site of the **Three Lesser Gorges** (Xiao Sanxia).

We disembarked to get a taste of the Yangzi's most scenic little tributary. Trips up and down the **Daning River,** first offered to tourists in

1985, are given on small motorized sampans. The river is so fierce, however, that at one point passengers must disembark and walk along the bank (lined with local vendors) while their boat struggles to overcome the rapids, the boatmen pushing their bamboo poles into the shallow streambed to gain enough leverage. The 20-mile trip upriver through the Three Little Gorges takes several hours, and many visitors find the scenery more impressive than that along the Yangzi, the peaks sharper, the current swifter and more violent. Sights along the way include bands of monkeys and old coffins suspended from holes carved into the cliff face—the famous hanging coffins of the Yangzi. Lunch is sometimes provided at Twin Dragons Village, where sampans turn around for a fast, water-splashed return downstream.

I myself happened to see plenty of monkeys on the trip, including several youngsters who slipped while running across the cliff faces and plunged into the water. The hanging coffins were still as difficult as ever to pick out, however. A new feature is gangs of roving vendors, some who proffer their wares to passengers in fishing nets on the end of long poles, others who charge the boats as they slow and bark at the windows, and some who even hurl themselves into the boats to make a sale (and are pushed back out into the river by the angry boatmen). Twin Dragon Village at the upper end of our little voyage will be submerged when the Three Gorges Dam is completed. So will the city of Wushan where we were anchored. Already its buildings are being torn down; a Wushan New Town is being erected at the top of the hills.

The Three Lesser Gorges pack the excitement of white-water rafting and the scenery of a deep river valley into one compact package, yet I prefer the bigger gorges, their massive scale emblematic of the great riverway dividing north and south China.

In the early afternoon we reached the westernmost gorge, **Qutang Gorge,** the shortest of the Three Gorges (just 5 miles long), but also the grandest and wildest. Here, the Yangzi narrows to as little as 300 feet (only one ship is allowed to pass at a time); the peaks rise upward of 3,700 feet; the water deepens, glistens, and charges like molten lava; and the wind itself is flattened and funneled through. As an ancient verse puts it, "Peaks pierce the sky as we course through the deep passage beneath." The mountains appear to have been split apart by the blade of a massive ax. Iron pillars, now submerged, were employed in Tang Dynasty times to string up defensive barriers, and later to tax barge traffic. A stone perched on the top of a black rock far overhead is aptly named **Rhinoceros Looking at the Moon.** At the upstream entrance, there's a series of zigzag square holes cut into the cliffs. Known as **Meng Jiang's Ladder,** after the exploits of a Song Dynasty soldier, it is actually the remains of a stairway to the top of the peak where a city once resided in the 6th century A.D. Wooden coffins suspended on this same cliff have been dated back to 1000 B.C.

At **Baidi Cheng** and **Fengjie,** cruise ships reach the upriver end of the Three Gorges. It was here that Zhuge Liang trained troops during the Three Kingdoms era and here that China's two greatest poets, Li Bai and Du Fu, both of the Tang Dynasty (A.D. 618–907), resided. Du Fu lived for 2 years in Fengjie, where he composed over 400 poems. At Baidi Cheng, Liu Bei, ruler of the Shu Kingdom, died of despair after failing to avenge his brother, Guan Yu. At **Baidi Temple,** these and other heroes of the Three Kingdoms are commemorated today.

Altogether, the Three Gorges occupy only a 125-mile section of the Yangzi, a mere fragment, but they form the central scenic gem of the riverway. On an upriver cruise, the gorges become the culmination of a slow battle against the great inland current that crosses China, its power reaching a crescendo as it funnels through the gorges as through an hourglass. Downriver, the gorges appear suddenly, dramatically, and are traversed in a fraction of the time. As Li Bai observed 1,200 years ago: "In the morning leaving Baidi Cheng, it was as if we went on clouds; from there to Jiangling is one thousand li, but in one day the racing waters brought us down." The *li* is an ancient unit of measurement; there are 3 li to 1 mile. Each way, although the sensation is different, the power of the river underlies the experience, its force so compelling that even a modern traveler can taste something of what the Yangzi was in centuries past. The paths of the trackers, harnessed by quarter-mile-long ropes of twisted bamboo to loaded junks and later steamboats, are still visible where they were carved into the sides of these massive canyons—traces of superhuman labor that will be submerged within a few years when the river itself is further tamed and modernized.

Fengdu/Wanxian (Day 10)

Our last full day on the river included the chance to stroll through a typical Yangzi village, either at Fengdu or at Wanxian, depending on the ship's timetable. On my most recent voyage, **Wanxian** was the stop, a very hilly, charming town, its wholesale districts near the wharves destined to drown. The shore tour took us up the terraced town in steep zigzags, past the new Government Center, the first building in town with elevators and central air-conditioning.

We stopped downtown twice, first for a stroll through a vibrant street market, where hundreds of live ducks were for sale, along with a thousand other fragrant, fresh foodstuffs. Then we were treated to a performance by local acrobats in the town auditorium. What makes this performance so charming is that the acrobats are children, students in the Wanxian academy devoted to this traditional entertainment. They are not only beautiful and innocent, but unabashed when they miss a trick or take a fall or drop a spinning plate.

Farther uptown is the **Wanxian Three Gorges Museum.** It has a new wing, but no signs in English, and its collection of artifacts from the Han to Qing dynasties is nothing special; the museum would not even exist were if not for the mummies and coffin on the second floor. This is a chance to see close-up a 2,000-year-old hanging coffin (made from a large tree sliced the long way in half), as well as its contents—the skeletons of a 15-year-old male and a 40-year-old female. They were buried together and suspended in a cave high up the sheer cliffs along the Yangzi. The boy died a natural death; the woman did not.

On other cruises I have stopped instead at **Fengdu,** China's "Ghost City," where a temple to the God of the Underworld, Yinwang, commands the summit of **Ming Shan Peak.** This is the place of final judgment in the Yangzi basin, making it an appropriate last stop on the way to Chongqing. At Fengdu you climb long rows of stairs, 600 steps in all, to meet Yinwang. There you must pass through all the stages—from a Ming Dynasty bridge to a Ghost Gate—that the soul is said to travel at the moment of death, as well as perform some feat: Cross a bridge in three steps, run up a flight of a hundred stairs in a single breath, or balance for 3 seconds on a round rock. If you fail, hell claims you (or so they say). Most visitors do survive this long journey to the top, where Daoist, Buddhist, and Confucian temples mingle, amusement-park statues of the Underworld line the courtyards, and Yinwang the King of Hell sits in judgment, assisted by four supreme judges. A Swiss-made chairlift whisks the nonbelievers and those in a hurry straight to the top, where the panorama of the Yangzi and the surrounding mountains is splendid.

Back in the park at the base of Ming Shan, the locals, along with the blind beggars, gathered in the afternoon. The elders practiced *tai ji quan* at such a slow pace, they seemed to be ghosts themselves. The fog on the water swirled like a weightless cloth, winding and unwinding. The banks of the river grew faint. We resumed our cruise. The last walls of the Three Gorges behind us rose like the sides of a stone crib. When we pulled out from the muddy banks of Fengdu, even the Mountain of the Underworld was lost in the mists.

Chongqing (Day 11)

At Chongqing, a city so hilly even bicycles are a rarity, a Yangzi cruise can either begin or end. Pulling upriver, one savors the power of the river, as irresistible as the flood of time, silted with the legends and hardships of the past. Speeding downriver, the flow is far swifter; the direction is toward the future, when the river's power will be harnessed by the walls of the world's largest hydroelectric plant, at the cost of the drowning of the Yangzi's famous towns. The hills are dotted with new billboards now, often placed above old villages, marking the 175-meter rim of the coming flood to end all floods.

Sailing downriver, the Three Gorges unroll twice as quickly, rushing by as in a dream. Coal factories drape the steep banks. Fishermen on small trawlers crank in their nets by hand. Women pound the day's laundry on the rocks. The Yangzi broadens. The mountains dissolve into fields so level and low one can't see over the border of the river. On one occasion I saw a long, low-laden barge, heaped with black coal, and on top of that coal, a dozen cows huddled together; someone remarked that it was a Chinese barbecue waiting to happen.

WHAT TO READ

Your Yangzi cruise will be enhanced if you read John Hersey's *A Single Pebble,* a novel about prerevolutionary, pretourism days on the river; and Richard McKenna's *The Sand Pebbles,* a gunboat epic that was made into a popular movie. Paul Theroux's *Sailing Through China* takes a sharp, personal look at cruising the Yangzi in the 1980s.

Probe International has published *Damming the Three Gorges,* a collection of essays by Chinese scholars and journalists who oppose the massive hydroelectric dam project. A general guide, filled with facts and lore, is Judy Bonavia's *The Yangzi River,* an Odyssey Illustrated Guide published in Hong Kong and available in many travel bookstores overseas.

PRACTICAL INFORMATION

WHEN TO GO

The best cruising months are September and October, since the rainy season in the Yangzi basin can extend from May through August. In March and April, too, the weather can be delightful.

CHINESE FERRIES & TOUR BOATS

Yangzi River **ferries** depart from Wuhan (for upriver trips) and from Chongqing (for downriver trips) year-round, but their facilities are crude. They function better as a means of inexpensive transport than as tour boats. They can be booked at wharves along the Yangzi.

Numerous Chinese **tour boats** operate March through November on the Yangzi, some of them with quite luxurious cabins and facilities, but management and staff are not used to foreign travelers. Chinese tour boats can be booked in Wuhan or Chongqing through **China International Travel Service (CITS)** outlets (☎ 027/ 281-6553 in Wuhan; 023/6385-0806 in Chongqing).

VICTORIA CRUISES

One of the few Western-managed Yangzi River cruise lines is Victoria Cruises, based in New York. Victoria meets the comfort and service expectations of Western travelers with well-appointed new ships and cruise directors. The quality of cruise directors is crucial on the Yangzi, and Victoria hires the best I've seen: English speakers who are fluent in Chinese, expert in Yangzi River history and sights, and dedicated to serving passengers. The Victoria fleet, built in the 1990s specially for cruising the Yangzi, accommodates about 154 passengers, all in outside staterooms and suites with picture windows, desks, closets, private bathrooms, air-conditioning, and closed-circuit televisions. The newest and most deluxe members of the fleet are the MV *Victoria Blue Whale* and the MV *Victoria Angel.* In many ways, a Victoria Cruise borrows from the luxury ocean cruise experience offered in the Caribbean and Mediterranean, but a closer analogy is to the more adventurous cruises operating in Alaska.

Victoria Cruises offers upriver departures from Wuhan to Chongqing (6 days/5 nights) and downriver departures from Chongqing to Wuhan (4 days/3 nights) from mid-March to the end of November. Prices per person, based on double occupancy, run from $680 to $760 for a standard cabin up to $1,890 for the largest suite, depending on the season. Upriver cruises, although longer, are actually cheaper. Children under 12 pay 67% of full fare; under 2, 10% of full fare. The April-to-May and September-to-October bookings are the most expensive. Shore excursions cost a total of $75 extra per person. The newest cruise options are Shanghai to Chongqing (11 days/10 nights) and Chongqing to Shanghai (8 days/7 nights), with per person prices (based on double occupancy) ranging from $1,240 to $1,520 for a standard cabin up to $3,780 for the largest suite, depending on the season. Shore excursions are $180 per person extra.

Victoria Cruises is able to book air flights as well. One couple I met from Philadelphia had come to the Yangzi strictly for the cruise. They booked the entire package, including round-trip airfare, from Victoria Cruises. For brochures and bookings, contact your local travel agent or **Victoria Cruises,** 57–08 39th Avenue, Woodside, New York 11377 (☎ 800/348-8084 or 212/ 818-1680; fax 212/818-9889; www.victoriacruises.com). The Victoria Cruise office in Chongqing is on the third floor at 3 Xinhua Lu (☎ 023/ 6381-5260 or 023/6380-4512; fax 023/6381-4474).

TRAVEL IN CHINA

WHILE VISITORS TO CHINA CAN now stay in five-star luxury hotels, dine in excellent restaurants, hire local guides fluent in English, book extravagant tours, board air-conditioned buses, fly aboard state-of-the-art aircraft, and use credit cards, and phone, fax, and e-mail, it is worthwhile remembering that China is still a third-world country. As the world's oldest continuous civilization and most populous modern nation, China also has its own way of doing things. Travel, especially on one's own, is not always a smooth, comfortable undertaking. It is best for a foreigner to approach China travel as a journey into a world that is both familiar and alien.

China Today

PEOPLE China is as spacious as the United States and its geography as various, but its people are overwhelmingly uniform. They belong primarily to one ethnic group, the Han Chinese, who constitute 93% of the nearly 1.3 billion population.

THE ECONOMY Despite China's relative poverty, it is becoming the economic powerhouse of Asia. About a third of the workforce is employed by prospering private firms (55 million workers in 25 million nongovernmental enterprises). Double-digit economic growth became routine during the 1990s, as did double-digit inflation. Growth slowed with the dawn of the new century, but continues to be vigorous. The economic improvements have changed the look of China. Taxis, which numbered just 60,000 in 1985, now number 10 times that many, and the streets, once filled with bicycles, are now clogged with motorized vehicles, most of them still burning leaded gas (although this is changing in the major cities). Heavy industries are on the upswing: China overtook Japan in 1996 as the world's largest steel producer. China's textile production and clothing exports are also immense. It's quite likely that the clothes you take to China will have been manufactured there. 60% of the shoes sold in America are made in China.

China's relatively prosperous cities offer many luxuries unavailable to previous generations. Nearly 90% of urban dwellers watch television daily. The latest pop music, high fashions, and electronic appliances from the West are sold in glitzy shops, boutiques, and department stores. Wal-Mart opened a Super Center and a Sam's Club Warehouse in Shenzhen, a Special Economic Zone near Canton. Amway, Avon, Mary Kay, and Sara Lee have established sales forces and factories across China. Coca-Cola sells 100 million cases annually.

A 40-hour, 5-day work week was mandated in 1995. Beijing has instituted a minimum wage ($35 a month) and unemployment benefits ($25 to $30 a month). China now has over 120 million telephone subscribers. International credit-card companies predict that by the year 2003, China will have 200 million card-carrying consumers (up from 20 million in the 1990s), accounting for one-fifth of the world's total. In response to rapidly rising consumer spending, the number of restaurants in major Chinese cities has been tripling every 5 years.

WAGES Despite China's recent economic boom, most people do not have wages or standards of living comparable to those in the West. The average income is about $700 per year, although it is about twice that in the big cities on the east coast (from Beijing down to Hong Kong). Actual wages vary widely, of course. College students in Shandong Province, for example, make about $10 a month at work-study jobs, while computer engineers and deputy general managers average over $13,000 per year. Rural residents, who constitute about 65% of the population, usually make less than $50 a month, sometimes far less. The commune system has been widely disbanded, enabling farmers to cultivate their own plots and sell surplus produce (after meeting state quotas and taxes) in the free market.

The distribution of wealth has become widely disparate since the egalitarian era of Chairman Mao ended almost 30 years ago. There are more than a million millionaires in China today, and nearly everyone dreams of getting rich as quickly as possible. Such dreams run up against the harsh reality of China's overwhelming population. While most Chinese have seen their wages and buying power soar over the last few years, they remain at a level that would be regarded as impoverished in the West. Large segments of the young, particularly in rural areas, are unemployed. Many drift into the overcrowded cities, lured by the chance to get rich. There are currently over a million maids (officially termed "home helpers") employed in China, including nearly 100,000 girls from the countryside in Beijing alone.

Perhaps the most startling fact is that the gap between the rich and poor in China is now greater than it was during the feudal days of the

1930s. The current notion that the newly rich will pull up the chronically poor is belied by other statistics, notably that 125 million Chinese people live below the poverty line as defined by the World Bank ($1 per day). China admits that 42 million of its citizens make less than $220 per year. The income gap in China today is greater than in the U.S. or Western Europe, greater even than in Indonesia or India.

POLLUTION With increased production and car traffic, pollution has become a serious problem. You'll notice the poor air quality in the cities, which can make the skies of Los Angeles seem downright pristine. China's cities can handle only 20% of their sewage and less than 50% of the garbage they produce.

CHINA'S PROSPECTS Whether China can continue to fuel its economic miracle is an open question. Major challenges looming on the horizon include large underemployment of the workforce, increasing immigration to the cities, unequal spheres of development across the country, pollution, mammoth money-losing state enterprises, and antiquated laws regulating business expansion and investment.

Nevertheless, the future looks rosy to most forecasters. In the 50th commemorative edition (October 1996) of the *Far Eastern Economic Review,* David K. P. Li of the Bank of East Asia envisioned the China of the year 2046 as the world's biggest economy (three times the size of the United States), the world's number one exporter and importer, and the largest consumer nation on Earth. China will then play a dominant role in world affairs, Li suggested, superseding the position held by the United States. After English, Mandarin Chinese will rank as the world's most important language—and Beijing will become the world's leading cultural center.

This expansion affects tourism as well. According to predictions from the nonprofit World Tourism Organization, mainland China will surpass the U.S., Spain, Italy, and Britain and replace France as the world's most popular tourist destination by the year 2020 (and Hong Kong by itself will rise from 18th to 5th during the same period).

Travel Basics

China may be the emerging superpower that will dominate this "Asian Century," but for the traveler it is not the easiest nation to understand or to visit. If you go on your own in China without a group or a government guide, you'll have difficulties nearly everywhere you go. There are few mechanisms set up for outsiders. If you don't read or speak Chinese and if you aren't familiar with how things are done by ordinary Chinese travelers, problems can arise.

A number of practical facts, tips, and strategies must be kept in mind before and during a journey to the East. What follows is my own list of facts, requirements, and tips for the China traveler.

VISITOR INFORMATION You can procure additional information on Chinese destinations and find answers to your questions by contacting branches of the **China National Tourist Office.** The American branches are in **New York** at 350 Fifth Ave. (Suite 6413, Empire State Building), New York, NY 10118 (☎ 212/760-8218 or 212/760-1710; fax 212/760-8809), and in **Glendale, California,** at 333 West Broadway, Suite 201, Glendale, CA 91204 (☎ 818/545-7505; fax 818/545-7506).

VISAS The People's Republic of China requires a current visa, stamped in a valid passport, before granting entry to any foreign national. You can apply for a visa from a Chinese consulate or embassy, although if you enter China first at Hong Kong (which I recommend) it is best to purchase your visa there (see below). If you are visiting China on a tour, including a cruise, the operator and your travel agent are responsible for putting you on the **group visa.** You'll need to provide them with a valid passport and other items they request. Check with them to be absolutely certain you are included on the group visa. Otherwise, you won't be admitted to China. The only drawback to a group visa is that you must stay with the group. Such a visa does not allow personal detours or extensions.

To **apply on your own** through a Chinese embassy or consulate, the first step is to request an application form. It's best to send the completed application back at least 30 days before departure, although embassies in the United States now say they need only a week to process and return applications. With the application, you must submit one or two passport photographs (as requested), a valid passport (good for at least 6 months after your visa expires), and the application fee. The tourist visa—coded L—is good for the number of days you requested and paid for, beginning with the actual entry date. Check your passport when it is returned from the embassy to be sure one of the pages has a PRC visa stamped in it.

In the past, dealing with these overseas bureaucracies could be a nightmare, but their efficiency has improved greatly. In the United States, the Chinese embassy is located in **Washington, D.C.,** at 2300 Connecticut Ave., NW, Washington, DC 20008 (☎ 202/328-2500 or 202/328-2517; fax 202/328-2564). The consulate in **Chicago** is located at 100 West Erie St., Chicago, IL 60610 (☎ 312/803-0095; fax 312/803-0122). The consulate in **Houston** is located at 3417 Montrose Blvd., Houston, TX 77066 (☎ 713/524-4311; fax 713/524-7656). The consulate in **Los Angeles** is located at 443 Shatto Place, Los Angeles, CA 90020 (☎ 213/380-2506 or 213/380-2507; fax 213/380-1961). The consulate in **New York** is located at 520 12th Ave., New York, NY 10036 (☎ 212/330-7409; fax 212/502-0245). The consulate in **San Francisco** is located at 1450 Laguna St., San Francisco, CA 94115 (☎ 415/563-4857 or 415/563-4885; fax 415/563-0494).

In Canada, the Chinese embassy is located in **Ottawa** at 515 St. Patrick St., Ottawa, Ontario K1N 5H3 (☎ 613/234-2706 or 613/234-2682). The consulate in **Toronto** is located at 240 St. George St., Toronto, Ontario M5R 2P4 (☎ 416/964-7260). The consulate in **Vancouver** is located at 3380 Granville St., Vancouver, British Columbia V6H 3K3 (☎ 604/736-3910).

In the United Kingdom, the Chinese consulates are located in **London** at 31 Portland Place, London W1N 3AG (☎ 0171/631-1430); in **Manchester** at Denison House, 49 Denison Rd., Rusholme, Manchester, M14 5RX (☎ 0161/224-8672); and in **Edinburgh** at 43 Station Rd., Edinburgh EH12 7AF (☎ 0131/316-4789).

The easiest place to apply for a visa is in **Hong Kong.** Entry to Hong Kong does not require a visa for citizens of most countries (including the United States and Canada). Once there, you have several China visa options. You can purchase a 30-day, 60-day, 90-day, or 6-month single-entry visa. You can also purchase multiple-entry visas of varying lengths. Unless you plan on making frequent trips in and out of China within a visa time period, multiple-entry visas are a waste of money (since they are much more expensive than single-entry visas). In Hong Kong, you get what you pay for. The longer the validity of the visa, the more expensive. The sooner you want it, the more expensive. The cheapest choice is a tourist visa good for 30 days, processed in 2 to 3 working days. That should cost from $25 to $35 (the price keeps rising). You can get a visa the same day if you're willing to pay several times that amount.

In Hong Kong I routinely purchase my visa at the **CTS (China Travel Service)** office in Kowloon, filling out the application (which is a mere formality), having passport photos taken, if necessary, and paying the fees (in cash only). This CTS branch is located a few doors west off bustling Nathan Road on Peking Road (despite its Nathan Road address), on the first floor (one floor above the ground floor) of Alpha House, 27–33 Nathan Rd. (☎ 852/2721-4481; fax 852/2721-6251). Nearly all travel agencies in Hong Kong can provide China visa service as well. Prices and visa options vary.

TRAVEL AGENTS In China, cities and towns with tourist attractions all have at least one branch of the official government travel agency set up to deal with foreign visitors. It is called **China International Travel Service**—CITS for short, *luxingshe* in Chinese. CITS can provide local tours; English-speaking guides; onward transportation tickets via air, rail, and road; and general information. Some offices are helpful and some are not. Another organization, **China Travel Service (CTS)** was set up by the government to help Chinese tourists from overseas, but it's now seeking non-Chinese customers as well. The travel agency business has become quite competitive in China, and government agencies must compete not only among themselves but with some new private travel agencies as well. Most hotels have their own travel desks (often branches of CITS) offering tours, guides, and ticket bookings, and these are usually the most convenient places to go when you want to book a local tour or make transportation arrangements.

Money

CURRENCY China's currency is called renminbi (RMB), meaning the people's money, and China is mainly a cash society. Few transactions are done with credit cards or personal checks. Renminbi comes in denominations ranging from RMB 1 to RMB 100, with smaller bills and coins for change. In the streets, RMB are called *yuan* or *kuai*. Numbers on most bills are in English.

TRAVELER'S CHECKS, CREDIT CARDS & ATMs Your best bet is to arrive in China with traveler's checks—plenty of them—mostly in U.S. $100 denominations, which you can easily cash in major hotels and at many branches of the official Bank of China. Remember that your passport is always required for currency exchanges. Major credit cards also work at the big international hotels to pay for room and restaurant charges. In some hotels, credit cards are only accepted during regular banking hours and not on weekends. Always take sufficient local currency when you leave the hotel for dining, shopping, or touring.

With the exception of Hong Kong, ATMs are still rare in most streets of China, although in downtown Beijing, Shanghai, and other large cities, they are spreading rapidly. Be advised that many ATMs only work for local credit and ATM cards, but some allow cash withdrawals (in RMB only) from foreign accounts. You can also perform cash withdrawals at special branches of the **Bank of China.** In most cities at least one branch of the Bank of China will do credit-card cash withdrawals (using Visa, MasterCard, and American Express). These transactions are limited to a maximum of $1,000 a day at present, with a 2% to 4% fee, and require about 30 minutes to complete. I recently conducted such a transaction in Xi'an, receiving over RMB 8,000 in cash. Since the

RMB 100 note is the largest in China, I was handed a stack of 80 bills. Walking out of the bank, I felt like a numbers runner making his rounds.

WHAT THINGS COST How much money to take? If you have purchased an all-inclusive package tour, take enough for shopping and miscellaneous purchases. You will be able to use your credit card at hotels and in major shopping centers. If you are traveling on your own, expenses depend on where you travel and what comfort level you select. Hotels and food can cost as much as in the West—far less if you can put up with very basic accommodation and inexpensive local food. Transportation can also be expensive if you rely on airplanes ($75 to $250 a trip, depending on distance); trains and buses are relatively cheap, and overnight trains serve as a night's lodging. I used to travel on far less than $50 a day (transport included), but these days only a dedicated and adventurous backpacker could travel that cheaply in much of urban China.

Allow **at least $150 per day,** more if you plan on staying in top international hotels and eating in their restaurants (although you can charge this to your credit card). Cities such as Hong Kong, Beijing, and Shanghai are quite expensive for lodging and dining, while the more remote cities are often quite cheap.

China has officially abolished its two-price system, in which visiting foreigners paid more than residents. Once in a while visitors find the two-price system in practice, at the admission gate to a remote attraction, for example, but this is no longer legal. Foreigners, always perceived as very rich, are of course gouged by some merchants and taxi drivers. Knowing the fair price for a given good or service and then driving a hard bargain is your best defense.

Health, Insurance & Packing

HEALTH Check with your doctor before departure. Except in remoter rural areas, inoculations and special vaccinations are not necessary. Make sure your tetanus shot is up-to-date, as well as your polio immunization. A flu shot is advisable, as are hepatitis A and typhoid vaccinations if you travel in rural or tropical regions. **The Centers for Disease Control (CDC)** maintains a hot line that updates health concerns for international travelers; call ☎ 888/232-3228.

Many travelers contract a cold along the way, often right after entry. Take your usual remedies with you. I carry a sterile syringe (issued with a note from my physician) in the event that I end up needing an injection in China. There's no guarantee that a given hospital in China uses sterile syringes in all cases, and disposable needles are not common except in large city hospitals (such in Shanghai, Beijing, and Hong Kong). It's also a good idea to take along any prescription medicines you may need—Western prescriptions can't always be filled in China.

In the larger cities, there are clinics that specialize in treating foreigners. If you need to see a doctor, advise the staff at your hotel. Western-style medical care is widespread in China, and many doctors in every region are fully competent.

Cautions: Chinese blood banks do not carry Rh-negative blood supplies. Also, you might want to have your teeth checked before departure and carry a small dental emergency kit.

INSURANCE Insurance is usually either included or presented as an option by tour operators outside China. If you are traveling on your own, the following carriers offer comprehensive travel insurance packages, including emergency medical evacuation: **Healthcare Abroad** (☎ 800/237-6615), **Mutual of Omaha** (☎ 800/228-9792), and **Travel Guard International** (☎ 800/826-1300).

PACKING The best advice is this: pack as little and as light as possible. You never know when or how far you might have to lug your own gear in China, even if you're on a group tour. I never take more than two pieces of luggage, one being a day pack I can strap on my back. In my youth, I traveled with a single bag, a backpack that converted into a handheld piece of luggage. In my advancing years, I've converted to a small roll-on that also has backpacking straps. Recently, I've been arriving in Hong Kong with old, cheap luggage, which I ditch in favor of a backpack/roll-on combination purchased for a pittance ($25 to $35) in one of Hong Kong's luggage shops. Although cheap, such a roll-on holds up for months at a time on the road. One roll-on and one stout day pack or shoulder bag is all you really need in China, where a traveler's wardrobe need not be extensive or formal.

The question is what to pack. The clothing you take should be simple, durable, and comfortable. Most of what I take are items for health and hygiene, as well as useful gadgets for life on the road. My wife and I have been keeping China packing lists for two decades. Here's a peek inside our luggage, with commentary:

Clothing

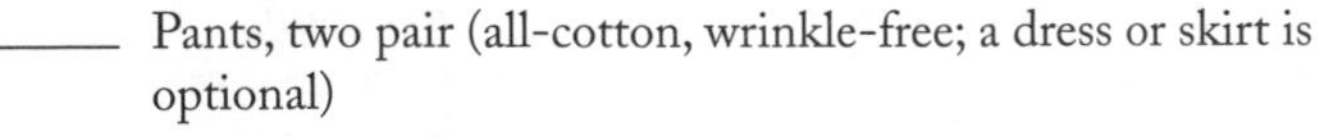

_____ Pants, two pair (all-cotton, wrinkle-free; a dress or skirt is optional)

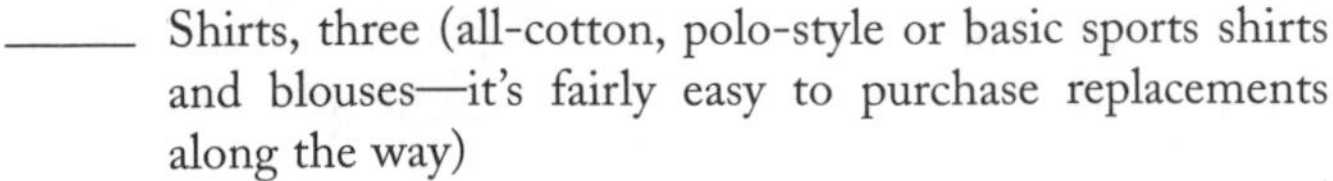

_____ Shirts, three (all-cotton, polo-style or basic sports shirts and blouses—it's fairly easy to purchase replacements along the way)

_____ Sweater or sweatshirt, one (to layer over shirts and blouses)

_____ Turtleneck, one (a layer for cold weather)

_____ Underwear, three or four sets (difficult to replace on trip; can be washed and dried overnight in hotel laundry or room sink)

_____ Socks, three or four pair (dark colors, can be laundered overnight)

_____ Raincoat or windbreaker, one (lightweight nylon)

_____ Hat, one (optional; keeps the sun out or head warm)

_____ Shoes, one extra pair (sturdy, comfortable, broken in)

_____ Thongs, one pair (for showers or as slippers)

Accessories & Gadgets

_____ Towel, one

_____ Umbrella

_____ Swiss army knife

_____ Flashlight

_____ Chopsticks, knife, spoon, fork

_____ Clothespins, clothesline, powdered detergent, flat "universal" sink stopper (for doing laundry in room sink)

_____ Clock or watch with alarm

_____ Sewing kit

Cosmetics & Medicines

Take your usual supplies. Be sure to include:

_____ Prescriptions

_____ Sterile syringe (in case medical injection is required)

_____ Cold tablets (lots of these—a cold is nearly guaranteed)

_____ Moist towelettes

_____ Glasses (extra pair)

_____ Contact lens supplies

_____ Sunglasses

We also take a passport/money pouch (which is worn almost all the time), a notebook and extra pens, an address book, a camera with film and extra batteries, cups and heating coil with coffee, copies of our passport and traveler's check receipts, and a supply of breakfast bars for use when meals are difficult to procure.

Getting There

AIRLINES The **Civil Aviation Administration of China (CAAC)** is a government-run organization that oversees more than two dozen domestic airlines, including its international carriers: **Air China, China Eastern,** and **China Southern.** Planes are up-to-date, and the in-flight services are improving. Tickets are usually booked through CITS (China International Travel Service). Hong Kong's airline, **Cathay Pacific Airlines** (☎ 800/233-2742), is one of the world's top airlines, and serves Hong Kong from North America. It is partly owned by CAAC and is the best choice if you want to fly the national carrier. Its subsidiary, **Dragonair** (same phone), connects Hong Kong to many destinations on the mainland, and it is the best choice for those routes.

The flight over the Pacific from the United States takes 11 to 16 hours. Of the many international airlines serving China, the best service from North America is offered by United and Northwest. **Northwest Airlines** (☎ 800/447-4747) offers flights several times a week to Hong Kong and Beijing, leaving from New York, Los Angeles, San Francisco, and Seattle, with a stop in Tokyo.

United Airlines (☎ 800/538-2929) offers two daily nonstop flights to Hong Kong from San Francisco and one daily nonstop flight to Hong Kong from Los Angeles, daily service (via Tokyo) to Beijing and Shanghai from San Francisco and Los Angeles, daily flights (via Tokyo) to Hong Kong from New York, and daily flights (via San Francisco and Los Angeles) from Chicago and Denver, including seasonal nonstop flights to Hong Kong from Chicago. United connects to these routes from about 100 cities and towns in the United States. The service is efficient, with plenty of amenities, including free drinks and movies in economy class, plenty of legroom in connoisseur class, and outright luxury in first class.

Other airlines offering good service from North America are **Asiana Airlines** (☎ 800/227-4262), **Canadian Airlines International** (☎ 800/426-7000), **China Air (Taiwan)** (☎ 800/227-5118), **China Southern Airlines** (☎ 888/338-8988), **EVA Airlines** (☎ 800/695-1188), **Finnair**

(☎ 800/950-5000), **Japan Airlines** (☎ 800/525-3663), **Korean Air** (☎ 800/438-5000), **Lufthansa** (☎ 800/645-3880), **Malaysia** (☎ 800/552-9264), **Philippine Airlines** (☎ 800/435-9725), **Singapore Airlines** (☎ 800/742-3333), **SAS World Airlines** (☎ 800/221-2350), **Swissair** (☎ 800/221-4750), and **Thai Airways International** (☎ 800/426-5204).

Getting Around

BY PLANE Air travel improvement has been remarkably fast in China. Clean, modern jets put even remote cities just a few hours away. Airline attendants provide basic services, often including a Chinese version of airline food (unfortunately, only on par or below par with that of the West). Most planes are chock-full; many leave on time, even before scheduled departures. You must check in early, since check-in windows commonly close 45 minutes before scheduled departures. On the other hand, many planes are delayed, sometimes for hours. The safety record has reached acceptable international levels (and flying is far safer than braving China's roads).

CAAC oversees commercial aviation inside China. In theory there are several dozen private airlines operating in China today, but they are all subject to the rules, regulations, and approval of CAAC, and function as regional branches of a monolithic airline system. Fares are fixed, and there's no real competition, although equipment is modern and the service is improving. Hong-Kong–based **Dragonair** (co-owned by CAAC and Cathay Pacific) is by far the best of the carriers for flights between Hong Kong and major cities inside China.

Tickets can be booked from the city of departure at leading hotel desks and through CITS. Round-trip tickets can sometimes be purchased. Most airports charge departure taxes, paid for at windows (labeled in English) before you go through luggage inspection; they're usually RMB 50 to RMB 100 ($6.25 to $12.50), payable only in Chinese currency.

BY TRAIN China has a vast rail network. If you travel by rail, it's easiest to have your hotel book the ticket, which can require up to 3 days' notice. A typical long-distance train has up to four classes: soft berth, soft seat, hard berth, and hard seat. Always request the best class. Dining cars often serve miserable fare; best to pack some edibles before departure.

Soft berth (ruanwo) is the top class. It consists of a special car with sleeping compartments. The compartments are small, with two bunk beds on either wall and a small table between. The beds always fill up, usually mixing foreigners with Chinese and sometimes men with women. You sleep under a quilt, with a hard pillow. During the day, compartment mates sit on the two lower beds. There is some overhead storage for luggage. Boiled hot water in a thermos is provided for each soft berth compartment; take a cup along. Toilets—often one squat style and one Western style at either end of these cars—are unbelievably filthy, and the communal sinks nearby aren't alluring either. Still, it's a wonderful way to mix with the Chinese and make new friends.

The other class of sleeper is called **hard berth (yingwo).** Hard berth consists of a car filled with triple bunk beds and no partitions or compartments. It's like sleeping in a packed dorm.

Some trains have an additional class, called **soft seat (ruanzuo),** in which you're assigned either a seat or spot on a bench. These are suitable for short day trips, although they can be noisy and crowded.

The lowest and cheapest class is called **hard seat (yingzuo).** Hard seat has some benches along the walls of a train car, but they are often free-for-all cattle cars, sometimes so crowded that only standing room is available. You get what you pay for. Many Chinese end up standing the entire trip, which can extend for days.

Trains are punctual, especially for departures. Train terminals are forbidding chambers, crowded with all sorts of people, including an occasional thief, so watch your luggage. Lines form for the departure of each train by destination. It's useful to know your train number and departure time. If you are traveling soft berth or soft seat, there is often a special waiting room in the terminal, worth finding. Waylay a train official and show your ticket if you need directions. Once on the train, conductors will assist you. After the train leaves the station, a conductor will come around to check your passport. For a full description of riding the rails in China, read Paul Theroux's *Riding the Iron Rooster.*

BY BUS **Long-distance buses** are usually a rugged challenge. Tickets can be bought in hotels. If you have to buy one at a bus station, you could be in for an ordeal—standing in long lines, often the wrong ones. But if you can pronounce your destination and ask the departure time in Chinese, and if you are determined, you should be able to buy your own ticket.

There are some decent express buses connecting cities these days, complete with padded seats, air-conditioning, and television monitors broadcasting noisy kung-fu films. Inquire at the hotel tour desk or CITS office, as these are the best buses operating in China, cheaper and faster than trains. Most long-distance buses, however, are crowded, bumpy, slow, and filthy—great places for an adventure, if not for one's kidneys. Overnight sleeper buses also operate on some long routes. In the last one I took, the condition of the road, the honking of the horn, and the smoking of the driver and passengers made sleep impossible, even though I had my own not-quite-long-enough reclining lounge.

City buses are frequently packed to the gills. Begin by procuring a city map, one with bus routes on it, if possible—one with Chinese and English is best of all. Have it in hand when you climb on. Chinese city buses will look familiar, if a bit beaten up. A conductor will approach you selling a small paper ticket. If you can't ask the price in Chinese, announce your destination and hand over an RMB 10 ($1.20) note. You'll get change back. Disembark when you see your stop.

BY TAXI The quickest way around cities, taxis are in plentiful supply. If you're on the street, stand on the edge of the sidewalk, stick out an arm, and lower it to hail a passing cab. Announce your destination. If there's no meter, don't get in. I've been cheated repeatedly by taxi drivers. When you have to bargain for a fare as a foreigner, you can be sure you're being bilked. This is frequently the case at airports and train terminals, where touts intercept you and drag you to an overpriced car. If possible, find a taxi queue or walk out of the terminal to the street, where your chances of finding an honest operator improve. Shanghai has instituted a system of taxi meters that print a receipt, and it helps keep cheating to a minimum. Elsewhere, there's a great deal of theft-on-wheels. Taxis in the city shouldn't charge more than $2 to $3 per trip. A good place to catch one is at the entrance to a major hotel, although I've even been ripped off there. Still, in recent days, overcharging has been less of a problem.

BY CAR Although more and more Chinese own their own private cars (or more commonly motorcycles), driving is largely a profession. Taxi drivers and others must be trained and licensed for the job. It is easy enough to hire a private car with driver through CITS or a hotel, or rent a taxi for the day. However, rental cars that you drive yourself are just at the experimental stage in some large cities; they either require enormous deposits or are simply outlawed for non-residents. Once you see how drivers use the streets in the cities and on highways, you probably won't want to try it yourself anyway, unless you're inclined toward car racing and demolition derbies. In a recent case, a thief in Beijing robbed a woman taxi driver of RMB 200 ($25), and then, hoping to use her taxi as a getaway car, forced her to teach him on the spot how to drive it; police apprehended him as he staggered away from the taxi.

ON FOOT Seeing a city on foot is the best means of getting around. Secure a map at your hotel or from a street vendor. You can use it to ask people directions if you get lost, particularly if the map contains Chinese labels. Blocks tend to be much longer than they look on these maps.

Moreover, most Chinese have difficulty making sense of any map in any language, and they often give vague or incorrect directions. It's always a good adventure, however, and it's the best way to get a feel for the city.

Walking does have its share of annoyances and dangers. The sidewalks are often filled with holes or stacked with garbage. Crowds can slow your progress to a standstill. Construction sites, parked cars, vendors, bicycle parks, and a host of other encroachments often make for slow passage or detours. Recently, the sidewalks have become runways for bicycles and even motorcycles in crowded cities, making mere walking a mortal challenge. And street signs aren't always obvious. When you find one, pray that it is written in *pinyin* (the alphabetic rendition of Chinese). Streets are often called *lu, jie,* or *dajie,* and the four directions are *bei* (north), *nan* (south), *dong* (east), and *xi* (west). It's easiest to navigate as the Chinese do, by landmarks rather than road signs and numbers—relying on towering buildings, public parks, and other big sites for orientation. If you really get turned around—as I have—flag down a cab.

BY BICYCLE Many hotels offer bicycle rentals, as do some private enterprises. Hourly and daily rates vary widely but are quite reasonable (a few dollars an hour at the most). Mountain bikes have replaced the once ubiquitous black, no-speed models. Check the tires and brakes—you'll need them. Bike riding looks difficult and chaotic, but once you get into the flow you'll be surprised at how easy it is, even in crowded cities. Bike-only lanes are a standard feature of most downtowns. On side streets, you simply have to barrel forward, confident that no cars or trucks will sweep you to one side (they don't). Use your bell at intersections.

Be sure you have a bike lock—bikes are often stolen. Try to find a bike parking lot. They usually fill part of a sidewalk. Park and lock next to other bikes. The bike keeper will charge you a small fee and give you a chit.

Tips on Accommodations

China now has a wide network of four-star and five-star international hotels that are as comfortable, efficient, and amenable as comparable hotels in the West. The prices are also comparable, at least in the biggest cities. Upon checking in, you'll be asked to present your passport and fill out a form. I keep vital numbers jotted down in my ever-present hand-sized notebook.

The two best chains in China are **Shangri-La International** (☎ 800/942-5050) and **Holiday Inns Worldwide** (☎ 800/465-4329). Shangri-La hotels in China are often the most luxurious in town, with standard room rates running from just $90 in Beihai to $295 in Beijing (and over $300 in Hong Kong), with $190 an average rate. Shangri-La also operates a top-flight four-star chain of hotels called **Traders.** Holiday Inn, which manages the largest number of hotels among international chains in China, has standard rooms from $80 in Xi'an to $190 in Beijing, with $120 an average rate. Holiday Inn has deluxe **Crowne Plaza** lodgings in Beijing, Chengdu, Shanghai, Xiamen, and Zhengzhou. All the better hotels in China now add at least 15% tax and surcharges to the room rates.

Other familiar chains operate a few hotels in China. In Beijing, Shanghai, and Hong Kong, you have a wide choice of lodgings, including hotels operated by **Sheraton International** (☎ 800/325-3535), **Hilton International** (☎ 800/445-8667), **Westin** (☎ 800/228-3000), and **Marriott** (☎ 800/321-2211), which uses the New World or Courtyard labels. Two fine Asian chains that have moved into China are **Marco Polo** (☎ 800/843-6664) and **Gloria** (☎ 800/821-0900), both of which maintain high Western standards.

The great lack in China is of moderately priced ($50 to $100 per room), clean, basic, and efficient hotels. There are many Chinese-run hotels rated by the government at two and three stars that could fit this bill. They have modern facilities and private bathrooms, but they routinely offer substandard levels of service and housekeeping and are seldom accustomed to the expectations of Western guests. Nevertheless, they are often the only choice in a given location and are certainly not nightmares. Even such cities as Hong Kong and Beijing have few moderately priced, comfortable, well-run hotels. Your choice is usually between a nice but expensive place or a hotel best described as modern but rundown.

Consult my listings for each destination. While I concentrate on the high end of the lodging spectrum, I also note more economical choices when they are ones I have tried myself, particularly when there are no better alternatives.

Tips on Dining

Chinese cuisine, including such renowned regional specialties as Sichuan and Cantonese, is fabulous. In the past, the best food and service was in hotel restaurants or at a few long-established cafes, but this is changing. Every week new independent cafes and restaurants are opening, offering good food and service at rates lower than in major hotel restaurants. Prices at top hotel restaurants, by the way, sometimes equal what you would pay in a fine Chinese restaurant back home.

Common "workers" restaurants are abundant, and some have good, cheap offerings, but their conditions can be a shock to foreign travelers and ordering is difficult without some knowledge of Chinese. Streetside vendors provide the cheapest dishes of all. Again, the chief barriers are language and hygiene, although it is not difficult to order something by gesturing and pantomime.

It's a good idea to practice using chopsticks before your departure. Except in the best hotel restaurants or Western-style cafes, chopsticks are the only utensils. It's advisable to carry your own chopsticks; local restaurants and vendors don't provide sanitary eating utensils.

China is not a good country for vegetarians, despite its Buddhist traditions. Dishes feature ample portions of vegetables, but these are often mixed with small bits of meat (meat being considered a luxury food). Vegetarian restaurants do exist, but they seldom cater to foreigners.

Good fruit, including bananas, oranges, and apples, are available from street vendors and at markets, as are boiled eggs and bottled water. Coke and other canned or bottled soft drinks are widely distributed, too. Ice-cream treats are safe when purchased from small stores, as long as they are packaged in protective wrappers. I've seen frozen treats in the streets that used twigs as sticks—to be avoided as hygienic risks, of course.

More and more small cafes with Western menus and Western dishes are opening across China. Fast-food chains such as Kentucky Fried Chicken and McDonald's are proliferating. They charge about the same as in the West and their products taste about the same, too.

Few restaurants, except in large international hotels, accept credit cards or traveler's checks, although this is beginning to change. Always carry enough local currency as a backup.

Tips on Nightlife

China after dark is still most often a Gobi Desert as far as entertainment for the traveler is concerned, with only a few small oases dotting the after-hours landscape. Cities and towns now have night markets in abundance, many within an easy walk of tourist hotels, and these provide fascinating evening strolls. The tourist hotels themselves offer the best (and often only) rendezvous points for foreigners interested in discos and bars. Cinemas are quite popular everywhere, but they usually cater strictly to a local audience. **Xi'an** has opened a dinner theater of Tang Dynasty song and dance for foreign guests; **Chengdu** has an excellent opera; and **Harbin** has its ice sculpture park in the heart of winter. You can find out about these and other evening entertainment at your hotel service desk or from your concierge. Special events and performances of interest to foreigners are also presented from time to time.

Three exceptions to these extremely limited nighttime possibilities are in the cities of Hong Kong, Beijing, and Shanghai. **Hong Kong** is the most startling exception, a neon city that snaps to life when the sun sets. Every conceivable form of nightlife is no more than a taxi ride away. Check the week's entertainment agenda in the English-language newspapers. The **Hong Kong Tourist Association (HKTA)** and the hotels can recommend a wide range of possibilities, from Chinese opera and Western classical concerts to all-night discos and regional dance performances.

Although the entertainment offerings in **Beijing** pale in comparison with those in Hong Kong, the capital no longer rolls up the streets at dusk. There are plenty of bars in the Sanlitun diplomatic district that cater to foreigners and locals alike, several cinemas that feature English-language films not seen elsewhere in China, and above all a number of nightly venues for traditional arts and entertainment. As always, check with the hotel desk for current offerings, tickets, and transportation. The English-language newspaper, *China Daily,* also has a listing of Beijing's top entertainment, both traditional and international.

The best bets for the traveler interested in Chinese culture are the **Beijing Opera** and the **Chinese Acrobats.** There are nightly performances in several theaters—your hotel should be able to book tickets. The **People's Art Theatre of Beijing** features Western plays. There's also a puppet theater, and dance performances. Perhaps the best place to sample a variety of traditional art forms is a **teahouse.** Beijing has several teahouses that present evenings of Chinese opera, acrobatics, martial arts, storytelling, and music and dance.

Shanghai also hosts an array of concerts and performances, including opera and acrobatics. Many of the top special events take place at the **Shanghai Centre** (1376 Nanjing Xi Lu), which also has its own deluxe cinema, not to mention the Long Bar, a favorite of expatriates, visitors, and Chinese yuppies. Entertainment is provided most nights by the **Shanghai Acrobatic Troupe** at the Shanghai Centre Theatre. The jazz band at the **Peace Hotel** is a nightly favorite and the **Great World Entertainment Centre** (downtown at 1 Xizang Zhong Lu) has four stories and two auditoriums of nonstop entertainment, including opera, puppetry, acrobatics, and traditional storytelling.

In Shanghai, Beijing, Hong Kong, and elsewhere in China, the place to find out about the latest offerings, book tickets, arrange transportation, and get advice is always your hotel service desk.

Other Basics

ELECTRICITY China uses a 220-volt 50-cycle AC system. Plugs come in a variety of shapes. I used to carry a set of adapters with various configurations of prongs, but I've found I don't use them much. Hotels provide plug converters. If you take a heating coil, be certain that it is a 220-volt model.

E-MAIL & INTERNET Computer communications are beginning to sweep China, and most of China's top hotels now offer state-of-the-art business centers where you can use e-mail or surf the Net. Many of these same hotels provide in-room hookups and data plugs for your laptop. Foreign businesspeople are bringing their laptops to China in growing numbers. Only in Hong Kong are e-mail and Internet links commonplace, although all across China now there are Internet cafes where e-mail can be sent and received.

FAXES China's main fax centers are the big hotels. You can easily send a fax from their business centers or front desks, although an international fax is rather expensive, rarely less than $6 for a one-page fax overseas. To date, there are few copy shops and business centers independent of the big hotels providing cheaper faxing services, except in Hong Kong.

HOLIDAYS Many cities and religious sites hold their own holidays and festivals on dates determined by the lunar calendar. Nationwide, the most important lunar festivals are **Chinese New Year's (Spring Festival),** falling on January 24 in 2001 and February 12 in 2002, followed 15 days later by the **Lantern Festival;** the **Qing Ming Festival (Grave-Sweeping Day),** falling on April 5 in 2001 and 2002; the **Dragon Boat Festival,** falling on June 25 in 2001 and June 15 in 2002; and the **Moon Festival (Mid-Autumn Festival),** falling on October 1 in 2001 and September 21 in 2002. Official state holidays, when offices and many shops close, follow the Western calendar: **Western New Year's** (January 1), **Arbor Day** (March 4), **International Working Women's Day** (March 8), **Labor Day** (May 1), **Chinese Youth Day** (May 4), **International Children's Day** (June 1), **Founding of the Communist Party Day** (July 1), **Army Day** (August 1), and **National Day** (October 1). National Day and Labor Day were recently declared 3-day holidays.

METRIC SYSTEM China employs the metric system for measurements (1 kilometer = 0.62 miles, 1 meter = 39.37 inches, 1 liter = about 1 quart) and the Celsius scale for temperature (each degree Celsius = $^9/_5$ degree Fahrenheit + 32).

SAFETY China is a safe country for a foreign traveler, with plenty of very honest people, but pickpockets, thieves, and muggers do target outsiders once in a while. China is the only place I have ever been robbed—it happened at knifepoint on a remote mountain trail.

TELEPHONES Most hotels in China now provide international direct dialing (IDD), meaning you can phone overseas from your room. The charge will appear on your hotel bill, with a service charge added. The telephone system has improved rapidly in the last decade. In nearly all instances, you will have clear connections. When phoning or faxing China from overseas, use the **China country code (86)** and drop the initial zero in the city code. When calling long distance within China, use the complete area code, beginning with the zero.

China is not filled with public phone booths, although many shops offer phones to the public for local calls. Unless you speak Chinese, making reservations or seeking information by phone is usually futile. Have the hotel desk make such calls on your behalf.

Caution: As China's telephone system expands, numbers change, often by adding digits. Even area codes are frequently altered.

TIME Despite spanning what would ordinarily be considered six time zones east to west, China has only one official time zone. Every location is on Beijing time, from Hong Kong to Kashgar. The time in China is GMT plus 8 hours, which means that wherever you are in China it is 16 hours earlier in Los Angeles, 15 hours earlier in Denver, 14 hours earlier in Chicago, and 13 hours earlier in New York. China does not use daylight saving time, so during those summer months it is 15 hours earlier in Los Angeles, 12 hours earlier in New York.

TIPPING Tips are still forbidden in China, but tipping is becoming a widespread custom in large cities. Porters expect RMB 5 to RMB 10 (about $1), guides RMB 15 to RMB 25 ($2 to $3) per day. Don't tip waiters and waitresses. There's a service charge included on most bills. Leave some change if you have a good taxi ride.

TOILETS The standard Asian-style toilet is a porcelain bowl in the floor. These are what you usually find in ordinary restaurants, public lavatories, train and bus terminals, sightseeing destinations, and parks. In public lavatories, where you usually purchase an inexpensive ticket of admission, there is little attention to hygiene and no toilet paper. Some Westerners carry their own spray disinfectants into these malodorous chambers. There's also little privacy. In the bigger hotels, the standard Western sit-down toilets, as opposed to squat-toilets, are used.

WATER **Don't drink the water in China.** It is not sanitary. Even the few hotels that now boast purification systems are suspect, in my opinion. Better safe than sorry. Bottled water is widely and cheaply available, even in remote areas. Use it for drinking and for brushing your teeth.

Parting Words of Advice

- Always book the best class possible on trains, buses, boats, and other modes of transport.
- Book transportation as far ahead as possible. Most flights are fully booked some days in advance.
- Inquire if more expensive rooms in Chinese-run budget hotels are available.
- Always carry your passport, traveler's checks, and other valuables in a concealed security pouch.
- Carry along an emergency snack, such as a breakfast bar, in case you can't find a suitable cafe, vendor, or grocer.
- If bad air quality is a serious threat, pack a dust mask. Many people in China wear them, particularly during dust storms.
- Take good, comfortable, durable walking shoes. Be sure they're well broken in before you leave home.
- Remember that the best small gifts are books and postcards.
- Camera film and batteries are available in shops and department stores in large cities, but it is best to carry plenty of both. Avoid X-raying at air terminals and train stations by handing film over for manual inspection. Put film in clear canisters and bag it in plastic.
- Be patient, flexible, open, and good-natured. China is a learning experience, not an escape; an adventure, not a getaway; a new challenge, not necessarily a holiday.

Customs, Attitudes & Enigmas: The Chinese Way

The Chinese way is not necessarily the Western way. Chinese culture was created in isolation from the West, just as Western culture was created without reference to the Chinese world. Customs, family relationships, and social interactions differ, sometimes only slightly, as modern China adjusts to Western ways. Here's my own list of differences the foreign traveler should expect to encounter while visiting China.

Worldview

CHINA & THE WORLD China has long conceived of itself as the center of the universe. The very name it gives to its nation, *Zhongguo,* means "Central Kingdom." At times, China takes an ethnocentric view of itself. All nations and peoples outside its ancient borders—all non–Han Chinese—traditionally have been regarded as "barbarians." Outsiders are, if not inferior, at last not real Chinese, and hence are forever at an unfortunate remove from the great motherland. Even today, there are millions of Chinese, even in the cities (though particularly those from the countryside), who have never seen a foreigner up close.

There may be occasions, at restaurants, in department stores, or at train and bus stations, when you will draw stares, openly curious rather than hostile. In Chinese eyes, foreigners have certain remarkable physical characteristics—big noses, curly hair, strange clothes and adornments. In such circumstances, return the stare or ignore it, as you please. Expressions of anger are useless. This is how a rock star or movie hero must feel. On one occasion I was walking with an American teacher and his 4-year-old daughter in the streets of Chengdu when a Chinese lady came over and in frank, open curiosity stroked the girl's blond bangs.

Having mastered the Sichuan dialect in 3 short months, the young girl told the admirer in no uncertain terms to desist.

The trick, if stares bother you, is to keep moving. When I first came to China, I used to be able to draw a silent circle of examiners every time I paused in the streets for more than 10 seconds. In large cities, people are more used to foreign businesspeople, students, and tourists in their midst and staring circles rarely form.

One consequence of the Central Kingdom mentality is that China clings proudly and fiercely to its own way of doing things, particularly when an outsider points out a "better" and more efficient way.

POLITICS You'll run across Chinese who can be surprisingly frank about their political situation. If they bring up these issues first, don't be shy about expressing your opinion. On the other hand, you will really be putting your well-intentioned hosts or acquaintances on the spot if you initiate criticisms of China in respect to its lack of political freedoms. Topics to avoid include freedom of the press, the Tibet situation, the status of Taiwan, the Tiananmen Square massacre, abortion, prison labor, and the handling of dissidents. Chinese tour guides get such questions all the time, and they have set answers, often quite defensive.

Society

SAVING FACE Fundamental to maintaining harmony in Chinese society is the ancient concept of "face," which on a personal level means one's self-respect. Personal status reflects on one's family, the paramount institution in China, and the family unit, in turn, is related to the greater society. To "lose face" is thus terribly humiliating, and the Chinese will go to great ends to avoid it. "Saving face" often comes through compromise, in which both sides in a disagreement receive a benefit. For the foreign traveler, the concept of "face" seems a matter of common sense, but it takes many unusual forms in China.

There is a reluctance, for example, to deny any request flat out, as this implies that one is not fulfilling one's duty as a host. Confronting a Chinese over poor service or demanding something difficult to deliver is often not the best way to reach the desired end. To save face, Chinese in a position to help could resort to making a promise they can't keep or to making a firm denial that seems absurd to an outsider. For example, many times in lesser hotels in China I've asked for a room and been told there was none. In an empty hotel, this seems absurd, but the clerk (aside from perhaps being lazy) may simply be saving face. Rooms may not yet be ready, floor staff may not be in position, or the boss may not have opened a block of rooms. In these cases, I simply retreat and wait in the lobby. Invariably something opens up.

The key in getting things done or corrected is not anger but *patience.* Patience is the primary virtue for a traveler in China, though it is not a foolproof device. There are many things, often very ordinary things, such as being seated in a restaurant, that sometimes are never resolved. Knowing the reason for a problem seldom helps, but treating the people who can get something done for you with respect and patience is your best bet. If your requests or complaints place a person in the position of embarrassment or of backing down, you have not scored a victory; rather, you've made an enemy, one whose "face" you have erased, whose integrity and worth you have besmirched.

COURTESY In Old China, especially among the cultured and educated, an elaborate set of social formalities and courtesies evolved. Most of these have disappeared from modern China, though many were adopted and are still practiced elsewhere, particularly in Japan. The Chinese do not bow, for example, nor do they remove their shoes upon entering houses or inns.

The Chinese are courteous and caring hosts. In general they conduct themselves straightforwardly, frankly, and with openness and good humor. They seldom express their thanks for small favors or transactions, although it is perfectly acceptable for foreigners to do so. When asking favors, however, it is best to be round about rather than direct, giving space for a host to refuse without embarrassment.

The Chinese are generally not overly forward or loud, except in gatherings of family and friends. Compliments are usually best directed to senior citizens, bosses, or children. Bragging about one's own accomplishments is not considered good form. Shaking hands has become the acceptable custom when meeting or parting. Kisses on the cheek are not part of Chinese culture, nor for that matter is kissing in public between lovers or partners accepted. On the other hand, the Chinese express their friendship and concern physically, often by placing an arm around the shoulders of the other person. Friends of the same sex sometimes hold hands when strolling.

QUESTIONS FROM STRANGERS It is perfectly acceptable for a stranger to ask you how much money you make. My response to this "impolite" query is to tell the truth and see the reaction. Wages even in the new, economically booming China are below what's standard in the West. When I taught English in China at a leading medical college, for example, I was paid more than the most skilled Chinese surgeons, more even than the college president, and yet the salary was 10 times less than I could have lived on in the United States.

It is also perfectly acceptable for a Chinese to ask you how many children you have. Since the family has always been the most important entity in China, this is a natural question. If you have no children, the Chinese reaction is likely to be one of bewilderment and concern. It's difficult for them to imagine the curse of a no-child family.

China's number one problem is its immense population, now at 1.2 billion, twice what it was when the Communists took power in 1949. Most Han Chinese have been slapped with a policy that allows them only one child. In a nation that puts an absolute value on the family as the primary unit, where traditionally boys are favored over girls, lecturing them on the "immorality" of this policy is rather insensitive. The Chinese feel its harshness and most of them deal with it courageously, patriotically, and sensibly, if not happily. After walking the streets of Shanghai or Beijing for a few days, ask yourself how China would be with 2 billion people. Even with severe controls on its population growth, China is adding 14 million people a year, more than enough new mouths to feed.

GUANXI (CONNECTIONS) During Chairman Mao's reign, 1949–76, and for a decade afterward, *guanxi,* the connections one forged with people in positions to get things done, was far more a measure of wealth and power than mere money. Nearly everyone might be paid a pittance and no one could afford a car or a house, but some were more equal than others in Mao's egalitarian society because they knew the person who could get something they wanted. The guanxi system worked on the basis of cultivated friendships and favors. This sort of "bribery by barter" permeated most aspects of life, from the political to the economic.

Guanxi is still how much of China operates, only today, as the economy booms, money often replaces favors, or pays for them "under the table." Petty bribery and official corruption have become so rampant at times that many ordinary people, from peasants to professionals, have become deeply upset. At least some of the demands of the Tiananmen Square protests issued from this widespread repugnance at the spread of corruption, particularly among officials. The government has repeatedly cracked down on corruption, often within its own ranks, and continues to do so.

MEN & WOMEN By law, there is complete equality between the sexes in the People's Republic of China, a great advance over centuries of feudal practice in which a woman was barely more than a father's or a husband's property. In theory, women today can enter any profession on an equal footing with men. Nevertheless, in daily practice, you will notice that women are still not as highly regarded, at least not as figures of power, in China. When it comes to field work or factory jobs, women are widely employed, but they are less numerous the higher up one goes in industry, business, education, and politics. The mandate to bear children and run the household still falls on women's shoulders, although perhaps with no more frequency than in most Western nations. This is a society where men are still in charge, but women are exercising increasing strength and freedom.

Nevertheless, it is still the dream of millions of Chinese to produce a male, rather than a female, heir. In all of pre-20th-century Chinese history, it was the man who carried on the family name, and in rural societies the man was the head of the clan. Modern education has gone a long way toward changing this perception, but the man is still most often the figure in charge.

WESTERNIZATION Most Chinese today seem quite enthusiastic about the modernization of their society; few express outrage at the adoption of Western architecture, business management, and popular culture. Yet most Chinese are deeply patriotic. The acceptance of Western ways does not mean an abandonment of Chinese ways and traditions. Westernization has struck so forcefully and suddenly in China that the term "culture shock" seems a bit mild. In many cases, the Chinese seem to be trying to use the best of the West to their own advantage, shaping it with Chinese traditions in mind.

The more negative aspects of Western influences cannot be ignored, however. The crime rate is rising; prostitution and drug addiction have returned from exile; the income gap is widening; the communal, communistic, and Confucian values are eroding; and even the fabric of family life at the center of the Central Kingdom is feeling the strain. For the first time retirement homes and senior centers are beginning to displace the extended family. Some couples are choosing not to have children; others are living together; and single-parent families are no longer a complete aberration—although there is still a stigma attached to anything but the conventional two-parent, one-child family with grandparents and other relatives nearby. China's divorce rate has accelerated, from 5% in 1978 to 7% in 1988 to 13% in 1998; it is said to be over 25% in Beijing and rising.

Family & Social Customs

CHINESE NAMES The Chinese give their names in the reverse order customary in the West. Fred Allen Smith becomes Smith Fred Allen. The Chinese refer to others by their family names, not their first names. Many educated Chinese also adopt English first names for use with foreigners. Women frequently hold on to their original family names after marriage. Family names in China—which are almost always one syllable in length—are in short supply. There are about 100 million people named Chang (or Chan in Cantonese) and nearly as many taking the next most popular names: Wang (Wong), Li (Lee), Chao, and Liu (Loo).

DINING CUSTOMS There are differences in the way meals are consumed and enjoyed in China. Slurping of soup, noodles, or rice from a small bowl held in one hand is not considered rude. Nor is scraping bones and other debris off the table onto the floor discouraged in common workers' restaurants. In nicer places, however, Western etiquette is observed.

Large meals and banquets are typically served on round tables, often with lazy Susans at the center. A series of common dishes are presented family style, with diners placing small portions on their plates using chopsticks, or, if provided, serving spoons. The host of a banquet will serve you the first portion of each dish. After that, you can serve yourself. It's considered childish to play with your chopsticks; for many foreigners, it's enough of a trial just to be able to use them. There are plenty of dishes served at a big meal or banquet. The first dishes are usually cold appetizers. Don't fill up on them. If you don't like a dish, try to take a taste and leave the rest on your plate. If you're a vegetarian, find out what's in each dish and politely decline those with meat. To the Chinese, meat is a luxury.

A Chinese host will usually propose a number of toasts during the meal. You can follow up with your own toast. The traditional salute is *gambei,* which once spoken obligates you to try to drain the cup. Many Chinese have limited capacities when it comes to drinking liquor and admire anyone who can drink a great deal. Watch yourself. Group meals are usually boisterous, happy affairs, where everyone is supposed to relax. In fact, eating is the chief Chinese pleasure, and many people spend large portions of their income on food. It is also customary to end a meal soon after the last dish, which is usually fruit, is served. The host will abruptly rise—no more socializing; the meal's at an end.

GIVING GIFTS Don't give clocks—the Chinese word sounds too much like the word for death. And don't wrap a gift in white paper—white is the Chinese color of death. Remember that what we consider rudeness the Chinese consider correct form. Many Chinese won't open a gift in front of you. And don't expect a thank you. Rather than thanking a gift giver and admiring the gift on the spot—thus ending the need to reciprocate in kind—the Chinese often say nothing and wait until they can give a comparable gift in return.

RESPECT FOR AGE By tradition, people of advanced years are highly respected for their wisdom. This respect, refreshing if you're older and from the youth-oriented West, harkens back to China's Confucian teachings. Just as fathers demand total obedience and respect from children, so anyone of advanced years expects respect from his or her juniors. Moreover, it is the responsibility of the young to care for the elderly. Retirement homes and nursing institutions are relatively new in China, and most families find it a loss of face not to be able to care for their own in their own homes. I've found, however, that many young people in China are beginning to resent this burden, and the movement to transfer the care of senior citizens to government programs and institutions is growing. Meanwhile, if you are over 60, you can assume that your younger hosts will treat you with deep respect.

Other Considerations

CLOTHING A decade or more ago, the Chinese all dressed in dull Mao jackets, matching trousers, and workers' caps. It was as if the whole nation were a vast private school, outfitted in the attire of the great headmaster. As the economy heated up and dire restrictions against "spiritual pollution" from the decadent West were eased—a modern version of China's traditional xenophobia and self-absorbing world view—the range of fashions broadened. In the big cities, the young dress in the latest Western fashions available (not so difficult, since much of the world's clothing seems to be made in China). Western attire, including business suits, is commonplace. Mao garb is rarely seen anymore, except in poorer towns and the countryside. Adults still tend to dress conservatively, in drab colors, while outfitting their children in the brightest outfits possible.

As a visitor, I find it best to blend in, selecting darker, duller colors, avoiding revealing clothes, and keeping jewelry to a minimum. Shorts are acceptable for outings, although few Chinese wear them. Bikinis, halter tops, plunging necklines, and short skirts are still too risqué for many Chinese. It's simply more comfortable for foreigners to blend in, avoiding calling attention to themselves as rich visitors willing to overpay for every meal and trinket.

SIESTAS The afternoon nap, once such a widespread custom in China that it was written into the constitution, is a practice out of fashion in the big bustling cities. Nevertheless, I still find an extraordinary number of offices and services that close their doors for an hour or two starting about noon. In smaller cities, towns, and villages, the noonday snooze is more often observed. Cafes and restaurants are always open, of course, to accommodate those taking "naps." When working in China in the 1980s, I became accustomed to a daily nap and I found it an invigorating custom, making one day seem like two. I still observe this custom when traveling in China, if possible, knowing that the Chinese, who go to bed late and rise early, understand why I need my midday rest.

SMOKING One in three cigarettes smoked today is lit up in China. The majority of men smoke. Few women do so in public. In many restaurants, diners smoke between courses and sometimes during them. For nonsmokers, this can become a gargantuan headache. In some cases, requesting that someone not smoke works wonders; in many cases, it does not. The former supreme leader of China, Deng Xiaoping, always smoked while meeting other heads of state, and he went so far as to claim it was a healthy addiction. As China grows more prosperous, smoking threatens to become even more widespread and continuous.

Nevertheless, health officials in China are aware of the dangers, annoyances, and ultimate price society must pay. Antismoking campaigns have recently been launched and severe restrictions have been placed on smoking in public places. As of May 1, 1997, smoking on public transport—on all trains, buses, planes, ships, and taxis, and in all waiting rooms as well—was banned by the order of six ministries. It had been determined that 60% of the one billion rail passengers in China were smokers. Instant fines of RMB 10 to RMB 50 ($1.25 to $6.25) can now be levied for anyone caught in the act of inhaling on trains, ships, planes, buses, subways, taxis, and terminals. Enforcement is now the difficulty, of course, but this "custom" of smoking in public places appears to be on its way out.

SPITTING Hawking and spitting in public used to be an institution, as common as breathing. The same went for clearing one's nose. People often spit from passing buses and in packed cafes. The practice was widespread and goes back centuries. Nevertheless, such activities are now illegal in most of China's cities, and public campaigns to improve hygiene and politeness have made large inroads in the last few years.

TAKING PHOTOS Taking photos of people in the streets of China is permitted, although many Chinese feel much as people in the West do—that it's an unwarranted invasion of privacy. If Chinese don't want their pictures taken, they'll wave their hands or shout. Many don't mind if you take a picture of their children. It's best to ask or motion with your camera. Photos are permitted in most temples and in all public sites except where prohibitions are posted. At some popular sites, there is now a charge for picture-taking, paid at the entrance gate.

TRAFFIC China has long been a nation of bicycles, but as motorized vehicles inundate the streets, traffic snarls and unregulated driving patterns have proliferated. You'll quickly notice that cabs, buses, trucks, and everything else on the road moves to a different drummer, that of sheer expediency. In fact, taxis often drive with as little regard for traffic lights and proper lanes as a bicycle might.

Such crazy driving and passing is certainly dangerous, but there's little you can do about it. Drivers, most of whom are still professionally trained, are quite skilled at avoiding collisions. Telling a driver to slow down or not to pass on a curve or hill usually falls on proud and deaf ears.

One lesson is worth mastering: When you cross intersections on foot, be extremely cautious, since vehicles take the right-of-way almost everywhere. Another annoyance you'll just have to get used to is the constant honking of horns. This has become the customary way that drivers communicate their presence and intentions to other drivers. In a few cities, such as Xiamen, this form of noise pollution has been outlawed.

To Sum Up

It's worth bearing in mind, above all, that Chinese society, despite its apparent chaos, is highly organized and hierarchical, that an individual's power is limited and rigidly defined, and that it is best to make a request or complaint with courtesy rather than in anger, exercising restraint and patience—mountains of patience. The Chinese put great stock in friendship, cultivating long-term personal relationships. Such investments smooth the way and often produce results that uncompromising demands, however rational and obvious they seem to the Western mind, may never yield.

A Quick History

CHINA IS THE PRODUCT OF A lengthy history conducted in proud isolation. Travelers seldom have time to master the intricacies of Chinese chronologies before stepping off the plane, but a basic briefing is useful. When I travel through China I always have in mind a simplified time line of China's major dynasties, a rough list of its famous figures, an outline of its major religions, and an acquaintance with its customs and cultural achievements. This background creates a context for much of what I see along the way, a context that is always expanded by direct experience.

The Early History

Bear in mind that Chinese scholars envision the history of their civilization as stretching back 5,000 years. However, it's unlikely that you'll see many sites or relics over 2,300 years old in your travels, with the exception of the Banpo Neolithic Village in Xi'an, which amply predates recorded Chinese history and the rise of imperial rule.

The earliest recorded societies in China rose during the **Xia period** (2200–1700 B.C.), continued through the **Shang period** (1700–1100 B.C.), and began to become more consolidated during the **Zhou period** (1100–221 B.C.), when various kingdoms fought to extend their domains. Archaeologists keep finding more relics from these early periods, although relatively little is known about them. Confucius (551–479 B.C.) lived during the Zhou period in the Kingdom of Chu, and the shadowy figure of Lao Zi, founder of Daoism, also dates from this era.

A Dynasty Primer

China's more recent history is usually—and quite usefully—divided into its successive dynasties. Sometimes it seems there are more dynasties than brain cells in which to store them. I've found, however, that most of the historical sites and treasures on display are the products of six major dynasties spanning the last 23 centuries. When I keep these six periods straight, I can usually come away from a museum display, temple, or historic monument with an understanding of how it fits into the larger picture.

China's two great imperial showcases, Xi'an and Beijing, roughly divide the history of these great dynasties between them. In the ancient capital of Xi'an, there are fine representatives of the art and monuments created during the Qin, Han, and Tang dynasties. In the modern capital of Beijing, the Ming and Qing dynasties hold sway. The creations of the earlier dynasties at Xi'an are simpler but powerful and graceful in style. The later dynasties, based in Beijing, took art and architecture to more elaborate and ornate extremes.

SIX MAJOR DYNASTIES

Qin	221–207 B.C.
Han	206 B.C.–A.D. 220
Tang	A.D. 618–907
Song	A.D. 960–1279
Ming	A.D. 1368–1644
Qing	A.D. 1644–1911

Viewing Chinese history simply as a succession of dynasties is, however, misleading on many counts. For long periods, centralized control was a dream rather than a reality. The four centuries between the Han and Tang dynasties, for example, which began with the romantic **Three Kingdoms** period (A.D. 220–280), was an age of division and strife among contending states. The **Northern Wei** (A.D. 386–534) managed to achieve a brief unification of power, first at Datong, where the Yungang Buddhist grottoes survive, then at Luoyang, where the Longmen Buddhist caves also remain.

Nor has China always been in the hands of the native Han Chinese. The **Yuan Dynasty** (1271–1368), the setting for Marco Polo's travels, was ruled by the Mongols. The Qing Dynasty (1644–1911), under which Western traders, missionaries, and scholars first entered China in large numbers, was ruled by the Manchus.

Inevitably, the decay and fall of the major dynasties led to massive destruction of relics and monuments. New ruling families often tried to make a clean break with the weighty past, razing the palaces, temples, and capitals of the predecessors they ousted. It's fortunate that anything at all survives today. Dozens of short-lived dynasties rose to power until more lasting central authority was again established. This cycle of creation and destruction seems to be the dynamic force underlying much of Chinese history, and it is repeated in modern Chinese history, too, which is marked by sudden gargantuan shifts in policy and wholesale elimination of the "evils" of the past.

Fortunately for travelers, historic relics, artworks, and monuments have survived in surprising abundance. Keeping straight to which dynasty each belongs is a formidable task, however, as there can be up to 60 or more periods and dynasties to keep in mind, depending on what source you consult. The six major dynasties of my simplified outline cover most of the ground, and they form a practical basis for expanding your knowledge as you see more of historical China.

Qin Dynasty (221–207 B.C.) The Chinese empire began with the unification of many warring states under the First Emperor, Qin Shi Huang Di, in 221 B.C. Qin's rule was brief and his successors could not hold the empire together, but the centralization of power, the bureaucratization of society, and the standardization of writing scripts, weights and measures, and chariot axles set the basis for later dynasties that sometimes ruled for centuries. The chief remains of this first dynasty are the First Emperor's terracotta army, unearthed in Xi'an.

Han Dynasty (206 B.C.–A.D. 220) After the first dynasty fell apart, a greater one emerged. The Han Dynasty extended the borders of the empire and cemented the institutions that would be the basis for Chinese civilization for 2,000 years. Some fine clay crafts and stone sculptures from the Han are found in China's museums, particularly in Xi'an, where the ruins of the Han capital are still visible.

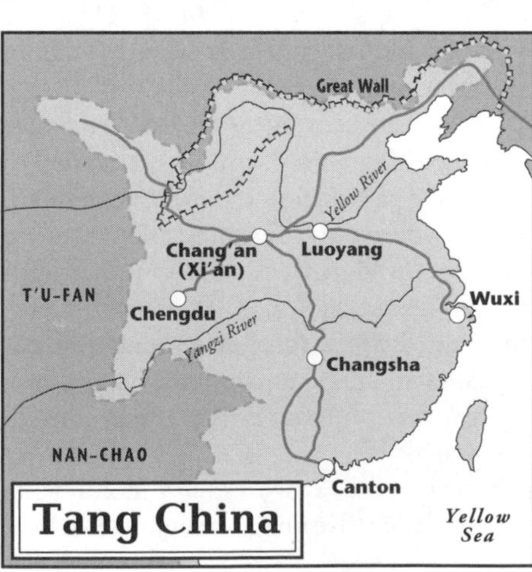

Tang Dynasty (A.D. 618–907) After 4 centuries of warfare and the waxing and waning of many minor dynasties, China's golden age began under a long succession of Tang rulers who lived in the capital of Xi'an (then known as Chang'an). The Tang traded by the Silk Road, and also by sea. Buddhism had entered China via India and under the Tang, rulers played a primary role in art and architecture. From this era we also have wood-block printing and the production of fine silk. Xi'an contains the richest repository of Tang art and architecture, but there are temples, pagodas, and artworks all over China that date from this prosperous period.

Song Dynasty (960–1279) After another period of unrest, the Song rulers reunified China and established a dynasty noted for its art and literature. The Song had the first paper money, movable type, the compass, gunpow-der, and rocket-propelled spears. The Northern Song Dynasty (960–1126) made Kaifeng its capital, while the Southern Song Dynasty (1127–1279) ruled from Hangzhou, then known as Qinsai. Both cities have many treasures and temples from the Song. Marco Polo found a prosperous empire when he first reached China at the end of the Song Dynasty.

Ming Dynasty (1368–1644) The invading Mongols, spearheaded by Genghis Khan and Kublai Khan, established the Yuan Dynasty (1271–1368), but after 2 centuries of Yuan rule, China reverted to a local line of rulers known as the Ming. The Ming capital was Beijing, and there

the Ming emperors built several of China's most famous monuments: the Forbidden City, the Temple of Heaven, and sections of the Great Wall that millions of tourists visit today. It was during this period that European ships began to arrive off the coast of China.

Qing (Manchu) Dynasty (1644–1911) China's final great dynasty, established by Manchu invaders from the north, brought about the last great flourishes of traditional Chinese art and architecture. The capital, Beijing, was graced with the Summer Palace. The empire was extended to include Tibet and Mongolia, but the Western powers made intrusions, establishing concessions in Canton, Shanghai, Qingdao, Beijing, and many other cities. In 1911, the Qing were overthrown by nationalistic forces led by Sun Yat-sen. The first Republic of China was then established, ending thousands of years of imperial rule and leading to the slow modernization of the country and the ascendancy of the Communists under Mao Zedong, who established the present People's Republic of China in 1949.

Modern Politics

In some ways, China underwent more changes in the 20th century than in the previous 20 centuries combined. The Republic of China, which replaced the last dynasty, proved weak and unstable. **Sun Yat-sen** led the powerful Guomindang, the Nationalist People's Party, until his death in 1925. His successor, **Chiang Kai-shek,** became head of China's government, but he was soon involved in violent struggles against two opponents: Japan, which conquered and occupied large areas of China as World War II neared, and the Chinese Communist Party, led by **Mao Zedong** and **Zhou Enlai.** In 1934, in the face of Chiang Kai-shek's military pressure, Mao's 100,000 supporters retreated to the north of China on the epic Long March. The Japanese, who had occupied Manchuria in 1933, went to war with China in 1937, occupying most of the east coast and pushing Chiang Kai-shek's capital all the way inland to Chongqing, where his troops were supplied by the legendary Flying Tigers and other American and British units.

With Japan's eventual defeat in 1945, the civil war in China intensified. Mao's People's Liberation Army (PLA) triumphed. Chiang Kai-shek's Guomindang fled to Taiwan. Mao proclaimed China a People's Republic in 1949 and set up his capital in Beijing. In a few violent decades, China had moved from an imperial dynasty to a modern republic to the largest Communist state on Earth.

Mao ruled Communist China as a new "emperor" until his death in 1976. His regime began on many promising notes. Many of the

CHINA TIMELINE

Xia Dynasty	2100–1600 B.C.
Shang Dynasty	1600–1100 B.C.
Zhou Dynasties	1100–476 B.C.
Western Zhou Dynasty	1100–771 B.C.
Eastern Zhou Dynasty	770–476 B.C.
Spring and Autumn Period	770–476 B.C.
Warring States Period	475–221 B.C.
Qin Dynasty	221–207 B.C.
Han Dynasty	206 B.C.–A.D. 220
Western Han	206 B.C.–A.D. 24
Eastern Han	A.D. 25–220
Three Kingdoms Period	A.D. 220–280
Wu Kingdom	A.D. 220–280
Shu Kingdom	A.D. 220–261
Wei Kingdom	A.D. 220–265
Jin Dynasties	A.D. 265–420
Western Jin	A.D. 265–316
Eastern Jin	A.D. 317–420
Sixteen Kingdoms Period	A.D. 304–439
Wei Dynasties	A.D. 386–557
Northern Wei	A.D. 386–534
Eastern Wei	A.D. 534–550
Western Wei	A.D. 535–557
Northern and Southern States	A.D. 420–589
Sui Dynasty	A.D. 581–618
Tang Dynasty	A.D. 618–907
Five Dynasties and Ten Kingdoms Period	A.D. 907–979
Liao Dynasty	A.D. 907–1125
Song Dynasty	A.D. 960–1279
Northern Song	A.D. 960–1127
Southern Song	A.D. 1127–1279
Western Xia Period	A.D. 1032–1227
Jin Period	A.D. 1115–1234
Yuan Dynasty	A.D. 1279–1368
Ming Dynasty	A.D. 1368–1644
Qing Dynasty	A.D. 1644–1911
Republic of China	A.D. 1912–1949
People's Republic of China	1949–present
Mao Period	1949–1976
Deng Period	1977–1997
Jiang Period	1997–

oppressive institutions of China's feudal past were simply eradicated. Prostitution, drugs, gambling, and other vices disappeared overnight. Peasants—the backbone of Mao's revolution—were given the land to work for the first time in centuries. Women were granted expanded rights. Electricity was spread across the country. Wealth was radically redistributed. For most Chinese, China had finally stood up to the world and was vigorously setting its own course, without outside interference, for the first time in generations. At the same time, landlords and other members of the "oppressive" classes were imprisoned, expelled, or murdered.

The idealism of the post-Liberation years eventually soured as Mao initiated a number of radical programs, many of which were extreme reversals of Chinese traditions. Intellectuals, highly esteemed in Confucian culture, were denounced and imprisoned in a number of political campaigns, starting with the Anti-Rightist Campaign in 1958. Peasants were forced into massive communes in the same year. Even more disastrous was the abortive **Great Leap Forward** of 1959, an attempt to industrialize the nation overnight that succeeded only in reducing agricultural output to the point where millions of people starved to death. In 1960, the Soviet Union, which had been China's chief supporter, advisor, and aid-giver, withdrew completely. China entered a period of isolation as severe as any during the great dynasties of the past.

The most ruinous campaign of all, the **Great Proletarian Cultural Revolution** (1966–76), turned China upside down and led to 10 years of self-destruction. Mao released millions of young people—who idolized him as a living god and swore by every word in his *Little Red Book*—to take control of China and cleanse it of all the old evils and ideals. Virtually anyone in power in 1966 would eventually be toppled by this wave of radical reform. Schools closed down and the economy ground to a halt as everyone engaged in political struggles. Unwavering loyalty to the latest politically correct line became the litmus test for keeping a job, a home, a family, life itself. Thousands, mainly the educated, were sent into the countryside where they worked as peasants in long programs of "reform through labor." The Red Guards went on campaigns to erase the past, trashing countless temples and other dynastic treasures of China's feudal days. Tourists still come across the legacies of the Cultural Revolution not only in ruins (many of which are being restored) but in the minds and hearts of Chinese people who suffered unspeakably and yet survived the ravages of this long nightmare.

The door to China remained closed to the outside world until 1972, when the United States, after a few rounds of "Ping-Pong diplomacy," recognized the People's Republic of China. But it wasn't until the death of Chairman Mao in 1976 that new leaders emerged to put China back on a rational and practical track. The Gang of Four, including Mao's wife, Jiang Qing, was put on public trial in 1980 for "crimes" perpetrated during the Cultural Revolution. **Deng Xiaoping,** several times removed from office and punished during the Cultural Revolution, assumed power and launched China on an entirely new course, away from radical experiments in egalitarianism and "pure" communism and toward a socialism "with Chinese characteristics" that yielded practical economic results.

China slowly recovered the ground it had lost during Mao's later reign, but a long shadow was again cast over the nation on June 4, 1989, when pro-democracy protesters who had seized **Tiananmen Square** in the heart of Beijing were evicted by force before the eyes of the world. China was instituting some economic and social reforms by this point, but political freedom was virtually nonexistent. The violent military crackdown on students and others in Tiananmen Square formed the most dramatic and lasting impression of China for millions of foreign viewers.

When I visited Canton, Shanghai, and Beijing the following year, I found a nation in shock. I also found almost no Western tourists. An invisible boycott had taken hold.

In 1992, Deng Xiaoping made a historic "southern tour" of China, during which he urged the nation to accelerate its economic liberalization. This set into motion a rapid **Westernization** of China. At times, China seemed the most capitalistic country on the planet, a freewheeling society whose motto echoed Deng Xiaoping's famous epitaph, "To get rich is glorious." Millionaires appeared overnight. Thousands of private enterprises were born in the streets. Greed replaced any lingering hopes for a rebirth of political idealism. The Communist Party, although widely discredited, remained firmly in power, and the people, given economic if not political freedom on a scale never before granted by any of its rulers, concentrated on helping build China into a superpower for the 21st century.

The death of senior leader Deng Xiaoping and the return of Hong Kong to Chinese sovereignty in 1997 marked the beginning of a third era in the history of China since Liberation in 1949. The economy of the 1990s boomed steadily onward. China hurtled through its own Industrial Revolution and beyond in a matter of months and years rather than the decades and centuries experienced by the West. Where this will lead, no one knows. China must initiate far greater, more perilous reforms to keep its economy running, and sooner or later it must liberalize its political system as well. But changes in all spheres do seem possible as a new century begins.

Not only are today's travelers able to feast on the splendors of Old China to a degree never before possible; they can also see this China of the future taking shape minute by minute, emerging from the deep shadows of the recent past into something surely brighter.

Portrait Gallery

China yesterday and today is a stage populated by thousands of actors well known to every Chinese but obscure to the outsider. It helps to have a thumbnail sketch of some of the leading members of the cast, as these names constantly come up as one travels across the country.

Chiang Kai-shek (1887–1975) Leader of the Guomindang (Nationalist People's Party) and president of China during the war against Japan (1933–45), Chiang fled to Taiwan after his forces were defeated by the Communists in 1949, establishing the Republic of China there in fierce opposition to the People's Republic of China on the mainland.

Empress Dowager Cixi (1835–1908) The power behind the throne during the last gasps of the Qing (Manchu) Dynasty and creator of the Summer Palace at Beijing, she is villainized in the popular imagination as an evil despot and conniving assassin.

Confucius (551–479 B.C.) This great philosopher, known as Kong Fuzi to the Chinese, is China's Socrates. His teachings, particularly about the strict relationships of leader to subject, man to woman, and parent to child, underlie the traditional organization of family and society in China.

Deng Xiaoping (1904–1997) A veteran of the Long March who later bobbed in and out of Mao's favor, Deng directed China's economic revolution in the 1980s and 1990s. He is blamed for ordering the military crackdown on Tiananmen Square in 1989. His most famous saying (applied to competing economic and political proposals) was, "It doesn't matter whether the cat is black or white, as long as it catches mice."

Du Fu (A.D. 712–770) Considered (along with Li Bai) China's greatest poet, Du Fu wrote powerful, personal lyrics that touch the major chords of Chinese history and human sadness. His "thatched cottage," where he lived in exile from the Tang Dynasty capital, is memorialized in a park in Chengdu.

Guanyin China's most popular Buddhist deity, usually regarded as a woman or a figure combining both sexes, Guanyin is the Goddess of Mercy, often petitioned to ensure the birth of a male heir. Her temple home in China is the holy island mountain of Putuo Shan.

Jiang Zemin (b. 1926) A master politician, Jiang has been paramount leader of China since the death of Deng Xiaoping in 1997. He is dedicated to economic reforms; all he lacks is charisma.

Kangxi (1654–1722) Second emperor of the Qing Dynasty and ruler of China from 1662 to 1722, Kangxi visited most of the important cities and mountains in China, restoring ancient temples and building many new ones. He built the imperial summer palace in Chengde (near Beijing), which still survives.

Lao Zi (circa 570–490 B.C.) Legendary founder of China's indigenous religion, Daoism, Lao Zi emphasized the essential way of nature and the inner, often magical powers of the individual.

Li Bai (A.D. 699–762) Considered (along with Du Fu) China's greatest poet, Li Bai wrote brilliant lyrics (often while drunk on wine) that celebrated individual power and the realm of the senses.

Mao Zedong (1893–1976) Chairman Mao helped create the Chinese Communist Party in 1921 and became the supreme ruler of China in 1949. Venerated as a living god in his lifetime, he led China out of its feudal past and initiated modern reforms, but he also devised campaigns and policies that destroyed the Chinese economy and educational system.

Marco Polo (1254–1324) Italian author of the West's most famous travel book about China, Marco Polo claimed to be an emissary of Kublai Khan during a 17-year residence in Old Cathay. Despite recent suggestions that Marco Polo never even set foot in China and merely recycled the accounts of Silk Road merchants who had, his name is synonymous with all that is exotic and mysterious in China.

Qin Shi Huang Di (259–210 B.C.) The First Emperor of unified China, Qin was known as the burner of books and the builder of the Great Wall. The terra-cotta warriors guarding his immense underground mausoleum at Xi'an are one of China's leading tourist attractions.

Sun Yat-sen (1866–1925) Patriarch of Chinese reform, democracy, and modernization, known as Sun Zhongshan to the Chinese, he headed the Guomindang movement that toppled the last dynasty and propelled China into the 20th century.

Empress Wu (A.D. 660–705) China's most powerful female ruler, Wu Zetian rose to empress of the Tang Dynasty from the position of a concubine and initiated thousands of Buddhist temples and works of art.

Xuan Zang (A.D. 602–664) China's most famous Buddhist monk, he made a 22-year pilgrimage to India to gather holy manuscripts *(sutras)*, which he translated at temples in Xi'an that still stand. He is the basis for the fantastical hero of *The Monkey: Or Journey to the West*, one of China's most popular epic novels.

Zhou Enlai (1898–1976) Confederate of Chairman Mao and one of the founders of the Chinese Communist Party, Zhou Enlai is remembered fondly by many Chinese because as premier during the nightmare years of the Cultural Revolution (1966–76) he intervened to save many lives as well as temples and historic treasures from the rampaging Red Guards.

Zhuge Liang (A.D. 181–234) During the Three Kingdoms Period (A.D. 220–280), he devised astonishing military strategies. His name is synonymous in China with wisdom and correct conduct. His memorial hall is located in Chengdu.

Temples, Mosques & Churches

Among the more interesting but often fatiguing sights in China are the temples. There are Daoist temples, Buddhist temples, even Confucian temples. Tourists, particularly on package tours, often get "templed out" after their third or fourth visit (in their third or fourth city) to these ancient shrines. Nevertheless, the religious architecture and art of China are among its most sublime creations, and temples and pagodas reflect much of the essence of Old China. Understanding the history of religion in China can pump some life and individual character into these monuments.

The Five Ways

Daoism (or Taoism), the most important indigenous religion, dates back 2,500 years. **Buddhism,** its chief rival among organized religions, is a transplant, introduced from India about 2,000 years ago. **Confucianism—** more a philosophy than a religion, although it does have its own rites and temples—is a way of conceiving of society and family in a series of hierarchical relationships. The Confucian is primarily interested in family, society, and education; the Daoist in nature, the individual, and magic; and the Buddhist in compassion, suffering, and transcendence.

These three ways of perceiving the world spiritually were blended over the centuries. Thus, at first blush it is not easy to tell a Daoist temple from a Buddhist shrine from a Confucian pavilion (or even from a royal palace). They share much in common, particularly their architecture. They also share worshippers. As an old adage puts it: "Go to work a Confucian, retire a Daoist, die a Buddhist."

In Old China, Daoism, Buddhism, and Confucianism played a large role in daily life. In modern China, it is quite a different story. Official estimates suggest that 70% of China's people are affiliated with no religion at all, 20% practice ancient folk religions, 6% percent are Buddhist, 2% are Muslim, 1% or less are Daoist or Christian.

Although you'll notice the Chinese thronging the old temples you visit, bowing and burning incense, devoted Buddhists and Daoists make up a tiny portion of the people. Chinese Muslims, actively devoted to **Islam,** also constitute a small minority. These days it is the Chinese **Christians** who are growing in strength, although again they do not constitute more than a small bloc of the Chinese people.

The temples, when toured with an understanding of China's past, are treasure houses, while China's mosques and churches are vital centers of worship for dedicated segments of the population. Both sorts of religious shrines, old and new, often provide moving experiences.

Daoism & Nature

Daoism is the metaphysical and naturalistic wing of Chinese religion and philosophy. In its pure form, as expounded in the writings of its legendary founder, Lao Zi, in the 6th century B.C., the Dao (or Tao) is the way—an absolute way, removed from space, time, society, and tradition, yet one with nature, that can only be discovered by the individual and cannot be described in words, except perhaps through paradox.

Daoism was not intended to be organized as a religion. Its most famous practitioners were usually hermits. The Daoist ideal is to retreat from society and learn from nature. All laws and rules are rejected. The individual cultivates a life of simplicity and withdrawal. Despite these antisocial ideals, Daoism did achieve an organized form, complete with temples, priests, and its own elaborate cosmology. Daoists became the alchemists of China, seeking the elixir of immortality; consuming gold flakes, cinnabar, and various poisons; practicing extreme methods of control over breathing and other bodily functions. Their history is filled with tales of the superhuman and the magical, and their living gods are the immortals who have achieved everlasting physical life and fly with the clouds. Many Chinese artists, particularly lyrical poets such as Li Bai, have been deeply influenced by Daoism.

There are Daoist temples in nearly all Chinese cities, along with Daoist priests and nuns who have returned in small numbers since their banishment during the Cultural Revolution (1966–76). Some of the more famous Daoist temples can be visited today on the Five Sacred Mountains of Old China: Song Shan, Heng Shan Bei, Heng Shan Nan, Hua Shan, and Tai Shan.

Buddhism & Art

Buddhism arrived from India by the same route as goods from the West, by the Silk Road. The new religion took hold in China's desert outposts during the Han Dynasty (206 B.C. to A.D. 220). At the oasis of

Dunhuang, devotees created China's greatest storehouse of Buddhist paintings and manuscripts in the caves of Mogao in the 4th century A.D. By the 9th century, Buddhism was so widely practiced and its temples so rich that the Tang emperor banished Buddhism altogether as an institution "foreign" to the Chinese way. The temples were reopened or rebuilt shortly after this edict, although Buddhism gradually lost its great power.

Buddhism's most important sites in China include the **Shao Lin Monastery** at Song Shan, where the fighting monks developed the martial arts and Chan Buddhism (known as Zen in Japan) originated; the two great **Tang Dynasty pagodas** and their temples in Xi'an, the ancient capital, where Buddhism exerted its strongest influence; and the temples on the **Four Famous Peaks of Buddhism:** Wutai Shan, Jiuhua Shan, Putuo Shan, and Emei Shan.

Buddhism's influence on art and architecture reached its zenith under the Tang and continued through later dynasties. Most of the temples, pagodas, and statues one sees all across China today are Buddhist.

Confucianism & Society

Confucius (Kong Fuzi), rather like Socrates, was a teacher whose ideas were written down by his students. Confucian ideas have had as far-reaching an influence on Chinese philosophy as Socratic ideas did on Western thought.

Confucius laid great stress on education, particularly on the study of ancient classics, since these depicted a more perfect society than what existed in the present, and on traditional rituals and rites, since these also came from an earlier, golden age. He also devised the image of the model gentleman, a highly educated public servant who fulfilled all duties and whose character and integrity were completely unassailable. All these notions became the basis of the Chinese educational system, with its imperial examinations, which were the route to a lucrative and influential career as a scholar-official in China's massive civil service system.

Even more profoundly, Confucius formulated the five relationships that all Chinese are traditionally expected to observe. Each relationship is between a superior and an inferior. Those relationships are between ruler and subject, father and son, husband and wife, elder brother and younger brother, and friend and friend. For society—indeed, for Heaven and Earth—to be in harmony, these relationships had to be strictly observed. They extended even beyond the grave: Recently departed family members had to be mourned and ancestors had to be "worshipped" at family shrines.

When the Confucians gained prominent positions in government during the early Han Dynasty in the 2nd century B.C. these ideas became state doctrines. The emperor was responsible for running human affairs in a virtuous and just manner or he could lose his "Mandate of Heaven," bringing disastrous consequences to the kingdom. The emperor's royal advisors were required to give their superior the best advice for the welfare of the state, regardless of its effect on an advisor's own career. These officials, in turn, were products of a rigorous state examination system that quizzed its students on the intricacies of Confucian classics. One long-term result still felt in China today is that the rule of law never gained a foothold. Conflicts were settled and policies were determined through negotiations conducted among a few powerful and presumably good and just men. Since they occupied a superior position, and were ideally of unquestionable integrity, their decisions could not properly be questioned by the masses.

In this century, Mao Zedong turned Confucianism on its head, making the masses superior to the scholar-elites. Ancestor worship, filial piety, respect for the past, deference to elders and the educated, unquestioning obedience to authority, the sanctity of the family—all these Confucian doctrines were for a time denounced as feudal and backward. But while many of these old ideas are not practiced today, they still underlie Chinese responses in subtle but profound ways. The need to "save face," for instance, originally prescribed as a way to protect the family, is still an everyday practice.

While mainly secular in its teachings, Confucianism gradually became China's state religion. The first temples to Confucius were built in the 7th century as shrines where the Great Scholar and his disciples could be worshipped as scholarly ancestors of the nation or at least of its bureaucracy. These Confucian temples can still be found in many cities in China. The Confucian Temple in **Beijing** is still quite active, and the one in **Xi'an** now serves as the lovely grounds for the old provincial museum.

Islam & Arabia

China's Muslim population numbers less than 20 million of China's 1.3 billion residents (about 2%), but their struggle to maintain an ethnic as well as religious identity is a major concern of China's leaders, who are wary of any sign of a burgeoning secessionist movement such as that in Tibet. Muslim minorities have therefore been granted many of the special rights enjoyed by China's other minorities, such as exemption from the one-family–one-child rule.

Arab sea traders and Silk Road merchants introduced Islam to the edges of the Chinese empire not long after the faith was born in the

7th century A.D. Today there are historic mosques worth visiting in Canton, Beijing, Xi'an, and the Silk Road cities of Gansu and Xinjiang provinces. Most of China's Muslim population resides in the northwest. Cities such as Xi'an have a Muslim quarter where the people, known as the Hui, are indistinguishable from Han Chinese, due to centuries of assimilation, but they strictly maintain many Muslim mandates, running their own schools, butcher shops, and restaurants. There are 6.5 million Hui in China.

In Xinjiang Province, the 5.5 million Uighur people, practicing Muslims, dominate the culture of a region that occupies one-sixth of China's territory. The mosques in **Kashgar** and other desert oases, dating from the Ming and Qing dynasties, are among the most fascinating religious sites in China.

Christianity & the West

Catholic missionaries first arrived in the 16th century in the person of Matteo Ricci of the Society of Jesus, but the Ming emperor was not so interested in Ricci's religious message as he was in the Jesuit's scientific knowledge. Protestant missionaries, making their mark in the mid-19th and early 20th centuries, made few converts while in China. Despite this failure and repeated episodes of persecution in more recent times, Christianity appears to be flourishing now as never before. In the 1990s an official census put the number of Christians in China at about 3 million—hardly enough to cause a blip on China's population radar—but in the last few years, and particularly with the addition of Hong Kong, this figure has soared. The government now counts 5 million Catholics and 6 million Protestants, and scholars would double these numbers, counting "underground" Christians who attend unofficial home churches. Even state statistics admit that China enrolls 60,000 new Catholic followers a year.

Most Chinese cities now have at least two officially sanctioned Christian churches in operation: one Protestant, one Catholic. The Protestant churches are controlled by the Three-Self Patriotic Movement and are not affiliated with any religious institutions in the West. The Catholic churches are controlled by the Catholic Patriotic Association, which does not recognize the authority of Rome. Catholic mass is still conducted in Latin. In addition, there are numerous illegal "home churches" throughout China that also have a growing membership, despite occasional crackdowns by local police.

I've attended dozens of services in Protestant and Catholic churches in many cities and towns in China. This is often a most interesting experience, even if you're not a Christian. Most of the churches were built in the late 19th or early 20th century in Western European styles. Few have any religious decorations left, but most have plenty of bibles and hymnals. Nearly all who attend Christian services today are Chinese. A decade ago, many of the worshippers were elderly, members who had attended churches before their closure either after Liberation (1949) or during the Cultural Revolution (1966–76). Now, more and more young people, perhaps curious about Western institutions of all kinds, are attending.

A traveler recently informed me that when she inquired at a hotel desk about attending Sunday services at a church in Xi'an, she was told that it didn't accept foreigners. This is nonsense. Foreigners are routinely welcomed with open arms in all the churches in China. Be persistent. The only difficulty in attending church in China is the same difficulty faced almost everywhere: breaking through the crowds and securing a seat inside.

How to Tour a Temple

Monumental Chinese architecture, from temples to cities, was traditionally laid out according to cosmological principles that became known as *feng shui*—a way of arranging objects to avoid or deflect the invasion of evil forces. In simple terms, this meant that everything from a temple to a city faced south (since evil forces galore swept in from the north), and was surrounded on four sides by a high wall to keep out bad spirits (not to mention ordinary thieves).

The Daoist, Buddhist, and Confucian temples you visit in China today adhere to this geomantically correct scheme. Protected by rectangular walls like a small city, the temple's main entrance faces south. The entrance gate is sealed off by huge wooden doors, near which novice monks collect the modern entrance fees. Immediately inside is a series of pavilions and courtyards lined on both sides by residence and administrative halls. The inner complex can be compact or vast, consisting of hundreds of buildings or a small handful. Usually, the deeper into the courtyards and pavilions you go, the more sacred the shrine.

The temple architecture is virtually identical regardless of the religion practiced within. Variations in style are a product of region and historical period, not the dictates of faith. The main support consists of interlocking wooden beams and enormous columns resting on raised platforms. The curving roof is paved in ceramic tiles. In the early Tang Dynasty, a system of cantilevered brackets enabled the eaves to become a more prominent and showy feature. Carved figures populated the gables. In southern China, ornamentation and increasingly upturned eaves became the fashion. In the north, temple architecture remained more restrained.

While Chinese temples are seldom multistoried, owing to restrictions inherent in their structural elements, the **pagodas** that often rise from temple grounds were deliberately designed to touch the heavens. Derived from religious towers in India, the Chinese versions served two primary purposes: as reliquaries for holy documents and other sacred relics, and as magical monuments to protect monasteries, cities, and the surrounding countryside from natural and man-made disasters. Some pagodas allow visitors to ascend the stairways inside, although many are closed. The Tang Dynasty pagodas in Xi'an can still be climbed and they are among the most important to survive in China.

In **Buddhist temples,** the grand entrance often contains two large statues of guardian kings, known as the Erwang, one on either side. The first buildings beyond the entrance are the bell and drum towers, once used to call the faithful to prayer. The first major hall is a holy military complex of sorts with large statues of the four heavenly kings, two on each side. Their task is to protect the sacred site, punish evil, and reward the good and just. The yellow Northern King, Duo Wen, carries the banner of sacred truth, which looks for all the world like an umbrella. The white Eastern King, Zhi Gui, has a lute to calm the tormented soul with his divine music. The blue Southern King, Zeng Zhang, is armed with a demon-defying sword. The red Western King, Guang Mu, clutches a snake for power over evil and a pearl for wisdom.

The first Buddha you usually encounter is Maitreya, the Laughing Buddha, with his trademark bulging belly. Maitreya is the Buddha of the Future, technically still a *bodhisattva* (enlightened follower remaining on Earth to help others). His belly is swollen by meditation. His earlobes are elongated by the heavy rings he once wore, signs that he was a respected teacher.

The Great Hall of most Buddhist temples often contains three large golden statues sitting on lotus flowers. These are the Buddhas of the Past, Present, and Future. Maitreya, the Buddha of the Future, you've already met. Sakyamuni, the Buddha of the Present, is the historical figure who attained enlightenment. Dipamkara, the Buddha of the Past, represents all who entered Nirvana before Sakyamuni, the 5th century B.C. northern Indian prince.

The walls of the Great Hall usually contain smaller statues of Buddha's divine followers, the 500 arhats (or luohans). Immediately behind the Great Buddhas is a statue of the Goddess of Mercy, Guanyin, who became the most popular Buddhist divinity in China. Guanyin is often portrayed as having "a thousand arms," representing her great capacity to reach out to others. She is also petitioned to grant a male heir.

The faithful temple-goer purchases prayer beads, amulets, and incense sticks from the temple vendors, placing a burning stick in the incense burners outside each hall and kneeling and praying on the cushions or rugs placed before the altar inside. If the temple has a large and active team of monks, they will often conduct chants inside the fenced-off area in front of the altar.

It's easy enough for a novice visitor to find the main altars in a temple complex: Just keep heading straight north from the entrance through the inner courtyards from hall to hall. Often the back door of a pavilion is open, so that visitors can walk around the altar and statues in the center and exit at the rear into the courtyard of the next pavilion.

In a **Daoist temple,** the layout is much the same but the gods have changed and the monks are wearing funny leggings. The red columns of a Buddhist temple are painted black and yin-yang symbols frequently appear on walls. The Three Buddhas are replaced by statues of the Three Immortals riding tiger, deer, and crane. Literary and historical figures, such as the Three Kingdom's Zhuge Liang, are often memorialized. One figure of adoration and petition that Daoist and Buddhist temples do share, however, is that of Guanyin, Goddess of Mercy.

Daoist temples tend to be more down-to-earth and eclectic than Buddhist temples. Most of the temples you'll visit in China are Buddhist, but there are plenty of Daoist temples as well. Those at the center of the city often opened their courtyards to Sunday marketplaces, and street markets still often surround Daoist temples. There are fewer **Confucian temples,** and they are seldom used by worshippers of the Great Sage these days. The Confucian temples in Beijing and Qu Fu, two of the most famous in China, employ the architecture of Buddhist and Daoist temples, but their stately interiors and altars are remarkably bare of the statues that other temples have in numbing abundance, save those of Confucius himself.

THE CHINESE LANGUAGE

THE CHINESE LANGUAGE IS ancient, complex, and quite alien to those who know only the languages of the West. All forms of written Chinese are the same, but there are many types of spoken Chinese. The most widely used is called *putonghua* or **Mandarin.** Most Chinese understand Mandarin. However, every city and region of China also has its own distinct form of Chinese, often completely unintelligible to outsiders. Cantonese and Mandarin are so different as to constitute different languages, though, again, their written form is the same. Mandarin is the dialect that students throughout China learn to speak in school.

Chinese students are also taught English, but not very well, and few Chinese (outside of the major hotels) can speak it. Therefore, knowing even just a few Chinese phrases is very useful. Unfortunately, Chinese is not an easy language to learn. In Mandarin, there are four basic tones: The first is high-pitched and even, the second is rising, the third falling then rising, and the fourth falling. The same "sound" spoken in each of these four different tones can have a completely different meaning.

Nevertheless, if travelers have time beforehand, it is fairly easy to learn a handful of useful basic spoken phrases. Correct pronunciation can be learned as one goes about in China through careful listening. Since few travelers have time to take a Chinese language course before visiting China, a **Mandarin phrase book,** especially one that has the words and phrases printed in Chinese characters, is essential.

The written form of Chinese is even more difficult to learn than the spoken form, since it does not employ an alphabetical system. Students must memorize the meaning (and pronunciation) of thousands of written characters, a time-consuming challenge even for native speakers. Travelers must rely on phrase books, bilingual maps, and hotel staff to unravel these enigmatic characters, although many visitors quickly learn to recognize some of the simpler and more common ones as they travel.

An easier form of written Chinese is **Pinyin,** the official transcription of Chinese into an alphabetical form. For example, a sign reading *Tiantanyuan* means Temple of Heaven Park. Street signs in major cities often have the name of the street in pinyin followed by the transcription

A GUIDE TO PINYIN PRONUNCIATION

a as in f**a**r	*l* as in **l**and
and as in l**unq**	*m* as in **me**
b as in **be**	*n* as in **n**ame
c as in ra**ts**	*o* as in l**aw**
ch as in **ch**ange	*p* as in **p**ar (aspirated)
d as in **d**o, **d**ay	*q* (ch) as in **ch**eek
e as in **er**	*r* as in 1) **r**ight or 2) a**z**ure
ei as in m**y**	*s* as in le**ss**
eong as in **ng** (nasal sound)	*sh* as in **sh**ore
er as in hon**or**	*t* as in **t**op (aspirated)
f as in **f**oot	*u* as in sh**oo**t
g as in **g**o	*w* as in **w**ant
h as in h**er**	*x* as in **sh**e
i as in **ea**t	*y* as in **y**et
j as in **j**eep	*z* as in su**ds**
k as in **k**ind (aspirated)	*zh* as in **j**ungle

of one of the words for street (such as *dajie*). Another help for travelers who don't speak Chinese are small cards offered at most hotels that have the name of the hotel and the name of your destination printed in Chinese characters. You can show the card to your taxi driver or to others along the way. These cards make getting to and returning from a site, restaurant, or shop quite easy.

Probably the most common question asked of travelers in Beijing is "Ni shi cong nar lai de?" or "Where are you from?" The answer is "Wo shi *Meiguo* lai da" if you're from America. *Meiguo* means America. *Aodaliya* means Australia, *Jianada* means Canada, *Yingguo* means England, *Faguo* means France, *Deguo* means Germany, *Helan* means Holland, *Aierlan* means Ireland, and *Riben* means Japan. China, by the way, is *Zhongguo* in Chinese.

Even if one's pronunciation is poor at first, it's worth making an attempt. Many Chinese are not only amused, but also impressed, when foreigners make a stab at using their language, which they regard as the world's most important.

English	Pinyin	Chinese
BEIJING	**Beijing**	**北京**
Ancient Observatory	Gugunxiangtai	观象台
Chairman Mao's Mausoleum	Mao Zhuxi Jiniantang	毛主席纪念堂
Forbidden City	Gugong	故宫
Lama Temple	Yonghegong	雍和宫
Old Summer Palace	Yuanminghyuan	圆明园
Summer Palace	Yiheyuan	颐和园
Temple of Heaven	Tiantan Gongyuan	天坛公园
Tiananmen Square	Tiananmen Guang Chang	天安门广场
BEIHAI	**Beihai**	**北海**
Old Town	Zhongshan Lu Laocheng Qu	中山路老城区
Silver Beach	Yintan	银滩
CANTON	**Guangzhou**	广州
Pear River	Zhujiang	珠江
Qingping Market	Qingping Shichang	清平市场
Shamian Island	Shamian	沙面
Sun Yat Sen Memorial Hall	Zhongshan Jiniantang	中山纪念堂
Temple of the Six Banyan Trees	Liurongsi	六榕寺
Yuexiu Park	Yuexiu Gongyuan	越秀公园
CHENGDE	**Chengde**	**成德**
Hammer Rock	Bangchui Shan	棒锤山
Imperial Summer Retreat	Bishushanzhuang	避暑山庄

English	Pinyin	Chinese
Mount Sumera Temple	Xumifushou Miao	须弥福寿庙
Small Potala Temple	Putuozongsheng Miao	普陀宗乘之庙
Temple of Universal Joy	Pule Si	普乐寺
CHENGDU	**Chengdu**	**成都**
Du Fu Cottage	Du Fu Caotang	杜甫草堂
Qingyang Temple	Qingyang Gong	青羊宫
Wenshu Monastery	Wenshu Yuan	文殊院
Zoo	Dongwuyuan	动物园
CHONQING	**Chonqing**	**重庆**
Chongqing Museum	Chongqing Bowuguan	重庆博物馆
Gate to Heaven	Chaotianmen	朝天门
Liberation Monument	Jiefang Bei	解放碑
Luohan Temple	Luohan Si	罗汉寺
Pipashan Park	Pipashan Gongyuan	枇杷山公园
DALI	**Dali**	**大理**
Erhai Lake	Erhai Hu	洱海湖
Shaping	Shaping	沙平
Temple of the Three Pogodas	San Ta Si	三塔寺
DATONG	**Datong**	**大同**
Huayan Monastery	Huayan Si	华严寺
Nine Dragon Screen	Jiu Long Bi	九龙壁
Temple Suspended in the Void	Xuan Kong Si	悬空寺

English	Pinyin	Chinese
Yungang Buddhist Caves	Yungang Shiku	云岗石窟
DAZU BUDDHIST CAVES	**Dazu Shiku**	**大足石窟**
Dragon Flower Bridge	Hua Long Qiao	花龙桥
Precious Mountain	Baoding Shan	保定山
DUNHUANG	**Dunhuang**	**敦煌**
Crescent Moon Lake	Yueyaquan	月牙泉
Mogao Buddhist Caves	Mogao Shiku	莫高石窟
Singing Sand Mountains	Mingshashan	鸣沙山
EMEI SHAN	**Emei Shan**	**峨眉山**
Clear Sound Pavilion	Qingyin Ge	清音阁
Elephant Bathing ` Pool	Xixiang Chi	洗象池
Golden Summit	Jinding	金顶
Golden Summit Temple	Jinding Si	金顶寺
Jieyan Hall	Jieyin Ge	接引阁
Peak of the Ten Thousand Buddhas	Wanfoding	万佛顶
Shrine of Limpid Waters	Jin Shui	金水
Temple of Ten Thousand Years	Wannian Si	万年寺
GRAND CANAL	**Da Yunhe**	**大运河**
GREAT WALL	**Wan Li Chang Cheng**	**万里长城**
Badaling	Badaling	八达岭

English	Pinyin	Chinese
Mutianyu	Mutianyu	慕田峪
Simatai	Simatai	司马台
GUILIN	**Guilin**	**桂林**
Banyan Lake	Rong Hu	榕湖
Brocade Hill	Diecaishan	迭采山
Cedar Lake	Shan Hu	杉湖
Crescent Moon Hill	Yueyashan	月牙山
Elephant Trunk Hill	Xiangbishan	象鼻山
Li River	Lijiang	漓江
Minorities Cultural Park	Feng Qing Yuan	丰庆园
Pierced Hill	Chuanshan	穿山
Reed Flute Cave	Ludi Yan	芦笛岩
Seven-Star Park	Qixing Yan Gongyuan	七星岩公园
Solitary Beauty Park	Duxiufeng	独秀峰
Whirlpool Hill	Fuboshan	伏波山
HANGZHOU	**Hangzhou**	**杭州**
China Tea Museum	Zhongguo Cha Bowuguan	中国茶博物馆
Dragon Well	Longjing	龙井
Lingyin Temple	Lingyin Si	灵隐寺
Three Pools Mirroring the Moon	Santan Yinyue	三潭印月
Solitary Island	Gushan	孤山
West Lake	Xi Hu	西湖
Zhejiang Provicial Museum	Zhejiang Bowuguan	浙江省博物馆

English	Pinyin	Chinese
HARBIN	**Harbin**	**哈尔滨**
Confusion Temple	Wen Miao	文庙
Japanese War Crimes Museum	Riben Xijun Shiyan Jidi Bowuguan	日本细菌试验基地博物馆
Old Town	Daoliqu	道里区
Siberia Tiger Park	Hu Yuan	虎园
Songhua River	Songhua Jiang	松花江
Stalin Park	Sidalin Gongyuan	斯大林公园
Sun Island	Taiyang Dao	太阳岛
Zhaolin Park	Zhaolin Gongyuan	兆麟公园
HENG SHAN BEI	**Heng Shan Bei**	**衡山北**
North Star Temple	Kui Xing Si	癸星寺
HENG SHAN NAN	**Heng Shan Nan**	**衡山南**
Fire God Temple	Zhurong Dian	祝融殿
Southern Gate of Heaven	Nantian Men	南天门
Temples of the Southern Mountain	Nanyue Miao	南岳庙
Zhurong Peak	Zhurong Feng	祝融峰
HONG KONG	**Xiang Gang**	**香港**
HUA SHAN	**Hua Shan**	**华山**
Eighteen Bends	Shiba Pan	十八盘
Jade Spring Temple	Yuquan Si	玉泉寺
Looking to Heaven Pool	Yangtian Chi	仰天池
HUANG SHAN	**Huang Shan**	**黄山**
Jade Screen Pavilion	Yuping Lou	玉屏楼
Lotus Flower Peak	Lianhua Feng	莲花峰

English	Pinyin	Chinese
Northern Sea of Clouds	Beihai	北海
Peach Blossom Hot Springs	Taoyuan Wenquan	桃源温泉
Stone That Flew from Afar	Feilai Feng	飞来峰
Turtle Summit	Aoyu Feng	鳌鱼峰
Western Sea of Clouds	Xihai	西海
HUANGPU RIVER	**Huangpu Jiang**	**黄浦江**
JIAYUGUAN	**Jiayuguan**	**嘉峪关**
Jiayuguan Fort	Jiayuguan Chenglou	嘉峪关城楼
Wei-Jin Tombs	Wiejin Ling	魏晋陵
JIHUA SHAN	**Jihua Shan**	**九华山**
Sweet Dew Monastery	Ganlu Si	甘露寺
Heavenly Terrace	Tiantai Shan	天台山
Minyuan Village	Minyuan	明园
KAIFENG	**Kaifeng**	**开封**
Dragon Pavilion Park	Longting Gongyuan	龙亭公园
Iron Tower	Tie Ta	铁塔
Kaifeng Museum	Kaifeng Bowuguan	开封博物馆
Lord Bao Lake	Baogong Hu	包公湖
Qingming Park	Qingming Yuan	清明园
Synagogue of Purity and Truth	Qing Zhen Si	清真寺
Xiangguo Monastery	Xiangguo Si	相国寺
KASHGAR	**Kashi**	**喀什**
Abakh Hoja Tomb	Xiangfei Mu	阿巴和家麻扎墓

English	Pinyin	Chinese
Id Kah Mosque	Aiti Ga'er Qingzhen Si	艾提尕 清真寺
People's Park	Renmin Gongyuan	人民公园
KUNMING	**Kunming**	**昆明**
Bamboo Temple	Qiongzhu Si	筇竹寺
Dragon's Gate	Longmen	龙门
Flower and Bird Market	Huaniao Shichang	花鸟市场
Grand View Park	Daguan Gongyuan	大观公园
Green Lake	Cuihu	翠湖
Lake Dian	Dianchi	滇池
Pavilion of the Three Purities	Sanqingge	三清阁
Stone Forest	Shi Lin	石林
Yauntong Temple	Yuantong Si	园通寺
Yunnan Nationalities Village	Yunnan Minzucun	云南民族村
LESHAN BUDDHA	**Leshan Dafo**	**乐山大佛**
LONGMEN BUDDHIST CAVES	**Longmen Shiku**	**龙门石窟**
LIJIANG	**Lijiang**	**漓江**
Old Market Square	Si Fang Jie	四方街
Dongba Museum	Dongba Bowuguan	东巴博物馆
LU SHAN	Lu Shan	庐山
Lushan Museum	Lu Shan Bowuguan	庐山博物馆
LUOYANG	**Luoyang**	**洛阳**

English	Pinyin	Chinese
MOGAO BUDDHIST CAVES	**Mogao Shiku**	**莫高石窟**
PUTUO SHAN	**Putuo Shan**	**普陀山**
Buddha's Head	Foding Shan	佛顶山
Southern Gate of Heaven	Nantian Men	南天门
Voice of the Tide Cave	Chaoyin Dong	潮音洞
QINGDAO	**Qingdao**	**青岛**
Badaguan	Badaguan	八达关
Catholic Church	Tianzhu Jiaotang	天主教堂
Lao Shan	Lao Shan	崂山
Little Fish Hill	Xiaoyushan	小鱼山
Marker Hill Park	Xinhaoshan Gongyuan	星号山公园
Qingdao Welcome Guest House	Qingdao Ying Binguan	青岛迎宾馆
Zhangqiao Pavilion	Qinhai Zhanqiao Ting	前海栈桥亭
QU FU	**Qu Fu**	**曲阜**
Confucian Mansion	Kong Miao	孔庙
SANJIANG	**Sanjiang**	三江
Bridge of Wind and Rain	Fengyu Qiao	风雨桥
SHANGHAI	**Shanghai**	**上海**
The Bund	Waitan	外滩
French Quarter	Faguo Zujie	法国租界
Huangpu River	Huangpu Jiang	黄浦江
Jade Buddha Temple	Yufo Si	玉佛寺

English	Pinyin	Chinese
Jinjiang Hotel	Jinjiang Fandian	锦江饭店
Nanjing Road	Nanjing Lu	南京路
Old Town	Nanshi	南市
Pudong Area	Pudong Xinqu	浦东新区
Shanghai Museum	Shanghai Bowuguan	上海博物馆
The Teahouse	Huxinting	湖心亭
Temple to the Town Gods	Cheng Huang Miao	城隍庙
Yu Garden	Yu Yuan	豫园
SONG SHANG	**Song Shang**	**嵩山**
Central Peak Temple	Zhong Yue Miao	中岳庙
Shao Lin Monastery	Shaolin Si	少林寺
Song Yue Pagoda	Song Yue Ta	嵩岳塔
SUZHOU	**Suzhou**	**苏州**
Forest of Lions Garden	Shi Zi Lin	狮子林
Humble Administrator's Garden	Zhuo Zheng Yuan	拙政苑
Lingering Garden	Liu Yuan	留园
Master of the Nets Garden	Wang Shi Yuan	网师园
Suzhou Silk Museum	Suzhou Sichou Bowuguan	苏州丝绸博物馆
Temple of Mystery	Xuan Miao Guan	玄妙观
Tiger Hill	Hu Qiu Shan	虎丘山
LAKE TAI	**Tai Hu**	**太湖**
Three Hills Island	San Shan Dao	三山岛
Turtle-Head Isle	Yuantouzhu	鼋头渚

English	Pinyin	Chinese
TAI SHAN	**Tai Shan**	**泰山**
First Gate	Yitianmen	一天门
Middle Gate	Zhongtianmen	中天门
South Gate	Nantianmen	南天门
Stele Without Inscription	Wu Zi Bei	无字碑
Tai'an Town	Tai'an	泰安
Temple of the Jade Emperor	Yu Huang Ding	玉皇顶
Temple of the Purple Dawn	Bixiao Si	碧晓寺
TERRA-COTTA WARRIORS	**Bingmayong**	**兵马俑**
TURPAN	**Tulufan**	**吐鲁番**
Astana Tombs	Asitana Gumuqu	阿斯塔那古墓
Bezeklik Thousand Buddha Caves	Bozikeli Qianfo Dong	柏孜克里克千佛洞
Suleiman's Minaret	Sugong Ta	苏公塔
Flaming Mountains	Huoyan Shan	火焰山
Gaochang Ancient City	Gaochang Gucheng	高昌故城
Karez Wells	Karez Er Jing	坎儿井
Jiaohe Ancient City	Jiaohe Gucheng	交河故城
Moon Lake	Aiding Hu	艾丁湖
URUMQI	**Wulumuqi**	**乌鲁木齐**
Heavenly Lake	Tianchi	天池
Hong Shan Park	Hong Shan Gongyuan	红山公园
People's Park	Renmin Gongyuan	人民公园

English	Pinyin	Chinese
Southern Mountains	Nan Shan	南山
WEIFANG	**Weifang**	**潍坊市**
Weifang Kite Museum	Weifang Fengzheng Bowuguan	潍坊风筝博物馆
Shijia Village	Shijia	石家庄民俗旅游村
WULINGYUAN	**Wulingyuan, Zhangjiajie**	**武陵源，张家界**
WUTAI SHAN	**Wutai Shan**	**五台山**
Pusa Ding Temple	Pusa Ding Si	菩萨顶寺
Southern Peak Temple	Nan Shan Si	南山寺
WUXI	**Wuxi**	**无锡**
Dragon Light Pagoda	Long Guang Ta	龙光塔
Jichang Garden	Jiachang Yuan	寄畅苑
Li Garden	Li Yuan	蠡园
Ling Shan Buddha	Ling Shan Dafo	灵山大佛
Xihui Park	Xihui Gongyuan	锡慧公园
XIAMEN	**Xiamen**	**厦门**
Gulangyu Island	Gulangyu	鼓浪屿
Nan Putuo Temple	Nan Putuo Si	南普陀寺
Shuzhuang Garden	Shuzhuang Yuan	菽庄公园
Sunlight Rock	Riguangyan	日光岩
Xiamen Museum	Xiamen Bowuguan	厦门博物馆
Xiamen University	Xiamen Daxue	厦门大学
XI'AN	**Xi An**	**西安**
Banpo Museum	Banpo Bowuguan	半坡博物馆
Baoqing Pagoda	Baoqing Ta	宝庆塔

English	Pinyin	Chinese
Bell Tower	Zhong Lou	钟楼
Big Wild Goose Pagoda	Dayanta	大雁塔
Catholic Church	Tianzhu Jiaotong	天主教堂
City Walls	Cheng Qiang	城墙
Daoist Temple of the Eight Immortals	Baxian Guan	八仙观
Drum Tower	Gu Lou	鼓楼
Eastern Mountain Temple	Dongyue Miao	东岳庙
Forest of Steles	Bei Lin	碑林
Great Mosque	Da Qingzhen Si	大清真寺
Lama Temple	Guangren Si	广仁寺
Protestant Church	Jidu Jiaotong	基督教堂
Reclining Dragon Zen Temple	Wolong Si	乌龙寺
Shaanxi History Museum	Shanxi Lishi Bowuguan	陕西历史博物馆
Small Wild Goose Pagoda	Xiaoyanta	小雁塔
Terra-Cotta Warriors	Bingmayong	兵马俑
YANGSHUO	**Yangshuo**	**阳朔**
Green Lotus Peak	Bilian Feng	碧莲峰
Moon Mountain	Yueliang Shan	月亮山
Xingping	Xingping	兴坪
YANGZI RIVER	**Chang Jiang**	**长江**
Fengdu	Fengdu	酆都
Red Cliff	Chibi	赤壁

English	Pinyin	Chinese
Three Gorges	San Xia	三峡
Three Little Gorges	Xiao San Xia	小三峡
Yueyang Tower	Yueyang Ta	岳阳塔
YIXING	**Yixing**	宜兴
Ceramic Village	Dingshu	鼎蜀
Shanjuan Cave	Shanjuan Dong	缮卷洞
Zhanggong Cave	Zhanggong Dong	张公洞
YUNGGANG BUDDHIST VACES	**Yungang Shiku**	云岗石窟

Terms & Useful Phrases

English	Pinyin	Chincsc
Useful Phrases		
Hello	Ni hao	你好
How are you?	Ni hao ma?	你好吗？
Good	Hen hao	很好
Bad	Bu hao	不好
I don't want	Wo bu yao	我不要
Good bye	Zai jian	再见
Thank you	Xie xie	谢谢
Yes	Dui	对
No	Bu dui	不对
How's it going?	Ni chi le ma?	你吃了吗？
When?	Shenme shihou?	什么时候？
Excuse me, I'm sorry	Dui bu qi	对不起
How much does it cost?	Duoshao qian?	多少钱？
Too expensive	Tai guile	太贵了
It's broken	Huaile	坏了

English	Pinyin	Chinese
May I take a look?	Wo neng bu neng kan yi kan?	我能不能看一看？
Do you speak English?	Ni shuo Yingwen ma?	你说英文吗？
What's your name?	Ni gui xing?	你贵姓？
My name is ____	Wo xing ____	我姓 ____
I'm lost	Wo milu le	我迷路了
I don't smoke	Wo bu chouyan	我不抽烟
I'm ill	Wo shengbing le	我生病了
Bill please!	Qing jiezhang!	请结帐！
I am vegetarian	Wo shi chisude	我是吃素的
Can I take a photograph?	Wo keyi zhao ge xiang ma?	我可以照个相吗？
I can't speak Chinese	Wo buhui shuo Zhongwen	我不会说中文
I don't understand	Wo ting bu dong	我听不懂
It doesn't matter	Mei guanxi	没关系
No problem	Mei wenti	没问题
Where are you from?	Ni shi cong nar lai de?	你是从哪来的？
I am from	Wo shi cong ___ lai de	我是从 ____ 来的
America	Meiguo	美国
Australia	Aodaliya	澳大利亚
Canada	Jianada	加拿大
England	Yingguo	英国
France	Faguo	法国
Germany	Deguo	德国
Holland	Helan	荷兰
Ireland	Aierlan	爱尔兰
Japan	Riben	日本
Do you have a ____?	Ni you mei you ____?	你有没有 ____ ？
Do you know ____?	Ni zhi bu zhidao? ____	你知不知道___ ？
What do you call this?	Zhe jiao shenme?	这叫什么？
I want to go to ____	Wo xiang qu ____	我想去 ____
Where is ____?	____ zai nar?	____ 在哪儿？
I want ____	Wo yao ____	我要 ____

English	Pinyin	Chinese
Airport	feji chang	飞机场
Bank	yinhang	银行
Beer	pijiu	啤酒
Bicycle	zixingche	自行车
Boiled water	kai shui	开水
Bus	gonggong qiche	公共汽车
Bus station	qiche zong zhan	汽车总站
Chinese "dollar" or renminbi	yuan or kuai	元，块
CITS	lüxingshe	旅行社
Credit card	xinyong ka	信用卡
Hot water	re shui	热水
Hotel	binguan, dajiudian, fandian	宾馆，大酒店，饭店
Map	ditu	地图
Mineral water	kuangquanshui	矿泉水
Passport	huzhao	护照
Police!	Jingcha!	警察！
Restaurant	fanguan	饭馆
Soft drink	qishui	汽水
Taxi	chuzu qiche	出租汽车
Telephone	dianhua	电话
Toilet	cesuo	厕所
Toilet paper	weisheng zhi	卫生纸
Train	huoche	火车
Train station	huoche zhan	火车站

English	Pinyin	Chinese
Telephone	dianhua	电话
Toilet	cesuo	厕所
Toilet paper	weisheng zhi	卫生纸
Train	huoche	火车
Train station	huoche zhan	火车站

English	Pinyin	Chinese
Zero	ling	零
One	yi	一
Two	er	二
Three	san	三
Four	si	四
Five	wu	五
Six	liu	六
Seven	qi	七
Eight	ba	八
Nine	jiu	九
Ten	shi	十
Eleven	shi yi	十一
Twelve	shi er	十二
Fifteen	shi wu	十五
Twenty	er shi	二十
Twenty-one	er shi yi (and so on)	二十一
Thirty	san shi	三十
Thirty-one	san shi yi (and so on)	三十一
One hundred	yi bai	一百
Two hundred	er bai	二百
Three hundred	san bai	三百
Four hundred	si bai	四百
One thousand	yi qian	一千
Two thousand	er qian	二千
Days of the Week		
Sunday	Xingqitian	星期天
Monday	Xingqiyi	星期一
Tuesday	Xingqier	星期二
Wednesday	Xingqisan	星期三
Thursday	Xingqisi	星期四
Friday	Xingqiwu	星期五
Saturday	Xingqiliu	星期六

English	Pinyin	Chinese
Yesterday	zuotian	昨天
Today	jintian	今天
Tomorrow	mingtian	明天

INDEX

I

J

T

Frommer's® Complete Travel Guides

Alaska
Amsterdam
Arizona
Atlanta
Australia
Austria
Bahamas
Barcelona, Madrid & Seville
Beijing
Belgium, Holland & Luxembourg
Bermuda
Boston
British Columbia & the Canadian Rockies
Budapest & the Best of Hungary
California
Canada
Cancún, Cozumel & the Yucatán
Cape Cod, Nantucket & Martha's Vineyard
Caribbean
Caribbean Cruises & Ports of Call
Caribbean Ports of Call
Carolinas & Georgia
Chicago
China
Colorado
Costa Rica
Denmark
Denver, Boulder & Colorado Springs
England
Europe
European Cruises & Ports of Call
Florida
France
Germany
Greece
Greek Islands
Hawaii
Hong Kong
Honolulu, Waikiki & Oahu
Ireland
Israel
Italy
Jamaica
Japan
Las Vegas
London
Los Angeles
Maryland & Delaware
Maui
Mexico
Miami & the Keys
Montana & Wyoming
Montréal & Québec City
Munich & the Bavarian Alps
Nashville & Memphis
Nepal
New England
New Mexico
New Orleans
New York City
New Zealand
Nova Scotia, New Brunswick & Prince Edward Island
Oregon
Paris
Philadelphia & the Amish Country
Portugal
Prague & the Best of the Czech Republic
Provence & the Riviera
Puerto Rico
Rome
San Antonio & Austin
San Diego
San Francisco
Santa Fe, Taos & Albuquerque
Scandinavia
Scotland
Seattle & Portland
Singapore & Malaysia
South Africa
Southeast Asia
South Pacific
Spain
Sweden
Switzerland
Thailand
Tokyo
Toronto
Tuscany & Umbria
USA
Utah
Vancouver & Victoria
Vermont, New Hampshire & Maine
Vienna & the Danube Valley
Virgin Islands
Virginia
Walt Disney World & Orlando
Washington, D.C.
Washington State

Frommer's® Dollar-a-Day Guides

Australia from $50 a Day
California from $60 a Day
Caribbean from $70 a Day
England from $70 a Day
Europe from $60 a Day
Florida from $60 a Day
Hawaii from $70 a Day
Ireland from $60 a Day
Italy from $70 a Day
London from $85 a Day
New York from $80 a Day
Paris from $85 a Day
San Francisco from $60 a Day
Washington, D.C., from $60 a Day

Frommer's® Portable Guides

Acapulco, Ixtapa & Zihuatanejo
Alaska Cruises & Ports of Call
Bahamas
Baja & Los Cabos
Berlin
California Wine Country
Charleston & Savannah
Chicago
Dublin
Hawaii: The Big Island
Las Vegas
London
Maine Coast
Maui
New Orleans
New York City
Paris
Puerto Vallarta, Manzanillo & Guadalajara
San Diego
San Francisco
Sydney
Tampa & St. Petersburg
Venice
Washington, D.C.

Frommer's® National Park Guides

Family Vacations in the National Parks
Grand Canyon
National Parks of the American West
Rocky Mountain
Yellowstone & Grand Teton
Yosemite & Sequoia/Kings Canyon
Zion & Bryce Canyon

Frommer's® Memorable Walks

Chicago
London
New York
Paris
San Francisco
Washington D.C.

Frommer's® Great Outdoor Guides

New England
Northern California
Southern California & Baja
Southern New England
Washington & Oregon

Frommer's® Born to Shop Guides

Born to Shop: China
Born to Shop: France
Born to Shop: Italy
Born to Shop: London
Born to Shop: New York
Born to Shop: Paris

Frommer's® Irreverent Guides

Amsterdam
Boston
Chicago
Las Vegas
London
Los Angeles
Manhattan
New Orleans
Paris
San Francisco
Seattle & Portland
Vancouver
Walt Disney World
Washington, D.C.

Frommer's® Best-Loved Driving Tours

America
Britain
California
Florida
France
Germany
Ireland
Italy
New England
Scotland
Spain
Western Europe

The Unofficial Guides®

Bed & Breakfasts in California
Bed & Breakfasts in New England
Bed & Breakfasts in the Northwest
Beyond Disney
Branson, Missouri
California with Kids
Chicago
Cruises
Disneyland
Florida with Kids
Golf Vacations in the Eastern U.S.
The Great Smoky & Blue Ridge Mountains
Inside Disney
Hawaii
Las Vegas
London
Miami & the Keys
Mini Las Vegas
Mini-Mickey
New Orleans
New York City
Paris
Safaris
San Francisco
Skiing in the West
Walt Disney World
Walt Disney World for Grown-ups
Walt Disney World for Kids
Washington, D.C.

Special-Interest Titles

Frommer's Britain's Best Bed & Breakfasts and Country Inns
Frommer's Britain's Best Bike Rides
The Civil War Trust's Official Guide to the Civil War Discovery Trail
Frommer's Caribbean Hideaways
Frommer's Food Lover's Companion to France
Frommer's Food Lover's Companion to Italy
Frommer's Gay & Lesbian Europe
Frommer's Exploring America by RV
Hanging Out in Europe
Israel Past & Present
Mad Monks' Guide to California
Mad Monks' Guide to New York City
Frommer's The Moon
Frommer's New York City with Kids
The New York Times' Unforgettable Weekends
Places Rated Almanac
Retirement Places Rated
Frommer's Road Atlas Britain
Frommer's Road Atlas Europe
Frommer's Washington, D.C., with Kids
Frommer's What the Airlines Never Tell You